P9-CQG-870

JOHN A. MACDONALD
The Young Politician

JOHN A. MACDONALD

The Young Politician

By

DONALD CREIGHTON

ON LOAN
MACMILLAN co

THE ONTARIO HISTORICAL SOCIETY

TORONTO
THE MACMILLAN COMPANY OF CANADA LIMITED

Copyright, Canada, 1952

by

DONALD G. CREIGHTON

All rights reserved—no part of this
book may be reproduced in any form
without permission in writing from the
publisher, except by a reviewer who
wishes to quote brief passages in connection with a review written for inclusion
in a magazine or newspaper.

Reprinted 1956, 1965, 1968

PRINTED IN CANADA

TO

HAROLD ADAMS INNIS

the two great
falls. A second
from 567

PREFACE

It is now nearly sixty years since Sir Joseph Pope published, in two volumes, his *Memoirs of the Right Honourable Sir John Alexander Macdonald, G.C.B., First Prime Minister of The Dominion of Canada.* Sir Joseph was Macdonald's literary executor; to him was entrusted the vast mass of the Macdonald correspondence; and his biography, solidly based upon these private papers, has long remained the standard work on the subject. Other biographies of Macdonald have been published, of course, since the *Memoirs* first appeared in 1894; but they were shorter and slighter works, and without independent authority. This was inevitable as long as the correspondence remained in the custody of Macdonald's literary executor; but in 1917 Sir Joseph Pope transferred the entire collection to the Public Archives of Canada. Since that time—thirty-five years ago now—the Macdonald Papers have certainly not been left unused. Historians have searched them—or, at least, parts of them—in pursuit of evidence on a variety of special topics. But, somewhat curiously, the principal subject of the collection, Macdonald himself, has never been made the main theme of an extended study. In view of the richness of the Papers, this neglect is surprising; and it is all the more surprising when one realizes how many other collections of original materials, relating in whole or in part to Canadian affairs during the long period of Macdonald's career, have been opened to students, in both Canada and Great Britain, during the past twenty-five years. It would seem, therefore, that the time has perhaps arrived for a re-examination of Macdonald's career in the light of all the evidence now available. That, at least is the excuse for the present study. The volume which is here presented covers the first of the two great periods into which Macdonald's career naturally falls. A second and concluding volume will deal with the years from 1867 to Macdonald's death in 1891.

I have to acknowledge Her Majesty's gracious permission to make use of material in the Royal Archives, Windsor Castle. I am indebted, for much kind assistance, to Dr. W. Kaye Lamb, Dominion Archivist, and his assistants in the Public Archives of Canada, especially Miss Norah Story and Mr. W. G. Ormsby of the Manuscript Division; to Dr. G. W. Spragge, Department of Public Records and Archives, Ontario; and to Mr. H. P. Gundy, Librarian, Queen's University, Kingston. For help in finding material in England, I am under obligation to Sir Campbell Stuart, Mr. R. L. Atkinson, of the Historical Manuscripts Commission, Colonel G. E. G. Malet, of the National Register of Archives, and Miss D. E. Eldred, representative of the Public Archives of Canada at the Public Record Office, London. I have also to thank the officials of the National Trust for permission to consult the Beaconsfield Papers at Hughenden Manor. Professor J. M. S. Careless, my colleague in the Department of History, University of Toronto, has verified a number of my references; and I should like to record my appreciation of his assistance.

Finally, I gratefully acknowledge my indebtedness to the University of Toronto, the Rockefeller Corporation, and the Nuffield Foundation for the grants which have enabled me to give my undivided attention to this work over considerable periods of time.

D. G. CREIGHTON

OXFORD, DOMINION DAY, 1952.

CONTENTS

ILLUSTRATIONS

JOHN A. MACDONALD

The Young Politician

Chapter One

The Immigrant Macdonalds

I

In those days they came usually by boat. A few immigrants may have made the long journey from Montreal by land, taking several weeks and stopping at a score of friendly farm-houses as they pushed their way through the green forest. But most people travelled westward by the river—either in *bateaux*, camping out at night on the shore under the stars, or by schooner, or by one of the new steamers which in the last few years had begun to chug noisily up and down the long stretches between the rapids. In its upper reaches, the St. Lawrence widened promisingly; but here the rocky formation of the Laurentian Plateau thrust a huge knotted fist southward, across the river into New York State; and the St. Lawrence was crowded with islands, big and little, long and low, or towering and crested with pine trees, which parted the vast expanse of water into innumerable channels and masked the approach to Lake Ontario. As the boats slipped at length past Howe Island, out of the river's last channel and into the lake itself, their destination was still hidden by a bulging promontory of mainland, dented with deep inlets, which jutted south into Lake Ontario. They passed Deadman Bay, and then Navy Bay—where Sir James Yeo had urged his shipwrights forward in the frantic struggle for the mastery of Lake Ontario during the War of 1812—and finally rounded Point Frederick. Here was another wide body of water, the estuary of the Cataraqui River, which drained into Lake Ontario from the rocky highland to the north.

And beyond that, on low land rising gently towards the west, was the town of Kingston.

From the site of Frontenac's old fort, the town's shore-line curved southward in a slow arc to Mississauga Point, with its battery and the blockhouse beyond. A paddle-wheel steamer, a half-dozen schooners were moored at Cartwright's and Forsyth's and the newer docks to the south; and behind them, the town lay like an outspread fan, its east-west streets, like ribs, converging on Store Street, less than a mile inland. In 1820 it was thirty-six years since Captain Michael Grass and his small company of United Empire Loyalists had drawn lots for their properties in the new town-site. Kingston had not done badly in the race for prominence and prestige which the little Loyalist villages had begun back in 1784. York had become the seat of government; York was already threatening to acquire the financial and commercial leadership of the province. But Kingston, with its three to four thousand inhabitants equalled, if it did not exceed, the population of the capital, and had far outstripped the other river and lake towns. Kingston, in fact, had been the real, though not the titular, capital of the early province of Upper Canada, the province of the Loyalists, with its concentration on the upper St. Lawrence. And the solid advantages which had given it this early pre-eminence lasted stubbornly on, long after settlement had begun to spill into the rich peninsula between Lakes Erie and Huron, and the whole centre of gravity of the province was shifted slowly westward.

The town stood at the head of the St. Lawrence, at the foot of the vast, interconnecting system of the Great Lakes; and this commanding position was important for all sorts of reasons, military and naval, as well as commercial and political. Like York, Kingston was one of the principal garrison towns in the upper province; but, in addition—and this was an unique advantage—it had since 1789 been the British naval base on Lake Ontario. It was true that the Peace of Ghent had silenced the busy activity of the dockyard at Point Henry. It was true, and more important, that the Rush-Bagot Treaty, limiting future naval construction on the Great Lakes, had seemed to drop the curtain on Kingston's briefly dramatic career as a naval base.

Those two giants, H.M.S. *Wolfe* and H.M.S. *Canada* lay unfinished on the stocks, just where they had been abruptly abandoned in 1815; and the *St. Lawrence* and the little flotilla of ships that had gained command of the lake in the last weeks of the war rode at anchor, in decaying splendour, in Navy Bay. Formally, peace had come; but it was a doubtful and uneasy period of tranquillity, during which the province waited, seized by recurring fits of apprehension; and Kingston, and other strategic centres, remained watchfully upon the defensive. East of the Cataraqui River, at the naval base, the decaying little fleet was not finally destroyed, and the "stone frigate", the largest structure yet built at Point Frederick, was erected in 1820. West of the river, in the town itself, the commandant still kept up his fine house, and the garrison occupied the site of Frontenac's old fort, just below where the scow ferry plied from one side to the other of the river. The town was full of soldiers. They were as familiar as the citizens; and some were becoming citizens themselves. Veterans of the Napoleonic and American Wars, they were settling down in the lands which they had fought to keep British; and along with them, or after them, there often came their sweethearts, wives, children, relations or friends. It was a characteristic episode of the period when, on a July day in 1820, a little group of Scottish immigrants arrived at the house of their kinsman, Lieutenant-Colonel Donald Macpherson, a retired British Army officer living in Kingston.

There were six of them—Hugh Macdonald, his wife Helen, and their four children, Margaret, John Alexander, James, and Louisa.[1] It was Helen Macdonald who provided the link with the Macpherson family and the claim upon the Colonel's benevolence. She was a big woman, sturdily built, with a firm, prominent nose, and wide-set, dark, intelligent eyes. She and Anna Macpherson, the Colonel's wife, were half-sisters. They were both members of a stout, intricate family connection of Macphersons, Clarks, Grants and Shaws, who inhabited a half-dozen tiny villages in Badenoch and Speyside, Inverness-shire. Their mother, Margaret Grant, had been twice married, first to William Shaw, of Dalnavert, and then to James Shaw, a clansman, but not a relation of her first husband, who came from Kinrara, a tiny neighbouring village in the same parish of Alvie. Anna and Margaret were daughters of the first marriage,[2] Helen of the second; and Helen's father, James Shaw, was a soldier who had fought for the Pretender at Culloden and who, like so many other more famous heads of Jacobite families, had taken service in the Hanoverian armies after the ruin of the Stuart cause.

Helen grew up in Dalnavert, in the house which her much older half-sisters had once occupied, in that professional military atmosphere which was common to so many Highland families in the two generations after Culloden. Her father had been a soldier; her elder half-sister, Anna Shaw, had married young Lieutenant Donald Macpherson; her younger half-sister, Margaret, had married another Highland officer, Alexander Clark. It might have been confidently expected that Helen, in her turn, would follow the example of her sisters and choose one of these men of high pride; and small means, and splendid courage, who had been fighting the battles of the British Empire in Europe and America since 1757. But she did nothing of the kind. Somewhere about 1811, she met and married Hugh Macdonald; and with him, as a sober merchant's wife, she settled down in Glasgow.

Hugh Macdonald introduced a distinct and novel strain into the Badenoch connection of Grants, Macphersons, Clarks, and Shaws. He came not from Inverness-shire but from Sutherland, and his family background lay not in military service with Stuart and Hanoverian armies, but in small farming and trade.[3] His father, John Macdonald, a tall, spare man, with abundant, black, curly hair, had been born in 1736 in Rogart; and Rogart was one of the few inland parishes, in the south-eastern part of the country, which had been carved out by occupation from the immense, sombre, treeless expanse of moorland which was Sutherland. Here, in little villages in the Strathfleet valley, he lived and worked; here in 1778 he married a clanswoman, Jean Macdonald; and here several of his children, including his second son, Hugh, were born. It was not until comparatively late in life that he made the great move of his career—a move that carried him only a few miles in space, but a considerable distance in opportunity—to the county town, Dornoch. In Dornoch, close to the edge of the North Sea, at the entrance to the long arm of Dornoch Firth, he slowly prospered. For a time he may have leased and farmed a part of the property known locally as "Fourpenny" in the vicinity of the borough; but he also kept a shop in town, apparently near the cathedral; and it was for these mercantile pursuits that he was evidently best known. For long afterward the old people of Dornoch used to remember him by his Gaelic title "the merchant Macdonald".[4]

John Macdonald's virtues were simple and solid ones; but his son, Hugh, was a much more complicated and unstable character. He had been born in 1782, and the new century was probably not very far advanced before he began to fret inside the grey walls of his father's shop. Amiable, a little indolent, he was fond of talk and company and the bottle; but he responded quickly to young faces, new landscapes, and fresh opportunities. He was at once ambitious and good-natured, restless yet fundamentally easy-going, enterprising and at the same time curiously lacking in persistence. He always seemed to believe that he was made for success, and he was in fact invariably susceptible to failure. Dornoch, a little northern county town, had proved ample enough for his father's ambition, and had generously repaid his father's hard work. But, once Hugh had attained his majority, nothing but the big city of Glasgow would satisfy him. In Glasgow, he set up in business with a partner as a manufacturer of cottons in a small way, and failed. He then tried a new and similar enterprise on his own account and succeeded no better. It was true that the times were scarcely propitious. The conclusion of the Napoleonic Wars was followed, after only a few years, by a depression which threw Glasgow, all Scotland, and the whole of the United Kingdom into a state of profound discouragement and unrest. Failure was epidemic; and so was the counter-contagion, emigration. After a long interval, the western movement of the British peoples was resumed once more; and, for the first time in their history, the northern provinces which had survived the American Revolution began to attract the interested attention of prospective migrants in the Motherland. It was only natural that the mercurial, avid, restless Hugh should think of emigration. It was inevitable, once the decision to leave Scotland was made, that he should get in touch with his wife's relatives, the Donald Macphersons, the one branch of the connection that had settled in British North America.

The Macphersons had been living in the Canadas for over twelve years, and the Colonel had spent an even longer portion of his agitated career in North America, defending British authority and British territory against bellicose republicans.[5] In 1775, when he was just a young man, he had joined the muster of Fraser's Highlanders, the 71st Regiment; and he had fought all through the American Revolutionary War until the surrender of Cornwallis's army at Yorktown. When, in 1783, Fraser's Highlanders were disbanded at Perth, and young Macpherson, a lieutenant on half-pay, returned to Inverness-shire, and settled down at Dalnavert, he may very well have assumed that his connection with North America was ended for ever. It was true that he did not remain very long in the Highlands, for when the war with Revolutionary France broke out in 1793, he at once resumed his old profession of soldiering; and if he had been a slightly younger man, he might have ended his long military career with his new regiment, the Gordon Highlanders, in the triumphs and endurances of the Peninsular and Waterloo campaigns. But one lifetime was too short to support active service in three wars which together covered a space of nearly forty years. In 1806—a major now—Macpherson was transferred to one of the veterans' units;[6] a year later he crossed the Atlantic for the third time to take up garrison duty in the distant yet supposedly far less hazardous theatre of action, British North America; and, on September 10, 1807, he landed at Quebec, with the Tenth Royal Veteran Battalion, commanded by Lieutenant-General Lowther Pennington.[7] When the War of 1812 broke out, five years later, he was stationed at Kingston; and the old man resumed the familiar exercise of fighting Americans. In 1813, as a reward of long service, he was promoted Lieutenant-Colonel. For a brief while he was apparently commandant of the garrison; and then, in 1815, the war came to an end.[8]

He did not return to Scotland. He retired on full pay, received an ample grant of land, and settled down in Kingston with a comfortable air of finality. His children were growing up. John Alexander, the eldest son, and his younger brother, Lowther Pennington, named in honour of the Colonel's old commander, were now lads in their teens; and there was a third boy, Evan, and four girls as well.[9] They were the children of Macpherson's mature years who, in effect, had known no home but Kingston and no country but Canada; and in Canada their circumstances were easy and their prospects promising. Kingston, in fact, had ceased to be a temporary advanced post from which soldiers of fortune inevitably returned. It had become a new home base round which a part, at least, of the vast Macpherson connection might be happily reunited. Back from this Upper Canadian household, solidly established in a promising wilderness, there flowed the encouragement, advice and assistance that were to lure the Macpherson clan from the old world to the new. Hugh Macdonald accepted it all eagerly. He was a born migrant whom failure and misfortune had made ready for travel again. In the early summer of 1820 he set sail for Canada; and on July 17, he and his wife, Helen, and their four children "entered Colonel Macpherson's house at Kingston".[10]

II

It could hardly have been a more pleasant introduction to Canada. The Macphersons lived in relative ease and dignity. The house was full of children, and the younger Macpherson boys and girls were much of an age with the Macdonald children. Anna Macpherson had a wealth of practical information to give to Helen Macdonald; and the Colonel, than whom nobody in Kingston was better known or more respected, had acquired a copious store of knowledge about the little town and its ways which was of immediate value to Hugh. For Hugh had determined to settle in Kingston. He had no intention whatever of submitting himself and his family to the terrible fatigues and privations of real pioneer life. The frontier homestead, won with incredible difficulty out of the bush in the remote north or west, the "improved farm" somewhere "out front" in the first row of townships—these hard destinies, which were the common lot of thousands of the first two generations of immigrants after Waterloo, were to form no part of the history of the Macdonald family. Hugh Macdonald knew village and town life. Commerce—petty trade and small-scale manufacturing—had formed the chief economic thread in the fortunes of his family for two decades. He had experience. He had some capital, not a great deal perhaps, but more, certainly, than the majority of his fellow-emigrants. And in the prosperous and benevolent Colonel Macpherson he possessed a commercial asset of high importance through which he could anticipate good will, make connections, and acquire credit.

Finally, he was fortunate in coming to the town of Kingston. Without any question, the commercial advantages of Kingston were superior to those of any other town in the eastern part of Upper Canada. The military barracks, the naval establishment at Point Frederick, the huge, if spasmodic, expenditures for defence, were all official endorsations of the basic importance of its position. Kingston was the capital of the Midland District; and, although the Midland District comprised only the four counties, Frontenac, Lennox and Addington, Prince Edward, and Hastings, these were very populous and prosperous counties. And, indeed, the prominence of the Midland District was such that people in other parts of Upper Canada often spoke and wrote of it, in a loose, inaccurate, but highly flattering fashion, as if it occupied the whole of the east-central part of the province. Even within its official boundaries, it extended over a vast and varied domain. To the north-east lay the plateau of the Precambrian shield, the gnarled and shaggy country of rock and forest and intricately connected waterways, from which the Cataraqui River brought the great red and white pine timbers down to the Kingston mills. It was true that the infertile rock-land crowded Kingston closely, a little oppressively, to the north-east, in somewhat the same way as the great moors of central Sutherland had crowded Rogart and Lairg and Dornoch, the little parishes of Hugh Macdonald's youth. But south-west of

Kingston, along the Bath and Napanee roads, the country broadened out comfortably in pleasant and fertile amplitudes; and across the narrow strait from Adolphustown lay the peninsula of Prince Edward county, nearly encircled by the warm, shallow waters of the Bay of Quinte, and rich with farms and barns and orchards. A score of villages and little towns—Bath, Ameliasburgh, Adolphustown, Hallowell, Napanee, and Belleville—looked up respectfully to Kingston as their local capital; and Kingston's economic hinterland extended far beyond the limits of its administrative authority. It had become the little commercial metropolis for all the eastern part of the province; and it was a major point of transhipment on the northern trade route which extended from England and the ports of Europe across the Atlantic, up the St. Lawrence and the Great Lakes system and far into the interior of the continent.

To Hugh Macdonald the town itself must have seemed not only novel and exciting, but also, in an odd way, vaguely familiar. There was a grey, sober, earnest, downright, yet not ungracious air about it which might have reminded him of the villages and towns of his youth. Many of the shops and houses of Kingston were built of limestone, which was obtained with ease in the ample quarries nearby; and the flat, grey shop fronts, with their rows of pleasantly spaced sashed windows, climbed in slowly ascending levels up Store Street from the harbour. Despite its smallness, the town had an eighteenth-century urban appearance, an old-fashioned inclination towards regularity and symmetry and perspectives, which was to yield only slowly and partially to the violent idiosyncrasies of Victorian stone- and brick-work. In the homely austerity of Lower Town, on the pavements of Store, Grass, Church and Grave Streets—grey thoroughfares which only later were to be given less hard-bitten names—Hugh might, at times, have thought himself back among the stone walls of Dornoch. And on autumn nights, when the wind blew chill from the west, and the waters of the huge, troubled lake roared outside the harbour he could have fancied himself looking out towards Dornoch Firth and the North Sea. He was done with big cities. His father had won his decent reputation and his sober success in a small town;

and, town for town, Kingston was infinitely more promising
than Dornoch. Hugh was not yet thirty-eight years old. He
had been unfortunate; but, in this new world, everything could
be, and would be, repaired. He arranged his credits, obtained
his stock, engaged a highly dubious assistant—an old soldier
named Kennedy, who drank in secret even more than his easy-
going master would have considered desirable—and, on October
16, 1820, almost exactly three months after his arrival, he opened
his first shop in Kingston.[11]

He and his wife and children lived above the shop, as did
the families of most merchants and professional men, even the
most affluent, in Kingston at the time. It was a relatively small
family, judged by the standards of that age, smaller certainly
than the Macpherson brood, and death, through disease and
accident, had been busy already with its members. Life was
uncertain enough for the adult population of the early nineteenth century. It was doubly precarious for children; and, of
the five sons and daughters born to Hugh and Helen, only
three survived the tragic disasters of childhood. William, apparently the eldest son, died in infancy long before they left
Scotland; and they had not been two years in Canada when
their second surviving boy, James, was killed in a frightful
accident. A little thing—he was not yet six years old when the
tragedy took place—he was left one spring evening in the care
of the old soldier, Kennedy, who, apparently, could be brutal
as well as bibulous; and Kennedy, either in impatience or anger,
struck him with such force that he fell, injuring himself fatally.[12]
Of the three children who remained, two were girls. Margaret
—"Moll"—was the elder, a gentle little girl, with a round, sweet,
serious countenance, and regular diminutive features. The
baby, Louisa—"Lou" she was called—was a sturdy, rather plain
child, not more than two years old when they arrived in Canada;
and, as she grew up, she came to resemble her brother very
closely.

Her brother, Hugh's only surviving son, was called John
Alexander. The third child, a year and a half younger than
his sister Margaret, he had been born on January 11, 1815, in
Glasgow. He remembered something of his native city, in the

queer disconnected flashes of childish recollection; and his accent and mode of speech were formed in a family and among relatives where broad Scots was continually spoken. But he was only five and a half years old when he was brought to Canada; and he grew up a typical Midland District boy, with the expressions and turns of phrase which were characteristic of the region.[13] Tall for his age, slight and yet sturdy, with an increasingly lanky and almost angular frame, he had his mother's prominent nose, her generous mouth, her wide-set dark eyes. These rugged lines, apparent already in the smooth countenance of early boyhood, were set off by another characteristic feature, a copious crop of dark, curly, almost frizzy hair—a legacy, apparently, of his paternal grandfather, old "merchant Macdonald" of Dornoch. In 1820, when his parents arrived in Canada, he had almost reached the end of the first free, happily unfettered phase of childhood. A rather quiet, thoughtful small boy—and yet, at times, full of exuberant fun and inventive mischief—, he must have learnt to read early, for he quickly became passionately interested in books. Now he was almost ready for school.

In the meantime, while Helen bore her domestic tragedy and coped with the thousand novelties of her new situation, things had not been going at all well with Hugh. The shop did not prosper—at least to his satisfaction. Its fortunes began to have a distressingly close resemblance to those of his abandoned enterprises in Glasgow. The fault, of course, must be a quite simple one, easily remedied. It was probably that his location was unfortunate—his shop inconvenient and remote from the main business of the town. He changed his location; but, strangely enough, he could not change his luck. And some time early in 1824, less than four years after he had arrived from Scotland, he came restlessly to the conclusion that he was through with the capital of the Midland District. There may have been talk, as he discussed the matter with his wife Helen, and with Donald and Anna Macpherson, of a move to one of the newer settlements, farther west along the shore of Lake Ontario, and an attempt at farming; but, in the end, Hugh made a much more modest and sensible choice, which had at least a definite relation with his training and previous experience.

He moved westward, indeed, but only a little westward, as the long ungainly province measured its distances; and on Hay Bay, one of the deep inlets of the Bay of Quinte, and in a small, clap-boarded building painted red, he opened his third shop.[14] Here, in the third concession of Adolphustown, the "Fourth Town" west of the capital of the Midland District, he was still in Kingston's economic hinterland, in long-settled country which had been occupied since the first coming of the Loyalists. In these pleasant surroundings, and in fairly short order, the third shop failed.

Even yet, Hugh was far from daunted. With his easy-going, well established migratory habits, he determined to abandon Lennox and Addington County as he had already abandoned Frontenac. A little to the south-west, across a narrow reach of water, lay the irregular peninsula of Prince Edward County, with a little settlement, later called Glenora, at its very edge. Immediately beyond Glenora, the land soared abruptly upward, in steep, wooded heights, to form a wide tableland, hundreds of feet above the level of Lake Ontario. High on this dominating plateau, set in thick woods, mysteriously suspended above the great stretch of water below, was a little lake, the "Lake on the Mountain". All around, to the north-east and north-west, lay spread out the immense, tranquil landscape of the Bay of Quinte and its counties, in an intricate pattern of deep bays and coves and reaches, of long projecting headlands, capes, and points, which, as they stretched away towards the horizon, became a succession of narrow, contrasting strokes of colour, blue water, dark woods, and yellowing farmlands. A small channel had been cut from the Lake on the Mountain to the cliff's edge, and from there a roaring stream of water tumbled down a wooden race-way to turn the machinery of a large stone mill, several storeys in height, which stood by the shore of Adolphus Reach.[15] This property, the "Stone Mills", as the place was known at the time, was Hugh Macdonald's last major investment. It was a grist-mill, where Hugh also carried on the carding of wool, and the fulling, dyeing and dressing of cloth.[16] An ill-fated but indomitable enterpriser, he had been both manufacturer and shop-keeper. Now he was to become a miller.

The stock of prudence and pertinacity which had been so laboriously accumulated during generations of hard living in Rogart and Dornoch parishes was apparently being frittered away during a single lifetime. It was true that Hugh Macdonald, unlike some of the gentlemen immigrants who lost everything, including the last shreds of their dignity, in the Canadian bush, never completely succumbed to his reverses. In his hopeful, amiable, ineffectual way, he managed, if but barely, to keep some kind of shaky foundation for his family's life. The mill was never more than a mediocre success; but at least, for a number of years, it avoided failure. And the countryside about the Stone Mills—the waters of Adolphus Reach, the wooded heights, the mountain, and its diminutive lake—all this formed an agreeable landscape through which John Alexander and his sisters rambled happily down the long, golden road of summer. Yet Hugh, though he always provided a house, and though, perhaps, he could teach his family some of the simplest arts of living, was never quite able to remove the uneasy sense of uncertainty and precariousness from his children's lives. It was Helen who succeeded in maintaining the family in effective being during those years of reverses and abandonments.[17] In her strong, solid frame there was an immense vitality and an immense power of endurance. Hugh grew rapidly older; for him the great hopes of immigration had failed. But Helen kept alive a family sense of purpose and direction. It was she who was always remembering the past. It was she who was planning for the future—for her children, for her only surviving son.

III

As far back, probably, as the winter of 1822, John Alexander had started to school in Kingston.[18] He was only nine years old when the family moved to Hay Bay, and probably for the first year he stayed at home, and tramped down the country roads to John Hughes's school at Adolphustown.[19] Then—and the change may have coincided with the move to the Stone Mills

—a different and more ambitious educational programme was
adopted; and he was sent back, for the winter months at least,
to continue his schooling at Kingston. It was a characteristic
Scottish decision. It meant long separations, and additional
expense, which Hugh could ill afford; but both he and Helen
—and perhaps particularly Helen—believed in their stubborn
way that it was essential; and, somehow or other, they managed to meet the fees and the charges for board and lodging.
John Hughes had a decent reputation as a teacher; but there
was probably no school within many miles of the Stone Mills;
and, in general, even in such old-established counties as Frontenac, Lennox and Addington and Prince Edward, the common
schools were few, badly equipped and even more badly taught.
The District Grammar Schools, usually established at the capital
of each administrative district, were the one great exception to
the general rule of poor and inadequate teaching. It was a
standing Radical grievance, repeatedly ventilated in the Legislative Assembly, that the provincial school system favoured the
rich of the towns at the expense of the poor of the countryside.
But the fact was that, at that time, Upper Canada could simply
not afford a substantial number of competent schools; and another twenty-five years elapsed before Egerton Ryerson began
to lay down the broad solid foundations of a truly provincial
educational system. In the meantime, the District Grammar
Schools, together with a few private academies, provided the
best education that the province could afford; and it was only
by unusual arrangements and some sacrifices that a country
boy like John Alexander could attend a good school.

He was, on the whole, lucky in the Midland District Grammar School. It was a small stone building, standing on the
north side of School Street, a little below Church, and kept by
two masters—the Reverend John Wilson, who was headmaster
from 1817 to the close of 1824, and his assistant George Baxter.[20]
Wilson was an old Oxonian, a member of Queen's College, and
a clergyman of the Established Church, whose reputation as a
scholar was not forgotten when he buried himself in the little
frontier Upper Canadian town; and the standard of teaching
at the Midland District Grammar School was probably pretty

high. John Alexander was well grounded in Latin; he was almost certainly taught some French, though what is likely to have been his first French grammar, still surviving, has a suspiciously unused appearance. And by 1827, when he was just twelve years old, he had worked his way through numbers and their properties, decimals, ratios and geometrical proportions, and was deep in square and cube root.[21] He wrote a round, clear, careful hand, which soon became easy and flowing. His books were neatly kept, with careful spacing, indentations, and headings; and it was only on the covers that he allowed himself to indulge in supplementary and unacademic expression—in repeated, grotesque representations of the human profile, in a few imaginary and euphonious appellations such as "Timothy Mudlark Toenail", and in the inspiring reflection, "God Save the King, and the Devil Take the Preacher".

He lodged and boarded in town, probably with several different landladies. But the Macpherson household was a second home, and he must have been in and out of it constantly. His uncle, the old Colonel, who had begun his fighting career over fifty years before, died at length in 1828. The citizens of Kingston shut their shops in honour of his memory, and the battery guns boomed out in a last salute. The two older Macpherson boys, John Alexander and Lowther Pennington, who by this time had reached their twenties, may already have left their home; and in 1826 one of the elder girls had married an able, pushing Scot named Francis Harper, who seemed to acquire capital and important friends with ease, and who was soon to become one of the financial standbys of the connection. The family circle shrank and altered; but Aunt Anna Macpherson kept the old household going, and the younger children, Helen and Catharine and Evan, were much of John Alexander's age and remained good friends with him. He used to slip into the Macpherson house after school, and Helen would supply him with slices of pudding and other delicacies not too frequently present on the table at his lodgings. Already he was a voracious reader, and he would sit for hours deep in a book, almost oblivious to what was going on, while the friendly tumult of the Macpherson household raged around him.[22] Then, when the summer came, he was away again to the Stone Mills for the long vacation.

He had profited from John Wilson's training in the first years of his schooling, before the family had left for Hay Bay. But, by the time he returned to Kingston, Wilson had resigned his headmastership and had returned to England to take up a post in his old university. The trustees of the Midland District Grammar School—the Archdeacon, George Okill Stuart, those two Loyalist worthies, John Macaulay and Thomas Markland, and the laconic Dr. Sampson, Kingston's principal physician for many years—pondered, at somewhat lengthy intervals, the question of Wilson's successor. Baxter was, of course, available. Baxter wanted the job; and Baxter, though it was regrettably true that he had once been a Presbyterian, was now definitely a member of the Church of England in good standing. Yet, the trustees, with the memory of Wilson's headmastership to inspire them, aimed at better talent. They wanted a man with an English university degree—a priest of the Church of England. This second requirement was included partly for reasons of religious conviction and considerations of prestige; but also partly on grounds of economy. The trustees could offer an annual salary of £350; but they believed that a clergyman could be more easily induced to accept it, since a clergyman would have the opportunity of increasing his income by doing a variety of odd jobs for the Archdeacon. In the end, however, these complicated and ambitious plans fell through. Baxter was made temporary headmaster, and then, in 1826, he was given the permanent appointment.[23] There may have been dissatisfaction with his principalship, or dissatisfaction with the grammar-school system in general, which some people, in places like Kingston, believed was certain to be injured by the large sums which Lieutenant-Governor Colborne seemed likely to divert to his pet project, Upper Canada College, at York. At any rate, the Kingston Scots began to be concerned about the education of their children.

The Protestant Scots community in Kingston had been growing fairly rapidly during these years. Scots had formed no important part of the original Loyalist settlement; but after the conclusion of the War of 1812 they began to come in increasing numbers. Up to 1820, they had lacked a church of their own; but in that year, the year in which the Macdonalds arrived in town, St. Andrews, in connection with the Church of Scotland, was built at the corner of Clergy and Store Streets. Its first minister, John Barclay, died in 1826, after only five years in Kingston; but again the Scottish community approached the Presbytery of Edinburgh, and the Presbytery of Edinburgh appointed John Machar, a young man from Forfarshire, a graduate of King's College, Aberdeen, and of Edinburgh University.[24] When he arrived in Kingston in the autumn of 1827, Machar was not yet thirty-one. He was a slight, rather frail man, with fine, fastidious features and thoughtful eyes, who combined a disciplined, intellectual faith with a gentle, non-combative tolerance. His congregation, he found on his arrival, was the "most numerous Protestant one in the place"; and aided by substantial elders like John Mowat and George Mackenzie, he took up its needs and interests with quiet but purposeful enthusiasm. One of these needs was education. St. Andrews was plainly dissatisfied with the management of the Midland District Grammar School. And it was not the last time that the sober Presbyterians were to show themselves ready to criticize and reject the leadership of the Anglican Loyalists who up to that time had run the province and the town.

The founding of the new school was the last important event in John Alexander's boyhood. Late in the autumn of 1828 another young Scotsman arrived in Kingston. He came with the encouragement, and probably at the invitation, of the Kingston Presbyterians; and everybody at St. Andrews was impressed with his credentials and recommendations. He was the Reverend John Cruickshank, a product, like Machar, of the Scottish universities, but younger than Machar by half-a-dozen years, a tall, handsome man, with curly hair, well-shaped nose and mouth, and clear intense eyes.[25] In January, 1829, he opened his school "for classical and general education" at Owen Macdougall's shop on Store Street.[26] Unlike the Midland District Grammar, it was a co-educational school, one of the first of such in the province. The Scots residents of Kingston hastened

to give it their support; and among others John Alexander Mac
donald was transferred to Cruickshank's care.

He sat in a small room, crowded with desks and forms, and
twenty or twenty-five children, of all ages from six to sixteen.
Some of them he would never see again; some would remain
mere acquaintances whose names he would make a point of
trying to remember in later years. But, by a curious chance,
he was to know two of them very well. Two of them were
to have careers as public and almost as prominent as his own,
and were to cross and re-cross his path repeatedly in future.
One was young Oliver Mowat, John Mowat's elder son, a
short, stocky boy, not yet ten years old, with a round cherubic
countenance. The other was John Hillyard Cameron. It was
almost by accident that John Hillyard attended Cruickshank's
school, for his father, Angus Cameron, quartermaster of the
79th Regiment, was soon to be posted to York, and young
Cameron was to become one of the earliest and most distinguished graduates of Upper Canada College. He was a tall
youth, with a broad, heavy, rather unprepossessing face which
was redeemed from unattractiveness by the friendly charm of
his smile and manner. Already there was an air about him of
precocious brilliance and easy accomplishment. His memory
and inventive powers were remarkable; and, with affable con-
descension he used to whisper jokes to the smaller boys, or tell
them long, fabulous stories to which Oliver Mowat listened with
round-eyed attention.[27]

The year 1829 drew to its close. John Alexander was nearly
fifteen, a "big boy" now, as the school population of Upper
Canada reckoned its ages; a promising boy too, fondly regarded,
no doubt, by Cruickshank, who long after kept a little sheaf of
his pupil's compositions. But, promising or not, John was
finished with formal education for ever when he walked for
the last time out of the classroom in Owen Macdougall's shop.
His was not an exceptionally unfortunate fate, for only a
favoured few of his contemporaries were permitted to continue
their studies much further. Richard Cartwright, legislative
councillor, chairman of the Quarter Sessions, and one of the
richest of Kingston's first generation of merchants, could afford

to send his twin sons to England for their education—Robert David to Oxford, and John Solomon to Lincoln's Inn.[28] But the Cartwrights lived an existence of inimitable splendour. Most boys, even the sons of fathers in comparatively comfortable circumstances, had to be content with the training which the Province of Upper Canada afforded; and, at that time, there were not even rough provincial substitutes for the venerable institutions of England. In 1830, it was a decade and more before King's College and Queen's College would open their doors to students; and, although the Law Society of Upper Canada examined pupils at the beginning and end of their legal training, there was no formal instruction in law in the province. Students were articled for both practical and theoretical training; and the old-established legal firms, together with the abler and more energetic of the younger lawyers, offered, in effect, the best professional education which could be had in the province. Many ambitious youths began in this way. They started early; even John Solomon Cartwright, long before he departed for Lincoln's Inn, had, as a boy of sixteen, begun his legal studies in John Beverley Robinson's office at York. The law was a broad, well-trodden path to comfort, influence, even to power; and back at the Stone Mills, after long and anxious conclaves, no doubt, it was decided that John Alexander should follow it. Hugh Macdonald had been a mediocre, ineffectual enterpriser; but the men of the Macpherson-Shaw-Clark connection had been successful professional soldiers. The professions were a part of the family tradition; the law was the obvious choice for a boy who seemed as attracted to study as he was uninterested in trade.

It was all settled in 1830. John was articled to a young Scottish lawyer, George Mackenzie, late of Ernesttown, and now of Kingston; and possibly in April of that year, when the assizes were on and the spring term in progress, he journeyed up by steamboat to York, the capital of the province, to confront the Benchers of the Law Society. He found lodgings at Osgoode Hall, or at one of the hotels or boarding-houses in its vicinity; dutifully he presented his petition and paid his fee of £10 to the secretary of the Society; and in a day or so, when

a quorum of the Benchers could be got together for the purpose,
he appeared formally to sit the examination required of a student
at law.[29] There was, inevitably, a passage of Latin to translate;
a little Latin parsing to do; some mathematical propositions to
expound and a few questions in history to answer; and then
the ordeal was over. In a few days John was given his certificate and formally admitted to the society as a student at
law. In a few days more, which he spent attending the courts
and watching the law officers of the Crown and the barristers
of the capital perform, the assizes came to an end and he had
"kept" the first of his four terms. He boarded the steamboat
back to Kingston and plunged at once into the work of his new
employer's office.

Chapter Two

The Lawyer's Apprentice

I

It was a highly respectable establishment, and also, in a sober, provincial fashion, distinguished. George Mackenzie, who reached the age of thirty-five in the year John began his apprenticeship, was still a comparatively young man, in the early stages of his career;[1] but already he occupied a place of special importance in the eyes of Kingston townsfolk in general and of his Scottish fellow-citizens in particular. John Machar of St. Andrews admired and respected him.[2] The long-headed merchants and lawyers of Store Street held his professional ability and integrity in the highest estimation. And throughout Kingston and its neighbourhood there was a growing opinion, which soon became a confident belief, that if Mackenzie wanted a parliamentary career, his knowledge, his interest in his own town, and his concern for the affairs of the whole province would easily win him a seat in the provincial legislature.[3] He was almost a model of virtue, certainly a pattern of professional rectitude. Yet, at the same time, he was a robust, genial, warm-hearted man, who, though he did not hesitate to correct and admonish those who served him, was quick to recognize ability and never niggardly in his praise.

In 1830 John took his inconspicuous place in George Mackenzie's office. It was a tumultuous year, with revolution in France, strikes and riots in England, and, even on the small stage of Upper Canadian affairs, a general election. But inside Mackenzie's busy establishment, the far-off dramatic clamour of international affairs, and even the more intimate homely argument of provincial politics must have sunk to a low, barely audible rumour. For John the demands of his own situation and his own future were loud and peremptory. He lodged and boarded with the Mackenzies; and, despite his professional articles, he was still very much the schoolboy, dependent upon authority and direction, hard to waken in the mornings, and watched over by Mrs. Mackenzie with kindly solicitude.⁴ All day he was at work, running errands, establishing titles, transcribing letters and documents, and making pressed copies of Mackenzie's correspondence on the wetted tissue leaves of the letter books. At night, under his master's benevolent direction, he began to read law. It was, no doubt, a tight routine of study, of small tasks and responsibilities, beyond which, as yet, he did not think to venture very far. His mother and father, his sisters, Margaret and Louisa, were a long journey away at the Stone Mills. The dispersal of the Macpherson family continued; and in 1830—the year in which he began his apprenticeship—Anna Macpherson married young Thomas Wilson, the Deputy Assistant Commissary-General of the garrison.⁵ But the old household which had served him as a second home all through his school-days was maintained for a few years longer, and he must often have visited it. Some of his earliest friendships—that with Charles Stuart, the grandson of Archdeacon George Okill Stuart, for example—probably date from this period. His reading broadened, and sometimes, of an evening, he would visit the precentor of St. Andrews—in secret a deplorable freethinker—and argue with him about religion.⁶

His place was small and inconspicuous. Yet—though this was perhaps apparent only to his elders at the moment—it was a position of considerable strategic importance. For Mackenzie was in touch with most affairs of any consequence in Kingston. His friends, associates, clients, and acquaintances formed a large and staunch company. His practice was already great and rapidly growing. Its main staple was, of course, the little contentions and affairs of farmers and small tradesmen scattered about in Kingston and its vicinity; but, in addition, there were a few of the luxuries of the profession—large accounts of merchants, and landowners, and forwarding companies, which Mackenzie already possessed, and still larger accounts which would come to him, if only the town prospered. Everybody believed it would prosper. The region of the lower lakes was being rapidly settled; and a struggle between the St. Lawrence and the New York routes for the prize of the western trade was now at hand. Already men were planning seriously for the first St. Lawrence canals; and far away, in the dense forests to the north-east, Lieutenant-Colonel John By was superintending the construction of the Rideau Canal, which was to link Kingston with the Ottawa, via the Rideau and the Cataraqui Rivers. The canal, which was designed as a military work to provide a route more northerly and safer than that of the exposed St. Lawrence, was certainly a fresh testimony to Kingston's strategic importance. But it was also a valuable addition to its commercial strength. It brought men, and money, and business to the town. And Kingston, busy and comfortably prosperous, began to desire the financial institutions appropriate to its new affluence. In January, 1830, the townsfolk assembled to petition the legislature for a new bank, their own bank, the future Commercial Bank of the Midland District.[7] For John and his employer, and the Macpherson-Macdonald clan, this project was charged with the greatest significance. Francis Harper, who had married John's cousin, was to be for many years the bank's cashier, or general manager; and George Mackenzie was its first solicitor.

During the next two years, while John sat soberly in his employer's office, performing his small tasks and learning something of the vast mysteries of the law, the Kingstonians, with Mackenzie in assiduous professional attendance, struggled earnestly for their bank. The first need, of course, was for an act of incorporation, which could be obtained only from the provincial legislature. But in 1830 the Kingstonians had the best of reasons for believing that the political way lay open and unobstructed before them. The bank's promoters were respectable Conservatives; George Mackenzie was a prominent Conservative; the general election of 1830 had returned a comfortable Conservative majority to the provincial Assembly; and—best of all—the newly elected member for Kingston, the tall, thickset, burly, overbearing Loyalist, Christopher Alexander Hagerman, had been appointed, one year earlier, to the post of Solicitor-General of the province. Yet for two years Kingston's hopes and expectations were denied by its old rival, York. For two years the supporters of York, entrenched in the Legislative Council, defended the monopoly of the Bank of Upper Canada, hitherto the one chartered bank in the province, which had its headquarters in the capital. In the end, however, the Conservatives grew tired of this unseemly and unprofitable controversy. The Assembly generously increased the capital stock of the Bank of Upper Canada; the Council handsomely accepted the charter of the Commercial Bank of the Midland District.[8] And Mackenzie received the most important company account in Kingston.

The years 1832 and 1833 were successful years for Mackenzie, for his firm, and for Kingston. Mackenzie's repute grew; and Kingston flourished. When young John and his fellow-Kingstonians read the newspapers or walked about the town and its environs with curious interest, they seemed to see on every hand the plain evidence of government favour and commercial prosperity. The completion of the Rideau Canal, the commencement of the great fortress on Point Henry, the government's decision to build the provincial penitentiary at Portsmouth, a little west of Kingston—all this appeared to show that the town was just at the beginning of a great new stage in its development. Kingston, with its busy new bank, its splendid public works, its obviously influential leaders in politics and finance, was re-asserting its old importance in the life of Upper Canada. Business flowed into it from the Midland District, from the whole eastern part of the province. Mackenzie's practice expanded, and he began to think seriously of setting up a small branch establishment, in the fashion of the time, a little to the west, in the Bay of Quinte region. Some time in 1832 he decided that Napanee was to be the new outpost and John Alexander was to be its manager.

In the late summer or early autumn of 1832 John set out. Napanee was nothing more than a little inland village which

had had its first beginnings in the early years of Loyalist settlement. A sawmill, a grist-mill, a carding-and-fulling mill, and
a tannery had been built on the banks of the Napanee River,
which, a few miles farther south, drained into the eastern end
of the Bay of Quinte; and around these prosaic little establishments—the inevitable first requirements of any pioneer community—there clustered a small group of shops and houses.[9]
Napanee was fewer than thirty miles away from Kingston,
and John was within reach—though not too readily within
reach—of his employer's advice and assistance. George Mackenzie promised to ride over that autumn to give his pupil's
quarters and activities a paternal inspection;[10] and a certain
Dier, who was, apparently, Napanee's solitary physician and
who occasionally travelled to Kingston "a horseback", used
sometimes to bring back letters, parcels and instructions. A
fundamental change in John's circumstances had taken place.
Napanee meant much more independence and much more
responsibility. For the first time he was nearly on his own.

One of the three or four shops at Napanee was kept by
Thomas Ramsay, a young man about John's age, and with all
John's bookish interests and love of literary conversations; and
it was here that young Macdonald established himself. He may
at times have helped Tom Ramsay behind the counter, weigh-
ing out the tea and sugar; and his first independent "office"
was probably nothing more than his own bedroom, or a corner
of the small shop, crowded with stoves and hardware, barrels
of pork, bolts of cloth, and kegs of beer and spirits. He was
seventeen now, at the perilous middle point of the journey
between boyhood and manhood, when the vagaries, the complications and the contradictions of adolescence were at their
most painful and baffling stage. The landscape of his character,
if it had passed through the first primitive period of upheaval
and subsidence, was still a new, unknown land, with hazy and
uncertain outlines. But to Mackenzie, peering with kindly interest through the obscurity, there were a few solid, rocky contours which were at once quite certain and entirely satisfactory.
Mackenzie, as in duty bound, used occasionally to write John
orthodox injunctions: "be industrious", "be assiduous"; but in

reality these platitudinous exhortations were unnecessary, and probably nobody was better aware of the fact than George Mackenzie himself. John was certainly quick and efficient and reliable. Only once, apparently, during that first perplexing autumn at Napanee, did he make a serious mistake. In casual and regrettably unprofessional conversation, he talked incautiously to a prospective client, "old Moore", about his pending suit, only to discover a little later, to his consternation, that "old Moore's" opponent had formally asked George Mackenzie to act for him. Mackenzie was annoyed to discover that he was likely to lose a paying client through the gift of free advice; but, with his stiff code of professional ethics, he saw no way out of the difficulty. He stood by his junior colleague's indiscreet commitments and informed Moore's opponent that he could not act for him "with propriety". In private he unburdened himself to John in what was less a reprimand than a little lecture on the economics of the legal profession. "This shows," he wrote, "the necessity you have to say nothing to anyone on business without receiving a fee in advance."[11]

Meanwhile John was getting ahead with the studies which formed the other important part of his job. He must have taken a few law books with him to Napanee; and when he applied to Mackenzie to forward a book, as he did at least once in the winter of 1833, it can hardly have been anything but a legal treatise. Yet these professional studies were evidently only a small part of his reading at this time. In the Macpherson household he had always been known as a bookworm; and now, when he was just turning eighteen, and with the literary Tom Ramsay to guide and inspire him, he plunged into a wide variety of reading—novels, history and biography, a sampling of the new books on economics and politics, and quantities of poetry. He wrote some verses; he may have tried his hand at other forms of literary composition. There was a touch of reserve about him, an evident relish in solitude, an occasional air of preoccupation in things very different from his immediate surroundings. His manner was often quiet; he could be laconic and a little stand-offish. His cousin, Helen Macpherson, noticed this, and it was, apparently, one of the few things about his pupil that bothered

Mackenzie. A genial, open-hearted, downright person himself, Mackenzie must have pondered over the mysterious complications of his pupil's character. John was a good boy—almost an exemplary boy, or he would never have been chosen for the important commission at Napanee. But was he, perhaps, a little too good—a little too quiet, reserved and bookish for his own welfare? "I do not think," he wrote in his abrupt, kindly fashion, "that you are so free and lively with the people as a young man eager for their good will should be. A dead-and-alive way with them never does." [12]

George Mackenzie knew best the boy who had lived respectfully with him at Kingston. But at Napanee, John became a young man, with all a young man's desired freedom, and at least some of his opportunities. His two best friends in the village—Tom Ramsay and the Highlander, Donald Stuart—were lively young men. The rest of the settlers—Andrew Quackenbush, the tavern-keeper, William Templeton who owned the tannery, and James Henry and Archie McNeil—were, no doubt, many of them young people, bachelors or newly married, the inevitable youthful and energetic enterprisers of a tiny pioneer community. Allan Macpherson, the "Laird of Napanee" who owned the saw- and grist-mill, and who watched over the little village with a kind of benevolent despotism, was Colonel Macpherson's eldest son by his first wife, and thus a connection of John's. He was very hospitable; and his large house, with its prim, pleasant Georgian lines, must have been opened freely and frequently to the young law student and his companions. There were parties and dances; there were long evenings of talk and jollification at Ramsay's and Quackenbush's. And on occasional Sundays, when Mr. Givens, the itinerant Anglican clergyman, visited the settlement and read service in the school-house—for there was no church—John used to sing in the choir. [13] Once out of his reserve, and in congenial company, he showed a lively and inventive gaiety. He was getting to be known for his store of anecdotes, for his burlesques and his absurdly comic improvisations. It began to seem probable that this tall, saturnine, rather ugly young man, with his reserved, studious manner, and off-hand, non-committal ways, might have a special talent for friendship, an almost creative ability for companionship and conviviality.

II

Some time in the spring or summer of 1833 John returned to Kingston. He found the town in an uproar, for during the winter the Colonial Office had made one of its sudden, well-intentioned but highly disconcerting interventions into Canadian politics. For some time past the imperial authorities had been gravely perturbed by certain actions of the legislature and government of Upper Canada. The new bank acts—the statutes which had enlarged the capital of the Bank of Upper Canada and established the Commercial Bank of the Midland District —were couched in terms which seemed inexcusably lax; and William Lyon Mackenzie, the new leader of the radical section of the Reform party, had been repeatedly expelled from the Assembly by its Conservative majority, in utter disregard of all the inconvenient precedents established by the case of John Wilkes. The Assembly, when mildly reproached about these and other matters, remained obstinately unrepentant; and the law officers of the Crown, who ought to have been anxious to support the wishes of the home government, blustered openly and defiantly against them. The Colonial Office, wearied by this insubordination and legislative incompetence, decided to act. Boulton and Hagerman, the Attorney-General and Solicitor-General, were dismissed; and it was announced that the bank acts, unless they were substantially amended, would be disallowed.

During the summer, when John had returned to Kingston, the excitement was still at its height. The town was aghast at the dismissal of its favourite son, its repeatedly elected member in the Legislative Assembly; while Francis Harper and George Mackenzie and their associates were seriously perturbed by the threatened disallowance of the charter of the Commercial Bank. Part of Kingston's resentment was almost immediately allayed, for the Colonial Office, with one of those important second

thoughts which made its name a byword for arbitrary inconsistency, reappointed Hagerman to his old post;[14] but the
danger of imperial cancellation still hung over the bank acts.
The Macpherson connection as well as Mackenzie's office was
deeply concerned in the outcome, and John must have shared
in the general perturbation. He was higher than ever in his
employer's esteem and confidence, and when, early in August,
after the assizes of the Midland District were over, Mackenzie
set out on a business trip down the river to Montreal and Quebec,
he left John in complete charge of the office. It was the most
important charge which the pupil had yet been given, and he
must have stuck closely to his task, performing the duties of
the practice with exactitude, and writing his employer a long
reassuring report which reached him at Brockville. "I am
sensible of your attention to the duties of the office," Mackenzie
replied, "and I trust that I may have it in my power to mark
my sense of your zeal and fidelity." [15]

Mackenzie's sincerity was not long to go untested. For in
that autumn of 1833 there came another small turn of John
Alexander's wheel of fortune. It was not so much an offer as
a request which he received, and it came out of the misfortunes
of the Macpherson family, the family who had given the
Macdonalds so much help, hospitality, and clannish friendliness
in the past. Lowther Pennington Macpherson, who had established himself as a lawyer in Hallowell, Prince Edward County,
became seriously ill. His malady was not one of those dreadful
and so often fatal diseases, such as cholera and tuberculosis,
which killed so many hundreds of Canadians during the migration period, but a supposedly far less dangerous illness, bron-
chitis.[16] But the provincial medical men proved mysteriously
unable to cure or even to relieve him. His cough grew chronic
and exhausting; his strength drained ominously away. There
was still assurance of recovery, if only he could obtain a period
of complete rest, if only he could find an able assistant who
would free him from the everlasting routine of the office. It was
inevitable that he should think of John. John was his cousin,
the pride of George Mackenzie's office, the successful founder
of the branch establishment at Napanee.

Mackenzie may well have hesitated. It was no time to be losing able assistants. The dreadful fate of undeserved extinction hovered over the Commercial Bank of the Midland District; and there was work and worry for all. Yet Mackenzie, as he himself had acknowledged, had a debt to pay to his pupil; and his pupil was evidently anxious to go, partly, perhaps, for financial reasons, partly for the zest of the job itself, but largely, it may be assumed, out of loyalty to his kinsmen, the Macphersons. George Mackenzie gave his consent and the way was open. Tom Ramsay wrote from Napanee, congratulating John on the "high compliment" paid to him, on "so positive a step to preferment", declaring that he didn't know which to praise more, Mackenzie's disinterestedness or Macpherson's generosity, and ending up with the rather pious hope that John would amply reward his new employer by "a vigorous employment of those talents in his service which you so fully possess".[17] The assignment was, in fact, a formidable one; Hallowell meant a good deal more responsibility than Napanee had done. For now John had a general practice, not a small branch office, to manage; and this for an employer who was ill, who needed rest, and who was soon to seek the milder air and more expert medical advice of England.

John could feel instantly and easily at home in Hallowell. The village, which stood at the end of the long narrow arm of Picton Bay, had by this time become the real centre of the Macpherson-Macdonald-Clark connection. John Alexander, the eldest Macpherson boy, who married Maria Clark in the following year,[18] lived at Hillier, a little way to the west. Hugh and Helen Macdonald were still established at the Stone Mills, which was even closer to Hallowell on the other side. And when, at about this time, old Mrs. Macpherson finally gave up the house at Kingston and took refuge in Hallowell with her married son, the family circle was virtually complete. It was pleasantly easy for the clan to gather at Hallowell under the presidency of the aged Mrs. Macpherson; easy, too, for John Alexander to slip down to the Stone Mills to visit his parents and his sisters, Moll and Lou. And the warm, intimate routine of family visits, and conferences, and occasions must have continued in much the same way as it used to do at Kingston, when the old Colonel was alive.

But, for John, Hallowell was interesting for other reasons than this. Though it was a smaller place than Kingston, it was definitely more important than the tiny pioneer village at Napanee. It was, in fact, composed of two fair-sized settlements, Hallowell and Picton, divided only by a small stream which flowed into the head of Picton Bay. Between these two sections of the same community there reigned the fiercest and most unremitting rivalry.[19] They competed for place and prominence in everything; and when, in due course, Prince Edward was made a separate judicial district, and it became necessary to build a court-house and a gaol, the two villages struggled valiantly and jealously for the possession of these important public works. In the end, through the unparalleled exertions of the Reverend William Macaulay, Picton's founder and principal squire, the smaller village won. The gaol and court-house were built in Picton and completed just about the time when John arrived to take over Lowther Pennington's practice;[20] and, despite all the wrangles they had occasioned, the new buildings were complacently regarded by the villagers as an appropriate sign of their community's coming-of-age. Hallowell was a growing place, full of bustle, and debate, and organized activity; and for these reasons all the more interesting to a young man with a zest for company and a developing interest in public affairs. At Hallowell—he turned nineteen there—his early uncertainty and diffidence began to wear off; at Hallowell, in a modest fashion, his career as an executive began. He became the first secretary of the Hallowell Young Men's Society. The Prince Edward District School Board appointed him secretary—it was his first municipal office—and he signed the board's advertisement inviting applications from prospective teachers. He even took part in an abortive effort to amalgamate the old rivals Picton and Hallowell and to christen the united village Port William, in honour of the Sailor King.[21]

Yet, despite the temporary attractions of Hallowell, the problem of his professional future became gradually more insistent. By the summer of 1834, Lowther Pennington Macpherson was back from England, still uncured of his malady and increasingly despairing about the future. "I am almost discouraged about my health," he wrote gloomily from Hillier, where he was visiting his brother. "Nothing now remains on my stomach and my cough is if anything worse. God only knows how it is to terminate." [22] John must have begun to suspect that his career as a *locum tenens* might be indefinitely prolonged. If he wished to, he might even establish himself permanently in Hallowell. But did he really want to stay? There was Kingston, as well as Hallowell—Kingston, the larger town, in which he had begun his apprenticeship, with which he was intimately associated; and at Kingston, during the summer of 1834 there occurred a tragic series of events which struck at his old employer and utterly changed his own professional prospects. The blow came at the very height of Mackenzie's career. The perplexities of 1833 were over. The Colonial Office, intimidated by the vast hubbub it had roused in Upper Canada, withdrew its threat of disallowance against the Commercial Bank. Mackenzie, victorious and successful, had achieved most of his ambitions. Was it not time now to fulfil those political expectations which his friends had held so long on his behalf? A general election—the first since 1830—was approaching, and Mackenzie was nominated as one of the Conservative candidates for Frontenac.[23] He never lived to contest the seat. In the last days of July, at the still middle point of the long hot summer, the Asiatic cholera returned to Canada, raging widely through the province, and killing with its appalling suddenness and terrible frequency. At Kingston the slaughter was at its height. There were eight burials in the Scots cemetery on the second day of the epidemic; John Machar stood waiting in the churchyard nearly the whole day for the dreary procession of coffins.[24] And a month later, when at last the violence of the plague was declining, the total dead in Kingston amounted to 265.[25] One of the long list of victims was George Mackenzie. On Sunday, August 3, a day of still, intense heat, he had sat as usual in his pew in St. Andrews Church. Before the day was out he was attacked with all the dread familiar symptoms, and by Monday morning he was dead.[26]

The tragedy helped in various ways to decide John Alexander's professional future. It must certainly have settled his immediate problem. There was no point now in an early return to Kingston, for his old master was gone and he could not recommence his apprenticeship. The only sensible thing was to stay on in Hallowell—as, indeed, his clannish loyalty prompted him to do—and round out his apprenticeship with what perfunctory supervision he could get from the ailing Lowther Pennington. For another year he stuck by his cousin's practice; he even tried to extend it, returning for a while to Napanee to recover some of the business which two years before he had tried to drum up for his old employer. And it was at Napanee, in the congenial company of Tom Ramsay and Donald Stuart, that he concocted the most elaborate of his serio-comic burlesques. The "Société de la Vache Rouge" had a political origin. In 1834 the Conservatives had lost the general elections in both Upper and Lower Canada; and in Lower Canada the victorious *Patriotes* were indulging in vaguely revolutionary gestures. The "Constitutionalists", as they called themselves, rallied pugnaciously in both provinces; and the "Société de la Vache Rouge", with its mock Gallic title and its curious mixture of medieval chivalry and Highland Scottish fervour, was, in its own absurd way, young John's riposte to the approaching revolution in the Canadas. Tom Ramsay, who was deeply read in heraldry, supplied the knightly organization with its necessary information. Donald Stuart, the young man with the royal name, was created "Lord Lyon, King of Arms"; and Helen Macpherson—"The Lady Helen o' that Ilk"—worked a banner "Sans Peur et Sans Reproche", which was presented with appropriate ceremonies at Allan Macpherson's house. That Christmas, the Christmas of 1834, John brought the whole company down with him to the Stone Mills for Christmas; and one night his mother, "Queen Helen", was enthroned with a long cardboard sword in her hand and the "Lady Helen" standing in attendance at her side, while the knights came forward one by one to do their obeisance and to make their vows.[27] Then, when it was all over and the knights were singing wassail songs, Helen Macdonald, who knew and loved Scots stories and legends, laughed until the tears ran down. It was the last Christmas but one that they were to spend at the Stone Mills. The fires burned brightly; and outside the dark trees rose behind them, tier on tier, to the crest of the mountain, and in front the waters of Adolphus Reach lay spread out still and white with ice.

By the summer of 1835 John Alexander was getting close to his majority—the solemn age at which he could be admitted to the bar. He made his decision to return to Kingston. It was true that at Hallowell he might soon be called upon—all too soon, it appeared—to succeed his cousin Lowther Pennington. But this was not the destiny he wanted. Hallowell, for all its bustle and pretensions, was only a large village. Kingston was the rival of York, the acknowledged capital of the eastern part of the province; and above all, at Kingston, there lay waiting the yet unclaimed inheritance of George Mackenzie. John, of course, was not the heir apparent. Mackenzie, dying in the brief agony of the cholera, could have made no provision for the future. But Mackenzie had liked him, valued his abilities, and given him responsible tasks; and, in the absence of any heirs of direct descent, the facts of his old employer's trust and approval were not bad credentials. And the inheritance was a prize worthy of real struggle! For Mackenzie had left not merely the obvious assets of his large practice and wide connections, but also the more intangible though no less real legacy of his genial distinction, his acknowledged prestige and the unrealized possibilities of his public career. Some time during the summer of 1835, John returned to Kingston, and on August 24 he wrote out and dated his first professional advertisement, which was printed two days later in the Kingston *Chronicle and Gazette*. "John A. Macdonald, attorney, &c," he announced, "has opened his office in the brick building belonging to Mr. Collar, opposite the shop of D. Prentiss, Esq., Quarry Street, where he will attend to all the duties of the profession."[28]

III

Store Street, which was Kingston's main avenue of commerce,

and which in due course changed itself into the through high-
way to Toronto and the West, was crossed, on its way up from
the harbour, by other streets, some of them nearly as long and
important as itself. Quarry Street was the third of these. It
was a lengthy thoroughfare which stretched from Brock Street
up to the northern suburbs, and, under the different name
of Grass Street—given in honour of Kingston's old Loyalist
founder—prolonged itself to the town limit on the south. The
shops and offices of Quarry Street were thickest towards the
centre of town; and it was here, on the east side of the short
section between Brock and Store Streets, and nearly midway
between the two, that the building belonging to Mr. Collar
stood. Unlike so many of the town's shops and houses, it was
built not of limestone, but of small neat bricks. It had the
flat, straight, severe front, the high-pitched roof, and the small
dormer windows which were characteristic of so much of Kingston's architecture. On the ground floor there were two small
shops, with a common entrance between, and twin doors set
at angles to each other.[29] And in one of these little low-ceilinged
rooms, with a window looking out on Quarry Street, young
Macdonald established his first office.

It was well situated. The coach from Toronto rattled past
him down Store Street to the post office; the market was held
a little to the south-west, on ground where the splendid municipal buildings were to be erected in the future; and the steamers
and schooners from Prescott, Port Hope, Toronto, and Hamilton lay moored at the foot of Brock and Clarence and Store
Streets. John had been away from Kingston—though not, of
course, continuously—for nearly three years; and, as he walked
about the streets, surveying his new office and the town he had
come back to conquer, he must have found a curious mixture
of hopeful and depressing portents. The great cholera epidemic
of 1834 had left Kingston in a state of numbed prostration.
The dreadful fire of November 1833[30] had been followed by
others almost equally destructive, and John did not have to
travel far from his Quarry Street office before he encountered
long stretches of desolate waste. Yet the town pulled itself
slowly together. The first year of the Quarry Street office was

a year of returning confidence and reviving hope.[31] And, from young Macdonald's point of view, the professional prospects were surely as promising as they had ever been. It was true that there were numerous lawyers, all of them senior to himself and better known. But nobody had yet incontestably occupied the proud place once held by George Mackenzie. It was a free field, full of uncertainties, but full of chances as well.

The young man who was to become so pleasantly familiar to Kingstonians in the next decade had now emerged from the awkward indecisions of adolescence. He was tall, as he had given promise of being, a lanky, loose-limbed young man, with alert, humorous eyes, a big, prominent nose, and a wide mouth that curved easily in an amused and disarming smile. He was at home, physically, in the fashions and conventions of the period. The close-cropped hair styles, so modish in the first decades of the century, with their affectation of republican simplicity, had given place to the more copious, flowing coiffures of the 1830's; but, on the other hand, whiskers and moustaches were still so rare that, to the country boys of the Midland District, they appeared almost as outlandish monstrosities. John's long, spare, oval face, with its wide cheek-bones and firm chin, was always shaven. His thick, black, curly hair rose to a crested wave on the top of his head and fell away in bushy amplitudes over his ears. He was far from being handsome; but, at the same time, he had his own odd air of distinction. He wore his best clothes—tall hat, black neckcloth, full-skirted, high-waisted coat, and checked or pale grey trousers—in a discreetly foppish manner. In his office, seated before his new desk, he fell easily into negligent, lounging postures; and outside, on Quarry Street, he carried himself in a confident, jaunty fashion.

In his first advertisement, he had described himself as an "attorney", a title he had acquired on February 5, 1835, when he was sworn in on the Attorneys' Roll, and announced that he was prepared to "attend to all the duties of the profession". The description was an aspiring one, but hardly accurate, for he had not yet been admitted to the bar. During that first autumn at Kingston, while he was waiting for the coming of his majority, he must have been busy with his books in preparation for the final ordeal; and he had scarcely passed his twenty-first birthday, on January 11, 1836, when the little office on Quarry Street achieved its proper status and took on a new air of professional consequence. Late in January or early in February he journeyed up to Toronto to confront the Benchers of the Law Society of Upper Canada; and shortly afterwards the official *Upper Canada Gazette* announced that on February 6, in the Hilary Term, 1836, John Alexander Macdonald had been admitted to the degree of Barrister at Law.[82] Less than a fortnight before, on January 27, the new barrister had acquired his first articled pupil. It was Oliver Mowat, John Mowat's eldest son.[83] The chubby boy, who had listened so attentively to John Hillyard Cameron's stories, had now become a slight, short youth of nearly sixteen, with a disarming smile and a cherubic countenance, whose expression of guileless and confiding innocence was accentuated by a pair of small circular spectacles. Small, neat, and quick, all intelligence, purpose, and assurance, Oliver Mowat was likely to be an asset in any office. But he brought much more than energy and ability to his new employer. His mere presence—the mere fact of a Mowat in the small room in Quarry Street—was, for Macdonald, a matter of incalculable importance. For John Mowat, though he would never attain to Mackenzie's eminence, was a man of some consequence in the Scottish community at Kingston. He inspired confidence and guaranteed respectability. And if he consented to send his son to Macdonald's office, did it not surely imply that Mowat and the Kingston Scots in general were coming to regard the new Quarry Street lawyer as their own professional man, the man to whom their bright boys and their business would be sent, just as they had been sent a few years before to the great George Mackenzie himself?

Moreover, Macdonald was not only a recognized professional man, but also a virtual householder. Only a year or two before, the Macpherson-Macdonald-Clark connection had seemed securely established in Prince Edward County; but now it began to shift its base back to Kingston, as a new strong centre of family unity made its appearance and as the old began noticeably to lose its cohesive power. Old Mrs. Macpherson, the Colonel's widow, had died in April, 1835, before Macdonald had left Hallowell.[34] Thomas Wilson, the Deputy Assistant Commissary-General, with his wife Anna, had set out on a series of missions which took him as far away as the West Indies, Central America and North Africa.[35] And it was while Wilson was in Jamaica, in November, 1835, that Lowther Pennington determined to visit his brother-in-law, in a last effort to seek a climate in which he could cure himself of his affliction. He never returned to Upper Canada.[36] His death and the break-up of his house and practice at Hallowell were signs that one phase of the family's history had ended; and an even more significant indication was the return of Hugh and his wife and daughters to Kingston. Hugh was only fifty-four; but his long, hopeful, erratic, and unsuccessful career had ended in the qualified failure of the Stone Mills. Francis Harper, the financial head of the connection, got him a small clerkship in the Commercial Bank; and the Macdonald family circle, which had been broken for so long by John's repeated and prolonged absences, was now again complete.[37] Yet its inner organization, if not its outward form, had been profoundly altered. Hugh was titular leader. But John was the family's real head. John was becoming an important member of the Macpherson-Macdonald-Clark connection, which, in exemplary Scottish fashion, was a tight, consciously united group organized for the protection, security, and advancement of its members.

The family was the first important association in young Macdonald's life; the second was the Scottish community at Kingston. Upper Canada was made up of such small, fairly distinct communities, for the settled homogeneous mixture of a new provincial society had not yet emerged out of the angry agitations of the migration period; and the new settlers, English, Scots, Irish, and Americans, who were almost as strange to each other as they were to their new physical environment, had yet to make their final peace with either. The Kingston Scots formed a group which was fairly typical of the others in the province, though perhaps better organized and more purposeful than most; and its Protestant members, who were in the majority, had their spiritual and intellectual centre in St. Andrews

Church. St. Andrews, which had been founded carefully "in connection with the Church of Scotland", regarded itself proudly as part of one of the two established churches of the Empire, with rights and privileges, guaranteed by the Act of Union of 1707, which were exactly coequal with those of the Church of England itself. Macdonald was made to feel that he was a member not of a dissenting sect, but of an ancient and venerable establishment, which emphasized the authority of law and history, and assumed the unity of the Empire as the basis of its claims. A son of the nineteenth, not of the eighteenth, century, he grew up in a Christian community which was mature in its organization, sober in temper, and proudly conscious of its historical traditions. If the sceptical detachment and rationalist absolutes of the Age of Reason formed no part of his experience, neither did the pious fervour and puritanical eccentricities of early nineteenth-century evangelism. He became a friend of the gentle and fastidious John Machar, who loaned him books and watched with interest over his welfare. And he was to take a modest part in promoting the interest and fighting the battles of the Kingston Presbyterians.

St. Andrews was not the only bond of union among the Kingston Scots. In the first years after Macdonald's return to the capital of the Midland District, they were founding secular organizations as well, of which the Celtic Society was the first. To a large extent these associations cut across religious divisions, and old Alexander Macdonell, the beloved Roman Catholic Bishop of Regiopolis, took an active part in their formation. Like the St. George's Societies and the Orange Order, the Scottish organizations were products of the increasingly disturbed political condition of the Canadas. The English, Scots, and Ulster settlers, worried by the growing truculence of the French Canadians and the republican demonstrations of the Upper Canadian Radicals, began to draw together for defence. At a later time, when a new "native" generation had made its appearance, their patriotism would have taken a different, more "nationalist" form; but in the 1830's, when the groups of new British immigrants, still strange to each other, were united mainly by their determination to defend British institutions against French and

American republicanism, it was natural, it was inevitable, that the old historic names should be used. The Celtic Society, like the Orange Order, which was much more powerful politically, was stoutly Conservative in politics; and when it met, in February, 1836, under president Bishop Macdonell, for its semi-annual celebration of the capture of Quebec, it toasted the Earl of Gosford, the new Governor of Lower Canada, and expressed the fervent hope that the British constitution would be "the sheet anchor of his administration".[38] Soon after Macdonald's return to Kingston, he became the Society's recording secretary; and it was he who signed its advertisement offering a gold medal for the best essay on Upper Canada as a guide for intending immigrants.[39]

Beyond the Macpherson-Macdonald connection, and St. Andrews and the Celtic Society, was Kingston as a whole and the wider world of Upper Canada. Macdonald was a young man with a lusty appetite for people, talk, debate, literary conversation, and conviviality; so it was as much his inclination as it was to his interest to increase his friendships and take a becoming part in public affairs. He had to begin modestly—even more modestly than he had at Hallowell. There were no small secretarial jobs that wanted doing; but he joined the Young Men's Society of Kingston, and debated the somewhat solemn subjects which its executive devised. And although he was too young and too little known to take a more prominent part, these small activities were making him pleasantly familiar to an increasing number of people in Kingston. The province, up to that time, had probably been a rather dim background in his life—a background only occasionally brought into sharp focus by the coming of a general election. But now, as a real political storm roared up over the horizon, Upper Canada and its affairs seemed all of a sudden to stand out with vivid clarity, lit by flashes of lightning. The political crisis in the province coincided almost exactly with his own coming-of-age, with the first beginnings of his professional life. In midwinter of 1836, when he had travelled up to Toronto to face the Benchers of the Law Society, the capital had been fluttering with excitement over the arrival of a new governor, a dapper little man with curly hair and a precise, opinionated mouth, called Sir Francis Bond Head. Within a few short months, Sir Francis had quarrelled with his Executive Council, quarrelled with the Reform Assembly, dissolved the House, and appealed, with grandiloquent gestures, to the whole province to join him in the defence of British institutions against ultra-democracy and republicanism.

The crisis was a real one, as the approaching rebellion proved; and it confirmed, beyond all doubt, the fundamental assumptions of Macdonald's political career. He had grown up in an environment in which there could be no trifling on these basic issues. Kingston, since it had been granted a separate seat in the Assembly, had invariably returned Conservative members. Old Colonel Macpherson had fought to preserve a united Empire, and there was no doubt about the political allegiance of the Macdonalds and Macphersons. George Mackenzie had been a Conservative; and St. Andrews Church and the Celtic Society, when it came to a plain question of the survival of the Canadas as British provinces, flung the full weight of their support in favour of the "Constitutional" cause. In the general election of June, 1836, the entire Midland District—Kingston itself, Frontenac, Lennox and Addington, Hastings, and Prince Edward—went solidly Conservative.[40] And on Thursday night, June 30, when it finally became certain that the Reform candidates in Lennox and Addington had gone down to defeat, the citizens of Kingston assembled on the commons to light triumphal bonfires and to cheer for their "glorious emancipation from the fangs of a ruthless and revolutionary party".[41]

And yet, though Kingston and the Kingston Scots stood squarely in support of constitutional rule and the British connection, they were not entirely comfortable inside the old Tory party, nor entirely submissive to its old leadership. And these reservations and qualifications—just as much as the basic loyalties which they modified—were an important part of the political tradition which Macdonald inherited. Kingston had never relished the political leadership of Toronto; the Kingston Scots had always been sensitively resentful of the ecclesiastical claims of the Church of England; and, to both town and kirk, the rule of the so-called "Family Compact", most of whose members were

both Torontonians and Anglicans, could, on occasion, be violently
objectionable. There came a day, in February, 1837, when
even Christopher Alexander Hagerman, Kingston's own member
in the Assembly, and Kingston's representative in the provincial government, turned savagely upon his old allies, the
Presbyterian Scots. Some of the Presbyterians had just presented
a new petition in which they had vindicated once more the
status of the Church of Scotland as one of the established
churches of the Empire, and reasserted its claim, along with that
of the Church of England, to a portion of the revenues of the
Clergy Reserves—the lands set apart by the Constitutional Act of
1791 for the support of a Protestant Clergy.[42] Hagerman, with a
pugnacious and pontifical manner reminiscent at once of the
pulpit, the schoolroom, and the parade ground, fell upon this
petition, overwhelmed it with invective, abuse, and ferocious
banter, and contemptuously reduced the Presbyterians to the
humiliating level of mere tolerated sectaries.[43] The Kingston
Scots were aghast. In March, St. Andrews met, in the greatest
agitation, to record its disapproval and restate its position.[44] In
April a general meeting of the Presbyterian churches—to which
Francis Harper was sent as the Kingston delegate—assembled
at Cobourg to take action; and William Morris was sent over
to England to plead the cause of the Church of Scotland at the
Colonial Office. Even the Quarry Street office took an unobtrusive part in this affair, for Oliver Mowat seconded one of
the resolutions passed at the meeting at St. Andrews; and, although Macdonald did not participate in this fashion, it was
not, as subsequent events clearly proved, because of any luke-
warmness in his support of the Presbyterian cause. He must
have shared the angry disappointment at Hagerman's betrayal
of his old friends. He had come of age in a community which
was British and Conservative yet sharply critical of Toronto
Toryism.

IV

During the summer of 1837, while the political situation in
the province went from bad to worse, and while the banking

crisis and the commercial depression heightened the ge
feeling of miserable uncertainty, Macdonald approached t
second anniversary of the opening of his office. For him, as
for any young ambitious lawyer at the time, it was essential to
make a name in the courts. But he had gone on for two years
now, relatively unnoticed, without the prestige or notoriety of
an exciting case; and to his cronies in the Young Men's Society
he was probably better known for his love of books and fondness
for conversation and debate than for the depth of his legal
knowledge or for the expertness of his court-room strategy.
Then, in the autumn of 1837, came a significant change. The
assizes of the Midland District opened; and in a long, rather
dull docket, the one really exciting item was a horrible case of
the rape of a child. William Henry Draper, the new Solicitor-
General—Hagerman had been promoted to the attorney-generalship—prosecuted for the Crown; and the defence of the accused
man, William Brass, fell to Henry Cassady and young Macdonald. In the circumstances, the outcome of the trial was almost
a certainty; and the accomplished Draper, sure of his verdict,
approached the prosecution with that air of restraint, of dignified moderation, and judicious impartiality which was so
characteristic of him. Macdonald could not save William Brass
from the death sentence; but he evidently made a prolonged
and adroit effort on his behalf. One of the local newspapers,
in a flattering paragraph, described the defence as "ingenious,
reflecting credit upon a young member of the bar".[45] And for
the first time, apparently, it began to be noticed that this tall,
ugly, genial young man seemed to possess a curiously winning
way with juries and a casual but cunning expertness in the
management of a case.

People still had time to be interested in this modest professional triumph, despite the rising clamour of political agitation in the province as a whole. Kingston itself seemed completely at peace. Early in August, in the presence of a great
crowd of officials and citizens, Richard Bullock, the sheriff of
the Midland District, proclaimed the accession of the young
Queen Victoria. The whole district—the entire eastern part of
the province—appeared settled in its loyalty, relatively unper-

...nously rising excitement about Toronto, and
...t the prospect of serious trouble in the sister
...ver Canada. On October 31, eight days after
...nadians had held their vast assemblies at Mon-
...Charles, over 250 grave and determined heads of
hou... ...Kingston, among them Hugh Macdonald, signed
a petition ...questing Richard Bullock to call a public meeting
in order that they might "take into consideration the peculiar
situation of affairs in Lower Canada".[46] Three days later the
meeting was held; and the assembled Kingstonians resolved that
"We cannot any longer defer the declaration of our determination to support with our lives and fortunes the supremacy of
the British Constitution and the just dependence of the Canadas
upon the British Crown".[47] It was Thursday, November 2;
and on the very next night the Kingston Young Men's Society,
with a fine independence of contemporary agitations, assembled
for its opening "soirée" of the autumn, elected Macdonald its
president and Oliver Mowat its recording secretary, and announced that the first subject of debate in the winter programme
would be: "Are the works of Nature sufficient in themselves to
prove the existence of a Supreme Being?"[48]

On Monday, November 6, before the Society ever got down
to its serious debate, the long-awaited clash between the *Patriotes*
and the Constitutionalists occurred in Montreal. All during
November, while the news of rebel concentrations and troop
movements drifted slowly in, the eyes of everybody in Kingston were fixed on Lower Canada, and all the regular troops in
the province had been sent there. The militia had not yet been
called up, and although the Frontenac Light Dragoons, a voluntary troop of horsemen, trotted with ostentatious loyalty through
the streets of Kingston, everybody expected that, if the Dragoons
were used at all, they would be used against the French Canadians. One editor reflected proudly that "if called into active
service under their gallant commander they will soon bring the
affairs of Jean Baptiste into a pretty narrow focus".[49] Even this
possibility seemed more and more unlikely as the troubled month
drew to its close. The news of the battles of St. Charles and
St. Denis, fought on November 23 and November 25, came

into town in confused but increasingly reassuring batches. By the beginning of December it seemed perfectly clear that the rebels had been routed and that their leaders had fled headlong into exile.

On Wednesday morning, December 6, in the midst of this satisfied calm, the regular stage coach from the west, which had left Toronto on Sunday, arrived in Kingston. It bore alarming news—all the more alarming since it was now three days old.[50] The Radicals—so the report ran—had been seen drilling, in large numbers, to the north of Toronto. An attack on the city had been feared on the previous Saturday and it was expected that on Monday the Lieutenant-Governor would issue a proclamation calling up the militia for duty. All day the news spread; all day the town waited anxiously; and the early December dark was already falling when another stage—an express direct from Toronto—clattered down Store Street to the post office.[51] This time the news was both definite and stupendous. The rebels to the number of about 400 had assembled with arms within a few miles of Toronto and an attack on the capital was hourly expected. Now, in peaceful Upper Canada, the revolt had broken out.

Chapter Three

First Public Appearances

I

That night, only an hour or so after the stage had brought the tidings of the rebellion, the magistrates called a meeting of the citizens at the court-house. The regular troops had left for Lower Canada. Apart from a few small detachments of Royal Artillery and Royal Engineers, there were no imperial soldiers in Kingston; and there, as elsewhere in the province, it was the plain citizens who rushed together, in a great spontaneous movement, to improvise their own defence. On the first night, in a strange atmosphere of ignorance, and worry and excitement, only the sketchiest arrangements could be made. The town was divided into wards for protective purposes; the townsmen were hurriedly enrolled and armed; and all night long, stout patrols, each headed by a magistrate, tramped through the echoing streets.[1] The next morning, Thursday, the steamboat *Traveller* arrived from Toronto, bringing the welcome news that the Gore Militia had landed at the capital the day before, and that the rapidly growing citizen army would probably soon take the offensive against the rebels. Arms, ammunition, and a couple of field pieces—all watched over by a strong, volunteer guard—were despatched back to Toronto by the *Traveller*.[2] But the first duty of Kingston, Frontenac County, and the Midland District generally was to defend Fort Henry and the naval base, and to secure the eastern part of the province. Actually, there was no danger east of Toronto; and at Toronto itself—on the day before the *Traveller* returned with its consignment of arms—the little amateur army of farmers, mechanics, and professional men which had gathered at the capital marched north up Yonge Street and easily scattered Mackenzie's dwindling forces. But in those first excited, bewildered days, precise news came slowly and vague rumours spread with incredible rapidity. And rebellion, which had not been seriously feared even at Toronto, was now expected almost anywhere and everywhere in the province.

Macdonald was, of course, a member of the Sedentary Militia. Every able-bodied male in the province, between the ages of eighteen and sixty, was, by law at least, a member of the Sedentary Militia. It was a vast, cumbrous, and, in many ways, a comically inefficient organization, which existed not so much to give the population an adequate military training—there was neither time nor money for that—as to acquaint the inhabitants with their responsibilities for the defence of the province and to muster them swiftly in times of actual danger. Once every year, on "training day"—June 4, George III's birthday—the awkward files of farmers and mechanics went through a few cheerfully simple manoeuvres in response to the uncertain orders of their amateur officers; and then everybody gratefully adjourned, in the pleasant June sunshine, for sports, picnics, robustious drinking, and general jollification.[8] Nothing could have been more chaotically unprofessional; but, at the same time, nothing could have been closer to the people of the small, half-organized province, or more suitable as a vehicle for their own angry determination, and the rough simple task they had in hand. In the ten days that followed the coming of the news of the rebellion, the two Frontenac regiments mustered companies; a company of Lennox and Addington Militia tramped into Kingston; and other eager citizens, not included in the regular militia formations, were joining independent companies, and volunteering as marines and artillerymen and civic guards. There were detachments at Fort Henry, at Point Frederick, at the Tête du Pont barracks, and at the blockhouses about the town; and in Kingston itself, the Frontenac Dragoons, careering about valiantly on horseback, were regarded complacently as "indefatigable".[4] Kingston was proud of its hastily collected, amateur army of over 500 men; and the "loyal ladies" of the town, meeting at Mrs. Harper's, at the Commercial Bank, quickly raised £44 to buy a set of colours for their husbands and sons in the Frontenac Militia.

Macdonald shouldered his musket with the rest. His professional friends, his cronies in the Young Men's Society, his relations, and his fellow-members of St. Andrews Church were prominent in Kingston's citizen army, some of them as officers.[5] Macdonald himself was considered for promotion when a new regiment, the Third or East Frontenac Regiment was formed in the following month, January, 1838. His name, with that of one of his best friends, Charles Stuart, immediately below, headed the list of those who were recommended as ensigns in the new regiment.[6] In the end, his appointment did not take place, for reasons which are unknown;[7] but it is possible that Macdonald—a virtual householder, with a family largely dependent upon him—may have pleaded his responsibilities as an excuse from the additional duty. In any event, he and fellow-privates and officers had comparatively little to do. There was, no doubt, some drill and target-practice, some marching and counter-marching; and long afterward Macdonald remembered vividly one gruelling march in which, though weary with the weight of his heavy musket, he had managed to keep up with his companion, "a grim old soldier who seemed impervious to fatigue".[8] But there was no fighting whatever, for the whole eastern part of the province was tranquilly loyal. West of Toronto, the disturbances continued for a little while longer, and there was some rather officious rebel-hunting; but, in effect, the rebellion collapsed on December 7, in the little skirmish on Yonge Street. Within a week the people of Upper Canada, by their own efforts and without the slightest professional military assistance, had overwhelmed a small internal revolt.

Yet, despite the conclusive defeat of the rebellion, the turmoil into which it had plunged the province lasted fully twelve months more. The tiny battle on Yonge Street, and the flight of Mackenzie and a few other fugitives across the border sufficed to rouse, in the northern United States, a mass of uninformed, credulous, and violently anti-British opinion, which for a year kept the international boundary in a state of actual or threatened violence. Inspired by the impulse to liberate the "oppressed" Canadians, to assist a republican movement which had scarcely ever had any real existence, large bodies of American citizens periodically assembled and armed themselves with little or no concealment, for the invasion of Canada. And on half a dozen occasions, while the military authorities of the northern states looked on with benevolent detachment, and while a few zealous American federal officers and a handful of federal troops struggled vainly to preserve their country's neutrality, these American "sympathizers"—these "pirates" or "bandits" as the Canadians called them—actually succeeded in carrying out raids on Canadian territory. The "rebellion", as a native uprising, had lasted only a matter of days; now it threatened to continue indefinitely as an undeclared guerilla war with the citizens of the northern United States. "It may be also safely affirmed," wrote the editor of one Kingston newspaper, "that had not some of the Americans taken by the hand a few discomfited leaders of the late rebellion, the inhabitants of Upper Canada would, within the short period of a week, without military aid, and almost without bloodshed, have extirpated this miserable faction, and have again returned to their peaceful and happy homes."[9]

The citizens of Kingston were not at first directly affected by these excitements on the frontier, for the first of the "pirate" bases was established, during December, 1837 and January, 1838, on Navy Island, in the Niagara River. But in February the danger began to spread eastward, towards the St. Lawrence River, directly threatening Kingston. During the third week of February, startling reports of the pillage of the Watertown arsenal, of "bandit" assemblies and drilling, began to filter into town;[10] and on February 22—what more appropriate day for the enterprise could have been chosen than Washington's birthday?—the "sympathizers" began to gather at the mouth of French Creek, a stream flowing into the St. Lawrence from the American side, nearly opposite to Gananoque. The Kingston garrison of British regulars had not yet returned, and once again the town was dependent upon its own citizen army. The whole Midland District rallied for the defence. The Frontenac Militia was called out, and militia regiments and volunteer companies from Hastings, and from Lennox and Addington moved into town to their support. Macdonald and his friends and relatives were almost certainly among the 1500 militiamen and armed civilians who assembled in Kingston on that February day; and, in the late afternoon, part of the little force marched out to occupy advanced positions along the shore and in some of the neighbouring Canadian islands.[11] In the gathering darkness the amateur soldiers waited in vain. The tiny "army" of American "sympathizers", watched by an enthusiastic crowd of spectators from New York State, did not finally get under way until the day was far advanced. It moved—only 300 to 500 strong—from Grindstone Island, safe in American jurisdiction, to Hickory Island, on the Canadian side. It was dark by now. The island was shelterless and it was February. The invaders fell back to the American side with such expedition that they left a good part of their supplies and accoutrements behind.[12]

For Macdonald and his generation, this was the first affair, since the troubles in the Canadas had begun, which had brought with it any real prospect of fighting. The danger had come not from their own discontented fellow-subjects, but from some bellicose citizens of northern New York State; and from then on, the "American sympathizer" became the chief object of the baffled indignation of the Kingstonians. In March, when the first round of raids was over, and when a great crowd assembled one evening in the Kingston market place to hang and burn their enemies in effigy, the symbolic figure of the United States was singled out for special treatment. At seven o'clock, eight stuffed figures were strung up on a tall gallows before an amused and satisfied crowd of thousands. It was a curious collection of criminals. The English Philosophical Radicals—Hume, Grote, Molesworth, Leader, and Roebuck—hung dangling beside the Canadian rebels Mackenzie and Papineau. A special place, outside the main gallows, was given to Uncle Sam or "Brother Jonathan the Sympathizer". He was "a tall, gaunt figure—real Connecticut phiz—green spectacles—white hat, with a streamer of black crape—a dapper cloak—in short, what our readers may readily consider a real republican of the old school, full of the recollections of the rebellion of '76, modernized into the infamous sympathizer, ready for pelf and plunder".[18] Dangling by himself, holding the placards "sham neutrality" and "authorized sympathy" in his limp hands, he was not even judged a fit participant of "honour among thieves" and even in this simple fact, as the editor carefully explained to his readers, there was exhibited that deep-seated sense of injury at the "vile conduct of our detestable neighbours".

II

In March and April, Macdonald, like the other young men of Kingston, could begin to think once more of his own affairs. The rebellion was over, and the border seemed quiet again. The night watches in Kingston were given up, and the zealous, inexpert militiamen returned to their homes. Sir Francis Bond Head, the Governor of the rebellion period, passed through Kingston on his way back to England; and everybody knew now that John George Lambton, Lord Durham, had been appointed Governor-in-Chief and High Commissioner to inquire into the affairs of British North America. Things were settling down to something like their old courses, amid a flurry of talk and speculation about the political future. Nobody knew, of course, what was going to happen to Upper Canada, though some of the Kingston Conservatives were already disturbed by slight misgivings; but Kingston, at any rate, was given a new and more appropriate status in the spring of 1838. In the opinion of the townsmen, it was high time. Other towns, far less important than Kingston, had recently been created municipalities, and it was four years now since the old rival York had been made a city and rechristened Toronto. Now, at length, Kingston was granted self-government, and on March 24, the first civic elections took place.[14] Macdonald was not a candidate —that would come later—but he was important enough to be associated, in a minor way, with this first stage in the history of the new municipality. He was appointed returning officer for Ward Three, and duly declared Edward Noble and Walter McCuniffe elected.[15]

As spring went on, the premature sense of returning peace and security grew stronger. Actually, it was during May that the Hunters' Lodges, the most formidable of all the secret associations formed for the forcible republicanization of Canada, began to spread outward from Vermont through the northern American states.[16] But the Canadians were, as yet, blissfully unaware of these developments, and in Kingston people went about their ways with confidence. Early in May, the 83rd Regiment, with Colonel the Honourable Henry Dundas in command, arrived in town to occupy Fort Henry; and when it turned out for its first church parade, the Kingstonians, listening to the splendid band and watching the long, reassuring lines of red-coats, felt agreeably confirmed in their new sense of security.[17] On May 17—it was one of the last sessions under Macdonald's presidency—the Young Men's Society met to debate the practical professional question: "How far is circumstantial evidence to be admitted as constituting satisfactory evidence, and what objections bear against the admission of circumstantial evidence generally?"[18]

Ten days later, on May 27, the *Hastings* dropped anchor off Quebec; and on May 29, Lord Durham, mounted on his fine white horse, rode up to the old Castle of St. Louis. The post rebellion settlement of the Canadas was obviously about to commence; and the Kingston Conservatives were impressed but not entirely reassured by the reputation of the nobleman who had been appointed to direct it. Lord Durham's record as a Radical Whig was certainly disquieting. The highly dubious morals of some of the members of his staff—Edward Gibbon Wakefield's elopements and Thomas Turton's infidelities—must have shocked the sober Christians of St. Andrews Church. And it was perturbing, as well as annoying, to see the jaunty confidence with which the Canadian Radicals tried to appropriate Lord Durham.[19] The doubts and misgivings grew; and, with Durham's first important public actions, they were turned into positive apprehensions. On June 28, which was observed throughout the province as Queen Victoria's coronation day, the citizens of Kingston assembled at block-house No. 3 to watch the "loyal ladies"—represented by Mrs. Smith, Mrs. Harper, and Mrs. Kirby—present the colours they had procured from England to the First Frontenac Regiment of Militia.[20] On the same day, at Quebec, Durham issued the famous Royal Proclamation which granted an amnesty to the great mass of the political prisoners in Lower Canada, and sentenced the small remainder to exile in Bermuda. The Conservatives were shocked by this prodigal clemency; a few newspapers ventured a mild protest. But in general the Upper Canadians choked back their alarms. They were waiting for Durham. It was most strange that he had not yet visited the province. It was July now and he had been in the Canadas two months.

In all this process of settlement, a young lawyer like Macdonald, with a small provincial practice, could expect to take only a very modest part. There was, of course, plenty of professional work—conspicuous, if not profitable, professional work —to be done. The gaols, particularly the Toronto gaols, were crowded—so crowded that the authorities despatched to Fort Henry at Kingston a small batch of political prisoners, including John Montgomery, the innkeeper at whose Yonge Street tavern Mackenzie's rebels had congregated. But the great political trials were Toronto trials, monopolized by the lawyers of the capital; and the Midland District, which had been relatively so unaffected by the rebellion, produced only one important treason case during the busy judicial summer of 1838. Macdonald took it, and took it this time alone. Eight men—residents apparently of Hastings, and Lennox and Addington Counties—were arraigned before Mr. Justice McLean in the first week in July.[21] The case against them looked dark enough. Some of them had been caught with arms in their hands; some had been persuaded or coerced by a vigorous, officious magistrate to sign affidavits in which they had sworn to their guilt. And the Kingston townsfolk clearly expected a verdict of guilty. But there was a new spirit of clemency abroad, affecting both courts and juries. John S. Cartwright, who prosecuted for the Crown, allowed the prisoners a good deal of indulgence; and Macdonald's defence was skilful. The compromising affidavits were summarily rejected as an outrage upon the administration of justice; the witnesses for the Crown, under close cross-examination, broke down and began to contradict each other; and the prosecution failed to establish any deliberate continuity of purpose on the part of the accused. To the very last, the outcome was uncertain. On the four most important of the cases, the jury was out from Saturday afternoon until Monday evening. But at last it brought in a verdict of not guilty, and in the end all the prisoners were acquitted. One young man sitting in the court and watching the trial's climax with absorbed interest remembered Macdonald's "marked triumph" long afterward;[22] and a Kingston newspaper informed its readers that "the prisoners were defended with much ingenuity and ability by Mr. J. A. Macdonald, who, though one of the youngest barristers in the Province, is rapidly rising in his profession".[23]

Macdonald could afford to feel pleasantly satisfied. For him, the post-rebellion settlement had not been very rich in professional chances. But he had been given one; he had taken it; and the result had perceptibly raised his prestige. The only trouble was that the period for such opportunities seemed now to be over; and, indeed, the whole grand investigation of Upper Canada, to which everybody had looked forward eagerly and anxiously, appeared to be coming to a sudden and unexpected end. For weeks the Upper Canadians had waited for Lord Durham; for weeks—for months—he had remained fixed in Quebec. And then, with almost unceremonious precipitation, he began to move west. On July 10, he left Montreal. On July 11, at about midnight, nearly twenty-four hours before he was expected, he arrived in Kingston by the steamer *Brockville* to find most of the town in darkness and a somewhat hastily improvised guard of honour drawn up on the dock to receive him. The next day it was rather better. At about the middle of the morning two barges, tastefully protected by awnings from the July sun, carried the Governor-General and his suite out from the Clarence Street dock for a tour of the harbour and its military and naval establishments. Lord Durham visited the dock-yard, inspected Fort Henry, cantered back across the penny bridge on his white horse, ate an expeditious lunch at the British American Hotel, and then, in the early afternoon, boarded the *Cobourg* and was off up the lake to Niagara.[24] What followed was even more disconcerting. The Kingstonians had barely time to learn that Her Majesty's High Commissioner had stayed a few days at Niagara, like any other tourist, and that he had cut short his visit to Toronto to twenty-four hours, when the vice-regal steamer, with Lord Durham on board, was back again in Kingston harbour! This time—it was Friday, July 20—Lady Durham did not trouble to go ashore, as a brief visit only was intended. A respectable guard of honour attended the Governor-General, and John S. Cartwright, Chairman of the Quarter Sessions, presented an address of welcome.[25] Then, after only a few hours delay, the *Cobourg* steamed off down the river for Prescott. The grand tour of Upper Canada was over, and Kingston sank back again into its midsummer repose.

It did not remain there long. Fewer than ten days later an astounding event occurred, which instantly revived all the old political excitement, and presented Macdonald with a curious, and slightly dangerous professional opportunity.

III

The night of Sunday, July 29, was violent with a prolonged summer thunderstorm. And when, after hours of blinding rain and crashing thunder, the summer day broke clear, wet and fresh, it was discovered that the fifteen political prisoners, newly incarcerated at Fort Henry, had broken out and had apparently got clear away. Their tortuous route out through the fortifications was easily traced. They had cleverly taken advantage of every characteristic feature of a building which was designed, not to keep people in, but to keep them out. It was a completely successful gaol-break. Yet it was obvious that it could not possibly have succeeded without somebody's assistance and advice.[26] The rough tools which the prisoners had used—a flat bar of iron, a long, poker-like spike, a makeshift lantern, and a primitive ladder constructed by cutting toeholds in a plank or "banquette"—could hardly have been secured without help; and when a rough plan of the fort and its underground passages was discovered in the prisoners' casemate, that put the matter beyond any possible doubt. There had been an accomplice, or accomplices, inside the fort. Somebody had helped the prisoners to escape.

This was the sub-plot inside the main drama of the gaol-break; and it was the sub-plot which involved Macdonald. Things happened fast on that Monday morning, July 23. Colonel Dundas, rushing to the fort in angry agitation, surveyed the evidence with mounting suspicion and quickly decided that the prisoners must have been aided and abetted in their escape. Almost as quickly—too quickly—he came to the conclusion that John Ashley, the gaoler whom the sheriff had appointed to look after these civilian prisoners, must be the guilty man. Ashley was arrested as soon as he appeared at the fort that morning. He spent almost eight hours in the guardhouse before a warrant was finally secured for his arrest; and very shortly after his detention was finally legalized, he was released by the magistrates on the ground that there was no case against him whatever.[27] Here the matter might have been dropped—an unfortunate accident, the consequence of legitimate, if excessive, zeal. But Ashley was not prepared to let it drop. He was a sober citizen, a respectable church-goer, who valued his reputation and had not enjoyed his eight hours' detention in the guardhouse. He promptly brought suit against Colonel Dundas for illegal arrest, and he engaged Henry Smith, Jr. and John Macdonald as his legal advisers.

The case came up at the autumn assizes of the Midland District before Mr. Justice McLean.[28] It was a major sensation in Kingston; and as he watched the crowded court-room on the evening of September 18, Macdonald may very well have wondered not merely whether success was possible, but also whether it was even desirable, in either Ashley's interest or his own. Arrayed against them were the two sacred symbolic figures of law and order. Dundas was the town's protector, the Commandant of the garrison; and for his counsel he had secured no less a person than Christopher Alexander Hagerman, the member for Kingston, the Attorney-General of the province, with all his prestige, his eloquence, and the pugnacious, masterful confidence of his manner. It was a formidable combination. Hagerman, the town's most distinguished legal authority, had a case in which he sincerely believed, both personally and professionally; and Dundas, Colonel of the 83rd, the regiment which had been welcomed with such relief and gratitude a few months before, was the indispensable military leader upon whom the whole of Kingston relied. Perhaps he had acted a little hastily —but out of excess of zeal, not malice. Perhaps he had failed for too long to secure the necessary warrant—but there were unfortunate circumstances which would amply account for the delay. He was a plain soldier, trying to do his duty in a sudden crisis, in the midst of a troubled period of rebellion and raids.

Yet, at the same time, Ashley undeniably had a case. His arrest had been ordered summarily, after what must have been a very cursory examination; and so solid was his reputation in Kingston that the three highly respectable magistrates—John S. Cartwright, John Mowat, and Alexander Pringle—who had accompanied him out to the fort, were astonished when he was suddenly torn from their midst and clapped in gaol. Their astonishment, moreover, was very quickly confirmed, when once they began an investigation into the escape. They discovered, beyond any possibility of doubt, that the guilty accessories to the gaol-break were two men employed in the engineering department at the fort, Organ, a master carpenter, and a casual labourer named Davis.[29] There never had been any basis for the Colonel's suspicions; there was no excuse—not even the need of organizing the pursuit of the escaped prisoners—which could justify his failure to seek a warrant, once the fatal order had been given. All day Ashley's lawyers sought to drive these points home. Macdonald, who acted in support of Smith, apparently pursued the military in general and Colonel Dundas in particular with a disrespectfully incisive vigour which was long remembered by at least one of the listeners in the courtroom;[30] and a Kingston newspaper remarked, with almost un-

willing admiration, that the young barrister "displayed much
ingenuity and legal knowledge during the trial".[81] This, however, did not greatly impress the court. Mr. Justice McLean, in
his summing up, tried to direct the attention of the jury to the
"true matter at issue" which, according to him, was "whether
the arrest was made by Colonel Dundas under a conviction that
he was faithfully discharging his duty, or whether he was
actuated by malicious or vindictive feelings". After that, every
unprejudiced person could hardly fail to reach the conclusion
that a verdict should be returned for the defendant. But the
jury—the jury of plain people whom Macdonald was learning
to influence and convince—decided otherwise. The original
arrest, they found, was justifiable. But the long, unwarranted
detention in the guardhouse was an excess for which Dundas
was ultimately responsible. And they awarded Ashley damages
of £200.

The trial was an important episode in Macdonald's career.
He was now a fairly conspicuous young man—noticed, and yet
not marked, for nothing could be said against him. He had
simply done his professional duty; he had acted a legitimate, a
necessary, part, in the venerable processes of British justice. The
officers at Fort Henry and Tête du Pont barracks might grind
their teeth at his irreverent treatment of soldiers; the sober,
conservative citizens of Kingston might shake their heads in
bewilderment, if not disapproval, at the decision in *Ashley* vs.
Dundas. But the finger of public scorn and indignation could
not be levelled at Macdonald. His professional reputation had
not been undermined; it had probably grown stronger and more
secure. Yet, at the same time, it had been slightly, subtly, but
unmistakably changed. He had been associated, if he had not
been identified, with the liberties of the subject, with the defence
of the plain people against the encroachments of military power.
The solid blue of his inherited conservatism was varied now,
in a pleasantly interesting fashion, with a few threads of a different and livelier colour.

IV

It was at this point, when the political trials were over and
when the first phase of the post-Rebellion reconstruction seemed
at an end, that the troubles of the Canadas recommenced. In
the very week in which the trial of *Ashley* vs. *Dundas* took
place, two highly significant events occurred. On September
19, the day after Smith and Macdonald had won their verdict,
Lord Durham received at Quebec the shattering news that his
ordinance, exiling the state prisoners to Bermuda, had been
disallowed by the Melbourne government in England; and on
Sunday, September 16, two days before the Ashley affair, the
Hunters' Society held the first session of its Cleveland convention, at which plans were adopted for concerted raids upon the
Canadas.[32] The news of Lord Durham's imminent return to
England, which very soon became public property, was bewailed
by almost everybody in the Canadas without distinction of race
or class or political affiliation; but the sense of resentment and
indignation at the Governor's betrayal, which even the Conservatives shared, was very quickly followed by other and graver
feelings of apprehension for the political future. Barely a week
had elapsed since the pro-Durham meeting at Kingston, before
the familiar, the too familiar, reports from the south began to
spread once more.[33] The whole border was in an ominous fer-
ment; and by October 10 the Kingston and Prescott newspapers were warning their readers that some of the most active
preparations for invasion were apparently going on along the
shore of Lake Ontario and the upper St. Lawrence River, in
the region between Syracuse and Ogdensburg. The Midland
District pulled itself together once again for defence. It was a
familiar exercise, which up to that time had been rather frustrating. But apparently it had not lost its zest.

The Sedentary Militia was not called out—even in part—
until October 23; but, in the meantime, there were various
ways in which young men like Macdonald could satisfy their
need for training and practice. During the troubled year 1838
a number of the militia regiments, particularly those in the
exposed border counties, organized so-called "flank companies",

which were kept as far as possible in a state of readiness for
instant action. And in addition, independent, volunteer companies, which served without pay and allowances, were formed
fairly frequently, some of them with official approval—such as
the Kingston company which the new Governor, Sir George
Arthur, sanctioned on October 15—and some, perhaps, without. The little, highly irregular unit, the "Société de la Vache
Rouge", was the first of these extra-official organizations to
which Macdonald belonged; the second, similar to the first in
its Scottish character, but far more resplendent, was organized
at Kingston in the autumn of 1838. It went by the resounding
name of the "Loyal Scotch Volunteer Independent Light In-
fantry Company", and its uniform was Highland feather bonnets, blue jackets, and Royal Stuart trews. Alexander McNabb,
a member in good standing of St. Andrews and an officer in the
Frontenac Militia, was the unofficial captain; and Macdonald
stood side by side in the ranks with Oliver Mowat and William
Gunn.[34]

By the last week in October, when the long, mild, rainy
autumn turned sharply to frost and snow, the reports of assemblies and drilling on the American side became more frequent and detailed. On November 1—the very day that
Durham boarded the *Inconstant* for England—the Kingstonians
assembled in public meeting, divided the town into five wards
for protective purposes and re-established the night watch which
had been formed first nearly a year before.[35] Four days later, Sir
George Arthur issued his proclamation warning the people of the
possibility of invasion, and attempting at the same time to appeal
to their patriotism and allay their fears.[36] The second regiment of
the Frontenac Militia was called out; the volunteer company of
artillery was stationed at Fort Henry; over 500 citizens were
armed; and at night the civic guard perambulated the town and
cavalry patrols trotted through the silent streets.[37] Still the days
went by and nothing happened. Periods of the wildest excitement alternated with periods of complete scepticism. And, as
late as Monday, November 12, a Kingston newspaper could
still predict that there would be no invasion from the United
States until the New Year. Actually it was on Sunday, the
previous day, that the steamer *United States*, crowded with a

suspiciously large number of male travellers and heavily freighted with bulky pieces of luggage, was moving down the river on her adventurous journey from Oswego to Ogdensburg, taking on passengers at every stop.[38] Kingston might have learnt the truth earlier. But the Americans detained the Wolfe Island Ferry at Cape Vincent, in order to prevent the news from reaching the Canadian side. And it was late on Monday before the Kingstonians began to realize the tremendous fact that the invasion was under way, and that the invaders had probably landed already, sixty miles down the river, at Prescott.

Late that night, Captain Sandom, R.N., set out for Prescott with his little armed flotilla, the steamer *Victoria* and the schooner *Cobourg*; and early next morning, Tuesday, the *Brockville* and *Kingston*, with Colonel Dundas and four companies of 83rd on board, moved off down the river from Kingston harbour.[39] Once more the Midland District was left to defend its own capital. Late on Tuesday, the clear, still weather broke, and snow came swirling out of the north-west in the wake of a stiff wind. But all day the Frontenac Militia was mustering; and on Wednesday, with snow and freezing rain still falling, companies of four Lennox and Addington regiments tramped into town.[40] By this time people knew that the Pirates, repulsed at Prescott town, had made a landing about a mile and a half farther down the river at Windmill Point, and that on Tuesday morning, before the arrival of Dundas and his reinforcements, the Johnstown Militia had marched out to meet them. Late Wednesday night, when Colonel Dundas and the companies of the 83rd returned unexpectedly to Kingston, the town learnt, in official detail, of the bloody little battle at the windmill and its outcome. The militia, with the assistance of a few regulars, had captured the outbuildings from the Pirates; but they had spent themselves in vain in futile charges against the ponderous stone walls of the windmill. About sixty of all ranks had been wounded, and sixteen killed; and one of the corpses, that of a Lieutenant Johnston, was subsequently discovered to have been mutilated, supposedly by the invaders. Dundas had determined not to risk any more lives; he had come back to Kingston to await the arrival of heavy artillery from Toronto. In the meantime—the Kingstonians learnt to their satisfaction—the Bandits

were cooped up in the mill and its stone outbuildings, closely
surrounded by the militia, without hope of release and without
prospect of reinforcement. At the appropriate moment they
could be destroyed.

Late Thursday afternoon—nearly twenty-four hours later—
the *Brockville* and *Kingston* churned their way out from the
docks once again, with Dundas, and the 83rd, and two eighteen-
pounders and a howitzer on board.[41] The town, crowded with
militia and tense with excitement, settled down to wait as best
it could. Friday passed by. The hours on Saturday crawled
along with heavy slowness; but by this time rumours of a victory
and the capture of the Bandits had begun to filter in from the
east and, long after night had fallen, the town stayed up, waiting
and expectant. It was nearly midnight when across the dark
harbour the citizens could see at last the twinkling lights of the
approaching steamers. The houses were illuminated; the crowd
rushed down Brock Street to Scobel's wharf. And then, between
guarding rows of red-coats, a long, double file of prisoners began
to wind its way down the dock to the street.[42] A tall, well-
formed, darkly handsome man strode at its head. His clothes
hung in ribbons around him; his shirt had been nearly torn off
his back. A great rope was knotted around his chest, and
behind him plodded his followers, in two long silent rows, each
with his right or left hand tied to the rope.[43] They marched
through streets which were lurid with lights and torches and
excited faces, and clamorous with exultant cheers. They marched
past the town and over the bridge, and out through the friendly
darkness to Fort Henry.

V

It was the trial of the captured American prisoners which
gave Macdonald his last important case of the year. The trial
was, of course, to be by court martial. A special statute, "An
Act to Protect the Inhabitants of this Province against Lawless
Aggressions from the Subjects of Foreign Countries at Peace
with Her Majesty", prescribed this summary form of trial for
invading American "sympathizers" found in arms. In a court

martial, civilian counsel had no status whatever and could not plead: they could do nothing more than advise and assist prisoners who quite literally had to conduct their own defence themselves. It was a poor, second-best kind of legal assistance; but one man in Kingston, who happened to be the brother-in-law of Daniel George, the paymaster of the Pirates, determined to secure it for his imprisoned relative. In the brief ten days which intervened before the opening of the trial, he tried at least twice to get help; and twice he was turned down. By now time was running short. And it may have been very shortly before the trial, and probably on the day of its opening, that the frantic brother-in-law knocked one morning early on the Macdonald door before John was even out of bed.[44]

Macdonald may very well have hesitated to take the case. It was a difficult, unprofessional, unpopular, and possibly danger-ous task. In a court martial, bereft of his usual status and pre-rogatives, he would be a nobody in an alien and perhaps hostile world. It would be almost impossible for him to secure an acquittal, or even to mitigate the death sentence, for the statute was clear and comprehensive enough, and the prisoners had been caught red-handed. Yet even an ineffectual defence might arouse the whole community against him. The prisoners were hated, as only foreigners who interfere by force in the affairs of others can be hated. The town was mad with grief and rage and horror. The futile enormity of the invasion itself, the long, needless list of dead and wounded at the Battle of the Wind-mill, the revolting mutilation of Lieutenant Johnston's body, and the heap of carved, double-edged bowie knives which had been taken from the Bandits and exhibited to the astounded Kingstonians—all worked like madness in the minds of the townspeople. Every circumstance seemed unfavourable. It was surely wisdom to have nothing to do with the whole affair. And yet, he took the case. Even he might have found it difficult to say why. A curious interest in people, a relish for cases which were odd and difficult, a jaunty recognition of the fact that professional prestige involved publicity, and, perhaps, a certain stubborn, independent conviction that these helpless and de-luded men deserved at least the bare minimum of assistance—

all these may have helped to move him to his decision. It was a solitary part that he had to play. Henry Smith, member for Frontenac, had shared with him the honours and the obloquy of the Dundas suit. But Macdonald went out to Fort Henry alone.

On Wednesday, November 28, when he arrived hurriedly at the fort, the court martial had already commenced its sombre business. John B. Marks, Colonel of the Third Frontenac Regiment, presided. The long, low casemate, with its bare, white-washed walls, was crowded with officers of the Midland District Militia, stiff in their scarlet and silver uniforms; and William Henry Draper, Solicitor-General of the province, who had been appointed Judge-Advocate for the occasion, had just concluded his first address to the court in the prosecution of Daniel George.[45] Urbane, learned, resourceful in the management of a case, yet not ungenerous to the prisoners, Draper had begun by setting out the terms of the governing statute, 1st Victoria, c. 3. The simple facts of the invasion were completely beyond dispute; but, by the statute, Draper was required to prove that the prisoners were citizens of a foreign country at peace with the United Kingdom, that they had associated themselves with traitorous and rebellious British subjects, and that they had made war against the Queen, and slain and wounded divers of her subjects. The second point was covered, but only barely covered; for not a solitary subject of the Queen had joined the American force after it landed at the windmill, and only three or four ex-Canadians had come with it from the United States. These people—Levi Chipman and two tearful French-Canadian lads—promptly turned Queen's evidence; and it was upon their testimony, and that of a little group of officers and men from the navy, the marines and the 83rd Regiment, that the Judge-Advocate chiefly relied. The first witness, Lieutenant Leary, R.N., had already begun his evidence, when Daniel George requested a brief delay, in order to obtain counsel. Macdonald arrived and the two held a hurried consultation. And then the trial went on.[46]

George was scarcely an heroic republican crusader. Actually he had attempted to "desert" the Pirate army immediately after

the Battle of the Windmill, leaving his companions to fight it
out on Canadian soil as best they could; and he had been picked
up in a small boat just off Windmill Point. The whole plan
of his hastily improvised defence was to dissociate himself as
completely as possible from the enterprise; and he concentrated
on the testimony by which the Judge-Advocate tried to identify
him as an American citizen, and on the evidence of his actually
levying war against the Queen. Prompted, no doubt, by Macdonald, he asked Lieutenant Leary a number of searching
questions; and he sought not unskilfully to break down the
credibility of the dishonourable Levi Chipman. "Has the witness ever stated that he would swear to anything to save himself?" he inquired. His trial lasted the whole of Wednesday;
and it was well into Thursday, November 29, when Draper
finished the case for the prosecution. George immediately requested a delay in which to prepare his defence, as he had
not had sufficient time to consult with his counsel.[47] The court
granted him until Saturday; and it then passed on at once to
the second case, the case of "General" Nils Szoltevcky Von
Schoultz.

Macdonald may have seen the dark, exotic Von Schoultz as
he strode proudly through the streets of Kingston on that wild
Saturday night ten days before, at the head of the long sullen
line of prisoners. Von Schoultz and the other "officer" of the
Pirate army, "Colonel" Dorethus Abbey, probably shared a casemate with Daniel George; and Macdonald almost certainly met
the "General" on Wednesday night as he talked over the case of
his first client. George and Abbey were colourless, if not spiritless,
characters, broken by the disasters which had overtaken them;
but the Pole, Von Schoultz, was purer and harder metal, tempered in really revolutionary fires.[48] His family, Swedish in
origin, cultivated, and distinguished in government service, had
for some time been established in Poland. His father, who
owned salt mines in the neighbourhood of Cracow, was a major
in a Polish regiment; and Nils Von Schoultz, brought up in an
atmosphere of ease and dignity, had been trained as a chemist
in the universities of northern Europe. In 1830, when the
Poles revolted to save their dwindling freedoms from the grasp

of Russia, this pleasant family existence was ended; and Nils, who had been elected to succeed his father as major in the defence of Warsaw, escaped, apparently alone among all the members of his family, and for half a dozen years wandered aimlessly over the face of Europe. He served in the French Foreign Legion, taught music in Florence, contracted a romantic but unfortunate marriage with an English girl; and then, in 1836, cutting himself clear from the past, he fled to the United States. His training as a chemist, his experience in salt manufacture, his experimental interest in the improvement of the refining process took him first to Virginia, and then to Salina, the salt-making town in northern New York State. Here, under the emphatic but dubious instruction of the Hunters, he reached the romantic conclusion that the Canadians were serfs groaning under an oppression indistinguishable from that of the Poles. He boarded the steamer *United States* on the fateful Sunday, November 11, without any very clear idea of what was going to happen; and the next day, to his consternation, he found himself the virtual leader of the little abandoned army of men who had been dumped down by their bragging compatriots at Windmill Point. Neither of the acknowledged "commanders" was with him. Bill Johnston, the river pirate, the self-styled "Commodore of the Navy of the Canadian Republic", with his picturesque belt of bowie knives and pistols, evidently decided that his duty lay with the "fleet"; and John W. Birge, the "General" of the land forces, resplendent with flashing sword and glittering gold braid, was suddenly afflicted with a stomachic disorder, which caused him unostentatiously to seek the seclusion of his cabin on the steamboat, and, as fast as possible, the safety of the United States. Von Schoultz bore himself well, with a vain, stoical bravery, in this last, grotesquely tragic episode of his career. A tall man, handsome and gentle-spoken, with fine manners, and an aristocratic reserve, he had about him a romantic air of strange tongues, and far countries, and lost causes. He consulted with Macdonald, he told the long, agitated story of his life. But Macdonald could do nothing for him. For the Pole had determined upon his course and nothing could swerve him from it.

He pleaded guilty. The answer to the fatal question was made with complete composure. While George and Abbey, the Canadian newspapers noted, were terrified men, Von Schoultz was "as unmoved as a rock".[49] Draper cautioned him against such a plea, pointing out its probable consequences; but the Pole tranquilly rejected the last slight opportunity offered him.[50] He had, he said, been terribly deceived; the whole enterprise had been conceived and carried out in ignorance and misrepresentation. But it was useless to deny that he had led the little army at Windmill Point. He persisted in his plea of guilty. The court, after a brief pause to consider the position, continued to take evidence. Von Schoultz listened to it with stoical impassivity. He asked the French-Canadian boys a perfunctory question or two; he inquired of the despicable Levi Chipman if he did not know that "General" Birge was the real leader of the expedition. But the witness who really shook him was Dr. Gardner, the surgeon of the 83rd, who told the court how he had examined the dead body of Lieutenant Johnston and had discovered its mutilation. Von Schoultz said nothing at the time, but he evidently brooded over this shameful revelation, to the exclusion of almost everything else. And when the trial was over, and he rose to address the court for the last time, it was the one subject on which he dwelt at any length. He spoke not, like George and Abbey, to save his life, but to clear his honour. He denied that he had treated the dead and wounded with inhumanity. He had done all he could to protect them; and he, and those about him, had spoken highly of Johnston as a brave man who deserved every honour.

On Friday, as soon as the court opened, Von Schoultz was condemned to death by hanging; and the next day, after George had read the written defence which Macdonald had prepared for him, he and Abbey were sentenced to the same fate. They were the first three of the principals who suffered the death penalty; and thereafter the trials became increasingly perfunctory and, in great batches, the rank-and-file were released. Macdonald apparently took no part in all these later proceedings. The court martial, despite its inevitable professional defeats, had been an important event in his career; and long afterwards it remained in his memory, though in an imperfect, uneven fashion, with vivid patches of clear recollection in the ambiguous shadow of forgetfulness, like a deep wood under strong summer sunlight. George and Abbey, the two rather nondescript Americans, made little permanent impression upon him, and in after years he could not even remember George's name. But Von Schoultz was an unforgettable person. Macdonald must have spent long and absorbed hours in his company. He drew the Pole's will; and Von Schoultz was evidently so grateful to the young lawyer, and so appreciative of his friendly counsel that he tried to leave him a small legacy, which Macdonald, of course, had to refuse. To the very last years of his life Macdonald remembered all the material details of the Pole's story with unfaded clarity.[51] Von Schoultz was one memory—a tragic memory—of the rebellion period. The Ashley affair was a comedy-drama which, in recollection, must have given him a certain acid amusement. The rebellion had made him as a lawyer; it had given him the reputation of a conservative who was not afraid to battle for liberal principles; and it had left him with one clear and uneffaceable general impression. For him, and for Kingston and the whole Midland District, the "rebellion" had been not so much a native uprising as a succession of American raids; and from then on he never quite lost a certain lingering anxiety for the problem of British North American defence.

waste and inefficiency of party rule; and with the engaging, peremptory address of a company promoter, he appealed to all sensible men to drop their meaningless debate over theoretical points of government and to unite in a great joint campaign for the improvement and prosperity of their province. The moderate Conservatives gasped with both relief and enthusiasm. The imperial connection was to remain undisturbed: the governor—no longer the tool of a clique, but the real leader of a province—was still to rule. Reassured, if not entirely satisfied, the moderates faced the future with more confidence, and prepared to accept the legislative union of Upper and Lower Canada, the basic political reform upon which Thomson had obviously set his heart. When in December, 1839, the Governor submitted the measure for the acceptance of the Upper Canadian legislature, the representatives of the old Toryism, Boulton and Sherwood of Toronto, and even Hagerman and Cartwright from the Midland District were opposed, or doubtful, or lukewarm; but it was significant that William Morris, the moderate Conservative who had been appointed to plead the cause of the Church of Scotland at the Colonial Office, declared his willingness to accept the union frankly and without conditions.[2] The Presbyterians throughout the province were prepared to follow him; and the Conservative papers in Kingston gave the union their support. During the early summer of 1840, the bill uniting the two provinces was pushed through the imperial Parliament; and in a special supplement of August 22, the *Chronicle and Gazette* printed the full text of the statute for the enlightenment of its Kingston readers. The union had come when Macdonald was only twenty-five; and it rigged the stage on which his political career was to be acted out for the next quarter-century and more.

He was almost, but not quite, ready to take his place. He had come a long way in a little while. In those days a young and ambitious man could legitimately expect to have accomplished a good deal by the time he was twenty-five; and, judged by those standards, Macdonald had not done at all badly. It was not yet five years since he had first opened the office in Quarry Street, and not yet six years since George Mackenzie's death. But could it not be said already that he had nearly won George Mackenzie's place? Without any question he was the preferred legal adviser of the Scots community; it might even be argued now that he was one of the most popular lawyers in the town as a whole. He was getting to be known professionally as an ingenious young man, persuasive with juries, adroitly clever in the management of cases—"a dangerous man to encounter in the courts", as one of his contemporaries phrased it long afterwards.[3] In his youthful readiness to take on cases which were difficult, or doubtful, or unpopular, there were pleasant signs of a professional adventurousness, a generous tolerance of attitude, a jaunty independence of mind. Yet nothing could be even hinted against the respectability of his associations or the soundness of his Conservative principles. He was gay, genial, even, perhaps, a little lightheartedly adventurous; but eminently safe. In 1839, the Commercial Bank of the Midland District affixed its broad impressive seal to the titles of his professional merit. In June—just six months after the Von Schoultz trial—he was elected a member of the Board of Directors;[4] and in the autumn, following the death of Henry Cassady, Kingston's second mayor, he became the bank's solicitor. Could anything prove more conclusively that George Mackenzie's old pupil had stepped firmly and decisively into his master's shoes?

With this increase in business and professional consequence, there came an augmentation of staff. Oliver Mowat had been Macdonald's first pupil; in the autumn of 1839, there came a second, Alexander Campbell, who had been articled to Henry Cassady.[5] A Scotsman by origin—though the Campbell family had lived for at least one generation in Yorkshire—young Alexander was a youth of seventeen when he joined Macdonald's office. He was slight in build, shorter than his youthful employer, with a reserved, serious face whose solemnity was accentuated by a slightly pendulous underlip. A sensitive and thoughtful young man, emotional yet scrupulous and cautious, Campbell was in many ways a more complex character than either his employer or his fellow-pupil. He brooded. He philosophized. His standards were obstinately high; he was rather dourly conscientious; he developed stubborn loyalties. And although Oliver Mowat was soon to abandon Kingston and to seek an independent career for himself in Toronto, the association between Macdonald and Campbell was never so summarily or so completely broken. With young Alexander's coming, the Macdonald establishment took on a size and grandeur which, except in the capital, were distinctly unusual at the time. Two articled pupils, when even the great George Mackenzie had had only one! Early that winter, in December, Macdonald gave up the tiny Quarry Street office, and moved to larger quarters, immediately adjoining the dry-goods shop of Douglas Prentiss, in the town's principal thoroughfare, Store Street.[6]

Things were going swimmingly. He was well on the way to becoming—what Alexander Campbell later claimed him to be—*facile princeps* of the Kingston bar. He was clever, and courageous, and friendly, and cheerfully resourceful. But he had had luck as well—luck, and good connections, and strong support. Back of him was the Macdonald clan, and back of that was the vigorous and cohesive Scots community of Kingston. His father, the agreeable and hopeful Hugh, his mother with her sturdy tranquillity and robust good humour, his sisters, Margaret and Louisa, the Macpherson boys and their wives, the Macpherson girls and their husbands and sweethearts were linked together, not only by the conventions, and affections, and small accepted antagonisms of family life, but also by the closest and most practical of material interests. The Commercial Bank was the main source of their welfare and the chief focus of their economic connections. The family had, indeed, moved into the bank solidly, bag and baggage, with a familiar, proprietorial air. Francis Archibald Harper continued to be its general manager. Appropriately enough, he lived on the premises in Kingston—though, it was true, he also owned a large and pleasant country residence, west of the town, along the lake front and close to Kingston's largest mansion, Alwington House. Hugh still kept his small clerkship in the institution. Thomas Wilson, the Deputy Assistant Commissary-General who had returned from his travels abroad and was soon to retire from the service with an injured arm, was appointed the Commercial Bank's representative in Montreal. And finally John Macdonald had

also become a director and the bank's solicitor. John S. Cartwright, the son of one of the town's founding fathers, the typical
representative of the Anglican Loyalist group, was still president
of the bank; but the firm hold which the Macpherson-Macdonald
group had secured upon it revealed only too clearly how the
new British immigrants who had come in since Waterloo were
effectively transferring the direction of affairs from the old
Loyalist leaders to themselves.

The Scottish community of Kingston was one of the strongest
of these immigrant groups. Macdonald was one of its chosen
younger representatives, clearly one of its favourite sons. And
Kingston, even, perhaps, more than Toronto, was becoming
recognized as the main citadel of Presbyterianism in Upper
Canada. St. Andrews Church had always been among the first
to urge the rights, and state the needs, and plan the future of
the Scottish community in the province. Kingston was frequently the meeting place of the synod; and it was soon to
become the permanent seat of the new Presbyterian university,
Queen's College. Macdonald, like Harper and other members
of the family, was closely identified with these causes and
enterprises. Back in the troubled autumn of 1838, when the
members of St. Andrews had met once more to take into consideration "the present state of the Presbyterian Church in
Canada", Macdonald, seconded by Harper, moved the first and
basic resolution which asserted that "the Church of Scotland,
in virtue of the Articles of Union between the two Kingdoms,
is as much an Established Church of the Empire as the Church
of England; and her Members, in every Colony acquired since
the Union, are entitled to the same religious liberty, and to an
equal participation in all rights and privileges with those of
the sister establishment".[7] Over a year later, in December, 1839,
just after Macdonald had moved to his new Store Street office,
the congregation met again to organize support for the new
Presbyterian college, which it was planned to establish in
Kingston. John Machar acted as chairman. Great "good feeling" prevailed; and before the meeting was over £1100 had been
subscribed. It was John Macdonald who seconded the first
resolution, proposed by Major Logie, which read "that this

meeting deeply regret the limited means afforded the youth of
this country, of acquiring a liberal education, founded on
Christian principles, and, more especially, the total want of an
institution for educating and preparing young men for the
Ministry in connection with the Church of Scotland".[8]

These public appearances were growing steadily more numerous. Up until the summer of 1840, they had been largely for
Presbyterian causes; but, after the Union Bill had finally passed
the imperial Parliament, Macdonald moved openly into the
general politics of his town. That summer everybody expected
that a general election—the first general election in the united
Province of Canada—would immediately take place; and in
Kingston it was clear that the growing influence of the Scottish
community, and of its representatives such as Macdonald,
could no longer be ignored or disregarded. In all probability
the Scots Conservatives would never again have willingly accepted Hagerman—Hagerman who had disgraced himself by his
terrible outburst of February, 1837, against the Presbyterian
Church; but, by a fortunate accident, they were spared the
embarrassment of open opposition to his candidature. Hagerman
could not run. His long professional career had been crowned
by an appointment to the bench. He was now definitely out
of politics and a successor to the Kingston constituency would
have to be found. Who was it to be? It was not really a controversy between Radicals and Tories, for no admitted Reform
candidate dared to present himself. It was really a question—
a delicate and fascinating question—of what kind of Conservative
the capital of the Midland District would send to the new,
united Assembly. The curious and significant fact was that
there was no generally acceptable representative of the Tory
and Anglican Loyalist group, which up to that time had so
largely controlled both the province and the town. Anthony
Manahan, a man in his forties, with some political experience,
who had been elected for Hastings county in 1836 along with
Edmund Murney, was put forward by one group in Kingston
as a possible candidate. But the Scots Presbyterians were plainly
no more satisfied with Manahan than they would have been
with a second edition of Hagerman. Manahan, it was true, was

a Conservative, a sensible moderate Conservative, who was turning into a good follower of Thomson. But he was also an Irishman and a Roman Catholic; and, from the point of view of the Kingston Scots, these were fatal defects. And, along with others of the same stubborn opinion, they set about obtaining a rival candidate.

Macdonald—it was a significant indication of his growing influence in politics—played a major part in these negotiations. He was one of a committee of two which interviewed Thomas Kirkpatrick, Kingston's first mayor, and begged him to run. And when Kirkpatrick finally declined, and the problem of a substitute was put before a general meeting of the Kingston electors early in August, 1840, Macdonald's competent general-ship was in evidence at every stage of the meeting.[9] The can-didate whom he and Thomas Kirkpatrick proposed to the little assembly was John Richardson Forsyth, a member of one of Kingston's oldest founding families, and related also, as his second name indicated, to the venerable commercial house of Richardson, in Montreal. The hereditary titles of Forsyth's conservatism were certainly good—so good that Radicals, and even moderates, might be disposed to look at them a little ask-ance. But, on the other hand, Forsyth was a young man, a Presbyterian, who, like Macdonald, had done his share of fighting for the rights of the Church of Scotland, and who therefore could hardly be regarded as too closely connected with the old Anglican governing set. The election address which he published, shortly after the meeting had accepted his can-didature, seemed to bear out this satisfactory impression. For-syth spoke with fitting impressiveness of the importance of the British connection; but he also showed himself a moderate, a follower of the popular Thomson, and he declared that he would give all the aid he could in the task of "leading the people of these colonies from fruitless and idle disputes upon theoretical points of government to the consideration of their real and practical interests".[10]

Yet the general election did not take place that summer, for Thomson—he had become Baron Sydenham now—had not yet issued the proclamation which would bring the union into effect and the new constitution into operation. All that autumn and winter of 1840-41, while the Canadians of the two old provinces waited expectantly for the official beginning of their new political existence, there was one topic, of inexhaustible fascination, upon which everybody's attention was focused. Where was the capital of this new, enormous, empire province to be? The imperial Act of Union, maintaining a discreet silence on this controversial subject, merely empowered the governor to select; and Sydenham had pressed to be permitted to exercise his leisurely discretion in the matter, on the plea that the selection was a very difficult problem, requiring prolonged and serious study.[11] In reality, he made up his mind quickly; but he did not choose to reveal it. And for long, dragging months, the province waited restlessly, in a state of agonized conjecture. The old capital cities, Quebec and Toronto, as well as the commercial metropolis, Montreal, and an odd little place on the Ottawa River called Bytown, all had their fervent partisans and their elaborate supporting arguments. But from the very beginning there was a strong, persistent, and confident rumour that Kingston would be the inevitable choice. As early as mid-August, 1840, the editor of one Kingston newspaper claimed that this decision was a certainty;[12] and when, a few days later, Sydenham visited the town for the second time, he received a rapturous greeting which differed markedly from the cool, reserved reception he had been accorded in the previous autumn. And young Macdonald, along with the other members of a select committee, presented him with a highly laudatory address.[18]

For another six months the matter of the capital slumbered. And then, one famous day in late January, it was suddenly discovered that Hamilton Killaly, the Chairman of the Board of Works, was in town, making a severely quiet inspection of all the available public buildings.[14] Hopes were raised at once to fever pitch; they were as quickly dashed by the doleful rumours that Kingston's accommodation had been found unsufficient; and they were raised once more when these rumours were indignantly and authoritatively denied. On Saturday, February 6, 1841, the Kingstonians were definitely informed that their town had been chosen as the seat of government;[15] and four days later the union, by Sydenham's proclamation, went into effect. A little town, of less than five thousand population, and fewer than five hundred houses, had suddenly become the capital of an enormous province, vastly larger than any which had existed in the nineteenth century in British North America; and Macdonald, a young man just turned twenty-six, discovered that provincial politics had been deposited on his own front door-step.

II

During these first years of Kingston's sudden greatness, Macdonald went through a period of illness more serious than he had experienced before. He had been ill during the winter of 1840;[16] there was, apparently, a return of the same trouble some time late in 1841. But these attacks came at intervals; and he was far too interested, and far too prominent, to sit back and watch others monopolize the arrangements for Kingston's reception of the new Canadian government. The town was busy with preparations and nearly frantic with excitement. Killaly, with the impressive authority of the Board of Works, hurried back and forward between Kingston and the temporary seat of government in Montreal. George Browne, the architect in charge of the reconstruction of the public buildings, was busy with plans and specifications. Down by the lake front, on the Penitentiary Road, about a mile from the centre of town, scores of labourers were remodelling the recently completed municipal hospital in preparation for its reception of the two Houses of Parliament and the government offices; and further west, another contingent of workmen was hurriedly constructing two additional and spacious wings for the handsome Grant mansion, Alwington House, which was to serve as the Governor's residence.[17] Accommodation—weeks before the parliamentarians and the civil servants could possibly arrive to occupy it—was suddenly found to be at a premium; rents went dramatically up. And, as early as February 17, barely ten days after the

wonderful announcement had been made public, a Kingston
editor found it necessary to rebuke his fellow-citizens for taking
undue advantage of their town's new-found glory.[18]

In the meantime, while Kingston waited for the Governor's
coming and the opening of the legislature, Macdonald had lots
to do. The Kingston election, for which all the preparations
had been made during the previous summer, was scheduled to
begin on Monday, March 22; and he acted as young Forsyth's
counsel and probably as his principal assistant in the campaign.
The election address—in which both young men no doubt had
a hand—seemed to strike exactly the right note of discreet mod-
ernity and forward-looking conservatism. Forsyth reminded the
electors of how long he had believed in the union, how loyally
he was prepared to follow Sydenham, and how anxious was
his determination to assist the parent government in carrying
out its beneficent intentions for Canada's welfare.[19] The Kingston newspapers, the *British Whig* and the *Chronicle and Gazette,* faced with two such equally acceptable Conservative candidates, seemed almost inclined to praise young Forsyth as much
as they did his senior, Manahan. And yet, from the beginning,
there were a few peevish criticisms, a few captious references to
Forsyth's family and its past. "If he has a drawback," declared
the *British Whig* of the Scottish candidate, "it is perhaps a too
intimate connection with the oligarchy of Upper Canada, who
have, by a long-continued series of successes, been led to consider the representation of certain towns and counties as their
own private property".[20] This was bad enough; but there was
worse to follow. For Forsyth, despite a well-meaning, rather
obvious effort to conciliate the Irish by pleasant references to
the hospitality he had received on a recent visit to Ireland, turned
out to be a lamentably poor speaker. On the fatal Monday,
March 22, while his stiff speech was received coolly, Manahan,
with his rich and tactful blarney, was repeatedly cheered. Forsyth lost; but he lost by only twenty votes.[21] And Macdonald,
contemplating the defeated young candidate, may very well
have wondered whether, if their roles had been reversed, the
decision would not have been altered also.

During late April and early May, when the workmen had

nearly finished their hasty alterations of the public buildings, a steady persistent avalanche of public officials, civil servants, records, papers, books and furniture began to descend upon Kingston. Down in the converted hospital building, in a situation which everybody agreed was "delightful and salubrious" in the extreme, the government offices were fitted out; and the Assembly room—a little exiguous, the newspapermen thought, for its full complement of legislators—was furnished with eighty-four handsome stuffed armchairs, of black walnut, covered in dark green moreen, with a small projection on the side to write upon.[22] Everything was now ready for the entrance of the principal; and, on a day in May, a little group of Kingstonians assembled in the town hall to make preparations for the final and crowning event—the arrival of the Governor—which would complete and validate everything that had gone before. Macdonald was there in his capacity as vice-president of the St. Andrews Society. On the previous November 30, in the absence of the president, he had taken the chair at the Society's great annual banquet. And now—the president being again out of town—he sat down with Dr. Sampson, Henry Smith, Jr., Thomas Kirkpatrick, and his friend Charles Stuart, to plan an imposing reception for Governor Sydenham.[23]

Friday, May 28, was a delightful day, clear and bright, with a gentle breeze, and a few white, comfortable clouds travelling with easy rapidity across a blue sky. It was nearly one o'clock, when the *Traveller*, commanded by Captain Sandom, the hero of the naval operations off Prescott nearly three years before, rounded Point Frederick into the harbour; and the guns of Fort Henry and the gaily decorated ships roared into the long official salute. The town was crammed with citizens and visitors, for all the shops were shut and people for miles around had come in to celebrate the general holiday. The crowd was packed thick by the Commercial Wharf, at the foot of Store Street, where Sydenham landed, attended by his guard of honour. And all the way up Store Street to the King Street intersection, along an avenue which was decorated and arched with evergreens, and gay with flags and defiant Britannic mottoes, there stood the Mayor and corporation, the local members of parliament and lawyers, the members of the national societies, of the Mechanics Institute and the Volunteer Fire Brigade, drawn up in two continuous ranks and cheering like mad. As Sydenham's carriage rolled slowly up Store Street, and under the festooned arch of evergreens, the citizens formed up behind him, with Macdonald and his St. Andrews Society among the first. A piper, Donald McKay, strode at their head. Macdonald and many of the members were in kilts; and a huge banner, with the red lion of Scotland, floated over their heads. In the brilliant spring sunshine, they marched along King Street and the lake front to Alwington House, to conduct their Governor home. Sydenham stood on the steps of the main entrance; and Macdonald and his Highlanders and the long cavalcade of citizens drew up in a great semicircle on the lawn before the Governor, with their banners to the front, and the pale green of the spring leaves and the dark blue of the lake behind them. The sheriff of the Midland District read the official address of welcome, to which Sydenham graciously replied. Then the procession paraded round the circular drive before the Governor, and down the road, and home.[24]

From that moment Macdonald drew back, an interested but relatively unimportant onlooker, while the stage was occupied by other and more commanding figures. Parliament, the first which Kingston had ever known, met early in June with impressive ceremonies. The opposition, under Baldwin and Lafontaine, massed themselves for a concerted attack on the government; but Sydenham, with his bland confidence and dexterity, divided and scattered his enemies. Kingston, the town, buzzed with interest in these national affairs; and Kingston the constituency—it seemed symbolic of the new capital's altered status —was swept out of the control of its local politicians and into the sphere of executive affairs. Shortly after the legislature met, Anthony Manahan, who had obligingly accepted an office of profit, was required to resign his seat; and Samuel Bealey Harrison, the Provincial Secretary in Sydenham's Cabinet, who up to that time had failed to win a constituency, intimated that he would be prepared to run. Obviously he would run without opposition. The Kingston newspapers, in a rather perfunctory effort to placate the surviving remnant of local independence, tried to convert Harrison into a Kingstonian by pointing out that he had purchased a lot on the outskirts of the town; but these efforts were clearly unnecessary, for pride and gratification in the possession of a cabinet minister as a member would certainly triumph over every other consideration.[25] Forsyth prudently declined to run again; and if the vague, pleasant thought had ever crossed Macdonald's mind that another rather more popular young man might succeed where Forsyth had unfortunately failed, he must now have tucked that thought away in the bottom drawer of his ambitions. In any case, he had enough to do during those spring and summer months. Oliver Mowat had left finally for Toronto, and the two remaining members of the firm were no doubt busy transferring masses of property to Kingston's new householders and arranging loans for Kingston's ambitious merchants. There was even a small amount of parliamentary business to be done; and in July Macdonald acted as counsel for Henry Smith, Jr., in the Frontenac contested election case.

In September, as the short summer slipped into autumn, there came a double tragedy, which flung a shadow over the radiance of Kingston's new political existence, and brought one phase of Macdonald's personal life to its close. On Saturday, September 4, while Sydenham was out riding unaccompanied he was thrown from his horse. And on Sunday, September 19, he died as a result of his injuries. His death must have come almost as a personal loss to Macdonald and the moderates; and it was only four days after he had been laid away in the earth of "Regiopolis", as he had once banteringly called Kingston, that the second, more intimate tragedy occurred, and the quiet, rather nondescript Scotsman, Hugh Macdonald, went off on the last long migration of his troubled career.[26] He was only fifty-nine. His life, which had ended in a mean little clerkship, seemed all too obviously a failure. But the small family which he had brought all the way from Glasgow had started promisingly in the New World. He had left an able son; and from him the son drew qualities important though not easily definable—

Public Archives

JOHN A. MACDONALD, 1842

a love of people, and their company and talk, a ready and courageous adaptability, an easy, generous tolerance for men and the infinite variety of their views and ways.

It was, apparently, shortly after his father's death that the most serious illness of Macdonald's young manhood occurred.[27] By the end of November he was so far recovered that he was able to take up police court work again and to appear at his place as vice-president at the annual St. Andrews dinner. In mid-December, when the town decided patriotically to plan a monster celebration of the birth of the Prince of Wales, Macdonald was, as usual, a member of the committee in charge. On December 22, while a sleigh dragged a huge roasted ox through the snow to the market place, and the whole of Kingston's poor sat down to a vast dinner of roast beef, mutton, ham, venison, coffee and beer, he and the other members of the "Committee of Bachelors" were coping with a cheerfully refractory mass of Kingston's children who were given a competitive banquet in the town hall.[28] He enjoyed these affairs, as his father would have, and was good at them. But from then on his public appearances grew fewer; and when, early in January, 1842, the new Governor, Sir Charles Bagot, was drawn across the ice from Cape Vincent in a racing "gig", Macdonald was not among the rather small informal company which gathered to meet Sydenham's successor. His illness had apparently trailed off in a long convalescence, which left him easily tired, without much appetite, and restless. He determined to go "home". Kingston, capital of Canada as well as of the Midland District, was satisfactory enough; but beyond Kingston, and Canada, and British North America, lay another world, imperial and international in scope, remote, and splendid, and vastly more exciting than anything he had yet known. From a practical point of view, there were probably family affairs to be settled in Scotland, following his father's death. In any case, he wanted the change and the rest, and the practice, which had certainly been booming during the last few years, could supply him with all the funds he needed for his travels.

John Machar recommended Butler's *Analogy of Natural and*

Revealed Religion and suggested that there was nothing so good as a sea voyage for serious and prolonged reflection.[29] For three nights—about the only three nights in his life when he tried cards for money—he played loo with John S. Cartwright, George W. Yarker of the Commercial Bank and two other fellow-spirits, and won with miraculous and unbroken consistency.[30] With his heavy winnings tucked in his pocket, along with John Machar's letter commending him to the protection of a gracious Providence, he set out from Kingston, some time late in January, 1842. He was accompanied by Tom Wilson, who was going back to England to interview the officials of the War Office in an effort to persuade them to take a serious view of the compensation which should be granted him for his injured arm. It was the depth of winter when they sailed from Boston. The ocean was white with tempest; and London, in February and March, was only doubtfully clement. But almost at once his health began miraculously to improve. He discovered, to his own astonishment, and to that of Tom Wilson and his well-to-do brother-in-law Edward Wanklyn, that he was eating plenteous breakfasts and even more bountiful dinners; and along with this suddenly voracious appetite, there went a surprised and delighted sensation of vitality, of conscious well-being, of easy and effortless strength. He went everywhere. Streets, shops, public buildings, theatres, exhibitions, dinners, parties, and balls were all crowded into an enormous programme which took his sleep, and tired his legs, and taxed his pocket-book. With intense interest, but without being moved to any very profound political or legal reflections, he watched the jury trials at the Guildhall, listened to a debate in the Lords, and heard Peel, Russell, Stanley, Goulburn and Sir James Graham in the Commons. And one bland, delightful day in late February, which was like a sweet breath of the coming spring, he visited Windsor, peeped, by special permission, into the Queen's private apartments while the pretty Margaret Wanklyn hung upon his arm, compared impressions of royal domesticity with his companion, and discovered, to his intense satisfaction, that they were in happily sympathetic agreement upon all the main points.[81] He lived in a state of continual high spirits. Amused, conscious of his amusement, conscious of things to be enjoyed and of his almost limitless capacity for quizzical enjoyment, he was realizing and perfecting his own style, his characteristic way with things and people, the easy, jaunty fashion in which he was to saunter through life.

There was some, but not much, evidence of practical purpose in his itinerary. London was pure fun. The projected tour of the Lake Country, and the visits to Oxford and Cambridge were all parts of a general programme of diversion and recuperation. Only occasionally was there some slight tangible sign of concern for the life which must soon be resumed in the far-off house and office in Kingston. In Chancery Lane, he bought a substantial law library which cost him a little over £160.[82] He wrote his mother that at Manchester he proposed to purchase a quantity of house furnishings—wall-paper, damask, ornaments, iron railings, and a kitchen stove—all intended for the house in Kingston, of which he had now become the proprietor. For the rest, there must certainly be visits with his British relatives. Evan Macpherson, a soldier like his father, the old Colonel, was now stationed at Chester; and at Arbroath were Major and Mrs. Bruce Gardyne—she had been Catharine Macpherson. In Scotland, other members of the family surrounded and claimed him. He met them all, and, among the rest, his first cousin, Isabella Clark, the second daughter of his Aunt Margaret Shaw, and the sister of that Maria Clark who back in 1834 had married John Alexander Macpherson in Hallowell.[83] Her gentle, tranquil features, her hair brushed smoothly away from its centre part in the demure fashion of the 1840's, have survived only in a faded picture whose blurred outlines seem to frustrate the enquirer with gently mocking modesty. When Macdonald left for Scotland, he was, and perhaps expected to remain for some time, a bachelor. Perhaps he carried with him back to Canada only the pleasant memory of her face. Perhaps, when he left, he had already secured from her at least one promise, that next year she might herself cross the ocean to visit her long-absent sister Maria in Kingston.

III

When Macdonald arrived home, some time in the summer of 1842, he was probably in much better health than he had been for years. Kingston also was prospering. Since the moment, in the summer of 1840, when the first intimations of its new grandeur had begun to circulate, the town had nearly doubled in population. The sense of well-being and vitality, which Macdonald had recovered so vividly in London, had been shared now for nearly two years by the moderate Liberal-Conservatives and by the new capital of the new province. For nearly two years the glittering but unsubstantial fabric reared by the magician Sydenham had lasted; and then in the autumn of 1842, almost without warning, it began to collapse. In September, the first parliament of the united Province of Canada met for its second session; and it had barely been sitting a week when the new Governor, Sir Charles Bagot, was obliged to reconstitute his Cabinet and to admit Robert Baldwin and his French-Canadian friends to office. The Tories were out; Draper, the principal hope of the moderate Conservatives, had gone. And yet, though some of the Kingston newspapers began to refer contemptuously to "Granny Bagot" and to print abusive burlesques on the subject of "Bagot, Hincks and Company, General Office Brokers and Cabinet Makers", public opinion in the town was inclined to be discreetly cautious in its attitude to the new government.[34] After all, Samuel Bealey Harrison, Secretary for Canada West and Kingston's own member in the provincial parliament, remained, with a few others, to provide a tenuous connection with the past. Surely Harrison would defend Kingston's interests? And surely it was common prudence for Kingston to give a decent welcome to the administration which governed in its midst?

Macdonald, who had no reason to qualify his known and definite Conservative position, was of course opposed to the political change which had just taken place. He must have been aware of the vague feeling of unease in the town, and must have watched with interest for the first sign of any policy which might render the new ministers objectionable to his fellow-townsmen. He had not long to wait. The new government had not been in office a week when a sinister rumour began to spread rapidly through Kingston that, at the determined instance of Lafontaine and the French Canadians, the seat of government was to be moved, probably to Montreal. The town waited in nervous apprehension. Late in September, Harrison read in the Assembly a despatch from the Colonial Office on the subject, a despatch in which Stanley, the Colonial Secretary, had poured a deluge of very cold water on the proposed removal, declaring that it could be done only under the "clearest necessity" and with "the general sense of the Province unequivocally expressed in its favour".[35] The government newspapers in Kingston drew a breath of relief. That settled the matter. Yet the ominous rumours persisted. "Our firm belief is," wrote one editor, "that in the arrangements lately effected, the interests of Kingston were actually and virtually sold."[36] As if to give point to this blunt assertion, the Assembly, a few days later, took up the embarrassing subject once again and, for some hours, expatiated offensively on Kingston's limitations as a capital. Even government supporters in the town now took alarm. The French Canadians were given downright warning not to abuse their power. "We do not know anything," wrote one government newspaper, "calculated to enter more deeply into the minds of the inhabitants of the Upper Province, than the removal of our Parliament to Lower Canada".[37]

All this was both alarming and encouraging. The transfer to Montreal would provide excellent political capital for the Conservative party; but, on the other hand, it would mean the certain ruin of the new-found prosperity of Kingston. Macdonald's feelings must have been mixed, for his political hopes grew bright as his professional prospects darkened. But the Kingston city fathers, who were responsible for the town's well-being, could naturally take only one view of the situation. They had realized for some time that their rapidly growing capital was badly in need of a new town hall and new market buildings; and they were aware also—and the thought hovered always at the back of their speculations—that the provincial legislature, completely ignoring the need of permanent provision, still occupied its avowedly temporary quarters, the four-storey limestone building which had been erected as a hospital. Contemplating these two necessities, the town council reached an audacious and grandiose decision. It would build an elegant, spacious, and splendid town hall, a town hall amply sufficient to accommodate not merely the offices and council rooms which a rising town like Kingston was certain to require, but also still larger chambers, fit, perhaps, for the deliberations of still greater and more august assemblies.[38] John Counter, thick-set, square-jawed, black-haired—Kingston's energetic and repeatedly elected Mayor—departed for England to raise the necessary funds, armed with £20,000 in corporation securities. The mission was a complete success and on his return in March John Counter was given a hero's reception. Ground was broken and the council's grand design marched steadily forward.[39] George Browne, who had supervised the alteration of the government buildings in Kingston, was the architect; and Browne had made an interesting and significant use of his space. The ground floor of the new building was to contain a variety of smaller rooms and offices; but upstairs, in the second storey, there were to be, not one, but two large and lofty chambers, larger certainly than any common council would presumably require, but not, on the other hand, too large for a provincial Legislative Council and a Legislative Assembly.

It was at this point, when the civic affairs of Kingston were taking on a new pomp and circumstance, that Macdonald decided to run as alderman. A municipal career, in and for itself, would be vastly more interesting than it would have been even a few years before. Also, though the fate of the Kingston constituency seemed settled for years to come, municipal office was in general a most suitable beginning for public life. He was certainly well known and popular. He had participated in the most intimate councils of the Conservative party and had taken part in every important civic affair for years. Moreover, during the previous autumn—it was a crowning honour for a member of the Scottish community—he had been elected president of the St. Andrews Society, with Harper and J. R. Forsyth as first and second vice-presidents.[40] Early in February, when he modestly announced that he proposed to run for the vacant seat in the Fourth Ward, the Kingston newspapers, of all political opinions, welcomed and supported his candidature with flattering unanimity. "We are not aware," said the editor of the *Chronicle and Gazette*, "that a more eligible person could offer. His experience in public business, his well-known talents and high character, render him peculiarly fit for the office, and we sincerely hope, for the sake of the Town, that he will be elected."[41] The *British Whig* assured the electors that they would never have cause to regret choosing Macdonald and his team-mate, Robert Anglen, who was running for the post of common councilman. The *Loyalist* wound up the chorus of praise with a soaring finale, when it confidently predicted that Macdonald would be returned with a triumphant majority. It proved to be exactly right. When, on March 28, the election finally took place, Macdonald and Anglen were returned with ease and were chaired in triumph through the town.[42]

Macdonald barely won his seat in council in time. For, on the very next day, March 29, one of the most important civic affairs of the year occurred. A new governor—the third since Kingston had been declared the seat of government—arrived in the capital. Sir Charles Bagot had fallen a victim to that curiously implacable fatality which seemed to hover over the lives of all the first representatives of the Crown who had tried to rule the united Province of Canada from Alwington House. Since December, 1842, he had been ill; and he still lingered, slipping daily closer to death, when his successor, Sir Charles Metcalfe, arrived to take over the governorship. Macdonald, as before, had met with others to plan a proper reception for their new ruler;[43] but the gloom at Alwington House made too great enthusiasm inappropriate, and with the arrival of the third governor in two years, it was a little hard to maintain the first thrill of novelty. The winter had been a terrible one; and the thousands of people who crowded into Kingston on that

late March day stood about uncomfortably in piles of deep
snow and slush. The ice was still feet thick in the river when
Sir Charles crossed from Cape Vincent in a carriage, changing,
just as he reached Kingston, into an open sleigh, with four fine
grey horses, which drew him through the capital.⁴⁴ The town
corporation—with the new alderman for Ward Four among
them—went over to the American side to greet the Governor;
and there Macdonald caught his first glimpse of the man who
was to have such a decisive effect upon the fortunes of the
Conservative party. He may not have been very impressed.
Metcalfe, a veteran colonial administrator with long and successful experience in the West Indies and India, was a stout, dumpy,
aging man, with iron-grey hair, and fat, rather pendulous
cheeks, upon one of which, already noticeable, was a frightening and venomous sore.

What was going on behind the grey and unrevealing exterior
of Government House when Metcalfe met his Reform ministers?
Macdonald, like most other people in Kingston, probably had
very little idea. But not even a fortnight had elapsed since the
new Governor's arrival, when the old horrible rumours about
the transfer of the seat of government were revived once more,
and this time with the most circumstantial particulars. It was
said in Montreal that Lafontaine, the Attorney-General for
Canada East, was decidedly in favour of a move to Montreal;⁴⁵
it was rumoured from Quebec that the French-Canadian members of the government had, in a body, threatened the Governor
with resignation, if their demands were not complied with.⁴⁶
In the midst of these depressing and unnerving rumours, and
in the vilest possible weather, the Kingstonians stubbornly continued to build their town hall. All that April and May it
rained and snowed, thawed and froze, with wearisome consistency; and on Monday, June 5—"Training Day"—when
Governor Metcalfe came down in state to the waterfront to lay
the cornerstone of the new municipal buildings, "the day was
cold and showery, which threw a damp upon the proceedings".⁴⁷
That evening Macdonald, the other members of the corporation,
and a long list of guests were entertained at dinner by the

Governor at the British American Hotel. A grey uneasiness, which matched the gloomy night outside, with its east wind and gusts of rain, may very well have fallen upon the company; and it must have been with a certain forced bravado that speaker after speaker arose to extol the glories of Kingston and to predict its prosperity in the future.

Yet, if the affairs of the province and the destiny of Kingston remained veiled in ominous ambiguity, Macdonald continued, unaffected, on his own cheerful way. Last year, in England, he had gained what seemed a long, strong, unshakable lease on life. He was a lawyer with a large practice, an alderman with a good deal of popularity, and a genial young man with quantities of friends. He was enjoying existence to the full; and that summer, which opened warmly and agreeably after the terrible prolonged winter, Isabella Clark arrived in Kingston. Her sister Maria, and her sister's husband, John Alexander Macpherson, who had lived in Hillier, in Prince Edward County, during the 1830's, had now migrated back to Kingston, like so many others of the Macpherson-Macdonald clan; and one of their children, a very small boy named James Pennington in memory of his uncle and in honour of his grandfather's old commander, remembered long afterwards how this strange, delightful aunt from overseas had captivated him with her sweetness, and gentleness, and tender sympathy.[48] "Cousin John" had always been a frequent visitor at the Macpherson household; now his visits became even more assiduous. And he and Isabella fell in love. This was first love, spontaneous, unpremeditated and impulsive; and within a few months, perhaps even a few weeks, it had brought the lovers to that quick, sure decision upon which happy marriages are based. On September 1, 1843, Macdonald did two things, accepted two contracts, the delicious incongruity of which may have amused his half-practical and half-romantic nature. He agreed to form a legal partnership with his old pupil Alexander Campbell, who had just recently been called to the bar;[49] and in St. Andrews Church, with John Machar as officiating clergyman and his two friends Tom Wilson and Charles Stuart as witnesses, he married his cousin, Isabella Clark.[50]

IV

1843

The young man was twenty-eight. He was married, an alderman, the senior partner in a young but flourishing firm, an
able practitioner who could work with ease and efficiency and
who now, after years of effort, had reached a comfortable level
of prosperity. On September 2, the day after the wedding had
been performed and the partnership sealed, Macdonald and
Campbell announced the opening of their office on what had
long been Store Street, but was now renamed Princess Street,
in honour of the Princess Royal.[51] A little later, when the
bridegroom and his bride had returned from their honeymoon,
they settled down in a house in Brock Street, spacious and
comfortable, replete with all the modern conveniences of a
wonderful mechanical age.[52] There was a library, for Macdonald had always bought and read books; there was a carriage
and a pair of horses, "Mohawk" and "Charlie". Sometimes the
young James Pennington Macpherson would be permitted the
enormous honour of sitting beside the coachman on his box.
Sometimes, coming home from school, he might meet his uncle
in the street, and his uncle, indulging the pleasant fiction that
he owed James vast sums of money, would proceed to liquidate
the debt with all the coppers in his pocket; and James Pennington would go on his happy ways, confirmed in the unshakable
conviction that his uncle was the richest and most generous
man in the world.

The Macdonalds were barely established in the handsome
house on Brock Street, when the crisis in the affairs of Kingston and the province, which had been gathering slowly for a
period of months, finally broke. The legislature was scheduled
to meet on September 28. A few days before, the town was
thrown into a state of angry excitement by a new and positive
rumour that Secretary Harrison and possibly one or two other
members of the Cabinet were about to resign in protest against
a definite official decision to transfer the seat of government
from Kingston to Montreal.[58] It was only too true. On September 30, Harrison's resignation was formally announced. Six
days later, the government introduced its proposal of removal;

and on November 3, after a long and acrimonious debate in which a growing opposition exhausted every device of obstruction, the transfer to Montreal was finally voted in principle. "And so, at the will of a few, and without any petitions or agitations . . . the hopes and means of many in Kingston are destroyed . . . the 600 houses erected here are to be left tenantless to moulder into ruin. The Market Building, than which nothing more noble has been erected in North America, is to be left a curse to the place."[54] Summarily, and—as it turned out—for ever, the political destiny of Kingston had been determined. And a profound sense of depression—of disappointment, injury, resentment and frustration—settled down upon the town.

Macdonald was affected as a Kingstonian, for his prospects were altered and injured, like those of every other townsman. He was affected also as a Conservative, for the Tory leaders, local and provincial—Sir Allan MacNab, John S. Cartwright, and Henry Smith, Jr.—at once leaped forward to direct the storm of protest to their profit. But what hope was there of upsetting the government, of ending—what now seemed to be a proved reality—the sinister, pervasive, and irresistible influence of Lafontaine and his French Canadians? It was true that the Seat of Government Bill was arousing a mass of opposition in Canada West. Undoubtedly, also, Baldwin's plan for a great, non-sectarian, provincial university was certain to alienate those who supported the small church colleges, Queen's, King's and Victoria, and who believed in the indissoluble union of "science and religion". And, finally, there could be no question that the Secret Societies Bill, a frank and undisguised effort—"unexampled in British legislation", Metcalfe called it—to destroy the Orange Order, had goaded the Grand Master, Ogle Robert Gowan, and his followers into a crusade more determined and furious than any which the Order had inspired since the election of 1836. But, though Harrison had resigned and a few other Reformers were now opposed or doubtful, the government still seemed to hold a commanding majority. The session went solidly forward. Then, suddenly, when nobody but a few initiates expected it, there came another sharp turn of Fortune's wheel. The year 1843, which had been an important one for Macdonald, full of new ventures and significant decisions, had one last, and more general, surprise in store. On Sunday, November 26, alleging a dispute over appointments and patronage, which they declared involved the principle of responsible government, nine out of the ten members of the provincial administration tendered their resignations to the Governor-General.

The crisis gave Macdonald his first great political chance. He rushed into the struggle—and in Kingston it was a popular struggle—for the defence of the legitimate prerogative of the Crown against the evils of extreme party government. On November 30, four days after the resignation of the ministers, when he presided once more at the annual dinner of the St. Andrews Society, the occasion took on an even more defiantly Conservative aspect than usual; and the guests and members sang "Charlie is my Darling" when they toasted the Governor-General.[55] The following Monday Macdonald and his Conservative friends were present and prominent at the public meeting which the Mayor called to take into consideration the question of an address to Metcalfe in the existing crisis. It was a rowdy meeting, in a packed hall, with a large preponderance of Metcalfe supporters; and for the first time Macdonald and the new generation of Kingston Conservatives appeared as popular leaders before a large crowd of their fellow-citizens. Charles Stuart moved the first resolution; Macdonald followed with a resolution which declared "that the firm, manly, and vigorous manner in which His Excellency has maintained the Prerogative of the Crown and at the same time upheld the just rights of all classes of the people, entitles him to our confidence". It was a fighting political speech which followed. With enthusiasm, and with a certain colloquial familiarity of address, he began his defence of the imperial connection, of the Governor who was its prime symbol, and of the Governor's just authority, outside the limits of responsible government as sanctioned by Sydenham in 1841, to protect the rights of both races and all classes of the population against the extremes of party rule.[56]

He started on a note which must have sounded real and

authentic, as nothing else could have done, to an audience
which, only six years before, had lived through the perils of
the rebellion and the American raids. The basic issue of the
controversy, he insisted, was the question of British supremacy.
He reminded his listeners of the benefits of the imperial connection, of the protection it could be counted upon to provide,
of the vitally necessary defence it had given in 1837 and 1838.
Most men in the crowd before him could remember well what
militant republicanism had meant. He told them roundly that
those who did not rally round the Governor were, in effect,
supporting republican principles. From these large generalities
in political theory, he pressed on, shrewdly, rapidly, to the more
intimate matters of local concern. The people, he declared,
had the right to expect a constructive programme from government; but all the ministry had done was to effect the ruin of
Kingston. The plea of the ministers, that they had resigned
in defence of the principle of responsible government, was so
much claptrap; it was no important political issue, but merely
the question of the party management of patronage, which had
caused them to resign. How could they be trusted now to fill
the offices in the Midland District appropriately, when, once
the legislature had been moved to Montreal, every place in the
government would be stuffed with the friends of Lafontaine?

The speech, and the meeting as a whole, which, to the annoyance of the Reformers, had been a triumphant success, thrust
Macdonald publicly and openly into the front rank of Kingston
Conservatives. From that moment he was certain to be one of
the leading figures, if not the central figure, in the popular
defence of Metcalfe in Kingston; and he and his fellow-
moderates must have looked with deepening anxiety to Government House for the first signs of the policy which could betray
them just as easily as it could invigorate their defence. On
December 7, parliament was suddenly prorogued. A few days
later, the Governor announced the first appointments to his new
Council. It was a curious collection of individuals—William
Henry Draper, the moderate Liberal-Conservative Englishman;
Denis Benjamin Viger, the repentant French-Canadian revolutionary; and Dominick Daly, the veteran, unpolitical Irish

bureaucrat, who had sat in Sydenham's government, and in Bagot's government, who saw no reason why he should ever surrender his job, and who must have regarded the whole disturbing business of responsible government with uncomprehending distaste. Incomplete, ill-assorted, incongruous—the new ministry was all of these; but it proved to Macdonald and the moderates that Metcalfe, in his sharp recoil from the Reformers, had not fallen automatically into the waiting arms of the old Tory Compact. The portly, commonplace-looking, stiffly formal man who had accepted the tragedy of his life with stoical resignation, and who knew now that he could never be cured of the hideous cancer that had eaten its way through his cheek, was determined never to yield to the extremes of either party. He embodied the spirit, not of Sir Francis Bond Head, but of Lord Sydenham. His aim from the first was a composite, moderate administration, representing both races and all groups. The moderates were mystified and embarrassed by the long delays in the completion of the Council. They could not know the details of those long months of unavailing negotiations, during which Metcalfe, still sticking obstinately to his plan, hawked the offices of government around with a frequency which was scarcely calculated to increase their prestige. But the few appointments which were made were highly satisfactory; and it became increasingly clear that the Toronto Tories, confident that the Governor must fall back upon them in the end, and furious that he had not done so already, were holding back their support with callous indifference.[57] Badgered from both sides, attacked by their enemies and betrayed by their friends, the moderates closed their ranks in the defence of Sir Charles.

During March, 1844, though the Governor's Council was still incomplete, and though parliament had not been dissolved, the Kingston Conservatives decided that it was time to begin preparations for the general election. Whom were they to choose as their candidate? Forsyth had failed, though not too badly, in 1841. Harrison, though he had resigned on the seat-of-government question, was suspected of having refused a place in Metcalfe's new Cabinet. The Kingstonians turned their backs on both these possibilities, and selected Macdonald; and

a little later their invitation, signed by 225 people, together
with Macdonald's reply, was printed in the *Kingston Herald.*[58]
The young lawyer's first political declaration was about as brief
and as laconically non-committal as Forsyth's had been. But,
amid vague benevolent professions of devotion to the interests
of Kingston, and of loyalty to "sound and liberal" principles of
public policy, there was one long and significant sentence. "In
a young country like Canada," declared Macdonald, "I am of
opinion that it is of more consequence to endeavour to develop
its resources and improve its physical advantages, than to waste
the time of the legislature and the money of the people in
fruitless discussions on abstract and theoretical questions of
government." Perhaps it was, in part, a real profession of faith.
Certainly, in the politics of the time, it was an instantly recognizable party label. It identified Macdonald as a moderate, as
a Sydenhamite, as a man who would support the Governor, but
who was not necessarily associated with the old Tory party.
Ten days later, on May 2, he and his friends met at the Court
House, to organize the United Empire Association, the electoral
organization by which they intended to fight the campaign.[59]

A long halt followed. For weeks, for months, the harassed
Governor made no significant move. And during the long summer, while the newspapers fired acrimonious editorials at each
other and while R. B. Sullivan and Egerton Ryerson, the heavy
guns of the Conservative and Reform parties, kept up their
long artillery duel over the meaning of responsible government,
Kingston was a dull and depressed place. By the middle of
June, most of the public officers, with their records and their
furniture, had left town for Montreal. On June 20, Metcalfe,
standing on the promenade deck of the steamer *Caledonia,*
waved a last farewell to the citizens of what had been, all too
briefly, the capital of united Canada.[60] Early in July, Macdonald and his wife left for the United States to visit one of
Isabella's sisters, Mrs. Greene; and they had probably been
back only a short time when, early in September, Metcalfe ended
the long political suspense with a decisive move. The names
of the new ministers were made public, and although some of
these qualified as moderates simply because they had been

political nonentities in the past, others, such as William Morris, had already proved the zeal and the quality of their moderate Conservatism. Obviously a dissolution of the Assembly was now imminent. It was time for Macdonald to act.

Towards the end of September, he called a meeting of his supporters at Metcalfe's Inn.[61] He explained his own position with ingratiating candour. The requisition of the previous spring was months old and he would hold no man bound to it. He would run if they wished; and if they wished, he would cheerfully retire. It was a polite and adroit move. But the minds of the Kingston Conservatives were made up now. When John Richardson Forsyth, the defeated principal of 1841, proposed Macdonald's name, it was voted by acclamation. On October 5, Macdonald published his first election manifesto, and four days later, at a crowded meeting in the court-house, he and Anthony Manahan were nominated as rival candidates.[62] Macdonald was far from underrating the generous, affable Manahan, with his solid Irish Roman Catholic support. He expected, as he said, to be "hard run by the Papishes".[63] He knew, too, that the Scots Presbyterians, upon whose united support he might have counted, had been divided by the "Great Disruption" between "Old Kirk" and "Free Kirk", with the Free Kirkers following the Reformist lead of George Brown and the Toronto *Globe*. It was all true. It was true also that Manahan, for all his good humour and his good stories, was a highly embarrassed man. He tried vainly to explain that he had resigned his seat in 1841 at Sydenham's own request; but he could never quite live down the imputation that he had sold the constituency for a job.

At nine o'clock on Monday, October 14, the voting began. These were the days of the open poll, when each vote was a blow which was known and cheered, and when the electors on both sides marched to the hustings like the men-at-arms of two medieval private armies. By noon of the first day, Manahan, overwhelmed with reverses, had retired under protest, and his discomforted and leaderless followers were scattered. But all that afternoon and all the next day, the Macdonald men continued to press forward, as if the contest were still on, and the issue yet in doubt.[64] At the close of the second day's poll, the vote stood 275 for Macdonald and 42 for Manahan. The election "terminated in a most peaceable and orderly manner, without the slightest attempt at disturbance".[65] It was true that Manahan's supporters, in a formal petition to the Returning Officer, protested the entire election, giving nine separate reasons why it should be declared invalid. But this was normal and rather routine procedure. The vote stood. Macdonald was member for Kingston.

Chapter Five

Minister of the Crown

I

Macdonald stayed in town long enough to attend the dinner in honour of the completion of the new municipal building, which was held on Thursday, November 21, in the town hall itself, in one of the spacious assembly halls which Kingston had vainly hoped would house the two branches of the provincial legislature.[1] Then, early in the next week, it was time to leave for the first session of the newly elected parliament in Montreal. The first great moment in his political career had come; and yet it is probable that he did not depart for Montreal in a mood of carefree triumph. His constituency, despite the drunken hilarity of the great civic dinner, was still sunk in depression and sullen resentment; and he was well aware of the fact that the new government could not possibly restore the town's artificial prosperity, for it did not dare to reverse the decision concerning the seat of government. The state of Kingston, and—intimately associated with it—the state of his own popularity, were problems which he carried away with him. And these worries were matched by other, more intimate, and more serious apprehensions concerning his own and his family affairs. It was true that he was leaving the practice in a most satisfactory state. The arrangement with Campbell, by which the junior partner was to have one-third of the profits of the practice, exclusive of the proceeds of Macdonald's retainer by the Commercial Bank of the Midland District, was an excellent arrangement which, from Macdonald's point of view, could hardly have been made more opportunely. Campbell, young, sober, conscientious, doggedly loyal, could be counted upon, as few men could have been, to maintain the practice which was Macdonald's one source of income and the necessary basis of his political career. The office was all right. If his family had been in as flourishing a condition, Macdonald would have been happy. But old Mrs. Macdonald, despite her iron will and her enormous vitality, was frailer now; and what was worse, infinitely worse, was that Isabella, "Isa", the healthy, happy bride of only a little over a year before, was suffering from occasional and debilitating attacks of illness.

Some time in the last week of November, Macdonald strolled down the streets of Montreal to take his first view of the new provincial parliament buildings. Kingston had built an extravagantly splendid town hall for the benefit of an ungrateful provincial legislature. But Montreal, well looked after by Providence, in the shape of Lafontaine and his impressive phalanx of French-Canadian votes, had not the slightest need to extend itself in this fashion; and all it did was to lease a market building to the Canadian government, which the Canadian government —with the advice, once again, of the inevitable architect, George Browne—proceeded to rearrange and redecorate at its own expense. The new parliament house—it had been called St. Ann's Market—stood just east of McGill Street in the wide irregular square since known as Place Youville. It was a long, low, narrow, two-storey building, with a pillared portico at each end, and a slight elevation in the centre which broke the roof-line without rising to the stature of a proper tower.[2] The ground floor, with its spacious hall in the centre of the building, and its long corridors running from end to end, was crowded with the offices of government. The first floor was occupied by the two assembly halls, the Council chamber in the east wing, the Legislative Assembly room in the west wing towards McGill Street, and each with its appropriate complement of robing-room, lounge, and bar. On the afternoon of Thursday, November 28, Macdonald took his seat for the first time in the Legislative Assembly, and shortly after, he and thirty-eight Conservatives elected Sir Allan Napier MacNab as their Speaker.[3]

As Macdonald sat, a relatively inconspicuous back-bencher, in his place in the St. Ann's Market building, two obvious things about the Conservative majority in the House must have struck him immediately. In the first place, the majority was very small; and in the second, it was almost exclusively English-speaking. The Conservatives elected MacNab to the Speaker's chair by thirty-nine to thirty-six votes; and though their majorities improved slightly during the next week or so, this first division was to remain an unhappily accurate revelation of the precarious margin of Tory power. The party drew almost no support from French Canada. Only a very few odd, unrepresentative French Canadians, who promptly forfeited the support of their old followers, and who were popularly despised by their compatriots as renegades and *vendus*, were to be found voting with the government in the first crucial divisions of the session. The towns—the "rotten boroughs" as the Reformers called them—had gone solidly Tory, with the exception of Quebec. In the far east, in the English-speaking districts of the Eastern Townships, the Conservatives had carried every seat; and in the far west, in the great peninsula between Lake Erie and Lake Huron, where American influences were regrettably strong and Reformist delusions notoriously influential, they had succeeded in taking Kent, Oxford, Middlesex, Huron, Simcoe, South Lincoln, and the two Haltons, East and West. In the main, however, the strength of the Conservative party lay, where it had always lain before, in the long narrow strip of farming country, homeland of the first Loyalist settlements, which stretched from Toronto eastward to the old interprovincial boundary. In fact, what the Conservatives had really done in the election of 1844 was to maximize their ancient strength.

The limitations of that strength were painfully apparent to Macdonald, as to others. He realized that the Conservative party, as then constituted, was a weak party. As time passed and he gradually acclimatized himself to the legislature and got to know his fellow party members, he became aware of another, and perhaps even more serious, defect in the structure of provincial Conservatism. The party was not only weak; it was also divided. It was struggling with difficulty through the first, perilous period of a great metamorphosis, and it hovered ambiguously, painfully, between its old and new selves, between the Toryism of the past and the Liberal Conservatism of the future. On the one hand were the Liberal Tories, distinctly the larger group in the party, but composed, for the most part, of men who were either young or relatively unknown. On the other hand were the surviving members of the Family Compact and the Chateau Clique—men like Badgeley, Hale, and Moffatt from Canada East, like MacNab, Boulton, Robinson, and the Sherwood brothers from Canada West. Despite everything that the moderates and the Governor could do, these relics of the past—surprisingly young, some of them, and surprisingly alive —had forced their way back into the centre of affairs. In the administration which Metcalfe had formed, back in September, 1844, not a single one of the old Conservative names had been included; but after the election, and after the upsurge of primitive Tory strength which it witnessed, the representatives of the old oligarchies could no longer be disregarded with impunity. Sir Allan MacNab, stout, hearty, emptily genial, was made Speaker; W. B. Robinson, brother of the old Chief Justice, Sir John Beverley Robinson, was given the portfolio of Inspector-General; and Henry Sherwood, one of the Toronto members, a young man, younger than Macdonald, with straight features, and curly hair, and an expression of arrogant assertiveness, was appointed to the solicitor-generalship, though without a seat at the Council board.

From the beginning, Macdonald must have regarded these men as doubtful and difficult friends. His background and all his early associations had made him a moderate, a Sydenhamite; and, once inside the Assembly, he gravitated immediately to the Liberal Conservative wing. Some of its members he knew already. William Morris, the defender of the Scottish Church and the patron of Queen's University, who held a seat in the Legislative Council, was probably an old acquaintance; and Ogle Robert Gowan, the Grand Master of the Orange Lodge, a man who combined the airs of a demagogue with the practices

of a cool realist, was one of the key members of the Assembly
with whom Macdonald quickly struck up a firm and lasting
association. But the man who, above all others in the party,
became Macdonald's leader and inspiration during the early
part of his career was William Henry Draper, the prophet of
Liberal Conservatism on Canadian earth, if Sydenham and
Metcalfe were its presiding deities in the imperial heaven.
Draper was an interesting and complex person who, despite
the unimpeachable respectability of his origins, views, and
habits, had had an adventurous career.[4] The son of a Church
of England clergyman, brought up in a remote rural parish in
Devon, he had run away to sea when he was a mere boy, had
served, for some years, in an East India merchantman, and
had turned up in Canada in 1820, when he was nineteen years
old. At first his activities in the New World seemed unremarkable and were certainly unnoticed. He taught school in Port
Hope. He studied law. And then, one fortunate day, shortly
after he had been admitted to the bar, he was noticed favourably at the Cobourg assizes by no less a person than the great
John Beverley Robinson himself, then Attorney-General of the
province. Robinson—a man not given to facile enthusiasms—
was impressed; he determined to persuade the clever young
man to enter his Toronto office. And from then on, Draper's
career was made. He became a Member of Parliament, the
colonel of a York militia regiment, Solicitor-General and then
Attorney-General in succession to Hagerman. And now, under
Governor Metcalfe, he was back at his old post of the attorney-
generalship once more.

Macdonald had met Draper for the first time professionally
at the autumn assizes of the Midland District in 1837. Draper
had acted also as Judge-Advocate in the trial of Von Schoultz
and the other "pirate" prisoners caught in the battle at Windmill Point in the autumn of 1838; and his physical presence
and public manner must have been perfectly familiar to Macdonald long before the opening of the first session of the new
parliament in 1844. Draper was a big man, with a rugged,
resilient frame, a capacity for brisk, long walks, and a considerable prowess at cricket which he played with zest until

he was quite old. To his followers, if not to all his contemporaries, he must have seemed a genuinely distinguished man. Cultivated, urbane, learned in the law, skilled in languages both ancient and modern, with a talent for lucid, if elaborate, exposition and a persuasive eloquence which earned him the title of "Sweet William", he might have seemed designed by Providence to lead the Tory party out of the old ways of routine and into the rewarding paths of experiment. Macdonald and the young moderates certainly accepted his leadership eagerly. Moreover, Draper's poise, his learning, his devout Anglicanism, and the irreproachable respectability of his professional connections in Toronto—all ought to have endeared him to the members of the Old Guard. Yet they obviously did not. The Toronto Tories may have been jealous of this successful young interloper from overseas. They certainly disliked him. They intrigued against him. And Macdonald had not been a member of the Legislative Assembly for more than a few weeks when it must have become perfectly clear to him that there could be no genuine negotiated peace between Draper and the Old Guard, and that the war between them—a war both of personalities and of principles—was certain to continue as a struggle for extermination. Macdonald became a devoted follower of Draper. He and the other moderates viewed their distinguished leader with a respect, a hope, and a confidence in which there was only one small flaw of doubt. Draper would infallibly succeed —if only he fought the struggle out to a conclusion. But could he be persuaded to continue? It was known that he had accepted office under Metcalfe reluctantly and as a matter of public duty. He was inclined to view the indecorous hurly-burly of democratic politics with an old-fashioned and fastidious aversion. He grew tired of the open quarrelling and the incessant subterranean intrigue. His eye wandered wistfully towards the seclusion of the bench and the legal library— towards the calm and unhurried composition of those elaborate judicial opinions, full of exact definitions, refined distinctions and learned allusions, which he did so well and enjoyed so much.

II

Macdonald had to familiarize himself with the large strategy of these conflicts between principles and personalities as well as with the detailed tactics of party manoeuvre inside the House. Newly elected, a humble back-bencher, inexperienced yet not intimidated, and never disposed to take himself or anybody else too seriously, he made his way slowly and cautiously through new and difficult situations. From the start he was a fairly good parliamentarian, sensibly obedient to party whips, present unfailingly at every important division. But during his first two sessions, he spoke only at rare intervals and with modest brevity. Yet he was by no means afraid to catch the Speaker's eye; and it was characteristic of him that he seemed even readier to enter the hurly-burly of debate, to take part, as few novices did, in the frightening business of exchange and parry, than to deliver a set prepared oration before a nodding House. The session was barely three weeks old when, on November 19, he made his first intervention.[5] The debate concerned a controverted election, an important election in the urban constituency of Montreal, and one by one the leaders on both sides had risen to attack or defend the petition which had been presented against it. The ample Baldwin, Reform leader for Canada West, with his solemn, slightly Pecksniffian air of conscious rectitude, had just sat down when the young member for Kingston arose to make his maiden speech. Macdonald knew the election law; he was well equipped with the precedents. Calmly, logically, in a brief speech of a few paragraphs, he proceeded to demolish the validity of the petition against the Montreal election. He was the only new member who had ventured to take part in a debate which had been almost monopolized by the great names on both sides; but curiously enough, he was not crowded back into obscurity and forgotten. "Mr. Macdonald, who moved the adjournment," wrote the reporter in the great *Montreal Gazette*, "is evidently not used to parliamentary debate, but he as evidently has the stuff in him. He gathered up the scattered strands of argument with great dexterity, and knitted them up like a man used to the work of reply."⁶

This was one Macdonald—the skilful practitioner of the Midland District courts, the adroit parliamentary tactician of the future. Yet there was another Macdonald, the student, the reader of learned reviews and books, the reasoning, theoretical conservative who had grounded his beliefs on history and philosophy; and this Macdonald, who, to Tom Ramsay, and Alex Campbell and Charles Stuart, must have seemed the real man, had at least one chance to show himself in the session of 1844-45. Late in January, when the House had nearly finished its debate on Roblin's bill for the equal distribution of intestate estates in Canada West, Macdonald rose to speak. To him, as to Burke, any serious change in the established law of private property implied, without any question, the utter subversion of the existing social and political order. His speech was an elaborate one, full of echoes of Burke, and references to *Blackwood's* and the learned reviews, and appeals to the great names of English history. "The great majority of the people," he declared, "were against this measure as anti-British and anti-Monarchical; it ought not to be introduced here, for the very reason that it had been introduced into the United States; and it was folly to raise a monarchical structure upon a republican foundation. The law of primogeniture was the great bulwark between the people and the Crown and the Crown and the people."⁷ Primogeniture was an essential basis of the constitution; it was a vital principle of political economy. The measure before the House, like all other such measures, was calculated to make "that which was a comfortable farmhouse in one generation, a cottage in the second, and a hovel in the third; and, under it, agriculture, instead of becoming a science, would be degraded, as it was in Ireland and France, to a mere means of life." The best economic authorities were opposed to such a division of lands; and the experience of the United States had amply demonstrated the evils of the partition law. "The greatness of England," Macdonald went on, rounding into his peroration, "was owing to its younger sons; it was they who had spread the name, the fame, and the glory of England all over the world—they formed its colonies, led its armies and navies—they were its statesmen and its scholars . . . What would have been the younger Pitt or Fox, if, instead of being sent forth to seek their fortunes, the estate of their father had been divided? They would have been mere country squires, instead of becoming, as they did, the lights of the world. What would the Duke of Wellington have been, if the paternal estate had been divided? It was fortunate for him, for his country, and the world, that he was left with his sword in his hand, and that sword all he had."[8]

This was a special effort, not repeated in the first session. He would never be famous for his oratory alone. Yet the gift for an occasional good speech was one item in the extended list of assets which was gradually making him known as a good parliamentarian. Rapidly he came to possess a cool and disconcertingly exact knowledge of the rules; and sometimes, when the Assembly became a turbulent verbal milling ground, he could intervene with devastating effect. On a day in mid-February, when Moffatt, goaded by Aylwin's repeated interruptions, had finally protested and when the House became at once a babel of excited controversy, it was Macdonald who gave generalship to the Tories and who gradually pushed Aylwin back from one humiliation to another.[9] He was at his best—cool and resourceful—in these encounters. He was efficient also in the more humdrum work of committee. The House—its rules, its ways, its members, and their varied interests and contrasted backgrounds—were all becoming an intimate part of his consciousness. Easily, almost effortlessly, he was compiling the first important pages of that vast catalogue of names, faces, personalities, constituencies, institutions, associations and churches, which he came to know so intimately, and which served him so well until the end.

He was an important acquisition for the party. As one of Draper's young men, he was an important addition to the ranks of the moderates. But Liberal Conservatism was still ringed round with enemies, Tories as well as Reformers; and as the session wore on it became lamentably clear how far the modernists were from dominating their party and how weak and dis-

tracted it still remained. Draper was determined to settle the
university question—the problem of King's College, with its
enormous endowment, and of the newer sectarian colleges,
Queen's, Victoria, and Regiopolis. This question of higher
education in the province, which involved the basic issues of
the relation of church and state and the connection between
science and religion, was the one thing, above all others, which
was almost certain to drive the Anglican Tories, the supporters
of King's and its vast exclusive endowment, into furious opposition against their moderate leaders. Yet the question was
an important one, long and violently agitated in the province,
clamouring for settlement; and Draper did not see how he
could possibly avoid it. In his urbane gentlemanly way, he tried
to compromise. The Reformers, under Baldwin, had hoped to
establish a single, great, non-sectarian university, completely
controlled by the state and its appointees; a university in which
the colleges were to be reduced to the level of divinity halls.
The Conservatives, who got their educational ideals from England rather than from Scotland and the Continent, believed
in colleges as well as in a university, in tutorials as much as
lectures, in academic management more than in external control,
and in church influence rather than in irreligious secular authority. Draper tried to steer a tactful course between these
two extremes. To placate the High Tories, he re-introduced a
moderate religious test, gave the colleges a larger place in the
life of the university, and strengthened its academic control.
To please his own moderate followers—and possibly also to gain
a few Reform votes—he kept all the main features of the Baldwin
measure, the unification and centralization of higher learning,
and the division of the university endowment, hitherto enjoyed
solely by King's.[10]

Macdonald had all Draper's interest in the university question.
Like Draper, he believed that the Conservative party should
tackle and settle the problem; and the debate which followed
the introduction of Draper's bill must, for him, have been a
dismaying revelation of the difficulties in the way. Robinson,
the Inspector-General, resigned his portfolio in protest against
the government's policy. W. H. Boulton and George Sherwood

of Brockville felt perfectly free, despite their recognized political
affiliations, to oppose the measure on the floor of the House,
and even dared, with insolent discourtesy, to move the six
months' hoist for the second reading.[11] Draper was furious.
Despite his mellifluous voice and his suave, urbane manner,
there was a strain of quick, combative emotionalism in the man
who long ago had run away to sea. " . . . To allow the bill to
be stopped before its second reading," he cried, "and to permit
the whole proceedings of the House to be stultified—never,
Sir, will I hold office on such terms."[12] Outwardly, it was a
bold defiance; and yet, in reality, Draper had been forced to
yield. The possibility—indeed, the probability—that a premature
and violent breach with the Toronto Tories might involve the
complete break-up of the party and the utter ruin of all his
hopes, hovered alarmingly before him. It was not yet time to
force the controversy to its climax. He drew back cautiously.
The University Bills were postponed. It was clear to Macdonald
and the moderates that the crisis had been an abortive one,
that the problem of leadership and direction was still unsolved,
and that the whole future of the Conservative party rested in
suspense.

III

Parliament was prorogued before the end of March and Macdonald was soon back in Kingston. The session, in many ways,
had been a disappointing one; but these small concerns for
the future of the party must have been quickly crowded from
his mind by a host of personal troubles which rushed in upon
him in the spring and early summer of 1845. His mother was
gravely ill. Late that spring she suffered one of the first of a
series of small apoplectic seizures which at intervals over a
long period of time wracked her strong and enduring frame.
"Oh, God," wrote Isabella, "it was dreadful to see her face so
twisted."[18] Yet the twisted face recovered its serene composure,
and the iron constitution survived; and it was not the indomitable old woman but the young wife who had caused

Macdonald's worries to grow so horribly out of nothing during the past few months. Isa was not well—far from well. She had been very ill indeed. And already, less than two years after her marriage, less than a year after her happy visit to her sister Margaret Greene in the summer of 1844, the pattern of this dreadful recurring illness had become established and known in all its details. Her attacks came at intervals, rising in spasms to terrible climaxes, which left her exhausted, sunk in complete prostration, incapable almost of moving, or of bearing the company of anybody but those she loved the most.

Yet, in the spring and early summer of 1845, she was, apparently, much better; and Macdonald planned to carry her off again to visit her sister, Margaret, who was living now in New Haven, and to whom she was very devoted. Old Mrs. Macdonald's seizure postponed the visit for some time, and then Macdonald had to go to Toronto on professional business. But it was all arranged that they would set out as soon as he returned; and on June 11, just at the beginning of summer, Isa was writing happily to her sister, giving her all the family news, chattering about lavender bonnets and yellow stockings, and promising that she and John would leave Kingston for the United States shortly after the 21st of the month.[14] She never finished and sealed the letter. The crisis came, and seemed to pass; and with its passing there followed the inevitable debility, which this time did not improve but deepened into an appalling exhaustion. On July 12, Macdonald faced the medical man, old Dr. Sampson, who had dealt with the troubles of so many Kingstonians; and Sampson told him that he could do no more. "God bless and protect both of you, my beloved sisters," Macdonald wrote to Margaret, "and enable you to meet the impending anguish with fortitude and resignation."[15] That day he expected her to die. And even if she did live, live at least for a little time, what chance did they really have of winning this race against time, this race for the warm air and the long sunlight of the south, which now, he had come to believe, held out the one real hope for her recovery? "It may be days—nay, weeks—before she has rallied sufficiently to attempt any journey. What to say or do, I know not. The summer is wearing away and may have nearly terminated before the invalid can be moved."[16]

The warm, pleasant edifice of his domestic happiness was crumbling towards utter ruin. He waited, planning and hoping, drawing on the cool, deep reserves of his fortitude. There was —or seemed to be—one last chance; and suddenly he took it, though the risks involved were frightful. Less than a week after the crisis, at the first fluttering, barely perceptible sign of Isabella's returning health, they set out by steamboat for Oswego, to New Haven and the south. Moll and Lou were with them, and there was work for all to do as they carried the exhausted Isabella down to the dock. At the last moment they almost turned back. They had risked everything. It was a chance, a wild, dangerous chance; but Macdonald was convinced that it was the one hope of survival which remained to Isa. The boat put out. That day the lake was violently stormy. Macdonald was sick, they were all sick, Isabella dreadfully so. "We thought she would die on the deck."[17] And it was not until the dead of night, an hour after midnight, that they finally reached the Welland House in Oswego.

And yet, as she lay on the couch that morning, she seemed— faintly, miraculously—to be improved. Her pulse, her whole appearance were better than they had been just before leaving Kingston. Now, with no thought of turning back, they pushed ahead slowly but hopefully. All the summer and early autumn were spent with Annie and Margaret at New Haven, in prolonged recuperation; but the doctor, as Macdonald had anticipated, ordered Isabella south for the winter, and they were determined to reach Savannah, which was their ultimate goal, before the real coming of the cold. Some time late in October, Macdonald and Isabella set out again. The journey was incredibly long and involved, but Isabella bore its tortuous difficulties with a tranquil and patient resignation which became habitual with her. Shifted from railway to steamboat and back again to railway, borne over cobbled streets in jolting hacks, carried in chairs up the steep, twisting steps of a long succession of hotels, and sleeping, often drugged with opium to dull her pain, through long exhausted days in order to prepare herself for the next stage of the journey, she passed, with Macdonald always at her side, in a dim, long confusion of movement, distress and torpor, through Jersey City, Philadelphia, Baltimore, Wilmington, Charleston, and finally, after over two weeks of broken travel, to "this city of sandy streets and circular squares"—Savannah.

It was a terrible journey. But Macdonald was always helpful, almost always hopeful, almost always light-heartedly ready to find something—even if it were only his own awkward attentions to his wife—which awoke his ready humour or prompted amused, ironic comment. ". . . Annie and I do our d——dest (as the Methodists say) to make her comfortable," he wrote.[18] At Philadelphia, seduced temporarily "from my allegiance to my petticoat government", and carried off by a Mr. Robinson to a highly intellectual conversazione, he found that the champagne and the terrapin supper lingered even more pleasantly in his memory than the scientific and literary discussion.[19] Penned up in dull little hotel parlours and bedrooms, he galloped through a strange variety of books—*Tom Burke, The Bible in Spain, Rookwood*, Carlyle's *Life of Schiller*, Bishop Moore's *Sermons*, and Lord Mahon's *History of England*, which he found "impartial and amusing".[20] He was charmed and delighted, he told his sister-in-law Margaret cheerfully, by the prettiness of the women friends to whom she had written, and who called occasionally on Isabella on their journey south. "By the way, sister," he wrote, "there is a Latin proverb 'Noscitur a sociis' which may be translated for the benefit of the Country Members 'birds of a feather flock together'. I always considered you a *charming woman*, but I did not calculate on all your friends being so. From those I have seen, I have only to say, that you will confer a great favour on me by sitting down and writing me Letters of Credence to *every one* of your Yankee lady friends, and it will go hard but I deliver most of them."[21]

At Savannah, he established Isabella in rooms and set about getting a more comfortable permanent boarding-house. Within a few nights of his arrival, he was taken off to a Whig political meeting; but his views of the two-hour oration delivered by

one of the local judges were a trifle mixed. "He is evidently
an able man, with great fluency and force of expression," he
wrote, "but he has the great fault of American speakers (with,
I believe, the single exception of Webster) of being too
theatrical in manner, and turgid in style."[22] He continued to
prefer English to Yankee oratory; but he found, that night,
that the Americans could, at any rate, concoct a most acceptable
kind of peach brandy. It was pleasant enough in Savannah,
and, if only there had been sufficient money, he would have
liked to stay and to have at least one "warm winter" in his life.
But that was quite impossible, and now he was impatient to be
away. Isabella was, of course, to remain with the southern sunlight which might cure her; and he comforted himself with the
thought that the faithful Margaret would soon come down
from New Haven to take his place beside the invalid. When
he first reached Savannah, late in November, he hoped and
expected to be able to leave by the beginning of the next month.
But Isabella's slow recovery from the terrible fatigues of the
journey must have delayed his departure. He was still in the
south on New Year's Day, and probably for some weeks thereafter. But some time early in February, back once more "among
the frosts and snows of Canada, sucking my paws like any other
bear", he was waiting for Isabella's letters, and reading with
pleasure Margaret's good news of the continued improvement
of her charge.[23]

IV

His absence had lasted six months. Altogether, counting his
long attendance at the first session of the provincial parliament,
he had been away from Kingston for by far the greater part
of 1845. The practice was undeniably suffering; and Campbell,
overburdened with work, was harried and inclined to be resentful. But though Macdonald's difficulties were accumulating,
and his expenses mounting in a frightening fashion, he showed
no sign of abandoning his parliamentary career; and when the
legislature met for the second time, late in March, he was in

TORONTO IN THE FIFTIES

his place as usual.[24] Outwardly his position and importance in
the House did not seem to have altered greatly; his speeches
were not more numerous nor very different in character. He
was, once again, the thoughtful young theorist, quoting freely
from Bentham and Sir James Mackintosh, when he defended
free trade in money against the old usury laws;[25] and his pro-
British nationalism reappeared in a new, economic dress when
he vigorously supported differential duties against imports from
the United States, claiming that it was American—not British—
manufacturers that the Canadians had to fear.[26] These infrequent public appearances were satisfactory enough; but they
were no index of the important place which he was gradually
and unostentatiously winning in the councils of the party. He
was one of Draper's most promising young men. Draper began
to realize it. And he looked upon the young member for Kingston with a fatherly benevolence.

It was at this point that Draper, weary, baffled, but indomitable, decided to make one more effort to strengthen the
government and to popularize the Conservative party. During
the previous summer he had attempted to gain the support of
the French Canadians by giving them a certain number of
places in the government. The attempt had finally failed. The
correspondence, betrayed to Lafontaine, was read triumphantly
to the House in April; and the whole affair had exploded in
the most lamentable and damaging publicity. Yet Draper was
not quite ready to give in. Even if the sullen, reluctant French
Canadians still remained unapproachable, he could at least
reorganize the existing government, secure the support of some
of the able young moderates, and openly dismiss the Tory in-
triguers who had successfully paralysed almost everything he
had tried to do. On June 10, 1846, the day after the Conservative government had finally pulled through its second,
lame parliamentary session, he wrote a long, confidential
memorandum to Lord Cathcart, the undistinguished nobleman
who had succeeded temporarily to the governor-generalship,
when Metcalfe, utterly overwhelmed by his terrible affliction,
had gone home to die.[27]

Only a "due infusion" of French Canadians, Draper insisted,

could make the government really strong; but, at any rate, it might be made less weak by the elimination of its inefficient and obstructive members, the incompetent Viger and the notoriously intriguing Sherwood. For the places thus left vacant, Draper made two definite recommendations: one was "a gentleman of great legal eminence, considerable talent, and irreproachable character"—later identified as John Hillyard Cameron, Macdonald's old fellow-pupil at John Cruickshank's school in Store Street. The other was John A. Macdonald himself. The Commissionership of Crown Lands—the office for which Draper recommended the member for Kingston—imperatively required "a man of activity of mind and familiar with business details". Macdonald's brisk efficiency, the easy swiftness with which, when it suited his purpose, he could get through masses of work must have impressed the harassed leader of the government; and if Draper had come to learn indirectly that, on an evening in the previous April, his prospective young lieutenant had spoken so disrespectfully of a member of the Boulton family that he had risked a duel with young William Henry Boulton, the Tory Toronto member,[28] he might have appeared outwardly shocked, but secretly he could hardly have helped being delighted. Macdonald was a good man—and sound on the Toronto "gang". But there was something else as well—something far more attractive and promising—the unmistakable first signs of charm and popularity, of political wisdom, and insight and tact—the accumulating, promising evidence, not only of open debate, of sober work in committee and caucus, but also of casual talks and convivial occasions, of little arrangements, and negotiations, and manoeuvres.

At the age of thirty-one, when he had had only two years' experience in parliament, Macdonald had been recommended for office under the Crown. Cathcart sanctioned the recommendation, writing to Draper that "the Governor-General has a very high opinion of Mr. J. A. Macdonald and his appointment to office in the administration would afford him much satisfaction".[29] But, for one reason or another, the appointment was not made at this time. Draper, still vainly pursuing his hoped-for alliance with the French, may have preferred to reserve the portfolio of the Crown Lands, pending a general reconstruction of his Cabinet; and it is just as likely that Macdonald himself was, at the moment, in no position to accept public office. He had overspent his income, overworked Campbell, and endangered the practice. The embarrassment of his position was plainly evident in September, 1846, when, after three years, the partnership arrangement came up for renewal.[80] Macdonald had to agree to pay his junior partner £500, in three annual instalments, as compensation for his own prolonged absences during the first period of the partnership. For the future, Campbell was to have one-third of the proceeds as before, but this time the third was to include the profits of the Commercial Bank business, hitherto reserved; and also—and this was a still more significant indication of Macdonald's vulnerable position—the head of the firm had to agree not to take more than £600 annually from the business during the next four years. Yet even these concessions were not all. For if, at the moment, Macdonald was obliged to forgo office, he was obviously thinking of it for the future—for a future not very far away. He agreed—and the concession was written formally into the new agreement—that if he accepted office, Campbell was to be allowed an additional annual payment of £250, beginning in June, 1847. Macdonald was in no position to drive a good bargain. He had piled a staggering burden of personal responsibilities and political ambitions on his neglected practice and long-suffering partner; and during the summer and autumn, he must have stuck closely to Kingston, slaving away at his desk. Isabella was still in the United States. During the greater part of 1846, she probably remained in Savannah, at Mrs. Hardie's boarding-house, improving slowly and with frequent setbacks; and then, possibly some time in the autumn, she was moved north to New York, with the object, no doubt, of obtaining more expert medical attention and more systematic treatment. There Macdonald visited her for the Christmas holiday season of 1846. They had been separated for very nearly a year.

On December 19, while he was away in New York, he was appointed Queen's Counsel, along with Thomas Kirkpatrick, one-time Mayor of Kingston, and Henry Smith, the member for Frontenac, who had acted with him in the famous Ashley-Dundas case. He treated his new honour with characteristic lightness of touch, informing Margaret Greene that it gave him "the *mighty* right of wearing a silk gown instead of a stuff one".[31] He was, however, pleased enough with the appointment, which came unsolicited and unexpected; and he must have read with interest the press comments on it, which, in their vituperative detail, were a sure indication of his growing consequence. "Mr. John A. Macdonald," declared the *Globe,* in its best vein of ferocious denigration, "stands some degrees below Mr. Kirkpatrick. Overlooking his short but discreditable political career, he is a man of perfect respectability—industrious, and successful in his profession—but far from possessing such talent as would warrant his being made a Queen's Counsel. He is, however, a Presbyterian Tory; of that species of respectable 'loose-fish' who denounce High Churchism and Family Compactism, and prate about opening King's College; who are guided more by *personal feeling* than by *principle,* and are prepared to *take office* under any administration, at the shortest notice".[32] Macdonald must have smiled with sardonic amusement. Overlooking (as the *Globe* would have said) the pert imputations and consistent depreciation, he had to admit that the picture of him which the Reform newspaper was industriously circulating, was both accurate and politically advantageous. Gradually, to both friends and foes alike, he was getting to be known as a moderate, as a "Presbyterian Tory", as a follower of William Henry Draper.

It was thus that Draper saw him. And Draper, approaching the final crisis of his political career, began to rely more and more upon his young subordinate, and to give him a larger and larger measure of his confidence. The position of the head of the government was becoming almost intolerable. Sherwood had been ejected from office; for the moment, the High Tories were held at bay; but the French Canadians, appealed to once more to join the government, had once more refused. Draper was sick of office. And then, before his longing eyes, he saw, slowly opening, the door of his escape. Judge Christopher

Alexander Hagerman, once Kingston's member and Attorney-General, was clearly at the point of death; and Draper, after all his services, could justly claim the right of succession. Yet he hesitated. "My thirst for relief from the responsibility of office . . . ," he wrote to Egerton Ryerson, "gets stronger and stronger. I should gladly avail myself of the first *just cause* to slake it, but I have not nerve enough to subject myself to the charge of weakening and perhaps breaking up the party Lord Metcalfe brought together by an act of personal desertion."[33] No! He would not leave yet. A new Governor, Lord Elgin, had arrived; and, under him, he would make one last effort to reorganize the government, to get the support of the French Canadians, and to strengthen the position of the moderates in the party. Macdonald would be useful to him—useful on his own account, useful also for his friendly association with Ogle Gowan, the Grand Master of the Orange Lodge, and one of the most popular and obstreperous opponents of the Family Compact in the party. He offered Macdonald the solicitor-generalship, which was refused. He begged Macdonald to pay a "flying visit" to Montreal, to persuade Gowan to accompany him, and to join with the Orangeman in the important work of convincing Lord Elgin that Conservatism did not necessarily mean ultra-Toryism.[34]

For Macdonald, all these political agitations—the arrival of Elgin, the threat of Draper's retirement, the approaching struggle within the party for the inheritance of leadership—coincided, with painful exactitude, with a crisis in his domestic affairs. He heard regularly from New York, for his own sister, Margaret, had gone down to look after Isabella; and early in January Isabella herself wrote him a note of congratulation, in her "trembling handwriting", for his birthday on the 11th. Then, just when she seemed to be improving, though slowly and with difficulty, a fresh complication was revealed. She had become pregnant. Late in March Margaret became so frightened at the state of her patient that she appealed for help. Macdonald rushed down to New York, taking with him Maria Macpherson, Isabella's sister, who, as the mother of a fine family, regarded herself as an expert in these matters, and who cheerfully volun-

teered to take Margaret's place. They found Isabella in a doubtful state. Her new medical adviser, Dr. Washington, reported
frankly that she was in a critical condition as a result of
repeated attacks of "uterine neuralgia". "These attacks . . . ,"
Macdonald wrote to Margaret Greene, "may bring on a premature confinement, and if so, God alone knows what may be
the consequence".[35] Isabella herself, lying all day in utter quiet,
was calm and resolute. Macdonald could not be always with
her, for the doctor would permit only one visitor at a time.
There was little he could do, besides. And, within a week, he
was on his way back to Kingston, carrying his consuming
anxiety with him.

When he arrived home, he found the Cabinet in the throes
of reconstruction and the opposition newspapers jubilantly
celebrating the embarrassments of the government and the
rivalries of the "Gowanites" and the "MacNabmen". Draper's
final effort to obtain the support of the French Canadians had
failed, like the others. But, inside the Cabinet, he and the
moderates were trying desperately to strengthen their position,
and, on May 6, William Morris wrote to Macdonald, offering
him the portfolio of Receiver-General, appealing for his assistance, and reminding him that "if you will not put your
shoulder to the wheel, you assist those who, it may be, desire to
regain power which you and I helped to deprive them of; I
mean the 'family'."[36] It was a cunningly worded appeal. And
Macdonald replied three days later, on the 9th. He accepted
office, on condition that Morris himself would remain in the
ministry, and with the hope that Draper might continue at least
until the end of the approaching session, and that his acquaintance, Gowan, might receive some political reward.[37] On May 11,
the perennial, unpolitical secretary, Dominick Daly, wrote, informing him that his commission had been issued on the same
day, and less than a fortnight later his appointment was
officially announced. The announcement created no great
uproar, either of delight or disapproval. The opposition papers
treated it with tolerant contempt. Macdonald was, the *Globe*
assured its readers, a "*harmless* man", a "third-class lawyer" who
had sat two sessions in parliament and "scarcely opened his

mouth during the whole time".[38] Yet Elgin, a fairly astute observer, was rather more flattering. "Since my last letter to you
was despatched," he wrote to Grey, "the prospects of the administration are brighter—a certain Mr. Macdonald, a person of
consideration among the *moderate Conservative, anti-Compact*
Party has consented to accept the office of Receiver-General
. . .".[39]

He accepted it at a moment when the government was in
the final agonies of reconstruction. During the last half of May,
the fortnight which preceded the long-delayed opening of the
legislature, the fortunes of the ultras and the moderates wavered
backwards and forwards across the trampled battleground of the
Conservative administration. Hagerman had died, Draper was
determined to resign. And for his post, the attorney-generalship,
the key post in the Cabinet, a successor would have to be found.
Who was it to be? John Hillyard Cameron, the first invited,
refused the office; and there was—or seemed to be—nobody else
but Sherwood.[40] Less than a year before, Sherwood had been
virtually dismissed from the office of solicitor-general. Now,
on the heels of Draper's retirement, he entered the ministry
again to occupy the post of leadership which his old rival had
just vacated. It looked like a complete victory for the ultras.
It looked as if the Tory party had openly and officially disavowed
Draper's Liberal-Conservatism. But nothing in that period of
Canadian Conservatism was ever conclusive or final. Draper
might have abdicated, but he had appointed his successor. And
Macdonald, as well as Morris, was there to carry on the fight
for his tradition.

On June 2, when parliament opened, Macdonald took his seat
on the treasury benches for the first time. He was badly worried
during the first ten days at Montreal, for Isabella was drawing
closer to her time, and he had no news from New York, except
a scrap which had been forwarded from Kingston.[41] He was
bothered too by the problems of his job, by the difficulties of
an embarrassing session; and it must have given him a certain
wry amusement to reflect that, just when he expected to become
a father, he was to appear in parliament as the principal author
of an important piece of government legislation. Back in May,

when he had written to Morris accepting office, he had insisted that the university question was the great stumbling-block in the path of the Conservatives, a stumbling-block which must in some way be removed. "Many questions of more real importance may arise," he pointed out, "but none which operates more strongly on the principles or prejudices of the public, and if the Conservatives hope to retain power, they must settle it before the general election." It was the first unmistakable sign of his purposeful sense of direction, of his sensitive alertness to popular demand. And for some reason, which can only be guessed at with difficulty, for the purposes of that erratic and distracted ministry are never easily explicable, he was given the chance of settling the matter once and for all.

On Friday, July 9, he was on his feet to sponsor the first government bills of his career.[42] His speech—brief, factual, straightforward—was in utter contrast to the elaborate eloquence of Draper.[43] Yet the terse, laconic exposition disclosed a policy which was a better compromise, a compromise potentially far more popular, than any that Draper had thought of. Daringly, Macdonald rejected the plans of his old chief, and of his old chief's great opponent, Baldwin. The idea of a unified, non-sectarian, provincial university was abandoned. The principle of collegiate organization and sectarian control, beloved of the High Tories, became the main basis of Macdonald's plan. King's College, which had been partly secularized by the amending statute of 1837, was to have its old charter restored to it almost unchanged, and was to become once more a strictly Church of England institution. All the colleges—King's, Queen's, Victoria, and Regiopolis—would thus conform roughly to the same pattern of clerical organization and management; and all —this was the great popular feature of Macdonald's bill—were to share in the splendid endowment. "Yet, in the division," Macdonald explained, "particular attention was to be paid to the Church of England, for they have just and equitable claims". Out of the annual revenue of the endowment, King's College, which had once had the whole, was to be given £3000, and the other colleges £1500 each. The plan was shrewd. More than shrewd, it was wise. It was based on the idea—the idea

which commanded widespread support for this and another
generation—that the union of science and religion was indissoluble. The claims of a wide variety of communions for government support in their educational work were generously recognized; and yet a fair preference had been given to the historic
rights of the Church of England.

For the moment, the success of the bills looked comfortably
certain. Macdonald appeared to have achieved the impossible:
he had united both sections of the Conservative party in the
support of his measure. John Hillyard Cameron, though he
gave a regretful glance backward to King's College as it once
had been, declared that the plan was just and that he was
prepared to accede to it.[44] Sherwood, who had opposed Draper's
bills so bitterly two years before, promised his support. Boulton,
the second of the Toronto Tories, amiably asserted that the
bills would satisfy all parties. And, on the other side, Ogle
Gowan, the anti-Compact moderate, had a flattering word of
praise for his friend, the man who "should feel proud at having
solved the problem that baffled so many others".[45] Yet had he
solved it, had he really settled it? "Settling the question, indeed,"
cried Baldwin, with sombre indignation, "by sweeping the University from the face of the earth, and giving the Country, in
its stead, a few paltry Institutions, in none of which could there
be any pretensions to those attributes which it was the highest
behest to a University to possess."[46] This kind of stuff might
be expected from the secular-minded Reformers, though Macdonald hoped to detach a few Methodists from their number.
But, when two supposedly faithful Conservatives unaccountably arose to make the same secular criticisms, then the young
member on the treasury bench began to feel uneasy.

Oddly enough, yet not so oddly in view of the violent
passions which the issue aroused, the debate had taken place on
the first reading of the bills. They were postponed for a while;
but they were due to come up again for consideration on July
26. And in the meantime, Macdonald, worried by the news
which kept arriving from New York, tried anxiously to consider the position. It was the old, endless problem of the feeble
Conservative majority, of the perilous insecurity of the govern-

ment. He wrote gloomily to the Principal of Victoria College that two Methodist Reformers, whose support he had hoped for, would vote against the bill; the Roman Catholic Reformers were also in opposition; and, what was even worse, the two Conservatives, Dickson and Wilson, refused obstinately to be won round.[47] Regretfully he decided that the bills would have to be postponed, and that he must wait for the organization of popular support in their favour. He had failed—almost as badly as Draper, and for much the same reasons.

On Wednesday, July 28, two days after the second reading of the University Bills had been perfunctorily discharged without debate, the legislature was prorogued. Immediately, with few or no explanations to his political colleagues, he hastened back to Kingston; and along with Mrs. Harper he set out for New York. The frantic travellers arrived on Saturday to find Isabella reasonably well, and Maria elated at their coming. But they were only just in time. For the next day Isabella became obviously distressed, and Dr. Washington, hastily summoned in the evening, declared that she was in labour. For some hours she continued to suffer. And then, in desperation, they called in another physician, a Dr. Rodgers, "celebrated for the use and application of the *Lethean* or somnific gas". But Isabella's weak and nervously disordered state intimidated him, and he did not dare to give her enough of the gas to put her comfortably asleep. All night, and far into the morning of August 2, the long agony went on. At length it became only too clear that Isabella was unable to deliver herself. The doctors determined to use forceps, and, at a little after 8 o'clock in the morning, her child, a boy, apparently strong and healthy, was born. "The first word the poor thing said," Macdonald wrote to his mother, "after being informed that the child was alive and not deformed, was to tell me to write you and to ask you to give it a name—which in her name and my own I now do."[48]

Chapter Six

The Twilight of the Tory Party

I

The boy was thin. As Maria said to Dr. Washington, that was scarcely to be wondered at, since he had been living on pills so long. But he was tall, and seemed strong and healthy.[1] His eyes, dark blue in colour, were very large, and his nose—his father's nose—was generous also. They had not much chance to admire him, for he was whisked off almost immediately to Kingston by Maria; and Macdonald settled down in New York to watch anxiously over his wife's convalescence. It was very slow. The neuralgic pains in her side and leg kept recurring; and Macdonald, impatiently sceptical of the leeching and blistering which had been prescribed for her, called in another physician who varied the treatment. She seemed slowly to improve. Yet her condition was so vulnerable, and the improvement so uncertain and precarious that when the doctor finally suggested that she might try to walk across the room, this little convalescent's adventure ended in a violent return of pain, and a recourse, once more, to the old anodyne, opium.[2]

The long, aching apprehensions, the sudden, recurring seizures of fear, like spurts of pain, seemed never to end or to subside. He scarcely knew what to do. Campbell and the practice would have to get along as best they could; but he was a minister of the Crown now, at a critical moment in the history of the government, and he could not stay away indefinitely. Cayley, the new Inspector-General, wrote him considerately from Montreal, assuring him "from our colleagues and myself that we will cheerfully submit to a longer deprivation of your services and assistance here should the continued illness of Mrs. Macdonald claim your care, rather than add to your anxiety by pressing your return".[3] These assurances were kind, but they could not be presumed upon. Obviously he would have to return, and obviously also—however much they might wish it—Isabella could not accompany him. How was he to leave her? The Macpherson-Clark women, who had come loyally to his assistance so often in the past, were now, for one reason or another, in no position to lend him aid. His sister Louisa was ill; his mother, attacked once again by an apoplectic seizure, and still weak and prostrate, required her daughter Margaret's constant attention. Maria Macpherson had enough to do to cope with her own children and to look after the infant John Alexander Macdonald, so called after his father. And Isabella's other sisters, including the faithful Margaret Greene, were far away and unable to come. He would have to leave his wife, for a time at least, with strangers. He said good-bye to her—ill, lonely, frightened at the thought of his departure—and tore himself away.

Back in Montreal, living in lodgings, "quite solitary and miserable" and comforted mainly by the news of young John Alexander's flourishing progress, he picked up departmental routine and political strategy once more. The arrears were cleared up with his usual expedition; and he found administrative work acceptable enough, for there was enough of it to keep him from boredom without absorbing all his attention. The really perplexing problem, which occupied the ministry at intervals during the greater part of the autumn, was the lamentable condition of the Conservative government. On the one hand, though the existing parliament still had some time to run, it would be difficult and very humiliating politically to stagger through yet another session with such a shaky majority. On the other hand, though Lord Elgin's consent to an early dissolution could probably be secured, the government would certainly run a very good chance of defeat at a general election. There was no doubt that the ministers were caught, partly by their own failures—the University Bills being the most notorious example—and partly by the general commercial depression, which neither they, nor anybody else in Canada, could conceivably have avoided. Already, during the whole of 1846, the timber trade had been seriously depressed. The first season which followed the repeal of the British Corn Laws was, to be sure, a good one for Canadian agriculture, for the terrible scarcity in the British Isles which had, indeed, dictated Peel's measure, created, for a time, an apparently bottomless demand for food-stuffs from North America. Prices kept up fairly well during the first few months of 1847; and then, with the dead weight of a stone, they dropped. By the autumn of the year, the whole province, and the whole of British North America, was becalmed in a windless commercial stagnation.

All autumn, Macdonald and his colleagues looked doubtfully at the problem, backed away from it, and returned to continue their morbid scrutiny. In the end they decided in favour of a dissolution. It was a choice between two evils, almost a choice between lingering and sudden death; but the ministry preferred the quick way, even though some of its members may have felt sure that their action amounted to political suicide. As early as October 30, Macdonald wrote H. D. Jessup of Grenville, informing him that a dissolution had already been under serious consideration;[4] and a few days later the first rumour of a general election began to appear in the Kingston newspapers. Parliament was not finally dissolved and the new writs issued until early in December; but at least a week before that Macdonald was back in Kingston, organizing his campaign. It was good to escape from his gloomy bachelor quarters and to be back with the family once again; and although Isabella still lingered in New York—for now it had been determined that she must spend another winter there—he could at least solace himself with the pleasant sight of young John Alexander, a sturdy little thing, nearly four months old. But he was very busy in Kingston. Now, it seemed, he might have a real fight on his hands.

Though the Reformers put up a candidate, a relatively unknown young man named Kenneth Mackenzie, this familiar type of opposition probably did not cause Macdonald a great deal of concern. What really gave him pause was the proposed candidature of Thomas Kirkpatrick—a disconcerting and preposterous candidature which threatened to divide the Conservative vote.[5] The trouble with Kirkpatrick was that he was —or would have been in other circumstances—such an unexceptionable candidate. A Conservative like Macdonald, quite as well known and apparently as popular—for at the time he was Kingston's Mayor—Kirkpatrick had, in addition, a special claim upon the Irish vote; and the Irish vote, as Manahan had demonstrated in 1841 in his contest with Forsyth, was important enough to cause the Conservative newspapers grave concern. The *Chronicle and News* reminded its readers that union was strength, deplored the possibility of an unnatural blow aimed "at the vitality of our existence as a Conservative Constituency", and roundly asserted that "no Conservative, who understands his duty, as such, will for a moment countenance a division as Mr. Kirkpatrick threatens".[6] Mr. Kirkpatrick began to realize that he had no press, but a good deal of opprobrium, in Kingston. He thought twice about the matter and retired.

Macdonald, as might have been expected, built most of his campaign around the University Bill. It was his bill, it was one of the government's most popular measures, and, above all, it had an intimate and direct connection with his constituency, for—by a special dispensation of Providence—two of the institutions, Queen's and Regiopolis, which were to be granted support under the new scheme, were actually situated in Kingston. The Radicals, uncomfortably aware of these circumstances, labelled Macdonald as a designing Tory "of the Draper, or crafty school", denounced his bill as a bill of "proscription, of injustice, and delusion", and tried to explain how it had deceived the Roman Catholics, Methodists, and Scots Presbyterians, and utterly proscribed the Baptists, Free Kirkers, and Episcopal Methodists.[7] These blows, watched by Kingstonians without much interest or alarm, did not drive Macdonald back upon the defensive. On December 20, when he addressed a large crowd of his supporters at one of the final meetings of the campaign, he was still dwelling proudly on the positive advantages which the lucky Kingston would derive from his measure.[8] He gave a brief, sidelong glance of disapproval at Baldwin's "great godless university, in which it was proposed to teach men everything but that which it most concerned them to know". Religion, the bond of social union, the preparation for the life hereafter, was the essential basis of all education. It was the basis of his plan; and his plan had secured the support of all religious authorities, Anglican, Presbyterian, Methodist, and Roman Catholic. No Christian communion was excluded from its benefits, as the Reformers had unjustly claimed; if other colleges, under other religious authorities, were established and obtained charters, they might participate, along with the original beneficiaries, in the proceeds of the endowment. His plan, which embraced all communions and all classes, was aimed at bringing education within the reach of the mass of the people. Earlier university bills had designed "one great institution at Toronto, inaccessible to the great body of the people"; but he, believing that parents would prefer to have their sons educated under their own supervision rather than to send them to Toronto from all parts of the province, had tried to place the advantages of an education within easy reach of all.

On December 22, at the nomination meeting, which was invaded by a large crowd of enthusiasts, many of them without votes, the show of hands seemed to be in favour of Mackenzie. "Mr. Macdonald is truly chop-fallen", exulted the *Kingston Herald*.[9] But Macdonald had suffered exactly the same small tactical defeat in his contest with Manahan; and as he said on the hustings, after the poll had been demanded, "he was quite content to take the voters, and to give his opponent all the advantage he could possess by enjoying the confidence of the remainder".[10] The voters in fact rolled up in impressive numbers in Macdonald's favour when the poll opened at 9 o'clock on December 28. And when, on the following day, it finally closed, the vote stood 386 for Macdonald to 84 for Mackenzie.[11] It was nearly, though not quite, as bad a defeat as Manahan's had been.

Yet, unfortunately, Macdonald's success was completely untypical of the fortunes of the Conservative party as a whole. Nearly two months later, on February 28, when the new par-

liament met in Montreal for its first session, the wastage of
Conservatism was apparent all too literally in the flesh. Many
of the leaders—MacNab, Cayley, Cameron, Robinson, Boulton,
the Sherwoods, as well as Macdonald himself—had all been
safely returned; but the truth was—there could be no denying
it—that the party had actually been cut to about half its strength
in the previous House. There were no French Canadians and
virtually no westerners who voted on the Conservative side in
the opening divisions. The party, now wholly English-speaking,
had been reduced to its primitive Loyalist nucleus; and for the
government there was no escape from defeat. In a few days,
it came. On February 25, MacNab failed of re-election as
Speaker by a vote of 54 to 19; and on March 3, Baldwin's amendment to the address in reply to the speech from the throne
was carried by 54 to 20.[12] The next day the entire ministry
resigned. Macdonald was a free man, and within a month—
for the rest of the brief, uninteresting session was over before
the end of March—he was back in Kingston again.

II

The first spring days had come by then, and the great event
of the early summer was the long-awaited return of Isabella.
It was in June, 1848, nearly three years after the terrible day
in July when they had set out for Oswego by the steamer, that
she finally arrived back in Kingston. Her longing for her husband and for young John Alexander, her desperate, continually
thwarted desire to begin the only life that mattered to her once
more, had sustained her to the end; and, as Macdonald reported,
"she bore the journey wonderfully well". But the reaction was
swift and disconcertingly severe. For days she lay in her half-
darkened room, sunk in lassitude and discomfort, overcome by
the excitements and fatigues of the journey, capable only of
the exertion of sitting up for about ten minutes each day, and
occasionally drugging her pain with opium. At first the boy
was shy with her. Weak as she was, "she could not dandle
him, or toss him about—a ceremony which the young gentleman

insists upon from all who approach him".[13] This strangeness must have hurt her a little, even in her torpor. But soon, as she grew slightly better, Macdonald reported that they had become great friends, and the baby used to sit "most contentedly in the bed with her, surrounded by his toys, which he throws about, much to her inconvenience, I am sure, though she will not allow it". She watched him with all the starved, fierce intensity of her emotional nature, watched him while he played with happy aimlessness beside her, bent over his small face when he fell so suddenly asleep. "Oh! darling, darling sister," she confessed, "my very soul is bound up in him. God pardon me if I sin in this. But did I not purchase him dearly?"[14] Now he was nearly a year old—a fine little boy "in high spirits and in capital condition". "Certainly," Macdonald reported proudly, "there never was a child who has got through his first year with less trouble or illness of any kind. God grant it may continue so."[15]

These were happy days of reunion. And yet as he watched Isabella and talked with her in the dim room, Macdonald grew more and more profoundly uneasy. The recurring neuralgia, the sudden violent attacks of pain, the opium, and the drear lassitude of recovery—all these, though dreadful, were known, familiar, even tolerable, for they had been borne so often before. But now there was something new—a small matter, perhaps, small at any rate in comparison with her accustomed miseries, but terrible in its sinister significance. Even before she had left New York she had been troubled by an occasional pain in her chest and a slight cough; and on her way up to Kingston, in the middle of June, she had unaccountably caught cold. For the first week after her arrival, the cough, though still not hacking or exhausting, was almost incessant; and although a new prescription which Dr. Hayward of Kingston supplied seemed for a while to give her some relief, the cough never completely disappeared. Once or twice, on the journey up from New York, she had discovered blood upon her handkerchief; and now at intervals, the small stains reappeared. The doctors conducted long examinations, failed to discover any signs of serious, permanent affection, and, for a while, talked soothingly about the fatigues and excitements of the journey. Her pulse was not feverish; there was no hectic flush on her cheek. But obviously, as the medical men admitted in the end, there must be some tenderness which time, and nature, and local remedies, it was hoped, would cure. Macdonald remained disquieted. "I fear," he wrote his sister-in-law, "I fear."[16]

If rest, and peace, and fresh air would help to cure her, he was determined that they should be hers. Some little distance from town, half-way down the long hill which sloped towards Lake Ontario, there stood a large, absurdly ornate "villa", with two long wings at right angles to each other, and, at the centre, a square, incongruous tower, which seemed almost to have a separate and disconnected existence of its own. The rent would certainly be heavy; and already—for there were servants and a nurse for the child—he was probably spending up to the limit of his income. But whatever financial worries he may have had were concealed under an easy flow of raillery at the expense of the architectural horror, "the most fantastic concern imaginable", which he proposed to rent. It had been built, he explained, by a retired grocer, who had dreamed romantically of an "Eyetalian Willar"; and in Kingston it was variously known—from the "laudable tho' rather prosaic pursuits of the worthy landlord"— as Tea Caddy Castle, Molasses Hall, and Muscovado Cottage.[17] Macdonald called it "Pekoe Pagoda" to his intimates and named it "Bellevue" for public consumption. They moved out towards the end of August. It was very quiet there, and the trees grew thick about the place, and a sweet fresh breeze blew in from Lake Ontario. The short journey—it was less than a mile from home—had exhausted Isabella and brought on a return of her neuralgia. But Macdonald was still sanguine that she would improve rapidly in the new surroundings. The boy was fine. "He sits by the hour now with his mother, as contentedly as possible," he wrote, "and smiles and crows away from one end of the day to the other."[18]

They had nearly a month of quiet happiness in Pekoe Pagoda. And then, on September 21, 1848, young John Alexander died. "Convulsions", a sudden, terrible fall—the accounts of the tragedy differ; and the newspaper notices simply announced the

death of "the infant son of the Hon. John A. Macdonald".[19]
He had lost his child; he never expected now to have another;
and the hope which still mitigated the enormous concern he
felt for his wife was sustained as much by his stubborn will as
by the warm, strong current of his sanguine temperament. That
dark autumn he and Isabella drew even closer together in their
loneliness. In October—far too sorn after the tragedy—he was
obliged to go to Toronto for a fortnight on professional business.
But Isabella, childishly eager to surprise and please him with
her improvement, practised sitting up a while each day during
his absence, and, the night he returned, a little table was brought
into her bedroom, and they dined in state together.[20] Gradually
the household began to approximate what still, after all their
misfortunes, must have seemed a delicious novelty—the ordinary
routine of family life. Macdonald became a typical, overworked
professional man, away to the office by nine o'clock in the
morning and absent until six at night; and Isabella, though she
was always confined to her room, and often—ill with pain—to
her bed, managed somehow, in her frail but persistent fashion,
to play the welcome role of housekeeper. And the house, under
her remote but methodical Scottish management, fell gracefully
into neat routines of order, regularity, and cleanliness. The
great event, the domestic climax of the day, was Macdonald's
dinner, "about which poor Isa takes the greatest pains". Sometimes he would draw her in on a chair to the table in the dining-
room; but often he sat there alone, eating a far too solitary meal.
Then, in the evening, he would read to her, while she lay with
a piece of sewing or knitting in her hand, and then it would
be tea-time and the day would be over.

The autumn passed with imperceptible and dismaying swiftness. It was December before they knew it, and parliament was
scheduled to meet in the following month. The very thought
of his absence, coming so swiftly after the death of their child,
distressed her pitiably. He almost decided not to go; but then
his stubborn loyalty to the party, in its period of trouble, reasserted itself, and he was not yet willing to abandon his own
political career. It was, he told his sister-in-law, "a matter of
necessity".[21] He would go; but not for long. And he set out

from Kingston, carrying the new waistcoat Isabella had made him, "which I am to sport as a winter vest".

III

He found his fellow-Conservatives in a black mood. In the Assembly, they were a pitiable minority, capable of mustering, at best, about twenty-five votes; and all over the province their old and stoutest supporters seemed crushed to earth by an accumulation of misfortunes. The depression, sullenly continuing, made the present almost unendurable; and the repeal of the British Corn Laws and Timber Duties, which at one stroke had ended Canada's old preferences in imperial markets, seemed to have cut short the hope of any real revival along traditional lines for the future. The Old Colonial System, to which the Tories had clung tenaciously in the past and which seemed at once the basis of their material success and the foundation of their old political supremacy, appeared to be tottering to its fall. The Canadian Conservatives acted like men who had been cheated of their inheritance and robbed of their faith. In the towns, and particularly in Montreal, where the depression was at its blackest, people began shamelessly to air strange, heterodox opinions and to bow down before outlandish pagan gods. There was discussion of protection to native industry, and a growing agitation for a wide reciprocal trade agreement with the United States, and even—this was the final apostasy—talk of annexation to the American republic. The Conservatives had reached these dangerous extremes, even before the meeting of parliament, even though they might have expected that there was more and worse to come. The ministry, now solidly Reform and backed by a solid Reform majority in the House, had been working out a great programme of new legislation ever since the brief perfunctory session of 1848. And one of the first measures to be introduced was Lafontaine's proposal to use public funds to compensate those persons in Lower Canada who had suffered property losses during the troubles of 1837 and 1838.

It was the Rebellion Losses Bill which completed the ruin of the old Tory philosophy and drove the Conservatives to the excesses of desperation. The bill, introduced first in the shape of seven resolutions, was a highly provocative measure, and, in all probability, intended as such by Lafontaine and his French-Canadian friends. The proposed benefits were apparently thrown open to everybody, without any defined exceptions whatever. Conceivably rebels who had sustained losses as a result of the action of the civil and military authorities might secure compensation just as easily as loyal citizens who had suffered at the hands of the rebels. To many people in Canada West, Reformers as well as Conservatives, the proposed bill meant, in effect, the formal annulment of the political decision of 1837 and the legitimization of the Lower Canadian revolts. The Tories were scandalized. This huge and shameless affront to their principles drove from their heads all prudent calculations of compromise with the French Canadians; and, without any reserves or qualifications or hesitations, they leaped upon what was for them the crucial point of the whole question. Did the government actually intend to compensate those who had taken part in the revolts? Did it—to take an embarrassing but pointed example—intend to pay over money to Dr. Wolfred Nelson, member for Richelieu, who had certainly, though ineffectually, tried to lead the rebels in 1837, and who afterwards, in 1845, had shyly presented a modest bill for £12,000 against the government he had defied by force of arms? All these interrogations and rhetorical questions were in vain. The government, either in embarrassment, or stubbornness, or complacency, remained silent. Even Dr. Nelson, who was occasionally goaded to reply by his tormentors, was scarcely more illuminating in his answers. Had not Nelson, inquired Sir Allan MacNab bluntly, been a "rank rebel" in 1837? "Not to my God," replied Dr. Nelson affectingly.[22] This removal of the whole question to the elevated plane of theology was scarcely calculated to advance its solution. Did Dr. Nelson's innocence before the Almighty entitle him to £12,000 from the government of the Province of Canada?

During two long sessions in committee while the debate centred, with ever mounting violence, upon the scandalous ambiguity of the measure, Macdonald maintained his accustomed silence. A fairly strict parliamentarian, not very much inclined to verbal heroics, he took no part in these emotional recriminations, these excited charges and counter-charges. But his temper was quick and occasionally it escaped from the cool control which he habitually imposed upon it; and his intervention in the debate of February 1849, when it finally came, was sudden and characteristic. It was William Hume Blake who goaded him to action. Blake, who came of a good family and who had been educated at Trinity College, Dublin, was a member of that cultivated and prosperous group of Anglo-Irish Reformers, led by the Baldwins, who repaid the supercilious disdain of the Family Compact with an equally cold and arrogant dislike. Elected for one of the York constituencies in the general election of 1847, he speedily came to be recognized as an acquisition of immense value to the Reform party; and on February 15, after MacNab, Sherwood, Gugy, and the other principal Tory speakers had had their prolonged say, he rose to attack the problem of Rebellion Losses. His speech, delivered in an assertive, dogmatic, passionate fashion, and with a prodigally copious flow of offensive Irish oratory, had lasted between two and three hours when it was suddenly interrupted. Blake, carried away by his invective, dared to call MacNab and his friends the real "rebels" of 1837! MacNab rose passionately to his feet. It was a falsehood, he shouted. The Speaker called him to order. MacNab insisted on repeating his statement, unless Blake would withdraw his. "Never!" cried Blake. A pandemonium of recriminations followed. The galleries erupted in fist fights; and the onlooking ladies, tumbling in charming disarray over the low barrier, were conducted by a gallant parliamentarian to the little island of safety behind the Speaker's chair.[23]

In this first skirmish, Macdonald took no part. But the events of February 15 were only a preliminary, for Blake had several thousand more words that he wanted to say; and next day, refreshed, and eager, and declamatory, he returned to the charge. Macdonald must have listened to him with rising impatience. Most parliamentary speeches left him tolerably unconcerned, if not cheerfully amused. But this was different. Blake's speech, which purported to be a long historical and legal review of the background of the rebellion, was so shamelessly vitiated by its evasions and omissions, and so grotesquely Irish in its rasping belligerency, that Macdonald grew white with Highland Scots fury. For long minutes he must have fidgeted and hesitated. And then, while Blake continued his interminable reading from old dispatches—garbling their contents, so the *Montreal Gazette* assured its readers, to "justify rebellion"—he could bear it no longer. He rose suddenly, to a point of order.[24]

"I should feel obliged," he remarked tensely, "by the honourable member reading all the words."

"What does the honourable member mean?" Blake inquired.

"I want the honourable member to read the whole of it," Macdonald explained. "I shall do it for him myself, if he wishes. Is it parliamentary, in reading documents, to leave out whole sentences and parts of sentences?"

MacNab jumped to his feet to support his lieutenant. Such a partial reading of documents, he declared, would certainly be considered irregular at Westminster.

Blake regarded them both with contemptuous defiance.

"I shall read any part I like," he declared.

The Speaker quieted the resulting uproar. Blake swept on his way, unchecked and unrepentant, and finished shortly after in a fierce peroration. The debate continued on a more humdrum and less provocative note. But, in the meantime, Macdonald had been busy. Duels, which had been a reality twenty-five years before, were still a diminishing possibility in the 1840's; and challenges, by which an explanation or an apology could frequently be extorted, were regarded with enormous seriousness. While the debate proceeded, Macdonald sent his challenge, his "threatening communication", and, shortly after, both he and Blake quietly left the Assembly hall. The Speaker was informed; the galleries were cleared of reporters and spectators; and the sergeant-at-arms, bearing the mace, went off solemnly to seek the culprits and to require their immediate attendance in the House. Macdonald was found, returned, and made his submission. But Blake, curiously enough, was not at home. Presumably, if the sergeant-at-arms was unable to find him, Macdonald's seconds would have been in a similar difficulty. It all ended happily on Monday, February 18, when the sergeant reported that he had also taken Mr. Blake into custody, and both repentant culprits bound themselves to keep the peace.[25]

The incident was over. And, as it turned out, the troubled passage of the Rebellion Losses Bill was nearly over as well. On February 22, Henry John Boulton, once a Conservative and now an independent Reformer eager for political preferment, introduced an important amendment to the resolutions—an amendment which he had actually persuaded Wolfred Nelson to second, and which had had the previous concurrence of the principal chiefs of the Reform party.[26] By the amendment, all those people in Lower Canada who had been convicted by the courts in 1837-38 or had been banished to Bermuda in accordance with Lord Durham's Ordinance, were excluded from the financial benefits of the proposed bill.[27] If the Conservatives had thought of this amendment, which was, in reality, the minimum amendment capable of satisfying Canada West, they might very well have overthrown the government. But Boulton, the busy, obsequious friend of the ministry, had forestalled them, and, once his device had been publicly accepted by the Reform leaders, the rank and file of the party, which up to that time had been dubious and reluctant, swung gratefully into line.

The passage of the Rebellion Losses Bill was now certain. Even so, the final debate on the subject lasted all through the night of Thursday, February 22, and on until nearly noon of Friday morning. Macdonald spoke late, when the long, all-night session was nearly over. This—his sole contribution of any length on the subject of Rebellion Losses—was a typical Macdonald speech, just as characteristic of his usual political strategy, as his brush with Blake had been typical of his hot Highland temperament. "They had been hurried into the consideration of the Resolutions," he declared, "without any notice, or without any explanation being given of the measure

. . .".[28] The ministers were now anxious to push the bill through in a hurry, because, if they waited, their supporters might be influenced by the rising popular clamour against it. The opposition, sure ultimately of popular support, would make no compromise; "they would speak when they liked, as long as they liked, and as often as they liked". Here the appeal was to popular opinion rather than to principle; and, indeed, Macdonald was one of the few leading Conservatives who did not take advantage of the Rebellion Losses Bill to fight the whole issue of the Rebellion all over again verbally.

He did not even witness—let alone participate in—the violent crisis which followed Lord Elgin's acceptance of the bill. Early in April, he secured leave of absence from the House. His ostensible reason was "urgent private business";[29] but it was probably Isabella as much as his practice that called him back. Although his leave, which was originally for fifteen days, does not seem to have been officially renewed, his name does not reappear in the proceedings until early in May. In the meantime Lord Elgin had signed the Rebellion Losses Bill, and the Conservatives were left in a mood of furious and self-destructive bewilderment. In their blind rage, they could not see that Lord Elgin had been wise and right to confirm responsible government by playing the constitutional role which it required of him; they only knew that they had relied upon a British governor to veto or reserve the bill, and that a British governor had failed them. Their unquestioned assumptions, their traditional beliefs, their hereditary loyalties, lay strewn about in the broken confusion of a rout; and grief and fury had planted their angry banners on the wreckage. For the Tories, "Elginism" had finished the dreadful work that "Cobdenism" had begun. The Rebellion Losses Bill was the political counterpart of the repeal of the Corn Laws; and the downfall of the Old Colonial System had been crowned and completed by the defeat of the Loyalists who had forfeited everything in its defence. After the passage of the Rebellion Losses Bill, Canada could no longer regard itself as a British province; and with the repeal of the Corn Laws, the reality of its membership in the British Empire had come to an end. It had become a foreign country, governed by an alien race. So the Conservatives felt rather than reasoned. And when, on April 25, Lord Elgin came in from Monklands to give his official acceptance to a number of measures, including the Rebellion Losses Bill, the Tory, anti-French mob of Montreal plunged into an orgy of violence and incendiarism which lasted for over a week. Macdonald did not, apparently, witness the blazing spectacle of the burning parliament buildings. He was absent on April 26, the morning after the fire, when the chastened Assembly met in the Bonsecours Market Place. Once again—though this time in an accidental fashion—he had been dissociated from the maddened extremism of his party.

IV

Yet he was far from being unaware of the baffled fury of the Conservatives, or indifferent to its serious implications. On May 1, when he was still at home on leave of absence, the Kingston Conservatives held a protest meeting in the city hall, with the Mayor in the chair. One by one Macdonald's friends and supporters—sober Tories such as J. R. Forsyth, John Counter, Major Logie, Joseph Bruce and his own partner, Alexander Campbell—arose to move strangely novel resolutions in strangely excited language.[30] It was true that they deplored the explosion of violence and the destruction of property at Montreal, and that they insisted that redress of grievances must be sought by legal and constitutional means only; but at the same time they resolved that the Governor-General had betrayed his trust and set at nought the wishes of the loyal inhabitants, that his recall was necessary, and that the only course now remaining was to petition the Queen to disallow the Rebellion Losses Act. All over the province such meetings were being held, such resolutions were being passed. All over the province, Conservatives, shaken in their old faith and absolved from their old loyalties, were groping, in angry perplexity, towards new policies and perhaps towards new principles. Already—and this was a significant indication of the general sense of political crisis—a new association, the British American League, had been formed, largely by Conservatives;[31] and from the beginning it was planned that the League should hold a great convention of delegates in order to determine its programme. A struggle began for the control of policy. On the one hand were the Conservatives apostates, the disillusioned extremists, with their terribly simple solution—annexation to the United States; on the other hand were the moderates, angry, confused, and anxious. What was their programme to be?

At the end of May, when the provincial parliament was prorogued and when the time for the convention of the British American League was rapidly approaching, Macdonald returned to Kingston. His own personal affairs, which during these years were almost never free from worries, had become tangled in a new knot of embarrassment and anxiety. It was true that Isabella had apparently thrown off the distressing symptoms of the previous year, and that all during the spring and early summer she had gained most promisingly. But, as he had come to realize, her improvement was always unstable, and this was proved true once again that summer when her brother John came to see them on a three weeks' visit. Although John was invariably careful not to overtire his sister himself, his presence naturally attracted Maria and a concourse of other relatives and friends, whom Isabella, with her hospitable instincts, felt she ought to see. The fatigue and the agitation were all too much for her, and when John had gone, she fell seriously ill with dysentery. "The whole gain of the spring is gone," wrote Macdonald morosely.[32] He was utterly despondent about his wife; and he was worried also about Campbell and the practice, for now at length the consequences of his heavy expenditures and enforced absences were coming back upon him. He had scarcely returned to Kingston, early in June, when Campbell began to broach the ominous question of a dissolution of their partnership. "The more I reflect on our conversations on the subject of a dissolution of our partnership," he wrote on June 8, "the more I am persuaded that it is desirable on very many grounds that it should take place".[33]

Yet, despite all these anxieties, Macdonald could not fail

to be deeply interested in the approaching convention of the British American League and in the unsolved problem of Conservative policy. From the beginning of his political career, he had been fighting extremists—first, the ultras of Toronto, who had tried to impose Anglican, Tory institutions upon the province, and now the ultras of Montreal, who were attempting to submerge it in the United States. This new extremism, which like that of the rebel Reformers of 1837 was directed towards continental union, was obviously by far the more crucial of the two, since it involved the total disappearance of a separate British North America. The first task of 1849, as Macdonald and the moderates saw it, was to defeat the desperate annexationist proposals. The convention was to be held at Kingston, symbolically the appropriate place. For if Montreal represented trade and Toronto government, Kingston, from the beginning, had stood for defence, and defence particularly against the United States. The convention "will, I think," wrote Macdonald hopefully, "put its foot on the idea of annexation".[34] It was his principal hope. But obviously the moderates would have to have some programme to substitute for the violent expedient they were determined to reject. During July, while Macdonald was busy trying to round up his moderate friends and associates and to persuade them to take part in the convention, he was already formulating alternative proposals. The programme which he sent to D. B. Stevenson, of Prince Edward County, was already fairly complete and specific: "Protection to native industry and home manufactures—connection with Great Britain—Reciprocity with the United States in agricultural products—and Repeal of the Municipal and Tariff monstrosities of last session. No French domination, but equal rights to all. *These* are the ruling principles of the League."[35]

On Wednesday, July 25, when the convention began its first session in one of the spacious upper chambers of Kingston's ambitious and slighted town hall, Macdonald joined the large but somewhat undistinguished crowd in attendance.[36] There was a small sprinkling of Conservative politicians, men like Edward Ermatinger, Rolland Macdonnell, Edmund Murney,

back-benchers, most of them, who had sat in the parliament of
1844-47 and who had not been re-elected. George Moffatt, the
ex-member for Montreal, and Ogle Gowan who had nearly
attained office in 1847, might be regarded as rather more important politically. But, of the leading members of the Conservative opposition—MacNab, Cayley, Boulton, Cameron and
the Sherwoods—not one had been tempted to put in an appearance. Macdonald was the only ex-minister of the Crown
present. It was a meeting of the interested rank and file, entirely
English-speaking, largely Conservative in its political leanings,
but with a few independents and worried Reformers, who helped
to give it a non-partisan character which was more apparent
than real. Macdonald, perhaps out of prudent regard for his
party, spoke little, even less than he might have been expected
to do; but from the start he was busy organizing the conference
and ensuring that it would run with smoothness. Perhaps, in
their very different ways, the unobtrusive Macdonald and the
talkative and theatrical Gowan were the two most important
people at the conference. It was one of the first illustrations
of a political partnership which was to last for years.

The next day the convention got down to a regular routine
of morning, afternoon, and evening sessions. In the main, it
followed the currently fashionable Conservative line. It spoke
with the outraged voice of English-speaking Canada, of Canada
West in particular, shouting its convictions in belligerent disregard of the susceptibilities of the French Canadians and of
the respect due to the representative of the Crown. The recall
of Lord Elgin was frankly demanded; the Rebellion Losses Bill
was vigorously denounced. The convention insisted at length,
and with gloomy particularity, upon the economic paralysis,
the feverish popular excitement, the social and moral instability,
and the decline and degradation of established authority, which
constituted, in its opinion, the chief distinguishing features of
the existing state of provincial affairs. But lamentations and
denunciations were not the only, nor the chief, part of its work.
With open talk of annexation and vague discussion of an elected
Legislative Council in the air, with Conservatives everywhere
subjected to the imputation of disloyalty, and the convention

itself regarded as a "Yankee League", it was vitally necessary
for the delegates to take their stand with decision on the major
issues of the day. Annexation was not even debated in the
Kingston town hall during those last days of July. The motion
for an elected Legislative Council was rejected. The convention affirmed its loyalty to the Crown, to the British connection,
to monarchical institutions, and the "mixed forms of government" of the parliamentary system.[37] Macdonald might well
have been satisfied. The convention had, indeed, "put its foot
on the idea of annexation" with decisive firmness.

He must have been equally pleased with the main motion on
economic policy. Here the convention was compelled, by force
of circumstances, to take an even more positive stand. The
Old Colonial System, with its tariff preferences and shipping
monopolies, to which Conservatives in Canada had clung
tenaciously for generations, had now been shattered by the
introduction of British free trade. The Canadians, for really
the first time in their collective history, were obliged to face
the basic economic problem of their existence as a separate
community in North America. In his letter to Stevenson,
Macdonald had spoken of protection to native industry and
home manufactures as well as of reciprocal free trade with
the United States in natural products. Both projects had been
discussed with rising interest during the black days of the
depression, as the Canadians sought worriedly for some escape
from the economic troubles which surrounded them. But, of
the two, protection was the more patently nationalist, the more
defiantly anti-American policy; and it was possibly for these
reasons that the convention accepted it and neglected to consider the idea of reciprocity. Gowan introduced the motion in
favour of protection; but Macdonald, as far back as 1846, when
he had been discussing Cayley's tariff, had sounded the note
of alarm at the dangers of American industrial competition.
The two of them were to argue strenuously in support of a
protective tariff in future; and the resolution in its favour is
perhaps one of the best illustrations of their co-operation in
the convention of the British American League.

In one respect, however,—and this in a matter of crucial im-

portance—the convention evidently went beyond anything that
Macdonald had intended or expected. On Saturday, July 28,
John Duggan and Rolland Macdonnell moved a resolution in
favour of the federal union of all the British North American
colonies.[38] It was true that, after the first wild enthusiasm had
expended itself, the conference drew back a little in prudent
hesitation; and all that it resolved in the end was that a scheme
of such immense magnitude must receive the most careful study,
and that a committee of ten should be appointed to discuss it
with representatives from the Maritime Provinces. Macdonald
was not made a member of the committee. In one of his very
few appearances before the convention, he suggested mildly
that the scheme was premature and impractical for the moment;
and his friend Gowan opposed and criticized Duggan's motion
with much greater fervour. Yet the debate may have accomplished an important stage in their political education. Duggan's motion was evidently a popular one, for speaker after
speaker arose to discuss it, and to support it with arguments
which anticipated those of a later date with curious exactitude.[39]
From the moment of this declaration by the British American
League, the Conservatives never lost a certain persistent, if
tenuous, interest in the federal union of British North America.

On Monday and Tuesday, July 30 and 31, when the convention met for the last times, Macdonald was at hand, nominat-
ing officers, providing for publicity, arranging for the re-
assembling of the convention, giving the final smooth, efficient
touches to the proceedings. He had been a member of the
committee which drafted the convention's address to the people
of Canada; but he was not elected an officer of the League nor
a member of the permanent executive committee. It was probably his own wish, for, at the moment, he did not dare to take
on any other commitments, even in the interests of the Conservative party. Isabella, thank God, was mending again. But
Campbell, with his all too legitimate feeling of resentment for
the injustices of the past, was obstinately bent on a separation,
and if the partnership were to survive, it would require all the
diplomacy of which Macdonald was capable. He was working
hard, no doubt, with his usual easy, tireless speed, in order to

make amends for the past, to propitiate Campbell, and to meet his own mounting obligations; but although, at the moment, he felt that he could give no more time to the British American League, he must have felt reasonably satisfied with what he had helped it to do at Kingston. It was true that the annexationist cry was still rising shrilly; and nobody, of course, could predict what the excited, irresponsible merchants of Montreal might yet do. But he had tried to ensure—and he must have thought successfully—that his own section of the province, Canada West, would stick to the idea of a separate, British future in North America.

Chapter Seven

Years of Recovery

I

Once the conference had ended, he could give himself without distraction to the task of pacifying Campbell. It was a formidable business. For Campbell, sensitive, warm-hearted, dourly cautious yet not unambitious in his shrewd way, was troubled not only by his own personal grievances, but also by his worries for the business as a whole. He certainly had a good deal to complain of. For years he had done by far the greater part of the work and had received only a third of the profits; and of the bonus which was supposed to have compensated him for his additional labours, £420 had not yet been paid. "So I feel," he wrote bluntly, "that I have been doing too much and getting too little."[1] It was the principal point of difference, for Campbell was stubborn in the defence of his own interests. But there were other, more general, and perhaps more fundamental differences, as well. The mere size of Macdonald's operations must have slightly intimidated his prudent colleague. Yet it was not size alone, for Campbell himself was keen enough where money was concerned; it was rather the complexity of the business, the embarrassments in which it was involved, and the almost cheerfully casual fashion in which Macdonald managed it, which created, in the junior partner, a dull, unappeasable sense of unease. Their bank account, Campbell pointed out accusingly, was overdrawn: the firm owed £1800, a debt which was a bad blot on their business escutcheon. And these painful embarrassments had been continued and ag-

gravated by Macdonald's long absences, by his political preoccupations, and by his easy-going habit of drawing upon the
firm's revenues to meet his own immediate financial needs.
"Your absence from home and your necessities," Campbell
wound up his case, "have been I think the *main* although not
by any means the only cause of the annoyances that have
arisen."[2]

As August passed rapidly along, as September, the anniversary
of the commencement of the partnership, drew closer and closer,
Macdonald struggled to overcome Campbell's timidities and
to appease his sense of injustice. For years now, the junior
partner had served him like a stout, serviceable, extremely
comfortable pair of boots, which had only occasionally squeaked
a little. He did not see how he could get along without Campbell. The practice—a big affair, now, despite the depression
and his debts—was supremely useful, perhaps even vital, to
the continuance of his parliamentary career. He used every
argument and every form of persuasion: he even pleaded with
Campbell not to desert him at this crucial moment; and Campbell, who, despite all his slow resentments and nagging worries,
never wavered in his belief in his friend's political future, was
particularly susceptible to such an appeal. "I am willing, indeed anxious," he wrote, "that your political career should not
be cut short at this moment . . .".[3] And, apparently at his own
suggestion, they succeeded, towards the end of August, in
working out a new agreement whereby the partnership was to
be continued, on the basis of a half share for each, for a further
experimental period of two years.[4] On August 30, the draft
agreement was ready. Then, at the last moment, Campbell
drew back. The new arrangement, he admitted generously, was
"fair and everything he could desire"; but, after dismal worries
and sleepless nights, he decided to reject it. He acknowledged
that he was probably sacrificing as much as £2000. "I do it
with a sore heart," he wrote, ". . . but after giving the matter
every consideration I have *finally* determined (with your permission) to abandon all the advantages it offered for the *comfort*
of a smaller business."[5] Comfort, security—he had diplomatically
identified these with a small practice; but he must have been

well aware of the fact that they were far from alien to a large
and lucrative practice, so long as it was under his own control.
He stuck to his decision. Macdonald agreed to buy him out
for £1250; and after September 1, when the partnership came
to an end, they commenced the painful and haggling business
of settling their complicated accounts.

Macdonald abandoned the Princess Street establishment
which he had shared with Campbell and moved into a new
and probably less expensive set of offices at 343 King Street.[6]
The loss of a partner, who had complemented and corrected
his own qualities so exactly and who had stood by him through
all their early difficulties with his own special kind of dogged,
complaining devotion, must have seemed an irremediable disaster. There was nobody, at the moment, whom he wanted, or
could persuade, to take Campbell's place; and all that autumn,
he must have stuck to his desk, working away at a mass of
humdrum, prosaic matters, to which he had grown unaccustomed during the easy years of the partnership and which probably irked him profoundly. He had little time for politics. And
yet, all the while, the state of politics grew steadily gloomier,
as the current of Tory extremism continued in its fatal, self-
destructive way. Early in October, the Montreal merchants,
utterly forgetting their city's long historic struggle to establish
a separate British commercial empire in North America, issued
their long-awaited, notorious manifesto, advocating the political
union of Canada with the United States.[7] The desperate action
had been finally taken, despite all that the moderates had tried
to do; and if the effect of the manifesto was to be counteracted,
and the feverish contagion of continentalism checked, it was
highly desirable that the British American League should carry
out its intention of holding a second meeting of the adjourned
convention. On November 1, when the agitation following the
publication of the manifesto was at its height, the League met
again, this time at Toronto. John Richardson Forsyth, the
defeated Conservative candidate of 1841, was Kingston's delegate. Macdonald, who in the autumn of 1849 had no time
for conventions, however much he might have wished to attend
this one, was forced to stay at home. He must have found the

news from Toronto puzzling—at once reassuring and disquieting. It was true that the convention disavowed annexation
once more, and with unqualified decisiveness: it was true also
that the project of an elected Legislative Council, raised a
second time, was again rejected, after a protracted wrangle.
But although these desperate courses, these republican innova-
tions, were pushed firmly aside, there was a good deal of evidence
that, even in this assembly of self-declared moderates, the current of extremism, restless, impatient, and exasperated, was still
running very strong. The original recommendations of the
League—retrenchment, protection to native industry, maintenance of the British connection—were, the delegates seemed to
say, all well enough, but inadequate in the existing crisis. Other
changes, more drastic and fundamental, were necessary for
colonies which had reached the extreme point of their endurance, which could not "continue in their present political or
commercial state". The Kingston meeting, to Macdonald's surprise and probably against his will, had advocated British North
American union; and it was upon this project, and the project
of constitutional change generally, that the delegates at Toronto
spent by far the greater part of their time. The League's committee, which had discussed federal union at Montreal with
a few representatives from New Brunswick, presented its report
to the convention. A torrent of vague, grandiose, irresponsible
constitution-making was immediately unloosed; and there were
repeated demands for a general convention of the people of
the whole of British North America to discuss the proposed
union.[8]

To Macdonald—busy, detached, and coolly sceptical—all this,
which went so far beyond his own modest, concrete proposals
of July, must have seemed mere theorizing, premature, nebulous,
and dangerous. The Conservatives had not closed their ranks
on a sensible and modest programme. They had continued to
fly apart, as if determined on dispersal and self-annihilation,
along various contrasted paths of hazardous eccentricity. And,
as the autumn wore on, and he continued his desultory bickering
with Campbell over the winding up of their joint affairs, there
was only one feature of the political situation to give him much

satisfaction. This was the fact—dimly apparent early in October and increasingly manifest as the autumn continued—that political division was not peculiar to the Conservatives alone, and that the unity of the huge and varied Reform party was threatened, much as Baldwin had earlier feared it would be,[9] by the revolt of its radical members. The first sign of trouble was the sudden political reappearance of Peter Perry, an "old Reformer", a gnarled veteran of the pre-Rebellion period in Upper Canadian politics, who, after a decade of oblivion, now came forward as a candidate for the third riding of York, in a by-election made necessary by the appointment of William Hume Blake to the chancellorship.[10] Perry was known to be dissatisfied with the "stale moderation" of the Reform government; he was suspected of favouring annexation to the United States; and to the Reform leaders, who wished on grounds of principle and political expediency to stamp annexationism as a purely Tory heresy, his candidature appeared particularly displeasing. Baldwin tried to discipline Perry publicly, but the attempt was a dismal failure. The "old Reformer" remained defiantly mutinous; he was elected to the vacant constituency without the slightest opposition. Before the autumn was out he had acquired a small but obstreperous following, a heterogeneous group of young Radicals and old Reformers, who drew their inspiration both from the tradition of the Rebellion of 1837 and from the new political philosophies of the 1840's, including Chartism. A new Radical movement, the "Clear Grit" movement, so called at first in derision by its opponents and then with complacent self-satisfaction by its own members, had arisen to trouble the comfortable well-being of the Reform party.

It was pleasant for Macdonald to observe these ructions going on in the large, ostentatiously affectionate family of the Reformers. It was gratifying to see a little of the annexationist mud sticking tenaciously to the respectable black broadcloth of Mr. Baldwin's trousers. These were the small consolations of an autumn which seemed full of nothing but work, of bickering over the past, and worry for the future. It was true that the settlement with Campbell, which had threatened on more than one occasion to become acrimonious, had reached a peaceful and satisfactory conclusion in the end. At one of their last conferences over a small contentious account, Campbell had characteristically pleaded for "a little forbearance on both sides". "It will never do," he wrote, "for us to disagree about the fag end of the affair, after escaping through so much."[11] They had indeed escaped through much—much which was ultimately Macdonald's responsibility; and in the end, after all the tangled, vexatious complexities of the partnership, they emerged good friends. It was something to have saved out of the wreck. But Macdonald was, as Campbell had shrewdly suspected, badly in debt. His political chances were jeopardized, for a time at least, and the practice, which had certainly declined in value since the beginning of the depression, now depended entirely upon his own exertions and tied him for long hours to his desk. But these were not his only worries. For a new crisis in his domestic affairs was looming up. Isabella had become pregnant once again.

When young John Alexander had died, a year ago in September, Macdonald had never expected to have another child. But the stoical, taciturn resignation, which was the last, invulnerable citadel of his spirit, offered no real refuge for Isabella from the tragedy of the nursery. The whole meaning of her painful existence lay centred in her own family, in her own household, in her husband and her child. Apart from the one brief setback, which had followed hard on her brother's visit in July, she had, on the whole, been better, a great deal better, during the spring and summer of 1849; and she must have realized her condition with a thrill of anxious, excited joy. From then on, despite her previous improvement, she became more than ever vulnerable to the slightest over-exertion, and to every crisis of her own febrile, emotional nature. When, early in December, the news arrived of the death of her sister Jane, who had been living with Margaret Greene in Athens, Georgia, she attempted desperately though vainly, for the sake of the child she carried, to control her overwhelming grief. But sleep, despite her feeble resolution, would not come to quiet her anguish, and the utter exhaustion into which she finally fell brought on a new and terrible attack of neuralgia, and the

familiar ominous bleeding at the mouth.[12] These were the old
familiar crises of her disease; and, as the old year ended and
her pregnancy drew toward its conclusion, a new and painful
set of symptoms, which she remembered dimly from the first
experience in New York, seemed to herald her approaching
confinement.[13] She bore the discomfort and the recurring pain
with less apprehension than on the first occasion and with
equal tranquillity and fortitude. All day long she lay in bed,
burdened with her body, often drugged with opiates, yet sensitively aware of every incident in the routine of her household,
and intent, with feeble but tenacious persistence, in imposing
her sense of order and decorum upon its operations. Macdonald,
as he watched and marvelled, compared her comically with the
"invisible lady" of the circuses of the day, who was "exhibited"
but did not "show" herself. "The invisible lady's voice, orders,
and behests," he wrote to Margaret Greene, "are heard and
obeyed all over the house, and are carried out as to cupboards
which she never sees, and pots and pans that have no acquaintance with her. Not a glass is broken, or a set of dishes
diminished, but she knows of, and calls the criminal to account
for. In fact she carries on the whole machinery as well, to
appearance, as if she were bustling from *but* to *ben* in person."[14]

Early in January of 1850, on the advice of the doctors,
Macdonald began to expect that the baby would be born within
a week or two. Everything was in readiness. One physician
was in constant attendance: another, a specialist in "midwifery",
was to be called in at the crucial moment; and a nurse was
already installed in the room adjoining Isabella's own.[15] "Isa
is in God's hands," wrote Macdonald, "and there we must
leave her." They waited miserably, while the weeks of January
and February went by, marked only by the increasing frequency
and increasing severity of Isabella's pain. At home, the agony
of suspense was almost unbearable for Macdonald; and, at the
office, the piled papers before him never seemed to diminish.
"Isa says I work too hard," he confessed, "and in truth I begin
to feel that I do, but like a thief on the treadmill, I *must* step
on, or be dragged."[16] So far as politics were concerned there
was some satisfaction in the now evident fact that the annexa-

tion cry had met with "very little encouragement". Also, it must have been agreeable to notice that Peter Perry's insurgent group was still receiving recruits, that a new Radical newspaper, the *North American*, had joined the *Examiner* in its crusade against the ministry, and that Caleb Hopkins, another unregenerate survival of the Radical past, had turned Clear Grit and was busily contesting East Halton against Wetenhall, the government candidate. But all these brief interests disappeared quickly in the dark, bottomless well of his concern for Isabella. He feared; and yet, in his characteristic fashion, and despite all the ominous recent tragedies in the family circle, he continued to hope. "The rod cannot be always smiting," he told himself. To cling to these hopes, to accept, at their face value, the repeated assurances of the doctors that all would be well in the end was a task almost beyond his capacity. For days and weeks, Isabella lay prostrate in a condition apparently unchanged; "she still lingers on, and suffers, and submits".[17] February passed, as January had slowly passed before it. He was still waiting, watching his wife's struggles and sufferings, still hoping for the best. And at last, on March 13, when it seemed as if Isabella could endure no longer, the child was born.[18]

II

"We have got Johnnie back again—almost his image," wrote Macdonald to his sister. "I don't think he is so pretty, but he is not so delicate."[19] The male parent, from the slight detachment of his position, could afford to make these realistic comparisons; but Isabella, who, in her state of emotional ecstasy, had almost brought herself to believe that her dead baby, purchased by her own suffering, had been restored to life by Providence, was anxious that the boy should be called John Alexander. Old Mrs. Macdonald, Maria Macpherson, and Margaret Greene—an impressive array of authoritative female opinion—looked doubtfully, with pursed apprehensive lips, at the ominous practice of giving a new baby his dead brother's name. In the end the child was christened Hugh John, after both his father and grandfather, and Hugh became the name by which he was usually called. It was comforting to realize that these simple, homely, family debates had mercifully succeeded to the agonizing worries of the winter; but the crisis which had passed had brought no real resolution of his troubles, and they continued, like a sombre formless story which had no meaning and could only have one end. Old Mrs. Macdonald, who had trudged stoutly through the snow to visit Isabella during the winter, had been attacked again with one of her seizures. Tom Wilson, his friend and relation in Montreal, the companion of his happy trip to England in 1843, had just lost his youngest child. And what was even harder to bear— for it touched his own youth and his earliest associations so closely—was the consumption which threatened at any moment now to end the life of his friend, Charles Stuart.[20] The friendship with Stuart went back to the time of his schooldays and apprenticeship, to the old days at Napanee and Hallowell; and it was Stuart who, in the first great meeting of his political career, had stood up beside him on that December day of 1843, to defend Sir Charles Metcalfe before the thrilling, cheering crowd of Kingstonians. All that was ended now. He knew it as he tried with joking, peremptory affection to play the doctor for a man who, with fatalistic obstinacy, refused all medicine and all advice. It was strange that so many of his earliest friends were gone or going. He could speak of this; but he would not admit the central tragedy of his life—the wreck of his marriage—which everybody about him knew and lamented. Isabella, he was writing, nearly a month after the birth of Hugh John, "still lingers very much in her recovery". Her recovery! He still believed in it with the same invincible gaiety of spirit with which he looked forward to the rebuilding of his practice and the success of his political career. But the troubles of the last year had taught him at least some sense of limitations, some realization that, with all his powers, there were choices which must be made. His wife, his small son, and the work which kept them all in existence—this was the real concern of the moment. Politics, and the future of the distracted Conservative party would have to wait.

Montreal had been punished for its incendiary violence by the removal of the government. It had been decided—and the decision had revealed clearly what a price in efficiency had to be paid by the Province of Canada for the blessings of its dual culture—that legislation and administration were to alternate, every few years, between Toronto and Quebec. Toronto had been selected as temporary capital for the fag end of the existing parliament; and when the legislature commenced its sittings there, on May 14, 1850, Macdonald was not in his place. For the first time in his political career he had missed an opening. He gave no excuses, sought and obtained no formal leave of absence; but it was not until early in June, nearly a month after the commencement of the session, that he finally took his seat.[21] The old parliament buildings of Upper Canada—three unpretentious, red-brick Georgian structures, with somewhat unsightly wooden passages connecting them, which stood, with their backs to Wellington Street, in a wide open space fronting on Toronto bay—were, of course, entirely new to him. The grounds around, which had been almost completely denuded of trees and shrubs, seemed incongruously bare and depressing in the early summer sunshine; but the setting, with its wide view of the bay, had real natural beauty. Inside the central building, the Council and Assembly chambers had been most sumptuously redecorated, with crimson carpets and crimson hangings, glittering chandeliers and desks with royal-blue covered tops, and black walnut armchairs with crimson morocco cushions.[22] For about ten days, worried and uneasy, Macdonald kept his place. He was present on June 18, when the resolutions proposed by J. H. Price precipitated a great debate on the Clergy Reserves, in which the hesitations and uncertainties of the moderate Reformers were revealed with painful clarity by the intransigent demands of the Clear Grits. It was the conviction of the Clear Grits that no support should be given by the state to any religious communion; and they now demanded that the revenues from the Clergy Reserves—the portion of the Crown lands reserved for the support of "a Protestant Clergy"

—should be appropriated to secular uses, and employed for
education or any other of the general purposes of the state.
Macdonald did not take any part in the debate; and it was
John Hillyard Cameron, his old fellow pupil at Cruickshank's
school, and his old rival for the affectionate approval of Draper,
who made, apparently, the most eloquent defence of the Tory
position, that the existing division of the Reserves among the
different Protestant communions should be left undisturbed.[23]
Macdonald sat the debate out; but a few days later the letters
from Kingston must have brought the dread familiar story of
a new crisis. He left at once; and on June 28, when a call of
the House was made, he was found absent and declared "ex-
cused on account of sickness in his family".[24]

It was not until after the end of the first week in July that he
was able to return. From then on he was a regular attendant;
but he had almost nothing to say on general issues—even those
issues in which he had been particularly active in the past. For
the moment, in the tight, difficult position in which he found
himself, it suited his purpose to become a typical, parochial
back-bencher, interested mainly in the concerns of his own
constituency. The case of the Trust and Loan Company of
Upper Canada revealed clearly how close the connection could
be between the interests of Kingston and the interests of John A.
Macdonald's law practice. Macdonald was determined, if possible, to revive the fortunes of the loan company. Ever since
it had been founded, back in 1844, he had been its solicitor;
and along with the Commercial Bank of the Midland District,
it had been one of the two most important company accounts
of the Macdonald and Campbell firm. The depression, which
had hit agricultural prices and farm properties so hard, had
brought about a grievous decline in the Trust and Loan Company's business; and in one of those lugubriously pessimistic
reviews of the prospects of the firm which Campbell had made
on the eve of the dissolution of the partnership, he had declared,
with terse finality, that the loan company account had been
"knocked on the head". In 1850, however, the directors of the
company, led by Oliver Mowat, attempted to revive it from
unconsciousness; and Macdonald sponsored a private bill which

was framed to amend the original terms of the incorporating statutes.[25] The bill, which was pushed briskly through parliament with the significant assistance of Francis Hincks, the Inspector-General, contained one small, inconspicuous, but immensely important change: it raised the limits on the rates which the company was permitted to charge for interest. As Elgin explained later, with much satisfaction, to Grey, the act had given "a thrust at our usury laws through its side".[26] The inevitable annual bill for the repeal of the usury laws, presented this time by Sherwood of Toronto, was, as usual, rejected by an overwhelming majority of French Canadians, with the addition of a few Clear Grits and Tories.[27] But the Trust Company Bill, with its tiny, significant amendment, had got clear through; and now, with better times and more attractive rates, there was a good prospect of acquiring a real supply of British capital.

There was one other local matter with which Macdonald busied himself in the closing days of the session of 1850. Outwardly it seemed to be of no direct interest to him whatever, for it merely concerned the provincial penitentiary at Portsmouth; but the sequel of his intervention in the affairs of the provincial penitentiary was of immense importance, for it brought him the personal enmity of George Brown. Until a little over a year before, Brown, in Macdonald's eyes, had simply been the too vigorous editor, the too successful publisher, of the Toronto *Globe,* a newspaper which, ever since its establishment in March, 1844, had been one of the most pugnaciously effective of the official journals on the Reform side. As a buzzing, waspish—though somewhat remote—journalistic nuisance, Brown could have been endured. But he was not destined to remain solely a journalist; and ever since the day, in the spring of 1843, when he had entered Samuel Thompson's office in Toronto with such healthy assurance and had begun his acquaintance with Canadian newspapermen and Canadian publishing,[28] he had been pushing himself steadily into a position from which he could exercise real influence and cause real trouble. He was an awkward, red-haired, extremely tall, extremely serious young Scotsman of firm views, great ambitions, and superabundant physical energy. In temperament, character, and convictions, he was almost the exact antithesis of Macdonald. A Reformer, a stiff Free Kirker, an ardent voluntarist who abominated any connection between church and state, a passionately serious dogmatist to whom all compromise and accommodation were alien and difficult, Brown contradicted Macdonald's instinctive habit of thought with the whole force of his downright, positive nature. The two men were almost certain to clash; and as Brown's popularity and prestige grew, as he became more discontented with the journalistic task of "puffing" the work of others and more determined to play a great political role himself,²⁹ the chances of such an encounter rapidly increased. It was fated to come; but it might have come without the bitterness of a savage personal enmity, if it had not been for Brown's first political appointment in the spring of 1848. The new Reform government, anxious to give some polite recognition to the editor of the *Globe,* and busy with the congenial task of sacking officials, investigating old abuses and planning new reforms, had decided to appoint a prison commission, and to make George Brown one of its members and its secretary. In the autumn of 1848, the commission had moved in upon the provincial penitentiary at Portsmouth with all the horrid purposefulness of an armoured regiment. It had carried out a minute, particular, uncompromising and exhaustive inquiry into the affairs of the penitentiary. The Warden, Henry Smith, Senior, had been suspended from office; and a huge indictment, consisting of eleven separate charges, divided into 121 distinct counts, and occupying 300 folio pages of manuscript, was finally preferred against him.

Macdonald had been immediately made aware of these scandalous happenings. He knew the Smiths well, for the Smiths were an old Kingston Conservative family. And since it was obviously impossible for Henry Smith, Junior, the Tory member for Frontenac, to intervene directly on his father's behalf in parliament, the main burden of the defence had fallen inevitably upon Macdonald. In the winter of 1849, immediately after the opening of the legislature, he had received a cascading series of letters from the senior Smith—one by almost every post—in which the injured Warden, vigorously denouncing his tormentors as "arrant scoundrels" and "unblushing liars", had attacked the malice, prejudice, and vindictive partiality which he discerned everywhere in the conduct of the investigation.[30] He had followed this up—once Brown had finished his voluminous report—with a lengthy, though not nearly so voluminous, refutation of its charges.[31] All these outraged effusions had been read by Macdonald with sympathetic attention. The penitentiary was in his bailiwick, the Smiths were his acquaintances and associates, and the investigation, with its secrecy and unprofessional informality, had revolted his lawyer's sense of the proprieties. Whatever the doubtful merits of the case may have been, he at least came to the definite conclusion that much of the evidence against Smith was of questionable origin, that a good deal of it had been scandalously manipulated and distorted, that Smith had never been given a reasonable chance to answer the charges against him, and that, in sum, a substantial injustice had been done. His complaint was, of course, against the commission as a whole. But, in his mind, the chief culprit was Brown, who, as the secretary of the commission and the chief author of the report, had systematically juggled the evidence. Once these conclusions had been formed, he clung to them with a peculiarly stubborn tenacity. He had brought one phase of the matter up before parliament early in the session of 1849.[32] And now, on August 5, as one of his last acts of the session, he presented Smith's petition—Smith in the meantime had been finally dismissed from office—and asked that it should be referred to a special committee of inquiry.[33] The request, of course, was voted down. Nothing resulted to the advantage of Smith. But Brown, sensitive and irascible, began to notice Macdonald's pertinacious attacks on his newspaper. The feud had begun.

At the moment, neither of the two contestants paid very much attention to it. Macdonald, anxious to exploit the new Trust and Loan Company's bill, was planning to leave for England as soon as the session ended. The recovery of his practice was evidently still his major preoccupation; and the prison controversy and political issues in general had declined in interest, perhaps because the Tory party still seemed so immovably stuck in futility. The annexationist cry, it was true, was dead; the extravagant excesses of 1849 were mercifully over; but the party, though chastened, had not found in its humiliation a new unity or a new sense of direction. If the Reformers had grown weaker through internal division, the Conservatives had not apparently increased in strength; and while the Clear Grits, at what was somewhat pompously described as the "Markham Convention", had drawn up a fashionably formidable list of Radical principles, the Tories had seemingly not even bothered to search the somewhat muddled proceedings of the British American League for a few new ideas. They did not press for protection to home industry, or urge the federal union of British North America, or even succeed in making the somewhat banal idea of "retrenchment" peculiarly their own. When they did take up a modish notion, it was likely to be some such highly questionable proposal as an elective Legislative Council, which the British American League had twice discussed, and twice rejected, and which the Clear Grits had appropriated as part of their general campaign for elective institutions. In the Conservative defence of the Clergy Reserves as a legitimate source of support for all recognized Protestant communions, there had been an appropriate appeal to British precedents and to old loyalties and affections; but it was apparently just as easy for some of the Tories to reject tradition completely, without any sense of incongruity, and with a commonplace North American contempt indistinguishable from that of the Clear Grits. There was a comic occasion on which William Henry Boulton, supposedly one of the old Family Compact Conservatives, brought two hammers and two adzes into the Assembly, one set British and one set American, and blandly proceeded, by an unflattering comparison, to prove the superiority of American enterprise, resourcefulness, and practical efficiency, and the consequent and inevitable superiority of American political institutions.[34] This attempt to substitute shirt-sleeves and galluses for neckcloths and sober Tory broadcloth, this effort to smarten up a roomful of Chippendale furniture by the introduction of an efficient American box-stove, was all slightly depressing; and the Conservative front-benchers—the bragging Sherwood, the timid Cayley, Mac-Nab with his tiresome geniality and tiresome rages, Boulton with his stage properties and conjuring tricks—were an uninspiring lot. They could not even stick together in public. And the session was still in mid-career when Boulton and Sherwood, the two Toronto members, began an unedifying controversy in the press.³⁵ Perhaps the best hope for the future was not in these men at all, but in their avowed enemies—in the prospect, now growing rapidly more certain, of a real break-up in the Reform party.

III

Late in the summer Macdonald sailed for England. It was eight years since he had last crossed the ocean; and now—for nearly a decade of disillusioning trouble had intervened—his plans were far more definite and practical than they had been before. He travelled as the accredited representative of the Trust and Loan Company of Upper Canada, and his main purpose was to secure new British capital for the concern and to carry out the enlargement and reorganization of its activities. It was highly desirable that he should gain admittance to British financial circles through the *porte cochère* of the governing class, and, despite his not altogether happy relations with Lord Elgin in the past, he had no hesitation in asking the Governor for a letter of introduction to the Colonial Secretary, Earl Grey. Elgin obligingly complied, describing his ex-minister somewhat patronizingly as "a respectable man and tolerably moderate in his views", and ending up with the comment—in itself an odd gloss upon his own vaunted political detachment—that Macdonald belonged to "the section of the Conservatives who are becoming reasonable".³⁶ Macdonald reached England some time in September, but Grey did not become aware of his presence until later, and November came before the Colonial Secretary invited the young solicitor of the Trust and Loan Company to dinner. It was quite a distinguished gathering, with Lord Lansdowne, the President of the Council, Sir Charles Wood, the Chancellor of the Exchequer, and another visiting Canadian, the Reverend Egerton Ryerson, Superintendent of Schools for Canada West, as guests. Ryerson, with his ready tongue, his copious store of knowledge, and his air of easy self-assurance, evidently outshone his fellow-colonial at dinner. Grey described the portly clergyman as "a very superior man", and had nothing at all to say about Macdonald.[37] But for all that he did not neglect the agent of the Trust and Loan Company, and the introductions and advice which he gave Macdonald probably helped him considerably in his task.[38] The mission was a triumphant success. The Trust and Loan Company, which Campbell had morosely regarded as defunct, rose again in splendid vitality with a capital of £500,000, an impressive set of British directors, and Thomas Baring and George Carr Glyn as trustees.

In the midst of these successes, Macdonald probably gave little thought to the subject of Canadian politics. But while he was still in England, busy with financial negotiations, there occurred a curious episode in British affairs which was to have violent repercussions in Canada, and which was to affect his new enemy, George Brown, and the Reform party, and even, indirectly, the Canadian Conservatives as well. On October 7, a few weeks before the dinner at Lord Grey's London house, Cardinal Wiseman, newly appointed Roman Catholic Archbishop of Westminster, had made public in a famous pastoral "From out the Flaminian Gate of Rome" a recent brief of the Papacy affecting Great Britain. The brief established the Roman Catholic hierarchy in England with, for the first time, English territorial titles, of which "Westminster" itself was obviously one of the most presumptuous and notorious. Englishmen, who for centuries had been unaccustomed to the sweeping rhetoric of papal pronouncements, learnt to their indignant astonishment that, as a result of this beneficent Roman brief, Catholic England, at length "restored to its orbit in the ecclesiastical firmament" was now to begin "its course of regularly adjusted action round the centre of unity", and that Cardinal Wiseman, the appointed emissary from this centre of unity, was to "govern the counties of Middlesex, Hertford, Essex, Surrey, Sussex, Kent, Berkshire, and Hampshire".[39] This parcelling off of English counties into Roman dioceses "with all the authority and minuteness of an Act of Parliament" aroused a storm of Protestant protest in England. The bishops and the press spluttered with indignation; and, on November 4, the Prime Minister, Lord John Russell, in a public letter to the Bishop of Durham, denounced the Pope's action as "insolent and insidious".[40] In Canada, as Macdonald knew very well, the first point in the dispute—the establishment of Roman Catholic dioceses with British territorial names—had really no meaning, since such titles had existed in British North America for a long time without any noticeable enslavement of the Protestant population. But Canada West was a cultural province of the United Kingdom, influenced by every important religious disturbance in the Mother Country, as the recent disruption of the Church of Scotland had proved once again. And the presence of the large, compact body of French-Canadian Roman Catholics helped to make the Upper Canadian Protestants peculiarly responsive to the charge of "papal usurpation". Somebody was almost bound to raise the "Protestant Cry", and fate had appointed the appropriate man and the appropriate megaphone through which it was to be sounded. On December 10 and December 19, 1850—fateful days for the Reform party and for George Brown—the *Globe* published two long and outspoken articles on the religious controversy in England.[41]

When Macdonald returned to Kingston, some time in the winter of 1851, the feverish symptoms of infection in the robust body of the Reform party were becoming more alarmingly conspicuous than they had ever been before. The Clear Grits, waxing stronger with every by-election, had recently published a revised and expanded edition of their reform programme in the *North American*;[42] but even their rising popularity, important as it was, could hardly have seemed more promising to Macdonald than the obviously growing estrangement between the leaders of the Reform party and their terrible newspaper ally, George Brown. To the dismay of the government, which now began to fear for its French-Canadian and Irish Roman

Catholic support, Brown had waged his anti-Catholic campaign all winter, with passionate conviction and complete disregard for all probable political consequences. Yet there were important consequences, as he was soon to discover. In April, 1851, in a by-election in Haldimand, he made his first attempt to enter parliament; and he was badly defeated by no less a person than William Lyon Mackenzie, the returned exile, the most notorious of all the "Old Reformers", who had attached himself loosely to the Clear Grits.[43] Brown was furious with Mackenzie and his associates; he blamed the interfering priesthood for his defeat. But his irritation with the Clear Grits and the Roman Catholics was little more than a weak reflection of his righteous anger with the official Reform leaders and the "party". The party, which owed him support both because of his principles and the services he had given in the past, had in fact let him down shamelessly out of a timorous and time-serving concern for the Roman Catholic vote.[44] He brooded sullenly over his accumulating wrongs. He had reached an ominous stage of rankling disappointment and angry determination.

It was in these rather more hopeful political circumstances that parliament met, late in May, for the last time before the approaching general election. Macdonald was present from the beginning. Since the terrible winter of 1849-50 his affairs had improved in almost every way. Isabella was better, despite her slow recovery after the birth of Hugh John. The return of good times and the beginnings of the railway boom had re-animated the law practice; and the Trust and Loan Company, firmly re-established in Canada with himself as solicitor and Francis Archibald Harper as one of the two Canadian commissioners, was preparing to enter the investment field once again in a vigorous fashion.[45] It was true that the Clear Grits, led by William Lyon Mackenzie, made a savage attack on the company's special privileges in the session of 1851; but both the Tory opposition and the government Reformers joined in defence of the now highly respectable financial institution, and Macdonald was not even required to say a word in its behalf.[46] His position was more secure than it had been; it seemed to be growing almost easy. There were no lengthy absences from

parliament, authorized or unauthorized, during the session of
1851. He had fewer preoccupations than before, and more time
and zest for politics. And as his experience grew and his confidence came back with a rush, he began to develop, with more
freedom, his own characteristic parliamentary style, his easy,
conversational, half-bantering manner, his terse, occasionally
flippant, and dangerously adroit method of attack. He could
put the virtuous Baldwin into a state of mild embarrassment
by supporting a transference of controverted elections to the
courts; and, when he sponsored a bill for the incorporation of
the medical profession, he made the House giggle with a tale
of his own amateur efforts to cope with a case of lumbago, as
a horrible example of the evils attending the activities of unauthorized practitioners.[47]

Yet the main task of the session was to encourage the divisions
in the Reform party, to promote by every possible means the
ill-concealed estrangement between George Brown and the
government leaders. Here Macdonald found that he could
make excellent use of the everlasting question of the report of
the Penitentiary Commission. On June 24 he rose to make his
annual demand for a parliamentary inquiry. He drew, of
course, an affecting picture of the senior Smith, a virtuous man,
"accused of the meanest peculation and the greatest cruelty",
condemned on the basis of garbled evidence which had been
originally supplied by "every unhanged scoundrel about the
penitentiary", and thrust forth, with vindictive unceremonious-
ness, from his office without a decent chance of reply. The injustice was patent and unquestionable, but Macdonald concentrated more upon the question of responsibility for Smith's
dismissal than upon the enormity of Smith's misfortunes. He
explained tolerantly that he did not believe the ministers had
nursed any real enmity against the luckless warden in the beginning; and although in the end they had certainly inflicted a grinding injustice, they had done so largely "from their cowardly fear
of George Brown, who had so completely bullied them".[48] In
the circumstance, this was a neat, calculated jab at the sensitive
quick of Brown's relations with the ministry, and its results
were highly satisfactory. Baldwin, opposing the inquiry, spoke

very temperately in reply. Lafontaine, defending the commissioners against the charge of falsifying the evidence, made, oddly enough, no reference at all to the secretary, thus "giving poor Brown the go-by, though a like charge had been made against him".[49] It was all a little tepid and unenthusiastic. Brown had sustained a fresh injury and had been given a new reason for resentment; and two days later, in the *Globe,* he printed an enormous editorial, three columns in length, in which he fell upon both his false friends and his open enemies, in a scandalized tone of shocked betrayal.[50] Macdonald must have been satisfied with the protean uses to which he had put the report of the Penitentiary Commission. The Reform leaders and the editor of the *Globe* had now one further reason for their open recriminations.

IV

Yet nobody—not even the hungry Tories—could really have expected that a disgruntled publisher and a handful of Clear Grits had much immediate chance of upsetting the "Great Ministry" of Baldwin and Lafontaine. And, in fact, the Cabinet would probably have continued calmly on its way for some months to come at least, if it had not been for Baldwin's weariness of office and the hypersensitivity of his temperament. On June 26, William Lyon Mackenzie proposed the abolition of the Court of Chancery, a court which Baldwin had reorganized two years before and which he regarded affectionately as one of his greatest achievements. A majority of the whole House rejected this intransigent proposal, but a majority of the members from Upper Canada supported it. Baldwin was wounded by the defection of his own followers in a matter where he thought he could count upon their loyalty. He at once resigned. Lafontaine followed with the announcement that he also would retire at the close of the present session; and in the fluid circumstances of Canadian politics, the imminent retirement of the two great leaders seemed almost certain to bring about a reshuffling of groups, and even a realignment of parties. The crisis—for which Macdonald and the Tories had hoped but which they had scarcely expected so soon—was now at hand. What profit could they possibly derive from it?

The essential basis of political power was an alliance with the main body of the French-Canadian members. Macdonald had inherited the idea of such a union from Draper, the father of Liberal Conservatism, who had tried three times in vain to carry it out. And despite Draper's repeated failures, the project still haunted the imaginations of the Conservatives with its tantalizing possibilities. They fortified their hopes by arguing that the existing coalition of the essentially Conservative French Canadians and the Radicals of Canada West was an unnatural coalition, an accident of history rather than a logical consequence of political realities.[51] Even Lord Elgin, though he dreaded the break-up of the existing Reform alliance, was convinced that it was only a recollection of their snubbing by the "old official set, and the fear that the union had been designed to swamp them" which kept the French Canadians away from their natural allies, the Conservatives of Canada West.[52] It was true that these old French-Canadian fears and grievances, slumbering peacefully away in the decade after the Rebellion, had been suddenly and violently reawakened by the excesses of the Conservatives during the controversy over the Rebellion Losses Bill. But if recent happenings in Canada had tended to revive the old fear and dislike of Conservative professions, the course of events on the continent of Europe was now bringing with it a rapid decline and discredit of the Liberal creed, both political and religious. Canada East, a French and Roman Catholic province, was bound to be influenced by the remarkable change which had come over European politics since the Revolutions of 1848, by the decline of the Second French Republic, the rise of Louis Napoleon, and the altered policies of the disillusioned Pius IX. Rome and Paris, which had so often contradicted each other in the past to the bewilderment of French Canadians, might now unite to proclaim a persuasive and authoritative anti-Liberal gospel. And if the Clear Grits grew too obstreperous, or if a radical, anti-clerical movement—similar to that of the Clear Grits—arose to embarrass the Reform party in Canada East, then the main body of French Canadians might be persuaded or frightened into an abandonment of their old alliance. They were already a little concerned over the intemperate politics of the western Radicals. Their concern might be judiciously heightened. And if, as seemed probable in the days that followed Baldwin's resignation, the Reformers could be kept in power only by a reunion of all their groups, however radical, and including the Clear Grits, the desertion of the French Canadians might come immediately.

Macdonald and the Conservatives, as they planned their campaign during the exciting summer of 1851, tried to take advantage of these vaguely discerned contours of the political landscape. They pointed to the ominous violence of George Brown's anti-Catholic campaign. They expatiated on the Clear Grits' dislike of clerical influence and unconcealed hatred of religious endowments. They repeated the solemn warning, made over a year ago by John Hillyard Cameron, that if the Roman Catholics of Canada East continued to act with the would-be spoliators of Protestant Church property, they would be endangering the principle by which their own ecclesiastical endowments were secured and that they might sow the wind and reap the whirlwind.[53] For a brief moment, these Tory manoeuvres may have had a chance of success; and through the thick murk, pierced feebly by flashes of rumour and conjecture, which still envelops the crisis of July, 1851, there are brief glimpses of the Conservatives, with Macdonald prominent in the foreground, making and receiving overtures for a *rapprochement* with the moderate Reformers, French and English. It was reported that Macdonald, with other Conservatives, had been sounded by the Ministerialists on the possibility of a coalition.[54] And McDougall, the editor of the *North American,* who was manoeuvring on behalf of the Clear Grits, declared that "the Tories have been making all sorts of humiliating overtures" to the French. "They thought they had the cherry in their mouths," he added, "but with the blessing of God we will disappoint them."[55]

And, at the last moment, the Conservatives were disappointed. The old feeling for unity among the Reformers, the urge towards the reconciliation of their recent unnatural feuds, was still too strong to be circumvented. By the end of July it was generally known that a new basis for the existing government had been laid in an alliance of the main body of Reformers with the Clear Grits; and in October the new Cabinet, headed by Francis Hincks and A. N. Morin, was formally constituted. Once again the Conservatives had failed to obtain power; once again they had failed to exploit successfully the admitted divisions of their opponents; and in the autumn of 1851 almost their sole consolation lay in the obvious fact that the new Reform coalition had been achieved with difficulty, that it was not really complete, and that its future career was uncertain. How would the Clear Grits enjoy the large concessions and compromises which their leaders now admitted must be made? How high a price would have to be paid by everybody in future embarrassments, frustrations, and perplexities? And what, above all, were the probable consequences of the sinister isolation of George Brown? For Brown—and herein lay the largest measure of consolation for the Conservatives—stood apart from the whole arrangement. Moody, resentful, jealous of Hincks, disappointed of an expected place in the new Cabinet, and determined to continue his struggle against the dark forces of the Roman Catholic hierarchy, he now broke openly and defiantly with the new government. And with his defection, the split in the Reform party, first noticed in the autumn of 1849, was continued in a different but possibly more dangerous fashion.

These cheerful circumstances, and the improvement of his own personal affairs, gave Macdonald fresh energy that autumn, despite the failure of the grand plan for a union with the French. The old zest in provincial politics had come back: and, as the general election steadily approached, he took the whole Midland District under his superintendence with easy and exuberant efficiency. In mid-September, though the formal reorganization of the government was still to come and the election months away, he was writing to his friend, D. B. Stevenson of Prince Edward County, warning him that "the Rads are working like blazes" and urging him "to take the

stump manfully" and at once.[56] It was not until late in November, to the accompaniment of mountainous snowfalls which
unfortunately blocked up the door of one of the Reform newspapers and prevented its appearance for a day, that the electoral
campaign in Kingston began to get under way. Then the
Conservatives discovered, to their shocked astonishment, that
the Radicals, despairing of finding a genuine candidate of their
own, had cunningly decided to requisition Kingston's popular
ex-Mayor, John Counter, in a last diabolical effort to "throw
John A. Macdonald overboard".[57] On December 6, at the hustings outside the city hall, Counter was actually nominated,
although he was not present at the meeting; but after the
crowd had pushed its way inside the hall to hear Macdonald's
speech, the ex-Mayor suddenly appeared. It was utterly impossible for him to accept the nomination, he explained, and
he must therefore decline it.[58] Despite this blunt disavowal, his
dubious friends persisted in their nomination and demanded a
poll on his behalf; but the opposition had now become so
obviously frivolous and fraudulent that Macdonald could afford
to treat it with benign contempt. Counter, he explained blandly
in his nomination speech, was not really a Reformer and had
been put up solely on the grounds that he, Macdonald, had not
paid sufficient attention to the local interests of Kingston in
parliament. For the first two-thirds of his speech he continued
in a severely parochial strain, dwelling upon his devotion and
his services to his own city; and it was only towards the end
of the usual lengthy nomination speech that he approached
really provincial affairs. There was an echo of the old programme of the British American League, in his demand for
protection to native industry; and he clung closely to Tory policy
in respect of religious endowments when he declared that "the
Clergy Reserves he would hold sacred to religious purposes
. . .".[59] He desired, he said, to see no inequality in the rights
of the different denominations of Christians, but he hoped to
establish equality, not by levelling down, but by raising up
those which were now in an inferior position to the enjoyment
of the privileges held by others.

On Monday, December 15, the poll opened. The vote was

light, partly because of the spurious nature of Counter's unwilling candidacy, and partly because of another terrific snowstorm, which began on Monday and continued in blinding
downfalls all the next day.[60] On Wednesday, at noon, when the
final totals were announced, Macdonald had received 291
votes and Counter 15. The entire Midland District, Kingston,
Frontenac, Hastings, and Lennox and Addington—everything
but Prince Edward County—had now been secured for the
Conservatives; and when he thanked his supporters briefly
from the steps of the city hall, Macdonald explained that there
was still work to be done for the party and that he was leaving
immediately for Picton to cast his vote for the Tory candidate,
Stevenson. Back in September, when he had written Stevenson, he had promised that he would bring over all the Kingston
Conservative voters who held property in Prince Edward; and
that afternoon he, and Alexander Campbell, John Richardson
Forsyth and Henry Smith, Jr., piled into a sleigh and were
driven off up the snow-choked road to the south-west.[61] They
stopped for the night at an inn at Adolphustown. The day
before, a far-seeing Reformer of the district had thoughtfully
collected all the small skiffs on the other side of Adolphus
Reach, by Macdonald's old home, the Stone Mills. The ruse
was simple, ingenious, but unnecessary; for a severe frost,
which followed the snowstorm, had frozen the Reach, and
immobilized everything, including the ferry, at Glenora. The
ice was too thin in places to bear a sleigh or horses; but the
cheerful and undaunted members of the voting party each
secured two planks and, pushing these tentatively ahead,
crawled slowly on their stomachs over the weakest parts of
the Reach towards the Stone Mills. There a sleigh whisked
them quickly over the snowy road to Picton, and they cast
their votes in time.

Stevenson was elected. The entire Midland District had now
been won for the Conservatives, and the drive back to the
Stone Mills, in the dark December evening, was a triumphal
progress. Down by Adolphus Reach, the inevitable crowd of
faithful Conservatives had assembled; and Macdonald, cheerful, irreverent, elated with whisky and triumph, mounted the

platform of Teddy McGuire's saloon to address the crowd. He was back in his old district, joking with his old neighbours, talking to old friends and acquaintances who already rolled his stories, and escapades, and burlesques about their palates like a well-loved spirit. For five minutes or so they shouted with laughter while he imitated the ridiculous sing-song manner in which a poor worthy Quaker clergyman, well known in the district, used to intone his interminable sermons. A young man, Canniff Haight, who had driven the sleigh back from Picton, stood watching the platform, and the flaring lights of the hotel, and the laughing faces of the spectators. Long afterwards he remembered: and it was out of episodes such as these —at ferries and by roadsides, in hotels and village inns, in city halls and on rural hustings—that the incredible Macdonald legend began to grow.

Chapter Eight

The Liberal-Conservative Coalition

I

In the new parliament—it was the third of which he had been a member—Macdonald stepped easily into a new prominence. He turned thirty-seven in January, 1852. His powers had matured; he had grown increasingly expert in their use; and he had kept his political good fortune in the midst of catastrophes which had eliminated, at least temporarily, so many of his rivals. The financial worries and emotional disturbances of the winter of 1849 were apparently a thing of the past. He stood on some admitted limitations and some abandoned hopes; but the ground, if less pleasant than it might have been, was still solid. He would never be a very great, or, perhaps, a very wealthy, lawyer; but money, or legal fame, was not his real ambition. With the Commercial Bank and the Trust Company accounts, he had enough to permit him to continue in politics and to keep his small family in reasonable ease and comfort. Hugh John, who would be two years old next March, had come through the first, anxious stage of babyhood. Isabella had crept slowly and painfully out of the never-to-be-repeated agonies of motherhood and into that feeble, uneasy state of convalescence which had come to be her best substitute for health. She could never be a normal wife, a normal mother, a normal mistress of a married establishment; and the house, which might have been crowded with company and talk and laughter, kept at its very centre a dim, hushed room, full of equivocal silences and nervous apprehensions. Isabella could

match Macdonald's silent, dogged fortitude; she could rival
the warmth of his emotional intensity; but it was beyond the
strength of her broken body and injured spirit to respond to
his gaiety, his buoyant vitality, his irrepressible genial interest
in a multitude of people and things. At the very heart of his
existence there was, not a denial—for Isabella never had the
opportunity to give or refuse her part—but the utter impossibility
of any real response. The long, hopeless years, with the familiar
crises, and recoveries, and relapses of the sick-room, never apparently calloused the tenderness of his anxious affection with
the hard skin of impatient familiarity. But there was a strong,
warm current of his nature which could find only a part of
its scope and encouragement in his own home and his own
office. He liked and understood people; he enjoyed the pace
and bustle of affairs; he had convictions; and he wanted power.
Politics could not absorb him completely. Politics was not yet
a vocation in Canada; and, even if it had been, he was probably
not yet ready to accept the tyranny which such a vocation
would certainly impose. He was a gifted amateur who had
not yet decided to become a professional. There was a new
confidence, as well as the old zest, in the way he played his
part.

The fortunes of politics favoured his sudden advance. He
had always been regarded as Draper's protégé and heir—as the
best of the possible moderates, as the potential leader of the
Liberal-Conservatives. And now a film of discredit, the discredit of defeat or of temporary political disfavour, had apparently dulled the prestige of his old rivals, the High Tories,
the survivors of the Family Compact group. He had kept his
tight, unshakable hold on Kingston and the Midland District,
while several among his more important colleagues had failed
to meet the basic political requirement of holding their ridings.
The party as a whole had done just as badly in the general
election of 1851 as it had in the general election of 1847; and
its few reinforcements—men like John Gamble from York
South and T. C. Street from Welland—were not enough to fill
the wide gaps where the veterans had fallen. William Cayley,
John Hillyard Cameron, George and Henry Sherwood, had all

been defeated. It was a wholesale clearance of the general staff. Henry Sherwood had been Attorney-General, titular leader of Canada West in the Conservative government in 1847; Cayley and Cameron had both held office; and all of them could have been regarded as potential successors to Sir Allan MacNab. They were all out of parliament now, and they were out at a time when the question of the succession to Sir Allan—a question propounded with hopeful frequency by the moderates in the party—was being raised once more. For nearly six years, ever since the retirement of Draper and the discredit of Sherwood in the election of 1847, MacNab had been the tacitly accepted Conservative leader. The son of a United Empire Loyalist, a soldier like his father, he had fought through the War of 1812 while still a boy in his teens, and had gained his knighthood for services in the Rebellion of 1837; and in his red-faced, jovial, downright fashion, he gave the philosophy of the Family Compact what was perhaps its most primitive military expression. He had long been odious to the "Gowanites"; he was becoming objectionably tiresome to larger sections of the party; and recently a new political disturbance had deposited a small cloud of disapproval about his ruddy, genial countenance.

The fact was that he appeared far too intimately connected with the government's ambitious railway policy.[1] A hearty, simple-minded soul who enjoyed every minute of his robust existence, and who alternated with genial ease between a rather ostentatious wealth and an unabashed impecuniosity, MacNab had always been a somewhat needy, greedy, not too scrupulous speculator. Now, in his older, more expansive years, he took to railways like a cheerful child to jam. He became president of the Great Western Railway. He was made chairman—though his party was in opposition—of the parliamentary committee on railways; and he was alleged to have said—and the newspapers frequently repeated the aphorism— "my politics now are railroads". As the summer of 1852 passed on, and the time for the opening of the first session of parliament drew closer and closer, it began to be hinted, with unpleasant openness, that the "gallant knight" was no longer free to oppose the government on any vital issue. From these insinuations some Conservative newspapers in both Toronto and Montreal went on to make the most damaging general assessments of Sir Allan's fitness for the post of leader.[2] Then, having pronounced judgment against him, they took the final step of advocating the claims of John A. Macdonald.

The chorus of approval was impressive and sustained. The *Montreal Gazette* referred regularly to the Conservatives of Canada West "led by Macdonald of Kingston".[3] "We believe it is now settled, with the unanimous consent of the party," wrote the editor of the Toronto *Patriot,* "that the Hon. John A. Macdonald, member for the city of Kingston, is to be the future parliamentary leader".[4] These calm assumptions and confident prophecies naturally aroused protests among some of the older Tories; and a long, unseemly dispute, in which a number of Conservative newspapers joined, went on for some weeks over the question of the leadership of the party. The *Globe,* which, though opposed to the government, still took the keenest relish in Tory squabbles, assured its readers, in a stern biblical metaphor, that "the Conservatives remind us just now of the inhabitants of Jerusalem when Titus was besieging their city".[5] Macdonald would probably have agreed that these demoralizing quarrels in the party simply emphasized its divisions and invited its defeat. The argument over the leadership had no doubt done him some good, but it was certainly doing the party harm. He had no wish to oust the still indispensable MacNab, and he was apparently one of a number of Conservative members of parliament who tried to put a stop to the controversy by signing a formal resolution in which they expressed confidence once more in their old leader.[6]

He was not yet head of the party, but it was significant that no other heir apparent had even been mentioned during the debate. These great expectations had apparently bred in him a greater sense of responsibility, a more becoming gravity. But even yet there was a certain light-hearted, amateurish inconsistency in his devotion to the party. In the first session of the new parliament, which began in Quebec in August, 1852, adjourned in November and reopened in the following February, he was certainly more prominent than ever before, but still not uniformly faithful in his attendance. At times, when the pressure of affairs was running strong at Quebec, he found he could not even spare the time for such important family occasions as the marriage of his sister Margaret to James Williamson, the Professor of Mathematics and Natural Philosophy at Queen's University.[7] "I wish that Moll should have a good kit," he wrote characteristically to his sister Louisa, "and I wish you to expend £25 for her on such things as you like. Don't say anything to her about it, but when I go up I will settle the bills. Get the things."[8] He added that he would "strain every nerve to be up on the 19th", which was the day in October fixed for the wedding. But on October 18 an important election petition came up for debate—he was a member of the election committee—and at the last moment it was impossible for him to get away.[9] Yet, despite these proofs of self-sacrificing zeal, his devotion was not consistent. He was nearly three weeks late when parliament met in the winter of 1853, after the long adjournment; and he left in the spring when the lengthy session had still a month to run.[10] His professional interests in Kingston, a certain cheerful casualness of attitude which some of the sterner members of the party were perhaps beginning to find a little exasperating, and a disinclination to commit himself too far to either the Conservative party or Canadian politics in general, all helped to keep him in a position of slight detachment. But when he was at Quebec—and for long months he stuck faithfully to his post—he was certainly busier than ever before, intervening more frequently in debate, making longer speeches, cultivating the French Canadians, drinking and dining with his fellow-members, and making plans and concocting plots and surprises for the day-by-day battle in the House.

As he grew better known to the Assembly and the country, the popular picture of his character as a politician, of his distinctive style as a public man, became filled out in detail and warmer in colour. Nobody, not even his most enthusiastic supporters, ever thought of complimenting him upon what were known in mid-nineteenth-century North America as the

JOHN A. MACDONALD, ABOUT 1856

Public Archives

"higher graces of oratory". But he had never liked and never tried to imitate the fashionable rhetoric of the period, with its ornate vocabulary and inflated periods. These turgid pomposities he had long regarded as characteristically American and highly undesirable. The easy, informal, rather conversational manner, rising occasionally and naturally to bursts of eloquence, which he had always regarded as the great traditional style of the British House of Commons, was his own instinctive preference. He was a debater by intention; and it was as a debater, as "an exceedingly close reasoner", laconic, cogent, persuasive, and entertaining, that he was getting to be known.[11] There was a touch of the old eighteenth-century manner in his occasional Latin tags, in his not infrequent quotations from satiric or comic literary classics such as *Hudibras*, in his appeals to the great traditions of Chatham, Pitt, Burke, Fox, and Wellington. He dealt frequently and easily in irony, in comic exaggeration; and the note of light-hearted humour which crept disconcertingly in and out of his speeches delighted his own followers and drove his opponents into a baffled state of half-amused exasperation. Drummond, Attorney-General for Canada East, who, on one occasion, had to admit to making an absurd error in the government's railway legislation, was pursued by Macdonald with such genial dexterity, that, in his blind rage, he scarcely knew where to turn. He began by accusing his tormentor of "flippancy"; then, with a brief effort to put the best face on the matter, went on to insist that Macdonald's "pleasant lecture" had really afforded him intense amusement; and ended up, in a badgered, truculent fashion, by demanding proof of the errors of omission and commission with which he had been charged. Macdonald blandly admitted that he always tried to be good-humoured in debate, noted how excessively disagreeable Drummond had found his pleasantries, wondered why a government whose politics were admittedly "railway politics" should be so ignorant of its own basic legislation, and finally advised Francis Hincks—the "Emperor Francis I" as the Conservative newspapers called him—never to be out of the House in view of the "awful messes" into which his colleagues got themselves during his absence.[12]

The manner was distinctive, characteristic and becoming increasingly well known. The matter—the sum total of his views on the constitutional and politico-religious questions of the day—was equally a typical expression of his character. Although, on occasion, he could quote authorities and appeal to abstract ideas, these references back to a fundamental political and social philosophy were usually implied rather than explicit. Unlike the formidable Brown, who appeared in parliament for the first time in the session of 1852-53, he was not a crusader with a mission. Equally he was not a rationalist who believed that government was a series of general objectives which could be attained by the application of timeless and universal rules. He thumped no tubs and banged no pulpits. He was far too concerned with the intricate details of concrete problems, far too interested in the curious and manifold complexities of human situations, to follow an ideal faithfully or to settle everything by scrupulous reference to a given set of rules. For him government was neither a quest for political justice nor an exercise in political arithmetic. Government was a craft, which one learnt chiefly by doing and by watching others do—a craft which consisted essentially in managing a small group of men which a far larger group of men had selected to govern them. There were no text-books and no divine revelations. The craft had its traditions, its conventions, its techniques, its stock of forms and variations—all of which were historical products. It found its raw material in the problems of a particular landscape and a particular people. It was the task of a politician to work within the tradition, and to respect the limitations and exploit the possibilities of the medium. He might remain a competent craftsman; he might become a great, creative artist. But he should never aspire to the alien roles of prophet, philosopher, or engineer.

In Macdonald's eyes, one of the main points of the tradition of his craft was the British parliamentary system of government. For him, the parliamentary system was, in fact, the grand style in which all his operations must be carried out. There was a slight, instinctive bias in his mind against any change in the system, even when change was clearly of native inspiration,

and when it amounted to little more than a modification of the style. The bias grew appreciably stronger when it became a question of alien borrowings, and particularly of imports from the exotic theory or practice of the congressional system in the United States. The old campaign for "elective institutions" which the Clear Grits had revived in 1851 had now dwindled away into a demand, fairly regularly repeated, for an elective Legislative Council. A number of Conservatives were, rather surprisingly, in favour of the change, for they believed that, if the upper chamber were elected on a stiff property franchise, they would have a good chance of wresting its control away from the Reformers. Macdonald had to treat these mild aberrations of his colleagues seriously; but he showed little interest, and took no part, in the campaign to smarten up the parliamentary system with a few day-before-yesterday republican improvements.[13] For him, responsible government, and the institutions out of which it had naturally developed, were amply sufficient. And when George Brown, who was in other respects a stout defender of the parliamentary system, proposed a fixed date for the annual meeting of the legislature, Macdonald objected that this would limit the use of the ancient royal prerogative to summon and prorogue parliament.[14] He looked with detachment on proposals to broaden the already fairly generous Canadian franchise; and even such an outwardly innocuous measure as the Representation Bill of 1853, which increased the representation of each section of the province to sixty-five members, found him dubious and critical. He had a number of debating points to make against the bill; he considered it unnecessary and uncalled for. "If there is one thing to be avoided," he declared, "it is meddling with the constitution of the country, which should not be altered till it is evident that the people are suffering from the effects of that constitution as it actually exists."[15]

If in politics he stressed the value of the constitutional inheritance, so in cultural matters he was prepared to recognize the strength and importance of the Christian tradition. His upbringing, his political experience, and the instinctive, easy-going tolerance of his nature all helped to make it easy for him

to realize how vital, and how endlessly varied, was the religious
life of early Victorian Canada. Confronted with this uniform
passion for religion, and these passionate religious differences,
both the secular-minded anticlerical and the deeply religious
"voluntarist" were accustomed to preach the doctrine of the
separation of church and state. But this simple and decisive
solution was not Macdonald's first choice. He was quite prepared to accept the old Conservative view that the state should
recognize and assist the religious and cultural activities of the
churches. He made, in fact, only one change—but a change of
enormous importance—in this venerable programme. From the
start he had tried to convince his Conservative associates that
they must liberalize and democratize the principles of recognition and assistance by extending their scope to all Christian
communions without distinction. The Constitutional Act of
1791 provided that one-seventh of all the public lands granted
by the Crown should be reserved for the support of a Protestant Clergy. The endless difficulties in the definition of the
term "a Protestant Clergy" had convinced many Christians that
it would be best to "secularize" the Clergy Reserves—to appropriate their revenues to the general purposes of government.
But Macdonald would have preferred to maintain the revised
settlement, established by the imperial statute of 1840, which
divided the proceeds of the Reserves among the principal Protestant churches. There were difficulties, of course, in the equitable division of state support—difficulties which were augmented
by the utter refusal of certain communions to accept any share
whatever: and these problems, which had led to the abandonment of the University Bills in 1847, might in the end force
the acceptance of the secularization of the Clergy Reserves. He
was better prepared than some of his associates to accept secularization, for his interest in the Reserves was not special privilege
but fair division. In his view, the Conservatives must learn to
recognize and respect not only the multiple religious divisions
of Canada West, but also the single basic cultural division
between English-speaking and French-speaking Canada.

It was this idea which governed his policy during the excited
politico-religious dispute of the early 1850's. He was prepared

to accept the cultural duality of Canadian life, to recognize that what was in form a unitary province was in fact a half-acknowledged federal state. The union could only be preserved by a series of compromises and conventions which sanctioned this cultural duality; and one of the most important of these compromises was the equal representation of the two sections of the province in the Assembly. Up until the session of 1852-53, the sectional political equality had not been very sharply questioned; but in March, 1853, George Brown first began his frontal attack on it by moving, in an amendment to the Representation Bill, that "the Representation of the people in Parliament should be based upon Population . . . and without regard to any separating line between Upper and Lower Canada".[16] This was the first emphatic and unambiguous expression of the principle of "Rep. by Pop."—the principle which, if adopted, was certain to upset the quasi-federal structure of the province, and to give Canada West, now rapidly surpassing the eastern section of the province in population, a dominant place in the union. Macdonald—a deplorably late arrival at Quebec that winter—was not in his place when Brown's amendment was debated:[17] but there can be little doubt that he eyed it very doubtfully from the start. For him, "Rep. by Pop." was an abstract idea, whose value could never be judged apart from the existing circumstances of time and place; and if, as the French Canadians insisted, the abandonment of sectional equality was tantamount to the dissolution of the union, then obviously the abstract idea was politically impossible. For the union of 1841 must be maintained. Macdonald did not, as yet, believe in the practicability of a general British North American federation; but at Kingston he had grown up into the conviction that the British lands bordering on the great river were indissolubly one. It was only through their union with each other and their connection with Great Britain that the St. Lawrence communities could hope to maintain their separate existence in North America. And for these reasons, the union, with all its necessary compromises, must be preserved.

II

This was the assortment of goods which Macdonald, now MacNab's principal assistant, could arrange inside the somewhat small and grimy panes of the Conservative shop window. To drum up trade among conservative Liberals and liberal Conservatives, to win the custom of the French Canadians—this was the old objective. And now that the Clear Grits were in the ministry, and the religious, cultural controversy in full swing, it was possible for the Conservatives to give a new and persuasive twist to the old propaganda by which they had tried to convince the French Canadians that they were taking their patronage to the wrong shop. In the speech which Macdonald delivered, early in September, 1852, on the address in reply to the speech from the throne, this new direction was at least vaguely indicated.[18] Already, he informed his listeners, the Radicals were jubilantly predicting that great and "progressive" reforms were bound to come, now that the "drag" of Baldwin and Lafontaine had been removed from the government. What could this possibly portend? Baldwin and Lafontaine, he informed Hincks reproachfully, "were the most upright men with whom the Inspector-General was ever allied". They had dignified the past of the Reform party. But now, with the Clear Grits in the government, who could safeguard its future? Macdonald glanced briefly, apprehensively, at that future. Possibly the Clergy Reserves question, now slumbering peacefully, would be revived. Possibly some equally fundamental attack on the established order would be begun. The future was dark with menace. The new alliance on the treasury bench was a preposterous and horrible partnership, a conspiracy merely to retain office, which could survive only through inconsistency, hypocrisy and deceit, and which promised to end in the treachery of the Clear Grits and the betrayal of the French Canadians.

On September 17, when, for the first time in his political career, Macdonald spoke at length on the subject of the Clergy Reserves, he took advantage of the occasion to picture the probable results of the alliance with the Clear Grits in still more horrifying detail. This, the third great debate on the

Reserves, marked another stage in the stumbling, erratic, and somewhat equivocal progress of the question. Lord John Russell's government, on receipt of the Canadian resolutions of 1850, had decided that it would repeal the imperial act of 1840 and permit the provincial parliament to legislate as it pleased on the subject. But the Russell government fell before it could carry out its expressed intention, and the Conservatives under Lord Derby succeeded to power. The Conservatives in England looked just as disapprovingly as the Conservatives in Canada upon any disturbance of the existing settlement of the Reserves; and the new Colonial Secretary, Sir John Pakington, informed Lord Elgin that his government was not disposed to touch the question. It was easy, fairly popular, and politically cheap for the Reformers to enter a valiant protest against this imperial veto.[19] It was equally easy for the Conservatives to take cover behind the Colonial Office, to justify the wisdom of its stand, and to deprecate the "collision" with the imperial authorities which the Canadian government seemed to threaten. Macdonald found Hincks's resolutions meaningless, insolent, and revolutionary. The imperial act of 1840 was, he insisted, a moderate, reasonable settlement of the problem. The deliberate resuscitation of the question of the Reserves, with a transparently fraudulent affectation of strong feeling, was a "solemn and discreditable mockery". Its one aim—for the ministers did not dare to pledge their followers to a policy of secularization—was simply to keep the country in an uproar. The interests of peace and equity required that this agitation should be stopped, and French Canadians had a special obligation to quiet a senseless and mischievous controversy which was full of peril for themselves. "They had it in their power," Macdonald declared deliberately, "to put a stop to the turmoil and the agitation and hypocrisy upon this question: and they should do it, as well to protect the constitutional rights of others, as to prevent the same violent hands being laid upon their own property and institutions in turn".[20] If they joined the spoliators of religious endowments in Canada West, they would inevitably endanger their own cultural institutions; and every French-Canadian member who voted for Hincks's resolutions "lent his influence

and support to a party who were seeking to destroy all ecclesiastical institutions, who would never rest until they tore down
every church establishment in British America".

Macdonald's dire predictions remained unsubstantiated during the first part of the session. But when the House met again,
in the middle of a snowy February, after a long adjournment,
it was at once evident that the question of the Clergy Reserves
had entered a new and still more exciting phase. In the interval,
the Derby ministry in England had been succeeded by a coalition of Whigs and Peelites under Lord Aberdeen; and the new
Colonial Secretary, the Duke of Newcastle, promptly informed
Lord Elgin that the new government was ready to honour the
pledge made by the previous Liberal administration. This despatch, read on February 15, the second evening after the opening, was listened to with "breathless attention".[21] Would the
Conservatives, now that the support of the Colonial Office had
been removed, continue their efforts to quiet the angry agitation
over the Reserves? Would the work of secularization and spolia-
tion now proceed unhindered to the satisfaction of those covetous
anticlericals, the Clear Grits? These were natural questions,
but they remained unanswered. Time went on, and nothing
seemed to happen. On the one hand, the government maintained a mysterious silence on the subject of the Reserves; on
the other, it seemed disposed to give every legislative assistance
to a great variety of religious groups and societies in French
Canada, who were covering the eastern section of the province
with a network of monasteries, nunneries, schools, colleges,
hospitals, and charities, all under ecclesiastical control. Was it
true that the favoured institutions of French Canada, far from
being menaced, were actually multiplying themselves with impunity? Could it be that the Clear Grits, and not the French
Canadians, were the real dupes of the coalition of 1851? And,
if so, how were Macdonald and the Conservatives to revise the
strategy by which they hoped to detach the French Canadians
from their "unnatural alliance", and thus attain political power
themselves?

One obvious device was at hand. Macdonald and his friends
could intensify their campaign to prove that these concessions

on the part of the Clear Grits were utterly insincere and calculating; they could redouble their efforts to reveal the Radicals as a group which was infinitely contemptible and yet infinitely dangerous. For months the Conservative newspapers made this form of caricature their favourite pastime. The Clear Grits were represented, in the first place, as an unsavoury and illiterate crew of yokels. "Coon" Cameron's hair resembled "a disarranged brush heap".[22] His followers occupied their leisure time in the Assembly in the "elegant operation" of picking their teeth and scratching their heads.[23] On formal occasions, they wore coats "evidently made when the broad-bottomed Dutch style was in vogue"; they acknowledged gracious salutations "with a picturesque chop of their heads and hoist of their heels"; and they found the parties at Government House a sad disappointment because the refreshments unfortunately contained no pork and beans, sauerkraut, or pumpkin pie.[24] Uncouth, ill-bred, bad-mannered, with nothing but a low animal cunning to serve them in the place of intelligence, they were just as morally reprehensible as they were physically dirty. Usually their convenient "sliding-scale" of principles permitted them to sit in the House and vote for anything the government demanded. But sometimes even their coarse radical stomachs were revolted by a strong and unchanging diet of ecclesiastical corporation bills. They sought refuge from humiliation in precipitate retreat; and Dr. Rolph, their second representative in the ministry, became known as "Old Dissolving Views" from the frantic haste with which he left the chamber, his coat-tails flying out, when a particularly embarrassing division was at hand.[25] All this transparent evasion and dissimulation was simply a device to permit the Clear Grits to enjoy the benefits of office. Their real views had not changed: their real views were indistinguishable from those of George Brown, the editor of the *Globe,* the newly elected member for Kent, who had carried into the Assembly his great campaign against the sinister forces of the Papacy, and who was now denouncing French and Roman Catholic domination in religious and cultural matters with terrific energy and passionate emotional conviction. "The spirit which the member for Kent has openly avowed through the columns of the *Globe* rankles in all their breasts and is only hidden now from motives of policy".[26]

Macdonald accepted these useful propagandist devices, but he must have realized that they had certain limitations. However much the Conservatives might denounce the unreality of the coalition of 1851, however much they might prophesy the eventual betrayal of the French Canadians, the fact remained that at the moment the government was pursuing a moderate policy in cultural and religious matters, a policy which could hardly have been anything but satisfactory to the French Canadians, and which was not very different from that which the Conservatives themselves would have followed. Yet if the Conservatives accepted the government programme too meekly they would forfeit their right to be regarded as a serious opposition, just as they would wreck the whole plan of a union with the moderates and French Canadians if they followed the intransigent opposition of Brown. It was a tight situation, and its difficulties were never better illustrated than by the so-called Ecclesiastical Corporations Bill of 1853. The government, wearied and perhaps embarrassed by the frequently repeated necessity of chartering individual Roman Catholic institutions, decided to introduce a general measure for the incorporation of such religious, charitable and educational bodies.[27] It was certain that George Brown would oppose the bill. But what of the Clear Grits, those restless, unhappy, conscience-stricken creatures, who listened dully, with one unwilling ear, to the orders of their government whips, and, with the other, hearkened yearningly to Brown's irrefutable logic? Obviously their vote was very uncertain; and after March 8, when Brown delivered his enormous, vituperative oration against the bill,[28] the rumours of dissatisfaction and impending revolt among the Clear Grits, the Baldwin Reformers, and even among the French Canadians began to grow and circulate rapidly.[29] Could it be that the government would be defeated on the measure? And in such a crisis, what policy should the Conservative party adopt?

Macdonald obviously enjoyed surprise, shock tactics—"plots" he called them to Captain Strachan; and it is not too difficult to see his guiding hand in the dispositions of the Conservatives on this occasion. The party waited developments in ambush. Not a single Conservative arose to debate Brown's amendment; and on March 10, when the debate was resumed, MacNab's entire following still remained fixed in mysterious and sinister silence. That night the galleries were crowded; rows of priests and Roman Catholic dignitaries sat watching anxiously for the result. And as Drummond, the Attorney-General for Canada East, ramblingly continued his protracted—perhaps deliberately protracted—speech, the desperate struggle for votes went on. Dr. Rolph, and Messrs. Richards and Cameron were observed "flying about the house, now soft-sawdering a refractory Grit, and again pulling the traces on the right side of the legs of a kicking French Canadian".[30] There was, a Tory correspondent noted with malicious satisfaction, a peculiar "goneness" in the stricken countenance of the Clear Grit David Christie as he contemplated the horrifying vision of his angry Free Kirk constituents back in Wentworth; and "as for poor Amos Wright, of East York, he was so flattered and fondled by great men in high offices, that he looked as bewildered with unexpected honours as an interesting young widow giving herself away in matrimony for the fourth time".[31] Then at last, when Drummond's long speech drew to its close, the vote came. The entire body of Conservatives, together with Brown and his few followers, and Cauchon, Sicotte, and a handful of French Canadians, voted for the amendment and against the bill. They mustered thirty-four votes. No, only thirty-three! For the once vigilant and terrible William Lyon Mackenzie, awakening in bewilderment out of a deep and stupefying sleep, voted for the amendment, then announced that he had made a mistake and voted the other way, while the House amused itself at the fretful old man's expense. Thirty-three votes! But the government had obtained thirty-nine. It had won; but only with the support and the humiliation of the Clear Grits.

Macdonald had now to talk his way out of the position in which the vote had placed the Conservative party. The opposition had done better than in any previous division in the new House. But the Conservative ruse had failed of its daring objective—the overthrow of the ministry. The party had voted as a body with Brown, and its course, to say the least, required some defence and explanation. Hincks rose, immediately after the vote, to taunt the "great Conservative party" with voting factiously for an amendment which it had not dared to support in debate. MacNab's defence was brief and rather feeble, and a good deal depended on Macdonald's reply. He did what probably nobody in the House beside himself would have thought of doing, or dared to do. He gave only the briefest of explanations, assuring the French Canadians, at the very end of his speech, that the Conservatives did not, of course, object to ecclesiastical corporations as such, but only to the generality and laxity of the present bill. He hardly bothered with a defence at all. Instead, he burlesqued the whole episode of the vote which the House had just recorded, covered the unhappy Grits with ridicule, and kept the whole House laughing over the preposterous divisions in the government.[82] Never before, he declared, had there been "such a whipping in" in Canadian parliamentary history. During the whole evening, ministers had been looking anxiously out into the corridors for skulkers; the President of the Council had been flitting restlessly about the room in search of recalcitrants. And yet, when, after all their efforts, they had got their last man in, they could muster a majority of only six votes—of only five "before the honourable member for Haldimand saw which way the wind was blowing and changed his mind". Poor Mackenzie, chattering with rage, got indignantly to his feet to refute this insinuation and to tell the humiliating story of his slumbers. But Brown retorted incisively that only the day before, Mackenzie had informed him that he would oppose the bill; and the resulting altercation between the member for Kent and the member for Haldimand continued for a moment or two, while the House rocked with laughter. Everybody was in a good humour when Macdonald resumed his description of the monstrous, hydra-headed government, whose agonized convulsions were so fascinating to behold that the Conservatives preferred to watch them in attentive silence. Office was the one thing that kept the government together; and office—and the well-filled purse of a developing young country—had brought the Clear Grits submissively to heel once again.

"These honourable gentlemen of more than common political virtue, these purists who would sweep everything away for their principles, these Clear Grits, the pure silica of Upper Canada, voted for the government against their principles".[33] Never again could they face their constituencies with impunity: "the member for Kent had ungritted them".

Macdonald's defence was ingenious, but it could not get the party out of the fundamental difficulty of its position. The fact was that the quarrel over cultural and religious institutions, over the relation of church and state, had aroused strong and conflicting opinions, which were inhibited and muffled by the existing divisions of the Canadian party system. Until recent times it had been chiefly the Conservatives who, for obvious reasons, had attacked the existing divisions; but now it was the turn of the Radicals to grow angry over the deceptions and frustrations of Canadian party politics. The secularization of the Clergy Reserves had been repeatedly and mysteriously postponed; the ecclesiastical institutions of Canada East had been steadily strengthened; the common school system of Canada West had been progressively modified to admit separate Roman Catholic schools. And all this had happened under a Reform government, of which the radical Clear Grits were a constituent party! William McDougall, the architect of the coalition of 1851, was now alarmed by the results of his handiwork.[34] The Radical leaders, Rolph and Cameron, steadily declined in prestige, and George Brown loomed larger and larger as the real leader of western Canadian discontent. He had become, in one short parliamentary session, a commanding figure in the House and the country. Humourless, blunt in diction, awkward in gesture—the stiff arm, jerking monotonously up and down like a dull saw on an obstinate log of hardwood, was the characteristic accompaniment of his speeches—he seemed, in the downright, purposeful simplicity of his thought and manner, to be the authentic, vital voice of Protestant Upper Canada. For him the existing party system was simply a sham. He had no doubt whatever that the Radicals, in accepting office with French-Canadian support, had debased their Liberalism and abandoned their entire programme of reform. The French Canadians, he insisted over and over again, were not real reformers at all: and "to think that the Liberals of Upper Canada can long continue in close alliance with the Lower Canadian party, as at present constituted, is absurd".[35] Once the unnatural union were broken, the western Liberals would be released from their thraldom, and the Ultramontanes of Canada East could make an appropriate alliance with the Tories of Canada West. "The two parties were in fact made for each other," he wrote bluntly, "and should embrace as soon as possible. Everybody is in a false position just now".[36]

Macdonald would have emphatically agreed that everybody was in a false position. It was natural that these two men, the coming Conservative and Reform leaders, the great political rivals of the future, should concur so nearly in their analysis of Canadian parties. Both men wished to break up the existing party system. Both hoped to establish great middle parties from which only a few extremists would be excluded. They were of one mind up to this point; but at this point their agreement ended. Macdonald believed that his Liberal-Conservative party could absorb the great body of the Reformers with the exception of a few radical Clear Grits from Canada West and a few *Rouges* from Canada East. Brown aspired to take over the majority of the Conservatives minus only an impotent handful of ultras and reactionaries. "It is the real Tory High-Churchmen of Upper Canada and the thorough ultramontanists of Lower Canada who must join," the *Globe* argued persuasively.[37] The two plans conflicted; the success of one meant inevitably the complete failure of the other. And from 1853 on, as the coalition of 1851 grew more insecure and the Hincks government more vulnerable, the two schemes began to stand out against each other with greater and greater clarity.

III

Early in May, when Macdonald left Quebec and returned to Kingston, the long, meandering session had still a month to run. It was probably the practice that drew him back; but a

weary discouragement with the results of the session may have
made it easier for him to leave. Back in Kingston, as he talked
over the probable future of the party with a friendly observer
like Alexander Campbell, he sometimes showed a cheerfully
cynical despair.[88] The fact was that the session, with its heavy
concentration on cultural and religious matters, had not advanced the fortunes of Conservatism nearly as much as he had
perhaps expected. In one way, the battles over schools, and
Clergy Reserves, and religious corporations had been useful
to the Conservatives, for they gave the party a chance of demon-
strating its basic sympathy with French-Canadian needs. But,
in another and equally important way, the cultural struggle
was dangerous to the Conservatives, and to any other political
group which was, in fact or by intention, a truly provincial
party. Disputes over schools and churches brought out into
the open the fundamental antagonism between the two divisions of the province. Cultural disputes emphasized the sectional rather than the provincial interest. They led to mutual
recriminations, to charges and counter-charges that one section
of the province was imposing a cultural domination on the other.
They supplied a cogent justification for George Brown's plan
of representation by population, and a plausible excuse for
George Brown's scheme of a great sectional crusade against
conservative French Canada. In such dangerous circumstances
it was difficult for Canadians to combine, as Canadians; and
it was altogether too easy for the Conservatives themselves to
hark back to their old anti-French prejudices of the past. The
party might not only fail to win the alliance of the French of
Canada East; it might also lose its following among the Protestant English of Canada West. The danger was real, and it
would almost certainly grow greater, if the cultural conflict
became more acrimonious. And the trouble was that in the
spring and early summer of 1853 religious and sectional antagonism reached a new and almost unexampled pitch of violence.

Partly it was the actions and inactions of the provincial
legislature—the new public school law and the failure to do
anything about the Clergy Reserves—which aggravated the
voluntarist and anti-Catholic grievances of Canada West. But,

to a very large extent, the emotional explosion of June and July was the result of the sudden appearance of a strange and exotic figure from abroad who, as not infrequently happens in provincial societies, touched off the charge of anger with an ease which no native could have approached. Towards the end of May, Father Alessandro Gavazzi, a veteran of the Italian Revolutions of 1848 and an ex-friar of the Roman Catholic Church, arrived in Toronto to begin a Canadian lecture tour. Gavazzi was a Liberal in politics who had become an evangelical Protestant in religion;[39] and after the collapse of the Roman Republic had driven him into exile in 1849, he had travelled about the English-speaking world, lecturing to large, responsive audiences on such currently exciting topics as the authority of the Bible, the doctrine of transubstantiation, and the evils of the Inquisition, ancient and modern.[40] His mission, he announced with grandiloquent comprehensiveness, was nothing less than the total destruction of the Pope and Popery. He was a tall, stout man, with a powerful voice, at once insinuating and commanding, and a strongly marked, extremely expressive countenance, radiating magnetic force and vehement conviction.[41] When he appeared before an audience, he wore a long, full, black robe, ornamented with a purple cross on the breast and left shoulder. His appearance was sufficiently startling; his platform manner was more than a little theatrical; and it seemed at first as if his Canadian tour was certain to be a triumphant success. On the last day of May and the first of June, 1853, he delivered two highly successful lectures to huge audiences in Toronto. From Toronto he travelled quickly eastward to Quebec, where the legislature was still sitting; and at Quebec, a riot occurred when he attempted to lecture in the Free Wesleyan Chapel in St. Ursula Street.[42] Almost immediately he left the capital; but instead of abandoning the province, as prudence might have suggested, he simply sailed up the river to Montreal. There, on the evening of June 8, at Zion Church in Haymarket Square, the tragedy occurred. A large crowd hostile to Gavazzi collected; a riot threatened, and the military were called out. The soldiers, acting in response to a fatal order, whose origin was hotly disputed afterwards, fired upon a section of the crowd, composed, as it happened, chiefly of the members of Gavazzi's audience, killing several people and fatally wounding others.[43]

This dreadful event put Macdonald, and the Conservatives, and indeed all the moderates, into a most embarrassing position. The tragedy was a terrible one, and its perpetrators seemed to have escaped with impunity from all consequences. No successful prosecutions were ever carried out in Montreal. Not even the thought of possible prosecution seemed to intimidate the rioters. For some time after June 8, so the newspapers alleged, crowds of Montrealers, completely contemptuous of the law, roamed the streets at will, breaking the windows of Protestant chapels and molesting and abusing evangelical Protestant clergymen.[44] And all the while, the governments, both municipal and provincial, seemed strangely unconcerned in the whole affair. No other series of events could have so effectively proved, in the excited popular mind, the justice of George Brown's crusade against the Roman Catholic domination of Canada East. Brown was a sectional leader—the defender of Upper Canadian sectional interests; but the tragedy of June 8—and this, for the Conservatives, was perhaps its most serious consequence—had invested his anti-Catholic crusade with a truly provincial significance and popularity. Down in Montreal, people began to argue hysterically that Protestants must combine to protect themselves with arms against the "thuggism" and "barbarism" which were "patronized by the legal authorities".[45] There was an ominous drift back towards the violence of 1849; there was an equally ominous tendency away from the compromises and accommodations which the dual culture seemed to require, and which Macdonald and some of the Conservatives had been trying to prove they were ready to accept. In these new and difficult circumstances, could the party hold to its chosen course, or would it slip back into the old anti-French direction, and so into the waiting arms of George Brown? In the weeks that followed the Gavazzi riots, the future seemed uncertain. Towards the end of June the Orange Order split. A minority of lodges, led by George Benjamin, withdrew in protest against the moderation of Ogle Gowan's pro-Catholic and pro-French policies: and it was significant that, in the political field, the "Benjaminites" preached a union with the Clear Grits to defeat Popery. In August, there came a dreadful day when even the *Montreal Gazette* admitted that the Conservative party, as then constituted, was moribund and incapable of resuscitation. A new party, the *Gazette* predicted, would arise—a new party which would labour to undo the iniquities of the past four years; and "this party," the prophetic editorial continued, "will demand equality for all sects and classes, gradual fusion of U.C. and L.C., free schools for the whole people, and Rep. by Pop.".[46] Was this not really the programme of the *Globe?* What was there to distinguish this "new party" from the party which George Brown was actually trying to create?

Macdonald's whole conception of the future of Conservatism was in danger. Some of his followers were ready to bolt; his policies had apparently been made meaningless by the horrors of the Gavazzi riots. He did not reappear in parliament for the last month of the session. He said and did little. He simply waited, hoping, no doubt, that the furious cultural and sectional antagonisms would wear themselves out through the very excess of their own violence. And, as the summer of 1853 passed slowly along, it began to seem possible that he had not waited entirely in vain. August was not ended before a new and very different political scandal began slowly and tantalizingly to be revealed to the fascinated gaze of the Canadians. It concerned no less a person than Francis Hincks himself, the Inspector-General, and the somewhat mysterious good fortune which had come to him in the last two years. For some weeks, the newspapers merely busied themselves with vague but interested inquiries into the source of Hincks's "sudden and inexplicable acquisition of great wealth";[47] and it was not until September, when the City of Toronto brought suit in chancery against its Mayor, John G. Bowes, that definite evidence of some of Hincks's financial operations at length became available. Then a tangled and curious story was revealed.[48] It appeared that the City of Toronto, wishing to aid the Toronto, Simcoe, and Huron Railway which was then in financial difficulties, had agreed to grant £50,000 in Toronto municipal debentures to the railway company. Sub-

sequently it was discovered that the authority by which the
city had made the grant was defective; and the debentures,
which had been paid out by the railway to its contractors, de-
preciated in value. The City of Toronto, moved by its Mayor,
John G. Bowes, now decided to consolidate the entire municipal debt with a refunding operation which would redeem all
its old or defective debentures at par; and the government of
Canada, with Francis Hincks as its finance minister, accommodatingly sponsored the consolidation act by which this operation was carried out. So far the case—a not unusual case of
Canadian municipal generosity and inefficiency—had not been
very remarkable. But there was more to come. It was now
revealed that Bowes and Hincks, the principals in the refunding operation were also the purchasers of the old and depre-
ciated debentures. They had bought the old bonds for £40,000;
they exchanged them for new bonds worth £50,000. They had
cleared £10,000 upon the deal.

This—the so-called "£10,000 job"—was a major sensation of
the autumn and winter of 1853-54. In September the chancery
suit began; in February three whole days were occupied in
receiving the testimony of Francis Hincks.[49] His evidence,
printed in long, close columns in the newspapers, almost competed in interest with the exciting despatches from England
which recounted the diplomatic prologue to the Crimean War.
A host of speculations and rumours, each clamouring for certainty, now gathered about the Inspector-General. Mr. Hincks,
the *Montreal Gazette* assured its readers, had been "financing
to a tune . . . of which the first notes are only now falling on
the public ear".[50] All that autumn and winter the public ear
was attentively cocked. What were the other high notes in
Mr. Hincks's soaring financial melody? Who had paid for the
1008 shares of stock with which he was credited in the books
of his own creation, the Grand Trunk Railway? Had he known,
when he speculated in the stock of the St. Lawrence and Atlantic Railway, that it was certain to be absorbed, on advantageous terms, by the Grand Trunk? By what means had he
possessed himself of a piece of government property which
happened to lie so conveniently close to the destined junction

of the railway at Point Levis? A clever little man—a typical sharp-eyed child of that unpleasantly prolific marriage between railways and responsible government, Hincks had gone about the business of furthering his own personal interests with the direct, uncomplicated ingenuity of a precocious infant. He had presented the public with a scandal so simple, so instantly comprehensible, so wholly malodorous that it brought unmitigated damage to the government and no embarrassment to the opposition. From the winter of 1854, it was almost certain that Hincks's political career was at an end; it was almost certain that the government which he had led would have to be reconstituted, and the only question, as William McDougall put it, was how were men to combine anew?[51]

Macdonald's objective remained exactly the same. He still hoped to build a party which would be liberal in its Conservatism and truly provincial in its scope. He still hoped to attract the bulk of the French Canadians and a large number of their associates, the Baldwin Reformers. For him the great political advantage of the Hincks scandals lay in the fact that they tended to direct attention away from the religious grievances and sectional resentments which for a year now had prejudiced this old Conservative programme. It was true that these resentments and grievances still rankled angrily in the minds of some Conservatives; and it was true too that George Brown, more openly than ever in the past, was seeking to seduce those waverers with his own special kind of blunt, argumentative wooing. "Between the great mass of the Reformers of Upper Canada and this largest or liberal section of the Conservatives," he argued, "there is little difference of opinion. Not one great principle divides them. Nothing but old recollections of antagonism, and a reluctance to yield up the Reserves, for which many of them have so long contended—prevents them working cordially together. When they do unite—when they unite on clearly defined, progressive principles—*French Canadian supremacy will be at an end,* and the political prospects of our country very different from now."[52] "French-Canadian supremacy will be at an end"—it was the old catch-cry, seductive and illusory, which the Conservatives had hearkened to long before. Macdonald had no desire to follow that mocking voice once more into the political wilderness. "I believe also," he wrote to Captain Strachan in February, 1854, "that there must be a change of ministry after the election, and from my friendly relations with the French, I am inclined to believe my assistance will be sought."[53] The French-Canadian alliance was still a main objective: so also was the liberalization of the old Conservative programme in Canada West. And although the Conservatives must never be led away into the fatal error of identifying their profession of faith with that of George Brown, yet they must struggle to convince moderate Reformers that there was a real prospect of progressive Reform in Liberal-Conservatism. "Our aim," Macdonald wrote to Captain Strachan, "should be to enlarge the bounds of our party so as to embrace every person desirous of being counted as a progressive Conservative, and who will join in a series of measures to put an end to the corruption which has ruined the present government and debauched all its followers."[54]

The theme of government corruption became the main theme of Macdonald's attack when parliament met again in June, 1854. In the meantime, the government of Canada, which, for nearly fifteen years, had been flitting unhappily about, like a distracted, migratory family of tenants, from one set of makeshift lodgings to another, had sustained a double tragedy in rapid succession. In the early morning of February 1, the old parliament buildings of Lower Canada, which had housed the government and legislature of the united provinces since their move from Toronto, were totally destroyed by fire;[55] and early in May, barely three months later, a second and equally spectacular conflagration wiped out the convent on the edge of the town which had been altered and redecorated at great expense for parliament's temporary accommodation.[56] It was the third time in five years that the lodgings of the luckless Canadian government had been burnt up by accident or arson; and, in this all too familiar emergency, the dwindling piles of books and records were packed up once more, the Legislative Council was transferred to the Quebec court-house, and the public Music Hall was hurriedly prepared for the reception of the

Assembly. The Assembly had barely met in these ironically incongruous surroundings when it became quite clear that even Macdonald had underestimated the amount of impatient disapproval which Hincks had aroused since the prorogation of the previous summer. Yet the Inspector-General apparently viewed this climbing wave of criticism with contemptuous unconcern. Badgered by many problems, and restrained by Elgin's cautionary advice, he presented only a very brief, perfunctory programme of legislation, which touched none of the controversial issues of the day; and he now surprisingly argued—echoing the arguments which the Governor-General had used to him—that, since the new representation bill was now upon the statute books, it would be better to seek the sense of the people again before beginning any radical changes. The House felt frustrated and irritated; the debate on the address in reply to the speech from the throne was prolonged and stormy; and when, on the night of Monday, June 19, Macdonald rose to speak, he may have believed that at last there was a real chance of doing something decisive. He began by attacking Hincks for the transparent self-interest which had dictated his change of attitude to a dissolution. Last year, when criticized for introducing a representation bill into the first session of a new parliament, the government had argued that the House, in passing such a measure, would not thereby confess itself to be an unrepresentative assembly which was incompetent to deal with serious matters. Last session, every government spokesman had insisted on the omnicompetence of the existing legislature; this session, with equal unanimity, they had proclaimed parliament's lack of moral authority to make law. It was an absurdly obvious contradiction, Macdonald argued, which arose solely from the government's desire to evade a parliamentary inquiry into its own misdeeds. Those corrupt misdeeds had been repudiated by everybody, including Reformers, including even the Inspector-General's own colleagues, for Malcolm Cameron, the Postmaster-General, had declared, at a public dinner in Perth, that he did not approve of the Point Levis purchase. The first, primitive duty of a member of any administration was not to speculate in public funds and public property. Pitt—

and here came one of Macdonald's characteristic appeals to the conduct of his favourite statesman—had for years remained completely unmoved by all the attacks made upon him; but, when once it was charged that he had speculated in public funds, then immediately he had filed suit in slander. Had the members of the present Canadian government been equally sensitive? They had not—and for a simple reason. They were terrified of the consequences which such a prosecution would entail.[57]

It was a particularly savage attack: and even the Toronto *Leader*, a government newspaper which the Conservative journals delighted to refer to as "Tsar Francis I's Court Circular", admitted rather wryly that Macdonald had "displayed more talent in the assault than the world usually gives him credit for possessing".[58] Hincks, pushed unceremoniously into an awkward corner, arose to give a somewhat laboured account of his purchase of the Point Levis property; Cameron got up to explain away his statement at the Perth dinner and to denounce Macdonald for repeating the falsehoods which foul-mouthed slanderers had been spreading for months against the government. Charges, recriminations and counter-charges were bandied about for a couple of hours between the alleged Reform railway plunderers of the present and the alleged Conservative land-grabbers of the past. The next day the debate was resumed with a new vigour and purposefulness. Cauchon, an ex-Reformer who had acted with Macdonald in the previous session, had already moved an amendment to the address, censuring the government for its failure to produce a bill for the "immediate settlement of the seigniorial question". Hartman, a Clear Grit, now produced a sub-amendment, which gave expression to the principal Upper Canadian grievance, and lamented the absence of a measure for "secularization of the Clergy Reserves". The horrid, definite word "secularization" was too much for the House: the Clear Grit sub-amendment was voted down. But where Hartman and Sicotte, the Clear Grit and the *Rouge*, had failed, it was possible for Sicotte and Cauchon, the Conservative, to succeed. Together they introduced a second sub-amendment which merely deplored the absence of a bill for the "immediate settlement of the Clergy Reserves". All the various, discontented sections of the House swung in behind this new, vaguely critical sub-amendment. It was passed by forty-two to twenty-nine votes; and Cauchon's main amendment, so altered, was accepted by the same majority.[59] The Hincks government had suddenly been defeated, and on two issues of major importance.

That night, when the long debate ended, Macdonald probably expected an immediate invitation to office. It was rumoured that next day, June 21, he and MacNab stayed patiently in their hotel rooms, waiting for a messenger from the Governor-General.[60] The House stood adjourned all day; all day the government debated its future course of action; but night fell and there was still no indication that Hincks had resigned and that a new government was about to be formed. It was not, apparently, until the morning of June 22 that the members began uneasily to suspect that Hincks had decided upon a very different course. Then, as the House assembled in the early afternoon, these suspicions were quickly converted into shocking certainties. Outside, the booming guns heralded the approach of the Governor-General to the nearby court-house; and inside the Music Hall, Hincks, in reply to a question from Sir Allan MacNab, calmly informed the House that the government had decided upon an immediate prorogation. At first the members seemed shocked into speechlessness. MacNab's brief protest was heard "amid a silence deep as death". Then William Lyon Mackenzie rose, somewhat more excitedly, to support the plea of the leader of the opposition that the Franchise Bill be passed immediately. But it was not until Black Rod had been admitted and the notice of prorogation given, that the House really seemed to realize what was happening, and then all order and decorum were suddenly blown into tatters as a furious storm of rage and disappointment swept through the Assembly. The hall was clamorous with cries and murmurs; a dozen members were struggling to voice their bitter protests; and the excitable Mackenzie, pointing a passionate finger at the ministers, screamed "shame on them, shame on them", over and over again. Yet it was Macdonald who seemed to ride over the whole enormous tumult as its principal avenging

fury. For the first time in his career he had become a fighter
in a parliamentary milling ground. He had always disliked
Elgin. And now Elgin and Hincks, by a too successful trick,
had defrauded him of office and robbed him of his revenge.
He was a political principal who was almost required to make
a protest. But he was also a furious Highlander who was ready
and willing for a fight. And for nearly a quarter of an hour he
stood in his place, his face contorted with excitement, gesticulating violently and shouting his denunciations at the top of his
voice.[61] Other angry voices succeeded to his. Drummond,
Robinson, Brown, and Langton took up the vehement argument. But these were briefer utterances, briefer exchanges,
which trailed away into ineffectuality, as the Speaker, and
the government members, and the whole body of the Reformers
began to move out of the room.

Within a fortnight the province was plunged into the excitement of an election. The Crimean War in which Great
Britain was now engaged had become stalled in its first phase
of laborious inactivity; and, for a moment at least, Canada
could give a nearly undivided attention to provincial politics.
It was the first general election since Macdonald had been
publicly accepted as MacNab's principal lieutenant; and although, in those days, a party could exercise only a feeble
control over its wayward and eccentric members, there were
more than a few signs of Macdonald's guiding hand in the
disposition of Conservative strategy. The ground for manoeuvre
was difficult in the highest degree. The great main object of
the campaign—the overthrow of the Hincks government—was
an object shared by a variety of political groups; and there was
inevitably some degree of association—desirable but dangerous
association—among the different sections of the opposition.
George Brown continued to make the most forthright and
indiscreet advances. He did not trouble to conceal his preference for certain Conservative candidates, even in his home
bailiwick, Toronto:[62] he announced publicly that the *Globe*
would have supported John A. Macdonald, if he had run against
Francis Hincks. The ministerial Reformers professed themselves
bewildered and scandalized by this preposterous behaviour.

"Either the Tory party are the only true Reformers," wrote the Toronto *Leader*, "or Mr. George Brown is no true Reformer but a Tory."[63] But Brown remained cheerfully unrepentant in the face of these rebukes. "Moreover," the *Globe* concluded a long editorial in explanation of its conduct during the general election, "we are free to admit that we have never failed to keep in view the small differences which now divide the Reformers and Conservatives of Upper Canada and the exceeding probability that ere long they will be found in the same harness working against the common enemy."[64] Macdonald believed also in the probability of a union—but on his own, not George Brown's, terms. And although the demonstrative expressions of Brown's rough wooing could not be rejected contemptuously, the Conservative party must set itself to prove that it had not compromised its independence by any too intimate political engagement.

Macdonald had tried to make the question of personal honesty in government the first issue in the campaign; and in the main the Conservative press followed him obediently. "Let us rid the country of its corrupt rulers," said the *Montreal Gazette*, "and ascertain how much damage they may have inflicted; and then, having repaired the leaks in the strong box, proceed to other reforms".[65] The nature of these "other reforms" was indicated vaguely with those moderate reforming gestures which Macdonald had been teaching his associates to employ. The Conservatives were not disposed to change their basic views on the relation of church and state; and they realized that the adoption of Brown's extreme voluntarist and anti-Catholic position would wreck their chances in Canada East. But, at the same time, they knew also that, if they wished to win moderate Reform support in Canada West, they must now show their willingness to compromise on the subject of the Clergy Reserves. They felt, and revealed, little enthusiasm for secularization; they announced simply that they were ready to face facts. The unpopularity of the Reserves must be conceded; and the vast hubbub, which, despite Conservative warnings, had been deliberately aroused over the settlement of 1840, could not be permitted to disturb society indefinitely. "Men

have become wearied of the perpetual jangle," observed the
Montreal Gazette temperately, "and are content to have the
thing got rid of in some way—in any way so far as the bulk of
the population were concerned . . .".[66] Badgley and Sherwood,
it was reported, were prepared for new legislation on the subject;[67] and even MacNab, though his opinions remained unchanged, was alleged to have declared that he "knew when to
bow to the voice of the country". It was rumoured, from
Quebec, that at their last caucus of the session, the Conservatives
had determined upon a fundamental change of policy with
respect to the Reserves.[68] Evidently the party as a whole was
preparing "to bow to the voice of the country".

So far as Macdonald's own election was concerned, the contest was a comparatively easy one. On July 17, at noon, outside
the Kingston town hall, while a broiling sun beat down on
the hustings and the perspiring crowd, Macdonald and John
Counter were nominated as the two candidates for the riding.[69]
Counter was, of course, the popular ex-mayor who had been
nominated back in 1851, but who had refused to run on that
occasion. With his hearty jokes and his bad grammar, he was
the same cheerful, loquacious partisan of Kingston that he had
always been. If he had any general politics they did not differ
materially from Macdonald's. But the main public concern of
his life had been Kingston; his principal interest in provincial
politics was Kingston; and he was prolific in criticisms of what
Macdonald had failed to do for the "good old town"—and
voluble with promises of what he himself would certainly ac-
complish if he were elected. A new post office, a new customs
house, the transfer of the "outer station" to the city, and even
the return of the seat of government to Kingston—these were
the spacious inducements in which Counter and his supporters
dealt. "We are told by these immaculate persons," said a
Conservative newspaper severely, "that Mr. Counter's politics
are expressed in the simple word 'Kingston'; that he knows
nothing but 'Kingston'; and that he will do anything and everything (if he *can* do anything) for 'Kingston'. If this has any
meaning at all, it means that, be the government radical, whig, or
tory . . . Kingston will be placed at its disposal, under any and all

circumstances, *for a consideration*."⁷⁰ This effort to disparage
poor Counter's politics as selfish and time-serving was apparently
all that was needed; and Macdonald won his seat again by
437 to 265 votes.⁷¹

It was a severely local contest, peculiar in its almost exclusive concern with parochial issues, and unusual also as an
easy Conservative success. The party, of course, won more
seats than it had possessed in the previous House, for, now that
the Representation Bill had gone into effect, there were many
more seats to win. But, in general, success fell far short of
Macdonald's hopeful expectations. The old, unreconciled disputes between the "progressive" Conservatives and the Tories
still continued; the split between the "Gowanites" and the
"Benjaminites" in the Orange Order was a serious weakness in
several constituencies; and Macdonald faced a long and disappointing string of defeats. The ministerial papers joyfully
announced that, after eight fruitless years of struggle, the Conservatives were now ready to "throw up the whole affair in
disgust". It was even rumoured that "one of their leaders has
made up his mind to resign his seat in Parliament, and leave
the deluded country to its fate".⁷² Whether the gossip-monger
had the member for Kingston in mind or not, the rumour was
apparently an all too accurate description of Macdonald's feelings during the dark weeks of July and August. He was sick of
the apparently profitless and hopeless struggle. "The party is
nowhere—damned everlastingly," he told Alexander Campbell
in his blunt, realistic way. "I will go down and get the bank
bill passed and retire. I am resolved upon it."⁷³

It was an odd declaration, in the light of what happened in
the first ten days of September. During the late summer Hincks
had tried in vain to strengthen the support of his government;⁷⁴
and on September 5, when he met the House, a large House
now of 130 members—"such immense shoals of loose fish were
never before witnessed"—it became immediately evident that
anything might happen, and happen quickly. On the first day
the government candidate for the speakership was defeated;
and on September 7, before the House ever really got down
to the debate on the speech from the throne, Hincks sustained

two tactical reverses in the case of the disputed Bagot election. On the morning of Friday, September 8, he and his colleagues resigned; and Lord Elgin sent at once for Sir Allan MacNab. Even then, and even among the Conservatives, the contradictory hopes and fears which had been bred of the bewildering confusion of Canadian party politics still continued to divide men; and the *Montreal Gazette* assured its readers that Sir Allan would probably fail in his task, and that then J. A. Macdonald and the "advanced Conservatives" would unite with the *Rouges* and the Brownites to form a government.[75] These confident calculations, so obviously copied from George Brown's exercise book in political arithmetic, could hardly have led to a more inaccurate conclusion. The next day MacNab saw Morin and Hincks; and Egerton Ryerson, who met him as he was coming out from his interview with the late Inspector-General, reported that Sir Allan was laughing heartily.[76] It was all arranged. The Conservatives were to unite with the moderates of the Reform party. The Lower Canadian section of the ministry was to continue unaltered; there were to be two Hincksite Reformers in the Upper Canadian section, and three Conservatives, MacNab, Cayley, and Macdonald. Macdonald was Attorney-General of Canada West, the office which both Draper and Baldwin had occupied. He was heir to the policies of both. He had won office with the support of a coalition which was provincial and moderate, rather than sectional and intransigent, in character. He, and not George Brown, had succeeded.

Chapter Nine

The Victory of the Progressive-Conservatives

I

Yet, in the autumn of 1854, the victory must have appeared doubtful and impermanent. Who could be certain that the coalition of 1854 was not simply one more of the many political arrangements and rearrangements of a troubled decade? And, in any case, had it not raised almost as many problems as it had solved? Even on the personal, the domestic, side, this sudden rise to office had certainly disturbed the rather genial, easy-going course of Macdonald's affairs. The new and welcome salary— it was £1250 a year[1]—had transformed him from a casual amateur into a responsible professional who, however hard or efficiently he worked at his duties, would have to spend at least a large part of the year away from Kingston, at the Canadian capital. The practice could be left with safety to his new, recently acquired partner, A. J. Macdonnell; but Isabella and the four-year-old Hugh John could not be disposed of so easily. Isabella was a woman who lived for her family, and who yet could not play her appropriate and desired role in family life. If she accompanied Macdonald to the capital, what could she bring but the burden of her invalidism; and if she stopped in Kingston with her female relatives, how could she support her husband's interminable absences? It was not easy to see a way through this new phase of an old anxiety, just as it was not easy to devise methods of consolidating the rather cramped position of political strength in which luck and astute management had suddenly landed him. How was he to strengthen and

preserve the Liberal-Conservative coalition, without either
affronting the old Tories or alienating the impatient Reformers,
and thus destroying the great, middle, constitutional party which
had always been his hope?

The first weeks of autumn were agitatedly busy. The by-
election in Kingston, made necessary by his acceptance of office,
came off late in September.² It was an easy formality, rather
than a contest; and early in October he was back in Quebec
once more.³ The House had adjourned for a week, to meet
again on October 10; and, during the brief interval, the ministers
feverishly planned their programme of legislation and doubtfully
considered the political future. In the Assembly, where a big
majority stood for the moment at their bidding, the position
seemed solid enough; but in the country as a whole it almost
appeared for a while as if the new coalition was being regarded,
not as a pleasant surprise, but as a painful shock. The outraged
comment of the *Globe*—"Never did politicians make a 'grab'
for office with less apparent regard for past professions than
these gentlemen"⁴—could, of course, be ascribed simply to the
fury of envious disappointment. But the cynical enjoyment of
George Brown's discomfiture, which the *Leader* and other
moderate newspapers exhibited, was not necessarily accompanied by any great enthusiasm for Macdonald's success.⁵ A
number of journals continued to regard the coalition with a
frigid, stand-offish curiosity, as if it were something artificial,
faintly discreditable, and inevitably temporary. It would take
time to win popular support, to create a respectable following
in the press; and there was a lamentable weakness even in those
journals which were ready to give the new government immediate and enthusiastic aid. Macdonald had not arrived back in
Quebec before importunate appeals began to arrive from Gowan
of the *Patriot* and Samuel Thompson of the *Colonist*.⁶ They had,
it appeared, huge debts and almost no money. The task of maintaining journalistic competition in Toronto with George Brown's
Globe was evidently going to be a formidable business.

But the first and main task faced the Conservatives at Quebec. They had to prove to the Assembly that the coalition of
1854 was not a factious combination of office-hungry politicians,

but a real union, based on a substantial identity of views, and fortified with a constructive programme for the future. Inevitably their sincerity was called in question. In consenting to enter the ministry, the Conservatives had accepted the elected Legislative Council, the secularization of the Clergy Reserves, and the abolition of the Seigniorial Tenure—policies which in the past they had opposed or sharply criticized, and which had formed the three main points in the late government's programme, as laid down in the speech from the throne. Charges of political opportunism and political inconsistency were certain to be hurled from both sides of the House—from outraged old Tories as well as jeering Radicals; and the session had barely recommenced after the adjournment, when Edmund Murney, the Loyalist member for Hastings, arose to deride his old friends for sacrificing their principles for power—for holding office "at the mere whim of those to whom they had been opposed all their lives".[7] Murney indignantly denied that the Conservative party had ever authorized its leaders to change their policy with respect to the Reserves: and Macdonald was obliged to tell in public the story of the caucus of the previous June— the caucus at which it had been decided that if the election registered a conclusive popular verdict in favour of secularization, the Conservatives would not oppose it any longer.[8] It was important for him, on purely personal grounds, to clear the party's record respecting the Reserves. Drummond, Attorney-General East, would sponsor the Seigniorial Tenure Bill; Morin would take up his old hobby of the elected Legislative Council; and MacNab, whose ancient martial valour had been reawakened by the opening of the war with Russia and by the allied landing in the Crimea, had already moved for a commission of four to report on the Canadian militia system. The Reserves—the most important item for Upper Canada in this first instalment of the new government's programme—were left for Macdonald.

Tuesday, October 17, 1854, was, for more than one reason, an exciting day. On the previous evening, vague garbled reports of a great action in the Crimea had reached Canadian cities by telegraph; and the men who sat down to listen to the

Public Archives

GEORGE ETIENNE CARTIER

Attorney-General West on the afternoon of the seventeenth had just finished reading the newspaper accounts of the Battle of the Alma. In such a tense atmosphere, it was well to be brief; and with such subject matter, at once highly technical and highly controversial, Macdonald evidently judged it best to return to the straightforward, matter-of-fact manner, and the serious tone which he had used long before in introducing his University Bills.[9] He reminded his listeners that the Canadian parliament had been permitted to legislate on the Reserves only on the express condition that the stipends or allowances actually being paid to the clergy of the different denominations should be continued until the death of these incumbents. The bill provided that these stipends were either to be continued annually, as a first charge upon the fund, or that, alternatively, they might be commuted or capitalized, with the consent of the ecclesiastical body to which the incumbent belonged. After these first charges and the expenses of collection had been met, the entire proceeds of the Reserves, divided into two funds, one for Canada East and one for Canada West, were to be apportioned yearly among the different municipalities of both sections of the province in accordance with population as determined by the last census. The bill was astonishingly brief: the introduction was equally laconic. Macdonald explained a few technical difficulties, countered the argument that the money ought to be transferred to consolidated revenue and used for education, and ended by appealing to all members to co-operate in making the bill as final and definitive as possible. Then MacNab moved "that in consideration of the news arrived this day from the theatre of war in the Crimea of a series of brilliant victories gained by the combined fleets and armies of France and England, it is the duty of this House to testify its high gratification at the event . . .".[10] The members poured tumultuously out of the House to celebrate.

The debates on the Clergy Reserves Bill, as they dragged on from second reading into committee, revealed only too clearly the nature of the double attack—from the right as well as from the left—which the Liberal-Conservative coalition would have to face. On November 2, John Hillyard Cameron, supporting himself with an elaborate, closely-reasoned legal argument, moved an amendment which would have saved a large portion of the Reserves for the churches. Other Conservatives—Powell, Bowes, Robinson, Gamble, and Murney—were expected to support this last diehard attempt to salvage something of the old rights of the Church of England.[11] But the members of this brave little band, including the obstreperous Murney, did not really need to be taken very seriously. "Is Murney as foolish as ever," Gowan inquired with heavy sarcasm, "or has he given up drinking?"[12] Murney, though he had been rather tiresomely talkative of late, was scarcely a dreaded opponent; but John Hillyard Cameron's opposition, as Macdonald knew very well, was a different and much more dangerous matter. Cameron was back in parliament once again, after an absence of three years. His political career, as brilliant as it was erratic and enigmatic, had been suddenly renewed. Macdonald's other contemporaries and rivals, Toronto Tories such as Henry Sherwood and William Henry Boulton, were dying or fading out of political life. But, at the last election, Cameron had been returned for Toronto at the head of the poll. A cultivated, prosperous, highly successful lawyer, who, as Samuel Thompson said, "ruled the Bench by force of argument and the jury by power of persuasion", Cameron was now nearly at the apex of his popularity, authority and influence.[13] It was no longer so easy to make fun, as the *Globe* had tried to do back in 1847, of his fluent rhetoric and elegant manner—to deride his "flute-like" voice, his "demnition-foin" vocabulary, and his affected, "dancing-master" attitude.[14] It was not good enough to write his abilities down—as Macdonald himself had done only six months before—to "a good memory and a vicious fluency of speech". Had Macdonald, in fact, not been betrayed, either by resentment or jealousy, into a serious undervaluation of his old rival's abilities? "Cameron was useful in legal matters when in the House," he had conceded rather patronizingly, "but he lacks general intelligence and is altogether devoid of political reading. . . . If he came in for Niagara, or fought some doubtful county, it would be all very well and he could be kept in his place."[15] Grotesquely vain assumptions! Cameron had not "come in for Niagara or fought some doubtful county". He had headed the poll in Toronto! Could he be "kept in his place"? He was a power in the Church of England, a growing force in the Orange association; and his professional income, magnified now by daring and successful speculations in real estate and foreign exchange transactions, was amply sufficient for him to play the patron to Samuel Thompson's *Colonist*. He had a press and a following. And he was dangerous to Liberal-Conservatism and the French alliance because he represented the old tradition of concern for Upper Canadian Protestantism and Upper Canadian sectional interests, which the old Tories had cherished in the past and which they had never yet distinctly repudiated.

On the other side of the House—and, if possible, still more dangerous politically—was the tall, ungainly and vehement figure of George Brown. On October 31, two days before John Hillyard Cameron spoke, Brown had led the Reform attack on the Clergy Reserves Bill. His criticisms, despite the pugnacity and portentous seriousness of his manner, were largely debating points; but there was nothing picayune in the formidable ascendancy which Brown seemed so rapidly to be establishing in the new Assembly. Two years ago he had been a loud but almost solitary and unapplauded voice in the Assembly, a would-be but unaccepted leader, a huge engine, with steam up, frantic to be going, and attached only to a pathetic string of carriages. Six months ago, in his desperate search for power and place, he had openly coquetted with the Conservative party. Another had won the game he tried to play, and Brown himself had been crushed beneath a load of humiliation and ridicule. For the moment it looked as if his—and all—opposition was in ruins. But no such assumption could have been more unreal. The new Liberal-Conservative coalition, despite the crowded regiment of its followers, had not, of course, ended opposition: it had merely ended, for the time at least, the frustrating ambiguities and unrealities which had bedevilled Canadian party politics for the last few years. Brown's own few faithful followers, the remnant of the Clear Grit party, and the few disgruntled Hincksites who had refused to join the coalition—the elements of a new Reform party were there, waiting to be welded together, and linked in some effective fashion with the *Rouges* of Canada East. Who could perform the task? Baldwin had long retired. Hincks was supporting the new coalition, and Malcolm Cameron and John Rolph, the two Clear Grit leaders of yesteryear, had been thoroughly discredited in Radical eyes by their compromising association with the defeated Inspector-General. There remained John Sandfield Macdonald, an ex-Speaker, an ex-minister in Baldwin's Cabinet, a veteran Reformer with obviously a good deal more experience than Brown could boast. But, apart from this diminutive pawky Scotsman, with his little "tail" of followers from the eastern counties of Canada West, who was there but Brown? More and more conspicuously, Brown's huge figure stood out from the ruck of his followers. And his rivalry with Macdonald, glimpsed for a long time only dimly through the confusing fog of Canadian party politics, now began to emerge as the central fact of the new parliament.

Macdonald took Brown's and Cameron's opposition seriously —at least in part. The easy levity which he used when countering attacks on the alleged opportunism and inconsistency of the Conservatives was dropped when he came to defend his principal measure, the Clergy Reserves Bill. His answer to Brown was a matter-of-fact, point-by-point rebuttal of specific criticisms;[16] his reply to Cameron was a deliberate, serious, almost emotional appeal from the new Conservatives to the old.[17] "I view this subject," he told the House frankly, "from the same point of view as the honourable gentleman . . . I have never disguised my opinion on that subject." At bottom, he insisted, he had always believed that in a country where the majority of people were of one religion, and that religion Christian, the state ought to acknowledge itself to be a Christian state, and to make provision accordingly for its church. The connection between church and state had been beneficial in England; but it had been most injurious in Ireland. He had been driven to the conclusion that the multiplicity of sects in Canada, and the uncertain division of the population among them, would make the connection equally injurious in Canada. He had reached this decision reluctantly, sorrowfully. But Cameron and his mistaken friends had refused to accept the irrefutable lesson of experience. They had prejudiced their own position and aroused a hideous public clamour by their protracted and stubborn resistance. "I believe it is a great mistake in politics and private life to resist when resistance is hopeless . . . ," Macdonald told the House. "There is no maxim which experience teaches more clearly than this, that you must yield to the times. Resistance may be protracted until it produces revolution. Resistance was protracted in this country until it produced rebellion." The immovability of the Family Compact could be copied, in this day and age, only at the risk of real peril: but the decision of the Duke of Wellington and Sir Robert Peel to accept Catholic Emancipation was an example, Macdonald declared, which had guided himself, and might very well guide the other members of his party.

The Clergy Reserves measure and the Seigniorial Tenure Bill marched nearly abreast through the legislature during November. On November 23, they were both read for the third time and passed by large majorities, the Clergy Reserves Bill receiving 62 to 39 votes.[18] For the government, the most important work of the first part of the session was ended; and a little over three weeks later, on December 18, the House was adjourned for the Christmas recess. Lord Elgin made his last public appearance at the adjournment. The next day, to the secret but probably immense delight of Macdonald and the Conservatives, he handed over the governorship of the Province of Canada to Sir Edmund Walker Head.[19]

II

Late in January, 1855, when Macdonald returned to Quebec, the general feeling that the province was settling down to a new phase of its political existence had perceptibly strengthened. A new Governor, a Governor very different from the last, was now in formal command of affairs. Head, who had been a Fellow of Merton College, and a Poor Law Commissioner in England before he accepted the lieutenant-governorship of New Brunswick, obviously did not belong to the exalted social and political circles which the eighth Earl of Elgin had entered freely by right of birth and marriage. The new Governor was a reserved and thoughtful man, a scholar with literary and artistic interests, who wrote verses and translated art histories from the German. There was a touch of the common-room in his manner, an echo of the lecture hall in his tentative yet architectonic speculations, an air of boards and committee rooms in his dry, unsentimental, bureaucratic precision. His life as a don and as a rather humdrum administrator had strengthened his native caution and sharpened his native efficiency for office work. It was these administrative powers which Macdonald naturally got to know first, and which, with his own nimble efficiency in administration, he was quick to appreciate. "I like Sir Edmund very much," he wrote laconically to his sister Louisa. "He is a thorough man of business and attends to the public interests *con amore.*"[20]

The coming of the new Governor was followed quickly by a partial reorganization of the new government. Morin and two undistinguished mediocrities disappeared from the Canada East section of the Cabinet. They were replaced by two equally undistinguished and, as it turned out, equally temporary mediocrities, and by a third French Canadian, a squat, solid, square-faced man, with immense physical powers, and an explosive, rapid, rather bullying manner in debate, called George Étienne Cartier. Macdonald remained blandly unaware of the fact that in Cartier he had found his most effective French-Canadian team-mate. He was temperately, almost tepidly, enthusiastic about the new Provincial Secretary. The district of Montreal, he explained carefully, required another representative in the Cabinet; and Cartier, "a Montrealer body and soul", was the obvious choice. The secretaryship required only "industry and method", both of which the new minister possessed in a remarkable degree.[21] "He is active—too active," Macdonald wrote a little patronizingly, "and will do his work."[22] Cartier, obviously, was still regarded as a diligent, slightly officious bureaucrat who could quite easily be kept in his place.

The triumvirate of the future—Head, Macdonald and Cartier—
had arrived on the stage which they were to occupy as principals. But the stage was still bewilderingly crowded with
personages, and the eminence of the three could not yet be
taken for granted. It was still possible to misjudge Cartier's
future position; and what Macdonald's place was to be, his
associates and even his closest political friends would perhaps
have found it difficult to say. His odd, ugly, memorable head,
with its pile of dark, curly hair, its big nose, its gay friendly
eyes and genially sardonic smile, did not inevitably suggest
the great political idealist or the great practical politician of the
future. In his speech, his easy-going manner, his whole youthful
appearance, he did not seem to conform exactly to any of the
plates in the political fashion book of the period. Certainly
his garments had not been cut from the sober, heavy black
broadcloth in which Canadian party leaders had usually appeared in the past. Draper had been a serious man, Baldwin
a very solemn man; and Hincks, though on occasion he had
displayed an acid wit, like that of a precociously knowledgeable
street-gamin, had been a bleakly clever, drably efficient administrator. Macdonald differed from all these predecessors
in a fashion at once puzzling and disarming. He obviously
enjoyed politics, just as he apparently enjoyed every other part
of life. His conviviality, his exuberant gaiety, his perpetual
flow of robust animal good spirits had by now become famous.
"I dare say," his old partner Alexander Campbell wrote, "you
are very busy from night until morning, and again from noon
'til night. The drinking the refractory members is in your
department, I take for granted. Another glass of champagne
and a *story of doubtful moral tendency* with a little of the Hon.
John Macdonald's peculiar 'sawder' are elements in the political
strength of a Canadian ministry not to be despised, as I have
no doubt all parties in the House are fully aware."[23] Undoubtedly, his smiling capacity for liquor, and his bawdy
stories, and his "soft sawder" were all elements of strength;
but he was occasionally a hard drinker, who took too much and
kept on taking too much; and the knowledge of these habits
strengthened the impression of easy-going conviviality, and

possibly helped to lead the undiscerning into a serious under-
estimate of his basic abilities. Yet there were some good qualities
which even the sceptics and the puritans were willing to concede him. "He can get through more work in a given time than
anybody I ever saw, and do it well," recorded John Langton, the
member for Peterborough whom Macdonald had just made the
new Auditor-General.[24] And it was the same caustic and critical
John Langton who generously insisted that Macdonald's "talent
was undoubted" and that "his character for integrity stood very
high". Almost everybody—opponents as well as friends—agreed
that Macdonald's conservative inheritance was qualified by a
genuine liberalism. Even William Lyon Mackenzie rather
grudgingly admitted that Macdonald had "something of the
liberal spirit" in him;[25] and Langton recalled that his "instincts
and associations were all with the Liberals, and people thought
that he had been thrown by circumstances on to the wrong
side of the house". These, for a man who wanted to modernize
and liberalize his party, were assets of a very high order. But
were they not, even so, outbalanced by those liabilities which
seemed so lamentable in the eyes of the provincial society of
early Victorian Canada? "He is fond of pleasure," Langton
wrote with grave severity, "and has an almost boyish exuberance
of animal spirits, and a poco-curantism, and want of earnestness in any pursuit which will always prevent him from being
a successful leader." What was to be done with such a
scandalously flippant creature? Could a man who did not even
bother to pretend to seriousness be taken very seriously? Langton did not believe so. In his judicious, tolerant but disapprov-
ing manner, he wrote Macdonald down. "His instincts are
all good," he summed up, "but he takes the world too easily to
be much depended on."

Macdonald was certainly taking the world of Canadian
politics very easily in this winter of 1855. "I am, thank God,
in good health and spirits," he wrote his sister Louisa in February, "and quite ready for the parliamentary campaign."[26] The
campaign that winter was an easy walkover, with the new
coalition, and its swollen army of followers, marching irresistibly
forward. The achievements of the session—the secularization

of the Reserves, the commutation of Seigniorial Tenure, the
elective Legislative Council, the reform of the Canadian militia
system, and the new Reciprocity Treaty with the United States
—formed an impressive total which seemed to prove, beyond
all doubt, that the new coalition was a genuinely liberal-minded
government which could settle old grievances and open up
new opportunities as no previous administration had been able
to do. For the moment, John Hillyard Cameron and the old
Tories were silenced; the Hincksite Reformers of Canada West
seemed genuinely satisfied; and Macdonald, confident that the
coalition was making its way, was zestfully eager to bury every
attack upon its sincerity and good faith with shovelfuls of raillery and ridicule. Sometimes he could not resist a joke for the
joke's own sake. "Did not the honourable gentleman drill *his*
men more than ten days?" he inquired urbanely of William
Lyon Mackenzie,[27] when that forlorn leader of the rebels at
Montgomery's Tavern objected to the amount of training imposed on the new volunteers by the Militia Bill. Sometimes,
when George Brown and John Sandfield Macdonald kept
reminding him of his attacks on the corruption of the Hincks
government and his criticisms of an elected Legislative Council,
he countered by jovially recalling how vigorously the *Globe* had
supported his own and MacNab's candidature in the election
of 1854. More and more frequently and lovingly he dwelt on
Brown himself—on his outstanding abilities, his increasingly
dominant position in the Reform party, and the monopolizing
authority of his newspaper. Poor feeble John Sandfield Macdonald had almost believed himself to be the real leader of the
opposition during the first days of the session; but once the
mighty member for Lambton had arrived, he had humbly abdicated this absurdly fancied eminence. Poor William Mc-
Dougall had once been the proprietor of a popular and aggressive
Reform newspaper the *North American*: but now, "like some
languishing lady falling into the arms of her admirer", the faint-
ing *North American* was "clinging to the strong and robust form
of his honourable friend opposite for support".[28] The continental *North American* had, in fact, become absorbed into
the universality of the *Globe*. The Reform press was Brown's:

the Reform party was Brown's. It was scarcely to be wondered
at that next day the *Globe* took occasion to rebuke the petty
way in which Macdonald had tried to sow personal jealousies
among the members of the opposition. "The harmony of the
Liberal party," it announced majestically, "is not to be disturbed
by the shabby manoeuvres of Mr. John Alexander Macdonald."[29]

Harmony had never been, and was not to be, a distinguishing
feature of the party which Brown was even then licking into
shape in his rough, imperious, but not unskilful, way. The session
rolled on, the coalition appeared impregnably popular, and it
was not until nearly the end of the year's proceedings that the
opposition found itself suddenly in possession of most acceptable grounds for attack. On May 12, when the long session
had less than three weeks to run, Dr. E. P. Taché introduced,
in the Legislative Council, a bill which clarified, confirmed
and, to some degree, extended the privileges of the Separate
Schools of Canada West.[30] The subject matter of the bill—
the educational privileges of Roman Catholics—was dangerously
delicate; the circumstances of its introduction seemed sinister
and suspicious in the highest degree. It had been introduced
in the fag-end of the session, in the Legislative Council and
not in the Assembly, by a French-Canadian minister from
Canada East and without the concurrence, or even the knowledge, of Egerton Ryerson, the superintendent of the school
system in the western part of the province. J. W. Gamble, one
of the Tories who had followed John Hillyard Cameron in his
defence of the Reserves, wired Ryerson, warning him of the
bill;[31] Brown, the old critic of Separate Schools, prepared himself again for his favourite battle; and by May 22, when Macdonald got up to introduce the bill in the Assembly, it was clear
that the great majority of the Upper Canadian contingent,
whether they were Tory, Conservative, moderate Reform, or
Clear Grit, regarded the bill with miserable uncertainty or
downright disapproval.

Macdonald did his best. He might have pointed out how
far short the bill fell of the demands which Charbonnel and the
other Roman Catholic bishops had been pressing upon the
government during the previous winter; but obviously this was

a suicidally dangerous course. Instead he tried to persuade his audience how faithfully the measure ran along established lines. He tried to prove that the clauses which facilitated the establishment of Roman Catholic Separate Schools and governed the calculation of their government grant were clauses which either made merely minor and formal changes in existing procedures, or embodied sensible principles which had been approved by Ryerson himself.[32] When attacks were made upon Separate Schools in principle—and Brown, of course, launched such attacks repeatedly and at enormous length— Macdonald simply took refuge behind the utter impossibility of destroying an establishment to which the province had already pledged its faith by repeated legislation. "If they could make the world all of one way of thinking it might work more harmoniously," he conceded with genially tolerant scepticism, "but yet he doubted very much if things would go on one bit better on that account. The severance of opinion, the right of private judgment tended to the elevation of man, and he should be sorry if a legislature, the majority of whose members were Protestants professing to recognize the great Protestant principle of the right of private judgment, should yet seek to deprive Roman Catholics of the power to educate their children according to their own principles. . . . "[33] The defence was not bad: and, although any, even the most innocuous, measure on such a subject would have been vulnerable, the bill was a defensible one. But the tactics of the government had been stupidly maladroit. The bill had been introduced in an equivocal, furtive, almost conspiratorial fashion. Had Macdonald been merely careless, or had his importunate Roman Catholic associates tried to be too clever by half? Now the Attorney-General West was acutely embarrassed. Gamble told the story of his telegram to Ryerson and of the Superintendent of Education's complete ignorance of the government's legislation. Langton, Hartman, Brown—the independent Conservative, the Clear Grit, and the Liberal Reformer—all pressed the case against the good faith of the administration. The remnant of the Upper Canadian members—for many of them had gone home believing the session over—looked on doubtfully or mutinously. The bill passed, but it passed by virtue of French-Canadian, Roman Catholic votes. A measure to amend the Separate School system of Canada West had been opposed by a majority of Western Canadian members. For the first time, on an issue of major importance, the government had given its enemies an excuse to argue that Canada West was still governed by the pressure and at the will of Canada East. Within a year of its establishment, the prestige and popularity of the coalition had received a profound shock in Protestant Upper Canada.

III

That autumn the unhappy peripatetic government moved again, back to Toronto. On Monday, October 8, the Governor-General, accompanied by his Western Canadian ministers, MacNab, Spence and Macdonald, bade farewell to Quebec and started out for his new capital. The vice-regal progress continued placidly, in a deliberate and dignified fashion, with loyal addresses, triumphal arches, and public dinners; there was an inspection of the provincial agricultural exhibition at Cobourg, a visit to Niagara Falls, and a triumphant reception at Hamilton, organized by MacNab, and unfortunately accompanied by a persistent drizzle of icy rain.[34] In the third week in October, the gubernatorial party swept westward still, in a leisurely tour of the peninsula between Lake Huron and Lake Erie. But Macdonald, leaving the superintending honours of these vice-regal perambulations to the eager and officious MacNab, remained behind in Toronto and began the task of settling in. There was a good deal to do. It was a question not only of organizing his department in new offices, but also of finding suitable quarters for an invalid wife and a small boy. He viewed the whole business of the family move from Kingston doubtfully. As late as a month before he had still been undecided as to whether Isabella and Hugh John should accompany him to Toronto.[35] There had, of course, been really no question of Isabella's going to Quebec. At Quebec, where the government's days were already numbered, she would have been in an unfamiliar world, with little opportunity to acquire a fresh set of friends. But Toronto was different for various and obvious reasons. And at Toronto, the government, and her husband with it, would be established for four clear years. Almost certainly she wanted to go to Toronto. And Macdonald agreed.

At Toronto, the little empire of provincial government and legislation was mainly centred in a long parallelogram of territory, bounded by Wellington Street on the south, King Street on the north, Simcoe Street on the east, and which, on the west, stretched out past isolated houses and summer villas into the open fields and orchards of the countryside. The heart of this administrative world—Government House and the parliament buildings—stood physically at its eastern frontier by Simcoe Street. The Attorney-General's office—the Crown Law Department, as it was called—was housed in an old building, once the town's general hospital, which stood on the north side of King Street, between John and Peter. King Street was mainly commercial and administrative in character, though there were a few, and some very splendid, private houses on it. Wellington Street was largely residential, and out west, at the town's outskirts, between Portland and Brock Streets, where the street changed its name to Wellington Place, Macdonald found the quarters he desired.[86] There could be no question of buying or leasing a private house, for Isabella was quite incapable of housekeeping. But one of the scattered buildings in Wellington Place was a boarding-house. And here the reunited Macdonald family was established.[87]

The place had its advantages. It was quiet for Isabella, for westward the town petered out rapidly, and all the noise and bustle and confusion of the city lay down Wellington Street to the east. The friendly houses of Macdonald's colleagues and acquaintances—John Hillyard Cameron, David Macpherson, and Philip Vankoughnet—at all of which were young children, were near enough for Hugh to visit frequently and with relative ease. Macdonald himself, once he had left his office, had but to walk a little way west on King Street, and down a block on Portland Street, to find himself at his lodgings. In its cramped, makeshift, unsatisfactory way, it was the nearest thing to a home together that they had had for years; and they had ventured much—more than they had dared to do since Isabella's return from the United States—to make it a success. It ought to have succeeded. But they had not been more than a month or so in Toronto before Macdonald knew in his heart that the enterprise was a tragic failure. For, in January of 1856, Isabella became terribly ill.[38] Janet, the nurse and companion who, Macdonald had no doubt expected, would help to look after five-year-old Hugh, had to give up the boy to slave over her spent and weary mistress; and Hugh was packed off almost unceremoniously in the mornings to spend the day under the kindly care of Rose Cameron at The Meadows, John Hillyard Cameron's pleasant house on Queen Street West. Macdonald hated to leave Wellington Place in the mornings. Once, fearing the very worst, the doctor had sent for him at the Crown Law Office; and afterwards he could hardly bear the sight of unfamiliar messengers. At night, when he walked homeward along King Street, the brief, sullen winter sunset had already faded in the west. A harsh wind roared along the road out of a blue-black sky; and such a grinding sense of foreboding and desolation overwhelmed him that he could hardly force his steps along the homeward way. A dozen times he really expected to find her dead when he arrived. A dozen times, in fact, she hovered upon the point of death. Yet, with her feeble but persistent resolution, she lived on. She waited for him in the dim sickroom; and there, night after night, he stayed with her. The town was busy with dances, dinners, and parties, with all the first events of the season, and all the preliminaries of the approaching parliamentary session. He was inundated with invitations; but he refused them all. Night after night, while the frost struck the desolate little street into icy stillness, he sat up with Isabella; and night after night the candle burned itself slowly downward to the socket.

There was something decidedly ominous also in the aspect of public affairs. The coalition had run through its first great programme of legislation and had used up its first supply of generous and uncritical support. The difficult passage of the Separate School Bill seemed to mark a turn by which the decline of government confidence and the rise of opposition hopes could be equally well dated. Ever since the prorogation of the summer, Brown had undeniably waxed in importance, as a journalist, as a party leader, as an accepted spokesman for injured Canada West. In February, 1855, the *Globe* had bought up William McDougall's *North American*; and this had been followed, in September of the same year, by the amalgamation of the *Globe* and the *Examiner*, the other principal Clear Grit newspaper in Toronto. McDougall joined the *Globe* staff; the erstwhile Clear Grit leaders admitted their own past political miscalculations and publicly admired the rugged consistency of George Brown. And all that summer and autumn, using the detested Separate School Bill of 1855 as a hideous example of French-Canadian tyranny, Brown was preaching a united Reform party for the defence of Upper Canadian sectional interests through the principle of representation by population in parliament. Macdonald at first affected a cheerful indifference to "Rep. by Pop.". It was, he had told Brown Chamberlin of the *Montreal Gazette*, back in August, "too abstract a question to be enthusiastic about".³⁹ Airily brave words! They were quite untrue. The "abstract principle" was an effective cure for real, substantial and sensitively felt grievances. For Upper Canadians, Conservatives as well as Reformers, it held a dangerously strong appeal. It not only meant the release of Canada West from the domination and exploitation of Roman Catholic Canada East; it also implied—what, indeed, George Brown made no pretence whatever to conceal—the "assimilation of the laws" of the two sections of the province, and therefore ultimately the extinction of the peculiar culture of French Canada, just as Lord Durham had foretold.

Macdonald was instinctively opposed to all this, as well because of temperament and personal conviction as because of party commitments. Once at least during that dreadful January of 1856, as he sat up beside his troubled wife, he tried to set out his own views in some detail. Isabella lay back exhausted, half glimpsed in the obscurity of the room: the "single dip" flamed feebly. He was writing to Brown Chamberlin, of the *Montreal Gazette,* one of the journalists whom

he was now beginning to cultivate, writing a long letter, full
of his jokes, his flippant pleasantries, his cunningly worded
appeals, and his fundamental tolerant sound sense.[40] The letter
was not addressed to George Brown, and it dealt only with
Canada East and its English-speaking minority; but it might
have served as a reply and a rebuke to the newly rebuilt Reform
party and its campaign for the "liberation" of Canada West
through "Rep. by Pop.". "The truth is," Macdonald argued,
"that you British Lower Canadians never can forget that you
were once supreme—that Jean Baptiste was your hewer of
wood and drawer of water. You struggle, like the Protestant
Irish in Ireland, like the Norman invaders in England, not for
equality, but *ascendancy*—the difference between you and those
interesting and amiable people being that you have not the
honesty to admit it. You can't and won't admit the principle
that the majority must govern. The Gallicans may fairly be
reckoned as two thirds against one third of all the other races
who are lumped together as Anglo-Saxons—Heaven save the
mark! . . . The only remedies are immigration and copulation
and these will work wonders. The laws are equally administered
to the British as the French, at least if we may judge by the
names of your judges it ought to be so. Lumping your judges
of the Queen's Bench, Supreme and Circuit courts, you have
full one half British. More than one half of the Revenue
officers, indeed of all offices of emolument, are held by men not
of French origin. It would surprise you to go over the names of
officials in a Lower Canada almanac and reckon the *ascendancy*
you yet hold of official positions. Take care the French don't
find it out and make a counter-cry. True, you suffer occasionally
from a Gavazzi riot or so, but in the first place you Anglo-
Saxons are not bad hands at a riot yourselves, and, in the second
place, the rioters are not Franco-Canadians, nor Canadians of
any kind. A proper jury law, if the present one does not suit,
is all you can want. But you must be represented in the
cabinet . . ."

His pen flowed on smoothly. The immediate and practical
note must now be sounded. The British of Canada East, split
into several contemptible fragments, must be convinced that

a united support of one party (and, of course, it could only
be the Liberal-Conservative party) would alone win them representation in the provincial government. He made the appeal
in his brief, rather off-hand, apparently disinterested fashion;
but the practical politics of government support and cabinet-
making did not detain him long; and he returned to the basic
cultural problem of Canada in a vein which, if he had been
noted for solemn speculation, might almost have been regarded
as prophetic. "No man in his senses," he wrote, "can suppose
that this country can for a century to come be governed by a
totally unfrenchified government. If a Lower Canadian British
desires to conquer he must 'stoop to conquer'. He must make
friends with the French, without sacrificing the status of his
race or language, he must respect their nationality. Treat them
as a nation and they will act as a free people generally do—
generously. Call them a faction and they become factious.
Supposing the numerical preponderance of British in Canada
becomes much greater than it is, I think the French would
give more trouble than they are said now to do. At present
they divide as we do, they are split up into several sections,
and are governed by more or less defined principles of action.
As they become smaller and feebler, so they will be more
united; from a sense of self-preservation, they will act as one
man and hold the balance of power. Look how in a house of
600 Pitt was supported through Dundas by the whole Scotch
vote, and remember that O'Connell with his tail absolutely
governed England after the Lichfield House bargain. So long
as the French have twenty votes they will be a power, and
must be conciliated. I doubt much however if the French will
lose their numerical majority in L. C. in a hurry. What with
the cessation of emigration from Europe, their own spread in
the Townships, the opening up of the Ottawa and St. Maurice,
and the certainty that they will ere long be the labourers in
our factories that are fast coming, I am inclined to think they
will hold their own for many a day yet."

He could discuss the future with Brown Chamberlin in this
jocular, laconic and curiously discerning fashion. But the
present, and the existing position of the Liberal-Conservative

government were very different matters, requiring different
arguments and different solutions. The long, unhappy Toronto
winter dragged on, and February 15, the day of the opening
of parliament, drew closer. It was bitterly cold, and he was
overwhelmed with work in preparation for the session; but this
was the kind of labour he dispatched with cheerful ease, and,
as he told his sister Louisa rather boastingly, "I thrive wonderfully under it".[41] His real trouble was totally different. The fact
was that the coalition had lost ground, and was still steadily
losing ground, in Canada West. The ministry and the party,
Liberal-Conservative by name, were also in reality an imperfect
combination of two rival elements, each of which was still
struggling for mastery. The scarcely concealed animosities
inside the Cabinet—between John Ross, the leader of the
Hincksite Liberals, and the genial, greedy, impecunious Sir
Allan MacNab, the titular chieftain of the Conservatives—
were repeated in the jarring ranks of the coalition as a whole.
A group of Conservatives, ranging themselves behind John
Hillyard Cameron, were reported to be sullenly opposed to the
continuance of Macdonald's influence in the party; and embarrassed Hincksite Liberals, smarting under Brown's charge
that the ministry had accepted the dictation of Canada East,
were drifting back into the swelling ranks of the reorganized
Reform party. Macdonald's political handiwork—the Liberal-
Conservative coalition—was falling apart in less than two years.
And back in Wellington Place, in a few rented rooms in a
boarding-house, all that remained of his domestic happiness
continued in hopeless jeopardy. His spirit was rasped raw by
worry and foreboding. Beneath his almost limitless good nature,
which was not a carefully cultivated pose but a cheerful instinct,
there lurked, far below, an uncertain temper—a temper which,
that winter, must often have struggled to be free. An outburst
was probably inevitable. And it came.

It came on Tuesday, February 26, when the debate on the
address in reply to the speech from the throne had droned
on for nearly a week. That night they were threshing over a
lot of singularly dry and brittle straw—the divisions in the Conservative government, the animosities in the Reform opposition,

the Conservative betrayal of their principles for the sake of office, and Brown's support of the Conservatives in the previous election for the sake of political power. Brown had already spoken in the debate at enormous length on the previous Thursday; but he was on his feet again on the fatal Tuesday evening, as provocative and belligerent as ever. When, towards midnight, Macdonald got up to speak, it soon became plain that he had been goaded too far. Yet he began quietly enough. His manner tense, his voice trembling a little, he started by exposing a few of what he said were the characteristic contradictions and inconsistencies of Brown's speech. Brown's assertions—and here the words began to come faster with excitement—were contradictory and inconsistent for the very simple reason that they were untrue. They always had been untrue. And how could people be expected to keep their tempers when they were assailed by the habitual untruths of a man who, years ago, at the very beginning of his public career, had abused his position on the Penitentiary Commission by perverting the testimony and falsifying the evidence! The words poured out in a furious torrent. The last restraints were gone now, the last inhibitions had been washed away. Macdonald was white with passion. All the old charges—the brutal intimidation of the aged Warden Smith, the suborning of convicted criminals as witnesses, the elaborate falsification of evidence, the calculated secrecy of the commission's proceedings, and Brown's resolute determination to prevent a parliamentary investigation of its work—all the accusations which dated back as far as the sessions of 1849 and 1850 were hurled again at Brown's head.[42] The House sat silent with shocked amazement. When Brown rose to reply, he was white with anger and excitement. But he was curiously brief as well. This was not to be one of his lusty, hard-hitting, long-winded attacks. He merely announced, in a low voice, that he would ask for a committee of inquiry into Macdonald's charges. There was a pause. The House got the ominous impression that something irremediable had happened, that the unforgettable and unforgivable had been said.

It was an unfortunate beginning. The session, which, unlike its predecessor, had no great programme of important practical reforms, seemed bereft of purpose and direction. It was the easy prey of bad temper and fortuitous accident; and the chief preoccupation of the House appeared to be its own chaotic condition—the disintegration of the coalition, the rivalries of Liberals and Conservatives, and the confused state of parties in the Assembly as a whole. Behind this confusion lay, as always, the central cultural division of the province; and, in the circumstances, a crisis could be precipitated by almost any revival of the old politico-religious disputes. The House had not long to wait. During the winter there occurred the trial of several Roman Catholics, Kelly and others, for the murder of an Irish Protestant, Edward Corrigan; and at the conclusion of the trial, the judge, Judge Duval, a French-Canadian Roman Catholic justice, delivered the accustomed final charge to the Roman Catholic French-Canadian jury. It was, as it was reported in the newspapers, a curious charge; and it was followed by what was, in the eyes of the Protestant Canada West, an inexplicable event—the acquittal of Kelly and the other Roman Catholic prisoners. Somebody in the Assembly was almost certain to raise the question of Judge Duval's charge. It ought, perhaps, to have been George Brown. But it was not George Brown. On Friday, March 7, John Hillyard Cameron moved, seconded by his faithful lieutenant Gamble, for an address to the Governor-General requesting a copy of the charge delivered to the jury by Judge Duval in the trial of Kelly and others for the murder of Edward Corrigan.[43]

IV

Macdonald, in all probability, had confidently expected some such move. In his mind, it was probably a question merely as to which of the two quarrelling divisions of the Liberal-Conservative coalition—the Progressive Conservatives or the Tories —would first begin the attack. He was well aware of the fact that Ross and Spence, the two Hincksite Liberals in the Cabinet, had become increasingly weary of Sir Allan MacNab, and his gout, and his absences, and the "infernal lot of hangers on" that he had to provide with jobs and militia commissions.[44] He may even have known that the Hincksites were now determined upon the gallant knight's removal. But, in a letter which he wrote to Brown Chamberlin late in January, he had still felt justified in deriding "the absurd grounds of suspicion that we want to get rid of MacNab";[45] and in the end it had been the Tories, and not the Progressive Conservatives, who had taken the initiative in the struggle. MacNab, racked with gout, had been absent from the House almost from the beginning of the session. But, from his sickbed, had he helped to inspire this movement of the ultras against a Francophile government of which he was the titular head? Was this supposedly bluff, hearty, downright old man secretly jealous of Macdonald and anxious to push John Hillyard Cameron forward as his own designated heir? For some time, Cameron's conduct itself had been curiously equivocal. Early in the session, he had called a meeting of his fellow-Tories, Murney, Powell, Gamble, Robinson and others, to discuss the government's educational policy; and from this meeting had sprung the rumour that the ultras were about to form a new party with Cameron as leader.[46] Equally curious speculations were provoked by the resolution of March 7. By putting himself forward so ostentatiously at the head of the insurgent group, Cameron seemed openly to be flirting with the invitation to accept its leadership. By moving the resolution in the Corrigan affair, he had opened an indirect but very real onslaught on the general policy of the Liberal-Conservative government; and, by choosing his ground for attack in the highly provocative field of race and religion, he had appeared frankly to invite the support of George Brown and the outraged Protestant radicals of Canada West. Cameron, "with his usual versatility," wrote one newspaper editor, "has served the double purpose of state physician to Sir Allan Mac-Nab and temporary leader of the anti-ministerial opposition in the House".[47] It looked as if Cameron had finally decided to precipitate a quarrel for the leadership of the coalition and the control of its policies, and that he had accepted the questionable alliance of the Reform opposition for the purpose.

Macdonald was determined to smother the quick flames of

this fire before Brown could fan it into another huge conflagration. The continuance of the Hincksite Liberals' support, the
very existence of the coalition, depended upon the rapid extinction of the insurgent blaze. On March 7, the opening date
of the debate, he argued long and learnedly with Hillyard
Cameron over the limits of the Crown's power to require
reports and information from the judges.[48] Even if the request
for the charge were not unconstitutional, he insisted, it was
still extremely inexpedient. It could not alter the course of
justice in the slightest degree, for the accused in the trial for
the murder of Edward Corrigan had already been irrevocably
acquitted: it could only deal a serious blow at the independence
of the bench. The House, listening with delight to Cameron's
elegantly expressed learning and Brown's Protestant moral
indignation, remained unimpressed by Macdonald's reasoned,
moderate appeal; and, on March 10, with virtually the entire
body of the members for Canada West voting in its favour,
the motion requiring the production of the charge to the jury
was passed by a vote of forty-eight to forty-four. This was
extremely serious. On March 11, the House was adjourned for
two days; and on March 13, when it met again, Drummond,
on behalf of the government, demanded that the resolution
requiring the production of Judge Duval's charge be formally
rescinded. J. S. Macdonald and A. A. Dorion promptly moved
the previous question, which was treated as a motion of want
of confidence and soundly defeated by seventy-five to forty-
two votes. Macdonald must have drawn a long breath of
relief. The government made no further difficulty about the
resolution to which, of course, it now advised the Governor-
General to refuse compliance. Head's reply denied that Duval's
charge could be "presumed to exist as a distinct document";
and it insisted that to call a judge to account for his words,
at the request of one branch of the legislature only, might
serve as a precedent for interference by the Crown with the
independence of the judiciary.[49] The request for the production of Duval's charge was politely refused. The House,
accepted the refusal passively; and although, a little later,
Dorion made a final attempt to defeat the government on the

issue, he was again unsuccessful. It looked as if Macdonald had won. The first effort of the Tories, backed by the questionable support of the Reformers, to upset the administration and break up the coalition had been a failure.

The Tories had begun the struggle. Who would finish it? The Hincksites, the few remaining Liberal supporters of the coalition in Canada West, grew more open in their opposition to MacNab and "fossilism", and more outspoken in their support of Macdonald. They were justified, so the editor of the *Leader* argued, by Cameron's provocative attempt to foist himself upon the party as its leader.[50] They may even have been justified by a shameless intrigue between the Tories and the Grits, for long afterwards Samuel Thompson, the editor of the *Colonist,* recollected how he had encountered George Brown in Sir Allan's house in Ritchie's Terrace, Adelaide Street, and how John Hillyard Cameron had burst in upon the conference with the announcement that the Liberal-Conservatives had elected Macdonald as their leader.[51] Certainly, towards the end of March, a circumstantial rumour began to run about town that the Liberal-Conservatives had assembled lately and had given their support to the Attorney-General West; and a few days later, the *Globe,* with a curiously affectionate interest in the fate of the doughty, stout-hearted old knight, began to refer openly to the campaign for the removal of Sir Allan and the substitution of a man who, it declared, was "scarcely known out of Kingston, save as a barrister of good standing, and what is called a jolly good fellow".[52] The whole matter had become public property, and questions had begun to be asked in the House. Macdonald finally decided to make a statement. "No such leadership was ever offered me," he declared, "and no such leadership was ever accepted by me." A deputation of three Liberal-Conservatives had, he admitted, come to him from a meeting of their fellows, held because of the growing rumours of a change of government. They did not, they said, desire a change: "but they wanted to state to me that if any change or reconstruction should take place under any exigency whatever, they had confidence in me, and they would support any reconstruction which I should advise. My answer was that

there was no truth in the rumours and that there was no chance
of any reconstruction at present."[53] Macdonald probably believed the matter would stop there. As he said himself, he was
prepared to follow as long as Sir Allan could lead. But it was
becoming increasingly difficult for the gallant knight to lead
at all, and impossible for him to lead the members of Canada
West. The western division of the party held another meeting
and determined that MacNab should be invited to retire. Macdonald intervened with decision and at once. The protest
movement was temporarily dropped. But it was renewed once
more; and finally the representatives of the remaining western
Reformers in the coalition announced that, if MacNab continued in the government, circumstances might compel them
to vote against it.[54] As soon as this notice was given, early in
April, John Ross, the senior Hincksite in the Cabinet, at once
resigned.

Obviously the climax of the whole confused affair was
rapidly approaching. It had been a terrible winter. And almost
nothing had occurred, either at his rooms or at the Crown Law
Office, to release Macdonald's real good nature from the prison
of its chronic, irritating anxiety. "Hugh is, thank God, in prime
health," he wrote his mother towards the end of March.[55] And
here, at least, was one source of unalloyed satisfaction. It was
pleasant to realize that Hugh had grown from a baby to a
healthy small boy of six, to watch him preside over a lively
assembly of his playmates at his birthday party on March 13,
and to note proudly that "he is quite tall now and is putting
on almost a manly appearance".[56] But Isabella was ill again
in March, this time with erysipelas. He was never really free
of the dull ache of his anxiety for her, and he was rasped and
irritated by the endless proceedings of the House committee
appointed to investigate his charges against George Brown.
"I am carrying on a war against that scoundrel George Brown,"
he told his mother, "and I will teach him a lesson he never
learnt before. I shall prove him a most dishonest, dishonourable fellow and in so doing I will only pay him a debt I owe
him for abusing me for months together in his newspaper."[57]
He was eager to pay off old scores, apt to take new offence

quickly, and ready to use his own bantering humour to drive others into fury. Early in the session George Brown had made him lose his temper; but, in the debate of April 16, it was he who provoked Colonel Arthur Rankin to outbursts of violent unparliamentary language.[58] Parliament was an almost continual verbal milling ground. As John Langton said, "the whole of this session has been a state of chronic crisis for the ministry".[59] The unresolved conflict in the Liberal-Conservative party continued; and the opposition, knowing this fact, pressed forward with their votes of want of confidence. It was almost too much for him. "John A. Macdonald is now the recognized leader," wrote Langton with cheerful harshness, "but he is anything but strong in reality."[60]

The long ordeal drew towards its close, as spring blossomed into summer. It was the question of the seat of government which brought the crisis to a head. Obviously the selection of a permanent capital for the united province was a question of deep cultural and sectional prestige to both English and French, to both Canada West and Canada East. It was only after the most protracted debate that the Assembly finally decided, on April 16, that Quebec was the most eligible place, that parliament be permanently established there after 1859, and that suitable buildings be commenced at once for the legislature and the government departments. Macdonald had expected the result. "The French will, I think, be too strong for us," he wrote his mother, "and we must submit to going to Lower Canada. . . . I am afraid that we have no chance for Kingston. We shall, however, make a fight for it."[61] He did, indeed, make a fight for it. He voted for Kingston, and for other towns in Canada West against Quebec: he even voted against the main motion declaring Quebec the most eligible town.[62] The issue was, in fact, not regarded as a "ministerial question", and members voted freely upon it; and it was this apparent exhibition of governmental irresponsibility which provided the opposition with its last great chance for a want-of-confidence debate. On Wednesday, May 14, just as the House was about to go into supply, Papin moved in amendment "that the position which His Excellency's administration have assumed up to the present

day, on the question of the seat of government, does not inspire
this House with the confidence necessary to entrust that administration with the moneys required for the construction
of the necessary buildings at the seat of government".[63] The
very next day, in further refinement of Papin's verbal attack,
Holton moved in amendment that "the course of the administration with reference to the question of the seat of government
and other important public questions has disappointed the just
expectations of the great majority of the people of this province".[64]

In the great debate which followed, a debate which lasted
almost exactly a week, Macdonald was most prominent. As he
himself proudly said afterward, "I fought the ship to the last".
Even after John Ross's resignation he had succeeded in patching up the government once again: he and Spence, the Postmaster-General, had between them persuaded J. C. Morrison,
another old Baldwin Reformer, to enter the Cabinet under
MacNab's leadership. But both Spence and Morrison had insisted they would resign if ever the remaining Hincksite Reformers carried out their implied threat and brought the verdict
of Canada West against the government. On Friday evening,
when the debate was adjourned for the week-end, it looked
as if the defection of the western Reformers was a certainty.
Even so, the ministers resumed the battle on Monday, May
19. The debate continued, before crowded, excited galleries,
without interruption, day and night, for over thirty hours; and
it was not until midnight on Tuesday that the final vote was
taken. Holton's sub-amendment was defeated, seventy to forty-
seven; Papin's amendment was voted down seventy-three to
forty-three.[65] The government had been sustained; but in Canada West it stood in a minority of six. Immediately the long-
awaited train of events began. The next day, when the House
assembled, the ministers were conspicuously absent. Spence,
Morrison and Macdonald, later joined by Cayley, had decided
to resign. They did not believe, they insisted, in the double
or sectional majority as an abstract principle; but Morrison
and Spence, who felt themselves to represent the Reform side
in the coalition, were dismayed by the defection of their old

followers; and Macdonald, who knew that if his colleagues
resigned they would take the last western Reform votes with
them, realized that the government and the coalition would
then be broken up.[66] MacNab, faced by the mass resignation
of the entire western division of his government, could do
nothing but place his own portfolio at the disposition of the
Governor-General; and Head found himself in the embarrassing
position of reorganizing a government which had not been
defeated, but which would have no peace with itself until it
had ejected Sir Allan.[67] On Saturday evening, May 24, the
new administration was constituted, with E. P. Taché, President of the Legislative Council, as first minister, and Macdonald
as Attorney-General West and leader of the government in the
Assembly. The new Cabinet, little changed otherwise, met the
House the following Monday, and four days later it pulled
through its first want-of-confidence debate with the narrow
majority of four.[68] The gallant old Sir Allan, crippled with
gout, swathed in flannel bandages, appearing heroically like
another Pitt to confront his successful enemies, was a pathetic
spectacle which the Grit opposition loved to exhibit.[69] But
many contemporaries, who knew some of the facts and suspected others, were not greatly impressed, and Macdonald,
when he was sufficiently provoked, grew openly defiant. "Heap
as many epithets and reproaches on me as you like," he declared,
"but this I contend, that having performed my portion of the
contract, having stuck to my leader, having tried every means
to keep the cabinet together, that I had a right as a gentleman
and a man of honour to go into a new government, with the
speaker of the Legislative Council, or anyone else."[70]

One great episode in his career was finished. The struggle
between the ultras and moderates in the Conservative party,
which had begun years before with the beginning of the union,
had ended at last. The moderates had triumphed, and Macdonald was the accepted leader of the Conservatives of Canada
West.

Chapter Ten

Double Shuffle

I

Draper—it had been a characteristic sign of the two equally authentic elements in his Liberal-Conservatism—had thought of both John Hillyard Cameron and John Alexander Macdonald as his possible successors. The decade which had elapsed since Draper's retirement in 1847, when regarded from the point of view of the Conservative party, had been, in effect, a long struggle between the principles represented by these two men. Indeed their rivalry itself was only the last phase of a conflict, which had begun before the Rebellion, between the High Toryism of the past and the Liberal-Conservatism of the future. The coalition of 1854 had marked the first great victory of Liberal-Conservatism. The extrusion of MacNab, and the rejection of his lieutenant, Cameron, had clinched it. Macdonald, and the philosophy he represented, had won. He had not, of course, finished with Toryism, for Toryism was to remain a strong constituent element in the party, without which Liberal-Conservatism would have lost its essential character. He had not even finished with John Hillyard Cameron, for Cameron was to appear again, with all his old prestige and following, though never—such was the tragedy of chance— with quite the same striking power. There would be insurgent groups and party divisions in the future; but they were never to be quite the same as those of the past. The Rebellion, and all the rancorous disputes which had preceded and accompanied it, was at last ended; and the secularization of the Clergy Reserves had been the last chapter in an old book of troubles. Macdonald was done with all that. He and the province were growing up. From then on, Canada was to become more continuously aware than it ever had been of its difficult position and uncertain future in North America; and Macdonald, at forty-one, was called upon to grapple with a new and interrelated set of problems, the problems of approaching maturity.

One of these problems had already appeared, in a brief, but sharply acute, fashion. The Crimean War, the first great war which the British Empire had fought since the Napoleonic conflict nearly forty years before, had compelled the province to think seriously about its defences; and the Conservative government, with Sir Allan MacNab taking the principal initiative, had overhauled the venerable militia system and established a small but fairly efficient volunteer force. A certain amount of military enthusiasm and reforming zeal was thus an early product of the war; but by the time it ended it had brought on something not very far removed from a panic, at least in the innermost circles of government. Once again, as had happened during the Napoleonic wars, a major military struggle in the Old World was accompanied by a crisis with the United States of America—a crisis in which Canada would inevitably be involved, though she had no responsibility whatever for its creation. It had been brought on by Great Britain, which, in the desperate need for men, had passed the Foreign Enlistment Act, and by the British minister to Washington, J. F. T. Crampton, and the Nova Scotian politician Joseph Howe, who, with imprudent patriotism, set out to apply the act in the United States, despite all the stringent American neutrality laws.[1] Howe, who was moving about the United States like a somewhat theatrical conspirator in his search for men, appealed to the Canadian government to accept recruits. But MacNab and his Cabinet, advised by the cautious Head, would have nothing to do with the whole affair; and a year later, when the United States exacted its delayed revenge, and dismissed Crampton and three British consuls, they could at least congratulate themselves on their caution. Yet inevitably the province became the innocent victim of the storm of anti-

British and annexationist rage which swept through the United States. Palmerston and the Secretary for War, Panmure, realizing the danger of an explosion, and freed now from the demands of the Crimean War, despatched five regiments to Canada and a vast quantity of military stores.[2] For a while the peril seemed real. "If I am carried off to Boston or New York," wrote Head cheerfully to a correspondent, "I will apprise you of the change in my address but I think we should have a fight for it first".[3] The fight never came, as it had never really come back in 1838; but the crisis brought back a sudden recollection of the old anxiety, which must have struck Macdonald like a blow. Within two years of accepting an important office in government, he had been compelled to take up the most basic of all Canadian problems, the problem of survival against the imperialist designs of the United States; and for the next fifteen years this was a problem which left him undisturbed for only the briefest of intervals.

Quickly he discovered that it lowered over most other problems like a huge, vague, sinister presence. It forced him, as it forced other people, to think in terms of a far-flung and daring strategy. Obviously the security of Canada was inseparable from the security of British North America as a whole. Canada could not be defended, it could not grow prosperous in isolation, but only as a part of a wider whole; and its relations with the other colonies and with the vast uncolonized west were certainly of prime importance for both opulence and defence. A whole host of absorbing and difficult questions had been raised by the Crimean War and the crisis with the United States. Was this the moment to revive the old idea of a general union of British North America, or was it wiser, for a while yet, to plan for a series of preliminary, regional unions? In the east, had the strategic necessity of the Intercolonial Railway been proved beyond a doubt by the threat of war with the United States? And, in the west, what was to be done with the Hudson's Bay Company, whose licence of exclusive trade in the North West Territories was soon to expire, and whose loose and uncertain hold over its enormous dominions might seem to justify some different and more effective provision

against the encroaching Americans? These questions were
asked, not only in Canada, which was nearly ready to expand
its interests, but also in Great Britain, which had already begun
to contract its obligations, so far as British North America was
concerned. In the late summer of 1856 Head was visited in
Toronto by Robert Lowe, the Vice-President of the Board of
Trade in Palmerston's Cabinet, a quick-tempered intellectual,
impatient of colonial commitments, and anxious that Canada
should become Great Britain's residuary legatee on the North
American continent. He and Head talked over a wide range
of British North American affairs;[4] and, as a result of these
discussions, Macdonald became aware that the imperial government was seriously considering several problems, including
that of the Hudson's Bay Company, which deeply affected
Canada. There was probably no very great surprise when,
towards the end of the year, the expected dispatch arrived from
Labouchere, the Colonial Secretary, informing the Canadian
administration that the imperial government had decided to
set up, at the next session of parliament, a committee of the
House of Commons to explore the whole subject of the Hudson's Bay Company.[5] The question of the renewal of the exclusive licence to trade in the North West Territories would
be the particular point at issue; but the inquiry was expected
to range freely over the present and future position of the company as a whole. Inevitably the interests of the Province of
Canada would be involved. Labouchere ended the dispatch
by politely requesting the Canadian government to send witnesses and make representations to the proposed committee.
There was no escaping the question. What policy was the
Canadian government to adopt?

This was one of the principal questions which faced Macdonald as he and his small family settled down again in Wellington Place for the winter session of 1857. There were many
confident voices, in the press as a whole and among the Reform
newspapers in particular, which urged that Canada should adopt
a vigorous policy of expansion. The Hudson's Bay Company
charter was dismissed contemptuously as invalid. Canada's
title to the entire territory was asserted with unabashed con-

viction, and the Canadian legislature was clamorously required
to take instant, practical steps to acquire what was properly
its own. Early in January, 1857, as a part of George Brown's
comprehensive drive for the reorganization of the Grit party,
a great convention of western Reformers was held at Toronto.
Among the half dozen basic planks in its new platform, the
convention adopted a resolution calling for the incorporation
of Hudson's Bay Company's territory in Canada.[6] The opposition, with the spacious irresponsibility which is the prerogative
of all oppositions, had pronounced in favour of western expansion; and, without any doubt, there was a good deal to be
said for the course which the Reformers had so hastily adopted.
It was popular in Canada at the moment, and it would very
likely be the course which Canada would adopt in the end.
But how could the province dare to undertake such a heavy
responsibility at present or in the immediate future? Macdonald and the Cabinet drew back cautiously. The newspapers,
even the *Globe*'s brassy voice of command, were all very well;
but there were other more intimate and more prudent councils
which were having their effect upon the willing Macdonald.

In the first place there was the influence of Head himself.
Head had made no secret of the fact that he preferred his new
government to the old one which MacNab had led. It was
true that Taché was the titular head of the new administration,
but Macdonald was now its principal Upper Canadian member.
In Toronto, he lived conveniently close to Government House.
He and the Governor saw a great deal of each other; they exchanged ideas and confidences; and their habits of mind,
which were not dissimilar, led them unerringly towards the
same general conclusions. Head distrusted popular clamour.
He was impatient with the idle "dreams and speculations" about
the west which he found "floating in the public mind here,
even among sober and good men".[7] He told people, a little
acidly, that Canada could not govern properly the dominions
which she already possessed; and he was convinced that the
Hudson's Bay Company's territories, even as a free gift, would
be far too great a responsibility for Canada to accept at the
present. The real point about territory was, not how to acquire

it, but how to administer it. Could Canada possibly cope with an empire which occupied a quarter of a continent?

This kind of advice was coming to Macdonald also from another and very different source, from a young Scotsman living in Montreal, named John Rose. Rose was half a dozen years younger than Macdonald, and he had arrived in Canada much more recently; but some time in the late 1840's or early 1850's they met and became close friends. They were light-hearted and still fairly irresponsible young men who enjoyed life to the full without taking it very seriously; and once, when Macdonald at least was old enough to know better, they went off on an absurd adventure in the United States, and wandered around as travelling showmen, with Rose caper-ing about as a dancing bear, and Macdonald playing some "rude instrument" in accompaniment.[8] In the meantime, back in the sedate professional circles of Montreal, Rose was build-ing up a very large and flourishing law practice. There was little likelihood that he would ever be Macdonald's rival. Am-bitious enough in his own way, and tranquilly assuming that the good things of life would come to him, Rose had no very great interest in public office or recognized political power. He preferred to do things unostentatiously and by indirection; he was born to conduct negotiations, to carry out delicate mis-sions, to make adroit and rewarding arrangements. He was an instinctive diplomatist who was by nature an urbane and charming man; and already, although he was still comparatively young, his sources of information were many and his influence wide. Rose knew Head and Macdonald and the other members of the Canadian government, and was well acquainted with the business and professional people in Montreal. He even seemed to possess a fairly large number of confidential correspondents in financial and governmental circles in England. One of them was Edward Ellice, old "Bear" Ellice, the veteran British fur trader, who had helped to bring about the union of the North West Company and the Hudson's Bay Company in 1821, and who ever since had been a potent influence in the amalgamated concern. Rose had become Ellice's legal adviser in Canada, and his agent for the Ellice seigniory at Beauharnois; and the old man, in a series of vigorous, cynically realistic letters, expounded to his Canadian subordinate the real position of the Hudson's Bay Company, as he saw it. It might have been—it obviously was—Hudson's Bay Company propaganda. But it also looked remarkably like good sense.

Ellice began by conceding—what Macdonald, Rose and other prudent Canadians were already prepared to admit— that in the end the Hudson's Bay Company would probably lose its chartered as well as its licensed territories. The lands would either become part of Canada, or they would be formed by Great Britain into new colonies, having, perhaps, some connection with Canada. Sooner or later they would probably gravitate to the St. Lawrence colony, for the sufficient reason that they could never be permitted to become a part of the United States. All this could be granted. It was not a question of principle, but a question of timing. When should the proposed change in administration take place? "It is neither the monopoly, nor the proprietary right of the Company, which is of much importance," old Edward Ellice argued shrewdly. "The great point is, how govern the territory. . . . Let anybody refer to the history and experience of the past, and they will be satisfied that these extensive and remote regions can only be governed by monopoly, and that the monopoly must be profitable to pay them who will undertake it. It is now profitable—it has never been more so—but if the Province of Canada, not having sufficient work on hand to govern themselves, covet this extension of their Dominion, its trade and its administration, nothing is as easy as to acquire it. For a million sterling, they may buy the fee simple of the whole territory north of forty-nine and between Canada and the Rocky Mountains, the whole trade and establishment of the Hudson's Bay Company, but they must saddle themselves at the same time with the expense, and what is of infinitely more importance, the responsibility of a territory extending some 6000 miles."[9] It was an intimidating prospect. Rose, who found it frankly terrifying, no doubt communicated the contents of Ellice's letter to Macdonald; and when the Governor next visited Montreal, he read a part of it to him. Head, Rose reported, was deeply impressed with the wisdom of Ellice's views. "I am sure he will exercise extreme caution," Rose wrote back to Ellice, "before he involves us in the heavy responsibility of protecting such an extent of territory, even were it given up to us for nothing."[10] Purchase or gift—it really made very little difference. If Canada were induced to accept major responsibility for the Hudson's Bay territories, would not Great Britain gladly and swiftly accelerate her withdrawal, certainly from the west, and perhaps even from British North America as a whole?

Yet, as Macdonald fully realized, some answer would have to be made to Labouchere's invitation. It would have to be a confident and perhaps assertive response, for public opinion in Canada obviously expected some clear declaration with respect to the Hudson's Bay Company's territories; but it need not be either very explicit or very compromising. And about the middle of January, Council got down to the business of concocting a suitable reply.[11] It began by asserting that the Canadian government "rejoiced" that the Hudson's Bay Company was about to be investigated. Then there was a reference to the unhappy uncertainty of the boundary between Canada and the United States, and another reference to the danger of encroaching American settlement. Canada, the order-in-council continued, had a natural interest in the affairs of every part of British North America; and, so far as her own claims were concerned, "the general feeling here is strongly that the western boundary of Canada extends to the Pacific Ocean". From all these rather vague and grandiose premises, Council drew the conclusion that Canada ought to be properly represented before the proposed parliamentary committee; and a few weeks later it decided that the proper representative could be none other than William Henry Draper, the first architect of the Liberal-Conservative party, and now the Chief Justice of Canada West. The instructions which Draper received were scarcely a great deal more definite than the language of the minute which had justified his appointment.[12] He was bidden to watch over the interests of Canada in the investigation and to assert her "legal and equitable claims"—whatever they might. be. The provision of tracts of land fit for settlement ought to be ensured in any settlement with the Hudson's Bay Company. Above all else, the international boundary must be defined and protected "against sudden and unauthorized immigration from the United States". But Draper was not to feel free to require, or conclude, any plan of settlement without reference back to the Canadian government. The Canadian government, in fact, had no very definite "plan of settlement" to press. It wished to protect Canadian interests for the future, but without serious obligations at the present.

II

By the time these decisions were taken, the Macdonalds John Alexander, Isabella, and Hugh John, were established once again in the rented apartments in the house on Wellington Place. It was a constricted, unhappy family existence. The narrow rooms were crowded with the paraphernalia of the sick-room and hushed by the presence of invalidism; it was almost like carrying on domestic life in all the depressing discomforts of a field-hospital tent. Isabella, it was true, had no recurrence of the terrible crisis of the previous winter. Sometimes Macdonald, in his letters back to Kingston, merely announced briefly that his wife was "as usual"; and once, towards the end of the winter, he was even able to report that she had been "in very unusual health and strength". But this, as everybody knew now, was only a brief interval of well-being in an incurable disease; and even so, the joy at Isabella's temporary improvement was darkened by concern for Hugh. The boy—he was seven years old in March—was ill most of the winter.[18] Afflicted with recurring but diminishing attacks of pain, treated with special diets and frequent hot baths, he was kept sternly in the house for weeks on end and permitted virtually no exercise. His education, which was obviously suffering, was already a concern to his parents. They worried over the fact that the seven-year-old was not able to attend a Toronto school; and a tutor was secured who, during the difficult period

of the winter, appeared daily for a token lesson of an hour.[14]
In March, when the sun climbed higher and the air grew
warmer, Hugh emerged to play in the open air. Now the tutor's
visits lengthened: Hugh "takes a two hours lesson every day and
is a wonderful arithmetician", Macdonald reported proudly to
his sister Louisa.[15] It was pleasant to record the small boy's
steady improvement; it was a hopeful episode in a family history which sometimes looked like an unbroken chronicle of
illness. Even Macdonald himself, who was usually so robustly
healthy, was ill that winter. The session began late, towards
the end of February; and a little after the opening, he gave
his arm a severe sprain—a sprain which shook him far more
than might have been expected. He kept the arm wrapped
up in flannel for some time; but he continued to feel weak
and depressed in spirit. It was a bad state in which to meet
parliament for what was destined to be the last session before
a general election.

It was an important session in other ways as well. The problems of Canada's approaching maturity emerged gradually out
of the haze of distance like the harsh, forbidding features of
some newly discovered and formidable landscape. The question
of defence against the United States, the problems of Canadian
westward expansion, of communications with the eastern seaboard, and of British North American union, were all important
matters which had jolted Macdonald and his colleagues out of
the rutted tracks of normal provincial speculation. They were
pushed further, protestingly, along the paths of invention and
experiment, by the very condition of their province itself, by
the incessantly recurring difficulties of a country which was
in form a unitary state, and in fact a half-acknowledged federal
system. The choice of a capital, the selection of the province's
spiritual centre symbolized, as perhaps nothing else could have
done, the irreconcilable conflict between unity and duality.
The debate on the "seat-of-government" question had been going
on almost without interruption from the moment that Sydenham had first selected Kingston back in 1841. For years it had
not been considered a "ministerial question". No recent government had dared to take up a decided stand on the issue; and

in the previous session, the MacNab administration had, ostensibly at least, permitted the debate on the subject to develop in complete freedom. The debate had resulted in the choice of Quebec. Macdonald and his colleagues, dutifully accepting the decision of the legislature, had included in the budget an appropriation for the construction of appropriate permanent buildings at the province's new capital. It looked as if the whole business was ended, when there came another odd turn in the erratic course of the provincial legislature. The Legislative Council threw out the appropriation for buildings. The whole affair had been deposited back again at the starting point.

The government was not quite nonplussed. The new session approached, and Macdonald was one of the originators of a completely new plan. He had probably not been very well pleased with the choice of Quebec, against which he had voted consistently in the last session. On the other hand, he disliked the ambulatory system even more, for the ambulatory system implied division, and he liked to believe in the continued existence of the united province, either by itself, or as part of a possible wider unity. Why not refer the whole perplexing issue to the Queen, and respectfully invite Her Majesty to make a decision which the Canadian legislature seemed incapable of making by itself? Surely this was an ingenious suggestion with a good deal to recommend it. In the first place, it would ensure delay, while Her Majesty deliberately made up her mind; and delay, which was always good anyway, could in this case be prolonged until after the next general election. In the second place, it was a patriotically unexceptionable course, which could only be criticized with difficulty, and which would probably end in a selection less easily disturbed than any which the Canadian legislature could make itself. The argument seemed sound and Macdonald launched the resolutions inviting the Queen's arbitrament early in the session. There was some criticism. John Hillyard Cameron attacked the government for its abandonment of responsibility. The request for the Queen's decision, he declared, was a retrograde step constitutionally, which would, of course, not prevent the Canadian ministers from offering surreptitious advice. "They will secretly exercise an influence," Cameron declared in his smoothest fashion, "the responsibility of which they are afraid openly to assume."[16] Macdonald jovially twitted the High Tory Cameron with being a late and doubtful convert to responsible government, insisted that the present administration, in proposing the reference to the Queen, had in fact assumed more responsibility than any previous government, and defended the course he proposed as the only remaining method of settling the contentious question. The baffled and weary House was inclined to agree with him. One last concession, it was true, had to be made to the Conservative supporters in Canada East. Macdonald, pressed by Alleyn and Lemieux, was forced to agree that the seat of government should be transferred for a last term to the city of Quebec before the final and permanent removal to the new capital, wherever it might be.[17] But this was a cheap price to pay for what might possibly be a lasting settlement, and what would certainly result in a welcome period of peace. Before March was out, Head had sent to the Colonial Office the reference to the Queen.[18] "It will not be expedient," he told Herman Merivale, the Permanent Under-Secretary, in a private letter dispatched the same day, "that any answer should be given for 8 or 10 months, *except the acceptance of the reference*. The sooner that comes the better." The Colonial Office acted with commendable promptitude. The Queen graciously accepted the reference. And Macdonald gratefully pushed the matter out of his mind as something which could be conveniently forgotten for nearly a twelvemonth.

He was not permitted to indulge his feeling of relief too long. The crisis with the United States in the spring of 1856 and the dispatch of the imperial reinforcements to Canada had raised the whole general question of British North American communications. In Canada a phase of the same problem was brought up again by the perennial difficulties of the Grand Trunk Railway. The Conservative government had not, of course, begun the Grand Trunk—that had been the work of Hincks; but from the beginning Liberal-Conservatives, as individuals, had played a conspicuous part in the financial melodrama of the railway age. MacNab, the first leader of the administration, was president of the Great Western Railway; Ross, the ex-President of the Council, was the president of the Grand Trunk Railway; and Cartier, the Attorney-General for Canada East and the effective leader of the French-Canadian bloc in the Assembly, was the Grand Trunk's principal solicitor. It was an intimate, all too vulnerable, personal connection; and it grew all the more easily open to attack as the Grand Trunk became an established fact, as its benefits tended to be taken for granted, and as its requirements and necessities rapidly became the subject of acrid public debate. A huge, though still incomplete, system, which stretched from Quebec and Portland in the east towards Sarnia and London in the west, the railway had in fact become the most important enterprise in Canada— an enterprise which was at once an economic and social asset to the province and a financial and political liability to the provincial government.[19] Repeatedly, the new Liberal-Conservative administration had had to rush to the assistance of the railway. Financial help had been given in 1855, and again in 1856; and with the opening of the session of 1857, it became perfectly clear that a new Grand Trunk aid bill would inevitably be an embarrassing item in the government's programme of legislation. The support of the government entailed the attack of the opposition; and resistance to the Grand Trunk and its financial exactions became an integral part of the new Liberalism which Brown and his associates were building up in Canada West. The railway was represented to the edified populace of Upper Canada as a malign creation of Montreal finance, which robbed the public treasury, debauched the country with the bribery of jobs and contracts, and impoverished the poor patient farmers of Canada West with exorbitant freight rates. The influence of the Grand Trunk, like the influence of the Roman Catholic priesthood, rested ultimately, the *Globe* explained to its readers, upon the votes of the French-Canadian bloc in parliament; and Rep. by Pop. would defeat both the despotism of the popish hierarchy and the financial tyranny of Montreal.

Macdonald, though he had never taken much interest in the detail of finance, found that he was being pushed more and more deeply into Grand Trunk affairs. It was, of course,

Cayley's job, as Inspector-General, to introduce the bill. But Cayley, with his diffident, gentlemanly manner, and weak voice, was ineffective in the House; and a good deal of the defence fell to Macdonald. Macdonald tried, as he always did, to avoid technical detail, and to confine himself to the broad basic considerations which would really determine the matter. The aid which the government proposed, he told the House, was not intended to relieve the shareholders, or to put money into anybody's pocket; it was designed simply to restore public confidence in the property, to facilitate the raising of fresh capital, and, above all else, to complete the road.[20] When, a few minutes later in the speech, Brown laughed cynically at the request that the bill be passed with as little delay as possible, Macdonald, in a moment of sheer exasperation, informed his tormentor savagely that he might very well laugh on the other side of his face, if, six months from then, he found himself at the head of a Reform administration, with the work on the Victoria Bridge suspended, the G.T.R. rolling stock handed over to the railway's creditors and the railway itself in bankruptcy. Nobody, Brown included, really believed that the railway could be abandoned. But, before this danger-point was even approached, criticism could be pushed a very long way indeed, for the financial history of the Grand Trunk was a tangled and somewhat questionable story. Brown exploited his advantage with his usual intemperate righteousness. He attacked the relief bill in violent diatribes; he secured a parliamentary committee for the investigation of the entire financial record of the Grand Trunk Railway Company; he flung accusations, insinuations, and reproaches in all directions. And at a certain point, which Macdonald saw approaching with delight, and which Brown himself seemed utterly incapable of anticipating, he went too far. His wholesale condemnations began to include the eastern members of his own party; the violent Upper Canadianism of his crusade began to awaken an indignant response even in Liberal Canada East. Alexander Tilloch Galt, the *Rouge* member for Sherbrooke, a railway promoter and contractor who had had a good deal to do with the Grand Trunk Railway, was subjected to a prolonged and merciless inquisition in Brown's

special committee of investigation. When Galt had the temerity
to interrupt Brown in the full flow of one of his speeches and
question him on a point of fact, Brown turned furiously upon
the member for Sherbrooke and screamed out his accusations
of bad faith and bribery to the whole House. When Luther
Holton, another *Rouge* who was also a railway contractor,
attempted to deny Brown's pet thesis and to argue that the
Grand Trunk was really of more benefit to Canada West than
to Canada East, Brown instantly attributed this infatuated
delusion to the basest of pecuniary motives. "There was a time,"
he told the House furiously, "when the honourable gentleman
opposed the Grand Trunk as strongly as I did; but that opposition ceased when he got a Grand Trunk directorship and
a Grand Trunk contract. There was a time when he professed
to act with the opposition, but his conduct on this question
has done more injury to the Liberal party than has been done
by all the efforts of the gentlemen opposite."[21] The situation
was comically grotesque. Brown, in one of his hysterias of
arrogant righteousness, seemed actually to be trying to read
Dorion, Galt, and Holton out of the party! But the *Rouges*
owed him no allegiance, and Dorion and the others were far
from being his submissive lieutenants. They protested indignantly, and the unseemly public row went on. It was a
good illustration of how difficult it was going to be to build a
provincial Reform party on the basis of militant sectionalism.

Macdonald amiably watched the opposition leaders indulging in the traditional Reform game of fighting with each other
in public. He tucked the idea away in his mind that this
might be a suitable moment to begin detaching Dorion, Holton,
and Galt from their censorious and dictatorial western colleague.
But this delicate operation would have to be postponed until
autumn, for he had other and still more urgent affairs on hand
for the summer. Early in the session he had reached the conclusion that railways in general and the Grand Trunk in particular would require him to go off to England as soon as
parliament rose. As the exacting session dragged on, his resolution wavered; he had become ill shortly after the opening and
his illness continued for most of the following three months.

He began to dream longingly of a real holiday at the seashore
for Isabella and Hugh and himself—a holiday such as they
had never had before. "On the rising of Parliament," he told
his sister Louisa towards the end of April, "I intend to go to
the seashore and not to England. I hope to have six weeks of
sea bathing which will put me all right again."[22] That was
in early spring; but by the middle of June, when the session
had at length ended, the earlier decision prevailed. The condition of the Grand Trunk—three times in succession rescued
by government—was desperate in the extreme; and both on
financial and political grounds the embarrassed government
was bound to make another effort to obtain imperial support.
Besides, the summer of 1857 was in many ways a suitable
moment for the mission. In London he would enjoy strong
Canadian support. Draper was already there on the business
of the Hudson's Bay investigation. Head, the Governor-General,
had sought and obtained leave to return home, partly on the
ground that his presence on the spot might be useful in the
Hudson's Bay matter and in the seat-of-government question.[23]
And Head and Macdonald were a formidable team in Canadian
affairs.

In mid-July, council authorized Macdonald's mission to
England;[24] and Eyre, the General Officer Commanding, who
acted as administrator in Head's absence, wrote a letter introducing the Attorney-General West to Labouchere at the Colonial
Office.[25] In its order of July 18, Council declared that Macdonald was to "have authority to call to his aid the services of
any gentleman whom he may deem necessary to the success
of the negotiations". At that late date the identity of the
"gentleman" was still apparently unknown; but, in reality,
Macdonald had made his choice some time before. It was John
Rose—the pleasant fellow, the good companion, with his affable
manner and his wide circle of influential London friends. Rose
wrote off to Edward Ellice that Macdonald had been begging
him to go. "I don't quite see my way to leave," he explained,
"nor do I quite relish the mission, but he, as well as others,
are so urgent that I may go."[26] He went indeed; and before
a fortnight had passed he and Macdonald were aboard the

Anglo-Saxon and bound for Liverpool. After the long grind of the session, Macdonald enjoyed the sea voyage. He admitted, in a letter to his mother, that he had felt a "little squeamish" at intervals for three days and had been decidedly sick one morning; but, he concluded proudly, "I never lost my dinner —a great and wonderful change for me".[27] It was a pleasant but uneventful voyage—"a couple of icebergs and a few whales being all our wonders"—and before the month was out he and Rose had docked at Liverpool, travelled down to London and were installed in the York Hotel, Albemarle Street. That first evening they went off together to the opera; but the next morning early he was "up to his eyes in business".[28]

It was, for him, a new kind of entrance to the capital of the Empire. He had come before as a young man on his travels or as the agent of a commercial company; now he appeared as the accredited representative of the senior colony in British North America. He appeared, moreover, with what could be defended as a practical scheme, which, far from laying all the burdens on Great Britain, would certainly place real and substantial obligations on the Province of Canada. They would be heavy obligations; but, according to the new plan, they would be somewhat differently distributed, and hence possibly more bearable. Canada had in fact determined to revive the old project of the Intercolonial Railway and to transfer some of its financial responsibilities from the provincial Grand Trunk to the interprovincial road. Macdonald and Rose proposed to the Colonial Office that if Great Britain should relieve Canada of the repayment of the £1,500,000 loan of 1841 and of the sinking fund established in connection with it, the province would agree to pay the entire cost of its share of the line from Rivière du Loup to Halifax.[29] During the first weeks of August, they were busy memorializing the British government and interviewing its various members. They saw Labouchere, the Colonial Secretary, Sir George Cornewall Lewis, the Chancellor of the Exchequer and Lord Panmure, the Secretary for War.[30] Head gave them his weighty assistance. Even Edward Ellice, "somewhat against my conscience", wrote to Lord Panmure to give what help he could towards "your military road".[31]

Everybody was very polite. Yet they seemed to make curiously little progress, as, indeed, Edward Ellice had anticipated. "You will be received with great civility," the old man had told Rose, "matters will be discussed with you, as if there was a disposition to assist you—'fair words butter no parsnips'—but when the real point of engagement comes on the tapis they will do nothing for you".[32] It soon began to look ominously as if Ellice's prophecy were only too correct; and, indeed, the circumstances of the summer of 1857 were unhappily unpropitious for Macdonald's proposal. The crisis with the United States of the summer of 1856 was a thing of the past; the Indian Mutiny had already broken out, and the whole focus of imperial concern had shifted from west to east. The Canadian mission, as a mission, was pretty obviously a failure; but as a diverting holiday for Macdonald, it had been a pronounced success. He found Rose, as he had anticipated, a pleasant companion, and they got on very well together. "I am, thank God," he wrote his mother, "in good health and spirits and enjoying myself amazingly."[33] He paid a series of visits to the members of the Macdonald-Macpherson connection, went off to Paris for an extra-official three-day visit, and bought a few things to take back to Canada, including a highland kilt for Hugh. "I have no doubt," he told his mother, "he will bare his bottom with due Celtic dignity."[34] Then it was September and time to return home. The problem of British North American transportation had not been solved in the brief summer of 1857.

III

That autumn he took up the delicate business of Cabinet reorganization. It was high time to be mending political fences. Parliament expired by the effluxion of time in the summer of 1858; and, as Head had anticipated, the government decided that it would be better to hold the election a little earlier, before the end of the current year. It was certainly not a particularly good moment to appeal to the constituencies, for the Crimean War boom broke in the autumn of 1857 and the province, like the rest of the western world, was soon deep in the pit of an economic depression. But there was not much point in delaying the election a few months, in the vain hope that things would improve. In any case, the reorganization of the Cabinet must take place immediately, for Colonel Taché, the titular head of the administration, was anxious to resign, and there were two other places to fill as well. Before he sailed for England Macdonald had been aware of the fact that an extensive shake-up in the Canada East section of the Cabinet was necessary; and in the autumn, after he had returned to the province, Head asked him to accept the major responsibility for making the new appointments.[35] At the age of forty-two, he was first minister of the government of the Province of Canada. Cartier, who had pushed his way rapidly to the front of the rather feeble and fluctuating group of French-Canadian politicians, was to be his principal assistant, almost his political equal; and Cartier's prodigious authority and influence in all that concerned Canada East could not be gainsaid. Together they sat down to recruit the eastern section of the Cabinet.

Macdonald knew the complicated rules well. And Cartier was always willing to expound them in his vigorous staccato style. Apart from the Solicitor-General, who was not formally a member of the Cabinet, there had to be in every self-respecting administration two members from the District of Quebec and three from the District of Montreal. One of these—it did not matter much from which district he came—had to be a "Britisher", not a French Canadian. There might even, at a pinch, be two Britishers, though Cartier looked very doubtfully at this augmentation of the English-speaking side. One of the Britishers was required to be a Protestant; the second—in case there unfortunately had to be a second—might very usefully be an Irish Roman Catholic. Macdonald left most of the details to Cartier, who every once in a while, like a minor prophet bursting into revelation, would be "delivered" of a fresh set of names.[36] Macdonald's principal purpose was to use the reorganization in such a way as to steal a little opposition support. He had divined the angry discontent of the *Rouges* with astonishing accuracy. The rift in the unhappy Liberal family was, in fact, very serious. "Have you and I any particular inducement," Holton inquired sourly of Galt, "to assist in playing the Opposition's game after the treatment we received last session?"[37] Macdonald pressed his sympathetic inducements in his most persuasive manner. Dorion was offered a Cabinet post; and when Dorion at length and somewhat hesitatingly declined, Galt was approached for his support in a jocularly friendly fashion. "You call yourself a *Rouge*," wrote Macdonald affably. "There may have been at one time a reddish tinge about you, but I could observe it becoming by degrees fainter. In fact you are like Byron's Dying Dolphin, exhibiting a series of colours—'the last still loveliest'—and that last is 'true blue', being the colour I affect. Seriously, you would make a decent Conservative, if you gave your own judgment a fair chance and cut loose from Holton and Dorion and those other beggars. So pray do become true blue at once: it is a good standing colour and bears washing."[38]

Galt did not become "true blue" at once. But it was significant that he had disapproved of Dorion's decision not to accept a Cabinet post; and in a little while he was to announce himself an Independent and to begin a vigorous attack upon his former colleagues in the opposition. The hope of obtaining the support of some of the prominent *Rouge* leaders had to be given up, at least temporarily; but Sicotte brought with him a Liberal flavour to the eastern division of the Cabinet and John Rose certainly raised the level of its intellectual ability. Rose was not very acceptable, as a second English-speaking member, to Cartier; but he was, if anything, even more objectionable to the ministers from Canada West, who looked on the Montreal lawyer as a very imperfectly disguised agent of the Hudson's Bay Company. "I will do almost anything to serve you," Philip Vankoughnet wrote to Macdonald, "but giving up to Lower Canada the Commissioner of Crown Lands and taking in John Rose also is too much. Rose will and must be regarded as the agent of Ellice . . . and as I have no doubt we will run the ship ashore with him it is as well to give it

up now with credit."³⁹ Macdonald blandly disregarded this
outspoken warning. Sicotte was made Commissioner of Crown
Lands, and John Rose became the Solicitor-General, Canada
East.

It remained to be seen whether they would run the ship
upon the rocks, as Vankoughnet had so gloomily prophesied.
After the reconstruction of the Cabinet was complete, Macdonald enjoyed a very brief holiday in Kingston; but on November 29 he left again for Toronto and by half-past nine that night
he was comfortably installed in the new Rossin House.⁴⁰ There
was no thought, at the moment, of Isabella and Hugh accompanying him or of a resumption of their life together in Toronto
lodgings. Isabella was seriously ill again; and next day, the
last day of November, he waited impatiently for the agreed-
upon telegram which would tell him that all was well at home.
The election was less than a fortnight away. The Reform
alliance, the new Reform organization which had been fashioned
at the convention in the previous January, was sweeping the
whole west in a boisterous campaign which extolled Rep. by
Pop. as the single sovereign remedy for all the cultural and
economic ills under which Canada West suffered and groaned.
The counter-campaign which Macdonald tried to organize from
Toronto was essentially defensive. He was unremittingly busy
—so busy that he could hardly spare a moment for the minor
engagement of his own election in Kingston. On December
9, he rushed down at the last moment and appeared the following day at the hustings before the city hall for the nomination
meeting. A local man, John Shaw, had been put up to oppose
him; but, as the local Conservative newspaper announced contemptuously, Shaw's candidature was so trivial that it was
generally believed to have been originated by wags for sport.⁴¹
And Macdonald, addressing the crowd in "his usual friendly
happy manner", hardly bothered to talk politics, either local or
general, in his election speech, and reminisced instead about
the old days in "the good old town".⁴² That very night he
returned to Toronto, announcing confidently that he "entrusted
his return to Parliament to the people of Kingston". The
confiding appeal could not be resisted. "Electors of Kingston,"

exhorted the editor of the *News*, "stand by your Political Child, and trample under foot the factious opposition that seeks to bring discredit upon our good old city".[43] On December 16, a mild day of dull, cloudy skies and muddy streets, the poll opened. Before the day was out John Shaw formally withdrew from the unequal contest; but his withdrawal did not prevent him from being burnt in effigy that night in the market place. And next evening, when the poll finally closed, Macdonald's total had mounted to 1189 votes, whilst poor Shaw had secured only nine.[44]

It was a walkover. But unfortunately it bore no resemblance to the results in the majority of the constituencies of Canada West. Three Conservative cabinet ministers—Cayley, Spence, and Morrison—were defeated; while George Brown was successful, not only in North Oxford, but actually in Toronto as well. Three years ago, when the Liberal-Conservative coalition had first faced parliament, John Hillyard Cameron, the Tory, had seemed almost as formidable an antagonist as the Reformer, George Brown; but now, in so short a time, their relative importance had completely altered. Cameron, who had not even sought re-election, had become one of the first and most tragic victims of the depression. The New York house through which he had carried on his ambitious exchange business had failed suddenly and its drafts on London were dishonoured. The securities which he had placed in the hands of his English bankers were sold at a loss of over £100,-000.[45] He was terribly, almost hopelessly, in debt. But he refused all financial compromises and swore he would pay twenty shillings on the pound. The great house on Queen Street was given up; the patronage of Samuel Thompson's *British Colonist* was abandoned; and he became the grimly willing slave of his profession. Never again would he be able to afford the time for a really active political career. He had fallen—fallen at almost exactly the same moment as Brown's most sudden and dramatic rise. Brown now towered above all his Radical rivals; he seemed to loom portentously over the whole Canadian political scene. For him the election had been a personal as well as a party triumph; it had demonstrated the justice of his convictions and the wisdom of his strategy. It was true that in Canada East the demoralized *Rouges* lost almost as heavily as the Grits gained in Canada West; but this, though it might save the Liberal-Conservative government, could not lessen Brown's feeling of triumph nor remove Macdonald's sense of personal defeat. Canada West was his own particular baili-wick; and in Canada West his party had now been put un-questionably in a minority.

The election had not yet finished when the holiday came. He had not intended to go home for Christmas; and he was still in Toronto, carrying on the battle for the last constituencies, when the message arrived from Kingston. There had been such messages before, and he had obeyed them instantly, hurrying home in a terror of apprehension as he had done from the Crown Law Office on that winter day almost a year before. In one sense his whole married life, ever since the terrible summer of 1845, had been one long frightened expectation of the tragic message which, in the end, must infallibly come. By Christmas night he was in Kingston, by Isabella's bedside, watching hope-fully as he had watched so often before. This time, as he must have seen immediately, there were no alternatives ahead. For three days more she dragged her broken existence along; and then on December 28, in the last exhaustion from which there was no recovery, she died.[46] It was the expected, inevitable end for what had been for almost a dozen years a grey, un-relieved tragedy. Life had cheated him terribly; he had given everything where, in the very nature of the case, there could never be a full and satisfying response. By the two supreme efforts of her life, Isabella had borne children, one of whom had lived; but for years she had been a bedridden invalid, who was physically incapable of giving him the love, the sup-port, and the companionship which he had craved. It was all over now—the agony of worry, the aching feeling of incom-pleteness, the patched habit of cheerful resignation. But for twelve years it had twisted his whole life. He had become a family man whose home was a hotel or a lodging-house; a bachelor husband who had to go for companionship to bars and lounges and smoking-rooms; a frustrated host who drank too much on occasion, partly because it was the only way he could entertain, and because it passed the empty time, and because it was an easy way to forget.

IV

He had spent the autumn reconstructing the Canada East section of the Cabinet. The first task of the dreary New Year was to recruit its broken contingent from Canada West. Two months before, he had cautiously felt out the discontented and half-rebellious forces of the enemy's eastern wing; and now, in the same kind of delicate manoeuvre, he sought tentatively for the weak spot on the western flank. John Sandfield Macdonald, the independent Reformer from the upper St. Lawrence valley, who had never accepted Brown's dictatorship, seemed to respond a little to these approaches; and late in January he was actually offered a choice of offices in the Cabinet. John Alexander Macdonald hoped for the telegraphic reply "All right" to his hastily written letters; what he received from his clansman was the equally laconic but unfortunately negative rejoinder "No go".[47] In the end John Ross returned to the Cabinet, and Sidney Smith, an authentic Reformer whose election the *Globe* had celebrated, was also persuaded to join. In some way the ranks were reformed. But it had been a difficult and disheartening task; and he was a depressed and lonely man during the winter of 1858 in Toronto. His wife was dead; his small son was a long day's journey away in Kingston; and now that the family apartments in Wellington Place had been given up for ever, he was living with a Mr. Salt, in bachelor quarters on Bay Street.

In the Assembly, George Brown led a clamorous and exultant opposition. Politically Macdonald lived from day to day, in a state of constant and irritating uncertainty. The House was a tossing ship in which, at almost any moment, he expected to lose his balance and fall headlong. During the first month of the long session he became ill, as he had done in the previous March; and for days of convalescence he dragged himself around with painful difficulty. It was pleasant to escape for week-ends to John Ross's house five miles out in the country on the Davenport Road, to have two good nights' rest, and to spend Sunday lounging in peaceful ease on the sofa. But this respite was very brief, and on Monday he found himself facing George Brown and his confident, truculent supporters once more. "We are having a hard fight in the House," he told his sister Margaret, "and shall beat them in the votes, but it will, I think, end in my retiring as soon as I can with honour. I find the work and annoyance too much for me."[48] He was depressed by weariness, by the continued drear sense of personal loss, by the unhappy realization of political defeat in his own old province of Upper Canada, and finally, perhaps, by a vague feeling that his own political mission was finished. He had formed the Liberal-Conservative party; and in the Clergy Reserves and Seigniorial Tenure measures he had helped to settle the outstanding issues of the past. But it was not the past that counted; it was the present and future. And here he could still not see a bold and easy course ahead.

For two years now the new and wider problems of approaching political maturity had been crowding about his government. For two years now his government had done little more than fumble with them cautiously and indecisively. It was true that he had thought of a new method, sensible as well as merely ingenious, for the solution of the seat-of-government question; and Sir Edmund Head's recommendation of Ottawa may very well have been his own private suggestion, though for many obvious reasons, he could hardly claim the credit for it. There were other quite different choices, from other advisers, civil and military, in the papers which were presented to the Queen.[49] But the Colonial Office, following Head, had decided for Ottawa; and General Grey, the Queen's secretary, drew the same conclusion from the evidence. "An attentive perusal of the papers relative to the seat of government in Canada," he wrote, "leads to the conviction that the choice of Ottawa will be the right and politic one."[50] It was all settled. The Queen had selected Ottawa, and the only remaining question was when the benevolent royal choice should

be communicated to the devoted Canadians. "Sir Edmund Head
is of opinion," wrote Labouchere to the Queen, "that the
decision had better arrive in Canada about Christmas."[51] It
was the Queen's Christmas present to the Province of Canada;
and the dispatch announcing it arrived early in January, a
little late for the holiday, but just after the elections, and
comfortably before the first session of the new parliament.[52]

As far as could be seen, Macdonald had cleared one problem out of the way with a dexterous flourish. But in other
matters, the government had either not been very adventurously
constructive, or, when it had tried to take a bold course, it had
not been very successful. The effort to persuade the imperial
government to give assistance in the construction of the Intercolonial Railway had turned out to be completely unsuccessful.
And the grand investigation of the Hudson's Bay Company,
about which there had been so much vainglorious talk in the
Canadian newspapers, had ended, not in the dramatic recognition of Canadian rights or the acquisition of new Canadian
territory, but in the virtual humdrum continuation of the
existing regime in the west. Worst of all, the Conservatives
seemed to have no solution whatever for the endless problems
created by the cultural division of the province. Almost every
other party, or fragment of a party, had a solution. They
represented all degrees of political decisiveness, from the completely catastrophic to the mildly reformist. Any one of them
could be made to look plausible; and all of them were given
lengthy hearing in the session of 1858, when the new parliament, weary with union yet frightened of separation, wore
down many doorsteps in its frantic search for a new and
comfortable shelter. Mackenzie, as of old the greatest ex-
tremist, advocated a simple dissolution of the union. Brown,
proudly conscious that he was the chosen mouthpiece for
the outraged and powerful voice of Canada West, presented
Rep. by Pop. once again, the official policy of the Reform Alliance. John Sandfield Macdonald, the invariable Liberal in-
dividualist, spoke up for the so-called Double Majority, a
scheme far more advocated than practised, which required any
truly legitimate government to have a parliamentary majority

in both sections of the province. And finally Alexander Tilloch
Galt, the one-time *Rouge* who had now broken with his old
associates, revived the old idea—advocated years before by the
British American League and by such Tories as Henry Sherwood—that the peculiar problems of the Canadian union could
best be solved in a federation of British North America.
At the moment Macdonald was willing to support none of
these proposals. On the subject of Galt's scheme, which was
the only broadly constructive one of the lot, he simply kept
his opinions in reserve; but all the others he opposed, for, in
his opinion, all the others were wholly negative and destructive.
Mackenzie would dissolve the union. Brown would break
it up equally effectively by destroying its peculiar character.
And Sandfield Macdonald would make it impossible to govern
by responsible government according to the parliamentary model.
Macdonald could do nothing more than stick by the union.[53]
It was a cautious, sensible, defensive policy—like so many other
of the government's policies; and, in the wild exasperation of
the moment, it could hardly be very popular.

Yet Macdonald somehow kept the weak, embarrassed, and
vulnerable government going. The winter and spring passed
slowly. Summer came, and still the interminable session prolonged itself. It was almost unthinkable that Brown would
fail to grasp what seemed to be his greatest opportunity. A
huge, earnest, clumsily vital man, he was now at the height
of his physical and mental powers; and his confident belief in
his own future and in the political destiny of Canada West
had become a fanatical conviction. Yet it was not until nearly
the end of the session that he and his followers were able to
precipitate the overthrow of the government, and even then
their sudden and almost unexpected success was achieved by
a method, which, if they had been less eager and over-confident,
they might have regarded as dubious if not dangerous. Clearly
the government's tenure of office was based upon its large
majority of members from Canada East; and clearly the government's defeat could be encompassed by the method of detaching,
if only temporarily, a considerable bloc of its Canada East
supporters. The simple—far too simple—way of accomplishing

this was obvious; it was by reviving the ancient seat-of-government question once more. Quebec and Montreal—and particularly Quebec which had had high hopes of becoming Canada's future capital—were resentfully disappointed at the Queen's choice of Ottawa. On this matter, if on no other, the members of Canada East might be moved by an irrepressible burst of local feeling to desert the government. This was the manoeuvre which the opposition finally decided to adopt. On Wednesday, July 28, an address to the Queen on the subject of the capital was mooted; amendments and still more ingenious amendments were suggested; and finally Piché moved that "in the opinion of this House the City of Ottawa ought not to be the permanent seat of government of this Province".[54] Macdonald intervened late in the debate. He reminded the House of the long acrimonious dispute which had moved the legislature itself to seek the royal intervention; he insisted that the Queen's choice had been made freely without the slightest advice from the Canadian government; and he condemned the resolution before the House as "a brusque and uncourteous insult to Her Majesty".[55] A few minutes later the vote came; and, as the Brownites had gleefully anticipated, the necessary bloc of French-Canadian votes changed sides. The government had been defeated sixty-four to fifty.

Flushed and excited Brown jumped to his feet at once. The vote which had just been carried, he explained triumphantly to the House, was in reality an express disapproval of the entire policy of the government; but, in order to put this interpretation of the event to the test, he would move the adjournment. Macdonald accepted the motion to adjourn as a deliberate challenge to his government; and the House, as most people, except the over-confident Grits, might have expected, immediately reversed itself.[56] The whole incident could have been dismissed as unimportant, but Macdonald decided at once that he would take it seriously. The appeal to the Queen, if it had not been his invention, had at least received his emphatic support. He may have intended merely to repudiate the vote as a reversal of his government's declared policy. He may have hoped to escape from a difficult position, to teach the irresponsible Assembly the consequences of its folly, to force a sobered House to take him back again on his own terms. And finally, was he not clearly aware from the beginning that the resignation of the Liberal-Conservative government would place before the blindly over-confident Brown the greatest temptation of his career—the temptation to accept office on the basis of a majority which, in the nature of the case, could only be ephemeral, the temptation to wreck his own future and the prospects of the Grit party by a premature grasp of power? That night, when a new and this time insignificant motion to adjourn had been passed, Macdonald called a late informal meeting of his colleagues in the Assembly. Before they went to bed, a majority of the ministers had decided to resign; and their decision, communicated next morning to their colleagues in the Legislative Council, was quickly made unanimous. Early in the forenoon of Thursday, July 29, the Macdonald-Cartier ministry tendered its collective resignation to Governor Head. A quarter of an hour later, when the Assembly opened at the unusual hour of 10 o'clock in the morning, Macdonald gave a lengthy explanation of the course he and his colleagues had taken.[57] After the adjournment, at his last brief conversation with Head, he learnt that the Governor had sent for Brown and that Brown had asked for time to consult his friends. "After that," Macdonald later concluded his account of the affair, "I had no conversation, direct or indirect, with His Excellency, of any kind, or by means of any agency."[58]

The next day, July 30, during a scene of odd and somewhat equivocal hilarity, the ex-ministers gave up their places on the treasury benches; and Macdonald seated himself comfortably on the opposition side to watch with interest what would happen. He had not long to wait for the denouement. The gods finished their sport with George Brown very quickly; and indeed they had little need to manipulate circumstances, for Brown's infatuated presumption had brought about his own swift undoing. He had, as he no doubt realized from the beginning, no chance whatever in the existing House. The members of his new Cabinet, in accepting office, would automatically forfeit their seats and be obliged to seek re-election;

and this would temporarily remove eight or ten stout Reformers from the Assembly. In a fairly evenly balanced House, where small numbers counted seriously, this temporary loss would be important; but far more important was the undoubted fact that the original majority on the seat-of-government question had been purely accidental, the result of special circumstances, unlikely to be repeated. Everything, then, depended upon Brown securing a dissolution; but here he came up against Governor Head, and the Crown's prerogative of the dissolution of parliament, and the Crown's necessary concern for the welfare of the country as a whole, irrespective of party. The present House had been elected only seven months previously; part of the supplies were still unvoted and several important measures awaited completion; and August, the harvest season, was the worst possible time for an appeal to the people.[59] For all these reasons Head hesitated to exercise the royal prerogative. Was he as impartial as he thought himself, or as his role required him to be? Was he influenced by distrusts and preferences which were inarticulate but compelling? The ground he stood on, at any rate, was solid; and his position was explained with complete candour. He warned Brown verbally, at their first meetings, that he could give no promise respecting a dissolution; he carefully repeated his warning in writing. But Brown swept on. "Some fish require to be toyed with," Macdonald explained amiably, a little later, to the House. "A prudent fish will play around with the bait some time before he takes it, but in this instance the fish scarcely waited till the bait was let down. He jumped out of the water to catch it."[60] Perhaps Brown expected that, in the end, the Governor would feel obliged to give way. In the lobbies and corridors of the legislature, the Grits were jubilantly predicting a dissolution; and Macdonald and his followers, in grave uncertainty, waited unhappily for the outcome. It came quickly. At noon on Monday, August 2, the Brown-Dorion government was sworn in; and a little after the House met for its afternoon session, one of the writs of election made necessary by the new appointments to office was proposed, and the motion immediately amended by a want-of-confidence resolution.

Before the House adjourned, at midnight, the amendment had been carried by the large majority of forty.[61] The next day, both verbally and in writing, the new ministers advised the Governor to dissolve the House and appeal to the people. Head refused; and on Wednesday, August 4, after having lasted almost exactly two days, the Brown-Dorion government ceased to exist.[62]

Macdonald waited a while longer. The Liberal-Conservatives had been defeated on a chance vote; the Reformers had been rejected far more decisively on a straight want-of-confidence amendment. To whom would the Governor turn? Head first invited Galt, a prominent independent, unconnected with either party, to form a government; but in short order Galt abandoned the task. The Governor then summoned Cartier, who immediately enlisted the help of Macdonald; and with little difficulty, the Macdonald-Cartier government was reconstituted, this time under the leadership of Cartier as first minister, and with only two changes of personnel, of which one, the substitution of Galt for Cayley as Inspector-General, was alone of real importance. The old government was back again; but when, on Friday, August 6, the ex-ministers were sworn in once more, each was appointed to an office different from that which he had held before. Somebody—it was more than probably Macdonald, the old master of manoeuvre in the courts—had conveniently recollected the seventh clause of the Independence of Parliament Act, passed the previous year, in 1857; and the seventh clause provided that if any one of the principal officers of government should resign his office and within one month accept another one, he should not be obliged thereby to vacate his seat in parliament.[63] It was not one month, it was only eight days, since Macdonald and his colleagues had tendered their resignations on July 29; and although clause seven had been pretty obviously designed to permit individual changes of portfolio without the expense of an election, there seemed no reason to believe that it would not validate a general shift of an entire ministry.

It was a clever device; in one way a little too clever, and in another not quite clever enough. It was not neat and finished;

in fact, it landed the ministers in a further difficulty. Did the words of the statute, "any other of the said offices", necessarily mean an office different from that previously occupied? There was some doubt on the subject; but the Cabinet decided that in a matter of this kind, it was far better to be on the safe side. On August 6, Macdonald was sworn in as Postmaster-General, and most, though not all, of his colleagues were similarly assigned to offices which they had no intention of occupying permanently. They occupied them, in fact, only one day; and on August 7 they all changed back to their proper portfolios once more.[64] By this time the device had become laboured and obvious and more than a little cheap. But it was none the less effective. The double shift—or, as it soon became popularly known, the "double shuffle"—permitted all the old members of the Macdonald-Cartier government to keep their seats in the Assembly at the very moment when the ex-ministers of the Brown-Dorion Cabinet had lost their parliamentary places as well as their political power. For the baffled and furious Grits, this was the last insufferable affront. They denounced it as a fraudulent evasion of the Independence of Parliament Act—an evasion made possible by an act of mass perjury on the part of the ministers, who had sworn to perform the duties of offices which they had no intention of occupying. It was an outrageous swindle—the last piece of knavery in a long and complicated plot, which had begun with the resignation of the Macdonald-Cartier government, which had involved the Governor and Macdonald in collusion, and which had been devised to defeat the innocent Reformers and defraud the long-suffering people of Canada.

Macdonald rejected this melodramatic invention with a sweeping denial. "It is a charge that I am a dishonourable man," he told the House, "a charge that the representative of our sovereign, myself, and all my colleagues, if they have any concern in the matter, are alike dishonourable conspirators, and here in my place in parliament, I say it is *false as Hell*."[65] It was fairly easy to dispose of the romantic horrors of Brown's excited imagination; but it was rather more difficult to brush off the dust which clung to him from the political mêlée of the summer. He had not been particularly anxious to retain power. For some time he had been considering hopefully the idea of resignation—of release from the "irritation" and "annoyance" of parliamentary life. But once the crisis was upon him, once he was engaged in the heat of the political battle, he had put forth all the resources of his cunning and experience. He had fought to win. On one occasion at least he had been guilty of sharp practice. He had paid his way back into power with some good money, and a few counterfeit coins. And his Governor, who had rejected the legitimate usage of the dissolution in such dignified terms, was obliged in the end to accept the contrivance of the "double shuffle". It was all a little unfortunate, and the trouble was that Macdonald could not tell at the moment just how unfortunate its consequences were likely to be.

But if Macdonald had been compromised, so also had George Brown. Macdonald had purchased success with a little cheap trickery; Brown had bought failure, humiliating and ridiculous, at the expense of his reputation for sincerity and consistency. There was no need for Macdonald to remain long upon the defensive. The comically pathetic performance of the two-day Brown-Dorion government—of "His Excellency's most ephemeral administration"—gave him an inexhaustible supply of material for raillery. What a curious spectacle that government had presented to the reflecting! Brown, the embodiment of militant Protestantism, had actually included six Roman Catholics in his Cabinet! Brown, the personification of the indignant sectionalism of Canada West, had apparently compromised all his main principles for the sake of office with a handful of Lower Canadian *Rouges*. It was true that he had not had time to frame and announce a programme; but, almost immediately after the resignation of his government, his ex-ministers and their friends and acquaintances began to make the most damaging revelations about the concessions he had apparently been prepared to make. Macdonald told the House jovially that it reminded him of a candidate in an election contest in Kingston, who had prudently equipped himself with a green handkerchief and an orange handkerchief which he flourished alternately before the beaming faces of the Irish Roman Catholics and the Protestant Orangemen.[66] Brown was never permitted to forget the "short administration". It had apparently existed for two days. But it did not really die on August 4, 1858. It lived on as a legend, at once sinister and ludicrous, which dragged a long, coiling tail of consequences for the Reform party.

There were to be consequences for both parties. And one of the first and most important of these was a dramatic change in the policy of the Liberal-Conservatives. Up to that time the party had devised no solution for the cultural problem of United Canada which it could oppose to the variety of other cures—Rep. by Pop., Double Majority, and Dissolution of the Union—currently being flaunted before the public. But now, in the last days of the troubled session, the ministers announced that they would attempt to initiate discussions for the federal union of British North America. Head had for some time been privately considering, in his speculative, academic fashion, the rival possibilities of a legislative union of the Maritime Provinces and a federal union of the whole of British North America. And Galt, the new Inspector-General, had advocated federal union during the great debates on the state of the province which had preceded the ministerial crisis at the end of July. Galt was a volatile and romantic character who took up new ideas with great ease, urged them with great persuasiveness, and altered them with great rapidity; and his inclusion in the Cabinet marked the adoption of the new policy and had probably helped to precipitate it. But the governing factor was different. What mattered most was the fact that Macdonald and Cartier, the two sectional leaders of the party, had been converted to the idea of a federal union. There can be little doubt that the crisis of July, with its peremptory warning of the growing difficulties of governing a divided and distracted Canada, had hastened their conversion. "I found him [Galt] and several of the gentlemen about to assume office," Head reported to the Colonial Secretary, "deeply impressed with the idea that in some such union alone could be found the ultimate solution of the great question which had been made a ground of agitation by Mr. Brown at the general election, viz.—the existing equality of representation of Upper and Lower Canada, and the alleged injustice inflicted on the former by such equality."[67] All the other solutions—Rep. by Pop. and the rest—Macdonald had openly and strongly opposed; but he had never opposed federation—at least in principle. He may, in 1849, have considered it impractical for the moment; in the years that followed he had simply not mentioned the subject at all. Whilst almost everybody had rushed impatiently forward with his solution, Macdonald had waited; and now he was free to commit himself and his party to the most ambitious and splendid solution of all.

In the explanations which he gave to the House on August 7, Cartier briefly alluded to the new policy; and on August 16, when he finally prorogued parliament, Head gave an even more formal announcement of the course which the new government proposed to follow. "I propose in the course of the recess," he told the House, "to communicate with Her Majesty's Government, and with the Governments of the sister Colonies, on another matter of very great importance. I am desirous of inviting them to discuss with us the principles on which a bond of a federal character, uniting the Provinces of British North America, may perhaps hereafter be practicable."[68] Less than three weeks later, on September 4, Council submitted a minute, which Head subsequently approved, outlining in some detail the steps which should be taken to start the discussions "with as little delay as possible".[69] On September 9, Head sent off this order-in-council, together with a covering letter, to the Colonial Secretary and to each of the British American Governors. A start, and a fairly quick one, had been made—so far as it could be made with letters and dispatches. But the government was not willing to rely solely on paper, and it decided to send a strong delegation to press the federation proposal upon the authorities in England. Macdonald was not to be a member of it. He was no longer the leader of the government, and the burden of the Canadian mission to England in the previous summer had been chiefly his. Cartier, the new first minister, John Ross, and Alexander Tilloch Galt were chosen as delegates; and early in October they set sail for England.

Chapter Eleven

The Humiliation of George Brown

I

The affairs with which Macdonald had been dealing for the past two years—communications, defence, and political reorganization—were by no means exclusively Canadian. They were imperial. They involved the other British North American colonies; they involved Great Britain itself: and their solution could only be reached through a complicated process of correspondence and discussions. The long series of pilgrimages to the Colonial Office, of conferences in British North America, had already commenced. During the previous summer Macdonald and Rose had joined forces with the Nova Scotians in an attempt to persuade the imperial government to support the Intercolonial Railway; and now, in the autumn of 1858, Canada had sent its federal proposal to all the capitals of British North America and had dispatched a strong contingent to press the plan upon the Colonial Office. Five different, highly individualistic, and largely unpredictable governments were concerned. What would Nova Scotia, New Brunswick, Prince Edward Island and Newfoundland think of the plan? How would they—and their Governors—enjoy being jerked out of the comfortable routine of provincial politics and required to consider an ambitious scheme proposed by their pushing and turbulent neighbour, Canada? Above all, and this was a crucial element in the general uncertainty, what impression would the plan make upon the Colonial Office and the British government?

In the short time which had elapsed since Macdonald's visit

in 1857, the political scene at Westminster had completely altered. Lord Palmerston's government had fallen; the Conservatives, under Derby and Disraeli, were in power once more; and the novelist, Sir Edward Bulwer Lytton, facile, versatile, charming, yet occasionally quick tempered, was installed at the Colonial Office. Lytton was genuinely interested in the colonies. He believed firmly in the continuation of the imperial tie; and, in his capricious, rather temperamental fashion, he realized, better than some of his contemporaries, the fact that the colonies were growing up and had become acutely sensitive to criticism and dictation. "To lecture any free Colony is dangerous," he told Disraeli bluntly, "to accuse the grand Province of Canada of corruption as the natural consequence of Democracy (which by the way is wrong in fact), would be madness."[1] Lytton had the novelist's gift of sympathetic understanding, and he was plentifully endowed with natural charm. But, at the same time, he was himself a sensitive, rather self-conscious person, who was by no means at ease in his new position. It was his first tenure of political office; and, although he had apparently been promised the colonial secretaryship some time before the Conservatives came into power, he got it only by reversion after Lord Stanley, the first Tory holder of the office, had been transferred to another department.[2] Lytton was justifiably annoyed. It was only natural that he should view his predecessor's policies with some distaste. It was equally natural that, as a novice, he should slightly resent the free and easy practices of the veterans in the colonial service. All the old hands knew that a good deal of the most important correspondence was by private letter and that a great governor like Head was sometimes a little late with the official dispatches. Lytton, who was not noticeably systematic in other things, desired more formality. He wanted to know. He wanted to control things. And he was uneasily conscious of the fact that about many matters he was still in the dark.

Thus, during that critical summer, while Macdonald had been coping with the ministerial crisis and devising the programme of his new government, an unmistakable grievance against Sir Edmund Head and the Canadian government had

Public Archives

GEORGE BROWN

been slowly building itself up in the sensitive mind of Sir Edward Bulwer Lytton. He convinced himself in the first place that Head's communications had, in general, been singularly "meagre" and "defective".[3] There was, for example, the Hudson's Bay Company question. On that matter Head had left the Colonial Office "wholly unenlightened" where he ought to have given "explicit information". There was also the whole business of the ministerial crisis—the "conditions" imposed on Brown and the "contrivance" by which the members of the Cartier-Macdonald ministry had managed to avoid the necessity of re-election; and although Carnarvon, the Under-Secretary, believed that Head had acted rightly in refusing to dissolve,[4] Lytton continued to have grave doubts about Head's "conduct throughout the recent transactions". These doubts were quickly magnified when the English newspapers, gaining their information from the somewhat dubious source of George Brown's *Globe*, began to criticize the course which the Governor had followed. Lytton foresaw questions in the House—perhaps a short debate—the very kind of thing in which he, with his set speeches, was poorest.[5] And he had nothing to fall back upon! There were private letters, but not a single public dispatch of explanation or justification—nothing which could be produced to satisfy a noisy and captious Commons.

It was at this point that the news of the Canadian federation proposal arrived in England. To the Colonial Office officials and to Sir Edward Bulwer Lytton, both the matter of the Canadian proposal and the manner of its introduction were alike astounding in the highest degree. The Canadian legislature had been notified of the new plan, not only by Cartier, but also by the Governor himself, who had referred to it in the last paragraph of the speech with which he closed the legislature on August 16. A matter of the utmost magnitude—a truly imperial matter which involved the other colonies and Great Britain—had been brought forward publicly by the Governor "already more than half impressed with the mark of his concurrence";[6] and before he could possibly have received any intimation of approval from the centre of Empire, his Executive Council had calmly proceeded to make arrangements

for the discussion of their daring proposal "just as if the consent
of the Queen and Her Government had been formally and
previously secured". The Colonial Office viewed this casual
conduct with the lifted eyebrows and pursed lips of disapproval.
"The last paragraph of the Governor's speech is, to me, very
startling," wrote Arthur Blackwood, one of the senior clerks;[7]
and Lytton, in his impulsive, theatrical fashion, was, of course,
far more outspoken. "It is absolutely necessary," he raged, "to
administer a reproof to Sir E. Head for his paragraph on Confederation. It has caused the greatest displeasure and I have
been even urged to recall him on account of it."[8] Heroic
action of this kind was clearly not in the tradition of the
Colonial Office; and even if it had been, there were reasons
why such a savage penalty could not possibly be applied to
Head. Herman Merivale, the Permanent Under-Secretary, recalled that Labouchere had "particularly" requested the Governor to take the matter of union in hand:[9] and Carnarvon
subsequently discovered that Lord Stanley's private letters also
gave undeniable support to the policy which Head had tried
to pursue.[10] Moreover, there was the undoubted fact that the
question of federal union had already been raised in the
Canadian legislature by Galt. Lord Carnarvon concluded that
Head's proposal to discuss the matter with the British government
and the other Colonies was not "entirely gratuitous". Still, the
Governor had been unwise. He had taken far too much for
granted. He had assumed that Lytton would concur in the
policies of his predecessors—an assumption which, in the circumstances, Lytton found peculiarly irritating. Yet the Colonial
Secretary's first spasm of annoyance had spent itself. He admitted that his views had been "modified".[11] He administered
a rather avuncular lecture to Head on the subject of private
correspondence and official dispatches. He reminded the Governor that the question of federation involved all the British
North American governments and that it therefore properly
belonged "to the executive authority of the Empire, and not
that of any separate province, to initiate".[12] And there, for the
moment, the matter rested.

Macdonald, of course, saw all public dispatches from the

Colonial Office. He was probably made aware of the gist of the private letters of each Colonial Secretary as well. And he and Head tried to divine what lay behind the carefully guarded sentences of these communications. The Colonial Office had criticized Canadian procedure; it had not touched principle. But the two were not entirely separable, and even before the delegation sailed for England in the early part of October, Macdonald may have begun to suspect that the federation proposal would not receive any very enthusiastic support from the London officials. Cartier, Ross, and Galt soon proved the truth of this surmise. Outwardly their reception was a flatteringly attentive one. They had an audience of the Queen. Lytton entertained them at Knebworth, and Carnarvon at Highclere Castle; but this agreeable procession of dinners and week-ends could not disguise the continuance of delay, nor quell the suspicion that delay was at least partly caused by uncertainty and doubt. In fact, the Colonial Office officials were in no position to be very enthusiastic about the Canadian proposal. They did not dare to commit the British government without some indication of a favourable response from all, or most, of the other British North American provinces; and the replies from the other British North American provinces, tepid and non-committal in character, did not begin to come in until the New Year. The only really prompt response came from New Brunswick. A highly negative and inconclusive document, it intimated that New Brunswick would like to consider a legislative, as well as a federative, union;[18] and it was followed, after only a brief interval, by a long argumentative dispatch in which Manners Sutton, New Brunswick's Lieutenant-Governor, attacked the Canadian proposal with great vigour and expatiated upon the advantages of yet a third type of union—a legislative union of the Maritime Provinces alone.[14]

In the most natural fashion, therefore, the Colonial Office was confirmed in its original suspicion that the federation scheme had been conceived in parochial selfishness, with the sole purpose of solving the peculiar difficulties of the Province of Canada, and in complete disregard of the interests and requirements of all the rest of British North America. From the beginning the London officials had been rather sharply critical of federal union. "In Canada, I suspect," wrote Herman Merivale, "it is chiefly popular with politicians, not with the community, and rather as a mode of getting out of the inextricable scrape in which they seem involved by the present union."[15] By the time T. F. Elliot drew up his lengthy memorandum on the subject for the consideration of the Cabinet, the Canadian scheme had come to be regarded unsympathetically as a gratuitous and barefaced attempt to drag the other colonies into the inextricable mess of Canadian politics.[16] Federal union had not been asked for by any other British North American government: it was not an answer to any really British North American problem. It was a purely Canadian remedy for a purely Canadian difficulty. Yet not even the Canadians appeared to agree upon its virtues: and certainly the Reformers had not hastened to embrace the new scheme in preference to that of Rep. by Pop. "At this moment," Lytton summed up, "Federation is really a question raised for the convenience of the present Canadian administration, and upon which the formidable Opposition, headed by Mr. Brown, have not decidedly committed their policy. An imperial interest of the utmost magnitude is, in short, in the crude state of a party question, embittered and obscured by fierce party passions. If the British Government were to take a pronounced course either way, it would thus appear to side with one party, be exposed to the assault of the other, and by participating in the contests of rival politicians, it would lose the character of a calm and impartial arbiter . . . "[17] At all costs, England must keep the "character of a calm and impartial arbiter"—an arbiter not only between Canadian parties, but also among the governments of the British North American provinces. "We think we should be wanting in proper consideration for those governments," Lytton wrote in a final rejection of the Canadian proposal, "if we were to authorize without any previous knowledge of their views, a meeting of delegates from the Executive Councils, and thus to commit them to a preliminary step towards the settlement of a momentous question, of which they have not yet signified their assent to the principle."[18] This dispatch, dated November 26, was given to Galt, who had waited in London to receive it;[19] and by the middle of December Macdonald and his colleagues had been made aware of the fate of their scheme. A meeting to discuss federal union could not be held without imperial authorization; and imperial authorization would not be given unless the colonies involved in the project had at least signified their willingness to discuss it. The Canadian proposal had not in the least been rejected by the imperial authorities; it had been temporarily postponed out of consideration for the other provinces. It could be taken up again. But the omens, so far, were not very favourable.

II

Yet, in the autumn and winter of 1858-59, Macdonald still confidently carried the ball which he had caught so unexpectedly in the political scrum of the previous summer. His audacity and cleverness seemed to have been rewarded rather than punished. It was true his government had received a check; but the check might be no more than temporary, and, in other and equally important respects, he had emerged triumphantly from the difficulties which had threatened him at first. Lytton and some of the Colonial Office officials had originally questioned the "contrivance" of the "double shuffle": George Brown and the *Globe* had denounced its flagrant illegality and hideous moral turpitude. The Reformers apparently believed that Providence would not permit such villainy to go unpunished. The courts, if appealed to, would surely deal in an exemplary fashion with this perjured and profligate government! Accordingly, three test legal actions were begun that autumn against Macdonald, Vankoughnet and Sidney Smith. The *Globe* invariably referred to them with awful solemnity as the "State Trials"; and the first, which concerned Macdonald, opened at Toronto on November 19, before Chief Justice Draper and Justice Richards.[20] John Hillyard Cameron headed the battery of lawyers who acted for Macdonald: and Cameron, in a speech which the *Globe* denounced as all too speciously fluent, approached the question from a severely legal point of view. "They had not to discuss here, as if the question was being debated in either branch of the legislature," he pointed out, "what would be the constitutional effect of the proceedings complained of. . . . Whatever they might desire as politicians, they could not as lawyers take any other view than the statute pointed out."[21] And the statute—the seventh clause of the Independence of Parliament Act (20 Vic. cap. 22)—pointed unmistakably and emphatically in Macdonald's direction.

Macdonald waited a month, not very uneasily in all likelihood, for his vindication. On December 18, when the judges' decision was read, Draper seemed to have very little difficulty in giving judgment for the defendant. The state of the facts, he thought, came expressly within the words of the seventh clause; and the only question in his mind was whether the section permitted more than one resignation and more than one appointment to a different office. If the court were at liberty to assume that the power to change offices frequently was a beneficial power tending to the good of the public service, then there would be no difficulty in construing the section so as to give the necessary permission. "I do not feel warranted in making that assumption," Draper continued smoothly, "but I am just as little warranted in making a contrary one; so that, after all, the construction must be made on the words used . . . and so taken, they are, in my humble judgment, so large as not to be confined to one change only, and therefore I feel bound to hold that the legislature meant to authorize more than one change, and, as a consequence, I am of opinion that the defendant should have the judgment. . . ."[22] On Monday, December 20, when this decision was made public, the *Globe* excelled even itself in vituperation. Up to that point Brown had maintained at least some slight check upon the violence of his newspaper. He may have indulged real hopes in the "State Trials": he knew at least that he must pretend to reserve judgment until they were finished. But now the last need for reserve had been swept away. All the accumulating, fermenting feelings of humiliation, disgust, anger and disillusionment suddenly vented themselves upon the "double shuffle" and its perpetrators. The deed itself was "the most shameful example of executive licentiousness ever perpetrated in Canada". It was a fraud to which the criminal ministers and the Governor-General were both parties: and it had been judicially condoned by a judge who had been "the pliant tool of Lord Metcalfe" and the "political father" of John A. Macdonald! "Mr. Draper," the *Globe* concluded savagely, "has mistaken the place and the age. He would have made a very fair Jeffreys, and might have served even for the Bloody Assize, but neither the governor who plays the part of James, nor his servile judge, are fit to breathe the free atmosphere of Canada in the middle of the nineteenth century."[23]

Macdonald may have noticed something else—something much more significant than these wild vituperative exaggerations. Brown was no longer content to criticize the "double shuffle" itself and its authors; he had begun to attack the constitution, the system of parliamentary government which apparently permitted such acts of ministerial knavery. "The unwritten constitution may do in England where rulers are scrupulous and careful," the *Globe* conceded, "but it is different here; and the decision in these cases will materially strengthen the hands of those who demand a written constitution, after the American model. With his unwarrantable exercise of the prerogative, and his tampering with the usages of the constitution, Sir Edmund has done more to Americanize our institutions than all other influences combined, although they have been both numerous and powerful. His reckless rule has weakened the confidence of even the most devoted advocates of the British model."[24] Brown himself, the old critic of the early "Yankee Grits", the old opponent of American "elective institutions", had certainly been one of the most sincere supporters of the British parliamentary system. And was not his strange mood of disillusionment in responsible government a most revealing sign of the state of moral collapse to which his party had been brought? The Reformers had tasted the extreme humiliation of defeat; and now, confirmed in their incapacity to win the game, they sought in desperation to change the rules. The ministerial crisis of 1858 was certainly having con-sequences—consequences perhaps more serious for the van-quished than for the victors. The Reformers had come perilously close to apostasy. Were they about to repeat, in another form, the Annexation Manifesto of 1849?

Macdonald could feel heartened. There had been a most laughable miscarriage of that frightful retribution which the Grits had been promising ever since the ministerial crisis. He was far from being out of the woods, but he kept to his chosen path with the serene stubbornness which was characteristic of him. In the summer his government had been overthrown and his party rocked to its foundations; and, in the months that followed, Liberal-Conservatism seemed for a while to meet nothing but obstacles and receive nothing but blows. But Macdonald was not much inclined to alter his direction. Others were ready for changes—were indeed anxious to alter the party's policy with respect to such notoriously dangerous matters as the seat-of-government question. "Oh that her Majesty had refused the reference," lamented John Rose to Edward Ellice, "or been advised to choose some other spot than the Romantic Hill we looked on!"[25] Rose himself was prepared to "modify" his opinions; and Sicotte, the Reformer who next to Cartier was the most important French Canadian in the Cabinet, insisted that the government should give up all attempts to defend the Queen's choice. The Attorney-General West opposed an urbane but flat refusal. " . . . Macdonald and those who had brought about the reference could not with honour recede," John Rose explained, "and the alternative offered was between breaking up the Government at *once* and without meeting the House, or taking the course we have."[26] Macdonald, who in any case was ready enough to escape from the tiresome burden of parliamentary life, was evidently quite prepared to resign upon the issue; but in the end it was Sicotte, the Commissioner of Public Works, and not the Attorney-General West who left the government.[27] The government pushed on sturdily. The address in reply to the speech from the throne, defiantly recog-nizing the Queen's choice and thus reversing the vote of the previous summer, was passed unaltered. "Cartier deserves great credit," Head explained to Herman Merivale; "he has parried abuse and odium from his civil supporters most manfully."[28] The Macdonald-Cartier combination was an efficient machine which was now reaching the apex of its smooth perfection.

Yet, if the Cabinet had at least held its ground on the seat-of-government issue, it had made no spectacular gains with the projects which had been taken up in the previous autumn. Cartier, Ross, and Galt had gone to London empowered to discuss two major schemes with the Colonial Office: one was the federation proposal and the other was a revised version of that favourite British North American plan—the plan of securing imperial support for the Intercolonial Railway. Lytton himself was ready to give some imperial aid to the railway. "I am of opinion," he told Disraeli, "that if we can do something we ought. . . ."[29] But a Conservative Chancellor of the Exchequer was just as little inclined as a Liberal Chancellor of the Exchequer to divert imperial funds to a public work which would always be physically remote and which would only occasionally become politically important. Lytton talked the matter over sympathetically with Galt, "who begged me for the sake of the imperial interest generally not to shut the door for ever in their faces";[30] and when the final negative reply came to be written, he composed it carefully "with a desire to soften as much as possible our refusal". The dispatch did handsomely admit the imperial interests and advantages of the Intercolonial Railway. "But still," it concluded, "the national expenditure must be regulated by the national resources."[31] There was no money for the Intercolonial Railway; and that was that. Cartier, Ross, and Galt had failed just as badly in 1858 as Macdonald and Rose had failed in 1857.

But, on the whole, the Confederation scheme was an even greater embarrassment to Macdonald. The Intercolonial Railway was a veteran, an almost tiresomely familiar, project, in which failure, by becoming habitual, had ceased to have much political significance. But Confederation was a brand new solution for an old and anguishing Canadian difficulty—a difficulty for which rival and much advertised remedies were constantly being pushed upon the market. The new remedy had certainly not been greeted with wild enthusiasm. But its virtues had not been very fully explained to its intended consumers either at home or in the Maritime Provinces; and obviously the first task of the Canadian government, which at this time had no thought of giving up its federal scheme, was to explain and justify the proposal to the phlegmatic and unresponsive Maritimers. In January, 1859, when the Canadian Council took the matter up in earnest, it was decided to acquaint the governments of the Lower Provinces fully with all the steps which had been taken in the matter, and, in particular, to send them copies of the elaborate letters which Cartier, Ross, and Galt had given to Lytton in the previous October.[32] The Maritime Provinces might respond in the end. But it would take time. Meanwhile, the Canadian opposition, sniffing eagerly for anything that might be used to disparage the government's new proposal, must be answered and silenced in some fashion. Dorion asked flatly whether the negotiations for federal union had been broken off. Macdonald denied this. The co-operation of the other colonies had been invited by Canada: but they were apparently not yet ready to take a decided course in the matter, and until all, or most, of them had accepted the invitation, further real progress must be delayed. The imperial government had certainly not rejected the proposal or stopped the negotiations. "But as the interests of all the British North American Provinces," Macdonald concluded, "as well as those of Canada and the mother country were involved, the answer of the Imperial Government was simply that until they were approached on the subject by the other colonies, they could give no answer in the matter."[33]

In the matter of federal union, Macdonald was compelled by circumstances to mark time: in the affair of the Hudson's Bay Company's territories he moved forward slowly by deliberate preference. Here, once again, he felt under no compulsion to change the policy of his government: it was exactly the same policy as before, cautious, realistic if not unambitious in character and completely unspectacular in results. It might, of course, have been very different if the project of federal union had made rapid progress, for federation could have provided the strength necessary for a more rapid westward expansion. Head had pointed out in one of his efforts to gain support for his union scheme that the new western colony or colonies might be "aggregated" to the federation: " . . . and it is, perhaps," he went on, "one great recommendation of this scheme at the present moment that it will thus admit of extending westward the body of our North American colonies."[84] New colonies could be "aggregated" to a federal union more easily and with less danger to Canada East than new territory could be "aggregated" to the existing Province of Canada. Cartier, as well as Macdonald, had no doubt appreciated this point; but it was useless to urge it, for the union scheme had come to a dead stop, and the Cabinet must think of some other way to still the vast hubbub over the Hudson's Bay Company. The Canadian newspapers were crowded with speculations about a vast array of romantic Western enterprises—settlements, colonies, staple trades, roads, telegraphs, and railways. But it was not merely the acquisitive clamour of the Reform press which embarrassed the Canadian government; it was also the somewhat irritated persistence of the Colonial Office. Time was getting on. The House of Commons committee on the Hudson's Bay Company had long ago finished its labours: the Company's licence for exclusive trade came to an end in 1859, and some legislation respecting the matter would have to be presented in the approaching session of the imperial Parliament. Yet Canada delayed, equivocated and remained unaccountably silent. It was the source of one of Lytton's chief irritations with Head. What did the province really want? She had seen fit vaguely to question the validity of the charter and had voiced certain equally vague claims to the territory over which it ran. Was she ready to test the charter by a reference to a judicial tribunal? Would she be prepared to acquire—which meant, of course, to govern and colonize—two new provinces on the Red and Saskatchewan Rivers?[35]

These, as Macdonald knew very well, were highly inconvenient questions. They had to be answered; and they could not be answered by aggressive yet academic claims for territory and grandiose yet unsubstantial projects for railways. The fact was, as Head explained to Lytton, there was a general belief that "the reversion of the fee of the colony ought to be vested in Canada". Ultimately the property must be hers. But not now. Now the inheritance would be too dangerous and too costly to be borne. It was not only, and certainly not mainly, a question of the expense of civil government. It was the inescapable consideration of defence—of protection against both Americans and Indians—which intimidated the Canadian government, not so much because of its cost as because of its dangers for a small and dependent power. "Canada," Head explained, "will not readily undertake the government of the Red River settlement as a charge on her own revenues. She will assert her claims and rights in the abstract, but she will object either to compensate the company, or pay continuously for the maintenance of military protection or civil government."[36] She objected to all these things, which were admittedly costly and might be very dangerous: she even hesitated to accept the rather inconsiderable undertaking of testing the Hudson's Bay Company's charter. Lytton had pressed this procedure upon the colony as an indispensable first step in assessing the value of the Hudson's Bay Company's titles. Canada agreed that, on the whole, the step was a sensible one, and ought to be made —by the imperial government. If the charter were proved invalid, then the lands which it covered would simply revert to the imperial Crown: if the validity of the charter were confirmed then the liquidation of the Hudson's Bay Company's rights was a task which only the imperial government could undertake.[37] From any and every point of view, the whole business was clearly an imperial affair, and even if the lands came to Canada gratis, Macdonald insisted that at the moment she would accept them at her peril. "If we obtained that territory," he told the House during the debate in April, "we would have no proper means of supervision over it—people would rush into it who from want of restraint would grow up into anything but a creditable population."[38]

All these obstacles and inhibitions had put the Conservative government in an inconclusive and uninspiring position. Macdonald knew it: but he had already begun to suspect that the state of the Reform party was even more miserable—that it had been dealt a far more shattering blow by the ministerial crisis of the previous summer. Macdonald had found a narrow, devious path through the blind thickets in which his party had been trapped. He had led his followers into the open. And was it not time now, and legitimately possible, for him to retire, as he had so often hoped to do during the previous twelve months? Surely the moment was appropriate? Isabella's death had altered things domestic in much the same drastic way as the ministerial crisis had changed affairs political. He was living in lodgings in Toronto and his nine-year-old son, Hugh, remained of course in Kingston with his grandmother and his aunts, Margaret and Louisa. Hugh had lost his mother and, as things stood, he might almost have lost his father as well. The three women relatives were all very well and all very necessary; but they could hardly take a male parent's place, even if they had been free, which they were not, from other preoccupations. Margaret, Mrs. Williamson, had of course her own separate domestic establishment. Old Mrs. Macdonald, who had now survived her husband Hugh for nearly twenty years, was shattered occasionally by apoplectic strokes;[39] and Louisa, tall, raw-boned and devoted, was obliged to look after her for lengthy periods. Obviously Hugh needed a father. And obviously also the father needed more leisure, and less annoyance, and more income. In September 1859 he would have completed five years of political power; and, at about the same time, the legislature and government were to move back to Quebec for a last period before the final transfer to Ottawa. Did he want to go to Quebec and start the whole business over again? Could he even contemplate settling down permanently with the government in Ottawa? In Kingston he was still the head of a prosperous and respected legal firm (Macdonald, Macdonnell, Draper and Wilkinson) which occupied a handsome apartment, lit by eight windows, in a pleasant little Renaissance-style building, which looked across Clarence Street to the post office.[40] Why not move back to Kingston, to his son, to his family and his practice, and lead the easy, comfortable life to which he had always meant to return?

And yet—could he really go? In the end all moments seemed inappropriate for a break so conclusive and so final. There was the province, and the Liberal-Conservative party, and his own small special band of Conservative followers who, since Cayley's departure, looked up to him as their only remaining leader, and who begged him not to desert them at this stage.[41] There was, despite all the sudden irritations and nagging annoyances, his own unquenchable interest in the game itself, in its puzzles and problems and solutions, in its devices and traps and surprises. And even if retirement in a session or two were certain, there was always the feeling, natural in a born and victorious commander, that only one more campaign was necessary to convert the defeat of the enemy into a complete annihilation. The truth was that in the session of 1859 the Reformers were a divided, confused, and irritable lot. Their brief two days' association in office seemed to have bred more animosities among them than a lifetime's partnership could possibly have done. It was their tragedy that in two days of power they had been able to sketch, but not to complete, a programme; and from this abortive reconciliation of their ideas came serious trouble. If they remained studiously vague about what they had intended to do in such vital matters as Separate Schools and electoral reform, they invited Conservative ridicule; and if, on the other hand, they made the fatal mistake of trying to be precise, they instantly revealed differences of opinion among themselves which quickly led to charges of deception and bad faith. Wiser heads such as Dorion and John Sandfield Macdonald might have steered safely clear of trouble; but between Brown and his late Lower Canadian colleagues there soon developed the most appalling disputes. Thibaudeau, who had been President of the Council in the Reform administration, announced, early in the session of 1859, that he would never have consented to accept office if he had not been perfectly assured that the Brown-Dorion government was prepared to do full justice to the Roman Catholics of Canada West.[42] Laberge, the two-day Solicitor-General East, informed the House that, according to his understanding, the Reform administration had intended to liquidate the remaining seigniorial obligations in

Canada East with moneys from the consolidated revenue of the province, and that therefore Brown's claim that his government would have relieved the *censitaires* "without taking money out of the pockets of the people of Upper Canada" was quite simply false.[43] All these arguments, contradictions and denials, all these miserable disputes over the dead body of a failure, were a pure gift to Macdonald. Almost every speech at the beginning of the session included a satirical passage at the expense of "His Excellency's most ephemeral administration". "They had intended to 'grapple' or rather to grope—and that in the dark too—" for a policy, he told the House, paraphrasing one of Brown's rather laboured explanations.[44] "There never was such an exhibition of political profligacy as in the formation of the Brown-Dorion Government."

No, he would stay as the leader of the Liberal-Conservatives for a while longer. He would stay for at least a session and complete the ruin of the great Liberal party which Brown had been labouring to create ever since the autumn of 1857. Already it was becoming apparent that the terrible fiasco of the two-day government had not been an ordinary unfortunate episode in the life of Brown or in the history of Grittism. It was much more: it was that kind of demoralizing crisis which can change a man's political philosophy or alter the whole direction of a party. Brown had been put into an abject position, and his deep personal humiliation had come at a time when he was physically and mentally least capable of sustaining it. For almost the first time in his life, the clumsy, impetuous giant was ill: and for the first time certainly in a career of unbroken commercial success in Canada, the robust publisher and promoter had become the prey of real financial worries. His prodigal energy had led him to take on too much. He had not been content to remain the proprietor of what was probably the most influential, and certainly the most popular, newspaper in Canada West: he had hoped to become an experimental land owner, a commercial farmer on the grand scale; and at Bothwell, in Kent county,[45] he had purchased very extensive holdings of land. For a few years, the "Laird of Bothwell" became a territorial magnate of some importance.

Then came the depression and the terrible fall in the prices of raw materials. The commercial collapse did not affect Brown so quickly and dramatically as it had John Hillyard Cameron; but, as 1858 dragged itself to an end, and a new and dismally unprosperous year began, he began to feel acutely embarrassed. The depression of 1857-58 had already virtually removed one rival from Macdonald's path. Was it about to remove his other rival and his greatest opponent?

Macdonald watched Brown's increasingly erratic course with curious interest. Surely the unhappy, frustrated publisher was being driven into ways of the most preposterous extremism! The reckless criticisms with which the *Globe* had greeted Draper's decisions in the "State Trials" were evidently not the products of a temporary outburst of temper; they were, it seemed, merely the first signs of a profound and permanent disillusionment with the existing political system. Beaten, humiliated, quarrelling with his friends and supporters, yet no doubt bitterly accusing himself, Brown must have felt disgust with Canadian parliamentarism rise in him like nausea. And he was at once too physically ill, too intellectually confused, too haunted by nervous worries, to direct his sense of deception into a critical and constructive assessment of the Canadian political system. He left that to others. He left it in particular to George Sheppard, a radical journalist from England, who now began to assume a sinister importance in the *Globe*'s editorial staff and who was the principal author of a long series of editorials advocating "organic changes" in the system of responsible government and parliamentary institutions.[46] Rep. by Pop., the *Globe*'s astonished readers were now told, was not enough! There must be a written constitution, a clear separation of executive and legislative functions, and definite checks upon the power of the provincial administration. There must even be, the *Globe* finally announced, a dissolution of the Canadian union! The Conservatives gasped with delight and surprise as they beheld Brown, like a huge, bewildered, wayward child, stumbling down the path which led past the dubious structure of "elective institutions" to the congressional system at Washington. "He has made the grand mistake," Spence wrote to Macdonald, "of assailing the system as well as the men working it out—charging as it were the hands with ineptitude and treachery and at the same time declaring that the ship's bottom was so rotten she must founder. . . . In no quarter, to any extent worth speaking of, will annexation leanings have any support—and changes of any kind will be looked upon with great distrust inasmuch as failure in constitutional tinkering might ultimately bring about such a result."[47]

Such a moment, when Brown seemed to be rushing precipitately towards political extinction and when all the signs pointed towards a commercial recovery, was no time to think about resigning. "Everything, my dear Macdonald," Spence wrote beseechingly, "looks well, and now, my old fellow, after five years' service, don't give up the ship when you and your colleagues are just nearing Port." No, he would stay a while longer, if only to see what would happen and to extract all possible advantage from it. Parliament came to the end of its session on a fine day early in May. The last prorogation that Toronto was to witness in a long time passed off to the accompaniment of royal salutes, crashing band music, and a flutter of gay spring dresses; and down in the Crown Law Office on King Street they began soberly to pack up in preparation for the move to Quebec. It could hardly be said that the summer was uneventful, for early in July Macdonald nearly lost his life when the *Ploughboy*, a steamer carrying him and a large party on an excursion to Sault Ste. Marie, drifted helplessly before a gale and was nearly lost upon the rocks.[48] In August, he got what he had wanted for some years now, a little sea-bathing off the coast of Maine; but he was called back to Toronto in the middle of the holiday and the imminent move to Quebec prevented him from returning and accompanying Hugh and his sister, Louisa, on their return journey to Kingston.[49] All that spring and summer, he—like every other Conservative—had been watching the columns of the *Globe* with unwearied attention. For a while everything seemed to go well. For a while the constitutional indiscretions of the newspaper reached and maintained a climax of awful impropriety.

And then something seemed to happen. It was as if Brown

had been suddenly awakened out of his mournful and bewildered apathy to realize with astonishment the commitments
that had already been made for him and for his party. From
somewhere, quietly but forcefully, the brakes were applied.
The *Globe*'s headlong career towards constitutional reform
perceptibly slackened. The articles in favour of "organic
changes" were fewer and more closely hedged by conditions
and ambiguities. Brown, a sobered and repentant Brown, was
plainly in control of his journal once again; and plainly also
he was determined to make another great effort to reorganize
the party which had been so morally shattered by the ministerial
crisis of 1858, and which—in part because of his own weariness
and preoccupation—had fallen into the control of Radicals and
Republicans. The great Reform convention of January, 1857,
had been the prelude to the triumphant Grit success in the
general election of the following December; and now another
great Reform convention would repair the ravages of the past
twelve months and prepare the way for the even greater electoral
triumph of the future. That autumn, on November 9, nearly
six hundred Reformers, coming from all parts of Canada West
—except, significantly, its eastern portion, where John Sandfield
Macdonald kept control—descended upon Toronto for a three-
day convention.[50] Macdonald, seizing upon what seemed to him
to be the essential point, tried to discover whether there had
been any incipient revolt against Brown. But Lindsey, of the
Toronto *Leader*, to whom he appealed for information, had to
confess that, so far as he could discover, the leadership had never
been mentioned, even in secret session. "Whatever was thought,"
he wrote, "nothing appears to have been said."[51] It was the
same all the way through the convention. The reawakened Brown
and his powerful directorate of Toronto Reform politicians
steered the convention smoothly and dexterously back towards
a moderate liberalism.[52] The Radicals and extremists—bred of
the crisis of 1858-59—were silenced or defeated. "Organic
Changes" were tacitly dismissed, and although Rep. by Pop.,
the sovereign remedy of 1857, was admitted now to be insufficient, its virtual successor, dissolution of union, was repudiated even more firmly. The convention decided upon a

federal union of Canada East and Canada West, with "some joint authority" connecting them, yet leaving each free for most purposes to go its own way. Alongside the Conservative plan—federation of British North America—there had now been competitively placed the Reform scheme for the federal union of Canada East and Canada West. Was the federal union of the Canadas a policy upon which the shattered forces of the Grit party could effectively reunite and by which they could win the next general election?

III

As the testing time—the session of 1860—rapidly approached, Macdonald may very well have had some apprehension. Once again he had comparatively little to offer parliament—at least in respect of the major problem of the constitution of the Canadas. Time had gone on. The Conservatives seemed to be making very little progress with their federal scheme. And, in the meantime, the project of the legislative union of the Maritime Provinces—a scheme which might be regarded either as the complement or the rival of the federal union of British North America—was being vigorously advocated once more. Manners Sutton, the Lieutenant-Governor of New Brunswick, had for some time been pressing it upon the attention of the Colonial Office; and even Head, who had, of course, supported both schemes, giving first one and then the other a slight emphasis of preference, now indicated that he thought the time was favourable for the undertaking of the smaller union.[53] With all these small regional plans—the federal union of the Canadas, the legislative union of the Maritime Provinces—in the air about them, the Canadian Conservatives may have felt somewhat intimidated about their own ambitious project. But they persevered for a while longer. Galt, the Minister of Finance (the old title of Inspector-General had been abandoned) had been perhaps the most ardent supporter of federation in the Cabinet; and since, in the autumn of 1859, he planned to visit the United Kingdom on the financial affairs

of the province, the ministry passed an order-in-council authorizing him to put himself in communication with the Colonial
Secretary "with the view of ascertaining what action has been
taken by the Imperial Government thereon, and what communications, if any, have passed between them and the other
Provinces on the subject. . . . "[54] The Canadians were anxious,
in the first place, to clear up a serious misconception which,
they suspected, had probably been created by Lytton's dispatch
of November 26, 1858, and which was no doubt having a most
unfortunate effect on the governments of the Maritime Provinces. Lytton's dispatch, Galt suggested, in a letter to the Duke
of Newcastle, the new Liberal Colonial Secretary, "has been
somewhat misunderstood as indicating a disinclination to entertain the question while it was, we believe, only intended to
express the unwillingness of the imperial authorities to initiate
discussion of the subject which it was conceived more properly
should proceed from the Colonies themselves."[55] This, Galt
intimated pleasantly, was a very acceptable attitude; it was a
gratifying further proof of the imperial government's firm adher-
ence to the well-tried colonial policy of self-government. Nevertheless, it had had somewhat unfortunate results. ". . . There
is no doubt that the dispatch has been misunderstood and an
objection to the mode of action has been construed into a
condemnation of the policy." Would the Colonial Secretary be
good enough to remove all doubt about Lytton's dispatch, and,
if the other provinces agreed to the proposal, would he authorize
a meeting of delegates to discuss British North American
union?

Faced with repeated and importunate demands to clarify the
imperial views and to support this or that scheme, the Duke
of Newcastle responded in a brief but classic explanation of
colonial policy. He had his own private ideas about the stages
through which British North American reorganization ought
to proceed; but he knew also—and it was the first principle of
his policy—that the imperial government must never be betrayed
into the premature expression of a preference for any particular
kind of union. "Her Majesty's Government," he informed all
the colonial governors in a circular dispatch, "see no reason to

depart from the general line of policy which they have hitherto pronounced it their intention to adopt if the occasion should arise. They do not think it their duty to initiate any movement towards such union, but they have no wish to impede any well considered scheme which may have the concurrence of the people of the provinces through their legislatures, assuming of course that it does not interfere with imperial interests."[56] It was a free field for all kinds of advocates and all types of union; and the only condition was that the governors, before authorizing delegates to a conference, must beforehand communicate with the Colonial Secretary. As late as the middle of February, 1860, the Canadian government was still interested in its scheme and disposed to press it.[57] But after that it was quietly laid on one side. Galt, in London, had probably been given the gist of the lukewarm replies of the other British North American provinces; and if the Canadian government had at first been eager to compete with their general federation scheme against the regional plan of the Grits, they soon began to see the dangers of such obvious competition. The two plans, and the reasons which justified each, could all too easily be confused and confounded in the public mind; and at the moment the strategy of the Conservatives was to isolate the Reformers' proposal as something scandalous, and to damn it as a device for breaking up the existing union. "It was true," Macdonald declared during the session of 1860, "that the government had proposed a Confederation of the British North American provinces—that they would like to take into it the Red River on the one side, and the Lower Provinces on the other, so as to make a great empire, stronger by wealth, position, and general standing than the parts could be while divided. But they were not prepared to admit that there were any internal grievances which could not be constitutionally remedied—cured without any alteration in the constitution whatever."[58]

Meanwhile, and some time before these words were uttered, Macdonald had begun to realize that it was probably not going to be very difficult to discredit and defeat the new Reform scheme. The Toronto convention had adopted it by a resounding majority; but it now began to appear that the Toronto

convention and the Reform caucus at Quebec were two quite
different things, with two quite different ideas of the wisdom
of a federal union of the Canadas. Back in the autumn there
had been most delicious rumours of the grumbling resentment
in Grit ranks at the dictatorial fashion in which Brown and
the Toronto gang had managed the Reform convention; and
the session had barely started when it began to be noised
abroad that the Reformers were quarrelling furiously—and
over the federal union of the Canadas, the very policy which
was supposed to have reunited their divided ranks! Foley's
no-confidence motion, which was intended to censure the government for its persistent minority rule in Canada West, gave
Macdonald an opportunity to exploit these rumours, to isolate
Brown as a brilliant but hated ruler, and to taunt his followers
with their abject submission to his rule. "No one knew better
than he (Mr. Brown) himself," he told the House, "that his
party was at the present moment breaking up. No one knew
better than he that the honourable members around and beside
him, while they feared him, did not love him. No one knew
better than he that they would like to remove him but dare
not face him. . . . By his superior will, by his superior ability,
he wielded them as he wished; he held the lash over them. . . .
The honourable gentleman was the Louis Napoleon of his
party, but he had an Austrian army. . . . There was the Italian
portion of it, and there was the Hungarian portion of it . . .
and horse, foot and artillery would find a common Solferino
in the next election."[59]

Macdonald could be embarrassingly contemporary in his
topical allusions, and the "Austrian army" speech was a delight
to his followers. ". . . you seem to have been in full force,"
wrote John Ross delightedly from London, "hitting out right
and left in splendid style."[60] Macdonald was enjoying himself
immensely. "We are having great fun just now with the
opposition," he wrote to Charles Lindsey of the Toronto Leader.
"They are quarrelling like fury and do not affect concealment.
I pat Brown on the back occasionally by calling him the only
man in the party worth *tuppence* and then I please his recal-
citrant followers by pitching into him as a dishonest and in-

consistent politician. In other words, I call him a 'knave' and them 'fools', an expression of which you will recognize the justice."[61] It was good fun and it was excellent value politically, for the Grits, whose private wrangles in caucus had now become notorious, were perilously close to the point of an open row in the House. On Monday, April 23, the explosion finally came.[62] For weeks Brown had been vainly attempting to speak to his constitutional resolutions—his version of the programme of the Toronto convention; and repeatedly, or so it seemed to him, his notice of motion had been postponed. On April 23, Cartier moved its postponement once again; and to Brown's amazement and indignation, Foley, the Grit member for Waterloo, arose to support the Conservative leader! It was the one thing needed to provoke Brown to another tirade of his scandalous accusations. Foley was no true Reformer. He had not given his leader proper support. He had a secret understanding with the members of the government! Foley replied hotly. There were excited replies and still more excited rejoinders; and it ended by Foley declaring furiously that he had been a Reformer long before Brown had even had a seat in the House, and that he did not doubt he would continue to be a Reformer long after Brown had ceased to vex and distress the party. At this felicitous point, Macdonald rose to intervene. The Reform party, he announced pleasantly, was in fragments: it "amounted to nothing more than a number of atoms accidentally placed together but without any principle of adhesion and indeed without any principle at all".

"You will see," Rose wrote to Edward Ellice, "that there is an open rupture between Brown and his followers—indeed the opposition is now a mere congeries of discordant opinions."[63] The divisions and the quarrelling were bad enough even while the main subject of Reform disagreement was still being postponed; but once Brown's constitutional resolutions began to be debated, the chances of a really serious rupture became much greater. McGee and John Sandfield Macdonald—the first principal Reform leaders to debate the resolutions after Brown had introduced them—showed themselves either unenthusiastic or opposed. But there was worse to come. On May 7, after the

debate had been going on with intervals for a week, Foley got
up to speak. He began by announcing bluntly that he had been
charged with infidelity to his party and with inconsistency in
his attitude to the constitutional resolutions. And he then proceeded to tell a curious story.[64] The whole Reform convention,
he charged, had been run by the Toronto Grits; the Toronto
Grits had packed the all-important resolutions committee and
dominated its proceedings. McDougall, a Toronto man, had
proposed the compromise federal scheme with "some joint authority" connecting the two sections of the province; and Brown,
the head of this small domineering cabal, had insisted, before
he had properly consulted the Reform caucus, on placing his
own version of the convention's resolutions upon the order
paper. Caucus had protested indignantly in a series of meetings;
and finally the public storm had burst. "From that day to
this," Foley concluded sombrely, "the members of the opposition
had never been called together to consult upon any subject."

No more was needed. By the time the session ended the
phrase "joint authority" had degenerated into a rather painful
joke and the Reform party had become a body of men united
chiefly by the emotional warmth of their antagonisms. Macdonald, for all his weariness with politics, must have felt elated.
It was very nearly two years now since the great ministerial
crisis of the summer of 1858; and, to all appearances, the
Liberal-Conservative party was stronger than ever. The long
months of the depression and the short week of political crisis
between July 29 and August 6, 1858, had between them ruined
his principal political rivals and enemies. The desperate efforts
of the Grits to recreate their organization and their programme
had apparently failed. The Reform party was broken in fragments; the depression had ended, and, best of all, the gangling,
growing, ambitious Province of Canada was to be honoured that
very summer by something entirely new in the history of
colonies, by the first of all the royal overseas tours, the visit of
Edward, Prince of Wales, to British North America. A year
before, in the summer of 1859, Henry Smith—son of the ex-
Warden of Kingston penitentiary and Speaker of the Legislative
Assembly—had carried an invitation to Queen Victoria to visit

Canada with her husband, the Prince Consort, and such other members of the Royal Family as might be selected to come. This novel and almost breath-taking request had produced scarcely less remarkable results. It was impossible, the Queen announced, for her to go herself; but she promised that within another year the Prince of Wales would pay Canada a visit. And on July 9, 1860, the Prince, accompanied by the Duke of Newcastle and a little contingent of minor functionaries, boarded the *Hero* at Southampton and set sail for British North America.[65] It was a thrilling but rather frightening thought that in about a month's time he would be actually sailing up the St. Lawrence River!

The excited members of the Canadian government redoubled their efforts; and poor John Rose discovered that there was a multiplicity of unusual tasks attached to the Commissionership of Public Works. "I am again the packhorse in this business," he told Ellice dolefully, "—all the work and arrangements falling to my department. . . ."[66] The drab legislative buildings at Quebec were converted into what the newspapers described rather grandly as a palace, with apartments for the Prince and his suite, a dining-room and a magnificent reception room with a yellow and purple flowered velvet carpet.[67] The Canadian ministers donned the British civil uniform appointed for the principal officers in Colonial governments. It was a handsome costume of dark blue cloth with gold braid, gold facings, a cocked hat and a sword. "A great deal of time," the *Globe* announced ironically, "has been wasted by John A. Macdonald in learning to walk, for the sword suspended to his waist has an awkward knack of getting between his legs, especially after dinner. . . . Galt is the best-looking footman of the whole lot. He advocated knee breeches, it is said, that he might show his fine calves; but John A. opposed the idea with great ferocity."[68] There was no doubt that they were all immensely excited, immensely proud, and more than a little nervous. The royal tour was to be the final authoritative rebuke to the constitutional tinkering of the Grits. It was to be a wreath of honour placed with truly imperial dignity upon the loyal achievements of the Conservative party.

At first all went superbly well. On Friday, August 10, Macdonald along with the Governor and the other members of the
Cabinet arrived at Gaspé harbour on board the Canadian
government steamer, *Queen Victoria*. Head had determined
to greet the Prince like some medieval sheriff, the moment he
entered the territorial limits of the Province of Canada; and he
waited for two days, in a frenzy of apprehension lest the royal
convoy should unhappily get past him and up the St. Lawrence.[69] At length, at 7 o'clock on the evening of Sunday,
just at the climax of a spectacular Canadian sunset, the *Hero*
and her little escort of ships sailed majestically into Gaspé
harbour. The next day, Macdonald and the other Canadian
ministers went on board and were presented. They lunched
and talked with the Prince;[70] and meanwhile the royal fleet
resumed its extremely deliberate way up the River of Canada.
It was Saturday, August 18—a dull, murky day, appallingly hot,
with not a breath of air stirring—when the Prince landed at
Quebec. On the platform were the Canadian ministers, perspiring profusely in their new uniforms, and looking, so the
Globe assured its readers, "as uncomfortable as so many pigs
in armour". Macdonald, no doubt, was nervously agitated as
the crucial moment approached; but he wore his clothes with
something of an air, as even his critics tacitly acknowledged.
"The thin, spare frame of John A. Macdonald was in ceaseless
motion," the *Globe* reported. "He put on a devil-may-care air,
managed to get his cocked hat stuck on one side and elevated
at the front in a most ridiculous fashion."[71] Then came the
procession through the hot streets, and presentations and addresses; and on Tuesday, August, 21—the climax of the royal
visit to Quebec—the Prince held a formal levee in the parliament buildings and knighted Narcisse Belleau, Speaker of
the Legislative Council, and the portly Henry Smith, Speaker
of the Commons. Then the royal party moved westward, in a
stately fashion, to Montreal, Sherbrooke and Ottawa; and, as
the Prince and his suite passed along, the Canadian rivers and
railway lines became avenues of almost uninterrupted jubilation. "Here is the universal programme," declared one newspaper correspondent sourly, "—spruce arches, cannon, procession,

levee, lunch, ball, departure; cheers, crowds, men, women, enthusiasm, militia, Sunday school children, illuminations, fire works, etcetera, etcetera, *ad infinitum*." The imposing Victoria Bridge, spanning the St. Lawrence at Montreal, was officially declared open; the cornerstone of the new parliament buildings at Ottawa was solemnly laid. On Monday, September 3, the royal party, accompanied by Macdonald and a number of the Canadian ministers, proceeded up the Ottawa River by steamer and canoe to Arnprior, drove inland to the village of Almonte and 'at Almonte boarded a special south-bound train on the Brockville and Ottawa Railway. It was dark by the time they reached Brockville. The loyal addresses had to be read with the aid of lamps, and they then drove at a foot's pace through dense crowds down to the St. Lawrence, where the steamer *Kingston* was waiting to receive them. "Our carriages," the Prince reported to his father, "were accompanied by firemen who carried lighted torches, and all the houses were illuminated, and the throng of people following cheering and hallooing gave it a very pretty effect."[7b]

It was superb. The Upper Canadian part of the tour could hardly have opened more auspiciously. Macdonald ought to have been completely satisfied. But he was not. As the train drove through the gathering darkness to Brockville, his worries and fears steadily deepened. All day he had known that at Brockville he would be given a last slim chance of averting what threatened to be a hideous contretemps. For days—ever since their visit to Montreal—he had seen it ominously approaching. He knew that he could not escape being involved. It concerned Kingston, which had been his faithful constituency since he had entered politics. It concerned the Orangemen, who under Gowan's leadership had gradually and largely become the zealous followers of the Conservative party. In Canada, the parades, banners, and insignia of the Orange Order were all perfectly legal; but in the United Kingdom they were not. The Duke of Newcastle, who accepted full responsibility for the actions of his royal charge, decided that the Prince could not be permitted to compromise himself by acknowledging an illegal organization; and he therefore wrote a formal letter

to the Governor, which Head forwarded to the mayors of
Kingston and Toronto, warning all concerned that there must
be no Orange banners or insignia along any route on which
the Prince would pass. Most of the Orangemen, wisely advised
by the new Grand Master, John Hillyard Cameron, grumblingly
accepted this incredible veto. But some did not. And among
these latter—to the discomfiture of Macdonald—were the Kingston Orangemen. A large and important body, nearly all stout
Conservatives, they clamoured so long and so loudly to be
permitted to parade under their Orange arch and in their
Orange costumes that in the end the corporation of Kingston
appointed a special delegation, which was to see the Duke and
beg him to modify his decision. The delegation—the Mayor,
Colonel Strange, Macdonald's old partner, Alexander Campbell,
and two other Kingston worthies—reached Brockville some time
before the Prince and his suite arrived.[74]

   It was eleven o'clock at night before the Duke was free to
see the Kingstonians. They boarded the steamer apprehensively;
Macdonald made the necessary introductions, and for two and
a half hours the fruitless discussion lasted. The Mayor reminded
the Duke that the Orange Order was entirely legal in Canada
and that its members could not be prevented from parading
as they pleased; and Macdonald argued that, since the favours
extended to Roman Catholics during the Prince's tour in
Canada East had been widely publicized, the Protestants of
Canada West would be correspondingly quick to resent a slight
offered to any part of their body.[75] It was all quite useless. The
Duke remained adamant. And so, as it turned out, did the
Orangemen. On the afternoon of Tuesday, September 4, as
the steamer drew close to Kingston harbour, the horrified members of the Prince's suite could plainly perceive an Orange arch,
Orange banners, and a "large concourse" of defiant Orangemen,
"occupying the street in great force so that the Prince could
not enter the Town without passing through the demonstration
they had prepared".[76] The Mayor was hurriedly sent for and
informed that the Orangemen would be given until the following morning to reconsider their scandalous conduct. The
Kingston, with offended dignity, remained all night in the

harbour, in the hope that a new day would bring repentance. But the new day had barely dawned when the incorrigible Orangemen began to reassemble. Once again, clad in their full regalia, they took up a position in the immediate neighbourhood of the landing-place, from which neither threats, remonstrances, nor supplications could move them. The Duke was affable but firm. In such circumstances the Prince could not be permitted to land and pay the town the expected visit. The *Kingston*, which had remained in the harbour for twenty-two embarrassing hours, now steamed away up the lake.

Macdonald was not on board. He had decided to stay with his injured constituents. He had actually abandoned the royal tour in mid-career! The opposition newspapers made the most of this conspicuous and astounding absence. "Where is John A.?" a *Globe* editorial began gaily. And from Toronto, whither the Prince had proceeded, Macdonald's colleagues and friends dispatched puzzled and importunate letters. "Your absence is very much remarked," John Ross wrote, "and I wish you would either come up or write and let us know what you propose to do."⁷⁷ The Governor-General, Philip Vankoughnet reported, felt very keenly about Macdonald's mortification. He had insisted that the decision was not his but the Duke's, and that the Duke would publicly accept full responsibility for it. "I think," he added, "that till the visit is over you should be here."⁷⁸ But it was no use. Macdonald, unmoved and unrepentant, continued to remain in Kingston for a few days more. No doubt he was worried by the political implications of the "Orange affair", but he was also genuinely annoyed that the Prince had been made publicly to disregard the laws of one of his own future dominions. It was not until later, towards the close of the Prince's tour, that he reappeared at a Hamilton celebration in "full fig", the newspapers noted, but "looking very hard".⁷⁹ He had much to think about. The royal tour had been expected to complete and crown the Liberal-Conservative recovery. But had it seriously miscarried? Were the Orangemen alienated? Had Protestant Upper Canada been given one more proof of its belief in the prevalence and power of Roman Catholic influence in Canada? These were serious questions: for within another year a new general election would have to be held.

IV

The more Macdonald and his colleagues considered the matter, the more likely it seemed that the consequences of the "Orange affair" would be deplorable. How rosy political prospects had appeared in the spring of 1860! How seriously they had been altered now! It was irritating to remember that all this had come about as the result of a stupid, meaningless contretemps. It was provoking for Macdonald to realize that his two old rivals, George Brown and John Hillyard Cameron, who, a few months ago, had seemed buried under an avalanche of misfortunes and humiliations, were now up and doing, and, in their different ways, exploiting the Orange affair to his disadvantage. Cameron, as leader of the Order, journeyed to England to present a monster petition, signed supposedly by 100,000 Orangemen, complaining of the Duke of Newcastle's decision and protesting their loyalty to the Crown. Acclaimed once more, brought suddenly back to something like his old prominence, Cameron was virtually leading an anti-ministerial wing of Conservative Orangemen; and George Brown, who had never ceased up to that moment to abuse the Order, now shyly revealed himself and the Grit party as the Orangemen's devoted champions! The part which Macdonald had played in the affair, and the extent to which his government was responsible for its outcome, were misunderstood by his friends and, of course, deliberately misrepresented by his opponents. Alexander Campbell, in one of his characteristically gloomy letters, begged his friend not to entertain the idea of an early dissolution of parliament. "To my mind," he wrote, "there is no room whatever to anticipate a result favourable to the existing government from that step."[80]

Macdonald agreed. Parliament could not be dissolved until much closer to the date of its legal expiration. But there was over a year, if need be, in which to make reparation and preparation: and the first task was obviously to explain his own course and the position of the government in the Orange affair. He decided to undertake something which was new in both his career and Canadian politics generally—a speaking tour. It began at Brantford on Friday, November 9, a few days after a famous and portentous electoral contest had resulted in the return of Abraham Lincoln to the presidency of the United States. November 9 was a dull, inauspicious, autumn day, gloomy with boisterous gales and heavy falls of rain; but at the Kirby House in Brantford nearly three hundred sat down to dinner, prepared to eat their way with pleasant deliberation through half a dozen courses, to drink eight or ten florid toasts, and to listen to nearly as many heavily political speeches.[81] Macdonald began with a long and careful account of the royal visit, of the constitutional conventions governing it, and of the responsibility accepted and exercised by the Duke of Newcastle. It was the most important part of his address; but during the time—literally hours—in which his admiring audience was prepared to listen to him, there was opportunity for a good many other topics. He reviewed the accomplishments of his six-year tenure of power, exposed the laughable absurdity of the very idea of "French Domination", lingered jocosely over the humours of the two-day Brown-Dorion ministry, and ended up with a stirring appeal for the preservation of the union against the machinations of the anti-unionist Grits. It was long after midnight that he got to bed, and next day, as had been promised during the dinner, he stayed at the Brantford hotel to meet a large company of the "intelligent yeomanry" of the country.

It was only the beginning. The success of the Brantford dinner inspired St. Thomas, London and Hamilton to send invitations; then, in a long procession, came Toronto, Guelph, Kingston, Belleville, Caledonia, St. Catharines, Simcoe, and Millbrook. Usually Macdonald was accompanied by some other member, or members, of the Liberal-Conservative government—by J. C. Morrison, Sidney Smith and Philip Vankoughnet; but invariably he was the chief speaker and the principal attraction. Hotel dining-rooms, town halls, mechanics institutes and athenaeums were hung with flags and streamers welcoming "John A." and honouring "the pilot that weathered the storm"; and over the gallery at the St. Lawrence Hall in Toronto, his name shone out in flaming gas jets. Invariably the crowd was stupendous. Such enthusiastic gatherings, according to Conservative newspapers, had never been seen in the history of the town or the county; they overflowed the available rooms and overtaxed the resources of the caterers. "The leading gentlemen of the district, the bone and sinew of the country", were present, 150, 300, 500, 800 strong; and the ladies, lending "a grace and brilliancy to the scene", watched the proceedings demurely from the gallery, or joined the company after the first toast had been given, while the diners, cheering enthusiastically, rose *en masse*, and the band played "Here's a health for all good lasses." Almost always there was a band—and sometimes two, for good measure of fellowship; and when Macdonald entered the room, or when the great moment arrived for him to respond to the toast "to the provincial administration", the big brass throats blared out into "For he's 'a right good fellow" and "See the conquering hero comes". At Simcoe they sang a song composed specially in his honour—a highly laudatory concoction, nine verses long and each verse ending "Nine cheers for Macdonald, hurra!", while at Guelph a Mr. Douglas, sticking firmly to the popular nautical motif, sang an original composition called, "The Pilot that stands by the Helm" in a good bass voice. Then came the speech, which might last for anything up to two hours; and then, when the toasts were all drunk, and the supplementary speeches finished, and the chairman duly thanked for "his able conduct in the chair", the long meeting at length broke up in a happy babel of greetings, introductions, recognitions, jokes and stories. Usually there was a "levee" the following day, if one had not already been held before the dinner, at which Macdonald met "the intelligent gentlemen and yeomen" of the county; and sometimes for hours the long file continued—lawyers, merchants, farmers, young men who were just learning to be fanatical Macdonald followers, and old men who had fought in a dozen political battles and bore the medals of the War of 1812 upon their chests.[82]

The series ended at length with the dinner at Millbrook on December 7. It had been a long affair—twelve meetings and twelve lengthy speeches—but surely it had been worth while.

Public Archives

JOHN A. MACDONALD, 1861

The opposition newspapers tried to make fun of the "lean and hungry" Attorney-General travelling about the country "looking for dinners", but the complete absence of any notices of these dinners in the columns of the opposition newspapers at least suggested a fear that they had been a success. It began to look as if the effort to accumulate a large amount of political capital out of the Orange affair was likely to be a dismal failure; and by the time the legislature assembled again, in March 1861, it had become clear that the Reform party was relapsing back again into its old state of division and weakness. When Mc-Dougall offered an amendment to the address, censuring the Cabinet for its conduct in the Orange affair and for the abdication of its functions as a responsible ministry, he could muster only a large handful of votes in support.[83] The "joint authority" federal scheme, the masterpiece of the great convention of 1859, had been hurriedly removed from sight as if it were something disreputable if not positively obscene. The western Grits returned for solace and inspiration to the old battle-cry of Rep. by Pop., and the unrepentant John Sandfield Macdonald was busy once again "trotting out his hobby", the Double Majority.[84] The old lamentable divisions were still there; but the old imperious master, who had at once provoked and dominated them, was not.

For the first time since 1852 George Brown was absent from his place in the legislature. For eight years he had led and captained the Reform party. He had even seemed to personify and represent Grittism, like a medieval champion riding out to do battle in single combat before his watching army. But now, when the legislature met in that uneasy March, a month after the southern states had founded the Confederacy, Brown was not in his accustomed place. He was ill, and worried, and sick at heart. For most of the session he was absent. And Michael Foley, who had been his principal critic in the previous session, and who had publicly exposed the shameful divisions of the Grit party, was destined to succeed him as leader in the House.

The Reformers had tacitly given up their federal scheme. And this abandonment was naturally followed by an imme-

diate revival of the old agitation for Rep. by Pop. After a
period in which they had pessimistically believed that Rep. by
Pop. was impossible of achievement, the Upper Canadian Reformers returned to it with greater determination than ever
before, and for a new and conclusive reason. The new decennial
census, published recently, had suddenly supplied a statistical
proof for all the old arguments based on alleged preponderance
of Upper Canada's population. It was revealed, beyond any
possibility of doubt or argument, that the citizens of Canada
West outnumbered those of Canada East by approximately
285,000.[85] This revelation profoundly startled Canada West,
whether Grit or Tory; it impelled a growing number of Conservatives to announce publicly that they wished to see "justice
done to Upper Canada". Sidney Smith in the Cabinet, Sir
Henry Smith, J. B. Robinson, and George Benjamin in the
Assembly, were plainly all in favour of electoral reform, and
Macdonald and Cartier, faced by the growing opposition, were
driven to agree that differences of opinion must be respected
and that the matter could not be regarded as a "ministerial
question". Superficially this decision seemed impartial, but
actually it was not, for, as Cartier announced candidly to the
House, the government had no intention of introducing a bill
which would disturb the electoral equality of the two sections.
Cartier, roused as he seldom was by any issue, spoke for nearly
five hours against any change in the existing system,[86] and
two weeks later, on April 19, Macdonald followed with a
speech which, if shorter than his chief's, was an equally lively
denunciation of the Grit resolution.

The date was significant. Exactly a week before, on April
12, the Confederate guns had opened fire upon Fort Sumter
in Charleston harbour; and the beginning of the American
Civil War was to mark an important stage in the development
of Macdonald's views on federalism. Cartier, in his speech,
had not even mentioned the Conservative plan for the federal
union of British North America; but Macdonald had returned
to it at least once during his speaking tour in the previous
autumn and now, as he faced the House on the night of April
19, he returned to it again—and with a new argument which

the troubles in the United States were already beginning to impress upon him. In his view, federation was still the only really acceptable solution for the difficulties of the Canadian union. Yet the future federation of British North America must not be a federation in the decentralized American sense. The failure of the American system, Macdonald told the House, had been proved by the present lamentable conflict in the United States. The Americans had committed the fatal error of making each state a distinct sovereignty and giving to each a distinct sovereign power. The Canadians, warned by the tragic consequences of this mistake, must realize that the true principle of Confederation lay in giving to the general government all the functions and powers of sovereignty. With such a powerful central government, Macdonald argued, British North America would be an important nation in its own right. Already Canada was fast ceasing to be a dependency, and was assuming the position of an ally of Great Britain. Great Britain, the centre of a vast interdependent organization, would be sustained by alliances with Australasia and British North America; and there would thus be formed "an immense confederation of free men, the greatest confederacy of civilized and intelligent men that had ever had an existence on the face of the globe."[87]

He had begun his speech late. Sidney Smith and others had already spoken and it was nearly eleven o'clock before he had got to his feet. "There was a general rush for places throughout the House," the correspondent of the *Leader* reported. "The Reporters' Gallery, lately empty, was overflowing in a moment, and everyone eagerly bent over to hear something good. It was without exception the best speech Mr. Macdonald ever delivered. Those who are acquainted with his style of delivery need not be told that he is not what is called a 'flowery orator'. There is no prepared introduction—no tragical allusions—no straining after effect."[88] It was a good, hard-hitting speech, a speech which was at once typical of him and exceptionally good of its kind, a speech which inspired his followers to rounds of uproarious applause. He sat down tense and excited. As the House gradually subsided, as he began to relax in the pleasant consciousness of his triumph, he was still in no state to endure the waspish note of a critic. And yet it was precisely at this unfortunate moment that a determined critic presented himself. It was Oliver Mowat, his old legal pupil, stocky, rotund, short-sighted, but completely self-assured, who rose to confront him. And Mowat had a grievance to air. During the course of his speech Macdonald had jovially twitted his old junior with inconsistency—inconsistency in now supporting Rep. by Pop. when he had abandoned it so conclusively at the Reform convention at Toronto. Mowat interrupted his tormentor briefly at the time to say that he had been misrepresented; but as soon as Macdonald had sat down he rose and read in full the actual words he had spoken at the convention. There must have been some provocation in his remarks —some charge that Macdonald had wilfully falsified his views. Macdonald gasped. These impertinences were actually coming from the fat boy who had been his inky junior at school and his respectful apprentice at law! Suddenly, as the plump, bespectacled, rather self-important little man finished his statement, Macdonald's brittle temper was shattered into splinters as at a blow. In a minute—as soon as the Speaker had left the chair—he walked quickly across the gangway. Blind rage in his heart, he confronted Mowat.[89]

"You damned pup," he roared, "I'll slap your chops!"

John Sandfield Macdonald quickly stepped between the antagonists. Others helped to pull them apart. It was over in a minute—an abortive encounter, which had ended without violence. But, nevertheless, it had what was almost certainly a deliberate and intended sequel. Mowat had publicly suffered an indignity, if not a humiliation. A short, round, physically negligible man, who had a lively sense of his own importance and a lusty urge towards domination, he was not likely to be above thoughts of revenge; and within a few weeks chance gave him what he must have thought was a gorgeous opportunity. The session was a short one, as Macdonald had hoped. It ended on May 18, and three days later Macdonald was writing to Samuel Amsden the warning which he had probably dispatched to all his principal followers that day: "Get ready for War!" "Get your voters' lists ready as soon as possible," he

continued three days later, "and begin your canvass. Act as
if the polling was to come on next week. . . . Keep all this
dark."⁹⁰ It could only, of course, be kept dark long enough to
give the Conservatives a good head start, and within another
week the province knew that parliament had been dissolved
and that writs had been issued for the new general election.
It was then that Mowat decided to spring the trap of his own
private surprise. He had a good safe seat in South Ontario,
and Macdonald's constituency in Kingston was so solid that
nobody of any political consequence had ever ventured to run
against him. But towards the end of the first week of June
a requisition requesting Mowat to offer himself as a candidate
against Macdonald was busily circulating through Kingston.⁹¹
By the end of the week, the stupendous news arrived that
Mowat would reach town on Monday, June 10, to see his
friends and investigate the situation.

Macdonald arrived at Kingston by the express on Sunday
morning. He was only twenty-four hours ahead of Mowat:
and from the very start Mowat or Mowat's men seemed always
ready to meet and check and embarrass his every movement.
He had, he thought, scored an initial advantage by reserving
the town hall for his first big public meeting on Monday
night, but Mowat countered this with a surprise manoeuvre
of the greatest cunning. The Reform candidate, preceded significantly by a large and proudly blaring Orange band, was
escorted directly to the town hall as soon as he arrived at
Kingston Monday morning;⁹² and at the town hall a large
crowd, composed principally of Grits, who had assembled
quietly according to plans, gave him a thunderous reception.
When night came and the hour of Macdonald's meeting arrived,
the Mowat supporters were free to marshal themselves *en masse*
again at the municipal buildings. The town hall was full of
hecklers; and when Macdonald began by saying, "Gentlemen, I
am on my trial—I feel that I am on my trial," the literal as well
as the metaphorical truth of his words was quickly proved.⁹³
There were groans, hisses, cheers, counter-cheers and constant
interruptions. When question time came, a particularly pugnacious heckler provoked Macdonald to an open altercation;

and the meeting was barely finished when the platform was invaded and a free fight began. The next day it was almost as bad. Mowat's large and successful meeting in the City Park was concluded before night fell and when Macdonald had finished only one of the series of ward meetings which he had planned for that evening. The second meeting, at the Grammar School House, where the voters of Sydenham and Victoria Wards were assembled, had barely begun when a sudden violent uproar outside announced the arrival of the Mowat men, fresh from the meeting at the Park where Mowat had announced his candidature; and for nearly an hour the little body of Conservative voters, penned in an upper room of the school-house, endured a kind of siege, rearing forms and desks against the windows to protect themselves against the fusillades of stones, and again and again hurling the charging Mowat men back down the staircase.[94] All this was new—surprisingly and intimidatingly new—in the usual placid and perfunctory history of Macdonald electoral contests. Now, for the first time, there was force and cunning on the other side. There was more. There was purpose and confidence.

Macdonald was uneasily conscious that his position had changed and that some of his strongest supporters were publicly admitting the fact. "While we feel confident," the News remarked editorially, "that his place in the affections of a majority of the electors is still unimpaired, we cannot conceal the fact that a good deal of the support which he has hitherto received is about to be withdrawn from him."[95] There was little uncertainty about the danger of this withdrawal and there could be no doubt at all that it was caused by Macdonald's recently expressed opposition to Rep. by Pop. Other Conservatives had bent themselves accommodatingly and adroitly before the weighty revelations of the new census. But he stood awkwardly apart. He had been committed once again by his speech of April 19, and in Kingston, during the campaign, he did nothing to modify his position. He defended the union—the union, apparently, as it was, with its conventional inequalities. As at Quebec, the only kind of political reorganization which he was prepared to support was a federal union of the British

North American provinces. Federation was one of the policies announced in the electoral manifesto which he addressed to the electors of Kingston;[96] and he advocated it again in his first great speech of the campaign, in the turbulent city hall. "It is the policy of the government," he told the noisy and quarrelling audience, "to try to secure the union of the Lower Provinces of New Brunswick and Nova Scotia and perhaps Newfoundland, but when unhappily we see the fratricidal strife which rages across the line, we must take advantage of the faults and defects in their constitution. We must take care that we will not, like them, have a weak central government. We must have local governments for local purposes only, and not run the risk in this country, which we see on the other side of the frontier, of one part of the country destroying the other part."[97] Union and strength—certainly for Canada, and, if possible, for British North America—these were theories which he had made peculiarly his own. But they were not very popular theories. Everybody was talking about the sectional grievances of Canada West.

Yet Macdonald continued resolutely on his way, and as the contest approached its climax, the outcome seemed to grow more and more doubtful. When, on Saturday, June 22, nomination day finally arrived, each side struggled desperately to provide its candidate with the larger escort to the hustings. Macdonald's procession, headed by two bands and by a long string of decorated waggons and carriages, was apparently the more numerous. But both sides were strong; there were continual interruptions and noisy exchanges; and Mowat, who gave the longer of the two speeches, seemed exhausted when he sat down after his great effort in the hot June sunlight.[98] Macdonald, using this most public occasion of the entire campaign, openly attacked Rep. by Pop. once more, insisting that the interests of Kingston were inseparably bound up with the St. Lawrence and the central Canadian region, and that it would be outrageous folly for such a constituency to assist in giving the West a numerical preponderance in parliament. For a while, after this daringly outspoken speech, Conservative support seemed to falter. The men of the Mowat party contemptuously resumed their rowdyism once more, and even the chief Conservative newspaper in the town rebuked Macdonald in a long and sorrowful editorial. The issue was still apparently uncertain when at length the poll opened on Monday, July 1. During the first day, which was clear and beautiful, the voters came forward in large numbers; but on Tuesday, a raw, chilly, rainy day, the totals mounted much more slowly. Yet, from the beginning, there was never really any doubt. Macdonald was ahead on the first day's polling; and by Tuesday night, when the poll closed, the vote stood 785 for Macdonald and 474 for Mowat.[99] He had won, by a majority of 311, over a man who had deliberately invaded his territory, looking for revenge.

This time, moreover, his success was no longer so exceptional. The Reform party, weakened by its unconcealed divisions, its frequent changes of programme, and its quarrelling and maladroit leadership, had received a sudden setback in Canada West. For the first time in five years the parties were almost exactly balanced: the Conservatives might even have a majority of one in the sixty-five Upper Canadian seats. Macdonald had apparently been rescued from his political dependence upon Canada East. He had recovered his pre-eminence in his own territory; and on Friday when the return of the Kingston election was formally declared at the court-house, a special effort was made to mark the joint victory of the candidate and his party. When he had given his thanks to the great crowd assembled at the hustings, Macdonald, along with a few of his principal supporters, got into a "beautifully decorated triumphal carriage, drawn by six horses". Followed by a long line of other carriages, it moved proudly through the city streets and out along the road to Portsmouth, where old Mrs. Macdonald and Hugh and Louisa lived. It was the last electoral triumph of her son which Helen Macdonald would ever see. She stood waiting for him in the summer sunlight, and beside her "a bountiful collation was spread on tables beneath the pleasant shade of the trees".

Chapter Twelve

Impasse

I

The famous victory had been adequately celebrated. It had been accompanied by so many blessings—including as a crowning mercy the defeat of George Brown in Toronto—that it might have seemed to have ended the very possibility of political worries and annoyances. But, in a curious and inexplicable fashion, they persisted. There were, of course, certain huge preoccupations, such as the problem of Anglo-American relations and the enigma of the political future of the North American continent, which had been raised by the American Civil War and which were beyond the healing power of even a Canadian general election. These large and sinister uncertainties might be expected to continue. The really disturbing fact was that the little annoyances, the petty irritations, of Canadian party politics should continue as well. But they did. In the complicated state to which politics had been reduced in the united Province of Canada almost no election could have a conclusive outcome. In accordance with what had now come to be regarded as a natural law of Canadian affairs, a party's gains in one section of the province were certain, or nearly certain, to be balanced by its losses in the other. The Conservatives had done badly in Canada East for the same reasons that they had done well in Canada West. The advocacy of Rep. by Pop., which had gained them constituencies in the west, had awakened a slight shudder of apprehension among their French-Canadian supporters. The

party, as a whole, had not improved its position. Numerically
it was about as large as it had been; and it was now split down
the middle on a really important issue. A number of western
Conservative members had definitely pledged themselves to their
constituents to uphold electoral reform. But the government
could not possibly bring in a measure which would really
establish representation by population throughout the province.
A section of its Upper Canadian supporters still opposed the
idea; and the entire body of its followers in Lower Canada
utterly abominated it. Yet, if humanly possible, the Radicals
in the party must be conciliated, for otherwise they would
certainly join George Brown. How could this fatality be
avoided?

This was the problem which Macdonald faced in the autumn
and winter of 1861. His problems had an unfortunate habit
of finding appropriate personifications, and this particular problem was no exception. It was embodied, so he discovered to
his rather bored annoyance, in the dignified person of John
Hillyard Cameron. This was not the kind of political resur-
rection which was likely to bring him to his knees in gratitude.
Everybody knew that Cameron was politically dead. A pathetic
victim of the depression of 1857, he had been buried under
an avalanche of debts and obligations; and if he were ever
again to revisit, in a fleeting fashion, his old political haunts,
it must surely be as a ghost, a spectral slave of his profession,
burdened with a long chain of briefs and law books. Yet here
he was once more miraculously restored to life, a very solid
political personality, and bowing gracefully to the plaudits
of an unexpectant but delighted audience. As Grand Master
of the Orange Lodge, he had made the most of the deplorable
affair at Kingston. He had returned, virtually a popular hero,
from his mission of dignified protest to the Queen. And when
he had decided to re-enter politics in the general election of
1861, he had scored an easy victory over his Grit antagonist
in Peel County. Back in the troubles of 1856, he had represented the Tory element in the Liberal-Conservative party—
the element which had always stood stoutly by the Protestant
religion and the sectional interests of Canada West. Now, by

publicly espousing electoral reform he had put himself once
more at the head of the little group of discontented Conservatives who were threatening to desert the ministry.

Macdonald hardly knew what to do. From all quarters news
of incipient revolts and impending desertions kept coming in;
and almost invariably at the centre of these disconcerting
rumours was the name of Cameron. "What is in the wind?"
George Allen enquired from Toronto. "William F. Powell
has been in Toronto abusing the ministry and holding conferences with J. H. Cameron. Dr. Clarke has also been down
and has been talking of 'independence'. . . . I am afraid there
is a party growing up amongst those for whom you have done
most, desirous of supplanting you. I therefore warn you."[1] It
was a warning that was repeated by others, including one
gentleman who had just enjoyed the fearful pleasure of an
interview with George Brown; and to him Brown had prophesied
confidently that Hillyard Cameron would detach a considerable
part of Macdonald's support.[2] How was he to cope with this
threat? Would it be best to attempt to pacify Cameron and
his Tories? Or should he try, as he had done in 1854 and
1856, to recoup his losses from the Reform side? After all,
if the Conservatives were divided, the Grits were also divided
and more seriously still. Rep. by Pop. was a solvent which
had left politics in a highly fluid state. And by a dexterous
movement he might scoop up quite as much as he spilled.

He had at hand an easy method of clinching the support
of possible new friends. There were places in the Cabinet
which would soon need to be filled; there were almost always
places in the Cabinet which were vacant or soon would be
vacant. Macdonald had never been able to build up a trained
and experienced team; he played most of his matches with
what amounted to a long procession of dubious substitutes.
Ministers were always resigning or thinking about resigning.
They were lusting irrepressibly to go back to their professions,
or on to the bench, or into business. Cayley, Spence, Drummond, John Rose and a long line of French Canadians had
already vanished, like the faces glimpsed momentarily in a crowd.
And now it was only too clear that Ross, who was tired of

politics, and Morrison, who never seemed able to get a seat, and Vankoughnet, who had an eye cocked in the direction of the vacant chancellorship, were all eagerly considering the question of resignation. Three places would probably be open soon. How should he fill them? If, on the one hand, he tried to make still another coalition with the moderate· Reformers, then, as one of his correspondents pointed out, it would be only too natural for Cameron "to ally himself with the remainder and more numerous body of the Grits". If, on the other hand, he attempted to make his peace with Cameron and the Conservative supporters of Rep. by Pop., then what changes of policy would have to be accepted to gain their support, and whom should he select to represent their views in the Cabinet? There was T. C. Street, or John Carling of London, or J. B. Robinson of Toronto, or Alexander Campbell of Kingston. There was even the great John Hillyard Cameron himself. But was Cameron in a position to accept office? George Brown had assured one of Macdonald's correspondents that Cameron was looking forward to power;[3] J. C. Morrison, another correspondent, informed Macdonald that Cameron had given up all hope of any real release from the tyranny of his debts and his profession.[4] This sounded conclusive. But was it really? Was Cameron simply trying to enhance his own value? And what price would have to be paid for the support of his followers? Cameron informed Morrison that he would be content with the smallest instalment of increase in the representation of Canada West. But some increase there would certainly have to be. Macdonald turned the matter over and over in his mind. Could he invent some scheme that Cartier could be induced to accept and which would yet enable the Conservative supporters of electoral reform to fulfil their election pledge?

No,the election had not ended the weaknesses and divisions of the Liberal-Conservative party, for it had not settled the basic politico-cultural problem of the Canadian union. It had left provincial politics in a state of uncertain equilibrium; and this at the very moment when the whole continent seemed rocked by the shocks of the American Civil War. From the

moment he had assumed power, back in 1857, Macdonald
had been only intermittently able to consider the Canadian
question by itself and in isolation. All too frequently the
problem of governing a united yet divided province had been
inextricably yet distractingly connected with other puzzles—with
the questions of western expansion, interprovincial union,
and external defence. In the past these complications had
been intermittent; but now, as a result of the American Civil
War, they threatened to become continuous. The peaceful
relations between England and Canada on the one hand and
the United States on the other might be endangered now at
any moment and for years to come. The war might end in a
division of the original republic and the independence of the
Confederacy. It might end in a political turmoil throughout
the entire continent, which would render meaningless all the old
divisions and boundaries. These obvious threats to the independence and separateness, to the very existence, of British
North America were a main consideration in the minds of
Macdonald and his contemporaries; but there were other and
more subtle ways in which the war influenced their speculations.
It brought up for re-examination the whole question of political
unions in general, and federal unions in particular. It raised
the still more fundamental problem of the validity of the
democratic and republican form of government.

Macdonald approached these matters with little prejudice
against the United States and with a good deal of respect for
the American character and American political experience.
Although Conservative opinion in Canada, as in the United
Kingdom, tended to sympathize with the Southern Confederacy, he gave little sign of a marked preference one way or the
other; and although, in the days which followed Great Britain's
recognition of the South as a belligerent power, the insulting
and provocative threats of a section of the American press
caused the deepest resentment in Canada, he was not very
apt to be disturbed by this kind of journalistic imperialism.[5]
In his great speech in April, at the beginning of the American
conflict, he had told the House that he regarded the apparent
break-up of the union, not with any sense of vindictive satis-

faction, but with feelings of sincere regret.[6] His belief in the
vigour of the Anglo-Saxon character, in the worth of Anglo-
Saxon institutions, whether in their British or American dress,
made it easy for him to sympathize with the misfortunes of
the republic. But, on the other hand, this sympathy did not
weaken his conviction that the war had its lessons which must
be heeded, and the American constitution its faults which must
be avoided at all costs. He dwelt on the fatal defect of state
sovereignty with growing emphasis in his speeches. But he
also shared the widely spread belief that the Civil War was,
in some sense, the inevitable bloody outcome of mob rule and
presidential despotism. To many English-speaking Canadians
of his generation, the American Civil War marked the final
stage in the discredit, not merely of federation, but also of
democracy and republicanism.[7] Since 1848, in both Europe
and North America, republican institutions had been in retreat.
The collapse of English Chartism, the defeat of the European
revolutions, marked the successive stages in their decline; and
now, in the United States, they were about to disappear in a
welter of blood and corruption.

Macdonald held a modified and highly particularized version
of this view. He had always believed in monarchical as
opposed to republican institutions and in responsible parliamentary government as opposed to divided powers and constitutional checks. In the 1850's, when "elective institutions" were
still popular with his own Conservative colleagues and followers, as well as with French-Canadian Reformers and Western Clear Grits, he had had to give way, at least to some
extent. But the introduction of the elected Legislative Council
in 1856 had been, in effect, the last victory of the supporters
of the "congressional system"; and thereafter the winds shifted
and began to blow with increasing strength the other way. The
Grit campaign for "organic changes"—a written constitution
and executive checks—had been disavowed by the Toronto
convention and disavowed even by those who later criticized
the work of the Toronto convention. It was possible now, as
it had not been before, for Macdonald to take the offensive on
behalf of British parliamentary institutions, and to blacken sug-

gested changes with the stigma of their alleged American paren-
tage. When the Grit, McDougall, describing with a rhetorical
flourish the desperate courses into which Canada West might
be forced by its accumulated wrongs, happened incautiously
to picture the Upper Canadians "looking for help to Washington",[8] Macdonald and his followers pounced on this fatal
remark as a particularly delectable piece of prey. They exhibited
it with telling effect to various shocked audiences during the
election of 1861; and, indeed, Macdonald in a private letter
to Egerton Ryerson declared that the election might "determine
the future of Canada, and whether it will be a limited Constitutional Monarchy or a Yankee democracy".[9] "Let these
people not look to Washington," he told one audience, "but
let them go thither. The loyal population will stay here,
happier that the others are away, and if they try to return,
with an army at their back, why, in the name of the militiamen
of Canada, let them come."[10] These heroics, which did heavy
duty in the election of 1861, were politically safer and more
effective than they had been. Morin, the original leader of
the French-Canadian division in the coalition of 1854, had
sponsored the first bill for making the Legislative Council
elective; but Cartier, who sometimes seemed to imply that the
American lack of responsible government was the sole cause
of the Civil War, was, if anything, an even more outspoken
critic of the "congressional system" than Macdonald. The Civil
War in the United States gave support both for those who
believed in British institutions and for those who desired a
strong federal union. If Canada survived, it would work for
Conservative principles. If Canada survived . . . . It was a
condition at the end of which the war itself had written a large
mark of interrogation.

II

It was the autumn of 1861, nearly four years after Isabella's
death. Time may have dulled what even in the beginning
must have been an old ache rather than a fresh wound of

grief; but his feelings for the dead, as for the living, Isabella, were kept securely within the firm wall of his reserve. People sometimes dimly suspected that he must have his unhappy moments—that there were thoughts which, with all his prodigal cameraderie, he had no intention of sharing with others. "I am of opinion," Spence wrote with rather ponderous kindness, "that with all your appearance of almost continual mirthfulness you are not without your seasons of serious reflection."[11] But these seasons he kept to himself. Then he was either a solitary or his one companion was a bottle. And to the little political world of Quebec he presented the appearance of a jocund widower, who was enjoying life to the full, who rose above the irritations of Canadian politics with careless ease, and who only occasionally astounded his friends by a sudden and unaccountable outburst of temper. He had apparently yielded, with smiling good humour, to the importunate appeals of his political friends. While everybody else wandered off in search of lucrative jobs or secure places, he remained at Quebec, an imperturbable fixture, a pleasant and approachable permanency, with whom one could always joke and on whom one could always rely. Little by little, Kingston and most of its affairs receded into the background of his mind; but Hughey, Lou, Moll and "the Parson" and his mother maintained their prominence in the light of his affection. Somehow, despite the long distances and the distracting preoccupations, he managed to hold them tenaciously close. He was a good son, who worried over the successive shocks which prostrated his mother, and a good father—interested, proud, generous and yet not over-indulgent. Hugh was to have the Shetland pony he desired; but he must ride it every day. "When it rains, let him wear the waterproof I sent him," he wrote to Louisa, "but he must ride daily."[12] He must also if possible do well at school; but equally his progress must be appreciated, and a good report from his master handsomely praised. ". . . in the first place," he wrote his sister, "tell Hugh that I am extremely pleased at the report of Mr. May. Tell him that I am quite proud of it and that I have shewn it to all my friends. Let him go on and prosper and he will make his mark in the country yet."[18]

November, which was to usher in such an exciting period for Canada, began with an appropriately important change. Sir Edmund Walker Head relinquished the office of Governor-General, and Viscount Monck, an Irish peer who had been a Member of Parliament for Portsmouth, arrived to take his place. Head had first assumed his duties nearly seven years before, when the Liberal-Conservative government was only a few months old; and except for the famous two days when Brown and his colleagues briefly supplanted the Conservatives, Macdonald had held office under him for the entire period. He had come to know and respect the Governor deeply. It was the kind of friendly acquaintanceship which could not easily be re-established with another person, and perhaps might never be established with Lord Monck. For Monck differed markedly from Sir Edmund. A large, comfortably built, heavily bearded man, less original, more sluggish, but perhaps more tenacious in his mental processes than his predecessor, he had little of Head's imaginative grasp or creative power in British North American affairs. Still, as Macdonald quickly discovered, he was a workmanlike efficient administrator; and, as the first events of his governorship soon proved, he was a man of wise prudence, of deep if somewhat narrow wisdom. No governor had ever had more need of these qualities. Monck had arrived and had taken the oaths of office in the last days of October. He had not been two weeks in his new position, when there occurred the "incident"—the incident almost doomed to happen by the ominous state of Anglo-American relations. On November 8, Captain Wilkes of the U.S.S. *San Jacinto* stopped the British mail packet *Trent,* and took from her by force two Confederate diplomatic agents, James Murray Mason and John Slidell. About a week later, this astounding piece of news became public property in the United States, where it was apparently greeted by the exultation of the people, and the complacent approval of the government. It became known in Canada about the same time, and, two weeks later, in England.

In both countries it aroused intense excitement. A British

note, modified by the faltering hand of the dying Prince Albert, demanded an apology and the instant return of the captured envoys. And Canadians, recollecting the awkward fact that their country was the inevitable battlefield of any Anglo-American struggle, wondered whether the jubilation of the American people would permit their government to give way. In those early days of December, 1861, Macdonald and his colleagues found that their private advices, as well as the public prints, were equally dismaying. On December 4, at the height of the crisis, Galt, who happened to be in Washington on business connected with the Reciprocity Treaty, had a private interview with President Lincoln.[14] He liked the President's sombre, strongly marked features, his simple, straightforward manner, and his remarkable fund of anecdotes. And yet the interview perturbed him. It was true that Lincoln suggested, in a reassuring off-hand fashion, that the Mason-Slidell affair would be "gotten along with" some way or other. But when Galt reproached him mildly for the rather formidable defensive measures that the government of the United States had already taken, the President replied significantly, "We must say something to satisfy the people."[15] It was not the first time that Canadians and British had heard the most provocative actions defended on the straight commercial grounds that there was a big demand for them in the home market of the United States; and Galt brought a doubtful report back to Macdonald and the Cabinet. All that December, Canadians and British worked feverishly to repair the defective defences of the province. Transports, bearing a total of nearly 14,000 imperial troops, raced for the St. Lawrence; and when the frost sealed the river and foiled them of their destination, they turned back to the Maritime ports, and the regiments they carried travelled laboriously over the snow-choked Temiscouata passage from northern New Brunswick to Canada East.[16] In the meantime, while a patriotic wave of enthusiasm swept through the entire province, the Conservative government decided to increase the volunteers, prepared to call up nearly 40,000 of the Sedentary Militia, and placed orders for 100,000 uniforms in the United Kingdom.[17] Finally—a last convincing proof that defence had suddenly become big government business—a new portfolio of Militia Affairs was created; and Macdonald, the Attorney-General West, was appointed the first minister.[18]

For a little while the new Minister of Militia Affairs expected to become very literally a Minister of War. But the United States decided to restore the captured diplomatists; Great Britain countermanded the dispatch of further troops to Canada; and Macdonald, a little breathless with excitement, was able to set down the biggest pack of his anxieties. The particular danger was apparently over. But the general problem of provincial defence in a highly troubled period remained; and the new Minister of Militia Affairs was not prepared to push it back into the lumber room of neglect, where it had been pushed so often before. If the first Conservative improvement of the militia had been justified by the necessities of the Crimean War, then the present crisis, so much closer and more dangerous, called imperatively for a still more thorough reorganization. Towards the end of January, 1862, the Governor appointed a militia commission, whose membership, significantly enough, included not only the expected imperial and colonial officers, but also such political figures as Cartier, the leader of the government, Galt, the Minister of Finance, and Macdonald himself, the new Minister of Militia Affairs.[19] The personnel of the new commission suggested an important change in policy: and so did the terms of reference which guided its labours. Its main assignment was to recommend a scheme for the reorganization of the militia and the building up of an efficient and economical system of defence. Finally, to bring all these investigations to a practical issue, it was commanded to prepare a bill on the subject for submission to the colonial legislature.

In the meantime, while these vast rumbling international disturbances kept the Canadian government in a state of continual agitation, Macdonald slowly pursued the business of the reorganization of his Cabinet. A tedious, provoking, yet immensely important affair, for on it depended the recruitment of political strength and the continuance of political power, its complications seemed never to be ended. The uncertainties, hesitations, conditions, scruples, and convictions of his retiring ministers and their possible successors—all had to be taken into consideration. He mystified and annoyed people with his changes and procrastinations. Gowan, protesting that this was "probably the last letter I shall ever address to you," stalked off in a tremendous sulk;[20] and Alexander Campbell, who had told Macdonald several times that he would not accept office unless the assistance of Street and Cameron were also secured, now bluntly informed his old partner that unless the originally suggested changes were made, "then with many thanks to you for the honour you have done me, I retire altogether from the field".[21] The problem seemed insoluble. The opening of parliament on March 20 steadily approached. The old ministers resigned; and still their places were unfilled. "One day more!" the *Globe* announced cheerily, "And no government yet. We advance. Van is gone. Joe is gone. Ross is gone. There is nobody left but John A., Sidney Smith, and George Sherwood. And parliament meets tomorrow."[22] It met tomorrow, and three days later, on March 23, Macdonald was still negotiating, through Hillyard Cameron, with Street, and Street was still "standing out on the representation question".[23]

Four days later, on March 27, when the appointments had at last been made, Macdonald rose to make the necessary explanations in the House. The new ministers—John Carling of London, and James Patton and John Beverley Robinson of Toronto—were all open and avowed supporters of Rep. by Pop.; but yet, as Macdonald announced firmly, the government was not prepared to introduce any measure which would disturb the existing sectional equality of representation. The question was not a ministerial question at all. "Every member of the Government," Macdonald told the House, "in his capacity as a member of Parliament could vote as his conscientious convictions induced him to do on that question."[24] It remained to be seen whether this promise was to be taken literally, and whether, even if it were taken literally, it would satisfy the large number of Conservative supporters of Rep. by Pop. The test came almost immediately, in the debate on the address, and therefore in its most difficult and politically embarrassing form; both McDougall, the Grit, and John Hillyard Cameron, the Tory, submitted amendments advocating a change in the system of parliamentary representation.[25] Faced with these two amendments—one of them introduced by a Tory of high standing and great influence—the Conservative supporters of electoral reform discovered that they had no choice at all. They would have to vote for the amendments. They were bound by their engagements to do so. Yet Macdonald was equally certain to look on their defection in the most serious light. Rep. by Pop. had not been placed before the House as a substantive motion, on which his followers could vote with the freedom he had promised them. It had been introduced as an amendment to the address, in effect a motion of want of confidence, which all Conservatives were bound to unite to resist. But they were not going to do so. And he was suddenly angry. Fretted and weary with a burden which everybody seemed to take for granted that he should carry indefinitely, he looked upon the inconveniently righteous convictions of his followers with cold annoyance. He may have intimated his displeasure. He may even, as the newspapers hinted, have threatened to resign.[26]

He must have been astounded at the result. True, the Mc-Dougall and Cameron amendments were defeated, for the bulk of the votes from Canada East were, of course, cast against them; but this outcome had already been expected and discounted as obvious. The really significant part of the vote—the part which would reveal the extent of the defection of Macdonald's English-speaking supporters—was the sectional vote of Canada West. On that night of April 1, forty-three Upper Canadian members voted for the two amendments and, in both cases, only sixteen voted against.[27] It was a sectional majority of twenty-seven in favour of Rep. by Pop.—a sectional majority of twenty-seven against the avowed policy of the government. The bulk of the western Conservatives had completely disregarded their leader's well-known preferences. They had voted exactly as they wanted to do with utter indifference for the interests of the party. He was furious; and that night everybody was aware of his fury. "The general talk on the ministerial side," the Globe reported complacently, "is of an immediate break-up." John Campbell, one of the Upper Canadian Conservatives who had voted for the amendments, hastened to write Macdonald a little letter of explanation and regret that very night.[28]

Next morning, a general assembly of the Upper Canadian supporters, a sobered and perhaps slightly frightened group of men, headed by John Hillyard Cameron, met to state their position and to appease the sudden wrath of their genial leader. "I have been directed by the unanimous voice of the meeting," George Benjamin wrote, "to state to you, that on the votes which were given on Mr. Cameron's motion on the question of representation, as well as on the motion of Mr. McDougall on the same question, it was not their intention to vote a want of confidence."[29] They believed, Benjamin went on to explain, that the government was quite safe. They felt that they must honour the solemn pledges made to their constituents. And they hoped—here the letter became a little pathetic—that Macdonald would sympathize with them. "I can only say," Benjamin concluded, "I never attended a more cordial meeting of friends, nor one where the feeling was more united in favour of yourself as their leader, and in confidence in your ability to conduct the affairs of the country." This was very handsome. And anyway Macdonald's anger had probably gone. It was a sparkling wine that left no sediment of resentment. Yet, when the whole episode was over, a certain sense of disillusionment and discouragement remained. Was it really possible to win at all in Canadian politics? Not a year had passed since the last general election, since his recovery of the majority in Canada West, and his great personal triumph over Mowat. Not a year had passed; and yet his support in Canada East had been sharply reduced and his followers in Canada West were divided. Could the problem of the Canadian union ever be solved? Would they ever escape from this apparently inevitable tendency towards a balance of parties, and from its inevitable consequences—political stalemate and governmental impotence?

He went ahead; but with, perhaps, a slightly more cynical recklessness than before. There was no attempt to renew the negotiations for Confederation; but, on the other hand, he had evidently determined upon something that was even more immediately hazardous—the radical reform of the Canadian militia system. On March 15, two weeks before the crisis over the McDougall and Cameron amendments, the commission on Canadian defence had presented its report;[80] and even in the circumstances of the moment—a crisis, barely over, in Anglo-American relations, and a mounting wave of patriotic fervour in the Province of Canada—this was a very formidable document indeed. The commissioners, after having briefly and somewhat pessimistically reviewed the primary factors which governed Canadian defence, went rapidly on to make their principal recommendations. "In order to provide an efficient force for the defence of the province," they declared, "we are of opinion that a far greater number of trained men will be required than have hitherto been sanctioned, and recommend the organization of an active force of 50,000 men of all arms, with a reserve of the same number." These were startling totals; and the means by which they were to be achieved were highly unusual as well. Yet the province was not given a very long time to accustom itself to these drastic recommendations. On Friday, May 2, Macdonald introduced the government Militia Bill—a bill which was frankly based upon the report.

It was a rather equivocal episode. The tone of the Minister of Militia Affairs was defensive, conciliatory, almost apologetic. His speech was an accomplished effort at extenuation, a masterly exercise in the difficult art of explaining away.[81] It was true that he began bravely enough by pointing out the dangerous position in which the province stood, and the wisdom and moderation of the recommendations of the report— "any honourable gentleman who looks at the map will admit the calculation to be a moderate one". He was frank enough also in the description of the composition of the new force, and of the methods by which it was to be recruited. In the cities and towns, the volunteer corps would simply be enlarged; but in the country districts active battalions of regular militia were to be raised from the old sedentary force, by voluntary enlistment, as far as possible, and if necessary by ballot or conscription. Drill would be carried on regularly in the evenings or the week-ends in the cities, where it was possible for the militiamen to assemble fairly regularly; but in the country, where such short, frequent drills were impracticable, a fairly long training period each year was proposed for the active militia battalions. All this looked definite enough. The reserved powers of conscription and the weeks of training were shockingly unusual; but there was no doubt what was meant. Still, the structure of the new system depended upon its details; and these, on investigation, turned out to be extremely hazy. Macdonald described the bill, a little too persuasively, as an "enabling bill". The Mutiny Act, it seemed, was an analogous measure. How many men would be called out under the new statute? That was for parliament to decide subsequently. How much would the first year's operations cost? That also was for parliament to decide. The whole bill was clearly "permissive"; and the new system could be expanded or contracted as the House thought best. These rather evasive explanations did not satisfy the critics. They pressed for concrete details and estimates, and Drummond complained that it was like drawing teeth to get governmental explanations. Macdonald relented a little; but it was not until four days later, when Galt announced that the government proposed, for the first year, to call out 30,000 men for fourteen days' training at an estimated cost of about $480,000, that the House really learnt the full truth.[82] It was a staggering revelation. "It is plainly and obviously our duty," Macdonald had argued in his peroration, "to provide a large and efficient force for the purpose of fighting upon our own soil, for our own possessions, our own privileges, and our own liberties." All very true, no doubt. But who had expected that a colony would be suddenly asked to do so much for defence?

The opposition to the bill began to mount. The French-Canadian supporters of government may have felt a lingering resentment at the ease with which their friends from Canada West had abandoned the principle of sectional equality in parliament. They may have been ready enough to desert their Upper Canadian colleagues and thus to get a little revenge for

the votes on the McDougall and Cameron amendments. And
in any case they firmly believed that the Militia Bill imposed
too large burdens and sacrifices upon a small colonial community. This conviction that the scheme was too absurdly
heroic was the main, but not the only, source of opposition to
the bill. The government, which had been in power continuously since 1854, had become old but not venerable. It
seemed almost a provincial oligarchy, determined to prolong
its rickety existence by the most dubious methods. It had
become distinctly unsavoury through what the *Globe* called the
"Ottawa jobberies" and other scandals; and its Finance Minister,
Galt, had just been obliged to disclose in his budget speech a
most unsatisfactory state of the finances. Monck actually
believed that parliament and the people in general were reluctant to trust the large amounts of money required by the
Militia Bill to such a suspect government;[33] and John Rose,
who had significantly resigned the Commissionership of Public Works some time before, was only a little less censorious in
a long letter of explanation which he wrote to Edward Ellice
immediately after the crisis was over. The government, he
explained—he was often a little sanctimoniously proper in his
letters to Ellice—"lived too long, resorted to too many shifts
to prolong existence, and people had begun to complain of
the political oligarchy that ruled the country. They were anxious to reform but *couldn't*—they were surrounded by place
hunters, jobbers, and had all manner of entangling antecedents.
Galt's budget disclosed an alarming state of the finances; and
all of us who had neither political regrets nor aspirations felt
that we must set the house in order."[34]

But even this was not all. Another event, at once comic
and awful, occurred. Macdonald suddenly ceased to be the
captain of the ship and became an irresponsible stowaway.
He was drinking heavily;[35] and he went on drinking heavily
in complete and cheerful disregard for the Militia Bill, the
Canadian government, the Conservative party, and the military
necessities of the British Empire. The bout may have been
accompanied or preceded by the depressing troubles of a real
illness; but there were other than physical reasons for this

prolonged relapse into irresponsibility. All that winter he had
been troubled by the realization that the government was weak
and the party divided. All that winter he had been growing
increasingly irritated by the bland assumption that he would
invariably continue at his post with patient fidelity, while
everybody else was happily free to vote, accept or reject office,
indulge all eccentric scruples and whimsical convictions exactly
as it pleased him. He was bored and sick and tired with the
whole business—with the endless deceptions and frustrations
of Canadian politics. He kept to his room; and on Tuesday,
May 13, nearly a week after the first debate on the Militia
Bill, the *Globe* reported that he was unwell. "He has one of
his old attacks," the correspondent continued jocosely. "It must
be confessed that Mr. Macdonald's 'illnesses' occur at very inconvenient times."[36] On Thursday, May 15, he was reported
still unwell. On Friday he was better; on Saturday he was
still unable to leave his bed; and on Monday, May 19, he
was said at last to be recovering. All during this deplorable
absence the opposition to the Militia Bill was steadily increasing. "Rumours are getting thick again . . . ," one correspondent
reported. "It is well known that the supporters of Government
are very much dissatisfied with the militia bill. Nobody makes
any secret of that."[37] Yet Macdonald was still not at his post.
"The Attorney General West, I am told," the *Globe* correspondent admitted, "has really been very ill—ill in earnest,
though at first the 'illness' was rather peculiar. Doubtless the
one illness was the consequence of the other."

He was back at length on May 20. In the meantime, "a
conviction is settling down in the minds of everybody that a
break-up is imminent".[38] Yet Macdonald apparently did little
to avoid it. He may even have welcomed it as the only way
out of an impossible situation. "There seems little reason to
doubt," one correspondent argued, "that Mr. Cartier and his
colleagues have known for some time that they could not get
through the session and that they elected to fall on the militia
bill."[39] It was—like the seat-of-government question—a highly
respectable, highly patriotic issue, an issue on which a slightly
disreputable government could make a most dignified exit.

It was, in fact, such a lordly form of withdrawal that the Conservative malcontents and the regular opposition hoped to compel departure by a more ignominious route. But Macdonald was too much for them. Within half an hour of the opening of the House on May 20, the second reading of the Militia Bill took place. A little group of French-Canadian votes changed sides; the measure was defeated by sixty-one to fifty-four votes; and the next day he and Cartier and the entire ministry resigned. Macdonald's first feeling was an overwhelming sense of relief; and the letter which he wrote a few days later to the family in Kingston glows with the joyous consciousness of freedom. "You complain of my not having written," he told his sister. "It is true, but I had the excuse of overwork. I have that no longer. You will have seen that I am out of office. I am at last free, thank God! and can now feel as a free man. I have longed for this hour and only a sense of honour has kept me chained to my post . . . I have now fulfilled my duty to my party and can begin to think of myself."[41]

III

Yet he did not begin to think of himself in what, for political men at that time, were the most obvious ways. Tradition, firmly established by a number of honourable examples, gave a retiring attorney-general the choice of all the vacant legal positions at the time; and retiring attorney-generals, even after only a brief term in office, were not infrequently in a hurry to press their claims. He had held the position—with the exception of a few days only—for nearly eight years. Two important offices had been open that winter, the chief justiceship and the chancellorship of Canada West; the one left vacant by the retirement of Sir John Beverley Robinson, and the other by the resignation of William H. Blake. Macdonald could have had either, and he refused them both. It was clear, at any rate, that he was not going to break dramatically and completely with politics, that he was not going to accept a position which would make it impossible to return. He finished out the session;

he did not resign his seat; he did not inform his followers that he would not take up the leadership of the opposition once more. His followers, of course, wanted one last great effort from him. They were out. They wanted to be in. Well, he would help them. He could hardly, if only for the sake of his own self-respect, leave the party at such an unfortunate moment. Privately he decided that he would not again accept office. That at least was settled. But the overthrow of the new government—there, surely, was an easier thing. Surely, in the light of all the savage divisions among the Reformers, it ought to be really easy?

In fact, the stage was rigged in such a fashion that the new government seemed destined for a tragic role. The terrible George Brown was still out of parliament; and his successor—the temporary leader at least of the Western Grits—was Brown's old critic, Michael Foley. But the portly and bibulous Foley did not stand out nearly so conspicuously as Brown had done from among his unfriendly associates, the other Reform leaders. It was possible to ignore him; and Monck, probably advised by Cartier, did ignore him, inviting John Sandfield Macdonald instead to form a government. John Sandfield Macdonald's cure for the political troubles of Canada was the so-called Double Majority; and L. V. Sicotte, who acted as the leader of the French-Canadian division in the new government, had supported the same principle. For the Conservatives, therefore, the elevation of Sicotte and John Sandfield Macdonald to power was an excellent form of political insurance. It ensured, in the first place, that no immediate effort would be made to introduce Rep. by Pop., and, in the second place, that the new government would be attacked with the greatest possible venom by George Brown and his die-hard followers. Sandfield Macdonald and Sicotte had set out on what seemed to be a most difficult and unpopular course. In Canada they were heartily disliked by an influential section of the Reform party, and in England they were regarded with outraged disapproval as unpatriotic colonials who had risen to political power on the wreck of that entirely necessary measure, the Militia Bill. "I have had two long interviews with the Duke

of Newcastle," Edward Watkin of the Grand Trunk Railway
wrote to John Sandfield Macdonald, "and found him at first
very angry and full of doubts as to the new ministry. He said
that he feared in the event of another danger the English
government dared not make the effort of last December over
again."[41] This was a very sad beginning in external relations.
But there was worse to come. Before the year ended, the
Macdonald-Sicotte government was to be dismally out of favour
with the colonial governments of Nova Scotia and New Brunswick as well as with Great Britain.

Macdonald did not believe that the new government would
last more than a twelvemonth. He told one of his correspondents, Samuel Amsden, that the policy of the party was
"to keep together and prepare for an election next year".
Probably not much effort would be necessary. The opposition
could forgo heroics and content itself with the most guilelessly
modest behaviour. "When Cartier and I crossed the floor,"
Macdonald told Amsden blandly, "we resolved to show the
country what a gentlemanlike and patriotic opposition was.
We resolved to give the new-comers fair play and offer no
factious opposition. Some hot-headed friends of ours were
dissatisfied with this, but I think they see now that we were
correct. We have shown that we did not wish to cling to office
for its own sake and we wish to show that we prefer the good
of the country to mere party triumph. . . . When the House
meets I will endeavour to prevent any vote of want of confidence. Let the Ministry have every chance to propose their
measures. If they are for the good of the country, pass them.
If not, oppose them. My opinion is that they are incapable
of satisfying the wishes of the country and that they must fall
from their own weakness and want of administrative ability.
Their absurd programme or platform with 'Double Majority',
etc., etc., must turn the country against them. Brown will
fight them on Rep. by Pop. and split them in two. If the
Government are defeated, it will be their own fault, and my
own opinion is that defeated they will be, but not by our
opposition. They will crumble to pieces before the end of the
session from their own weakness."[42]

In one way, there was nothing very daring about these prophecies. They were based, not on any little-known, special weaknesses of the Reform party, but on the general and notorious defects of all Canadian parties in the third decade of the union. John Sandfield Macdonald's administration might, indeed, fall within a year. But if John Alexander Macdonald's government succeeded, what guarantee was there, in the existing state of things, that it could last any longer? "I will play the party game if allowed to do so . . . ," he had told Samuel Amsden. But would he be allowed to do so? Had the time not arrived when he, and everybody else, must stop playing the party game for a while—when all parties, or, at least, the bigger, more responsible parties, must unite to bring about a radical change in the constitution? That summer he had several long and significant conversations with a curious, apparently self-appointed intermediary named David Shaw, who, in a strictly private fashion, was trying to promote a union of parties to carry constitutional reform. Shaw saw George Brown and then Macdonald. He reported to Brown that Macdonald was prepared to support Rep. by Pop. as a less serious evil than the Double Majority; he told Macdonald that Brown would be prepared to join with him in a union government pledged to carry that great measure.[43] But like a good many intermediaries, before and since, Shaw found himself quickly disavowed by his principals. He probably misrepresented Macdonald; he certainly misrepresented Brown; and Brown wrote in some heat to say that his remarks had been entirely misconceived, that he had never suggested such a demoralizing thing as a coalition of parties, and that he did not contemplate for a moment renewing friendly personal intercourse with Macdonald, who had made charges against him of such a character "that until entirely withdrawn must debar any other than Parliamentary intercourse between us".[44] After this, Shaw's negotiations rather languished; but their life, however brief, had had a certain cloudy significance. Macdonald may merely have been trying to trap Brown into giving open assistance in the attack on the Macdonald-Sicotte administration; but, on the other hand, he may have been genuinely prepared to sink

party differences for the sake of radical but necessary reform.
He could look at the matter disinterestedly, at any rate, for
his own ambitions were not involved. And Shaw grasped this
fact clearly. ". . . My intention," Macdonald wrote privately
to another correspondent at this time, "is *entre nous* to keep out
of the government myself. I have had enough of it and must
set to work to make a little money."[45]

This feeling, that the year 1862 would mark a firm period
in his career, must have been greatly strengthened by another
event which took place that autumn. On October 24, his
mother died. It was almost exactly forty-two years since she
and her husband had opened the first of their shops in Kingston,
and slightly over twenty-one years since Hugh himself had
died. Despite the shocks which, for years now, had racked and
prostrated her body, she had lived sturdily on. She had clung
tenaciously to her independence, to her own separate establishment—the house at Portsmouth—where she and Louisa and
Hugh lived, and where a room was always kept in readiness
for the return of her famous son. She was gone now, and with
her went a good deal of the past—the old stories of Scotland,
the clearest recollections of his father, of his own childhood,
of the shops in Kingston, and the long summers at the Stone
Mills. His wife was dead. His mother was dead. He had
lost political power, and all these conclusions, big and little,
seemed to combine to mark the end of a definite period of
his existence. He was still only forty-seven. With a good
third of his life still to come, he could resume his lucrative
practice and pick up all the other interests that he had had
to drop so largely during the last eight years. That autumn,
shortly after his mother's death, he sailed for England. There
may have been matters connected with the maternal estate in
Scotland which had to be attended to. But now he was free
to investigate the prospects of the future as well as to wind up
the affairs of the past. He could discuss the business of the
Trust and Loan Company in a leisurely fashion with Frederick
Fearon. He could talk over possible speculations with Edward
Watkin—and at a fortunate moment, too, for Watkin and his

pushing friends were already negotiating for the purchase of the Hudson's Bay Company.

It was over twelve years since he had last visited England in an unofficial capacity. His reception this time was very different. He was, of course, far better known than he had been; and he could hardly have been more favourably known than he was at that very moment. To official London, he appeared as the patriotic sponsor of the Militia Bill, while his opponents, two of whom happened to be in London at the same time, were naturally distrusted as the authors of its defeat. Sicotte and Howland, together with representatives from Nova Scotia and New Brunswick, had come over to complete the financial arrangements for the Intercolonial Railway. At last, after years of vain negotiations, this project seemed actually to be under way. Great Britain, alarmed by the transport difficulties at the time of the *Trent* crisis, had offered to guarantee a provincial loan to be used for the purpose of the railway; and, in September, the three provinces concerned had finally agreed on a division of the costs. Everything appeared to be settled when the delegates assembled in London. But the Canadians, refusing to accept the sinking fund which the British government had insisted upon as the indispensable condition of its financial guarantee, suddenly and completely broke off the negotiations. They were now in bad odour with everybody; and they flung angrily away almost at the moment that Macdonald arrived. His appearance could hardly have been better timed. His reception, though unofficial, could hardly have been more pleasant. He was given a temporary membership at the Athenaeum. Various people competed for his company at week-ends; and the Duke of Newcastle himself was graciously pleased to grant him an interview. "I shall be very glad," wrote C. B. Adderley, one of the sternest of the "anti-colonials" in Parliament, "to let you see in me the lamentable ignorance prevailing here of Canada and to get you to cure it as far as possible in my case."[46]

He reached Quebec again on February 18, only a few days after the session opened. Outwardly his role was very much what it had been before. "I find our friends in the House—

indeed in both Houses—in very good health and spirits and eager for the fray," he told Samuel Amsden.[47] Apparently he was still "playing the party game", making the usual small moves on the battered political chessboard, guarding with jealous fondness every piece that could possibly be pressed into service in the attack against Macdonald and Sicotte. Even the old animosities—the venerable rivalry with John Hillyard Cameron and the irreconcilable quarrel with George Brown— were now discovered to be luxuries too costly to keep up during the rigorous poverty of opposition. At a dinner, which was given to Macdonald at Russell's Hotel the day after he arrived in Quebec, Cameron told the delighted company that the hatchet—if it had ever been lifted between Macdonald and himself—was now solemnly buried.[48] And when George Brown at last sought to re-enter parliament by contesting the vacant seat in North Oxford, the local Conservatives decided to repay his slashing attacks on the Macdonald-Sicotte government by giving him their enthusiastic support.[49] Secretly Macdonald was going a good deal further. At his instigation, no doubt, Malcolm Cameron, the old leader of the Clear Grits, renewed the delicate conversations with George Brown, which David Shaw had taken it upon himself to begin the previous summer. "I saw Brown," he reported to Macdonald, "and nothing is nearer to his heart than to upset the ship, but it is to him impossible unless Rep. by Pop. is in some way got over, and he says he understands the Cartier party was prepared to give two or three members to the West."[50] This was a big affair, very unlike the small change of party manoeuvres. He still could not see his way through it; and, in the meantime, the Conservative rank and file grew more impatient for a final, frontal assault. "We can put the ministry out whenever we like," Macdonald wrote to Amsden, "but the pear is not yet ripe." What was he to do? Where would a new and stable government get its support? Who was to lead it and what were its policies to be? The great difficulty, Rose wrote to Ellice, was to know what to put in the place of the Macdonald-Sicotte administration. "Your old friend Cartier is unbecomingly eager to get back to power, but there are very great objections to him, and yet there is hardly a Frenchmen to take his place. If he would but show himself superior to office, and agree to support some friendly government for a time, he would do himself lasting credit and the country a service. Macdonald—the late Attorney-General—is all for taking this course and anxious that Cartier should."[51]

Macdonald held his hand for a while yet. He had told Amsden that he fully expected the Macdonald-Sicotte government to ruin itself; and it suited his purpose to wait while the ministry reeled onward on its career of prodigal ineptitude. Already, within a year of taking office, it had chalked up a fairly consistent record of disavowed engagements and abandoned principles. It had, as John Rose put it, "shuffled out" of its responsibilities for defence and its railway engagements. And what was perhaps even worse, several of its members from Canada West, the old followers of Brown, had most obviously "shuffled out" of their Grit principles. From the very beginning it had been clear, from their mere acceptance of office in a government whose avowed policy was the Double Majority, that they had abandoned Rep. by Pop.; and during the session of 1863 it became equally apparent, as a result of the debates on R. W. Scott's Separate School Bill, that they had given up their old beliefs in non-sectarian schools. The whole history of the Scott bill was, in itself, a faltering, unhappy confession of weakness. The ministry as a whole, fearful of losing its strong support in Canada West, had not dared to introduce the bill as a government measure; but the ministers individually, worried by the prospect of arraying the whole of Canada East against them, had decided that they must give it their support. McDougall, the first leader of the Clear Grits, the author of the revolutionary Grit programme of 1851, actually voted in favour of Separate Schools; and for an amusing quarter of an hour Macdonald read maddeningly from the official journals of the Assembly to prove how frequently and consistently the poor Commissioner of Crown Lands had voted, while in opposition, against their extension, and in favour of their total abolition.[52] Yet even ignominious reversals such as this were not the end of the government's humiliations. The Scott

Separate School Bill passed, but in a fashion characteristic of such measures. A majority of the whole House voted in its favour; a majority of the members from Canada West voted against it. It was, in other words, a sectional, a "single", majority. Yet Double Majority was professedly the fundamental guiding principle of the government. What would it do? What explanation could it possibly give? It did nothing. It said nothing. It gave no explanations, yet it continued in office.

Macdonald decided that it would not remain in office much longer. As early as March 3, Rose had prophesied that the ministry would be turned out by a direct vote of want of confidence shortly after the Easter recess. The Easter recess came and went. The House reassembled and the Conservatives grew hourly more impatient. James Patton wrote from Toronto to ask how long Macdonald intended to keep McDougall, Foley and Co. in suspense. "Have they not had enough rope yet?" he enquired.[53] It was Friday, May 1, before Macdonald finally rose to address the House on his want-of-confidence motion.[54] He spoke for two hours—a long attack on the government's failure to live up to its professions. Almost exactly a week later—at 1.25 a.m. on the morning of Friday, May 8 —the vote finally came. The government was defeated by sixty-four to fifty-nine votes. John Sandfield Macdonald asked for a dissolution; and unlike Brown, he got it. A short while after, the seventh parliament of the Province of Canada ceased to exist.

IV

On Tuesday, May 19, Macdonald arrived in Kingston by the late night train, and the next day he appeared in the streets, talking with friends and acquaintances and "looking in most excellent health and evidently in the best of spirits".[55] He viewed the election—as he viewed all elections—with a cynically jocular smile. For him they had only some of the excitement, and all of the uncertainty, of a horse race; and he had to admit that in the last few hours of the old parliament the odds against him had perceptibly lengthened. Sandfield Macdonald had abandoned the now obviously untenable principle of Double Majority and had made his peace with George Brown. In the Cabinet, Oliver Mowat, a zealous follower of Brown, had been substituted for Michael Foley, his fat and frequently inebriated critic; and the places which Sicotte and the moderates from Canada East had once occupied were now filled by Dorion and his more radical followers. It was as clear as it could be that Sandfield Macdonald, now strengthened by George Brown's vehement support, was bent, at all costs, upon the recovery of Canada West. Electoral reform, which, of course, had been proscribed before, was now to be treated as an open question; and the Separate School Bill, which was law in any case, was in some sense redeemed by the grace of George Brown's forgiveness. The angry floodwaters seemed to be returning to their original channels. There was no longer any opportunity, for John A. Macdonald, of new alliances and new and radical policies. It was a straight party fight of the old kind. And he was far less fitted to win a straight party fight in Canada West in 1863 than he had been in 1861. Then the Conservatives had campaigned freely with Rep. by Pop. as an open question. Now they were committed by their stand on Scott's Separate School Bill. Most of the Conservatives had followed Macdonald and voted for the bill, while the Reformers had rejected the leadership of McDougall and others and voted against it. The rank and file of Grits were free from stigma, and their party was united as it had not been for years.

Macdonald once again accepted the inescapable burden of leadership. There was no way out of it. He knew everybody and everybody looked to him. Weeks before the election commenced he was busily writing his innumerable little letters to his political correspondents in each riding, recommending candidates, advising about strategy and tactics, pleading for reconciliations and unity—"let there be no splits". Everybody wrote to him in return. Everybody confided in him, appealed to him, demanded his presence, and drew upon his campaign money. "I can get them to do absolutely nothing," John

Duggan wrote from Toronto, ". . . they say, 'we'll wait till John A. comes up . . .'."[56] He was so bothered and driven by these ceaseless importunities—by these repeated and rather peremptory requests to raise drooping spirits and to unravel angry political tangles—that he must have been relieved at the prospect of a comparatively easy contest in Kingston. This time it was not an important secondary politician such as Oliver Mowat, but another one of those worthy, respectable, unknown Kingstonians, O. S. Gildersleeve, who was put up to oppose him. When nomination day came on June 12, poor Gildersleeve's single flag and tiny troop of followers contrasted comically with Macdonald's three bands, gaily decorated waggons and carriages, and hundreds of defiantly marching Conservatives.[57] "As for Kingston," Patton wrote from Toronto, "everyone laughs at Gildersleeve's vanity in supposing that he could rob you of your old and tried friends. . . ."[58] Gildersleeve was, of course, infinitely ridiculous. Gildersleeve, unlike Oliver Mowat, was not to be taken seriously. Yet, when the votes were counted, it was discovered that Gildersleeve had received only one vote less than Mowat and that Macdonald had barely bettered his majority. It was a shock; and other and worse shocks were to follow it. The defeats began to accumulate. Sometimes, of course, failure was expected and discounted in advance—as it was, for example, in the case of poor Ephraim Cook, who campaigned valiantly against George Brown in South Oxford. "It is impossible to meet such a man in a back country as this," Cook told Macdonald lugubriously, "—500 devils could not begin to tell the yarns he does—and not one word of truth."[59] Yet in other ridings, untroubled by Brown's furious presence, where the Conservatives imagined they had a real chance, the toll of casualties grew longer and longer. The Conservatives went down. But they went down battling. "We had a fight," T. M. Daly reported from Stratford, "and twenty of the Grits are under medical treatment yet, only two of my men got hurt and they were up next day."[60]

It was impossible to escape the plain facts. The Conservatives had done badly in Canada West. The scant victory of 1861 had been converted into a defeat as serious as that of

1857. It was bad; but it was, quite literally, only half bad. For in Canadian elections there was always another, and a very different, side of the story. The thesis of Canada West invariably provoked the antithesis of Canada East; the Upper Canadian action was followed automatically by the Lower Canadian reaction. In exactly the same fashion as the Conservatives in 1861, the Reformers had won in the west and lost in the east. The Lower Canadian Conservatives were almost jubilant. "Things have not gone so well as you expected in U. Canada," Cauchon wrote to Macdonald. "Nevertheless there is no cause for despair and your only duty now is to gather your scattered soldiers and to bring them in good spirits with our Lower Canadian troops on the field of battle."[61] With good management, Cauchon thought, and a little judicious yielding on Cartier's part, they could muster fifty votes from Canada East; and Macdonald's reduced contingent from Canada West would number another twenty at least. "That would make seventy in all," Cauchon concluded hopefully, "and more than necessary to upset the fellows." The old game was about to begin again, and on almost exactly the same terms. The old and rather ignominious search for allies had already recommenced. Cartier was sounding out Sicotte. Patton—so he wrote Macdonald—was listening with sympathetic attentiveness while Foley unburdened his mind on the "damned treachery" of Sandfield Macdonald.

"I leave here for Quebec on Friday," Macdonald wrote a friend from Kingston on August 5, "so as to be early on the ground."[62] An autumn meeting of the new parliament was necessary because the sudden dissolution had prevented the completion of a good deal of business; and later in August the Assembly met with the two parties in an exquisitely dangerous state of near balance. "We are going to upset these fellows, I think, this week," Macdonald wrote in September.[63] But at the last moment the government collected sufficient votes to defeat a want-of-confidence motion; and when the session closed on October 15, Sandfield Macdonald was still precariously in power. This kind of thing could apparently go on for ever. It was not exactly stalemate. There were always

a few small moves that could be made. There were always a
few votes that might be won. John A. Macdonald had gained
the increasingly popular McGee, and, as the autumn wore on,
it looked also as if he were going to capture Foley. The
ousted Reform leader had already begun to write plaintively ingratiating letters to him; and now he redoubled the fervour
of his professions. He would turn over an absolutely new leaf![64]
He had already joined the Sons of Temperance! He would
soon declare himself unreservedly a supporter of the Conservative party. One vote more! It would almost do it. Two—
and the thing would be a certainty! And, as everybody had
known all autumn, the second vote would soon be open for
competition. The government had not yet appointed a Solicitor-
General for Canada West; and the appointment, which would
require the new official to seek re-election, would instantly
open a solitary seat for contest. "If they lose this election in
U.C.," wrote Macdonald, appealing for funds to Brown Chamberlin of Montreal, "it will be Sandfield's coup de grace. Herein
fail not an thou lovest me!"[65] Everybody was on the alert. Who
would get the appointment? What seat would be thrown open?
There were repeated rumours. And towards the last of December, 1863, the government finally made its move. A. N.
Richards was appointed Solicitor-General; and the open constituency was South Leeds.

It might have been a general election. "If you decide on
war to the knife," wrote Alleyn, "draw on me at seven days'
sight for five hundred dollars. I regret it is not five thousand."[66]
It was to be, Macdonald decided, "war to the knife", and the
whole party began to roll into action. D. F. Jones, the Conservative candidate opposing Richards, wrote from Gananoque,
modestly suggesting that if Macdonald, McGee, Campbell,
and one or two others would range through the riding following his opponent, a great deal would be gained. "Chrysler
says," he wrote, "they want to see John A.—and I think if
he shewed himself in the county, and at the nomination, etc.,
it would have a good effect—but the great thing will be the
needful."[67] The "needful" poured in in fairly copious quantities. It was true that at first there was a dreadful rumour

that the Bank of Montreal was secretly aiding Richards; but John Rose went quickly to interview the president and the general manager, and the rumour turned out happily to be false. Railwaymen such as Brydges of the Grand Trunk, and contractors such as David Macpherson, who wished to get ahead with the Intercolonial Railway, contributed readily enough in support of the Conservative cause. "As long as the present men remain in power," Brydges wrote, "we can do nothing and the Lower Provinces will be driven to connect with Portland instead of Quebec."⁶⁸ Armed with these resources, Macdonald and his new ally, Thomas D'Arcy McGee, plunged into the riding on an extended speaking tour. These two "outsiders", as the *Globe* called them contemptuously—the "pretended" Orangeman and the "pretended" Roman Catholic— together accomplished the defeat of poor Mr. Richards, and in the last days of January the letters and telegrams of congratulation began to flow in.

"We have no difficulty in acknowledging," the *Globe* declared editorially with a somewhat odd, detached realism, "that the defeat of Mr. Richards is a serious blow to the administration. After the defection of Mr. Foley, parties being so nearly balanced last session, they could ill afford to lose the vote of the Solicitor-General."⁶⁹ The Conservatives were, of course, triumphant. Everybody was suddenly talking about preparing for a new general election, and building a new political organization, and taking "the Grits in the hour of their prostration". It was all very well, and Macdonald himself had been talking about the need of organization as recently as December; but as the prospect of the defeat of the government grew clearer and clearer, the old questions—which he had been asking himself for years now—came back with renewed force. Upon what basis could a really stable government be formed? And who was to assume the leadership that he had grown so tired of? Back in the previous spring, Rose had suggested that Campbell, who had had no part in the history of the old Conservative government, might suitably take over; and others, of only less importance, agreed that the Grits might be robbed of half their powers of attack if the Conservatives could only

present themselves to the public under a different name.
Campbell would certainly make a respectable titular head:
but would the Conservatives ever accept him as the actual
leader? Macpherson thought not. He told Macdonald that he
did not believe it would be possible for him to transfer his
command to another:[70] and James Patton of Toronto—another
correspondent to whom Macdonald had confided his plan of
retirement—rejected the idea even more conclusively. "I believe," he wrote, "that a Ministry formed on our side, without
you and Cartier as the master minds, *would not hold together*."
Macdonald must not even suggest the possibility of resigning.
He could not effectively play Brown's role; and if he abandoned
the leadership in the Assembly, the party would simply break
up piecemeal. "No!" Patton concluded forcibly. "Your position
is such, by common consent, that proper deference would
always be paid to your advice, for it is felt that your generalship
can carry the Party through when another man—no matter
how able—would fail. *You* bring to bear the experience of a
quarter century in Parliamentary warfare and *no man* on our
side *can take your place*."[71]

Well, he would see. But obviously the moment in which a
decision would have to be made was coming closer and closer.
And the question of leadership was inextricably bound up
with the question of policy—policy for the Province of Canada,
and perhaps for British North America as a whole. For months,
almost for years now, he and his opponents had gone on
making these small adjustments, fighting these mimic battles,
rejoicing over these insignificant victories; but the time was
surely coming when some government—a government in which
he might exercise an influence if he did not play a leading
part—would have to grapple at last with the really big issues.
During the American Civil War, these problems had grown
more serious; and ever since the summer of 1863, when the
loss of the battle of Gettysburg had put the southern Confederacy upon the defensive, they had become more urgent
still. What was to be done about this knotted tangle of problems—defence, the West, British North American communications and British North American political reorganization? The

Americans, irritated with both Great Britain and her colonies, were threatening to abrogate the Reciprocity Treaty and to repeal the bonding laws which made possible the free transit of Canadian goods through the republic. Great Britain, which had already sent one group of military experts to investigate and report upon Canadian defences, might be expected soon to raise the military problem in a more acute form. The newly reorganized Hudson's Bay Company was making great plans for the development of the West. The Grand Trunk authorities, worried at the prospect of a connection between the Maritime and American railways, were anxiously promoting the old Intercolonial once more. Nothing whatever had been done about the central difficulty of the Canadian union. It had left everybody baffled and exhausted. The plan for a federal union of the Canadas, and the rival plan for a federal union of British North America, were both apparently dead. And in the meantime, down in Halifax and Fredericton, they were beginning to talk seriously of a legislative union of the Maritime Provinces.

Could anything be done without a coalition of major parties? It was over eighteen months now since the officious Shaw had first begun the very tentative overtures to Brown. Was it possible that the time had arrived to renew them, even more hopefully? Later in December he noted with interest that the *Globe* had been "pitching into" McDougall for his abandonment of Rep. by Pop. Was the reconciliation between Brown and the members of the Sandfield Macdonald government already wearing a little thin? These were questions which he must have pondered deeply during the long three-day journey from Kingston to Quebec through the snow-piled landscape of winter. C. J. Brydges, who, as a promoter of the Intercolonial, had his own reasons for being interested in Brown and the *Globe*, agreed to see the western Grit leader when he was in Quebec on railway business and to report back to Macdonald. Brydges, who suspected that the post office, under the pure administration of Sandfield Macdonald, was systematically tampering with his correspondence, was careful to send his reports through an intermediary. He had a curiously interest-

ing but inconclusive story to tell. Brown, he reported, was
certainly angry with the Sandfield Macdonald government and
fully expected its immediate fall. The great editor was prepared
to talk future politics, and even to consider Brydges' offers in
a gingerly fashion; but, as Brydges admitted sadly, "it did not
go as far as could be wished", for Brown would not give him
the opening. "I offered him the chair of the Canada Board
of Hudson's Bay," the manager of the Grand Trunk wrote
Macdonald, "at which I think he was a good deal impressed,
but would not say positively. . . . I showed him that nothing
could be done about Northwest without the Intercolonial. On
the latter point he is much mollified—thinks that the action of
the Yankees about reciprocity and bonding has put an entirely
new phase on the question, and that it ought now to be seriously
taken into consideration. . . . He does not object I think to the
marrying of Northwest and Intercolonial but wants the number of items enlarged. He wishes an omnibus arrangement
to include Northwest, Intercolonial, Representation, and change
of tariff by lowering duties."[72] Brown, Brydges reported, would
support such a programme and believed that it could be carried;
but that was as far as the editor of the *Globe* was prepared
to go. "He could not be secured at the moment," Brydges
admitted, "but you can now judge if it is best to press him
further now."[73]

No, it would not be best, Macdonald decided, to press him
any further at the moment. It would be useless, as well as
undignified, to follow that faint but tantalizing trail any longer.
As the session opened, he settled down in Quebec without
any clear plan for the future. His new quarters, which were
much nearer the legislature than the old, were comfortable
enough; and, as he told his sister, Louisa, "I am pretty well
just now, barring an occasional colic, which sticks to me with
wonderful pertinacity."[74] His health was all right, he was
in the best of spirits; and, amid the general fog of uncertainty,
there were at least some desired objectives that he could see
clearly. A broad coalition government, in which the old Liberal-
Conservatives would be fittingly represented, must be formed,
capable of dealing at last with the really big issues. He himself,

having assisted in its formation and given it his blessing, would gracefully retire. All this—and his retirement in particular— was quite clear. It was like a far hill lit by a single shaft of sunlight. But all around was dark with shadow. And, like everybody else, he was frightened of losing his way, frightened of bumping into difficulties, frightened of taking positive steps in any direction. He had always stood for the unity of the British lands bordering on the St. Lawrence River system. He had always held that, if the legislative union of Upper and Lower Canada were to be given up, it must be surrendered only for a really strong union of the whole of British North America; and, from the very beginning of the American Civil War, he had repeatedly warned his fellow-countrymen that in their proposed general union, they must at all costs avoid the manifest weaknesses of American federalism. With this important change of emphasis, he had still stuck to the Conservative plan of 1858. But in the meantime his unhappy doubts had been growing stronger. Was it possible to frame a plan of federal union which would be immune from the dangers which American experience had revealed?

He could no longer be certain. His first objective was the strength of real unity; and if federation could not ensure that strength, then another and safer form of union might have to be substituted for federation. He must have realized that these vigorous conclusions would embarrass the unity of the party; but that did not prevent him from speaking his mind when, on March 14, Brown moved for a select committee of nineteen on the problem of the constitution. Galt, who spoke early in the debate, insisted that the plan of the Liberal-Conservative government had been, and remained, Confederation, and that the proposed legislative union of the Maritime Provinces was an important preliminary step towards it. Scoble, who followed Galt, declared roundly that he did not believe in federal union, and did not wish to see repeated in Canada a plan which had so manifestly failed in the United States. Macdonald called out, "hear, hear", and later, when he himself was on his feet, he told the House that British North American union, if it ever came, must be a complete union.

"The sad experience on the other side," he continued, "proved it must not be merely a federal one; that instead of having a federal one, we should have a Legislative Union in fact, in principle and in practice."[75] This, in view of the past, was an oddly independent pronouncement; and Brown inquired satirically whether that was the policy which the Liberal-Conservative government had previously announced. "That is not my policy," Cartier said grimly, and the House laughed. It was a tempting opportunity for the Reformers; and Brown promptly denounced Macdonald as a man who had proved his want of fixed principles by a total abandonment of the Conservative Confederation scheme of 1858. Macdonald, who had already attacked Brown in much the same fashion for his apparently waning interest in Rep. by Pop., might have retorted that his old antagonist relied far too much on principles, programmes, and resolutions, and far too little on the humdrum but necessary machinery of cabinet government. Macdonald realized at any rate that a broad coalition government could alone tackle the enigma of the Canadian constitution. But what was the solution to be? Once he had thought he knew. And he still believed that above all else a strong union was necessary. That was the most important principle and he clung to it.

In the meantime, the desired and dreaded event which he had anticipated so long drew rapidly closer. The Conservatives massed their full strength for the defeat of the government; and on March 21, without even waiting for the vote on the want-of-confidence motion, John Sandfield Macdonald and his Cabinet resigned. Now was the moment for which he had hoped. Years ago he had told his sister, Margaret, that he intended to give up politics as soon as he could "with honour". Surely now he could honourably retire! Surely this was the moment to form that broad administration composed of the veteran moderates of both parties! For obvious reasons, the Governor shared these views and was prepared to act on them. The old leaders of both old parties had failed him. He could legitimately look elsewhere. And the search for new men began. Monck turned first to Fergusson Blair, who had been a member of the Sandfield Macdonald government. When Fergusson

Blair reported his failure, he then invited Alexander Campbell to undertake the task. For months the Conservatives had been grooming Macdonald's old partner for this very role; and now that his moment had arrived Campbell struggled long and desperately to gain the necessary support. Yet he failed as well. There was still no government. The days went by; and, as time passed fruitlessly, the pressure upon Macdonald steadily increased. It came from all directions, from both circumstances and persons, from ex-cabinet ministers, Members of Parliament, and from obscure followers of the Liberal-Conservative party who wrote or spoke to him, begging him not to desert them. "If you take the helm all is well," one of them wrote, "if not, disaster is certain to follow . . . Surely all our conquests, our fights, our triumphs are not to end in this way. John A. not the U.C. leader!—bosh, the Government won't stand."[76] It was this very argument, couched, no doubt, in more literary terms, that old Dr. Etienne Taché was now pressing upon him; and to Taché, as a last resort, the now nearly frantic Governor had turned. Macdonald gave in, as he had given in so often before. He would make one last effort. On March 30, after nine days of interregnum, the Taché government was formed; and the next day the weary House adjourned.

A stiff north-west wind had filled the St. Lawrence opposite Quebec with drifting ice. The steamer which carried passengers across the river to the Grand Trunk station at Levis—there was no North Shore Railway then—was stopped; and Macdonald and Campbell, who dared, like a few others, to cross in a canoe, were driven through drifting ice to a point far below their destination.[77] There was need for haste. So much had to be done in the brief interval of the adjournment. So much; and yet what, after all, would it possibly avail? The old government had, in effect, come back again. Dr. Taché had admittedly been out of politics for a few years; but everybody remembered that he had been first minister of the Liberal-Conservative government as recently as 1857. Campbell, who had accepted the post of Commissioner of Crown Lands, was known as a respected semi-independent, and Foley and McGee, who had also joined the new government, had been Reformers of some prominence in the past; but, whatever their previous affiliations, they could not bring with them sufficient support to change the character of the Taché government in any essential. It would stand as a Liberal-Conservative government; and—what was even more important—it would probably fall as a Liberal-Conservative government, and in short order. When parliament met again on May 3 after the adjournment, Macdonald doubtless had very little hope. The poor, unfortunate Foley had already been defeated in his by-election, and in the House the two sides were almost in perfect balance. The government stuck it out for nearly a month; but at last, on June 14, it was defeated by a majority of two.⁷⁸ Macdonald told the House next day that, as a result of the vote, he and his colleagues had decided that it was their duty to communicate with the Governor. What would happen he had, as yet, almost no idea. But he knew at least that the last card in the old game had been played.

Chapter Thirteen

British North America in Conference

I

Yet, even on Wednesday, June 15, there were a few slight signs that this "ministerial crisis" would not end as all ministerial crises had done before. When Macdonald had finished his announcement, John Sandfield Macdonald got up immediately to demand further information. It was the usual opposition request. But George Brown did not give it exactly the usual support that might have been expected of him. He agreed, of course, that the House had a right to information; but he felt "that in the position of great gravity in which the honourable gentlemen opposite were now placed, they should be allowed every fair opportunity to consider what course they should pursue".[1] A new attitude of concern and conciliation was faintly suggested even in this public pronouncement. In private Brown had already gone much further. On Tuesday evening and Wednesday morning he had spoken to several Conservatives, urging strongly that the present crisis should be used to settle the Canadian constitutional problem for ever, and stating that he was prepared to co-operate with the existing, or any other, government that would deal with that problem promptly and firmly. These words were, by permission, communicated to John A. Macdonald and Galt; and Macdonald immediately changed the direction which his baffled government had already taken. The ministers, in despair of achieving a stable government in the existing House, had advised a dissolution and an appeal to the people. But there was no guarantee that a new general election would give either party a solid majority, and no hope whatever that it could end the sectional difficulty. Brown's words implied something quite different and infinitely more promising. It was what Macdonald had been hoping and working for, through tentative, indirect approaches, ever since the summer of 1862. He had made advances himself in the past. Now he was ready to respond to the advances of others. On Thursday, just before three o'clock in the afternoon, when the galleries were rapidly filling up with eager spectators, and the members were chatting idly in the Assembly room, waiting for the Speaker to take the chair, he approached the member for South Oxford. Would Brown have any objection to meeting Galt and himself to talk the matter over? And Brown replied, "Certainly not."[2]

On Friday, at about one o'clock, Macdonald and Galt called on Brown at the St. Louis Hotel. Only three days before, Macdonald had still felt at liberty to record his theoretical preference for legislative union. On June 14, the very day of the defeat of his government, Brown's constitutional committee had reported that "a strong feeling was found to exist among the members of the committee in favour of changes in the direction of a federative system, applied either to Canada alone, or to the whole British North American Provinces. . . ."[3] And Macdonald had publicly dissented. He had stuck to his own private convictions, in their extremest form, as long as the issue remained an academic question. But now it had been transferred from the debating society of a committee to the practical politics of government; and as he and Galt walked that day into the lobby of the St. Louis Hotel, he realized that he must give way. When Brown inquired courteously what remedy the government proposed for the constitutional difficulty, Macdonald and Galt replied that their remedy was a federal union of British North America. And when Brown, in his turn, was asked what solution he preferred, he answered that he advocated parliamentary reform based on population. Each side rejected the other's initial proposal with equal firmness; and the preliminary exchange of diplomatic courtesies was over. Then the two Conservatives made the obvious sug-

gestion that the recommendations of Brown's constitutional
committee offered the best basis for an agreement; and "after
much discussion on both sides, it was found that a compromise
might probably be had in the adoption either of the federal
principle for all British North American Provinces, as the larger
question, or for Canada alone. . . ."⁴ The two policies, Conservatives and Reform, were to be combined as alternatives in
a single programme. But which was to come first? For obviously
no government could pursue both policies together. It was
the crucial question. They were still discussing it, and Brown
was still insisting "that the Canadian Federation should be
constituted first", when they all realized that their time was
almost up. It was nearly three o'clock. They would have to
meet the House. But they could confidently ask it for a
further and longer adjournment, now that there was a real hope
of an agreement.

The galleries were crowded once again when Macdonald
rose to make his announcement. He told the House that the
Governor had, that very morning, given the Cabinet permission
to dissolve. He informed the eagerly listening members that
the ministry, reserving the newly granted authority, had already
begun discussions with the member for Oxford in the hope of
finding a basis for a stronger government in the existing House.⁵
Dorion complained that the government was using the power
of dissolution to coerce the Assembly. John Sandfield Macdonald supported his objections. It was clear that the little
group of *Rouges* from Canada East, and the still smaller "tail"
of Sandfield Macdonald Reformers from the Ottawa valley,
would certainly oppose any agreement that might be made
in the next few days. But that hardly mattered. For Brown
was now on his feet, making the most dramatic announcement
of his political career. He was sure, he said, that the members
would acquit him of any desire to aid the government in
coercing the House. Only the pressure of most extreme circumstances could have justified the government in making
its approaches to him; and only the force of the same extreme
circumstances could have justified him in meeting men to
whom he had been so long and strongly opposed. He paid

tribute to the spirit in which the members of the government had made their advances; and he promised that there would be no secrecy. Then he sat down. In another minute the Speaker rose. There was a great roar of applause from either side; and Dufresne, one of the members for Montreal, walked quickly across the floor of the House to shake Brown's hand. Then they were all shaking hands. And, in spirit at least, the new coalition was made.

After this, the principals could hardly fail. Next day, Saturday, June 18, they got down to it in earnest. There were repeated conferences between Brown on the one hand, and Macdonald, Galt, and Cartier on the other. Brown had an interview with the Governor-General, and saw a number of his own followers. Macdonald called a ministerial caucus, and sought, and obtained, approval for the course which he and Cartier were pursuing. At night, when the third of the conferences ended, they had at least agreed upon the main point of policy. Brown had made a vain last attempt to insist upon the immediate federation of the Canadas, with a provision for the future admission of the Maritime Provinces and the North West Territories. But Macdonald and his colleagues had declared that they would not consent to waive the larger issue; and in the verbal formula which was finally adopted as an alleged compromise, there was no doubt that the coalition would be committed to an immediate attempt to seek a general federation.[6] On this matter, Brown had had to give way; and, when the conference closed on Saturday night, Macdonald and Cartier were contending that he must also abandon his extreme demand that the Reformers should be given one-half the places in the coalition Cabinet. On Monday, when the discussions were resumed, with Sir E. P. Taché in attendance, this question of Grit representation in the coalition ministry had become the principal subject. Macdonald said that he was ready and willing to resign if his resignation would help matters. But he made it clear that if he remained in the Cabinet, he would not be content with any serious alteration in his position; and he refused to concede more than three places—exactly half the Upper Canadian division in the ministry—to the Reformers.

This was the arrangement which, after a good deal of further debate, was finally accepted on Tuesday. And this was the result which Macdonald communicated to the House in his "ministerial explanations" on Wednesday, June 22. A week later, on June 30, the House was finally prorogued. On the same day, George Brown, Oliver Mowat, and William Mc-Dougall were sworn into the Executive Council of the Province of Canada.

It had happened. The hopes held stubbornly for years had been realized. The union with George Brown was a fact; the broad coalition government had been brought into actual being; and its declared policy, though admittedly a compromise, was the compromise which Macdonald had proposed from the first. He had committed the new administration not to a division, but to an enlargement, of Canada, in a general federal union of British North America. It was his task now—the task for which he had clung to a place in the Cabinet—to see that the proposed federation was as strong as it could possibly be made. At the moment, circumstances seemed propitious—more propitious certainly than they had been back in 1858. On at least two occasions in the last few years, Newcastle, the recent Colonial Secretary, had declared that he was ready to consider sympathetically any scheme of union, regional or general, which had the consent of the parties concerned. The American Civil War had strengthened a mental attitude favourable to Macdonald's scheme; and the approaching conference of the Maritime Provinces supplied an occasion on which to launch it. This conference, which the Canadians had, of course, known about since the winter, could hardly help but be an important element in all their calculations. It was true that the Maritimers were scheduled to discuss only a union of their own legislatures. But, from the reports of the debates and from other more confidential sources of information, Macdonald may have begun to suspect that Maritime union, by itself, was a somewhat academic subject, which had aroused very little public enthusiasm, and which was favoured more by Maritime governors than it was by Maritime politicians. In any case, the delegates at the conference would probably be willing to interrupt their official discussions to listen while the Canadians presented unofficially the advantages of a different type of union.

It was in this sense that Monck wrote, on June 30, to the Governors of Nova Scotia, New Brunswick and Prince Edward Island. Would a delegation from the new coalition government of Canada be permitted to attend the proposed Maritime Conference to present a plan for a general federal union of British North America? This polite but unexpected request revealed an odd state of unpreparedness in the Maritime governments, which scarcely suggested any great zeal for legislative union. The three provincial legislatures had authorized their governments to appoint delegates to the approaching conference; but no delegates had in fact been appointed by any colony, and the very date and place of the conference were still unsettled.[7] The Maritime governments, jarred somewhat from their curious lethargy, answered courteously that of course the Canadians would be welcome. But two of the replies stressed the fact that Canadian participation must be entirely unofficial; and one Governor, Sir Richard Graves MacDonnell of Nova Scotia, was so uncertain about the matter, and so troubled about his own power to appoint any delegates without previous authorization from the imperial government, that he wrote back for reassurance to the Colonial Office.[8] By the end of July, the dilatory Maritime governments had at last decided on the time and place of their proposed meeting. It was to be at Charlottetown, Prince Edward Island, on September 1. At least there was to be a conference for the Canadians to attend.

Obviously the Maritime attitude to the general question of union was very different from what it had been back in 1858. That, as Macdonald knew very well from experience, was one very important point gained. But what of the Colonial Office? Had the rather cold neutrality that was so evident in Lytton's day altered for the better? There were several good reasons for believing that it had. In the first place, the very readiness of the Maritime governments to welcome a visit from the Canadians was sufficient in itself to remove one of Lytton's chief objections. It was true, although Macdonald had probably no means of knowing this, that the Duke of Newcastle had always privately believed that Maritime union ought to precede Confederation, and that the Intercolonial Railway ought to precede both.⁹ It was also true that the permanent officials of the Colonial Office, converted by the persuasive dispatches of a succession of Maritime governors, had come to believe devoutly in the wisdom and expediency of a legislative union of the three Lower Provinces. But Newcastle had never for a moment imagined that the imperial government should take the initiative in the matter, or that the private preferences of imperial officers should be permitted to disturb that attitude of benevolent neutrality which the Mother Country should maintain until the colonists had made up their minds. Moreover—a point of some importance—Newcastle was no longer at the Colonial Office. He had been succeeded by Edward Cardwell. There was no particular reason to assume in advance that Cardwell's private preferences on the subject of British North American unions would be the same as Newcastle's. There was, in short order, a good deal of reason to be certain that they were quite different.

During that July of 1864 the new Colonial Secretary was particularly preoccupied with Canadian affairs. There was Monck's laconic dispatch announcing the formation of the coalition government; there was Sir Richard MacDonnell's puzzled communication, with its news of the Canadian request to attend the Maritime Conference. Above all, there were the protracted discussions in the imperial Cabinet on the question of British North American, and particularly Canadian, defence —a question raised once more by the report of the military expert, Lieutenant-Colonel Jervois, who had made a tour of Canada and the Maritime Provinces in the autumn of 1863. There were members in the Cabinet—Gladstone by his own confession was the most prominent among them—who wished to make serious changes, "to shift the centre of responsibility", in the matter of British North American defence.¹⁰ But these members, though they voiced the currently fashionable dogmas on the subject, did not yet form the most numerous or influential body in the Cabinet. "I cannot admit," Palmerston wrote in a lengthy minute on a suggested change in Cardwell's proposed dispatch to Monck, "that it is a question for consideration or division whether our North American Provinces are to be fought for or abandoned. There may be much to be said for the theory put forward by some, that our Colonies are an encumbrance and an expense, and that we should be better without them, but that is not the opinion of England, and it is not mine."[11] It was not, indeed. And Palmerston's opinions, in a somewhat less robust form, were shared by other members of the Cabinet. Even Gladstone acknowledged that "the Cabinet as a whole is not prepared at the present time, and perhaps never may be prepared, to proceed upon such a basis" as he had laid down. The dispatch which Cardwell sent to Monck on August 6 assumed the continuance of imperial military help; but it also asserted the principle that the security of Canada must depend largely on the efforts and courage of its own people; and it invited the Canadian government to make definite proposals for the improvement of its defences in the light of the Jervois report.[12] A little later, towards the end of August, the British government also decided to send Colonel Jervois, the author of this disturbing document, back to Canada to assist the colonial authorities in making their decisions.

At the end of July, when these discussions of Canadian defence were going on, Cardwell was already well aware of the new Canadian coalition government and its project of a general British North American federation. In the minutes and letters which the ministers exchanged on the military question, there was no connection drawn between federation and defence, and no suggestion made that the former would promote the effectiveness of the latter. Yet the Colonial Office was obviously interested, in a speculative, academic way, in the Canadian proposal; and Gordon, the Lieutenant-Governor of New Brunswick, who was in London on leave during July, later recalled a conversation he had had on the subject with Cardwell and T. F. Elliot.[13] As might have been expected, the Colonial Office officials were a little bit jealous for the success of their pet project, Maritime union. The copious comments which they made on MacDonnell's dispatch, announcing the Canadian request, showed quite clearly that even Frederic

Rogers, the Permanent Under-Secretary, and Fortescue, the
Parliamentary Under-Secretary, were very insistent that "the
smaller union may not be imperilled or delayed by the discussion of a larger union. . . ."[14] But Cardwell obviously did
not share these apprehensions. There was no sign of them
in the minute which he himself wrote on Sir Richard's communication or in the reassuring dispatch which was sent back
to him on August 9.[15] There was equally little sign of displeasure at the presumption of the Canadians in the dispatch
which was written, after a few more leisurely days, to Monck,
asking for further information about Canada's request to attend
the Maritime Conference. It was not until September 10,
when the delegates had actually left Charlottetown, that
Monck's explanatory reply reached the Colonial Office. The
clerks were plainly dissatisfied. Monck ought to have done this.
He most certainly should have done that. It was all most
regrettably informal. But Cardwell was evidently not much
impressed with their strictures. "Put by," he wrote briefly on
the dispatch.[16]

II

On Monday, August 29, Macdonald boarded the Canadian
government steamer, *Queen Victoria,* at Quebec.[17] With him
was a large company of people. There were the seniors in
the Cabinet, Cartier, Brown and Galt, and their junior colleagues, McDougall, McGee, Campbell and Langevin; and
—what was distinctly unusual in British North American conferences—a secretarial staff of three. It was, for the times, a
large, determined, and well-equipped delegation that set out
from Quebec. But it had only the vaguest notion of what
its reception was likely to be at Charlottetown. The letters
from the Maritime government had been polite—but very
formally polite. The Maritimers might be simply annoyed by
this uninvited Canadian intrusion. The whole affair might
have a most deplorable ending. And yet, at the same time,
it was impossible not to regard the meeting at Charlottetown

as a divinely granted opportunity. The Canadians might succeed, though their mission was strictly unofficial; and if at
the end of the conference there it seemed a reasonable prospect
that a general federal union could be formed, then it would
be easy to call a formal conference on the subject.[18] The great
thing was to convince the Maritimers; and, as the *Queen
Victoria* travelled slowly down the Gulf of the St. Lawrence
towards Prince Edward Island, the Canadians must have been
frantically busy, putting the last touches to their federal plan
and deciding who had best speak on this or that phase of it.
It was late Wednesday night, the last day of August, when
the steamer began slowly to approach Charlottetown. The
somewhat incurious citizens of the capital city of Prince
Edward Island casually noticed a strange vessel just off the
harbour that night; and next morning the strange vessel, which
was without benefit of pilot, came timidly up the harbour,
casting the lead for safety at every few feet.[19] The exciting
news spread that the Canadians had arrived; and W. H. Pope,
a member of the Prince Edward Island government, procured
a small boat and rowed manfully out to the steamer to greet
them. The *Queen Victoria* hoisted its flag. The breathless
Pope presented the greetings of Charlottetown and Prince
Edward Island. And shortly after, while it was still morning,
the formidable Canadian delegation came ashore.

Charlottetown was crowded with a sudden influx of visitors.
The *Heather Belle* had brought the Nova Scotian delegation
on the afternoon of August 31; the New Brunswickers had
arrived on the *Prince of Wales* a little before midnight on the
same day. But the conference on Maritime union was not the
only, nor, indeed, the main, attraction which drew people towards the somnolent little town of Charlottetown on the last
day of August, 1864. There was also a circus, the first circus
to visit the Island, it was said, in twenty-one years, and people
were travelling eagerly from sixty miles away to behold it.
"What is the cause of this 'wonderful migration'?" the correspondent of the Saint John *Morning Telegraph* enquired
satirically. "The circus, Sir, the circus," came the answer from
a dozen throats as the "surging throng" swept past him.[20] The

circus not only attracted people from all over the Island; it also
apparently attracted a good many members of the Prince Edward
Island government. At any rate they were not on the dock to
greet the delegates. Not a soul was on hand to give an official
welcome to the Nova Scotians. There was not even a carriage
or a waggon, so it was said, to take them or their belongings
to hotels.[21] Pope, the indefatigable Provincial Secretary, hurried
out alone to welcome the New Brunswickers, and the Canadians. And after this rather meagre reception, it was discovered
that there was difficulty about lodging. The New Brunswickers
could be put up at the Mansion House; but there was not
enough room for the Canadians at the Franklin. The embarrassed Islanders subsequently tried to excuse themselves for
this unfortunate lack of accommodation by pointing out that
Monck had indicated a Canadian delegation of only four.[22] In
the end, some of the Canadians stayed in town at the Franklin
House; but most of them remained in the *Queen Victoria,*
and among these, with his secretaries, was Macdonald.

It was an awkward beginning. Was it an unhappy symbol
of the Canadians' real position? Physically their delegation was
half in town and half out in the harbour; morally, they were
a part, yet not a real part, of the conference. Was the whole
enterprise to end in embarrassment, irritation, and defeat? The
first hour or so after the landing at Charlottetown must have
been full of painful uncertainties. And yet, though the Canadians were, of course, unaware of it, their problem was already
solved in a fashion which could hardly have been more favourable. On Thursday morning, September 1, as the *Queen Victoria* was moving deliberately up the harbour towards Charlottetown, the Maritime Conference had held its first meeting. The
delegates had scarcely assembled when the news of the imminent arrival of the Canadians was announced. And then an
odd but revealing event occurred. With a unanimity and
alacrity which almost suggested a general sense of mental
relief, the conference decided that it would postpone the discussion of Maritime union until the unofficial visitors, the
Canadians, had had a chance to present their very different
plan.[23] This was the wonderful news that greeted the ad-

venturers from the *Queen Victoria*. They may have heard it
first at about twelve o'clock when all the delegates went out
to Government House, on the outskirts of the town, to pay
an official visit to Lieutenant-Governor Dundas. They were
to be heard at once! The conference had cleared its agenda
for them! Everybody was ready to give immediate attention
to what they had to say. It could hardly have been a more
courteous reception. And that evening, when the Canadians
went out again to Government House for the opening dinner
of the conference, they must have been in a pleased and excited
frame of mind.

Next day, Friday, at a little past ten o'clock in the morning,
Cartier began the presentation of their case for federal union.
He spoke for some time—a fairly carefully prepared address—
and then, for the rest of the session, a general discussion followed, with the Maritimers asking questions, and the Canadians attempting to supply satisfactory answers.[24] It was the
pattern which the meetings were to follow for the next few
days. Cartier had given a general survey of the advantages
which union might be expected to bring. Macdonald, in all
probability, had planned to analyse the general character of
the proposed federation; and next morning he got up to face
the conference.[25] He was, in appearance, though not in age,
nearly the youngest of the delegates. His pearl-grey trousers
contrasted almost frivolously with the funereal expanse of black
broadcloth around him. He was clean-shaven in the midst
of a grizzled and rather forbidding forest of beards, side-
whiskers, and moustaches. And the spare lines of his long,
oval face, his high forehead, and the graceful mass of his
dark curly hair gave him a sensitive, thoughtful, even vaguely
poetic expression. He could be earnest and persuasive; but his
frequent smile, which was charming, belied any suggestion of
undue gravity. He was full of his subject. British history and
constitutional practice, the precedents in the other colonies of
the Empire, the tragic experience of the United States, and
the brief experiments of the Southern Confederacy—he knew
them all. His speech—probably the longest given at the conference, and certainly one of the most serious efforts he had

ever made—lasted most of that day's session. He was a good
advocate. But, as the Canadians knew very well, he was also
a convivial host; and it was only appropriate that his speech
should be followed by a lavish exhibition of Canadian hospitality. At three o'clock in the afternoon, all the delegates—
thirty-three in number—adjourned to the *Queen Victoria* for
an elaborate luncheon. They were still there, talking and
drinking toasts, until late in the evening.

On Monday, after Brown and Galt had spoken at length
on the economic and financial aspects of the proposed federation, a definite impression began to form rapidly in the minds
of the delegates. The conference had almost ceased to be a
meeting for the consideration of a Maritime legislative union;
it was becoming a conference for the promotion of British
North American federation. Everything that subsequently occurred seemed to confirm this tacitly accepted view. On Tuesday
—before the Maritime delegates had devoted so much as a
single session to their own separate project—the conference
decided that it would adjourn two days later and proceed to
Halifax. On Wednesday—when at long last the Maritimers
got down to the subject for which the conference had ostensibly
been called—a complete impasse was quickly reached as a
result of Prince Edward Island's impossible demand that the
capital of the united province should be established at Charlottetown. It was not that Macdonald and the Canadians were
hostile to Maritime union—so long, of course, as it did not get
in the way of federation. According to a rumour which the
correspondent of the Halifax *Morning Chronicle* retailed to
his readers, the Canadians were reported to be quite indifferent
as to whether the Maritime Provinces should enter their
proposed federation as one government or three.[26] But the
Maritimers simply could not agree. And now the best chance
of reaching an agreement had gone by. The conference was
on the move. On Thursday, September 8, the delegates went
off on an excursion to the northern part of the Island; and
that night, when they returned, came the final ball.

The Province Building, where the conference had held its
sittings, had been hurriedly prepared for the festivities during

the brief absence of the delegates. The Legislative Council chamber had been fitted up as a reception room. In the legislative library—now a refreshment room of a rather different character—tea, coffee, sherry, claret, and champagne were available in copious quantities; and the Assembly, where the dancing was to take place, had been decorated with flags, flowers, and evergreens, with tall and cunningly placed mirrors, and with the most brilliant lighting effects which the superintendent of the local gas works could produce.[27] Macdonald was paired off with Mrs. Dundas, the wife of the Island's Lieutenant-Governor, for the first quadrille. And at one o'clock, when supper-time came, he took his seat to the right of the chairman, Colonel John Hamilton Gray of Prince Edward Island. In the eyes of everybody he had come to represent the visitors, and he responded first to the toast in their honour. He was beginning to win the Maritimers, as he had already won the Canadians and, from his point of view, the conference could hardly have been a more complete success. But now he was anxious for the next move, and ready to be gone. It was after three o'clock in the morning. The Canadians had agreed to carry the entire conference across the straits to the Nova Scotia mainland in their steamer; and the delegates, having torn themselves away from the ball, packed their bags frantically and hurried down to the harbour in the early hours of the morning. By Saturday they were supposed to be in Halifax.

The *Queen Victoria*—the "Confederate Cruiser" as the Islanders jocularly called her—was lying in the harbour, with steam up. But for some hours yet she could not stir. A dense fog—the like of which, the Maritimers assured their visitors, had not been seen in a matter of ten years—settled down over the Island and Northumberland Strait, obscuring everything. It was eight o'clock in the morning, and the delegates, who had had little, if any, rest in the previous twenty-four hours, were just about to sit down to a substantial breakfast, when at last the mist cleared sufficiently to permit the *Queen Victoria* to get away. Now it promised to be a fine day. The sea was smooth, the sky clear. A little after midday they reached

Pictou where most of the party disembarked, and started off
on a long overland excursion, by carriage and railway train,
which would show them something of the sights of Nova
Scotia. But Macdonald, along with McGee, Langevin, and
the secretaries, remained on board the steamer.²⁸ He enjoyed
a welcome rest and a good night's sleep as the *Queen Victoria*
ploughed her deliberate way along the North Shore and around
Cape Canso. It was noon on Saturday, September 10, before
they reached Halifax; but even so they were half an hour
earlier than the overland party.²⁹ That afternoon, at four
o'clock, the conference reconvened. As they discussed plans
and problems fully, with "visitors" and official delegates taking
an equal part in the debate, it began to look as if the ultimate
purpose which had brought the Canadians down to Charlottetown was about to be achieved. On Monday these hopes
were at last confirmed. At ten o'clock on the morning of that
day, the Maritime delegates held another meeting by themselves, in a final effort to come to some conclusion about Maritime union. The attempt failed; and within another hour, the
doors were opened and the Canadians admitted once more.
By the time the session adjourned at half-past one it had
reached the stupendous decision that a new conference, to
discuss a federal union for the whole of British North America,
was to be held at Quebec, beginning October 10. Macdonald
and his secretaries immediately began their hurried preparations.
A telegram was sent off to the premier of Newfoundland inviting that island to send representatives to the Quebec Conference. Another telegram was dispatched to Sir E. P. Taché
informing him of the decision that had been taken and promising that the *Queen Victoria* would be back in Quebec by
Sunday, September 18.³⁰ Now the matter was clinched.

That night, September 12, a dinner in honour of the
"Colonial Delegates" was given at the Halifax Hotel. Tupper
was in the chair. Macdonald sat next to the Lieutenant-
Governor of Nova Scotia; and it was he who responded to
the toast given by Tupper to "Colonial Union". His theme—
the theme which he had made peculiarly his own for the last
three years—was the need of a strong federation. He began

with the constitution of the United States. He praised its
wisdom; he admitted its defects; "and it is for us," he told the
great audience of Haligonians, "to take advantage by experience,
and endeavour to see if we cannot arrive by careful study at
such a plan as will avoid the mistakes of our neighbours." The
British North American provinces could avoid the mistakes
of their neighbours if only they could agree upon forming a
strong federal union which would have all the rights of
sovereignty except those that were specifically reserved to the
local governments. "If we can only attain that object—a
vigorous general government—we shall not be New Brunswickers, nor Nova Scotians, nor Canadians, but British Americans, under the sway of the British sovereign."[31] It was true,
of course, he hastened to add, that they would have to consider what was practicable as well as what was desirable, that
they must consult local ambitions, and that they should try
to preserve the identity of the separate provinces. But this
was not the note on which he ended. He told his audience
that they could make British North America a great nation
capable of defending itself. He reminded his listeners of "the
gallant defence that is being made by the Southern Republic
—at this moment they have not much more than four millions
of men—not much exceeding our own numbers—yet what a
brave fight they have made. . . ." The purpose of the British
North American federalists was a noble one. Theirs was the
object of "founding a great British Monarchy, in connection
with the British Empire, and under the British Queen".[32]

The conference was over. The Canadians had achieved
their original purpose; and, in their anxiety to prepare for
Quebec, the last of their Maritime travels may have seemed a
little superfluous. But they had visited both Prince Edward
Island and Nova Scotia. It was extremely important, even
from the point of view of the federation they were trying to
create, to pay New Brunswick the courtesy of a visit as well;
and on Wednesday, September 14, after a complete day of
welcome rest, they set out on their travels once more. Most
of the party went by rail to Windsor, and across the Bay of
Fundy by the steamer *Emperor* to Saint John;[33] but once again

Macdonald adroitly dodged the public excursion for the peaceful quiet of the half-empty steamer *Queen Victoria*.[34] It was foggy when they set out for the North Shore—a less unusual circumstance at Halifax than it was at Charlottetown. The ship was late in arriving at Shediac. He missed the train, missed the big public dinner at Saint John, and only caught up with the perambulating conference at Fredericton. By the late afternoon of Friday the whole party was back once more in Saint John, and there at last the delegations separated. The Canadians left town for Shediac on a special train, and late that night they finally boarded the *Queen Victoria* and were off up the St. Lawrence.[35]

Once back in Quebec there was time only for the briefest of rests. By the middle of the week the Cabinet was reunited and hard at work again; and on September 22 Macdonald wired Charles Tupper, the premier of Nova Scotia, that the formal invitations to the Quebec Conference had been sanctioned and would go out the following day.[36] There was no doubt about the answers. That had been decided at Halifax. All the Maritime Provinces would certainly send delegations. Their authority—as the Canadian ministry was careful to point out in the order-in-council of September 23—was that invaluable document, the dispatch of July 6, 1862, from the Duke of Newcastle to the Lieutenant-Governor of Nova Scotia.[37]

The Canadians thought they could assume the permission of the Colonial Secretary; and if, as seems probable, Macdonald knew something of the private correspondence between Monck and Cardwell, he doubtless realized that he could assume something a good deal more cordial than permission. For Cardwell was being converted to the Canadian plan; and, as the promising Quebec Conference drew nearer, he was not in a mood to be interested in the points of procedure raised by the officials in the Colonial Office, or in the doubts and criticisms of the Governors of Nova Scotia or New Brunswick. MacDonnell, of Nova Scotia, who had doubted his own authority to appoint delegates to the Charlottetown Conference, was similarly uncertain about his power to send representatives to Quebec, and wrote in to the Colonial Office asking for permission. Cardwell,

Public Archives

CAPT. RETALLACK HON. A. H. GORDON VISCOUNT MONCK CAPT. MOODY EARL OF MULGRAVE D. GODLEY

GOVERNORS OF BRITISH NORTH AMERICA AND STAFF, QUEBEC, AUGUST, 1862

in the comments which he made on this request, noted that time was important, and added, "I have no hesitation in giving the required permission."[88] Three days later, in a private letter to Gordon of New Brunswick, he revealed much more clearly how far he had already been won over to the Canadian scheme. Gordon had written as quickly as possible, giving his criticisms of the proposed union. Cardwell, in his reply, defended federation against this stout partisan of Maritime legislative union. "Monck assures me," he wrote, "that there is no idea of that feeble legislature which you so justly object to; that they wish a strong central legislature with subordinate municipal Institutions."[89]

III

By Saturday, October 8, Macdonald was ready. The Canadian ministers, with the exception of McDougall and Cockburn, were all at their posts at Quebec; and it was hoped that the preparations for the guests were complete. Russell, the proprietor of one of the biggest hotels in Quebec, had been persuaded to keep his establishment open much later in the season than was usual, with the idea of avoiding the shortage of accommodation experienced at Charlottetown; and the Canadian Cabinet had planned a long series of dinners, *déjeuners* and balls. Before midnight on Saturday a number of the visitors had arrived.[40] The Newfoundland and Prince Edward Island delegations, and Tilley and a few of the New Brunswickers, were already there. On Sunday the *Queen Victoria*, which the Canadians had hospitably sent down east for the transport of their guests, reached Quebec, with Sir Richard MacDonnell and the remainder of the Maritime delegates on board.[41] The conference was now complete. It was a large company, considerably larger than that which had assembled at Charlottetown, for the entire Canadian Executive Council attended; and Newfoundland had, for the first time, sent a delegation of two, and both Prince Edward Island and New Brunswick were represented by two additional delegates. They

were all greeted with attentive and flattering welcomes, and
were barely installed in their lodgings, when the parade of
entertainments began. There was a dinner at the St. Louis
Hotel on Saturday night, and on Sunday night both Monck
and his Executive Council were entertaining again.

On Monday morning, October 10, the Quebec Conference
assembled for its first official session. Its quarters were adequate,
though hardly splendid. The original parliament buildings at
Quebec had been burnt down over ten years before; and
since then the government of Canada had had to be content
with makeshift accommodation. The building which they
then occupied had been constructed originally as a general
post office.[42] It was an unpretentious, yet not undignified structure, three storeys in height, built of grey stone and in a
simplified Renaissance style. Its situation was magnificent.
Perched near the edge of the high cliff of the Upper Town,
it commanded an immense perspective; and from the tall round-
arched windows of the room on the second storey where the
conference met, the delegates could see the wide river and its
lofty banks recede slowly in tones of diminishing blue towards
the remote horizon. It was a noble prospect. If only it had
not rained so much! The weather, on the whole, had been
fine for the Charlottetown Conference. But it broke at Quebec.
The rain drummed relentlessly on the tall windows; it drowned
the curves of the river and the long line of the Laurentians in
pale washes of indigo.

From the start Macdonald exercised a directing control over
affairs. He had had twenty years of parliamentary experience.
Hewitt Bernard, the chief clerk in the office of the Attorney-
General, Canada West, was appointed executive secretary to
the conference on its second day; and the master and his
confidential servant were an efficient, smoothly working machine. Other members of the Canadian delegation apparently
took little active part in the proceedings; and even Cartier,
who was often so voluble, remained relatively silent. But the
easy pressure of Macdonald's guidance can be felt in a long
list of motions, in a thick bundle of slips of paper on which
the principal resolutions of the conference are set out in his

clear, flowing hand. It was true that the plan was a Canadian one, the submission of the Canadian Cabinet as a whole; but he alone, of all the ministers, seemed to have a truly architectonic view of the entire structure. During the first two days he worked his hardest to get things going smoothly. They were critical days—days of formalities, of rather stiff beginnings, when it was essential to create an atmosphere of ease and friendly concord, and when an awkward motion or an unfortunate wrangle might prove absolutely fatal. Once, on the very first day, he barely avoided serious trouble. As soon as the conference was properly constituted, Edward Palmer of Prince Edward Island and Robert Dickey of Nova Scotia moved that in all questions but those of order each delegation should have one vote.[43] It was a clever manoeuvre on the part of these two men, who were so soon to become known as outspoken champions of provincial rights. The Canadians were at once put into a distinctly awkward position, for they could not possibly accept an arrangement which would give Canada only one vote as against the four possessed by the Atlantic provinces. At the very start, they were forced to argue—to insist upon the exceptional importance of their province. The debate was unfortunate, and it went on. It threatened—on the first day of the conference—to become a serious altercation. But Macdonald intervened. It was essential to divert the attention of the delegates—to awaken their enthusiasm, if possible. He moved, with Tilley seconding the motion, "that the best interests and present and future prosperity of British North America will be promoted by a Federal Union under the Crown of Great Britain, provided such union can be effected on principles just to the several provinces."[44]

Next morning, when the second session was well advanced, he got up to speak to this key resolution. Already, on that second day, he had been busy enough. He had sponsored a successful amendment to Palmer's motion, providing that Canada should have two votes, in virtue of its two historic divisions, Canada East and Canada West.[45] And, with Tilley seconding as on the previous day, he moved a series of six sensible resolutions for the order of proceedings.[46] The tension relaxed. The

conference was warming up like a social function which people
were now ready to make go. And yet, as he got to his feet to
begin what was undoubtedly one of the greatest efforts of his
career, he could have no certainty whatever as to the outcome.
This was not the Canadian legislature. The men facing him
were not his faithful and devoted Conservatives, willing to do
almost anything at his bidding. They were virtually strangers,
at best mere acquaintances, some of whom he had met for the
first time as late as the previous Saturday, and only a very
few of whom he had known before the Charlottetown Conference. As he looked at the rows of heavily bearded faces,
the serious, non-committal faces of men who had come to hear
and to judge, he could probably detect only a few which he
knew already to be sympathetic. There was Charles Tupper,
the premier of Nova Scotia, with his round youthful face
encircled in a glossy frame of black hair and beard; there was
Samuel Leonard Tilley, premier of New Brunswick, a short,
neat man, with small, sharp features and bright eyes. These,
and some of their followers, were already half converted; but in
the eyes of others he could read the unmistakable signs of
watchful hostility. Dickey, with his grey head set at an opinionated angle, might be the only determined sceptic in the approv-
ing Nova Scotia delegation; but the prevailing attitude of
the group from Prince Edward Island was distinctly more
unsympathetic. George Coles and Edward Palmer—a tall man
with huge features and a bushy, ragged beard—had already been
making embarrassing motions and awkward criticisms. They
—and how many others?—might prove troublesome. Yet somehow
a majority of delegates in a majority of delegations must be
won. Among them the Atlantic provinces had four votes. If
they wanted to, they could out-vote Canada two to one.

He began to talk. It was the speech for which he had been
consciously preparing for the last five years, for which, indeed,
his entire career had been an unconscious preparation.[47] All
the material was ready in his mind. He could state the leading
themes with precision and emphasis; he could develop them
with the rich variations of detail and example. And two *motifs*
which kept coming back and back, and sounding emphatically

as if with the authority of the horns and percussion, were the need of a strong central government, and the desirability of maintaining British institutions and British parliamentary government. Their constitution, he told the delegates, must, in the words of Governor Simcoe, be an image and transcript of the British constitution; and their federal system must avoid those fatal errors which had wrecked the American experiment. By the existing practice of responsible government under the Crown, the British North American provinces had already escaped most of the defects of the American constitution; and the elected Legislative Council—the only feature of the congressional system which had been adopted, and that by two colonies only—might now be abandoned as a well-meaning but mistaken departure from British parliamentary rule. So far as basic institutions were concerned, only a few minor corrections and modifications were needed. They had but to return to the original purity of a well-known and well-loved system. But, for the federal aspects of their future constitution, a more sustained and comprehensive attempt must be made, Macdonald insisted, to create a central government strong enough to withstand the shocks that had divided the United States. The provinces, as parts of the British Empire, could not, of course, regard themselves as separate and distinct sovereignties; and, in the new constitution which was to unite them, nothing should be done to encourage these absurd pretensions. There should be regional, not provincial, equality, in the federal Upper House, or Legislative Council; and in the division of legislative authority, all powers—except the few granted to the local governments for local purposes only—should be reserved to strengthen the central government.

Macdonald finished his speech at a little after one o'clock; and before the day's session was over, his general motion, in favour of a British North American federation, had been carried unanimously and with a burst of applause that could be heard outside the hall.[48] It would be some time before such a united enthusiasm would be voiced again. The expositions and the generalities were over. It was time to come to particulars and debate. Macdonald brought up the subject of the composition of the Legislative Council; and at once the little provinces by the sea began a determined and protracted resistance. For them the importance of the federal Upper House was very great. They knew very well—from what had been said at Charlottetown—that the Canadians would propose a federal Assembly based on representation by population; and they were sadly aware of the fact that in such an Assembly the Maritime members would be heavily outnumbered. Their one hope of redressing the political balance lay in the Legislative Council. Why should they not demand provincial equality there, as the small American states had at Philadelphia? But it was precisely this unfortunate American precedent which Macdonald was determined to avoid if he possibly could; and his resolution divided British North America into three divisions or sections—Canada West, Canada East, and the four Atlantic provinces together—and gave each section an equal number of representatives in the federal Upper House.[49] This arrangement left the Maritime delegates deeply dissatisfied. In their view such representation was pitiably inadequate. They hungrily wanted more members in the Legislative Council. And yet—in somewhat the same fashion as the Canadians— they did not think in terms of the Philadelphia precedent, and did not dream of asserting their demand for larger representation as a right based on provincial sovereignty. A. A. Macdonald of Prince Edward Island hinted at the principle; but even he did not draw the logical conclusions from his premises.[50] The delegates from the east exhausted their ingenuity in producing a great variety of resolutions, all aimed at giving the Maritime Provinces a larger membership in the Council, and all unfortunately failing to win the united support of the Maritime delegations. Yet the debate continued—through Thursday, Friday, Saturday, and on into Monday, October 17. The Canadians tried to maintain an atmosphere of hearty conviviality by frequent dinners and balls; but the rain never seemed to stop falling, and, by the weekend, everybody was depressed by the weather and irritated by the standstill to which the conference seemed to have been brought.[51] Yet the Canadians stuck to their plan of sectional equality. And finally, on Monday, they won their point—though only by dint of a concession which certainly modified the rigour of the original scheme. Newfoundland was removed from the list of provinces making up the third, or Maritime, division and given four additional members in the Council in her own right.[52]

Macdonald had saved his principle. This compromise was nothing like provincial equality. But the victory had been purchased at the cost of a concession, and even the concession had not satisfied all the delegates. Several of the Prince Edward Islanders—Coles, Palmer and A. A. Macdonald—remained resentfully unconvinced; and the entire delegation may, as A. A. Macdonald claimed, have voted against the compromise. Regional equality in the Legislative Council—with four seats for Prince Edward Island—was bad enough; and the next Canadian resolution, which provided that the legislative councillors were to be appointed for life by the Crown under the great seal of the general government, was almost as objectionable.[53] Appointment by the federal power would surely make meaningless any remaining belief that the Legislative Council could act as the defender of regional, let alone provincial, rights; and Coles and A. A. Macdonald apparently opposed Macdonald's resolution, demanding instead appointment by the provincial legislatures.[54] The anger, and the number, of the Prince Edward Island malcontents was growing; but they still could not invariably swing their delegation. Macdonald's resolution was unanimously accepted; and, by the close of the Wednesday morning session, the remaining problems of the Legislative Council were satisfactorily settled. It was not until the evening of Wednesday, October 19, when the conference had already been in session for nearly nine days, that it finally reached the question of the composition of the federal Assembly. Then, at a stroke, the disgust of the Prince Edward Island delegation became general and complete. George Brown, appropriately enough, introduced a series of resolutions providing for representation by population in the new Lower House. Canada East was to have sixty-five seats, its existing strength in the legislature of United Canada, and the other provinces in proportion. This would give Canada West, the most populous province, a total of eighty-nine seats, and Prince Edward Island, the smallest numerically, a total of five. The entire Island delegation revolted against this contemptible number. The delegates—Reformers and Conservatives—were obviously quarrelling among themselves; but this did not prevent them from uniting in their outraged demand for more representation. They begged—basing their appeal on nothing much better than the difficulty of dividing the Island's three counties into five constituencies—for one more seat. But even this electoral morsel was denied them. And with this denial Prince Edward Island settled down into a state of sullen, permanent opposition.

The conference was nearing the end of its second week, and already the chances of making a comprehensive British North American union had grown slight indeed. Newfoundland, a little-known colony which so far had taken almost no part in the union movement, could certainly not be counted upon to join; and Prince Edward Island, whose delegation had now relapsed into a state of chronic negativism, would probably remain aloof. But, after all, the scheme would not fail from the absence of one or both of the two island colonies. The mainland provinces were the important provinces; and both Nova Scotia and New Brunswick had accepted the compromise over the Legislative Council, and had supported Canada consistently in the battle for representation by population in the Lower House. The first part of the new structure—the federal institutions of government—was almost finished, and finished, in the main, as Macdonald wanted it.

Yet the division of legislative powers—the most important part of the whole work, from his point of view—was still to come. For years he had been arguing that, above all else, British North America must reject the theory of the United States, and grant residuary power to the central government; and on Friday, October 21, when he got up to move a series of resolutions on the powers of the federal legislature, this major principle of his scheme came up for acceptance or rejection.[55] No crucial objections appeared in Friday's debate; and on Monday, October 24, Mowat, for the Canadians,

introduced a complementary set of resolutions on the powers
of the local legislatures. At this point trouble broke out. George
Coles moved that "the local legislatures shall have power to
make all laws not given by this conference to the General
Legislature expressly".[56] It was the exact opposite of Macdonald's principle.

Prince Edward Island had done it again. Though most of
the members of its delegation were morally outside the conference, they were still physically a part of it. They could
still perplex its proceedings. They could fight for the sheer
pleasure of fighting, though victory would scarcely have mollified
them; and Coles, once again, had been successful in putting
the issue in its sharpest form. Yet if Coles and the Prince
Edward Island malcontents had been alone, it would not have
mattered so much, for their attitude was now notorious. But
Coles was not alone. He was joined by E. B. Chandler, a
member of the New Brunswick delegation, who argued strongly
that the subjects given to the provincial legislatures were so
insignificant that the union would, in effect, be a legislative
union. Tupper, of Nova Scotia, got up to answer him. Macdonald must have been pleased by Tupper's support. It was
better that, if possible, Maritimers should reply to Maritimers,
and Tupper argued in his best downright style, asserting stoutly
that the closer the approximation to legislative union, the better
pleased he would be.[57] Yet the debate dragged on with angry
inconclusiveness. Chandler complained that his argument was
being answered, not on its merits, but on the basis of what
was alleged to have been decided at Charlottetown. Macdonald
saw that the case for his sacred principle had not really been
made and, late in the long evening of discussion, he got up
to reply. He was desperately serious. There was a strange
note of extreme vehemence in his phrases. He drove Coles's
resolution back to its origin in the American constitution. He
told the conference that to grant residuary powers to the local
legislatures would be to adopt the worst error of the American
constitution, the error upon which all writers had expatiated,
the error whose awful consequences de Tocqueville had foretold. "A source of radical weakness" would be introduced into

the new constitution of British North America. "It would ruin us," Macdonald declared emphatically, "in the eyes of the civilized world."[58]

The appeal succeeded. In the end, no provincial delegation, not even that of Prince Edward Island, voted against Macdonald's principle. It was his last great triumph in the conference. Galt carried the main burden of presenting and defending the Canadian government's financial proposals; and although Macdonald was deeply preoccupied with the delicate problems of uniting the common-law provinces with Canada East and its very different legal tradition, these were settled fairly easily, without any serious disagreement in public. By Wednesday, the delegates, although still considering fresh items, were already engaged in the task of reviewing and rounding out their work; and on the late afternoon of Thursday, October 27, the conference drew to a hurried close. The room, with its tall windows and its magnificent view, now darkening rapidly in the late October twilight, was full of lassitude, of scarcely concealed impatience, of a sense of impending departure. Yet also present, and perhaps even dominant, was a surprised, excited realization of accomplishment. Less than two months before, Macdonald had set out, a self-invited guest, for Charlottetown. Now all the provinces, with the doubtful exception of Prince Edward Island, had apparently agreed to the Canadian scheme for federation. The union was to embrace not only the existing provinces but, in the end, the whole of British North America; in the ambitious plans of the delegates, it was to become a transcontinental federation. During the last hours of the last session, the conference declared that the communications with the North West Territories, and the improvements required for the development of its trade with the seaboard, were subjects of the highest importance which should be attacked as soon as the finances of the new federation would permit; and it was provided that British Columbia and Vancouver Island, as well as the North West, should be admitted into the union upon terms agreeable to all parties. Then, amid a flurry of last moment revisions and formalities, the conference came to an end. Already, at

four o'clock, a large party, chiefly Maritimers, had left in a
special train provided by Brydges. A second group, including
about half the members of the Canadian Cabinet, departed
by the regular Grand Trunk Railway night express at nine
o'clock.[59] Among them was Macdonald. In the mass of papers
which weighted his luggage were all but three of the seventy-
two resolutions which subsequently came to be known as the
"Quebec Plan". The conference was over.

IV

Yet it was obvious, of course, that the real work of making
Confederation had barely begun. The provincial legislatures
would have to accept the plan; the Colonial Office would have
to approve it; and the elaborate bill necessary for carrying out
the decisions of the conference would have to be drafted and
pushed through the imperial Parliament. As Macdonald faced
the future, a long, grim line of dispatches, interviews, speeches,
debates, elections and conferences seemed to stretch forward
interminably until it disappeared at length over the edge of
his mental horizon. Yet one small but pressing need stood
out in the immediate foreground. The Quebec Conference,
like the Charlottetown Conference before it, had met behind
closed doors; and unless something were done fairly quickly
to enlighten and conciliate public opinion, it would be all
too easy to disparage the federal plan as the work of a gang
of guilty conspirators. The Canadians had already been presented to Maritime audiences in the tour which followed the
Charlottetown Conference. Now a similarly modest triumphal
progress was to introduce the Maritime delegates to the Canadian public, and to disclose, in discreet generalities, the main
provisions of the Quebec plan. Brown hurried back to Toronto
to make preparations for the reception there; Macdonald was
selected to preside over the proceedings at the new capital,
Ottawa; and Cartier was the obvious choice as master of ceremonies at Montreal. At Montreal, which was the first port
of call, the delegates found time to hold a final official session

of the conference, and to pass the three supplementary Montreal resolutions, in one of which the Queen was requested "to determine the rank and name of the Federated Provinces". This, appropriately enough, was almost the last official action of the conference, and the rest of the proceedings were purely social. Macdonald, clad in his dark-blue civil uniform, attended the ball on Friday night. But he was apparently not present at the long-drawn-out *déjeuner* on Saturday afternoon, and Cartier gave the formal reply to the toast to the Canadian ministry.[60]

Macdonald was worn out. For two months he had been almost continuously under pressure; and during the last three weeks, his work had been incessant. By far the biggest part of the burden at the conference had fallen upon his straining shoulders; and the inevitable reaction had already set in when the steamer carrying the touring delegates started up the Ottawa River early in the morning of Monday, October 31. The day was crisply cool. There were only a few hours of fitful sunshine, and the chill autumn night had fallen long before the steamer reached Ottawa, where a shouting, welcoming crowd of citizens had carried the delegates off in triumph to Russell's Hotel. Macdonald had not visited the broad promontory, which was soon to be known as Parliament Hill, for some time at least, and possibly not since the Prince of Wales had laid the cornerstone of the central building back in the late summer of 1860. Now the lines of the three great structures were beginning to emerge clearly from the chaos of scaffoldings and building material. But the roof of the Legislative Council chamber was only half finished, the roof of the Assembly room was as yet untouched; and next day, when the delegates sat down to a luncheon given by the contractors, they had to be accommodated in the future "picture gallery", which at least had a covering, and which was decorated bravely, for all the cool, autumnal weather, with wreaths of flowers.

Yet the buildings were—as Brown had declared them to be during the summer—"surpassingly fine". The site was magnificent. From the edge of Parliament Hill, Macdonald was able to show his visitors another enormous perspective. Below, down an almost sheer drop, lay the Ottawa River. A little distance to the west, it plunged into the vast agitations of the Chaudière Falls, recovered itself, and swept serenely past Parliament Hill and away to the north-east. On the other side, the green lush river meadows ended abruptly in dense masses of pine trees, which climbed up, in tier after tier of darkening green, to the long, low, blue line of the Laurentian Plateau. Here geography confronted politics. Here the men who had made a federal union on paper came face to face with the ancient geological system which covered nearly half of British North America, and which in some way must be conquered before a transcontinental federation could be achieved in fact. Macdonald was to spend the rest of his life in these tasks; but now he could not finish the first speech he ever tried to make in the Canadian parliament. He was supposed to have been sickening with the illness that kept him away from the rest of the triumphal tour. Perhaps he had been drinking. He managed to get out a few of his casual, friendly phrases. And then, without warning, he stopped. He could not continue, and, after an awkward pause, Galt got up to reply in his place to the toast to the Canadian ministry.[61]

At the conference, he had carried almost everything. Now he was wearied of it all. Next day, Wednesday, November 2, while the special train carrying the delegates continued westward towards Toronto, he got off gratefully at Kingston. The sight-seeing and the speech-making went on without him. He stayed where he was, needing the relaxation; and the only trouble was that he had such a few days in which to lounge about and recruit his strength. By Sunday the last of the Maritime delegates were on their way back east; and on Tuesday, November 8, the Canadian Cabinet began to reassemble at Quebec. There was a great deal still to be done. And the first task, which must be completed before the union scheme was submitted to the provincial legislatures, was to secure the approval of the Colonial Office. Monck had already sent the Seventy-two Resolutions over to the imperial government, and had written a long, confidential dispatch in their support.[62] But from the first it had been planned to send a confidential envoy to consult with the imperial authorities on the question of union, and, as far back as the coalition negotiations in June, Brown had been selected for the mission. Brown's departure had been several times postponed while the Charlottetown and Quebec Conferences dragged on; and it was postponed a last time to permit the Cabinet to assemble once again and to come to some conclusions on the problems of Rupert's Land and of defence—two problems which were intimately related to each other and to Confederation, and which were certain to come up in the discussions at the Colonial Office. Answers must be sent back to Cardwell. Brown must be briefed for his mission. On the night of November 9, the special train bearing Macdonald pulled in at the railway station at Levis.[63]

The near prospect of a general federal union of British North America certainly had its influence on the Cabinet's decisions. It was true that in the matter of the Hudson's Bay Company the ministers still kept on coolly insisting that all the cost of extinguishing the monopoly must be borne by the imperial government; but, on the other hand, they showed a livelier enthusiasm for westward expansion, and a new readiness to co-operate with the British government in opening up communications with the Territories, and in promoting their settlement and providing for their local government.[64] These western gestures were still rather vaguely hearty; but in the matter of defence, the Canadians evidently felt obliged to be a good deal more definite. Cardwell's dispatch of August 6, which had asked the government of Canada to set out its military proposals, had lain for months unanswered; and Colonel Jervois, the author of the report which had prompted Cardwell's inquiries, had travelled across the ocean again expressly to help the Canadian ministers make up their minds. On October 12, when the Quebec Conference had barely begun, he had had a long interview with them. He had gone away to work out answers to a series of practical questions put to him by the Cabinet. But before he had finished this supplementary report, an event occurred which suddenly sharpened everybody's interest in defence. Early on the morning of Thursday, October

20, when the delegates were just about to begin their last attempt to persuade the offended Prince Edward Islanders to accept five seats in the federal Assembly, Monck received a highly excited telegram from Gregory Smith, the Governor of the State of Vermont, which seemed to suggest that a small-sized army of desperadoes from Canada had been committing wholesale murder in the town of St. Albans.[65] Subsequently, when this intelligence had been somewhat deflated, it turned out that on October 19 a small party of about twenty-five ununiformed Confederate soldiers had indeed descended from Canadian territory upon the town of St. Albans in Vermont. There they destroyed a little property, robbed the banks, wounded two people, one of them fatally, and escaped over the border again into Canada.

Macdonald must have been reminded of the American invasions of his young manhood. In one alone of these invasions —the American descent on the stone windmill near Prescott— the Canadians had suffered as many casualties as they had in the Battle of Queenston Heights; and to regard the trifling incidents of the St. Albans "raid" in the same light as this wholesale and gratuitous slaughter must have seemed, to the men of Macdonald's generation, to be a monstrous impertinence. Yet the St. Albans raid, whatever its real significance, was certain to be politically important. For one thing it came at a time when American dislike of British, and British American, behaviour during the Civil War had already reached alarming proportions; and, for another, it unfortunately happened to occur when the American presidential election was only three weeks away. "We must be prepared," Lyons wrote from Washington to Earl Russell, "for demonstrations of a 'spirited foreign policy' by Mr. Seward during the next fortnight, for electioneering purposes."[66] And, indeed, for the next few days there was a tremendous hubbub in the United States. General Dix, the American Commander on the north-eastern frontier, ordered his men to pursue the St. Albans raiders, if necessary, into Canadian territory. And, a little later, Seward instructed Adams, the American minister in London, to give the six-months' notice required for the abrogation of the Convention of 1817, limiting naval forces on the Great Lakes. "In conversation both with Mr. Burnley and me," Lyons reported to Russell, "he [Seward] said it would be impossible to resist the pressure which would be put upon the Government to abrogate the Reciprocity Treaty also, if these invasions from Canada continued."[67] All this—and most of it was known unofficially in Quebec at an early date—must certainly have seemed serious to Macdonald. Yet, on the other hand, the signals were not all for danger. In short order the Canadian police captured thirteen of the raiders; and Monck was thanked by Seward for the zeal and efficiency which his government had shown. In a very few days the commotion in the United States died down.

The Canadian ministry, therefore, took up the subject of defence in circumstances which were certainly pressing—they had been that for years—but which had not yet become unusually urgent. On November 10, the day after Macdonald had arrived at Quebec, Jervois presented his supplementary report.[68] This formidable document called for an armed force of 110,000 men, and the construction of large fortifications at Quebec, Montreal, and Kingston, at an estimated cost of £1,754,000. As they contemplated these monstrous figures, Macdonald and the other members of the Cabinet must have experienced a sudden access of colonial feeling. Wars, they insisted in a long minute of Council, were the result of imperial policy.[69] Defence, they argued, was properly an imperial concern. Canada was totally incapable of providing the enormous forces and footing the huge bills which Jervois thought necessary; and federal union, which promised in the end to strengthen British North American defences, was at the moment largely an embarrassment, for it would be dangerous to prejudice the Quebec scheme with heavy military commitments. Much of this argument was in the traditional Canadian manner. Yet the whole minute of Council was far from being an exercise in colonial irresponsibility and procrastination. The Cabinet agreed to construct the works at Montreal, the cost of which Jervois had estimated at £443,000, provided Great Britain would undertake the Quebec fortifications and supply the armament for both. In addition, the ministers promised to propose a vote of a million dollars for the militia in the next session of parliament.

The programme was complete. Brown was well armed, surely very acceptably armed, for his encounter with the Colonial Office; and on Wednesday, November 16, he sailed from New York for England. There was nothing that could be done now but wait and hope for the best from the Colonial Office. In the meantime, Macdonald kept himself occupied in clearing off the arrears of his departmental work and in preparing for the next session of the provincial parliament. The main business of the session would certainly be the consideration of the Quebec Resolutions. At the conference the delegates had generally agreed that it would be best to follow British practice and to submit the resolutions to the provincial legislature rather than to the people. And Macdonald was only occasionally called upon to reassure some of his followers who had perhaps expected a plebiscite. "It would be unconstitutional and anti-British to have a plebiscite," he told Samuel Amsden. "If by petitions and public meetings Parliament is satisfied that the Country do not want the measure, they will refuse to adopt it. If on the other hand Parliament sees that the country is in favour of the Federation, there is no use in an appeal to it. Submission of the complicated details to the Country is an obvious absurdity."[70] No, parliament would have to settle the matter; and they decided to call it, a little earlier than usual, for January 19, 1865. He noted that Dorion had rushed into print with a manifesto against the Quebec scheme, and that the *Rouges* and John Sandfield Macdonald were "beating up for recruits everywhere".[71] But he had very little doubt about the easy passage of the resolutions through the Canadian legislature. Yet what was done at Quebec was now only a beginning. He was already learning to think of the other provinces; and the news from the other provinces was far from reassuring. Not a word had come from Prince Edward Island. Shea, of Newfoundland, had written optimistically but somewhat vaguely, about the prospects in the other island colony. Tupper, who was usually so sanguine, admitted frankly that he and his colleagues had met "a strong opposition" in Nova Scotia.[72] But the very worst news of all came from New Brunswick. Tilley wrote briefly to say that the feeling in his province against the Quebec plan was so strong that he had been obliged to promise that the government would not press the resolutions in the existing House.[73] The New Brunswick Assembly was due to expire shortly in any case; now it was decided to dissolve it within a few months. Almost at once the Quebec plan would have to stand the rough passage of a provincial election.

"Will you let me know what you hear from the British government?" Tupper inquired anxiously of Macdonald. As their difficulties grew, the provincial leaders naturally looked to London for encouragement and support. What would the Colonial Office think of their federal scheme? The Maritime premiers may have been quite uncertain; but Macdonald very probably knew, for Cardwell, in his private letters, had been at no pains to conceal his views. The Colonial Secretary had, in fact, made up his mind fairly quickly, and yet independently of the pressure of unusual circumstances. The real crisis in the affair of the St. Albans raid did not begin until the middle of December. The first news of the raid itself did not reach the Colonial Office until November 10, and long before that time Cardwell's declared preferences were quite definite. He had reached them, indeed, at a time when, in his own view, Anglo-American relations were in a much better state than had been previously expected. "If McClellan had carried the Presidency," he wrote to Gladstone on October 27, "and peace had been made on Southern and pro-slavery conditions: which was a sufficiently possible contingency not to be excluded from our view—the immediate danger to our small force in Canada might have been considerable. That hazard does not seem to be great now."[74] It continued to seem only a small hazard for a few weeks longer. On November 23, Adams gave notice of the abrogation of the Rush-Bagot Convention; but this, by itself, was not sufficient to cause any great alarm, and in any case it came too late to have any appreciable effect on the Cabinet's decision on British American union. The Quebec Resolutions arrived at the Colonial Office on November 22, and four days later, in a private letter to Gordon of New Brunswick, Cardwell was predicting the government's unanimous and enthusiastic approval.[75]

Earl Russell, the Foreign Secretary, had expressed his preference for a federal union of British America over two years before, while Newcastle was still at the Colonial Office.[76] And Cardwell seems never to have believed in any other solution but the strong federation which Macdonald and Monck desired. "My principal fear," he wrote to Gladstone on October 27, "is that the selfish interests of the men in the smaller Provinces should lead them to insist on *federation* as against *union*:— on the policy of Jefferson as against that of Washington and Hamilton;—on a policy which would run B.N. America upon the rock on which the Union has gone to pieces." He was ready to admit in advance all the criticisms which could be brought against federations in general. But, like Macdonald and Monck, he had come to believe that a federation might be made sufficiently strong and centralized so as to approximate to a legislative union. "Of course," he wrote realistically to Gordon, "it signifies very little what name is employed. What we wish is a central and strong government as distinguished from a number of small states united by a feeble bond."[77] Monck had convinced him that this was what the Canadians intended. He was prepared to accept their plan in advance; and in a private letter of November 14—over a week before the Quebec Resolutions reached the Colonial Office—Monck thanked him for the consistent support that the Colonial Secretary had afforded.[78] Cardwell was not only giving the Canadians direct encouragement at every stage; he was also defending them indirectly by rebuking their critics. Usually he was polite enough with Gordon, the fervent advocate of Maritime union; but once he ventured a sardonic reference to the "selfish interests" of the Maritimers. "The bold, ambitious leaders of public opinion in Canada," he wrote on October 14, "are more likely to wish for a complete fusion, which would extend their powers, than are the ministry and parliament men of New Brunswick, whose occupation would in that case be ended."[79]

His conclusions had already been reached. There was no hesitation or delay. On December 3, the Colonial Secretary sent off the public dispatch which, in almost enthusiastic terms, announced Great Britain's warm acceptance of the Quebec Resolutions.

Chapter Fourteen

Checkmate

I

Yet before Cardwell's inspiring dispatch arrived, real trouble
had broken out for Canada. It had been coming closer, despite
the false appearances of calm, ever since the St. Albans raid
on October 19. The American people had, it was true, temporarily dismissed the thoughts of the raid from their minds
and had returned to the gorgeous excitement of the presidential
election; but they had done so on the evident assumption that
a savage retribution would be meted out to the raiders. "There
can be no doubt," Burnley wrote to Russell from Washington,
"that considerable irritation exists in the minds of the American people on the general subject of these repeated raids from
Canada, and I am afraid that if the Canadian Law Courts
should look upon the men concerned in the St. Albans affair
as regular commissioned Belligerents rather than as criminals
to be given up under the Extradition Treaty that we may
expect a very serious outburst of feeling against Her Majesty's
Government."[1] Seward had, of course, peremptorily demanded
that the "criminals" be given up to his government; and
Monck had temperately replied that as soon as the proofs required by the extradition treaty had been furnished, the prisoners
would be handed over to the American authorities.[2] Yet, on
December 13, when the question of the extradition of the
raiders at last came up for a preliminary hearing before Magistrate Coursol of Montreal, a most unexpected and astounding
event occurred. Coursol never got to the crucial point of whether

the raiders were extraditable criminals or regularly commissioned
officers of a country whose belligerent rights Great Britain
had recognized. He simply asserted want of jurisdiction on
the ground of technical defects in the British and Canadian
statutes implementing the Ashburton Treaty.[3] And he dismissed the raiders, who promptly walked out of the court free
men.

Both as a lawyer and as a politician, Macdonald was seriously
annoyed with this judgment. "The unhappy and mistaken
decision of Coursol at Montreal," he wrote, "has had a most
unfortunate tendency. From the fact of his being called 'Judge'
Coursol, his decision is considered a judicial one in the United
States. He was however merely acting in his capacity as
police magistrate, and altogether mistook his duty, when he
presumed to judge as to his right to discharge those prisoners.
It was his duty to assume that he had the authority under the
statute, and the question of jurisdiction should only have
been brought up to be solemnly decided by the Superior
Courts."[4] It was all very regrettable, and, as Macdonald
realized, its consequences were likely to be extremely unfortunate. But even he may possibly not have been prepared for
the violence of the reaction in the United States. The American press returned at once to that continental military imperialism which was one of its best loved themes. The conquest
of Canada was earnestly advocated as a suitable small exercise
for the victorious union army after the conclusion of the
American Civil War. The American executive and the American Congress, which had just reassembled, revealed the national
displeasure in actions which were almost as pugnacious as the
words of the newspapers. On December 17, for the first time
in the relations of British North America and the United
States, the American executive issued an order requiring pass-
ports from all persons entering the republic from the provinces.
In his message to Congress at the opening of the session,
Lincoln had already revealed the fact that the United States
had given the required notice for the abrogation of the Rush-
Bagot Convention; and almost at once both the Senate and
the House of Representatives took up the question of the

Reciprocity Treaty.[5] There was, unfortunately, not the slightest doubt that the treaty would be abrogated just as soon as it was legally possible for the United States to terminate it. The sky was by now nearly opaque with threatening gloom. And the one pale gleam of hope lay in the fact that General Dix's order had been disavowed at Washington—a disavowal which certainly came belatedly, but at a fortunate moment, in the end.

Macdonald watched all these developments with his accustomed calm. He was not inclined to get excited. He refused to be hustled by circumstances into heroics of one kind or another. "We must perform our duty, however, irrespective of the smiles or frowns of any foreign body," he told one correspondent, "and will never be hurried into extra exertions by proclamations like those of General Dix, or prevented by any feeling of indignation from carrying our laws into full force."[6] In a few rapid and energetic moves, the government tried to cope with the new situation. The released St. Albans raiders were pursued once more and most of them were recaptured in New Brunswick. To prevent a recurrence of the raids, nearly 2,000 volunteers were called up and stationed at appropriate points along the border. In addition—and this was the most novel of Macdonald's measures—it was decided "to organize a detective and preventive police force, for the purpose of watching and patrolling the whole frontier from Toronto to Sarnia. . . ." This force which was soon in its modest fashion to become a most efficient instrument of counter-espionage and prevention, was put under the control of a newly appointed stipendiary magistrate, Gilbert McMicken. "He is a shrewd, cool, and determined man," Macdonald wrote, "who won't easily lose his head, and who will fearlessly perform his duty."[7] McMicken was to deserve every word of the encomium which Macdonald wrote for him.

"I think," wrote Burnley to Russell, "we have got safely out of the Canadian troubles thanks to Lord Monck's extremely energetic and conciliatory policy towards this country, which has been duly appreciated by Mr. Seward and the cabinet. . . ."[8] There was no doubt whatever about Canadian effort. But as Burnley observed, it was equally true that "with all this there is a general latent feeling of dislike to the English which it would be useless to disguise. . . ." Macdonald was well aware of this old animosity. He realized that the new passport regulations and the threatened abrogation of the Rush-Bagot Convention and the Reciprocity Treaty had all been prompted largely by the desire for political retaliation. It was useless to hope that commercial considerations, or any kind of reasoned argument, would have the slightest effect. At the moment, the republic was like an aged and irritable female relative, who had been deeply offended by behaviour lacking in deference, and whom it was quite impossible to propitiate. Thomas Swinyard, of the Great Western Railway, and Brydges, of the Grand Trunk, were in despair at the effect of the passports on their traffic; and Swinyard wanted an immediate effort made at Washington to have the restriction removed. Macdonald thought such a proposal quite unwise. He believed that, so far as immediate steps were concerned, it would be best to appoint agents on the Canadian side who would make it their business to establish friendly relations with the American passport officers. As for the future, the right policy would be to put up with the annoyance, and try to bring private influences to bear at Washington.⁹ "I think," he wrote to Swinyard, "it would be extremely impolitic and, indeed, defeat our object, if the Canadian Government went on its knees to the United States Government for the purpose of procuring a revocation of the late order. It would give Mr. Seward an exaggerated idea of the inconvenience and the loss sustained by Canada and would be kept up as a means of punishment or for purposes of coercion. The true way to succeed is for the Canadian Government to assume an indifferent tone in the matter, leaving it to the Western States and private solicitation to effect the purpose."¹⁰

In the meantime, while relations with the United States still remained in this state of worrying uncertainty, the Confederation scheme had run into several large snags. Tilley's unhappy admission that he had agreed not to submit the Quebec Resolutions to the existing House in New Brunswick was the most disturbing piece of news. But the advices, public and

private, which now began to reach Macdonald from Nova
Scotia, were almost as bad. At Quebec, the cheerful Tupper
had been fairly confident of the success of the scheme in his
native province. He felt that he could count not only upon
the united support of his government and his party, but also
upon the favourable influence of A. G. Archibald and Jonathan
McCully, two prominent members of the Reform party, who
had been delegates to the Quebec Conference and who were
enthusiastic supporters of the Seventy-two Resolutions. The
fact that McCully was the editor of the Halifax *Morning
Chronicle* served to ensure that this most important of the
Reform newspapers would be on the side of Confederation.
And as for Joseph Howe, the leader of the Reform party and
prime minister of the previous government, Tupper assumed,
with some justification at least, that the old tribune's appointment as imperial Fisheries Commissioner would neutralize him
fairly effectively, particularly if the imperial government could
be persuaded to give vigorous support to the Quebec scheme.[11]
These confident expectations lasted for a little while after
Tupper's return from Quebec to Halifax. He was still fairly
complacently optimistic at the end of the second week in
December. He admitted the existence of "a strong opposition";
but he was frankly delighted with the success of its first public
meeting for Confederation, and full of hope for the future.
By the beginning of January this note of lusty confidence had
changed. "We have had hard work here," he confessed to
Macdonald. "A great body of the leading men comprising the
most wealthy merchants in the city are exerting themselves to
the utmost to defeat the scheme. Archibald and McCully have
stood by me like trumps and I hope we will carry the day."[12]
Hope—a little battered—was still surviving. Archibald and
McCully were a stout support. But their old leader, Joseph
Howe, had tossed away his neutrality as a civil servant and
had flung himself into the struggle against the Quebec scheme.
As Tupper confessed ruefully, his old opponent had become
overnight the chief centre of the opposition to Confederation
in Nova Scotia.

As the circle of Macdonald's influence widened the number

and variety of his enemies increased. He probably knew something about Howe's career, for he made it his business to
inform himself generally about British North American politics.
He may even have met Howe briefly in London on one of his
expeditions to the Colonial Office. But in 1864 the two men can
hardly have been more than mere acquaintances at best. And
then, almost overnight, a virtual stranger, a blurred recollection,
a name in the papers, became one of the most important figures
in Macdonald's career. The two men belonged almost to two
different political generations, though in age they were separated
by only a little over ten years. That winter, on December 13,
Howe turned sixty. It was not a great age, though he had
always used and abused his strength with careless prodigality.
But it was an age at which, in the life of any man, a settled
and inescapable sense of dissatisfaction might at length become
an agonizing conviction of failure. His consciousness of his
own powers, his relish for important people and great affairs,
his everlasting and grinding need for money, had kept him
fluttering around the bright flame of office and position like
a moth, at once attracted, wounded and repelled. Three years
before, he had attained the premiership—the highest executive
office in the province then open to a colonial—but without
exhilaration, and without much conviction of great work still
to be done. For a long time now he had manoeuvred and
struggled and humiliated himself for the sake of an imperial
appointment which would be commensurate with his talents;
and at long last he had been awarded the Commissionership
of Fisheries, a post not indeed completely insignificant, but of
an appalling mediocrity, a mediocrity made all the more emphatic by a salary which was just big enough to compel him
to accept it. Cooped up in H.M.S. *Greyhound* or H.M.S. *Lily*
for two or three months of every year, with nothing but the
company of the captain and his own drunken secretary, fishing,
shooting ducks and curlew, writing unimportant reports which
nobody of any political importance would ever consider for
a moment—this was the mean way in which he was dragging
out the last years of his life.[13] This was the almost sordid
duty which had kept him from accepting the invitation to

From Bengough: "Caricature History of Canadian Politics". (Public Archives)

CROSS ROADS

SHALL WE GO TO WASHINGTON FIRST, OR HOW(E)?

attend the conference on Maritime union. It had been Charles Tupper, and not Joseph Howe, who had gone to Charlotte-town and Quebec, who had argued, debated and resolved, who had spoken for Nova Scotia and accepted the honours due to her. Others had always occupied the commanding positions at the crucial moments; others had known how to bring the dream and the reality together. He brooded, his big face, with its rather coarse features, once ennobled by vitality and conviction, now dulled and heavy with care and disillusionment and fatigue. In his absence, without his help, without his knowledge, others had dared to rearrange British North America to their liking. Well, they could not. They could not, for he, Joseph Howe, would prevent them.

He did not believe in Confederation. It was true that in his facile—too facile—way, he had spoken rhetorically of a British North American dominion stretching from the Atlantic to the Pacific Ocean. But he was so much a Nova Scotian, so spiritually a part of the old British maritime world of "ships, colonies, and commerce", that these visions of transcontinental empires could be only transitory and artificial. The federation which was closest to his heart was a federation of the whole British Empire, with a great federal imperial parliament at Westminster.[14] It was this old belief, sharpened now by his haunting sense of neglect and failure and, perhaps, by the tormented urge to undo the work of others more successful than himself, that drove him into the last unhappy crusade of his career. Once his decision was taken, events followed rapidly. McCully was deposed from the editorship of the *Morning Chronicle*. Annand, a stout anti-Confederationist, reigned in his place; and early in January the first of a series of articles by Howe called *The Botheration Scheme*, attacking Confederation, appeared in Annand's newspaper. Rallied and emboldened by Howe's leadership, the anti-Confederation forces drew together in an imposing array, and Tupper suddenly found himself upon the defensive. Howe demanded that an appeal should be made to the people on the Quebec scheme. It was, in the circumstances, an extremely adroit move, which took advantage of the weakness of Tupper's position—a weakness which had been caused by Tilley's reluctant consent to dissolve the New Brunswick Assembly and go to the country.

If only Tilley could be persuaded not to give the anti-Confederationists everywhere the benefit of this fatal example! "I hope you will assist me," Tupper wrote to Macdonald, "in pressing Tilley to put it through without going first to the people."[15] Macdonald was thoroughly convinced of the unwisdom of Tilley's decision. He always maintained that Tilley should have held a final session of the legislature, and had the Quebec scheme discussed, so that the subject would at least have been understood by the people. "It would have been much better, as you say," he wrote later to a correspondent in New Brunswick, "to have called the House together, and to have had the subject thoroughly ventilated, and then to have tried the vote. If the vote had been carried, all well, if not, you still had recourse to the people."[16] There was, in short, almost everything to gain and nothing to lose in submitting the Quebec Resolutions to the House in a final session. Macdonald certainly considered Tilley's plan of campaign timorous and inept. But, at the same time, he characteristically assumed that Tilley must make his own decisions, for Tilley alone was in full possession of all the relevant facts. And, indeed, the premier of New Brunswick was already hard pressed: by his own colleagues and followers; by an opposition which was already exploiting the growing dislike of the Quebec scheme; and, last but not least, by the Governor himself, Arthur Hamilton Gordon.

Gordon was another one of the personalities from the Maritime Provinces who played an important part in the troubled passage of the Quebec scheme. Macdonald had met him first at Charlottetown, where Gordon had appeared for the early part of the conference. In 1864, he was still a comparatively young man, thirty-five years old, with a long, lugubrious, bearded face and sad, heavily-lidded eyes. The son of the Earl of Aberdeen, Prime Minister of Great Britain from 1852 to 1855, young Gordon had been private secretary, first to his father, and then to that increasingly important architect of the new Liberalism, William Ewart Gladstone; and Gladstone, who kept up an intermittent correspondence with his protégé, always saluted him affectionately as "Arthur". New Brunswick was Arthur's first colonial appointment. He cannot be said to have liked it. He was not long in Fredericton before he conceived a marked distaste for colonial politicians in general, whom he regarded as uncouth, illiterate, corrupt, and curiously obstinate in holding opinions different from his own. When Cardwell, hoping to mollify him, reported the flattering tribute that George Brown had paid to the Lieutenant-Governor of New Brunswick during his visit to the Colonial Office, Gordon was not greatly impressed by Brown's compliments. "They at least shew," he conceded tartly, "that I succeeded in carefully concealing from him my true opinion—viz., that he is the most dangerous and most unscrupulous demagogue in British North America."[17] On the whole, however, he held a relatively high opinion of the Canadians. Cartier, at all events, was a "thorough gentleman", Galt "a remarkably clever fellow", and "Macdonald (when not drunk) is a really powerful man".[18] But as for the provincial politicians of New Brunswick, they were, with the exception of Tilley, almost contemptible. And to Gordon it was insufferably galling that creatures like this should actually rule in fact whilst he merely governed in form. When Cardwell mildly reminded him that government in one of the democratic colonies was very much like government in the constitutional monarchy of Great Britain, Gordon indignantly rejected this respectable analogy. "I hold," he wrote, "that . . . the position of the Governor is less like that of the Queen than that of Louis XVI during the Constitution of 1791."[19] He wanted to be free from this degrading servitude. He wanted more power, or, as he rather quaintly put it, more "opportunity for usefulness". He dreamed longingly of an appointment to a submissive Crown Colony, with a nice climate, and a nice salary, and, above all, no Assembly and no "parliamentary eloquences".

Gordon had been an ardent believer in Maritime union. At every stage in the proceedings of the Charlottetown and Quebec Conferences, he had attacked the federal scheme, and impugned the motives of its authors, the Canadians. Card-

well's dispatch of December 3 announcing the British government's hearty support for the Seventy-two Resolutions must have
come to him as a profound disappointment, a personally mor-
tifying disappointment. In his complaining, argumentative
fashion, he kept on reiterating his criticisms of federations in
general and the Quebec plan in particular; but he at least
indicated that he would "act in conformity with Her Majesty's
gracious commands".[20] He did more. All of a sudden, almost
without warning, he was eager for immediate action. Could
it be that those veiled sardonic eyes had already discerned an
appropriate revenge for the shameful neglect with which he
and his opinions had been treated by both British and colonials?
Had he realized that he could embarrass Confederation even
more by clumsy and inept support than he possibly could by
outright opposition? Or was he merely trying once again to
assert himself, to show that he was not under Tilley's thumb,
to demonstrate that he was not a contemptible cipher in the
government of New Brunswick? At all events, he was all
haste and all confidence, where Tilley, who ought to have
been the best judge of the situation, was plainly hesitant and
doubtful. Tilley had promised not to submit the Quebec
scheme to the expiring House; but he was anxious, nevertheless, to hold a final session of the legislature, to postpone the
general election until June, when the legal term of the parliament was up. He wanted time—time to complete the speaking tour on which he was then engaged—time to explain the
merits of the Quebec scheme and to weaken the prejudice
against it. But time was the very thing that the Governor was
unwilling to concede. He wanted an immediate dissolution
and a winter election. He saw, apparently, no reason for Tilley's
programme of education; he gauged public opinion with a
strangely optimistic eye. It was not until January 16 that he
admitted in a dispatch to Cardwell that the apathetic attitude
of New Brunswick to the Quebec scheme had of late been
somewhat altered and that it had been replaced "by a sentiment
more decidedly hostile to the proposed arrangement".[21] But
even then—even later—he showed no alarm for the safety of
Confederation at the polls. While Tilley hesitated, he pressed

him vigorously with arguments; and in the end the Governor got his way. On January 19, 1865, the Executive Council decided in favour of an immediate dissolution. Tilley acquiesced. But he permitted himself one last reproachful remark. "I cannot refrain, however, from stating," he wrote, "that our chances of success would have been increased by adhering to our original design."[22]

II

The disturbing news of the imminent New Brunswick election reached Macdonald only a little after the Canadian legislature had assembled for its winter session. He arrived in Quebec on January 22, three days late for the opening.[23] He had been ill; and when, on the cold evening of Monday, February 6, he rose in the Assembly to move the adoption of the Quebec Resolutions, his voice was still a little weak from the effects of ill health. It was not a new speech. He had given much of it before, in various forms, at Charlottetown, at Halifax, and, above all, at Quebec. But the rank and file of the Canadian legislature had not heard it yet; and never before had it been given in such a full and finished form, and with such a wealth of illustrative detail. Yet the main themes —the need of a strong central government, and the importance of maintaining British institutions, and British principles of government—stood out as clearly as before. The imperial Parliament, he told the House, would have to decide the title which the federal Legislative Assembly would bear. But the Canadians hoped it would be "House of Commons", with all that that historic name implied; and as for the Upper House, with its councillors appointed by the central government on a regional basis, it had been designed "in accordance with the British system as nearly as circumstances would allow". Executive authority was vested, as it always had been, in the Crown, and administered "according to the well understood principles of the British Constitution". Responsible government under the Crown had served the colonies well in the past; and, in

Courtesy Confederation Life Association

THE FATHERS OF CONFEDERATION, LONDON, 1866

(See key on page 525)

their new federal state, they could still avoid the despotic powers and party label of the American presidency by sticking firmly to the monarchical principle. "I believe," Macdonald went on, "that it is of the utmost importance to have that principle recognized, so that we shall have a sovereign who is placed above the region of party—to whom all parties look up —who is not elevated by the action of one party nor depressed by the action of another, who is the common head and sovereign of all."[24]

Yet the lessons of the British constitution, Macdonald implied, were not confined to the sphere of political institutions and principles of government. The British constitution was an almost equally valuable guide in the purely federal parts of the projected union. For the Empire, with its sovereign imperial Parliament and dependent colonial legislatures, was itself an informal federal system; and the rules which had governed the old imperial connection could be easily transferred to regulate the relationships of the central and local governments in British North America. "As this is to be one united province," Macdonald explained, "with the local governments and legislatures subordinate to the General Government and Legislature, it is obvious that the chief executive officer in each of the provinces must be subordinate as well."[25] In the Old Colonial System, the governors and lieutenant-governors had been appointed by the imperial authorities; in the new federation, the lieutenant-governors of the subordinate provinces were to be nominated by the central government. "The General Government," said Macdonald, appealing directly to the imperial analogy, "assumes towards the local governments precisely the same position as the Imperial Government holds with respect to each of the colonies now."[26] The main origins of the Quebec scheme, in short, were British origins. The federation had been planned to achieve that close unity which was symbolized by the imperial Crown; it had been designed to avoid the fatally divided sovereignties of the United States. "We have strengthened the General Government," Macdonald declared. "We have given the General Legislature all the great subjects of legislation." Above all, they had given it—and not the local legislatures—the residuary power. "We thereby strengthen the Central Parliament," Macdonald went on, "and make the Confederation one people and one government, instead of five peoples and five governments, with merely a point of authority connecting us to a limited and insufficient extent."[27]

Cartier followed the next night, Tuesday, February 7; and on Wednesday Brown held a crowded House for over four hours. The debate, which promised to last until virtually every member of the legislature had said his say on the subject of the Quebec Resolutions, was now well under way; and, unfortunately for the success of both, it coincided almost exactly with the New Brunswick election campaign. Macdonald was worried by the possible influence that each might have upon the other. He had far more doubts about the result of the election than he had about the outcome of the debate; but he realized that Tilley and the New Brunswickers would be watching with interest the reports in the Canadian newspapers, drawing ammunition and confidence from the course of the argument. Yet even with his awareness of the growing interdependence of British North American politics, he was betrayed into a fairly serious mistake. The *Rouges* and John Sandfield Macdonald, who together constituted the only opposition in the House, were loftily contemptuous of number sixty-eight of the Quebec Resolutions, which declared that the general government of the new federation would complete the Intercolonial Railway without delay. Macdonald, in reply to a question from Holton, admitted that the guarantee of the Intercolonial could hardly form a part of the new federal constitution proper. In a few days this statement was public property in New Brunswick. It created the greatest consternation in government circles. From Tilley's point of view, the Intercolonial was one of the few immediate and practical benefits which he could claim that Confederation would bring to his province. Why, asked his anti-Confederate opponents, was a doubt now cast upon the formality of the guarantee? Were the Canadians getting ready to betray the New Brunswickers once again, as they had betrayed them back in 1862? Tilley, bombarded with questions and jibes, wrote immediately to Macdonald. "Now

I can assure you," he declared emphatically, "that no Delegate from this Province will consent to Union unless we have this guarantee. And we will certainly fail in all our elections unless I have word by you, and to be in time must be by telegraph, saying that this security will be given us. All will be lost without this. . . ."[28] This nearly frantic appeal drew an immediate reply from Macdonald. "My remark," he telegraphed back, "was that an agreement to build a Railroad could not be a portion of a Constitution. In our case it was one of the conditions on which Constitution was adopted. Such condition will of course be inserted in the Imperial Act."[29]

In the meantime, the diplomatic bag had brought another, and an only slightly less disturbing, communication. It was a dispatch from Cardwell, in which the Colonial Secretary reported the reply of his government to the long Canadian Council minute of the previous November on the subject of defence. On January 19 and 20—at the very moment when the Canadian parliament was assembling again—the British Cabinet had been considering the fortifications of Quebec. Gladstone, still eager to "shift the centre of responsibility" in colonial defences and still confronting his impatient colleagues with long, involved paragraphs of argument, had been, in Lord Palmerston's words, particularly "troublesome and wrong-headed".[30] With equal prolixity and tenacity he had objected to the fortification of Quebec and urged a reduction of 500 men in the navy. He had been overborne, of course; and the decision of the majority of the Cabinet was "that the best security against a conflict with the United States will be found in an adequate defensive force". Yet the conclusions drawn from this general principle were curiously meagre. Jervois had estimated the total cost of the Quebec fortifications at £200,000. The Cabinet merely decided to put an item of £50,000 in the army estimates for the current year, towards the construction of the works. As for the general problem of the organization of Canadian defences, Cardwell agreed, almost too readily, to postpone the whole business until after Confederation.[31] At this leisurely rate of progress it would be years before anything solid was done. There was remarkably little evidence of a sense of acute peril, of desperate urgency, in Great Britain; but in Canada there was certainly a greater feeling of apprehension than there had been back in the previous November. The fate of the St. Albans prisoners was not yet determined. The passport nuisance still continued. Worst of all, the Americans were evidently in dead earnest about the abrogation of the Reciprocity Treaty.

There was a good deal to worry about. Macdonald was ill, also, with a severe cold; and for the last week in February he obeyed doctor's orders and stayed away from the House.[82] The New Brunswick election drew closer and closer; and his convalescence was not yet over when on Saturday, March 4, the news began to come in over the telegraph wires. The halls of the legislature in Quebec were crowded. The little knot of *Rouges* and Sandfield Macdonald Grits were excited and triumphant.[83] Tilley and Watters, the two Confederate candidates in Saint John, were both defeated; and, before Saturday was out, the downfall of the union government was conceded. The Quebec scheme was not only stopped; it was derailed. On Monday Dorion's followers were predicting a crisis for the Canadian ministers. The Cabinet met early that morning. Macdonald was back at his post again; and when the House met for the afternoon session, he rose to make the expected statement of government policy.

He began by admitting frankly that the New Brunswick election had been "a declaration against the policy of Confederation".[84] But, he went on—and the argument was far from being merely specious—, Confederation was by no means the only issue involved in the contest. What was at stake in this, as in all other elections under the British system, was the total record of the government. To a very large extent, the contest was simply the usual battle between the ins and the outs. It was also a battle between the rival railway policies competing for the favour of the New Brunswick electorate. Macdonald was well aware—though he took no time to deal with this in his brief explanation—of the basic division of interest between the North Shore of New Brunswick, which identified itself with the St. Lawrence and British North

America, and the Saint John and Bay of Fundy region, which often sought its prosperity in trade with the United States. The Intercolonial Railway was an essentially Laurentian, British North American enterprise. "Western Extension", which meant the extension of the existing New Brunswick railway— the European and North American—south-westward, so as to connect with the railway lines of the United States, was an equally good expression of the urge towards the American market. Tilley's opponents, led by a group of Saint John merchants, had, of course, taken up "Western Extension". But back of the Saint John merchants was a still more powerful group, the railway capitalists of the north-eastern United States, who had for years been competing with Watkin and Brydges for the control of the Maritime Provinces, and who were ready to put a good deal of money into the election for the sake of defeating the Intercolonial Railway. "It was a fair stand-up fight," D'Arcy McGee said bluntly, "of Yankee interests on the one side and British interests on the other."[35] Macdonald was rather less outspoken. He merely hinted at the widespread suspicion that American money had helped materially to decide the New Brunswick election.

His main task was to explain government policy for the future. The ministers, he told the House, wished it to be "most distinctly understood" that they regarded the New Brunswick election not as a reason for changing direction, but as an additional cause for perseverance in their original course. Since the previous June, when the coalition government was formed, a scheme of union had been worked out, had been sanctioned by all the governments of British North America, and approved by the Colonial Office. The project, on the whole, had been a success, rather than a failure. The Canadian government had no intention of abandoning it. The ministers proposed, Macdonald announced crisply, to put the Quebec Resolutions to a vote as soon as possible, to prorogue the House as soon as possible, and then to send a mission to England to discuss Confederation and related questions with the British government.[36] One of these questions was the unsatisfactory state of trade relations with the United States, and

the other was defence. Last autumn it had been hoped that
a new federal government would soon be able to deal with
the question of British North American defence in general.
But now, since the New Brunswick election, there was no
immediate prospect of united action; and the Canadian military
problem could be postponed no longer. This was Macdonald's
defiantly energetic announcement to Dorion, Sandfield Macdonald, and their followers; and, having made it, he sat down.

III

On Tuesday and Wednesday, March 21 and 22, the Canadian Cabinet held two long sessions which lasted on until
after six o'clock at night.[37] Everybody knew that the personnel
and programme of the delegation to England was up for discussion. Macdonald did not want to go. He had accepted
office in the previous June as an emergency task. But now
the temporary emergency seemed to be aging into a permanent
ordeal. He had been ill again, for the third time since the
New Year, and he would have been perfectly content to stay
at home and let his colleagues have the excitement and the
honour of the negotiations in England. Yet this was perhaps
the most important mission that Canada had ever sent to the
imperial government. The other members of the Cabinet pressed
him to go; and, once a rumour of his reluctance got abroad,
others added their appeals to the pressure of the ministers. "I
pray you go to England," wrote Brown Chamberlin of the
Montreal Gazette. "There are many true hearts will not rest
satisfied unless you do. If the wit of men can help it, there
must be no failure to come to an agreement with the Mother
Country. . . . The greatest interests, the very birthright of
Britons in Canada are in your keeping. . . . Five years hence
we shall be more truly British or altogether Yankee. Whose
will be the fault if the latter should be our fate?"[38]

No, it was impossible for him to stay at home. He would
have to go to England. He would have to try to give direction and
encouragement to the union movement everywhere, to watch

over the different provinces of British North America as he
had watched over the constituencies of Canada West for the
last fifteen years. Everywhere things seemed to have gone
wrong. There was still no word from Newfoundland. The
legislature of Prince Edward had rejected Confederation and
Maritime union with equal decisiveness and announced firmly
that it wished to be left alone. From the defeated unionists
in New Brunswick—Tilley, Charles Fisher, and Colonel J. H.
Gray—there came a series of unhappy letters, bewailing the
catastrophe of the election, and trying miserably to account
for it. Even Nova Scotia was involved in the general retreat. The
magic of Howe's name and the evil spell of the New Brunswick
defeat had between them confounded Charles Tupper. He told
Macdonald that, if Tilley had only succeeded, he might have
got the Quebec Resolutions through the Nova Scotian Assembly
with a bare majority; "but the moment he failed," he went on
dismally, "I found that all my ingenuity would be required
to avert the passage of a hostile Resolution."[39] Since the anti-
unionists were professing an unreal love for Maritime union,
Tupper was forced to adopt the defensive manoeuvre of taking
up that defunct project himself. On April 10, he moved that
"whereas under existing circumstances an immediate Union of
the British North American Colonies has become impracticable",
the negotiations for a legislative union of the three Maritime
Provinces should be renewed.[40] In every province but Canada
Confederation had been brought to a dead stop. From every
province the gloomy news kept coming in during March and
April as Macdonald made his preparations for the mission to
England. He tried to keep his correspondents in good heart.
The tactics in New Brunswick had been wrong, he said frankly;
but it was "easy to be wise after the event", and for the future
he promised assistance. "I do not at all despair," he wrote to
one of the faithful delegates in Prince Edward Island, "of
carrying out our great project sooner or later."[41]

The prospect abroad was almost as bad as the outlook at
home. It was true that early in March—just after the New
Brunswick election—there had come a slight relaxation in the
portentous displeasure of the American Secretary of State. On

March 10, the Canadian papers reported that the hated pass-ports were no longer being required at the American border;[42] and two days earlier Seward had instructed Adams, the Ameri-can minister in London, to notify Earl Russell that the United States was willing to let the Rush-Bagot Convention remain "practically in force".[43] The irritating annoyances, the direct threats seemed to be disappearing; but now a huge though vague peril was taking their place. Spring had come, and early in April Grant was pursuing Lee down the last twisting turns of that desperate flight that ended at Appomattox Court House. In a few weeks the Civil War would be over. In a few weeks the victorious north would be able to give its undivided atten-tion to its grievances against Great Britain and British America, and the Grand Army of the Republic would be free to win any military objective that was set for it in the continent of North America. Macdonald was fearful of a revival of Ameri-can military imperialism; but he was even more worried by the state of Canadian defences and Canadian morale, and by the half-hearted response that the British government and the British Parliament seemed to be making to the Canadian danger. "The indiscreet publication of Colonel Jervois' report in Eng-land," he wrote to J. H. Gray of New Brunswick, "has at the present caused a panic in Western Canada, as it shows the defencelessness of most of our Province, unless protected by permanent works, and the wretched debate in the House of Lords has not diminished the dread of forced annexation and abandonment by Great Britain. Fancy the British Empire for the purpose of defending Canada and the British Flag from an impending war voting £200,000 in all, to be expended at £50,000 a year! . . . In order to shame them we carried the vote for a million of dollars, and we go home with that sum in our hands."[44] This was frank enough; but to Watkin, of the Grand Trunk Railway and the Hudson's Bay Company, he was even more reproachfully downright. "But if England," he wrote, "can do nothing better for us than to vote £50,000 a year for four years to fortify Quebec, we may give up the idea of resistance as hopeless. . . ."[45]

In any case, it was time to be away. On April 20, five days after Galt and Cartier had departed, he sailed with Brown on the *China* for England.[46] Only eight years before, they had had their fearful row in the House—a row which had made Brown swear a deep and passionate oath that never again would there be anything but purely "parliamentary intercourse" between them. Yet here they were sailing in the same ship and bound on the same mission! It was certainly a delicate, precious relationship, which Macdonald treated in a gingerly, almost deferential, fashion. He even appeared to regard Brown as his senior. Although the proprietor of the *Globe* was, in fact, five years younger than himself, he referred to him blandly as "the old fellow", and "the covenanting old chap". There was, indeed, a strain of intense, brooding seriousness in Brown which made his companion's high spirits seem almost frivolously youthful. The Reform leader was a difficult colleague: reserved, sensitive, moody, and impulsive; touchy about everything that concerned seniority and precedence, and already quite obviously jealous of Galt. But the coalition had lasted now for nearly a year without any serious trouble; and the long voyage across the Atlantic to England was one of its most pleasant incidents. The wind blew steadily from the east, and there was scarcely ever any point in hoisting their auxiliary sails; but the *China* ploughed steadily ahead, making a regular twelve miles an hour all the way.[47] It was a gay company on board. They played round games, fenced for exercise, and got up balls and parties and concerts. There was only a brief stop in the Mersey for quarantine, and then they were off by the night mail for London. Next morning—the morning of May 3—they walked into the Westminster Palace Hotel. Macdonald was to become almost wearisomely familiar with the Westminster Palace Hotel in the next two years.

Its doorway must have seemed, in the days that followed, like a triumphal arch into the heart of imperial London. The London press had given a good welcome to Confederation;[48] and now its chief authors, the four principal members of the Canadian Cabinet, were honoured with a fatherly greeting from *The Times*. On May 16, they were presented to the

Queen (with Galt confessing a slight doubt as to the tenacity
of the trousers of his new uniform).⁴⁹ In the days that followed,
the members of the royal family, cabinet ministers, titled personages, railway magnates and London livery companies all
seemed to be competing with a flattering enthusiasm for even a
few hours of the delegates' time; and for over a month they
travelled round the circuit of the West End houses through
a pleasant succession of balls, dinner parties and receptions.
Macdonald enjoyed it all—less naïvely than Cartier, who frankly
delighted in big and splendid affairs, but more wholeheartedly
than his two introspective Scots colleagues, Brown and Galt.
Brown, the most recently married of the lot, a most passionately
devoted family man, was always fretting to be back to his
wife and little daughters in Toronto. Galt, who, in his own
way, was just as temperamental as Brown, was very much the
self-conscious colonial, doubtfully analysing his sensations in
London society, and occasionally reminding himself of the
obvious fact that if he had not been Finance Minister of
Canada, not one of these pleasant hosts and hostesses would
have paid the slightest attention to him.

The political reception of the delegates was quite as impressive as the social accolade with which they were received.
They began with informal talks with Cardwell, the Colonial
Secretary, and went on to more official discussions with a committee of the Cabinet, which included Gladstone—still arguing
interminably over "this most formidable Canadian question"—
as one of its principal members. The committee had decided,
as Gladstone later explained privately to Gordon of New Brunswick, to treat with Canada "as morally in the attitude of an
independent Power".⁵⁰ Galt, who regarded himself very gravely
as a virtual "independent"—and who would have been far
more furious if the delegation had received a condescending
reception—brooded darkly, with suspicious colonial misgivings,
over this ceremonious treatment. The British, on their part,
were puzzled by the new note of desperate urgency which the
Canadians sounded, and by the unprecedented scope of Galt's
first defence proposals. What had happened to the Canadians?
Were they in deadly earnest? Or were they simply presenting

views which they imagined would be highly acceptable in London? Gladstone, who continued to wrestle heroically with his enormous doubts, suspected that some of the Canadian views were "derivative and factitious". He wanted to make quite sure that the Canadian proposals were "spontaneous and not mere reflections of imaginary wishes here".[51]

By the time Macdonald and Brown arrived, Cardwell and his colleagues had already given their promise to use all the influence they possessed to forward the Quebec scheme, and Galt's first gigantic programme of defence measures had been tacitly dropped. The Canadians abandoned their rather melodramatic manner; and, basing their representations on the Jervois reports and on a new report which was furnished by the imperial defence committee, they returned pretty much to their suggestions of the previous November. They offered to build the fortifications west of Quebec, to improve the provincial canals, and to spend up to $1,000,000 annually on the training of the militia—provided the imperial government would guarantee the loans necessary to finance these works, and would also supply a naval force for the defence of the Great Lakes.[52] The guarantee, they demanded with reiterated insistence, must be granted at once. It must be authorized in the current session of the imperial Parliament. Without it the fortifications west of Quebec would have to be postponed a year, to a time when heavy military commitments would merely embarrass the project of Confederation. The demand was a rather peremptory one, awkward for the British to concede, for the army estimates for the year were already passed; and, as May drew to its close, they and the Canadians were still arguing about the matter.

The last day of May was Derby Day. Business was suspended. Everybody was out of town. The Canadians made up a party of eleven, with Russell of *The Times*, Grant and Brydges of the Grand Trunk, and D'Arcy McGee, the Canadian Minister of Agriculture, who had also arrived in London. They set out for Epsom at nine o'clock, in two stout carriages with postillions, and with a huge basket of food and wines from Fortnum and Mason's tucked away inside.[53] The road was jammed with an unending stream of vehicles. They took hours to

cover the sixteen miles to the Downs; and it was twelve o'clock
before they had established their carriage in a good position
and were washing away the dust of the journey with sherry
and seltzer water. The crowd thickened every minute. Macdonald and Galt walked about for a bit, with Russell as their
guide, and when they turned back could scarcely discover
their own carriages in the dense mass of vehicles. Somebody
suggested a pool at a guinea a draw. Galt—he was always a
person to whom things happened—drew the favourite, the
French horse, Gladiateur. Macdonald drew the field.

"You are a lucky fellow," said Macdonald.

Galt gazed at his ticket doubtfully. He would have gazed
doubtfully at any ticket he could possibly have drawn. "I do not
know about that," he said slowly. "There are fourteen horses
running, and it is a great chance if one of them does not come
in ahead."

"Well," said Macdonald, "I will swop and give you a guinea
to boot."[54]

They swopped and then it was time for Macdonald and
Galt to go. Russell, who knew everybody, had got the pair an
invitation to the pavilion and stand, just opposite the royal
party, which was provided by Todd Heatly, the wine merchant,
for his race-going patrons and friends. Inside the pavilion
there was turtle soup, "and all the delicacies and substantials
of the season", and a brimming fountain of champagne. Outside, on the stand, was an uninterrupted and magnificent view
of the entire course. There were a dozen false breaks, and then,
just at two minutes to four, the horses were off at last and
streaming up the hill. Wild Charley, Christmas Carol, Eltham,
Broomielaw, and Oppressor were out in front; and somewhere
in the ruck, almost unnoticed at first, were the blue and red
sleeves of the "Frenchman", with Harry Grimshaw up, carrying
Macdonald's guineas as a part of his enormous baggage of
metal. It was the crowd, rather than the race, that fascinated
Macdonald. As the horses pounded round Tattenham Corner,
the enormous black mass of spectators turned as one man;
and—it was like a flash of lightning—a multitude of white
staring faces rushed in a second into view. Now the horses

were into the straight. Broomielaw was still going very fast; but soon "those light back ribs could do no more". The two "magpie jackets", Eltham and Christmas Carol, shot out together; but deep on the inside was a stealing blur of blue and red that swept into a lead, "and nothing else was in it".[55] Macdonald could have dropped his handkerchief on Gladiateur's head, as the horse passed the post, a winner by two lengths. Then it was all over; and the crowd, shouting, pushing, gesticulating, and fighting, poured out onto the course.

"The Road", the creeping cavalcade back from Epsom to London, was a licensed saturnalia of horse-play and broad good humour. The Canadians buttoned up their greatcoats tightly, crammed their hats down on their heads, and armed themselves with peas, pea-shooters, pincushions of bran and little bags of flour. Macdonald, greatly daring, even bought a bag of peas for the "old chap", George Brown; and Brown, for a few wild, uncovenanting hours, developed an unexpected zeal for the pea-shooter. Galt thought himself lucky to be in the same carriage with Macdonald and Russell, who were "past masters at the art of chaffing". Macdonald kept up a constant raillery with the strangers on every side; and once, when they were blocked for an hour at a railway bridge, Russell got up on his seat and addressed the crowd in an eloquent extempore election speech. Assaulted in turn with cheers, jeers, peas, flour, and uproarious abuse, their carriage maintained its reputation for originality and high spirits all the way to London. It took them five hours to reach the capital. They were tired out when they walked into the Westminster Palace Hotel, and white as millers with dust and pelted flour.

The next day, June 1, they were back in conference once more. It was clear by now that the prospect of a comprehensive military settlement had faded. Macdonald and his colleagues wanted to start the defence construction programme during the current season. The British ministers could not understand the frantic haste of the Canadians and did not believe it was justified by the state of relations with the United States. "I frankly own my entire inability," Gladstone wrote to Cardwell, "to comprehend the feverish impatience of the Deputation, and their repeated declarations that the spring of 1866 is the crisis of their danger."[56] It was difficult for the British to grant the financial guarantee immediately, and equally hard, now that the Rush-Bagot Convention had just been restored, to start planning for a force of small ships in the Great Lakes. Yet the Canadians attached an enormous importance to their conditions; and Macdonald argued that if they could not be met, then the whole plan, including the expenditure of the $1,000,-000 already voted for the militia, would become politically difficult and embarrassing, and would have to be delayed beyond a year.[57] The British ministers, taking these arguments very literally indeed, proposed, in their turn, that the entire question of Canadian defences should be postponed once more until after Confederation. In the end, after all the investigations, reports, and proposals of the past eighteen months, this was what was decided. It was not quite all that was decided, however, for Great Britain and Canada exchanged pledges to assist each other with all their resources, in the event of war; and this British promise, though in fact it pledged nothing new, cleared at a stroke the unhappy uncertainty of the past few months. Yet the big Canadian armament programme had come to nothing. Defence, like Confederation, had ended in delay and postponement. And once again there was that depressing feeling of unfulfilment, of spiritual deflation.

The conference was over, and on June 17 Galt and Brown sailed for Canada. Macdonald waited another week. He had, he told his sister Louisa, a good deal of private business to attend to; besides, Oxford University had invited him to accept the honorary degree of D.C.L. "This is the greatest honour they can confer," he told his sister, "and is much sought after by the first men, so that I of course was only too happy to wait for it."[58] He stayed the last week-end at Strawberry Hill, Horace Walpole's old house, as a guest of the Countess Waldegrave; and on Tuesday, June 20, he travelled up to Oxford. That evening the Vice-Chancellor gave a dinner party, to which he was invited; and early next day—a morning of cloudless skies and brilliant sun—the "saturnalia of undergraduate Oxford", "the well-known melodrama of grave ceremony and

uproarious fun was once more enacted" at the Sheldonian
Theatre.[59] The undergraduates, who had taken their seats first,
enlivened the wait by giving alternate cheers and groans for a
long list of public figures and members of the audience. This
had just begun to pall, and a loud voice had suggested that a
policeman be sent to fetch the Vice-Chancellor in, when the
organ struck up the national anthem, and the academic procession entered. Macdonald was in distinguished, though hardly
splendid, company: Lord Lyons, the Minister to the United
States, who had just returned from Washington, Sir Hugh
Rose, late Commander-in-Chief in India, Henry Maine, Regius
Professor of Law at Cambridge, and three more British and
foreign scholars were the other recipients of degrees. Lord
Lyons and Sir Hugh Rose were most loudly cheered, "the
next in popularity being Mr. Macdonald".[60] He sat in his
gorgeous robes and listened to the public orator trying to complete a Latin oration which one undergraduate invited him "to
finish off tonight over a bottle of port". The prize essayists read
their English and Latin compositions amid a hubbub of genial
undergraduate comment, and the Newdigate poet fumbled
feebly through his verses on "Mexico". Then the young gentlemen of the University gave a final cheer "to ourselves for being
so good" and *Encaenia* was over. Macdonald carried away
pleasant memories of Oxford in the June sunshine; and three
days later, on June 24, he sailed for Boston on the *China*.

IV

He arrived in Montreal on July 7. Monck wrote him a
friendly note of greeting, congratulating him on his reception
in England. "I hope," he added, "you were as well pleased
with H.M. Ministers as they—from all I hear—were with you."[61]
It was amusing to be announced as "Dr. Macdonald" by
Monck's butler, Lambkin, as he went in for his first interview
with the Governor-General on reaching Quebec. But Monck
was anxious for a variety of reasons, public and private, to
reassemble the legislature as quickly as possible, and Macdonald

found himself plunged at once into public affairs. The Cabinet met on July 12; and the next day a proclamation was issued calling parliament for August 8. Then the ministers separated and, at long last, Macdonald went back for a brief holiday to Kingston.

He was not permitted to enjoy as much rest as he had hoped or expected. On July 30, old Sir Etienne Taché, the titular head of the Canadian ministry, died at his home at Montmagny. It was a shock, in more ways than one. Taché was a link with the past—a necessary link in the present, also, for he helped to bind the disparate elements of the coalition government together. Back in 1856 he had succeeded Sir Allan MacNab as the second head of the Liberal-Conservative government; and he had presided over the deliberations of the Quebec Conference, a benevolent old chairman, with his round friendly countenance and his nimbus of white hair. He had been very fond of Macdonald. Two days after the ministers had separated, when he already knew that his end was close, he had written a last little note on public business to the Attorney-General West, begging Macdonald to let him know as soon as he returned to Quebec. "J'aimerais à vous voir encore une fois," he wrote, "avant le long voyage que je vais bientôt entreprendre."[62] Now that last meeting could never take place. Taché was gone. And his going produced a political crisis of the first importance. A magnanimous old neutral who had no political ambitions and of whom nobody could be jealous, he had held the coalition together. Who was to succeed him?

Early in the morning of Thursday, August 3—the day after he had gone out to Montmagny for Taché's funeral—Macdonald received a note from the Governor-General. Could he come out that very morning to Spencer Wood for breakfast?[63] There could be only one meaning in such an invitation and within an hour it was made plain. At Spencer Wood, Monck invited him to take Taché's place as first minister and to form a new administration. Ever since June, 1864, he had been, in reality, the effective head of the government. Now he was asked to become its formal leader. He probably wanted the leadership. He knew that, in fact, nobody deserved it more than he. But, as he accepted the Governor-General's commission, he realized that nothing could be more conditional than his acceptance. He would have to confront Brown. And Brown was almost certain to make difficulties. Nobody could be more generous in his enthusiasms, more willing in his sacrifices, than Brown; but nobody also was more acutely sensitive, more prone to irritations, jealousies, and resentments, more apt to take offence, to stand upon his dignity, or to stick upon some absurd point of punctilio as if it were a major question of principle. In Brown's view, the Cabinet had been a triumvirate of equals—Macdonald, Cartier, and Brown—with Taché as merely nominal head. But, as time went on, it seemed to him that his own position was being threatened by a long and calculated succession of slights and indignities. He became convinced that Macdonald was ambitious to rise above this senior committee of three, and that Galt was intent upon thrusting his way into it from below. He had given up much. He knew it; and behind those sunken, smouldering eyes there now lay a sullen determination to yield no more. When Macdonald met him on the morning of August 3, with the Governor-General's commission, he would have nothing to do with it.[64] He refused to accept Macdonald as titular leader.

The crisis lasted for three indecisive days. Yet its outcome, as Macdonald must have realized, was inevitable from the beginning. He wanted the leadership—yes. But he was content to wait; then, and always, he was content to wait—for, in all the larger strategy of his career, he was gifted with a limitless patience. At that moment, nothing must be done which would permanently alienate Brown. With the movement for federal union stopped in apparent frustration, with Canada's whole future in a state of dangerous uncertainty, the coalition government could not possibly be permitted to dissolve. At first he suggested Cartier as Taché's successor; and then, since Brown still hesitated and demurred, he proposed that Sir Narcisse Belleau, a much less important member of the Legislative Council than old Taché had been, should be elevated to the empty honour of leadership, leaving the equality of the triumvirate, Macdonald, Cartier, and Brown, undisturbed.[65] Sir

Narcisse was not anxious for political office of any kind; but he yielded to the solicitations of Macdonald and Cartier. Brown accepted the arrangement. And on Tuesday, August 8, one day after Belleau had been sworn in, parliament met. It had been done in the nick of time.

Back in March, when it had been first announced, the summer meeting of parliament had seemed almost like an emergency session. But by now ministers might have been willing to dispense with it altogether, if only they had been able to do so. They had little to communicate and even less to propose. Though the British had promised to do all they could to forward Confederation, it would take time for their influence, and all other influences, to have any effect whatever; and although the fundamental pledges of military assistance given at London had profoundly reassured the Canadians, the big defence programme had been postponed once more. The seven-point statement of government policy which Cartier read to the House on August 15 was singularly negative and indecisive.[66] The government proposed no further action on the plan of federal union, no immediate construction of works for the defence of the province, no votes of money for the Intercolonial Railway, and no revisions of the tariff. The whole problem of the militia would have to wait for a further government investigation. The question of the Reciprocity Treaty and of foreign trade in general would have to be postponed until after the meeting of the interprovincial conference, which was scheduled for the autumn. Very evidently, and rather wearily, the government was marking time. It was a lame session. And, for a good part of it, Macdonald was absent. He was ill and for a while under doctor's orders.[67]

A sense of bafflement and suspense, a feeling of uncertainty and frustration seemed to infect the Canadians like a low fever. What could, or should, be done about defence, about their external relations with the United States? On the one hand, that enormous and dreaded fighting force, the Union army, was now being rapidly demobilized; but, on the other, the undiminished American resentment at Great Britain and her colonies seemed to promise, at least, a long period of diplomatic

fights and economic retaliations. The Americans had never
been satisfied with the dragging inconclusiveness of the St.
Albans trials. They now proceeded to vie with each other in
suggesting outrageous totals for the damages which the United
States must demand of Great Britain for the havoc wrought
by the *Alabama,* the cruiser which had been built in a British
shipyard and acquired by the Confederate States. It was true
that most of the retaliatory moves which had been so far
prompted by these grievances had not lasted very long. But
the notice of the abrogation of the Reciprocity Treaty had
never been cancelled; and Galt and Howland, who had gone
down to Washington in July to discuss with Sir Frederick
Bruce the prospects of renewal, returned with a very pessimistic
report. It looked now as if, in less than a year, the international
border would be closed to the free passage of Canadian raw
materials.

All this was bad enough. Now there was one thing more.
The Union army was, indeed, being demobilized; but a fairly
large number of its Irish veterans were promptly re-enlisting
in the unofficial forces of a new militant organization, the
Fenian Brotherhood. The Brotherhood dated back to 1858.
Its original objective had been the liberation of Ireland from
English "tyranny" and its establishment as a free and independent republic. It was perhaps too much to expect that an
Irish revolutionary society should remain very long united on
a single objective. At any rate its members in the United
States soon began to quarrel bitterly over high policy. One
lot, led by John O'Mahony, the original "Head Centre" of
the movement, continued to preach the pure, original evangel
of revolution in Ireland. Another group, captained by W. R.
Roberts and R. W. Sweeny, now began to advocate the invasion and occupation of British North America, as a base for
future heroic but unspecified operations against Great Britain.[68]
Macdonald, on the death of Taché, had taken over the Department of Militia Affairs once again; and by the autumn he
was receiving a good deal of information about the Fenians
and their activities through the espionage organization which
Gilbert McMicken had built up. "I am watching them very

closely with his assistance," Macdonald wrote to Monck, "and think that the movement must not be despised, either in America or Ireland. I am so strongly of that opinion that I shall spare no expense in watching them on both sides of the line."[69]

There were all sorts of reasons for Macdonald's anxiety and uncertainty, for the delays and embarrassments of the Canadian government's policy. But, without any doubt, the most important of them all was the impasse into which Confederation had blundered. So much was bound up with Confederation—was dependent upon Confederation; and its abrupt stoppage not merely held up the entire programme, but also filled everyone with a discouraged, paralysing feeling of futility and exasperation. Nothing whatever could be done until the decision in New Brunswick was reversed. But what chance was there yet of upsetting the apparently powerful new government, led by A. J. Smith and R. D. Wilmot, which had come into office only six months before as a result of a triumphant victory at the polls? The British government had done its part nobly. Cardwell and his colleagues, who believed that union was desirable on general imperial grounds, British as well as British North American, were quite ready, without any prompting from Canada, to push Confederation with all their power. "I wish to avoid all appearance of *undue* pressure or of dictation," Cardwell wrote to Gordon during his conversations with the Canadians in May, "but at the same time to let it be thoroughly understood that this question of Confederation is one in which the Home Government is quite in earnest; and considers that its wishes ought to have and will have great weight in the Provinces."[70] On June 24, when he wrote again to the Lieutenant-Governor of New Brunswick, transmitting the results of the conference with the Canadian ministers, the Colonial Secretary stated these wishes once more without ambiguity and in a tone of earnest admonition.[71] Later in the summer, Smith and Allen, the New Brunswick delegates, arrived in England in an attempt to counteract the evil influence of the Canadians. But they were received at the Colonial Office by men whose minds were firmly made up and who politely refused to be budged an inch. As for the opposition in Nova Scotia, Cardwell wrote a private letter to Earl Russell, at the Foreign Office, suggesting that "anything you could do to bring round Mr. Howe might help exceedingly".[72]

Surely all that could be done had been done. What further action was possible, unless the British government resorted frankly to coercion? There were some at least who were willing to consider even this. Russell, in the gloomy days in early September, when everything in British North America seemed to have reached a standstill, wrote Cardwell that he thought the colonies must be united for their own preservation, and that "some coercion" would be necessary. "The question will be," he went on, "whether the Maritime Provinces should be coerced in order to form a Federal Union, or whether the Province of Lower Canada should be forced to consent to a Legislative Union, with their separate privileges and laws being secured to them in the Act of Union. I incline to the latter plan."[73] It could scarcely be called a "plan", for drastic deeds of this kind still lay in the realm of speculation. And so long as they remained in the realm of speculation, the British government had clearly reached the end of its influence. The "earnestness and just authority" of Her Majesty's imperial ministers had not availed very much. "My present information about the prospect of Confederation is not very favourable," Cardwell wrote to Russell late in the summer. Everything possible had been done to win over A. J. Smith. "Yet I fear," Cardwell went on sadly, "he is unshaken in his determination to oppose to the uttermost."[74]

The gloom appeared unbroken. Yet back in British North America, where everything effective would have to originate in any case, there seemed suddenly to be a small gap in the curtain. In August Charles Fisher wrote quite optimistically to Macdonald from Fredericton.[75] Early in September Tilley came up to Quebec and spent two days talking over the situation in his native province with Monck and Macdonald and the other members of the Canadian ministry.[76] The fact was, as Tilley and Fisher had already begun to appreciate, that the Smith government, despite its appearance of strength, was already pretty seriously weakened and divided. A common dislike of the Quebec scheme was the one thing that had drawn this odd collection of Liberals and Conservatives together; and they found it almost impossible to discover an alternative policy which was at all practicable, and upon which they could agree. Maritime union, despite Prince Edward Island's obstinate refusal to consider the matter further, was a faint possibility; but the members of the Smith government had not really the slightest interest in Maritime union. The one positive plank in their programme was the promotion of railway and commercial relations with the United States. But the province was too poor to build "Western Extension" itself; and it could not offer sufficiently attractive terms to persuade private capitalists to undertake the project. Finally—and this in itself was a fatal blow—the approaching end of the Reciprocity Treaty would certainly make meaningless the whole pro-American commercial policy for which Smith and his friends stood. The government began to lose confidence and direction. It was becoming vulnerable. "We will watch the moment," Tilley wrote to Macdonald, "and be ready to strike a blow if there appears to be a chance of success."[77] Now the chance appeared. A by-election in York county was necessary. Fisher himself believed he could win. "I am quite certain," Tilley wrote to Macdonald, "Fisher can be returned under any circumstances, with an expenditure of eight or ten thousand dollars. If this should be considered necessary, is there any chance of the friends in Canada providing half the expenditure, not to exceed five thousand dollars, for their share?"

Macdonald promised Canadian aid. He told Fisher that if he went into the York election, he must go in to win at any cost. Now there was something to hope for. But the New Brunswick contest was nearly two months away; and meanwhile there was nothing to do but mark time. Monck left on the morning of September 26 for a brief holiday in England; and the Canadian government was already on the move to its new home in Ottawa.[78] As soon as he had said good-bye to Monck, Macdonald hurried off to seek quarters in the new capital. At Ottawa he found Parliament Hill still littered with unsightly masses of building materials. The steam-heating system, one of the wonders of the new buildings, was in good working order. There was a plentiful supply of water; but oil lamps flared in the rooms in the late afternoon, for Parliament Hill had not yet been connected with the municipal gas-works. In the streets—streets which seemed so curiously wide and empty after the crowded thoroughfares of Quebec—the civil servants tramped about, looking for flats and houses. Macdonald himself found a house, one of a terrace at the south-west corner of Daly and Cumberland Streets. A day later, as the steamer carried him down the river again to Montreal, he was writing to Louisa, inquiring about bed and table linen.[79] Yet for some time the house on Daly Street—the "Quadrilateral" as it came to be called—was only a somewhat temporary resting place. Ottawa itself was like a handsome new residence which its owner had formally purchased, but which was still unfinished and unfit for tranquil occupation. Ottawa, in fact, was very much like Confederation.

V

On November 6, Charles Fisher defeated John Pickard in the York by-election. Macdonald learnt the news the same day; and, a few days later, he received a long jubilant letter from Fisher recounting his victory.[80] The precise value of that victory to Confederation was more than a little obscure. For Fisher, in his election campaign, had said as little as he could on the subject of federal union, and at one point had been driven publicly to declare that Confederation could not be proceeded with until the people of New Brunswick had had another chance to pronounce their will on the subject at the polls.[81] But, despite all these tactical reservations, the meaning of Fisher's election was clear and very heartening. He had been a delegate to the Quebec Conference and was a known admirer of the Quebec scheme. He had cleverly tried to identify Smith and his pro-American policies with the growing menace of Fenianism, and he had aroused the Loyalists and the Orangemen of the province by an appeal to the British connection. Monck, to whom Macdonald wrote as soon as he had received the news from York, was suddenly all confidence again. "I think," he wrote back from England, "this is the most important thing that has happened since the Quebec Conference and if followed up judicially affords a good omen of success in our spring campaign."[82]

Of course, it could be, and would be, followed up by other judicious Canadian moves. Yet by themselves these Canadian efforts would have been ineffectual. What gave them their value was the persistent deterioration of the Smith government. The defeat of Pickard in York was merely the outward sign of serious inward decay. Two weeks later, T. W. Anglin, one of the staunchest supporters of "Western Extension" in the administration, resigned as a result of the failure to proceed with his favourite scheme. The policies which gave the Smith-Wilmot government its only meaning and justification were breaking against immovable obstacles; and as Smith and his colleagues grew more muddled and divided, the Canadian government rushed in to take up the position of an unofficial opposition. "We look to you to help us out of the scrape," Fisher wrote to Macdonald, presenting his bill of expenses in York, "for if every dollar is not paid it will kill us at the general election. . . . Do not allow us to want now or we are all gone together." The Canadian ministers prepared to honour Macdonald's pledge; and in November, when George Brown visited Fredericton on business connected with the Reciprocity Treaty, he and the now confident Gordon laid plans for the triumph of Confederation in New Brunswick. "We confidentially settled the whole course of operations to be pursued here," Gordon confided to Cardwell, "and found ourselves almost perfectly agreed. I am convinced I can make (or buy) a union majority in the Legislature. . . ."[83]

The feeling of anxiety and frustration which had got on everybody's nerves during the summer had magically vanished. The York by-election—an equivocal victory by itself—had, in some strange fashion, changed everything. The Canadian government was stronger morally than it had been at any time since the news of Tilley's defeat in the previous March. It was strong enough even to survive George Brown's resignation, which, if it had come five months earlier at the time of Taché's death, would in all probability have wrecked the coalition. Brown had disagreed with the policy which Galt and the rest of the Cabinet wished to pursue in a last effort to persuade the United States to continue the Reciprocity Treaty; but this disagreement, while it was not simply an occasion or an excuse for his resignation, was at the same time not its only cause. There were incompatibilities of temperament in the coalition which had been endured only by a supreme effort of patience and good will on all sides; and when Brown finally left, everybody, including Brown himself, must have felt a profound sense of relief. Yet the original political agreements of the coalition had remained unbroken. The rather strained cordiality of its members had lasted to the end; and when the break finally came, Brown's last letters, addressed to Cartier, not Macdonald, were friendly and even generous.[84] He promised that if the government stuck to the policies already agreed upon, he would give it his "best aid". He offered $500 towards the New Brunswick fund and pledged himself to give more if further help was required. The continued support of the Grits was assured. Macdonald accepted it gratefully, making the necessary promises to Howland, now the senior Reformer in the Cabinet. And the coalition went on. Yet the time in which it could achieve its first objective was now running out. In August, when Belleau had been appointed, it had been agreed that if a general British North American union should be still impracticable by the time the Canadian parliament met for its next session, then the government must proceed immediately with the federal union of Canada East and Canada West alone. The meeting of the Canadian legislature could not be delayed beyond the summer of 1866. Macdonald had about six months left.

Yet by now he was beginning to believe that scarcely half that time would be necessary. "Mr. Cardwell showed me his private communications from Mr. Gordon," Monck wrote confidently from London, "and from them I have come to the

conclusion that the success of the Union next spring in New
Brunswick may be looked upon as *certain*."⁸⁵ All the news
from Fredericton seemed to confirm Macdonald's impression
that the disintegration of the Smith government was proceed-
ing apace; and early in January the rickety administration
received the worst blow it had yet sustained. R. D. Wilmot
sent in his resignation. From the start Wilmot and Smith had
been regarded as the joint leaders of the anti-Confederate
Cabinet. Even by itself, Wilmot's resignation would have been
serious enough; but its significance was magnified by the
reasons which had caused it. For Wilmot, the anti-Confederate,
had been converted to Confederation. A delegate to the interprovincial conference on trade, held at Quebec in September,
1865, he had come to believe in the prospects of a united
British North American commerce; and, at the same time, he
had come to recognize the hopelessness of all attempts to renew
the Reciprocity Treaty.⁸⁶ His resignation was, in essence, a
public admission of the fact that the policies of the Wilmot-
Smith government had now been invalidated by circumstances.
Within a few weeks, his interpretation of the facts was proved
correct. Galt and Howland of Canada, Henry of Nova Scotia,
and Smith of New Brunswick journeyed down to Washington
in January, 1866, to make a last attempt to continue the Reciprocity Treaty. But the one offer which they finally received
from the members of the Ways and Means Committee of the
House of Representatives could hardly have been more derisory
if it had been intended as a deliberate insult. The Reciprocity
Treaty had gone. And with it went the main policy, and one
of the two leaders, of the Smith-Wilmot government.

What would Gordon do with his wonderful opportunity?
Macdonald knew, from what Brown and Monck had told him,
that the Lieutenant-Governor had counted much on Wilmot's
support in his plans for gaining a union majority in the legislature. But could he not derive even more advantage from
Wilmot's retirement from the ministry than from his presence
in it? Could he not use it to break up the existing government completely and to replace it by a new administration
really favourable to Confederation? At first, from the news

that Macdonald received from Tilley, it seemed that this was precisely the course that Gordon intended to follow. "I have had one or two interviews of late with our Governor," Tilley wrote, describing the approaching crisis, "and find that he is determined to put matters through without delay. He has declined to accept Wilmot's resignation and it is probable that one or two members of the Government beside Wilmot will take ground in favour of Confederation and that a break up will be the result."[87] Obviously this final, happy denouement could not take place until Smith had returned from the Reciprocity Treaty negotiations in Washington. On February 15, 1866, the day after he reached Fredericton, the Governor tackled him firmly. And then occurred the most astounding episode in the whole ambiguous and tortuous history of the Smith-Wilmot government. Smith, though still intensely disliking the Quebec Resolutions, professed himself not opposed in principle to British North American union. He consented to a paragraph on the subject being inserted in the speech from the throne. He even promised that in due course, and in a somewhat indirect, face-saving fashion, his government would carry out the union policy which the imperial authorities had so strongly recommended.[88] In the end the Lieutenant-Governor closed with this curious offer. The crisis passed. And Smith and most of his colleagues remained in power.

What had happened? Were both the principals in this strange compact acting in good faith? Or, if not, who was deceiving whom? Fisher, who had always suspected that the Governor was determined to injure Confederation in every possible way, naturally doubted Gordon's sincerity. Tilley, who was a good deal closer to the centre of affairs than Fisher, never believed that Smith and his colleagues really intended to carry out their promises. To Macdonald, far away in Canada, the whole course of the affair must have seemed tangled and equivocal to the last degree. On March 8, the New Brunswick legislature met. The paragraph on Confederation in the speech from the throne seemed non-committal and innocuous; but, on the other hand, it certainly had the effect of indicating to Smith's diehard anti-Confederate followers that a change in policy was imminent.[89] The debate on the address began in both Houses, while the Governor waited impatiently for the new policy to be declared. In the Assembly, days and weeks dragged by in an inconclusive argument prompted by Fisher's want-of-confidence amendment; but in the Legislative Council, where a strong pro-Confederation majority had existed from the start, the outcome was quick and decisive. Early in April the telegrams from Fredericton began to warn Macdonald that a crisis was at hand. "Address to Queen for Confederation on basis of Quebec Conference carried in Legislative Council thirteen to five," Peter Mitchell wired on April 7. "Government opposed but powerless. They cannot stand long."[90] Macdonald may have wondered how the passage of an address in the Legislative Council could cause the downfall of a government; but he was soon enlightened. For Gordon had determined to answer the address of the Council at once; and he had determined also, despite the delays and evasions of the past few weeks, to answer it in the favourable sense which he thought was justified as a result of his agreement with Smith. He prepared an answer expressing satisfaction. Smith and his colleagues objected to it. They refused to accept responsibility. But the Governor had decided to "brusquer les choses". He read his prepared reply to the legislative councillors; and three days later he briefly announced its consequences to the Canadians. "My answer to Legislative Council address," he wired Monck, "proved too strong for my government who have resigned today."[91]

Chapter Fifteen

Triumph

I

Macdonald's first feeling was one of enormous relief. "The *Telegraph* of yesterday informed me," he wrote to Peter Mitchell on the morning of April 10, before Gordon's telegram had arrived, "that you have not yet got through your vote of want of confidence in the Lower House, but that you are in the midst of a ministerial crisis, in consequence of Mr. Gordon's reply to the address from your branch of the Legislature. I hope this is correct, and that you will be able to form an administration that will at once carry Confederation."[1] These hopes were strong—stronger now than they had been for months; but even so, they were still mixed with apprehensions and doubts. For months the handling of affairs in New Brunswick had seemed to him curiously clumsy and inept. What he thought of Gordon's conduct he kept carefully to himself. But he had criticized Tilley for promising not to submit the Quebec scheme to the legislature in a final session; and he was very suspicious of Fisher's want-of-confidence amendment to the address, which the Assembly had still been debating when the ministerial crisis occurred. He suspected that Fisher was "playing Mr. Smith's game". He was certain, at any rate, that everybody down in New Brunswick had been playing party politics a great deal too much. If Smith were, indeed, half converted to federal union, why was it not possible to form a coalition of both parties and to carry Confederation through the present House without a general election? What was needed in New

Brunswick, after all these devious meanderings, was a little straightforward action. "Can Mr. Gordon not be moved," he wired Monck on April 11, "to form coalition ministry so as to secure passage of address without waiting for re-election of ministers?"[2]

These early impressions vanished quickly. Tilley's letters—cool, realistic, yet resolute—supplied a full analysis of the "ministerial crisis" and of the awkward position in which it had left all the New Brunswick unionists. There was no doubt whatever—Gordon had put his foot into it most decisively. The long-faced, sad-eyed young man, with his unsubdued preference for Maritime union, his cold contempt for colonial politicians, and his secret longings for a nice biddable Crown colony, had chosen to "forward" Confederation by the brusque action of a benevolent despot. Even if all the worst suspicions of him had been true, even if he had been really trying to injure Confederation by his maladroit championship, he could hardly have acted with more tragic ineptitude. "In the particular case of your reply to the Legislative Council," Cardwell wrote privately a little later, "you made, as I thought and as you said yourself, a great mistake in acting alone and giving occasion for complaint which might easily have been avoided."[3] The indignant clamour raised immediately by Smith and his colleagues against the "arbitrary" action of the Lieutenant-Governor introduced a new and difficult element into the contest, and utterly changed the campaign which Tilley and the unionists would have to fight. "It is unfortunate for the cause of Confederation," Tilley explained to Macdonald, "that the break up was brought about in the manner in which it has been. . . . The Governor was indiscreet in dealing with his advisers on one point, though I think we can make a fair defence of him. Smith and the Antis now desire to make the issue one of a violation of the principles of Responsible Government, not a test of Confederation. Had the case not come up in this shape, we could have beaten them with great ease, but this new issue arising, it complicates matters."[4]

It did indeed. And Macdonald, up in Canada, hardly knew how to cope with the complications. What they had all hoped

and longed for had come, but it had come in such a questionable shape as to be hardly recognizable. Yet out of this disappointing and dangerous opportunity, an advantage must be
plucked, and at once. Time was rapidly running out. In
another three months at most, the Canadian parliament would
have to be called. And if, at the time it reassembled, there
was not an absolutely clear course for Confederation, then he
would have to do what he had repeatedly promised Brown
that he would do—he would have to deal with the constitutional problem of the Province of Canada alone. "If we fail
this year in New Brunswick," Monck wrote to him ominously
at the height of the crisis in Fredericton, "would it be possible
to pass Representation by Population for Canada on the basis
proposed at Quebec, with effective guarantees to Lower Canada
for her peculiar institutions and laws?"[5] The time was coming
fast when he would have to consider these desperate alternatives seriously. But not yet. The game was not quite played
out yet. Down in the Maritime Provinces there was now a
chance, as well as a hazard. And if Tilley and his new ministry
could only get the existing New Brunswick House to sanction
renewed negotiations for union, then they would be through in
safety. In Nova Scotia, where the legislature was also sitting,
Tupper had introduced a non-committal resolution, which,
while it said nothing whatever about the Quebec scheme,
did authorize the provincial government to continue the
negotiations for a federal union of British North America.
If Tupper could get his resolution passed, there would be a
clear way for Confederation. And Tupper, with his skill and
robust confidence, would probably succeed, if only his doubtful and restless Assembly were not panicked by the news of
an impending general election in New Brunswick. Tilley, if
he could possibly avoid it, must not risk another dissolution.
Macdonald telegraphed to him, begging him to get a union
resolution passed without going again to the country.

But this was precisely what Tilley could not do. If the
break-up of the late government had come over the issue of
Confederation, it might perhaps have been fairly easy for him
to have picked up a good deal of support from among Smith's

divided and bewildered followers. But Smith and his colleagues had resigned in protest against what they termed a "gross violation" of the principles of responsible government; and before adjournment of the House, which took place only a few days after the formation of the new government, the leader of the "Antis" had succeeded in reuniting his followers in an attack on the Governor for his arbitrary conduct. After this, Tilley could scarcely meet the same House again. If he did, the same majority would commence its constitutional tirade all over again; and the unionists would be prevented from getting at the question of Confederation.[6] No, it was obvious—there was no way of avoiding another general election in New Brunswick. It would be a difficult contest—just how difficult Macdonald began to realize as the long letters from Tilley kept coming in. It was rumoured that Howe would come over from Nova Scotia to aid the New Brunswick anti-Confederates; and there was no doubt, Tilley reported, that the American imperialists would supply Smith with money as generously as they had in the election of 1865. "The opposition are raising Heaven and Earth . . ." he told Macdonald gloomily. "Smith and his friends now attempt to keep Confederation out of sight and make it a constitutional test, and you know how the masses of the people view any supposed infringement of their constitutional rights."[7]

Macdonald realized that the Canadians must now make their supreme effort. In September, 1865, when Tilley had visited Quebec, they had discussed the possibility of Canadian assistance in the event of another New Brunswick election. Already the Canadians had paid over a good bit on account. The bills for Fisher's contest in York had come in; and early in January, Brydges had reported that he had "sent the needful to Tilley and kept all our names here off the document".[8] Now—from the estimates which kept coming in from Fredericton—it was clear that a much bigger effort was required. "I think we can with good management and with means," Tilley reported realistically, "carry a majority in the province. . . . If you can give us funds, we can send a responsible man (such as Mr. Wright of Saint John, one of our wealthiest merchants) to

Portland where he might meet Brydges or some other person
to arrange finances. It will require some $40,000 or $50,000
to do the work in all our counties. . . ."⁹ The sum was not unusually large for a provincial general election in mid-Victorian
times; but the Canadians had to find it largely among themselves and their closest friends, for the rank and file of party
contributors could not be expected to have a very lively interest
in New Brunswick politics. Everybody—including the Governor-
General—was agreed that aid should be sent and at once.
"Cartier and Galt both think that someone in the confidence
of the Canadian ministry should have an interview with Mr.
Tilley," Monck reported to Macdonald. "I think if Galt were
to go to Portland and get Tilley to meet him there it would
be the best plan."¹⁰

When the money had been scraped together and Galt, or
someone else, had gone down to Portland to give it to the New
Brunswickers, the Canadians would have done all they could.
The rest was up to Tilley and his followers. The election had
been fixed for the last days of May and the first of June; and
Macdonald was ready to delay the meeting of the Canadian
parliament until the verdict in New Brunswick had been
given. There was still time; and he was prepared to wait a
little longer for certainty. But he had not reckoned with the
unexpected, the unprecedented zeal of the Governor-General,
Lord Monck. Monck may not have been a very profound or
a very original political philosopher—"though the Prince of
good fellows," said Gordon caustically, "he never appears to
me to see anything with his own eyes or to look below the
surface."¹¹ But, up to that moment at any rate, he had been
—in his comfortable, rather sluggish fashion—a very sensible
and cautious guide. Now the news that came up from the
Maritime Provinces seemed to electrify him with a frantic
zeal for instant action. On April 17 the union resolution had
successfully passed the Nova Scotian Assembly; and, at about
the same time, letters arrived from the Lieutenant-Governors
of both Newfoundland and Prince Edward Island, speaking
in optimistic terms of the prospects of Confederation in these
provinces.¹² "I think the time has come," Monck wrote to

Macdonald, "when we ought to call our Parliament together."[18] It must meet, he thought, almost immediately, in the first week in May. The local constitutions for Canada East and Canada West—the last part of the Confederation settlement which still remained to be completed—must be framed and passed as quickly as possible, without even waiting for the longed-for action in Fredericton. Then, whether the results of the New Brunswick elections were good or bad, they must hurry over to London in time to get the required legislation passed in the present session of the imperial Parliament. Legislation by the imperial Parliament was, of course, absolutely essential. In no other way could the British North American Provinces be constitutionally joined together in a federal union. The northern provinces were not independent states; they had never renounced their allegiance to the Crown; and as Colonel Gray had pointed out, "they still recognized a paramount and sovereign authority, without whose consent and legislative sanction the Union could not be framed". Obviously the independent making of such a union required the exercise of two essential sovereign powers which the provinces had not acquired, and never even thought of claiming; they could not formally amend their own constitutions, and they could not negotiate formal agreements among themselves or with foreign powers. Legislation by the imperial Parliament was necessary—particularly necessary in the case of the Province of Canada, for there a long series of imperial statutes, of which the Quebec Act, the Constitutional Act, and the Act of Union were the most important, had established the constitution; and what had been done by the imperial Parliament only the imperial Parliament itself could alter. Everybody took for granted that the Quebec Resolutions, and their possible amendments, were simply the basis of a bill which would have to be drafted in Whitehall, sponsored by the British government, and passed by Lords and Commons at Westminster. This, in fact, was the final goal of the whole union movement. And now Monck was all impatience to reach it. "To use a phrase of your own," he wrote persuasively to Macdonald, "the thing should be completed *per saltum*. . . . If we are ready and present ourselves

at the Colonial Office in time I am very much inclined to think
that New Brunswick—particularly divided as she now is—would
not be allowed to stop the way."[14]

It was a question of tactics. It was a delicate problem in
timing. And Macdonald did not want to be hustled into
precipitate action. There were half a dozen different parliaments
—including the imperial Parliament—to be considered. Newfoundland and Prince Edward Island, where the prospects of
success were still very vague, could be dismissed without
much attention; but the others counted seriously, and each
was a problem in itself. The Nova Scotian parliament would
expire by law in the spring of 1867; and unless Confederation
were completed before that date, it would run the grave risk
of another defeat in another provincial general election. In
Great Britain, the government was obviously in serious difficulties with its Reform Bill; and if the legislation uniting British
North America were not presented at once, there might be
a change of government, or a dissolution and an appeal to the
people, which would delay the whole business for months.
Both these considerations were important. They both suggested
speed. But there was a third factor in the problem—the New
Brunswick general election; and, for an equally important
reason, it invited delay. The Canadian parliament had formally
accepted the Quebec Resolutions without amendment. But in
Nova Scotia and New Brunswick it was hardly possible to
talk in public about the Quebec Resolutions without a storm.
The most that could be hoped for in these provinces was a
general resolution authorizing the continuation of the negotiations for union; but the passage of these resolutions would
certainly be imperilled if the Canadian legislature met at once.
If parliament met for its first session in Ottawa before the
New Brunswick general election, Dorion and John Sandfield
Macdonald would hardly neglect the delightful opportunity
of asking the coalition government whether it still adhered
to the Quebec scheme. "Had we answered in the affirmative,"
Macdonald later explained to Tilley, "you would have been
defeated, as you were never in a position to go to the polls on
those resolutions. Had we replied in the negative, and stated

that it was an open question, and that the resolutions were liable to alteration, Lower Canada would have risen as one man, and good-bye to Federation."¹⁵ No, it would be fatal to run such a risk before the New Brunswick election had taken place. But the Canadians could meet as soon after as possible, if only to quiet Monck's feverish impatience. And it was decided to call parliament for June.

In the meantime, another matter, which was to reach a crisis before the Canadian parliament assembled and which was to have a profound effect upon the general election in New Brunswick, had already begun to take up a very large amount of Macdonald's time. This was the Fenian Brotherhood which, in the spring of 1866, seemed to be working itself into a paroxysm of crazy activity. As far back as the late autumn of 1865, the two provinces with long land frontiers had become so alarmed by the threats of Fenian raids that Canada had called out nine companies of volunteers for service and New Brunswick had set about enrolling a home guard. During the winter the Fenian advocates of the plan of invading British North America had been stirred into even more frenzied demonstrations by the controversy over high policy which was still convulsing the Brotherhood. A Fenian convention, called in January, vindicated O'Mahony and the old gospel of revolution in Ireland. A second Fenian convention, called in February, upheld Sweeny and Roberts and their new revelation of "on to Canada". Sweeny and Roberts were, by their own confession, the more intrepid crusaders. Theirs was the more immediate objective. It was obviously up to them to do something spectacular. And, as March 17 drew closer and closer, reports began to come in from all along the border that the Brotherhood had chosen the symbolic occasion of St. Patrick's Day for the great adventure of their attack on Canada. "Be at all times on the lookout," "Oliver", the spy, wrote to McMicken at Windsor. "A desperate advance and attack will be made along the whole of the frontier on or about the 17th instant. You may depend that a struggle is at hand. . . ."¹⁶

As Attorney-General West and Minister of Militia Affairs, Macdonald had to accept the main responsibility of preparing

for the Fenians. He accumulated masses of material about
them. The Fenians themselves always advertised their proceedings in public with vainglorious garrulity. Moreover, news
of their plans and doings poured in from the British minister
at Washington, from British consuls in the various cities of
the republic, and above all from Gilbert McMicken, the stipendiary magistrate at Windsor, who had organized an excellent detective force along the frontier, and who had a wide
acquaintance of spies and informers. Macdonald usually knew
more about the plans of the Fenians than the Fenians did
themselves. This, to be sure, did not mean a great deal. But
it may have meant too much. For Macdonald was usually
inclined, in a laudable spirit of prudence, to give the Fenians
credit for more sanity than they possessed, and to invest the
kaleidoscopic chaos of their plans with a degree of order and
coherence never remotely approached. On March 7, ten days
before the dreaded attack was expected to take place, he insisted, despite the doubts of several members of the Canadian
ministry, on calling out 10,000 of the Canadian militia.[17] When
the famous day came, the volunteers were strung out along
the frontier, waiting for raids; and the police of Toronto—
where a riot of St. Patrick's Day demonstrators was expected—
were watching the streets with apprehension. Yet nothing
happened. March 17 had passed in complete and baffling
peace. It began to look as if the only real result of all the
machinations of the Fenians would be a remarkable outburst
of British North American patriotism, a remarkable demonstration of the new British North American national feeling.

There was, however, another result—a result of still more
immediate and practical value. New Brunswick, as well as
Canada, was embraced in the comic grand strategy of the
Fenians. "At the moment I am writing this letter," Macdonald
observed in his brief note to Mitchell of April 10, "you are,
I fancy, in great excitement about the Fenians. I really would
not be surprised if these rascals gave you some trouble."[18] In
fact, the "ministerial crisis" in New Brunswick coincided almost
exactly with the threat of a great Fenian invasion—a threat
which ended in a few characteristically dirty deeds of incen-

diarism—and the coincidence was highly unfortunate for Smith. Smith and his followers were already upon the defensive. As Tilley had foretold, the leader of the anti-unionists had tried to shift the main issue of the election away from Confederation and back to the sacred principles of "responsible government". The attempt was not much of a success. The Governor, defending himself with a good deal of force and plausibility, publicly revealed his agreement with Smith; and Smith was obliged to admit, in his own elegant phraseology, that he had told the Governor that he "would go for a union provided one could be obtained upon fair and equitable terms".[19] Convicted at the worst of double dealing and at the best of wavering procrastination, Smith was a highly damaged man. His policies —"Western Extension" and increased trade with the United States—had proved impossible to carry out. Worst of all, the whole pro-American attitude of his government had now become doubly suspect and unpopular as a result of the Fenian raids.

Both sides, of course, tried to draw political capital out of the raids. But the Confederates were by far the more successful. "The Fenian excitement continues on our borders," Tilley reported to Macdonald on April 21, "and you will laugh when you see that the Antis are endeavouring to make the people believe that you Canadians have sent them here to aid Confederation."[20] There was, indeed, something of the quality of bad amateur theatricals about the Fenian movement, but there ran through it also a very real strain of vicious gangsterism; and the attempt to explain away the Irish-American menace as a clumsy Canadian imposture had the natural effect of increasing the public suspicion of Smith and his colleagues. Timothy Anglin, an original member of the Smith government who had fled from Ireland after the Rebellion of 1848, was declared to be in daily communication with the Fenians; and it was reported that Smith himself had become an enthusiastic convert to the movement during his visit to Washington on the business of the Reciprocity Treaty. The unionists, in their campaign, used the bogey of external danger to the limit. The

Fenian threat aroused doubts of their opponents' loyalty. It gave a new meaning to the grave warning of the British government that Confederation was necessary for effective defence.

Up in Ottawa, where everybody was now getting ready for the approaching session of the Canadian parliament, Macdonald waited with growing confidence for the outcome of the New Brunswick elections. Towards the end of May, the news began to come in over the telegraph wires. As was usual at that time, the elections were spread out over about a fortnight; and it was not until June 12 that the returns from the last constituencies came in. But there was no doubt, from the beginning, that the decision of the previous year had been completely reversed and that Tilley and the unionists were victorious. Only two of the ex-ministers of the Smith government survived the general defeat; only six of the twenty-two members of the old House who had signed the protest against the "unconstitutional" action of Gordon had been re-elected to the new parliament. This time, everything, including even the Fenian menace, had worked together to produce a smashing success. The Fenians almost deserved Macdonald's and Tilley's gratitude. The nuisance had a value. But it was an interminable nuisance, nevertheless; and just at the very moment when the news of Tilley's triumph was reaching Ottawa, the rumours of Fenian movements along the Canadian frontier were beginning to pour in once more, growing more precise and ominous with every passing minute. On May 31, the government called out 14,000 volunteers. These youthful, half-trained companies might have encountered nothing but the peaceful calm which had reigned on March 17; but chance decided differently. In the cowardly incompetence of Fenianism there was still the Irish element of the unpredictable; and among all the vainglorious "head centres", "generals" and "grand organizers" who had shouted for the capture of Canada, there was one man— John O'Neill—who was not afraid to fight. On the night of May 31, he led a body of Fenians across the Niagara River into Canada; and two days later he drove back a detached column of Canadian volunteers at Ridgeway. By the night of June 2, the invaders had hurriedly retreated to the United States; but they left behind them nine dead and thirty wounded Canadian militiamen.

II

It had all happened before, as Macdonald knew very well. There had been the large American invasions of his young manhood, and, much more recently, the tiny Confederate raid on St. Albans in Vermont. But this gratuitous act of mass murder had not even the justification of the feeblest of rebellions, of the smallest of internal disturbances. The St. Albans raiders had been native Americans, the commissioned officers of a power whose belligerent rights had been recognized, and which was engaged in fighting a great war. But there was no civil war going on in Canada and the Fenians were not Canadians; they were Irish Americans who had crossed an international border to bring death and havoc to a completely peaceful land. The incredible wantonness of their attack, which seemed to imply that a large section of the American people regarded the mere separate existence of British North America as a permanent offence, provoked, in response, an angry outburst of genuine national feeling. The entire body of the volunteers—over 20,000 strong—turned out eagerly to guard the frontiers; the Canadian parliament, meeting in the exciting atmosphere of an emergency, proceeded to suspend habeas corpus, vote lavish credits for defence, and re-enact the old law by which Von Schoultz and the other officers of the invading American force had been executed back in 1838. "The autonomy of British America," declared the *Globe*, "its independence of all control save that to which its people willingly submit, is cemented by the blood shed in battle on the 2nd June."[21] Macdonald's profoundest purpose in political life was to preserve that autonomy, in co-operation with Great Britain, and against the United States. Confederation, his most ambitious political project, was in essence a design for the defence of that separateness. And the Fenian raids had given a new significance and meaning to the federal scheme. They clothed the bare bones of the Quebec Resolutions with the living tissue of popular enthusiasm and popular will.

But this was not all. The raids, which in one way were a positive inspiration to the new nationality, were in another a mere added complication in the already difficult time-table of Confederation. How, while the Fenian crisis continued, could the necessary delegation leave Canada for England to help prepare the legislation which would unite British North America? Yet the whole constitutional process must be completed within a year or infinite trouble would certainly result. The New Brunswick anti-Confederates had been thoroughly silenced by the overwhelming defeat of June. But in Nova Scotia, Howe was still vigorously at work, gaining converts at every stage of his passionate anti-unionist crusade, and threatening almost certain defeat for Tupper, if the old constitution should last long enough to permit another general election. Archibald and Tupper were becoming almost frantic. "We *must* obtain action during the present session of the Imperial Parliament," Tupper wrote in great excitement, "or all may be lost. Our House expires by law in May next when a general election must be held and for reasons which it is not necessary to enter into here the result would be most disastrous to Confederation and probably defeat it altogether. I am sure I need not add a word more to convince you of the necessity of prompt and immediate action."[22] Further words might have been quite unnecessary but within three days Tupper added them.[23] And his importunate appeals for haste were reinforced by Lord Monck who, although the session of the Canadian parliament had not lasted more than a fortnight, was already fretting with impatience for the completion of the local constitutions of Canada East and Canada West.[24] Badgered by importunities and scarcely veiled threats, Macdonald kept his temper fairly well. He had always intended to have the local constitutions passed at the summer session, and he knew very well that the Nova Scotian legislature expired in the following May. It was a question now, not of strategy, but of tactics, he told Lord Monck; and he politely reminded the Governor-General that "somewhat" should be left to the Canadian parliamentary experience of his principal minister.[25] Yet on the main point he yielded to combined pressure. Tupper and Archibald came up to Ottawa towards the end of June to press their case; and it was decided that an effort should be made to get legislation through the present session of the imperial Parliament. The Maritime delegates were to leave for England on July 19. The Canadians—Fenians or no Fenians —would sail two days later.

Everything now depended on the continuation of the present session of the imperial Parliament, and on the survival of the Whig government under whose benevolent supervision the whole union scheme had been worked out. Yet it was at this highly unfortunate moment that the long-awaited crisis in British politics occurred. Lord Russell's government, defeated on its Reform Bill, resigned; and on July 7 Cardwell wrote regretfully to Monck announcing that he had left office the day before, and that he could no longer look forward to moving the British North America Bill in the House of Commons.[26] Only a week later, on July 14, the first news of the English crisis reached Canada. Its effects were shattering. What was to be done? With the prospect of the session in England being wound up almost immediately, whatever party was in power, was there any point in trying to carry out the plan that had been agreed upon with Tupper at the end of June? Monck and Macdonald decided that it would be useless at the moment to send delegates to London. They reached agreement easily. But it soon became clear that the Maritimers took a completely different view. They were determined to sail for England so long as there remained the shadow of a hope of legislation in the current session of Parliament; and Tupper gave a peremptory answer to Monck's first telegram, politely intimating the Canadian desire for delay. "Nova Scotia and New Brunswick delegates," he announced very firmly, "will leave on nineteenth as agreed with you. Any delay on the part of Canada for reasons personally explained will undoubtedly be fatal to Confederation."[27] Monck wired back the same day

to Sir Fenwick Williams, the Lieutenant-Governor of Nova
Scotia, arguing that it would be "simply absurd to send delegates home until we have some communication with the new
Secretary of State", and begging Williams to "keep your people
quiet if you can".[28] But it was difficult to keep the strong-
minded and voluble Tupper quiet, and impossible to persuade
him and Tilley to alter their decision. "New Brunswick and
Nova Scotia delegates go by steamer tonight," they telegraphed
Macdonald peremptorily on the fatal July 19, "and rely upon
Canadian delegates meeting them promptly in London as agreed
on."[29] But the Canadians had no intention of meeting their
fellow British Americans in London promptly. Monck refused
to stir himself and refused to authorize the appointment of a
delegation.[30] The Canadians and the Maritimers were already
out of step. They were also extremely annoyed with one
another.

Meanwhile, the new Conservative government in England,
underestimating the effect of an imperial political crisis on
colonial plans, was going ahead on the assumption that all
the British North American delegates would be arriving in
England early in August. Lord Carnarvon, the new Colonial
Secretary—he had been Under-Secretary during the Bulwer
Lytton regime eight years before—was just as eager as Cardwell
had been to complete the Quebec scheme in the current year.
The session was very far advanced; but he believed it would
just be possible, if he could count on the hearty support of
the opposition, to get the required legislation through before
the House prorogued. It would have to be a very odd, rudi-
mentary bill, a mere legislative framework, which would leave
most things—even the division of powers itself—to be settled
by order-in-council, after they had been thrashed out with the
delegates. He appealed to Cardwell.[31] Would the Liberals
consent to help? Cardwell, of course, was sympathetic, and
he reported that Earl Russell was most eager to have the
Confederation Bill "ratified" that year by parliament.[32] It was
true that the ex-ministers were very anxious that nothing
should be done until the arrival of the delegates, and that they
were a little perturbed at the amount of important matter that

was to be left for order-in-council.[33] But an agreement was
quite within the range of probability. On July 21, Cardwell
had a long interview with Carnarvon; and on July 27 he
pledged the support of the Liberals for the bill, on two conditions which could have easily been met. It was all useless.
The very next day the news arrived that the North American
steamer was in with the Maritimers, but not the Canadians,
on board. There was, moreover, not the slightest indication
of when they might be expected.

Carnarvon instantly gave up the idea of legislation in the
current session;[34] and the Maritime delegates reached London
breathlessly to discover that the cup of political security had
been quite literally dashed from their lips. They had felt
vexed and injured before. Now they were almost seething
with exasperation. If the Canadians had only kept to the
agreement and sailed on July 21 as they had promised to do,
the union of British North America might have been made
irrevocable by the end of the first week in August. Now everything must be postponed again—how long? In a long, complaining, and foreboding letter to Galt, Tilley mingled his
angry reproaches with the darkest prophecies for the future.[35]
The imperial Parliament, he informed the Canadians, was
expected to be prorogued on August 10; and even when it
reassembled, there was no certainty of the passage of the
British North America Bill. A want-of-confidence motion might
be carried against the unsteady Conservative government. There
would be a dissolution and a general election. Months would
be lost in these interminable delays. And all the time the
fatal hour of the demise of the Nova Scotia parliament would
be drawing closer and closer.

Macdonald remained unconvinced by these arguments and
unimpressed by this show of moral indignation. "As the English Parliament has risen by this time," he wrote briefly to
Oliver Mowat, "there is no use in my going home just now,
and probably I shall not leave until the end of October or
beginning of November."[36] He reminded Tilley that the Maritime delegates had sailed in the full knowledge that the Canadians had no intention of following them; and he could never

be convinced that, even if the Canadians had yielded and
followed in the next boat, the British North America Bill
could have been pushed through in the fag end of the session
of 1866. "The settlement of the terms of the Bill is not the
work of a day," he reminded Tilley a little tartly, "—it must
take weeks of anxious and constant labour."[37] The British
Parliament could not meet again until January or February of
the New Year; and if the British North American delegates
assembled in London in the autumn, there would be ample
time to prepare the bill. Tilley protested in outraged astonishment at this suggestion, and threatened that the Maritime delegates would come home. But the Canadians stayed in Ottawa.
They had found, in the meantime, another and an excellent
reason for delay. Once again the rumours of a Fenian raid
began to multiply; and a wave of panic excitement swept over
the entire province.

Macdonald, who had considered early in July that "the Fenians
are thoroughly disheartened," refused to be over-excited by these
threats.[38] "The *Globe*'s idea about calling out all the volunteers is all nonsense," he wrote to Gilbert McMicken on August
25, "and no one knows better than Brown that it is so, but
he desires to make a fuss and cause discontent."[39] Without
much doubt, the opposition newspapers were exploiting the
public fear. But, during the next few days, the rumours
became more circumstantial and alarming hour by hour. On
August 27, Monck and Sir John Michel, the General Officer
Commanding the imperial forces in Canada, suddenly sent off
an appeal to the British government for reinforcements. Only
a very little while before, the appeal would have gone by diplomatic bag in the next Atlantic mail; but this message sped
over to England through the newly laid cable; and the very
next day Carnarvon was himself telegraphing Disraeli at Hughenden Manor, trying to arrange for an immediate meeting of
the Cabinet on the Canadian crisis.[40] There was no doubt about
what the imperial government would do in such an emergency.
Carnarvon acted with speed and efficiency;[41] and in the last
days of the month he was seeking ocean transports for the
troops, while Macdonald was writing to Michel about the

barracks in which they were to be accommodated when they
reached Canada.⁴² In the next few weeks there was a vast
amount of work for a Canadian Minister of Militia to do. It
began to seem almost providential that the Canadians had
decided to stay in Ottawa. And in Ottawa they would certainly have to remain, until the approach of winter made
Fenian military "operations" impossible. Monck, in the midst
of the crisis, reported that he had received a dispatch from
Carnarvon, inviting the Canadians to be in England by the
end of September. "The present Fenian excitement has given
me the opportunity of telling him," Monck confided to Macdonald, "that it is impossible for the leading members of the
Government to leave until the season is so far advanced as
to render an attack impossible."⁴³

It was all very sensible, but its immediate consequences were
unfortunate. The Maritime delegates, despite their threats,
were still in London, kicking their heels resentfully; and what
was still worse, Joseph Howe, who had followed them over to
England, was busily employing the interval of their enforced
inactivity in presenting the case of the anti-Confederates of
Nova Scotia in long and persuasively rhetorical papers. He
and his fellow-delegate, Annand, were writing something else
as well—some more intimate, more decidedly personal communications—to the new Colonial Secretary. Macdonald was
the principal subject of these effusions; and they were prompted
by a shower of mingled eulogy and abuse which had fallen
on the Attorney-General West in Canada during the last weeks
of the summer of 1866. Late in August the *Globe* began an
open attack against what it claimed was Macdonald's disgrace-
ful intemperance. Macdonald, it assured its readers in scandalized tones, had been drunk at the time of the Fenian raid
in June, and repeatedly intoxicated during the final fortnight
of the summer session. The Attorney-General, his "utterance
so thick as to be almost incomprehensible", had had to cling
to his desk in the House to prevent himself from falling; and
what was even more deplorable, he had been utterly incapable
of performing his duty as Minister of Militia at the perilous

moment when the enemy was on Canadian soil. On September 6, after several weeks of this abusive campaign, and as if in answer to it, the city of Kingston gave a dinner in Macdonald's honour; and, on that occasion, D'Arcy McGee paid tribute to his leader as the principal author of the Quebec Resolutions, and as the resolute defender of Canada during the Fenian raid. On the very day before the dinner, and with the apparent intention of discounting in advance all possible eulogies that might be made at it, the *Globe* amplified and summed up its lofty indictment of Macdonald's "weakness".[44] These charges were widely reprinted and commented on in Canada West; and in due course the Canadian newspapers reached England. Howe was deeply impressed. How better could he employ his time than in communicating this sad intelligence about Macdonald to the Colonial Secretary? He felt it his duty, he told Carnarvon gravely, to call his attention to the "impropriety and peril" of entrusting the defence of the Maritime Provinces to a man who could not govern himself. This gentleman, "whose habits and gross neglect of important public duties have been thus rendered notorious by the Canadian and English Press", was—so D'Arcy McGee asserted—the author of fifty of the seventy-two Quebec Resolutions. "Assuming the statement to be accurate," Howe went on jocularly, "the undersigned, while charitably attributing to the inveterate habits referred to the incoherent and defective character of the whole scheme, would respectfully submit to Her Majesty's Government whether the knowledge of its paternity is likely to make it more acceptable to the Imperial Parliament, or to the people of the Maritime Provinces whose institutions it is proposed to disturb."[45]

Macdonald and the Canadians were hardly enjoying a good press in London. Carnarvon wrote very sorrowfully to Monck, enclosing Howe's charges. Howe himself continued his indefatigable lobbying against Confederation, and the Maritime delegates had nothing to do but watch his activities apprehensively and nurse their grievances against the Canadian government. Brydges, who had received an extremely gloomy letter from London about the Maritimers, reported that they were completely disgusted with the long delay and on the point of abandoning the enterprise and returning home.[46] Macdonald did not believe it. Tilley and Tupper had committed themselves too far. They would have to wait. And, despite all these minor irritations and misunderstandings, Confederation was safe now —provided, of course, that there was no major political upheaval in England during the next six months. Yet it was bad politics to alienate Tilley and Tupper, with whom he had already made a defensive and offensive compact for the future. He wrote a long, frank, but conciliatory letter of explanation to Tilley, and Monck wired to Carnarvon that the Canadians would positively sail on November 7. "I think," the Governor-General wrote jocularly to Macdonald, "it is of very great importance that this arrangement should now be carried into effect and that the *feelings* of these gentlemen should not be further 'trifled with'!!"[47] Macdonald, who had carried the main burden both of Confederation and the Fenian crisis, was hurriedly preparing for the departure in the last weeks of October. "I have been working night and day to get ready for England," he told Thomas White, "and scarcely know how I shall be through in time. The Fenian prisoners and their fate may perhaps keep me for a while, but this is strictly *entre nous* for I am supposed to sail on the 7th without fail."[48] Actually, he was still frantically writing to Gilbert McMicken about the Fenians on November 8, and it was not until November 14 that he finally sailed from New York. There was still ample time, he was convinced; and a little before his departure, he and Monck carefully worked out a time-table for the next few months.[49] The three or four weeks between the time of Macdonald's arrival in London and the Christmas holidays could be spent in the last crucial discussions with the Nova Scotians and New Brunswickers. Before the Christmas break-up the delegates would be able to present their plan, in its final form, to Carnarvon. The conferences with Carnarvon and the Colonial Office officials could be begun with the New Year; and by the time the imperial Parliament opened, at the end of January or the beginning of February, the British North America Bill would be ready for presentation.

III

All the delegates were staying at the Westminster Palace Hotel. It stood at the junction of Victoria and Tothill Streets, a long, narrow, wedge-shaped building, which overlooked Westminster Abbey, and St. Margaret's, and the Houses of Parliament beyond. The entrance was on Victoria Street; and beyond the reception desk a short passage led to a long, handsome room—rather ornately decorated in the Corinthian style—which was then used as a lecture hall or concert room. Here, on the morning of Tuesday, December 4, 1866, the "London Conference" opened its sessions. It was a much smaller company than that which had assembled at either Charlottetown or Quebec. Neither Prince Edward Island nor Newfoundland had sent delegates, for neither island was as yet prepared to enter Confederation. Five Nova Scotians, five New Brunswickers, and six Canadians made up the group that settled down on December 4 to decide the last details of the federal union of their governments.

On the very first day, Tupper and Tilley proposed that Macdonald should be chairman of the conference.[50] Sir Narcisse Belleau, the amiable figurehead of the Canadian administration, had stayed at home; and there was no George Brown to deny to Macdonald the pre-eminence that everybody else was so willing to concede him. The chairmanship at the Westminster Palace Hotel was delicate and exacting, but not a really dangerous task. The men facing him were already convinced and had already committed themselves; and everybody knew that whatever their differences of opinion might be, a final set of resolutions would certainly be sent off to Lord Carnarvon in a few weeks. But the Quebec scheme, which had been accepted without amendment by the Canadian parliament, had never even been presented to the legislatures of the Maritime Provinces. The Canadians were bound, in theory at least, to stick to the letter of the Seventy-two Resolutions; the Maritimers felt themselves equally obliged to stress the changes which, they hoped, would make the plan more popular back in Nova Scotia and New Brunswick. They did not, of course, want any very serious alterations. The Quebec scheme, which was partly their own creation, was still fundamentally their own preference. But they were convinced that, at the very least, something must be done to make the scheme financially more acceptable—a "better bargain"—for the small provinces. On the very first day they announced bluntly that their authority to act was contingent upon a guarantee of the construction of the Intercolonial Railway; and a fortnight later Galt complained rather sadly that "our friends from the Maritime Provinces are excessively fond of talking, and very naturally wish to have some changes made in their interest."[51] Macdonald dealt in an easy off-hand fashion with the theoretically conflicting authorities of the different delegations. "We are quite free to discuss points as if they were open," he announced with bland inconsistency, "although we may be bound to adhere to the Quebec scheme."[52] On December 4, the conference began a rapid preliminary survey of the Seventy-two Resolutions as a whole, leaving difficult and contentious items for further consideration; and by the end of the first day they had got down as far as resolution twenty-nine.

While the discussions were going on inside the Westminster Palace Hotel, Macdonald was getting to know Carnarvon and renewing his acquaintance with the Colonial Office officials. The new Secretary, Henry Howard Molyneux Herbert, fourth Earl of Carnarvon, was still, at thirty-six, a comparatively young man. A gracious and cultivated person, at once urbane in manner and chivalrous in spirit, Carnarvon nevertheless clung strongly to his basic convictions. One of those convictions was a well-grounded belief in the wisdom of the Quebec scheme. Like Cardwell before him, he had an emphatic theoretical preference for a federal union with a strong central government. In July, when, for a brief while, he had hoped to push the British North America Bill through parliament in the last days of the session, he had confessed to Cardwell that his "foremost object would be to strengthen, as far as practicable, the central Government against the excessive power or the encroachments of the local administrations".[53] The new Colonial Secretary, just like the old, had been con-

verted in advance to Macdonald's plan. Macdonald was fortunate in this; but he was lucky in having Carnarvon for a
more general, and perhaps more important reason. Unlike
the coldly intellectual Cardwell—who had looked upon the
colonies with a little of Gladstone's calculating detachment—
Carnarvon believed in the continuance of the Empire, and
the future greatness of its principal colonies, with a warm
emotional conviction. Macdonald always remembered this
generous enthusiasm; and long afterwards he still believed that
Carnarvon, almost alone of the men of his generation, had
had a real and splendid vision of the great nation he was
helping to create.

Highclere Castle, with its lovely setting of gently rolling
parkland and noble beech trees, became, in its own pleasantly
informal fashion, a drafting-room for the British North America
Bill. On Tuesday, December 11, when Macdonald, Cartier,
and Galt travelled down to Newbury as guests of the Colonial
Secretary, the conference had already, after a week's work,
completed its preliminary survey of the Quebec Resolutions
and was deep in the consideration of the reserved contentious
points. They stayed overnight at Highclere, had a long talk
with Carnarvon on the problems of Confederation, and enjoyed their day's relaxation in the country.

It was late on Wednesday night before they got back to the
Westminster Palace Hotel. Macdonald was already tired out
and sleepy by the time he got into bed, gathered the newspapers about him, and began that final reading of the day's
political news which was his invariable custom before he blew
out the light. In a few minutes he was asleep with the candle
still burning beside him: and—how long later he knew not—
he was suddenly awakened by a sensation of intense heat, and
started up to discover that the bed, bed-clothes, and curtains
were blazing about him. He pulled the curtains down, emptied
the water jug upon them, yanked the burning bed-clothes on
to the floor, and, ripping open bolster and pillows, "poured
an avalanche of feathers on the blazing mass". The flames
were very nearly under control by this time; but he hurried
into Cartier's room and then into Galt's—the three had ad-

joining bedrooms and a common sitting-room—and waked his companions. Together, collecting all the water available, they put out the fire.[54]

It was only then, after the excitement was all over, that he discovered that he himself had been scorched about the head and hands, and that his right shoulder-blade was badly burnt. "So I got it dressed," he told his sister Louisa, "and thought no more of it." On the very next day—Thursday, December 13—the old problem of the Legislative Council, which had caused so much trouble at Quebec, came up once more. What was to be done with the twenty-four seats in the Maritime division, now divided equally between Nova Scotia and New Brunswick, if and when Prince Edward Island came in? And, even more important, should not some method be devised of increasing the membership of this body of immovable oligarchs, if it should get into a serious deadlock with the House of Commons? The conference debated a long time.[55] Provision was made for the entrance of Prince Edward Island; but otherwise the clauses on the Legislative Council were not disturbed. Indeed, there were relatively few changes in the whole plan, and none at all that affected its fundamental character. The conference emphatically bound the general government to build the Intercolonial Railway, substantially increased the subsidies which were to be paid to the local governments, and amplified the educational clauses in the interests of religious minorities. By December 19—two weeks after the conference had begun—the delegates had pretty well finished their work. It was just in time, for Macdonald at the moment could no longer act as chairman. The burn on his right shoulder, which he had characteristically made light of, was not healing at all. It had suddenly taken on an ugly look, and he had to submit himself to a doctor. For three days he stayed in bed, stubbornly reading. For eight days—while Christmas came and went—he was kept firmly inside the Westminster Palace Hotel. "I had a merry Xmas alone in my own room," he told Louisa, "and my dinner of tea and toast. I drank all your healths in Bohea though you didn't deserve it."

On the day before Christmas, he reported to Carnarvon that

the delegates had finished their preliminary discussions and on Christmas Day he dispatched the London Resolutions to the Colonial Office.[56] Almost at once, Carnarvon replied from Highclere Castle, saying that he had sent the resolutions off to London to be printed for the benefit of the Cabinet and the officials in the Colonial Office. Everything looked to be well in train, and Macdonald, who was tired with his work at the conference and bored with ten days of enforced seclusion in the Westminster Palace Hotel, badly wanted a holiday before the difficult business of drafting the bill began. But, at the back of his mind, he was always conscious of the inevitable approach of spring and the equally inevitable expiration of the Nova Scotian legislature. The bill, if possible, must be completely ready by the opening of the imperial Parliament. Was there time enough, he wondered unhappily, and wrote off to Monck, confiding some of his apprehensions. Monck, who had already followed him across the ocean and had reached his house, Charleville, at Enniskerry, replied comfortably that the imperial Parliament would not meet until February 5, and that there would be ample time before that date. He himself, he told Macdonald, expected to reach London on January 7. Carnarvon would probably return to town on the same day, and nothing much could happen until his arrival.[57] The coast was obviously clear, and Macdonald decided to take advantage of the respite. He hurried off to France for a few days' holiday.

It was his last holiday alone. His wife had died a little over nine years before; and now he was about to marry again. At fifty-two, he was very far from being the young barrister who had made his vows at St. Andrews Church, Kingston, back in 1843, and Susan Agnes Bernard belonged to a world very different from that which the simple and devoted Isabella had inhabited. Her father had been a member of the Privy Council for Jamaica; her brother, Lieutenant-Colonel Hewitt Bernard became a senior official in the office of the Attorney-General, Canada West, shortly after the family migrated to Canada in the middle 1850's. Macdonald came to rely a great deal upon the tall, handsome colonel, and for a time they shared bachelors' quarters together in the "Quadrilateral" in Ottawa. But, despite this close acquaintanceship, he saw very little of Susan Agnes; and it was not until late in the autumn of 1866 that the rapid courtship began. Mrs. Bernard and her daughter had returned to England to live, over a year before; and Macdonald met them, quite by accident, in Bond Street, during the early days of the London Conference. Though she was, of course, considerably younger than Macdonald, Agnes Bernard was a mature woman, tall and handsome like her brother, with a good deal of natural poise and dignity and a fair amount of social experience. She would make a charming companion, a distinguished chatelaine; and now that Hugh had nearly reached seventeen and was far less dependent upon him, his sense of loneliness may have increased. Before the end of the year he had proposed to Susan Agnes and had been accepted. They decided that they would be married very shortly, after only a brief engagement, while the delegates were still in London awaiting the passage of the British North America Bill.[58]

It began to look as if the marriage ceremony might coincide with the most important debate on the bill. By the beginning of the second week in January, Carnarvon had come back to town and Monck was installing himself in his house in Hill Street, Berkeley Square. There was a series of discussions and conferences with the Colonial Office officials and, in the meantime, F. S. Reilly, the professional legal expert, worked on the first draft of the measure. Carnarvon had hoped to be able to send Macdonald a copy of the first draft by January 20;[59] but there were the usual delays in drafting and printing, and Carnarvon himself was ill with influenza and preoccupied with his stand in the matter of the projected Conservative Reform Bill. It was Thursday, January 24, before Macdonald and his colleagues had received their copies of the draft; and another two days passed before they sat down, at Carnarvon's house in Grosvenor Street, with the Colonial Secretary, Adderley, Rogers, and Reilly, to go through its provisions systematically.[60] Carnarvon was in the chair, and he and his subordinates had only one really important criticism to make of the draft that lay before them. They did not object to the appointment of the senators by the central government, nor even, in principle, to their tenure of office for life. What worried them was the fact that this body of immovable life members was fixed at a total of seventy-two. They argued, as some of the delegates had already argued in the discussions at the Westminster Palace Hotel, that there was at least the possibility of a serious deadlock between the Senate and the House of Commons; and the draft on the table provided no method of escape from it.[61] In Great Britain, the Crown could always increase the number of peers and thus overcome the obstinate resistance of the House of Lords. But, in the proposed constitution of Canada, there was no comparable means of ensuring the ultimate triumph of the popular branch of the legislature.

Macdonald must have groaned inwardly as he saw this venerable difficulty coming up once again. The problem of the Upper House had very nearly wrecked the Quebec Conference and had preoccupied the London Conference with further long hours of argument. The plan, for which he had fought so hard and so long, must now be altered in a small but important particular; and to carry out even the tiniest of changes in the clauses relating to the Senate was an operation almost as delicate as the removal of a thorn from the injured paw of a lion. He took up the task once more, while the delegates and the Colonial Office officials watched him with a jealous or an anxious scrutiny. "Macdonald was the ruling genius and spokesman," Sir Frederic Rogers wrote later, "and I was very greatly struck by his power of management and adroitness. The French delegates were keenly on the watch for anything which weakened their securities; on the contrary, the Nova Scotia and New Brunswick delegates were very jealous of concession to the *arriérée* province. . . . Macdonald had to argue the question with the Home Government on a point on which the slightest divergence from the narrow line already agreed on in Canada was watched for—here by the French, and there by the English—as eager dogs watch a rat hole; a snap on one side might have provoked a snap on the other, and put an end to the concord. He stated and argued the case with cool, ready fluency, while at the same time you saw that

every word was measured, and that while he was making for
a point ahead, he was never for a moment unconscious of any of
the rocks among which he had to steer."[62] There were indeed, a
good many rocks ahead; but in the end the very variety of the
conflicting interests involved became a help rather than a
hindrance. The different objections cancelled each other out;
and what might have been a complicated compromise ended
by becoming a fairly simple one. They had not quite finished
with the difficulty by the end of the month, but on February
2 Macdonald wrote to Carnarvon enclosing a final draft of
the clause.[63] On the recommendation of the Governor-General,
the Queen might direct the appointment of three or six additional senators, representing equally the three divisions of
Canada. And there, at last, the matter rested.

Macdonald, on his part, had another and a quite different
criticism to make of the first draft of the bill. Reilly had throughout described the product of the proposed union as the "United
Province". He was thinking, naturally enough, in the old provincial terms; but Macdonald believed in the national stature
of the country he was creating. He had spoken more than once
of founding "a great Kingdom, in connection with the British
monarchy and under the British flag": and the title "Kingdom
of Canada", which was undoubtedly his own preference, was
written into the delegates' revision of the first draft of the
bill.[64] It might very probably have been accepted by Carnarvon,
for nobody believed more sincerely than he in the dignity of
the country he was helping to create. But Carnarvon was not
the only member of the Cabinet. There were others more important; and one of them was Lord Stanley, the son of
the Prime Minister, who was Foreign Secretary. Derby, whom
Disraeli later unkindly described as living "in a region of perpetual funk", was frightened of the possible international consequences of this defiant monarchical title.[65] Would it wound
the republican sensibilities of the United States? Derby decided
that it would; and the accuracy of his assumption was soon
borne out by the facts. On February 27, H. J. Raymond of
New York tried to introduce a resolution requesting the president to inform the House of Representatives "whether any

remonstrance has been made by this Government against the
proposed consolidation of all the British North American Provinces into a single confederation under the imperial rule of
an English prince. . . ."⁶⁶ The Raymond resolution did not
provoke much discussion in the House; even its sublime
arrogance was apparently regarded as quite unremarkable. But
Sir Frederick Bruce, the British Minister at Washington, sent
a copy of Raymond's enquiry to the Foreign Office. The title
"Kingdom of Canada" had, he informed Lord Derby, aroused
"much remark of an unfriendly character in the United States".⁶⁷

Although the preferred title had been rejected and Canadian hopes had been sacrificed once more to the fear of a
dangerous outburst of American dislike, the delegates and the
Colonial Office officials quickly found an alternative designation upon which they were all agreed. The name "Canada"
proposed by one of the representatives of the Maritime Provinces, had already been unanimously accepted by all the delegates;⁶⁸ and they now proceeded to link it with the designation
"Dominion" to complete the title. "The North American delegates are anxious," Carnarvon explained to the Queen, "that
the United Provinces should be designated as the 'Dominion
of Canada'. It is a new title: but intended on their part as a
tribute to the monarchical principle which they earnestly desire
to uphold. . . . It will give greater dignity to the commencement
of this great scheme and consequently greater self-respect to
those who take part in the administration of affairs there."⁶⁹
The Queen graciously accepted the proposal. She had been
invited, by the second last of the Quebec Resolutions to
"determine the rank and name" of the new nation; and when
she had confirmed the title *Dominion of Canada,* the British
North America Bill was at last complete. It was only just in
time. Parliament had opened on February 5; but the next
day, Rogers was still begging Macdonald for some important
details for a few of the sections of the bill; and the Queen's
final answer to Lord Carnarvon on the subject of the title
probably did not come in until Friday or Saturday of that
week. The last clauses were completed over the week-end;

and on Tuesday, February 12, the bill was read for the first
time in the House of Lords.

Macdonald's last-minute delays with the material for the
educational clauses and the powers of the local legislatures may
very well have had their explanation in his frantic preparations
for matrimony. On Saturday, February 16, four days after
the first reading of the British North America Bill, the marriage ceremony was performed at St. George's Church, Hanover
Square.[70] The Bishop of Montreal, Metropolitan of Canada,
read the service; and four of the daughters of the delegates,
the Misses McDougall, McGee, Tupper and Archibald, attended the bride. Seventy people sat down to the wedding
breakfast at the Westminster Palace Hotel; and Francis Hincks,
Governor of British Guiana, Macdonald's great opponent in
times past, proposed the toast to the bride. It was mid-afternoon
before the newly married couple left for what could only be
called with some courtesy their honeymoon. It could not be
longer than two or three days at most; for the second and
crucial reading of the bill was scheduled to come up in the
House of Lords on the following Tuesday, and Macdonald
knew that he could not possibly miss it. Before the short February day had ended they were in Oxford. The university city
was scarcely at its best in the middle of the dull Hilary
term. But Macdonald could now regard Oxford as his Alma
Mater; and the memories that he had carried away from it
on the previous June were very pleasant ones.

He was back in London on Tuesday in time for Carnarvon's
great effort. Surely the whole business was as good as finished
now. There could be hardly any doubt as to the outcome; and
yet, as he watched the operations of a Parliament in which
he had no part or influence whatever, he could hardly quiet
his nervous apprehensions. All this time Howe and Annand
had been continuing their lobbying and propaganda against
the British North America Bill. It was known that they were
about to present a monster petition, signed supposedly by thirty
thousand people, begging the imperial Parliament to delay the
consideration of the bill until after the approaching general
election in Nova Scotia. In the present state of affairs at

Westminster, with a ministry holding office precariously and
a House almost distracted by the question of electoral reform,
it was still possible for a sudden catastrophe to overwhelm the
bill. Yet the debate on Tuesday night was unquestionably
reassuring. Carnarvon, who was at the height of his form,
gave the best speech that anybody was to give on the measure
in the imperial Parliament. Normanby, Monck and Lyveden
supported him; and Russell, though he again gave expression
to his old preference for a legislative as opposed to a federal
union, practically committed the opposition to an acceptance
of the bill. It was comforting to hear how effectively Carnarvon
dealt in advance with the case which Howe had been building
up against the measure. And it must have been a moving experience to listen while the Colonial Secretary pictured the
future which Macdonald himself had dreamed for his country.
"We are laying the foundation of a great State," Carnarvon
declared in the last eloquent sentences of his speech, "—perhaps
one which at a future day may even overshadow this country.
But, come what may, we shall rejoice that we have shown
neither indifference to their wishes nor jealousy of their aspirations, but that we honestly and sincerely, to the utmost of
our power and knowledge, fostered their growth, recognizing
in it the conditions of our own greatness."[71]

From his uneasy position on the side-lines, Macdonald
watched the rapid passage of the measure through the House
of Lords. On Friday, February 22, the bill slipped easily
through the committee stage, with only a brief reference to
the petition which was expected from the dissentients in Nova
Scotia. The third reading was to come up on the following
Tuesday: but already Macdonald was worried about a different
and even more exacting test—the decision in the House of
Commons—that lay ahead. Could an appeal be made to Gladstone and Cardwell for their support, he asked Carnarvon
unhappily? Carnarvon tried to soothe him as best he could;[72]
but Carnarvon himself was now struggling, in agonies of in-
decision, to determine his own course in a political crisis which
threatened to divide, and possibly to upset, the government.
On Saturday, the day after the British North America Bill

had got safely through committee in the House of Lords, Disraeli proposed to the Cabinet a new and more radical scheme of electoral reform in place of the moderate measure which had been so coldly received at the beginning of the session. Over the week-end, Lord Cranborne, the future Marquess of Salisbury, Carnarvon and General Peel decided that they could not accept the revised plan; and, early on Monday morning, they demanded another Cabinet for reconsideration.[73] "The enclosed, just received, is utter ruin," Derby wrote in a hastily scribbled note to Disraeli. "What on earth are we to do?"[74] Another Cabinet was called. In frantic haste, a new moderate compromise—the "Ten Minutes Bill"—was put together. Disraeli went down to the House of Commons with it, and Carnarvon and the others stood by their posts. But the compromise was received with noisy dissatisfaction; the Cabinet was obviously divided; and the mind of the whole Parliament was centred on nothing but electoral reform. What could be more sensible than to decide that the British North America Bill should be delayed? "A more unhappy moment could not be selected for sending the Bill to the other House of Parliament," Lord Campbell declared weightily at the third reading in the House of Lords, "unless the avowed object is to bar deliberation and make a chorus to repeat the statement of a Minister, or tribunal to register the edicts of his office. Distracted by a prospect which affects its own existence, the House of Commons cannot give its mind to British North America."[75]

Yet Carnarvon was determined that it must give its mind to British North America. With only a few days or a few hours of office left, he was fighting hard to get his bill through in time. On Tuesday, February 26, the bill finally passed the House of Lords, despite Lord Campbell's plea for delay; and immediately it was transferred to the House of Commons. It had its first reading on Wednesday; the second, crucial, reading was scheduled for Thursday. Wednesday, with a fine though unwitting sense of dramatic appropriateness, was the day selected for the presentation of Macdonald and the four other principal delegates to the Queen. It was, as he carefully pointed out to his sister, a special court, at which only those specially summoned appeared; and before it took place, at half-past twelve in the afternoon, the colonial ministers had, in succession, a private audience of the Queen. Macdonald, as chairman of the conference, went in first. There was nobody in the big room but Princess Louise, and Lord Carnarvon, and the small figure with the grave face and the sombre garments. He knelt and kissed the Queen's hand. She told him that she was glad to see him on this mission, that she realized the importance of the bill he was sponsoring, and that she was aware of the loyalty that the British Americans had shown. "We have desired in this measure," he replied, "to declare in the most solemn and emphatic manner our resolve to be under the Sovereignty of Your Majesty and your family for ever."[76] It was only a sentence; but if he had been asked to state the political purpose of his life in a single sentence he could hardly have done better. Then the audience was over, and he bowed his way out.

The next day, with Agnes at his side, he watched while Adderley moved the second reading of the British North America Bill. Already there were small signs of restiveness in the Commons. On the preceding day Hadfield had demanded an explanation of the curious haste with which the bill was being rushed through the House. It was known that Howe had received some kind of assurance from John Bright; and there was good reason to fear that the proposed imperial guaran-tee for the Intercolonial Railway loan—a guarantee fairly clearly foreshadowed in the bill itself—would provoke some caustic criticism from the inveterate anti-colonials. Adderley's speech, which had nothing of the eloquence of Carnarvon's, was prac-tically designed to meet these criticisms and to stave off the demand for delay in the interests of the anti-Confederate minor-ity in Nova Scotia. It looked for a while as if he had succeeded. Cardwell, who followed immediately afterwards and who spoke strongly in favour of the bill, committed the Liberal rank-and-file to its support in the same way as Russell had already done in the House of Lords. But the Radical voice of Birmingham was not governed by these commitments; and, in a few moments,

Bright rose to make his expected attack. He told the familiar story of the opposition in Nova Scotia. He made the familiar charge of indecent haste, and the familiar demand for delay. But it soon became apparent that his main concern was not for Nova Scotia or British North America, but for the financial and military assistance which Great Britain had so far granted them. "But if," he told the House, with that unctuous mixture of pecuniary considerations and moral values which was so characteristic of his school, "they are to be constantly applying to us for guarantees for railways and for fortresses and for works of defence . . . then I think it would be better for them and for us—cheaper for us and less demoralizing for them— that they should become an independent State—and maintain their own fortresses, fight their own cause, and build up their own future without relying on us."[77]

Yet, as Macdonald and the watching delegates were quick to notice, Bright ended on a somewhat lame and indecisive note. Nobody of any importance supported him in his attack; and after only a relatively brief debate, in which most of the participants spoke strongly in favour of the bill, it passed the second reading with triumphant ease. The detailed consideration in committee was expected to come up at the beginning of the next week; and Monck reported that on Friday night, in an attempt to ease the way for the committee stage, he had had a long discussion with Cardwell and Robert Lowe.[78] Lowe, another notorious anti-colonial who had not yet spoken on the subject, was expected to oppose the bill out of dislike for the Intercolonial Railway loan; and on Monday, March 4, when the House went into committee, he and Roebuck repeated their familiar arguments. Yet the bill went through with only trifling amendments, and Macdonald could draw a long breath of relief. They had taken almost all the fences. Now they were nearly out into the clear. Carnarvon had done his work and done it well. And it had been finished just in time. For on Friday Disraeli had again presented his radical scheme of reform to the Cabinet, and it had been accepted. Cranborne, Carnarvon and Peel had at once resigned; and on Monday, the very day that the British North America Bill passed through

committee in the House of Commons, Carnarvon revealed his
resignation in the Lords. The next day Macdonald sat down
to write to him. He lamented Carnarvon's resignation, hoped
that he would be soon back again at his old post at the
Colonial Office, and ended by thanking him "as a Canadian
for the sincere and great heartiness with which you addressed
yourself to the object of our mission and for the able manner
in which you ensured its success."[79]

Carnarvon had gone; but Macdonald knew now that "their"
measure was safe. Adderley was worried that when the amended
bill came up for consideration, Hadfield would move for delay
until after the forthcoming general election in Nova Scotia.
But, in the end, no protest was made, and the bill passed
third reading on Friday, March 8, without a word of debate.
The work that Macdonald had begun nearly three years before
was finished. After all the fears and frustrations of the past
months, he had completed it on time; and nothing remained
now but the final problem of the guaranteed loan. "Pray tell
Mr. Watkin," Adderley wrote to Macdonald, "that I shall be
much obliged to him if he will speak in defence of the proposed guarantee which I hear is to be attacked strongly."[80] It
was attacked strongly, by Lowe and others, with their accustomed arguments. But Gladstone, though he echoed some of
these anti-colonial banalities in a long and characteristically involved speech, came down heavily in the end in favour of the
guarantee, and its success was assured. The imperial Parliament
had finished its work for the new Dominion of Canada. It
had done, and done generously, all that had been asked of it
by the British North Americans; and its members might, in
Carnarvon's own words, "rejoice that we have shown neither
indifference to their wishes nor jealousy of their aspirations,
but that we honestly and sincerely, to the utmost of our power
and knowledge, fostered their growth, recognizing in it the
conditions of our own greatness."

Epilogue

The First of July, 1867

I

The day was his, if it was anybody's. He, above all others, had ensured its coming, and he had prescribed the order of its celebration. But the actual day—July 1—was not his first choice. For simple and practical reasons—he did not believe the preparations could be completed earlier—he would have preferred a date a fortnight later. But he was far away from London when the matter was finally settled; and on May 22 a royal proclamation announced that the union of British North America was to come into effect two weeks before his chosen date. "So you see," he wrote off to Fisher of New Brunswick, "we are to be united in Holy Matrimony on 1st July—just a fortnight too soon."[1] There was certainly not a great deal of time to make the necessary arrangements. "Much has to be done before then—," he told Tilley, "the members of the cabinet to be determined, the offices distributed, the policy considered, and the whole machinery set in motion."[2] But even with the weight of all these practical, political matters, he found time to give some attention to the day itself. Others would expatiate eloquently upon its significance—after he had done the work of bringing it about. He was neither an orator nor a prophet. And it was characteristic of him to speak of what was so largely his own creation with jocular understatement rather than with rhetorical hyperbole. "By the exercise of common sense and a limited amount of that patriotism which goes by the name of self-interest," he wrote frankly to Shea

of Newfoundland, "I have no doubt that the Union will be
for the common weal."[3] He would never exaggerate any occasion
or glorify any future; but he had the conservative's feeling for
historical continuity, for the stages in the process of national
growth; and from the first he had determined that the day
of the Dominion's beginning should have its appropriate celebration. "On the 1st July, as you know," he wrote Denis Godley,
Monck's secretary, "Confederation will be a fixed fact and we
think it well that some ceremony should be used in inaugurat-
ing the new system."[4] It was decided to make the day a general
holiday. The volunteers were to turn out; and Sir John Michel,
the Commander of the Forces, was requested to make sure
that, in the various garrisons throughout the country, "Royal
salutes should be fired, and the Royal standard hoisted, with
such other military show as is usual on festive occasions."

He could prescribe the order of the day; but he could not
determine the weather. Yet it did not disappoint him. Officially
the northern hemisphere was ten days away from the summer
solstice; but in the Maritime Provinces and along the St.
Lawrence River valley there were as yet almost no signs that
this long six-months' period, in which the sun's power had
daily and majestically increased, had ended at last in its appointed fashion. The first of July belonged, by natural right,
to the little group of the richest days of the year; and in 1867
no accident occurred to rob it of its birthright. On the previous
night certain Canadians, watching the sky anxiously, had been
disturbed by the appearance of a few ominous clouds; but
by the morning these threats had vanished completely. All
through the federation, the day dawned fair and warm, with
a clear, cobalt-blue sky, and a little breeze that took the hottest
edge off the bright sun. Everybody noticed the beauty of the
day; everybody observed how auspicious was its splendour. "On
aimera à se rappeler," declared the editor of the *Journal des
Trois Rivières*, "quand la Confédération aura subi l'épreuve du
temps, combien a été beau le jour de son inauguration."[5]

The day began long before Macdonald was up; in Ottawa
it probably began even before he had gone to bed. Just after
midnight struck, a long salute of 101 guns was fired, while

all the church bells pealed, and a huge bonfire was kindled.[6]
Then, presumably, the people of Ottawa went to bed; but
neither they nor Her Majesty's loyal subjects in other parts
of the new Dominion were permitted to enjoy too long a rest
on that short summer night. Early in the morning, when the
sky was hardly yet paling with the approach of sunrise, the
royal salutes began. At Saint John, New Brunswick, the
twenty-one guns in "honour of this greatest of all modern
marriages" were fired off at four o'clock.[7] At six, they sounded
out from Fort Henry, just across the river from Kingston.
And at eight, when it was now full day, the Volunteer Artillery
of Halifax discharged a long salvo from the Grand Parade,
which came back, as if in booming echoes, from the guns of
the naval brigade on the Dartmouth side of the harbour.[8] The
bells were ringing also, in town halls, and clock towers, and
church steeples. High Mass was sung in the cathedral at
Three Rivers at seven o'clock in the morning; and all over
the country, people dressed in their Sunday best were walking
soberly along the streets to pray, in early church services, for
the welfare of the Dominion.

By nine o'clock, the sun was already high. The air was
warm; the sky's benignant promise was unqualified. People
thronged the streets of their own cities and towns, or crowded
into excursion trains and steamers to join in the celebrations
of their neighbours. The steamer *America* brought nearly 300
visitors across the lake from St. Catharines to swell the crowds
in Toronto. And down in the Eastern Townships, the little
villages of Missisquoi—Philipsburg, Bedford, Dunham, and Fre-
lighsburg—arranged a common celebration to which people
flocked from all over the county. All the shops were shut; the
streets were bright with flags and bunting. "Bientôt," wrote
one correspondent of a French-Canadian town, "St. Jean dis-
parut dans les drapeaux et les pavillons."[9] Down in the Maritime Provinces, where the anti-Confederates watched the bright
day with sullen disapproval, a few shops stayed ostentatiously
open; a few doors were hung with bunches of funereal black
crepe; and in Saint John, New Brunswick, a certain doctor

defiantly flew his flag at half-mast until a party of volunteers
happened to come along, offered politely to assist him in raising it, and, on receiving a furious refusal, raised it anyway
and went on their way rejoicing. But there were few enough
such incidents; and everywhere it was a good-humoured crowd
that pressed along, on foot and in carriages, under the banners,
and triumphal arches and the great inscriptions and trans-
parencies which, in English and French, offered "success to
the Confederacy" and "Bienvenue à la nouvelle puissance".

It was mid-morning—nearly eleven o'clock. The crowds were
thicker now, and they pushed their way along more purpose-
fully, as if towards an important objective. The day marked
the greatest state occasion in the history of British North
America, and now its solemn, official climax was at hand. The
Grand Parade at Halifax, Barrack Square at Saint John, Queen's
Park at Toronto, and Victoria Square and the Place d'Armes
in Montreal were rapidly filling up with waiting citizens. And
all over the country, in scores of market squares, parks, and
parade grounds, the little officials of Canada, the mayors, and
town clerks, and reeves, and wardens, were about to read the
Queen's proclamation, bringing the new federation into official
existence. In Kingston, the mayor and committee stood on a
great scaffolding which workmen had been busily erecting in
the market square since early morning.[10] The town clerk of
Sarnia carried the proclamation honourably in a carriage, while
the Sarnia band and the volunteers paraded proudly in front,
and behind came another carriage and four, with four young
girls, all in white, representing the four provinces of the new
Dominion.[11] At the parade ground in Montreal, the troops,
regulars and militia, formed the three sides of a great square.
Sir John Michel, the Commander of the Forces, waited with
his officers in its centre; and then the Mayor and the Recorder,
bearing the proclamation, arrived resplendently in a fine carriage drawn by six white horses. The proclamation was read;
the bands crashed into "God Save the Queen"; there were
cheers for the Queen and the new Dominion. Then the Volunteer Field Battery began another royal salute; down on the

river the guns of the *Wolverine* boomed their response. And, at every seventh explosion, the *feu de joie* "cracked deafeningly along, up and down the lines, from the new breach-loaders".[12]

II

In Ottawa also, it had just turned eleven o'clock when the Mayor appeared at the entrance of the City Hall on Elgin Street to read the proclamation. There was a little crowd of listeners to applaud him; but most of the citizens of the capital were making their way along Rideau and Wellington Streets, and up Metcalfe and O'Connor, towards Parliament Hill. Macdonald, an early traveller along Rideau Street, had reached the parliament buildings in good time; and long before eleven o'clock approached he was ready and waiting in his office in the Eastern Departmental Building. The official inauguration was about to take place. He hoped everything was in order. It had taken him nearly three years to get the British North America Act passed, and over a month to prepare for the day when it was to go into effect. The work had been barely finished in time and his had been the major responsibility for its completion. The old thoughts of retirement had vanished now. He was to be the first Prime Minister of the new Canada. As far back as March 21, he had confided to his sister Louisa that Lord Monck had charged him "with the formation of the first Government as Premier". He was the obvious choice. There was no method of discovering what individual possessed the confidence of a parliament which did not yet exist; and Monck had fallen back upon the fact that the delegates of all the British North American provinces, assembled in conference at London, had unanimously chosen Macdonald as their chairman. "In authorizing you to undertake the duty of forming an administration for the Dominion of Canada," Monck wrote to him formally on May 24, "I desire to express my strong opinion that, in future, it shall be distinctly understood that the position of First Minister shall be held by *one* person, who shall be responsible to the Governor-General for the appointment of the other ministers, and that the system of dual First Ministers, which has hitherto prevailed, shall be put an end to."[13] The Provinces of Ontario and Quebec had replaced the old united Province of Canada; and with its passing had gone all those dual offices and dual departments which were the mark of its half-acknowledged federal system. Now, for really the first time, he was Prime Minister in form as well as in fact.

From the end of May, when Monck's commission and the news of the royal proclamation had reached him from London, he had been struggling to complete the arrangements for his Cabinet. It was the old task—a little larger and more complicated than it had been, but essentially the same. A few more jagged and intractable pieces had simply been added to the original heap of the Canadian puzzle. There were, as there always had been, racial interests, religious interests, and territorial interests to be considered; and there was the additional and vastly complicating fact that the new government could only be a government of Confederates, a government which drew its support and its leadership from the unionists of both parties in every province of the Dominion. It was true that in Nova Scotia there was a certain unreality about this assumption of concord. And in Ontario, the great coalition, which had been an inspiring fact three years before, was now rapidly degenerating into a rather dubious fiction. George Brown, who had left the government eighteen months earlier, was now busily reorganizing the Grits for the coming struggle against the coalition; and at the great Reform convention, held in Toronto early in June, Howland and McDougall—the two ministers who were supposed to represent the Grits in the coalition government—were excommunicated and overwhelmed with anathemas, in the lavish manner of an early Christian council. To his colleagues, Macdonald tried to put the best face on these depressing developments. "McDougall and Howland have returned from Toronto in good spirits," he wrote to one correspondent. "It is believed that they have made a great impression upon the members of the convention by their manly conduct there. The split in the Reform ranks seems to be permanent. . . ."[14] A split was all he could hope for now, whereas Brown had brought a united party with him in June, 1864; and it must often have seemed that to regard Howland and McDougall as effective Grit leaders was simply to alienate good Liberal-Conservatives without even the hope of gaining much Reform support. Yet McDougall and Howland had fought for him as best they could. He was pledged to them —and to everyone, Grit or Tory, who had supported Confederation. And the coalition must go on.

At first it had seemed relatively easy to maintain its impartial spirit so far as the Maritime appointments to the Cabinet were concerned. Tupper was a Conservative; and Archibald, who had come to be recognized as his principal lieutenant, was a Reformer. "You will of course come on with Tupper," Macdonald wrote to Archibald, urging both of them to be at hand in Ottawa for the first meeting of the future Cabinet on June 15.[15] Tilley, another Reformer, was also a certainty; and there was only a small hesitation about the other New Brunswick representative. "I note your suggestion to bring an associate with me," Tilley answered Macdonald's letter of invitation. "At this moment I am a little puzzled who to ask."[16] It was a choice between two people only—Fisher and Mitchell; and Mitchell, who, to do him justice, probably had no very great desire for office, settled the matter by reminding Macdonald and Tilley that his section of the province, the northeastern section, which had always given its support to Confederation and the Intercolonial Railway, must have some representation in the Cabinet. Where was the Intercolonial Railway to run—by the St. John River valley or by the North Shore? Macdonald could easily appreciate Mitchell's argument that his constituents would expect an advocate for their interests in the government. "It would certainly appear to me, on the first impression, as the lawyers say," Macdonald wrote back to Mitchell, "that it would be politic to select a St. John's river man and a northern route man for the Cabinet."[17] Tilley agreed. The Maritime contingent was complete; and towards the end of June, Tupper, Tilley, Mitchell and Archibald had arrived in Ottawa.

To their surprise, they found the whole matter of the Cabinet

chaotically unsettled and Macdonald almost in despair of
effecting a settlement. As far back as May 30, he had told
Tilley that he had already made preliminary arrangements for
Ontario and Quebec; but possibly even he did not expect the
variety and the truculent strength of the demands that were
made of him. Though McDougall could always fall back
upon the need of maintaining the principle of the coalition,
his bargaining power, as a Reform leader, was obviously in
decline. Yet he demanded no fewer than three places for
himself and his associates in the Cabinet. "You admitted,"
he reminded Macdonald, "that if Ontario should be represented by five members in the Cabinet, the Liberal party
should have three, your position as Premier equalizing the preponderance of Liberals in that Province."[18] This would leave
Macdonald only two places for his faithful Liberal-Conservatives. He was anxious to have Alexander Campbell, his old
partner, in the Cabinet. But Campbell had always been regarded as a moderate "Rep.-by-Pop." Conservative; and his
inclusion would leave no room for a representative of the old
Tories, the followers of MacNab and Hillyard Cameron, who
up to a few years before had been such an important factor in
the party. Still, as McDougall said, he would himself be
Prime Minister. He had forced the poor Tories to accept a
good many unpleasant things in the past two decades. Perhaps
they would follow him grumblingly still.

The real difficulty was not in Ontario at all, but in Quebec.
McDougall and Howland had insisted not only that Ontario
must have five seats, and that three of the five should be given
to Reformers, but also that Quebec would have to be content
with one seat fewer than her sister province. This somewhat
perverted application of Rep. by Pop. to the business of cabinet-
making instantly created the most awful difficulties. Cartier
was ready to agree that Quebec could have only four cabinet
ministers; but he would not consider for even a minute the
suggestion that the French-Canadian membership should be
reduced by one. Whatever happened, he and Hector Langevin
and Jean Charles Chapais must be ministers. That would
leave only one seat. But there were still two important interests

in the province which were unrepresented—the English-speaking, Protestant minority, which had long looked up to Galt of Sherbrooke as its leader, and the Irish Roman Catholics, who had grown greatly in numbers in the past few decades, and who had fixed their affections upon Thomas D'Arcy McGee. Galt, however wayward and temperamental he might be, was undeniably one of the ablest men in Canadian politics. But McGee had been the chief public prophet of Confederation; and he was quite conscious of his enormous popularity. "I certainly have no desire to embarrass future arrangements which will naturally be under your direction," he had written Macdonald as early as April 9, "but in a Confederation Government, founded on principles which I have always zealously advocated, I will, if in Parliament, give way neither to Galt, nor to a third Frenchman, 'nor to any other man'."[19]

There were demands, stubborn and unyielding demands, on all sides. How could he satisfy them? He was almost ready to throw the whole business up in disgust, when at nearly the last moment—it was one week away from July 1—a way out was found. Charles Tupper, with his robust optimism and friendly good nature, was a man more generous in spirit than many of those who had gathered at Ottawa. He offered to give up his own strong claim to office, and suggested a method by which his withdrawal could be used to settle the difficulty. In his place there might be appointed another Nova Scotian who was also a Roman Catholic, a Nova Scotian who might thus satisfy both the claims of his own province and the aspirations of his co-religionists in Canada as a whole. Tupper's resignation was essential to the success of this plan; but so also was McGee's; and McGee, despite his pugnacious protestations of a few weeks ago, yielded his personal claims. On June 24 Macdonald wired offering a seat in the new Cabinet to Edward Kenny, who happened to be both a Nova Scotian and a Roman Catholic. He had few other claims to distinction or to office; but in the circumstances, he was apparently worth both the veterans, Tupper and McGee. The first Confederate government was complete.

III

As eleven o'clock drew close, they were all waiting—all except Edward Kenny, of course, who had hardly had time to collect his senses and his luggage, let alone make the long journey between Nova Scotia and Ottawa. A crowd of Ottawa citizens had gathered outside the Eastern Departmental Building, and people had even pushed their way along the corridors to the doors of the Privy Council chamber. Monck was expected at almost any minute. The Governor-General, in his characteristic easy-going fashion, had not sailed from England until the last possible moment, and had reached Quebec on June 25. "I bring out with me," he wrote reassuringly to Macdonald, "my new commission and the Great Seal of Canada, Ontario, and Quebec, so that everything is ready to start the new coach on Monday next."[20] The new coach was indeed ready; but Monck was apparently unaware that he should contribute anything special to the pomp and circumstance of its send-off. "I hope the people of Ottawa," he wrote anxiously to Macdonald, "will be satisfied to postpone any *demonstration* until I come to remain at Rideau Hall as I should like that my present visit should be considered one for business only." To be told that the inauguration of Confederation was "business only" was a little depressing to the spirit. Yet Monck had some justification for looking rather coolly upon the visit to Ottawa that he was about to undertake. It was nearly three years ago that George Brown had described Rideau Hall as a "miserable little house". "To patch up that building," he had insisted to Macdonald, "will cost more than a new one. . . ."[21] But, despite this advice, the government had decided to "patch up" instead of building anew, and even after three years the "patching up" process was not complete. Monck could camp out for a night or two at Rideau Hall; but permanent residence would certainly have to be deferred till later. He may have been slightly annoyed. He would hardly have been human if he had not been. But there was more than a little temporary irritation back of his casual attitude to July first. He had believed firmly in Confederation, and had done all in

his power to strengthen it and forward its progress. But
Carnarvon's visions would have been quickly dissipated in
his practical, workaday mind. A "good man", Macdonald
described him later, but quite unable, from the constitution
of his mind, "to rise to the occasion".

Along with a large crowd of people, Macdonald had waited
on the dock for the steamer *Queen Victoria*, which had borne
Monck up to Ottawa on Friday, June 28. He would have liked
to see Lord Monck, as head now of the new state, in a role more
imposing than his former one. In April, after the British North
America Act had been passed, he had suggested that it would
be gratifying to the people of Canada if the Governor-General
could be styled Viceroy as in India.[22] But such touches of
purple had not been applied; if Canada could not be a kingdom,
presumably she could not have a viceroy. And it was simply
a very typical mid-Victorian gentleman, in civilian clothes, and
with only his private secretary, Godley, as attendant, who had
landed at Ottawa and driven away in a carriage to Rideau
Hall.[23] There had been no reception on Friday night, and no
ceremony; and now, as he waited anxiously for the Governor
on the morning of July 1, Macdonald knew very well that he
could expect a repetition of the same kind of gentlemanly
informality. He was not disappointed. Monck drove up to the
East Block in plain clothes and with Godley as his only companion.[24] The crowd of waiting people was hardly aware of
his arrival, and there was no demonstration. He walked along
the corridors to the Privy Council chamber. The prospective
councillors, the judges, and a few officers in uniform were
waiting for him there; and after he had entered the room, the
doors were thrown open to the public.

The brief, business-like ceremony began. Godley read
Monck's new commission; and the judges—Chief Justice Draper,
Chief Justice Richards, and Justices Mondelet, Hagarty, and
Wilson—administered the oaths.[25] The Governor, his hand
resting on the Bible, spoke the solemn words in a clear, firm
voice; and then, having shaken hands with the judges, he
seated himself in the chair of state. Up to this point the proceedings had been unremarkable, and could easily have been

anticipated; but now came an announcement which Macdonald could have foretold in only the most general fashion. Monck had determined that the coming of Confederation should be marked by the distribution of honours; and, in conformity with a custom which up to that time had been invariable, he and the Colonial Office officials had among them decided what the honours were to be. Cartier, Galt, Tupper, Tilley, McDougall, and Howland were to be made Companions of the Bath—there was no doubt about that. There was equally no doubt that Macdonald should be given a superior honour, for in Monck's opinion he had unquestionably been the principal architect of federal union. But what form should this special royal favour take? At first Monck thought of a Baronetcy; but in the end he agreed with the new Colonial Secretary, the Duke of Buckingham and Chandos, that Macdonald should be made a Knight Commander of the Bath.[26] It was a sharp distinction between the new Prime Minister and his colleagues; and, as Macdonald heard Monck make the announcement that morning, he must have realized instantly that it would be regarded as an invidious distinction as well. In one minute a grave political mistake had been made. But the public session was over; the onlookers withdrew from the Privy Council chamber—the newspaper correspondents among them; and in a few minutes the news of the awards would be speeding over the telegraph wires. The thing had been done; and a little while later Monck and his new councillors, including his new Knight, adjourned their meeting to review the troops on Parliament Hill.

It was high noon now, and for the last hour and a half, all through the four provinces, the military parades and reviews had been going on. At an early hour in the morning the citizens of Kingston had been streaming across the Cataraqui Bridge and up to the Barriefield Common to secure the choicest positions for the spectacle; and before half-past ten, when the review began in Toronto, the Torontonians had gathered in an "immense circle" round the reviewing grounds to the north-west of the city.[27] In little places like Cayuga, where the 37th Battalion of Haldimand Rifles paraded—"the 37th

cannot be surpassed by any Battalion in Canada"—it was the
volunteers, of course, who made up the review.[28] But in
the larger towns of Halifax, Quebec, and Montreal, where
there were imperial garrisons, the regular soldiers gave a smart
professional air to the exercises; and at Toronto the most
romantic feature of the whole day's entertainment was the
presence of the 13th Hussars, the "Noble Six Hundred" of
Balaclava, who had newly arrived in town. For a couple of
hours, while the bright day grew rapidly warmer, and the
vendors of soda water, ice cream and confectionery did a
roaring trade, the troops marched, and drilled and fought
mimic battles. Cavalry crashed against hollow squares and
"thin red lines"; the Hussars went by at the gallop in a blur
of blue and silver; and everybody admired the wonders of the
new Snider-Enfield breech-loading rifles. Then came the grand
march past, and the general salute, and the review was over.

IV

In Ottawa, the last of the troops marched down Parliament
Hill and away, and the crowd, in search of its midday meal,
began slowly to disperse. The square, with the fountain playing in the middle, was nearly empty. But Monck, Macdonald,
and the other ministers, after only a brief interval, returned
to the Privy Council chamber to complete the list of essential
actions, without which government in Canada and its provinces could not have functioned at all. It was early afternoon
—the climax of the long summer's day. In the height of the
sky, the sun seemed scarcely to have moved; and the whole
earth sunned itself luxuriously in the careless assurance of the
long hours of warmth that lay ahead. From the windows of
the Privy Council chamber, one could watch the river, all
splashed with sunshine, flowing smoothly away past the high
cliffs of Major Hill Park towards the north-east. Beyond the
far bank stretched the pale green river flats, and beyond them,
rising abruptly in wave after long, low wave of pine trees,
were the Laurentian hills. In that far country where all the

colours seemed to darken so swiftly into sombre blues, there was, on most days and in most lights, the harsh suggestion of something vast and gnarled and forbiddingly inhospitable. But on this day of brilliant sunshine, the colours of the whole ragged landscape had mysteriously lightened and freshened; the dull blue had narrowed to a thin line at the horizon, and it was possible to distinguish clearings, and perhaps a village or a winding road—the signs of indomitable human life. It was warmer now—the heat of an unruffled summer's day. And they must have felt it in the Privy Council office as they worked away, swearing in the ministers to their respective offices, appointing the Lieutenant-Governors of the different provinces, setting the coach in motion, in Monck's own phrase.

In the meantime, most of the population of Canada had gone on holiday. The parades were over; the proclamation had been read; everything official—civil or military—was finished. And the people had packed up, left their houses, and gone off to sports, games and picnics. At Three Rivers, a large crowd of spectators watched the Union Club and the Canadian Club play "une partie de cricket". There were games in the cricket grounds at Kingston, while the band of the Royal Canadian Rifles played faithfully on during the long afternoon; and out on the waters of the bay the competing sailboats moved gracefully along the course round Garden Island and back. The citizens of Barrie turned out to Kempenfelt Bay to watch the sailing and sculling races, and to amuse themselves at the comic efforts of successive competitors to "walk the greasy pole" which extended thirty feet beyond the railway wharf, with a small flag fluttering at its end.[29] At Dunnville, down in the Niagara peninsula, a new race-course had just been laid out. People came from all around "to witness the birthday of the course as well as that of the nation"; and while "the Dunnville and Wellandport brass bands discoursed sweet music to the multitude", the spectators watched the exciting harness race between Black Bess and Jenny Lind.

In dozens of small villages, where there were no bands or race-courses, and where there could be no water sports, the farmers and their wives and children thronged out early in

the afternoon to the local fair grounds or picnic place. Sometimes this common occupied a piece of high ground just outside the village, where a great grove of maple trees gave a
pleasant shelter from the heat; and sometimes it lay a mile
or two away—a broad, flat stretch of meadowland, through
which a shallow river ran. The waggons and buggies stood
together in a row; the unharnessed horses were tethered in the
shade of a group of tall elm trees; and out in the sunshine the
young people and the children played their games and ran off
their sports. For an hour or two the small boys who were
later to drive the Canadian Pacific Railway across their country
and who were to found the first homesteads in the remote
prairies, jumped across bars and ran races. The long shadows
were creeping rapidly across the turf when they all sat down
to a substantial supper at the trestle tables underneath the
trees. Afterwards they gossiped and chattered idly in the still
calm evening. Then it grew slowly darker, and the children
became sleepy; and they drove home over the dusty summer
roads.

By nine o'clock, the public buildings and many large houses
were illuminated all across Canada. And in Toronto the
Queen's Park and the grounds of the private houses surround-
ing it were transformed by hundreds of Chinese lanterns hung
through the trees. When the true darkness had at last fallen,
the firework displays began; and simultaneously throughout
the four provinces, the night was assaulted by minute explosions
of coloured light, as the roman candles popped away, and the
rockets raced up into the sky. In the cities and large towns,
the spectacle always concluded with elaborate set pieces. The
Montrealers arranged an intricate design with emblems representing the three uniting provinces—a beaver for Canada, a
mayflower for Nova Scotia, and a pine for New Brunswick.
At Toronto the words "God Save the Queen" were surrounded
by a twined wreath of roses, thistles, shamrocks, and *fleur-de-lys*;
and at Hamilton, while the last set pieces were blazing, four
huge bonfires were kindled on the crest of the mountain. In
Ottawa, long before this, Monck and Macdonald and the other
ministers had quitted the Privy Council chamber; and Par-

liament Hill was crowded once again with people who had come to watch the last spectacle of the day. The parliament buildings were illuminated. They stood out boldly against the sky; and far behind them, hidden in darkness, were the ridges of the Laurentians, stretching away, mile after mile, towards the north-west.

A NOTE ON AUTHORITIES

This book is based on materials contemporary with the events described in the text. The principal sources are collections of manuscripts, which are to be found in a number of different archives and libraries in Canada and Great Britain.

Of these repositories, the richest in material relating to Macdonald is undoubtedly the Public Archives of Canada, at Ottawa. At the Public Archives are the Macdonald Papers, a magnificent collection of letters and documents, bound in 545 portfolios. The Macdonald Papers are more voluminous for the latter part of Macdonald's career than for the period covered by this volume; but the correspondence up to 1867 is considerable in quantity and high in quality. Obviously this collection has been of unique importance in the making of this book.

A number of other manuscript collections at the Public Archives of Canada have proved useful. The state papers of the different provinces of British North America are indispensable for an understanding of the period. The G series, which contains the dispatches from the Secretary of State for the Colonies to the Governor-General of Canada, is of obvious importance for a study which centres in Canadian politics; and the similar collections of the official correspondence of the Maritime Provinces, the Nova Scotia and New Brunswick Dispatches, are necessary sources for the history of British North American federation. The Minutes of the Executive Council of the Province of Canada are an essential record of government policy during the periods of Macdonald's tenure of office. Other collections of Canadian state papers—the C series, the J series, and the Upper Canada Sundries—have also provided occasional pieces of valuable material. In addition there are also at the Public Archives of Canada numerous collections of private papers, of which the Baring Papers, the Brown Chamberlin Papers, and the John Sandfield Macdonald Papers have been the most useful.

The other principal Canadian libraries and archives, from which material was obtained, are at Toronto. The John Langton Papers, at the University of Toronto Library, and the Baldwin Papers, at the Toronto Public Reference Library, yielded a few items of interest. At the Public Records and Archives of Ontario, there are several relatively small collections of private papers which have proved useful. Of these the most important are the Hodgins Papers, the Clarke Papers, the Buell Papers, the Stevenson Papers, and the Alexander Campbell Papers.

For the student of Canadian affairs during the pre-Confederation period, the Public Record Office is the most important repository of material in Great Britain. Here is to be found the other side of the official correspondence between the colonial governments and the imperial authorities—the dispatches from Canada and the other North American provinces to the Secretary of State for the Colonies. These state papers—series C.O. 42 for Canada, C.O. 188 for New Brunswick, and C.O. 217 for Nova Scotia—have been extensively used; and the dispatches from the British Minister at Washington to the Foreign Secretary, contained in series F.O. 5, have also been consulted for particular periods. In addition, the Public Record Office has acquired a number of collections of private papers, of which several—the Russell Papers, Carnarvon Papers, and Cardwell Papers—have been significant sources of material for this book. In particular these collections are essential to an understanding of British policy on Canadian federation.

In addition to the Public Record Office, several other British archives and libraries contain material important for this study. At the Royal Archives, Windsor Castle, a number of interesting letters were found. The Beaconsfield Collection, at Hughenden Manor, High Wycombe, and the Gladstone Papers, at the British Museum, illustrate British colonial policy as it was developed under both Conservative and Liberal governments. Finally, the Ellice Papers, at the National Library of Scotland, contributed some valuable information.

Contemporary printed material, of which there is a great quantity, has also been extensively used. The *Journals* of the Legislative Assembly and the Legislative Council provide essential information on parliamentary proceedings and government activities. The newspapers of the period are an indispensable source. Since there was no official *Hansard* at that time, they supply the only record of the debates in the Canadian legislature; and they also contain a good deal of useful information on electoral campaigns and public affairs in general. Valuable files of newspapers were found at the Public Archives of Canada and the Parliamentary Library, Ottawa; Queen's University Library, Kingston; the Legislative Library, Toronto; and the Toronto Public Reference Library.

NOTES

CHAPTER ONE: *The Immigrant Macdonalds*
(Pages 1 to 20)

[1] Public Archives of Canada, Macdonald Papers, vol. 540, Hugh Macdonald's Memorandum Book.

[2] *Ibid.*, vol. 538, Louisa Macdonald to Macdonald, 28 March, 1879.

[3] Joseph Pope, *Memoirs of the Right Honourable Sir John Alexander Macdonald, G.C.B., First Prime Minister of the Dominion of Canada* (London, 1894), vol. 1, pp. 1-2.

[4] Gilbert Gunn, "Sir John Alexander Macdonald of Canada and his Sutherland Forbears", *Northern Times* (Sutherland, Scotland), 27 September, 1923.

[5] J. P. Macpherson, *Life of the Right Hon. Sir John A. Macdonald* (Saint John, 1891), vol. 1, pp. 78-80.

[6] *A List of All the Officers of the Army and Royal Marines* (London, 1807), p. 369.

[7] *Quebec Gazette*, 17 September, 1807.

[8] Macpherson, *Macdonald*, vol. 1, pp. 79-80.

[9] Macdonald Papers, vol. 540, Hugh Macdonald's Memorandum Book.

[10] *Ibid.*

[11] *Ibid.*

[12] *Chronicle* (Kingston), 3 May, 1822.

[13] Public Records and Archives of Ontario, Alexander Campbell Papers. Undated Memorandum on Campbell's early association with Macdonald.

[14] *Chronicle*, 30 July, 1824. H. Macdonald is listed as the agent of *The Chronicle* at Hay Bay; Canniff Haight, *Country Life in Canada Fifty Years Ago: Personal Recollections and Reminiscences of a Sexagenarian* (Toronto, 1885), p. 296.

[15] *Chronicle and Gazette* (Kingston), 16 August, 1834, contains a contemporary description of the Stone Mills.

[16] *Hallowell Free Press*, 4 June, 1833.

[17] Macpherson, *Macdonald*, vol. 1, pp. 80-81.

[18] T. S. Webster, John A. Macdonald and Kingston (M.A. Thesis, Queen's University, 1944), pp. 1-5.

[19] W. S. Herrington, *History of the County of Lennox and Addington* (Toronto, 1913), pp. 98-99. The inscription on the fly-leaf of Macdonald's French grammar is dated Kingston, 23 May, 1825, which suggests that he did not attend school at Adolphustown for more than a year at most. The French grammar is in the possession of Percy Ghent, Esq., of Toronto, who kindly supplied the author with information concerning it.

[20] D. A. Lapp, The Schools of Kingston, their First Hundred and Fifty Years (M.A. Thesis, Queen's University, 1937), pp. 69-79.

[21] Macdonald Papers, vol. 540, John Alexander Macdonald's Exercise Book.

[22] Macpherson, *Macdonald*, vol. 1, pp. 80-81.

[23] Lapp, The Schools of Kingston, pp. 69-79.

[24] Memorials of the Life and Ministry of the Rev. John Machar, D.D., Late Minister of St. Andrew's Church, Kingston, ed. by Members of his Family (Toronto, 1873), pp. 11-37.

[25] J. Carnochan, Centennial, St. Andrews, Niagara, 1794-1894 (Toronto, 1895), pp. 47-48. This volume contains Sir Oliver Mowat's reminiscences of his school days. There is a photograph of Cruickshank.

[26] Chronicle, 17 January, 1829.

[27] Carnochan, Centennial, St. Andrews, pp. 48-49.

[28] A Shortt, "Founders of Canadian Banking: John Solomon Cartwright, Banker, Legislator, and Judge", Journal of the Canadian Bankers Association, vol. 30 (July, 1923), pp. 475-487.

[29] No record of Macdonald's appearance before the Benchers of the Law Society exists; but the procedure described in the text was evidently required of all legal students at the time, and is described in some detail in the diary of Patrick MacGregor, M.A. (Edin.), 1815-1882, who was a candidate at the spring examination of 1834. A typescript copy of the original diary is in the possession of Professor D. C. MacGregor, University of Toronto, who kindly brought it to the author's attention. As the diary makes clear, Patrick MacGregor was accompanied to Toronto by Macdonald, who, in the spring of 1834, was evidently keeping another of the four terms required of students at law.

CHAPTER TWO: *The Lawyer's Apprentice*

(Pages 21 to 45)

[1] Notice of his marriage was given in the Chronicle, 23 May, 1829.

[2] Memorials of the Life and Ministry of John Machar, p. 56.

[3] Carnochan, Centennial, St. Andrews, p. 48.

[4] Macpherson, Macdonald, vol. 1, p. 81.

[5] Chronicle, 4 December, 1830.

[6] Macpherson, Macdonald, vol. 1, p. 81.

[7] Shortt, "Founders of Canadian Banking: John Solomon Cartwright", Journal of the Canadian Bankers Association, vol. 30, pp. 475-487.

[8] D. G. Creighton, The Commercial Empire of the St. Lawrence, 1760-1850 (New Haven and Toronto, 1937), p. 280.

[9] Herrington, History of the County of Lennox and Addington, pp. 208-233.

[10] Macdonald Papers, vol. 336, Mackenzie to Macdonald, 29 September, 1832.

[11] Ibid., Mackenzie to Macdonald, 17 December, 1832.

[12] Ibid.

[13] Herrington, History of the County of Lennox and Addington, pp. 214-215.

[14] Chronicle and Gazette, 3 August, 1833.

[15] Macdonald Papers, vol. 336, Mackenzie to Macdonald, 19 August, 1833.

[16] Macpherson, Macdonald, vol. 1, p. 82.

[17] Macdonald Papers, vol. 336, Ramsay to Macdonald, 3 December, 1833.

[18] *Chronicle and Gazette*, 25 October, 1834.

[19] *Illustrated Historical Atlas of the Counties of Hastings and Prince Edward, Ont.* (Toronto, 1878), pp. xiv-xv.

[20] *Hallowell Free Press*, 30 July, 1833.

[21] *Picton Gazette*, 11 March, 1931, contains an article on Macdonald's activities in Hallowell, based on the early files of the *Hallowell Free Press.*

[22] Macdonald Papers, vol. 336, Macpherson to Macdonald, 1 August, 1834.

[23] *Chronicle and Gazette*, 12 July, 1834.

[24] *Memorials of the Life and Ministry of John Machar*, pp. 55-56.

[25] *Chronicle and Gazette*, 6 September, 1834.

[26] *Ibid.*, 9 August, 1834.

[27] Macpherson, *Macdonald*, vol. 1, pp. 82-83.

[28] *Chronicle and Gazette*, 26 August, 1835.

[29] E. E. Horsey, *Sir John Alexander Macdonald, His School Days and Law Offices* (Typescript pamphlet, Queen's University Library, 1942), p. 3.

[30] *Hallowell Free Press*, 11 November, 1833.

[31] *Chronicle and Gazette*, 20 April, 1836.

[32] *Ibid.*, 9 March, 1836.

[33] C. R. W. Biggar, *Sir Oliver Mowat: a Biographical Study* (Toronto, 1905), vol. 1, pp. 6-18.

[34] *Chronicle and Gazette*, 30 May, 1835.

[35] Public Archives of Canada, C, vol. 148, pp. 355-356.

[36] *Chronicle and Gazette*, 27 April, 1836.

[37] Macpherson, *Macdonald*, vol. 1, p. 78.

[38] *Chronicle and Gazette*, 17 February, 1836.

[39] *Ibid.*, 6 February, 1836.

[40] *Quebec Gazette*, 15 July, 1836.

[41] *Ibid.*, 8 July, 1836.

[42] *Journals of the House of Assembly of Upper Canada* (1836-1837), p. 157.

[43] *Chronicle and Gazette*, 22, 25 February, 1837.

[44] *Ibid.*, 29 March, 1837.

[45] *Ibid.*, 11 October, 1837.

[46] *Ibid.*, 1 November, 1837.

[47] *Ibid.*, 4 November, 1837.

[48] *Ibid.*, 11 November, 1837.

[49] *Ibid.*, 22 November, 1837.

[50] *Ibid.*, 6 December, 1837.

[51] *Ibid.*, 9 December, 1837.

CHAPTER THREE: *First Public Appearances*

(Pages 46 to 68)

[1] *Chronicle and Gazette*, 9 December, 1837.

[2] *Ibid.*

[3] A. Jameson, *Winter Studies and Summer Rambles in Canada* (London, 1838), vol. 1, pp. 300-303.

[4] *Chronicle and Gazette*, 18 December, 1837.

[5] C, vol. 1968A, pp. 18-19; *ibid.*, vol. 1968C, pp. 25-27.

[6] *Upper Canada Gazette*, 15 February, 1838.
[7] *Ibid.*, 22 February, 1838.
[8] Pope, *Memoirs*, vol. 1, p. 9.
[9] *Chronicle and Gazette*, 10 January, 1838.
[10] *Ibid.*, 21 February, 1838.
[11] *Ibid.*, 24 February, 1838.
[12] A. B. Corey, *The Crisis of 1830-1842 in Canadian-American Relations* (New Haven and Toronto, 1941), p. 41.
[13] *Chronicle and Gazette*, 21 March, 1838.
[14] E. E. Horsey, *Kingston a Century Ago* (Kingston, 1938), pp. 16-19.
[15] *Chronicle and Gazette*, 28 March, 1838.
[16] Corey, *The Crisis of 1830-1842*, pp. 75-76.
[17] *Chronicle and Gazette*, 16 May, 1838.
[18] *Ibid.*, 19 May, 1838.
[19] For example see the *Mirror* (Toronto), 16 June, 1838.
[20] *Chronicle and Gazette*, 30 June, 1838.
[21] *Ibid.*, 11 July, 1838.
[22] Alexander Campbell Papers, Undated Memorandum on Campbell's early association with Macdonald.
[23] *Chronicle and Gazette*, 11 July, 1838.
[24] *Ibid.*, 14 July, 1838.
[25] *Ibid.*, 21 July, 1838.
[26] C, vol. 611, pp. 24-30, Bonnycastle to Wright, 30 July, 1838.
[27] Public Archives of Canada, Upper Canada Sundries, Cartwright to Macaulay, 8 August, 1838. This is the complete report of the Kingston magistrates on the escape of the state prisoners. It contains depositions by eleven persons, including John Ashley.
[28] *Chronicle and Gazette*, 19 September, 1838.
[29] Upper Canada Sundries, Cartwright to Macaulay, 8 August, 1838.
[30] Macpherson, *Macdonald*, vol. 1, p. 88.
[31] *Chronicle and Gazette*, 19 September, 1838.
[32] Corey, *The Crisis of 1830-1842*, pp. 77-78.
[33] *Chronicle and Gazette*, 10 October, 1838.
[34] Macdonald Papers, vol. 538, William Gunn to Joseph Pope, 11 July, 1891.
[35] *Quebec Gazette*, 12 November, 1838.
[36] *Upper Canada Gazette*, 6 November, 1838.
[37] *Quebec Gazette*, 18 November, 1838.
[38] C. Carmer, *Dark Trees to the Wind, a Cycle of York State Years* (New York, 1949), pp. 225-226.
[39] *Chronicle and Gazette*, 14 November, 1838.
[40] *Ibid.*
[41] *Ibid.*, 17 November, 1838.
[42] *Ibid.*
[43] Macpherson, *Macdonald*, vol. 1, p. 88.
[44] Macdonald Papers, vol. 538, Memorandum by Pope of a Conversation with Macdonald about Von Schoultz, 17 May, 1890.
[45] Public Archives of Canada, R.G. 5, B. 41. Copy of proceedings of the Militia General Court Martial, Fort Henry, 1838.
[46] *Ibid.*; Cobourg Star, 12 December, 1838.
[47] R.G. 5, B. 41, Court Martial of Daniel George.

[48] Carmer, *Dark Trees to the Wind*, pp. 218-225.

[49] *Cobourg Star*, 12 December, 1838.

[50] R.G. 5, B. 41, Copy of The Proceedings of a Militia General Court Martial, holden at Fort Henry, at Kingston, for the trial of Nils Szoltevcky Von Schoultz.

[51] Macdonald Papers, vol. 538, Macdonald to Overlander, 8 December, 1890.

CHAPTER FOUR: *The New Conservative Candidate*

(Pages 69 to 99)

[1] *Journals of the House of Assembly of Upper Canada* (1839), Appendix, Report on the State of the Province, 30 April, 1839.

[2] *Cobourg Star*, 25 December, 1839, 1 January, 1840.

[3] Alexander Campbell Papers, Undated Memorandum on Campbell's early association with Macdonald.

[4] *Chronicle and Gazette*, 12 June, 1839.

[5] Webster, Macdonald and Kingston, p. 14.

[6] *Chronicle and Gazette*, 18 December, 1839.

[7] *Quebec Gazette*, 22 October, 1838.

[8] *Chronicle and Gazette*, 18 December, 1839.

[9] *Ibid.*, 8 August, 1840.

[10] *Ibid.*

[11] D. J. Pierce and J. P. Pritchett, "The Choice of Kingston as the Capital of Canada", *Canadian Historical Association Report* (1929), pp. 57-63.

[12] *Chronicle and Gazette*, 15 August, 1840.

[13] *Ibid.*, 22 August, 1840.

[14] *Ibid.*, 3 February, 1841.

[15] *Ibid.*, 6 February, 1841.

[16] Macdonald Papers, vol. 336, Wilson to Macdonald, 23 March, 1840.

[17] *Chronicle and Gazette*, 27 February, 3 March, 1841.

[18] *Ibid.*, 17 February, 1841.

[19] *Ibid.*, 27 February, 1841.

[20] *Ibid.*, 8 August, 1840.

[21] *Ibid.*, 24 March, 1841.

[22] *Montreal Gazette*, 21 May, 1841.

[23] *Chronicle and Gazette*, 8 May, 1841.

[24] *Montreal Gazette*, 31 May, 1841.

[25] *Chronicle and Gazette*, 19 June, 1841.

[26] *Ibid.*, 29 September, 1841.

[27] Macpherson, *Macdonald*, vol. 1, p. 85.

[28] *Chronicle and Gazette*, 24 December, 1841.

[29] Macdonald Papers, vol. 336, Machar to Macdonald, n.d.

[30] Pope, *Memoirs*, vol. 2, p. 270.

[31] Macdonald Papers, vol. 539, Macdonald to his Mother, 3 March, 1842.

[32] *Ibid.*, vol. 336, Account of H. Sweet, Chancery Lane, 27 April, 1842.

[33] Macpherson, *Macdonald*, vol. 1, pp. 85-86.

[34] *British Whig* (Kingston), 17 September, 1842.

[35] *Chronicle and Gazette*, 28 September, 1842.

[36] *British Whig*, 20 September, 1842.
[37] *Chronicle and Gazette*, 8 October, 1842.
[38] Horsey, *Kingston a Century Ago*, p. 23.
[39] *Ibid.*, pp. 23-24.
[40] *British Whig*, 21 November, 1842.
[41] *Chronicle and Gazette*, 4 February, 1843.
[42] *Ibid.*, 29 March, 1843.
[43] *Quebec Gazette*, 24 March, 1843.
[44] *Ibid.*, 3 April, 1843.
[45] *Chronicle and Gazette*, 8 April, 1843.
[46] *Quebec Gazette*, 12 April, 1843.
[47] *Ibid.*, 9 June, 1843.
[48] Macpherson, *Macdonald*, vol. 1, p. v.
[49] Macdonald Papers, vol. 194, Memorandum of the Terms of Co-partnership between Macdonald and Campbell, n.d.
[50] Macdonald Papers, vol. 545, Macdonald's Marriage Certificate, 1 September, 1843.
[51] *Chronicle and Gazette*, 2 September, 1843.
[52] Macpherson, *Macdonald*, vol. 1, pp. v-vi.
[53] *Chronicle and Gazette*, 27 September, 1843.
[54] *Ibid.*, 11 October, 1843.
[55] *Ibid.*, 6 November, 1843.
[56] *Ibid.*, 6 December, 1843.
[57] C. B. Sissons, "Letters of 1844 and 1846 from Scobie to Ryerson", *Canadian Historical Review*, vol. 29 (Dec. 1948), pp. 393-411.
[58] *Herald* (Kingston), 23 April, 1844.
[59] *British Whig*, 3 May, 1844.
[60] *Chronicle and Gazette*, 22 June, 1844.
[61] *News* (Kingston), 3 October, 1844, quoted in Macpherson, *Macdonald*, vol. 1, pp. 92-93.
[62] *British Whig*, 11 October, 1844.
[63] Macdonald Papers, Macdonald to Thirkell, 10 October, 1844.
[64] *British Whig*, 15 October, 1844.
[65] *Chronicle and Gazette*, 16 October, 1844.

CHAPTER FIVE: *Minister of the Crown*

(Pages 100 to 124)

[1] *Chronicle and Gazette*, 23 November, 1844.
[2] N. Bosworth, *Hochelaga Depicta* (Montreal, 1839), pp. 149-150.
[3] *Journals of the Legislative Assembly of the Province of Canada* (1844-1845), p. 1.
[4] D. B. Read, *The Lives of the Judges of Upper Canada and Ontario* (Toronto, 1888) pp. 222-236.
[5] *Montreal Gazette*, 21 December, 1844.
[6] *Ibid.*
[7] *Ibid.*, 1 February, 1845.
[8] *Ibid.*

[9] *Ibid.*, 20 February, 1845.

[10] J. G. Hodgins, *Documentary History of Education in Upper Canada from the Passing of the Constitutional Act in 1791, to the Close of the Reverend Doctor Ryerson's Administration of the Education Department in 1876* (Toronto), vol. 5, pp. 159-164.

[11] *Christian Guardian* (Toronto), 26 March, 1845; *Journals of the Assembly* (1844-1845), p. 374.

[12] Hodgins, *Documentary History*, vol. 5, pp. 191-192.

[13] Macdonald Papers, vol. 545, Isabella Macdonald to Margaret Greene, 11 June, 1845.

[14] *Ibid.*

[15] *Ibid.*, Macdonald to Margaret Greene, 12 July, 1845.

[16] *Ibid.*, Macdonald to Margaret Greene, 11 July, 1845.

[17] *Ibid.*, Macdonald to Margaret Greene, 18 July, 1845.

[18] *Ibid.*, Macdonald to Margaret Greene, 31 October, 1845.

[19] *Ibid.*, Macdonald to Margaret Greene, 3 November, 1845.

[20] *Ibid.*, Macdonald to Margaret Greene, 15 November, 1845. Macdonald was fairly up-to-date in his reading. George Borrow's *The Bible in Spain* appeared in 1843, Charles Lever's *Tom Burke of Ours* in 1844, and Harrison Ainsworth's *Rookwood* in 1834. A new edition of Carlyle's *Life of Schiller* was published in 1845. *The History of England from the Peace of Utrecht to the Peace of Versailles, 1713-1783*, was a work in seven volumes which appeared at intervals in the years 1836-1853. Its author, Philip Henry Stanhope, Viscount Mahon, later fifth Earl of Stanhope, was an historian whom Macdonald much admired; Stanhope's *Life of William Pitt* (1861) later became one of Macdonald's favourite biographies. The *Sermons* were probably those of John Moore, Bishop of Ely; they were published early in the eighteenth century.

[21] *Ibid.*, Macdonald to Margaret Greene, 3 November, 1845.

[22] *Ibid.*, Macdonald to Margaret Greene, 20 November, 1845.

[23] *Ibid.*, Macdonald to Margaret Greene, 27 February, 1846.

[24] *Journals of the Legislative Assembly of the Province of Canada* (1846), p. 6.

[25] *Mirror of Parliament of the Province of Canada* (Montreal, 1846), pp. 104-105.

[26] *Ibid.*, pp. 109-110.

[27] Macdonald Papers, vol. 209, Draper to Cathcart, 10 June, 1846, quoted in Pope, *Memoirs*, vol. 1, pp. 43-44.

[28] *Ibid.*, vol. 336, W. H. Boulton to R. Maitland, 10 May, 1846.

[29] *Ibid.*, vol. 209, Draper to Cathcart, 10 June, 1846.

[30] *Ibid.*, vol. 194, Memorandum of the Terms of Co-partnership between Macdonald and Campbell.

[31] *Ibid.*, vol. 539, Macdonald to Margaret Greene, 20 January, 1847.

[32] *Globe* (Toronto), 9 January, 1847.

[33] Public Records and Archives of Ontario, Hodgins Papers, Draper to Ryerson, 22 February, 1847.

[34] Macdonald Papers, vol. 209, Draper to Macdonald, 4 March, 1847.

[35] *Ibid.*, vol. 545, Macdonald to Margaret Greene, 5 April, 1847.

[36] *Ibid.*, vol. 336, Morris to Macdonald, 6 May, 1847.

[37] *Ibid.*, Macdonald to Morris, 9 May, 1847.

[38] *Globe*, 22 May, 1847.

89 Sir A. G. Doughty, (ed.) *The Elgin-Grey Papers, 1846-1852* (Ottawa, 1937), vol. 1, pp. 39-40, Elgin to Grey, 18 May, 1847.

40 Macdonald Papers, vol. 336, Cayley to Macdonald, 22 May, 1847.

41 *Ibid.*, vol. 539, Macdonald to his Mother, 10 June, 1847.

42 Hodgins, *Documentary History*, vol. 7, pp. 4-6.

43 *Ibid.*, pp. 6-7.

44 *Christian Guardian*, 21 July, 1847.

45 *Ibid.*

46 Hodgins, *Documentary History*, vol. 7, p. 8.

47 *Ibid.*, p. 52.

48 Macdonald Papers, vol. 539, Macdonald to his Mother, 2 August, 1847.

CHAPTER SIX: *The Twilight of the Tory Party*
(Pages 125 to 146)

1 Macdonald Papers, vol. 545, Macdonald to Margaret Greene, 31 August, 1847.

2 *Ibid.*, Macdonald to Margaret Greene, 28 September, 1847.

3 *Ibid.*, vol. 336, Cayley to Macdonald, 4 September, 1847.

4 *Ibid.*, additional, vol. 1, Macdonald to Jessup, 30 October, 1847.

5 *Herald*, 3 November, 1847.

6 *Chronicle and Gazette*, 27 November, 1 December, 1847.

7 *Herald*, 8 December, 1847.

8 *Chronicle and Gazette*, 22 December, 1847.

9 *Herald*, 22 December, 1847.

10 *Chronicle and Gazette*, 24 December, 1847.

11 *Ibid.*, 29 December, 1847, 1 January, 1848.

12 *Journals of the Legislative Assembly of the Province of Canada* (1848), p. 17.

13 Macdonald Papers, vol. 545, Macdonald to Margaret Greene, 9 July, 1848.

14 *Ibid.*, Isabella Macdonald to Margaret Greene, n.d.

15 *Ibid.*, Macdonald to Margaret Greene, 1 August, 1848.

16 *Ibid.*

17 *Ibid.*, Macdonald to Margaret Greene, 15 August, 1848.

18 *Ibid.*, Macdonald to Margaret Greene, 29 August, 1848.

19 *Chronicle and Gazette*, 23 September, 1848.

20 Macdonald Papers, vol. 545, Macdonald to Margaret Greene, 3 December, 1848.

21 *Ibid.*, Macdonald to Margaret Greene, 17 December, 1848.

22 *Montreal Gazette*, 16 February, 1849.

23 *Examiner* (Toronto) 21, 28 February, 1849.

24 *Montreal Gazette*, 19 February, 1849.

25 *Journals of the Legislative Assembly of the Province of Canada* (1849), p. 88.

26 Toronto Public Libraries, Baldwin Papers, H. J. Boulton to Baldwin, 2 January, 1850.

27 *Montreal Gazette*, 26 February, 1849.

28 *Ibid.*

[29] *Journals of the Legislative Assembly of the Province of Canada* (1849), p. 219.

[30] Macpherson, *Macdonald*, vol. 1, pp. 148-149.

[31] C. D. Allin and G. M. Jones, *Annexation, Preferential Trade and Reciprocity, an Outline of the Canadian Annexation Movement of 1849-50, with Special Reference to the Questions of Preferential Trade and Reciprocity* (Toronto, n.d.), pp. 49-60.

[32] Macdonald Papers, vol. 545, Macdonald to Margaret Greene, 24 July, 1849.

[33] *Ibid.*, vol. 194, Campbell to Macdonald, 8 June, 1849.

[34] *Ibid.*, vol. 545, Macdonald to Margaret Greene, 24 July, 1849.

[35] Public Records and Archives of Ontario, Miscellaneous Papers, 1849, Macdonald to Stevenson, 5 July, 1849.

[36] *Montreal Gazette*, 28 July, 1849.

[37] *Minutes of the Proceedings of a Convention of Delegates of the British American League held at Kingston (Canada West) on the 25th, and by Adjournment on the 26th, 27th, 28th, and 31st Days of July, 1849* (Kingston, 1849), pp. 7-8.

[38] *Ibid.*, pp. 11-12.

[39] *Montreal Gazette*, 31 July, 1849.

CHAPTER SEVEN: *Years of Recovery*

(Pages 147 to 173)

[1] Macdonald Papers, vol. 194, Campbell to Macdonald, 8 June, 1849.

[2] *Ibid.*

[3] *Ibid.*, Campbell to Macdonald, n.d.

[4] *Ibid.*, New Terms of Agreement, 30 August, 1849.

[5] *Ibid.*, Campbell to Macdonald, n.d.

[6] Horsey, *Macdonald, His School Days and Law Offices*, p. 4.

[7] G. N. Tucker, *The Canadian Commercial Revolution, 1845-1851* (New Haven, 1936), pp. 178-201, 227-233.

[8] *Minutes of the Proceedings of the Second Convention of Delegates of the British American League held at Toronto, C.W., on Thursday, November 1, and by Adjournment on the 2nd, 3rd, 5th, 6th and 7th of November, 1849* (Toronto, 1849).

[9] Public Archives of Canada, John Sandfield Macdonald Papers, Baldwin to Macdonald, 1 February, 1848.

[10] G. M. Jones, "The Peter Perry Election and the Rise of the Clear Grit Party", *Ontario Historical Society Papers and Records*, vol. 12 (1914), pp. 164-175.

[11] Macdonald Papers, vol. 194, Campbell to Macdonald, n.d.

[12] *Ibid.*, vol. 545, Macdonald to Margaret Greene, 9 December, 1849.

[13] *Ibid.*, Macdonald to Margaret Greene, 6 January, 1850.

[14] *Ibid.*, Macdonald to Margaret Greene, 20 January, 1850.

[15] *Ibid.*, Macdonald to Margaret Greene, 27 January, 1850.

[16] *Ibid.*, Macdonald to Margaret Greene, 20 January, 1850.

[17] *Ibid.*, Macdonald to Margaret Greene, 2 February, 1850.

[18] *Ibid.*, vol. 540, Hugh Macdonald's Memorandum Book.

[19] *Ibid.*, vol. 539, Macdonald to Margaret Macdonald, 2 April, 1850.

[20] *Ibid.*

[21] *Journals of the Legislative Assembly of the Province of Canada* (1850), p. 63.

[22] *Montreal Gazette*, 18, 21 May, 1850.

[23] *Globe*, 22 June, 1850.

[24] *Journals of the Legislative Assembly of the Province of Canada* (1850), p. 106.

[25] *Ibid.*, pp. 158, 165.

[26] Doughty, *Elgin-Grey Papers*, vol. 2, p. 715, Elgin to Grey, 27 September, 1850.

[27] *Globe*, 29 June, 1850.

[28] Samuel Thompson, *Reminiscences of a Canadian Pioneer, for the Last Fifty Years, an Autobiography* (Toronto, 1884), pp. 215-216.

[29] Baldwin Papers, Brown to Baldwin, 9 October, 1848.

[30] Macdonald Papers, vol. 297, Smith to Macdonald, 23, 26, 28, 29 January, 1 February, 1849.

[31] *Ibid.*, Statement of Charges preferred by the Penitentiary Commission against the Warden, with his Comments, 15 February, 1849.

[32] *Montreal Gazette*, 26 January, 1849.

[33] Macdonald Papers, vol. 297, Humble Petition of Henry Smith, late Warden of the Provincial Penitentiary; *North American* (Toronto), 9 August, 1850.

[34] *Globe*, 27 June, 1850.

[35] *British Colonist* (Toronto), 5 July, 1850.

[36] Doughty, *Elgin-Grey Papers*, vol. 2, p. 715, Elgin to Grey, 27 September, 1850.

[37] *Ibid.*, p. 736, Grey to Elgin, 15 November, 1850.

[38] *Ibid.*, p. 748, Grey to Elgin, 13 December, 1850.

[39] W. Ward, *The Life and Times of Cardinal Wiseman* (London, 1912), vol. 1, pp. 542-543.

[40] *Ibid.*, pp. 547-548.

[41] *Globe*, 10, 19 December, 1850.

[42] Charles Clarke, *Sixty Years in Upper Canada, with Autobiographical Recollections* (Toronto, 1908), p. 65.

[43] *Globe*, 8, 17 April, 1851.

[44] *Ibid.*, 19 April, 1851.

[45] *News* (Kingston), 2 January, 1852.

[46] *Globe*, 27 May, 1851; *Montreal Gazette*, 30 May, 1851.

[47] *Montreal Gazette*, 25 July, 1851.

[48] *Globe*, 26 June, 1851.

[49] *Montreal Gazette*, 30 June, 1851.

[50] *Globe*, 26 June, 1851.

[51] *Montreal Gazette*, 1 August, 1851.

[52] Doughty, *Elgin-Grey Papers*, vol. 2, pp. 745-747, Elgin to Grey, 22 November, 1850.

[53] *Globe*, 22 June, 1850.

[54] *Montreal Gazette*, 11 August, 1851.

[55] Public Records and Archives of Ontario, Clarke Papers, McDougall to Clarke, 26 July, 1851.

56 Public Records and Archives of Ontario, Stevenson Papers, Macdonald to Stevenson, 14 September, 1851.
57 *News*, 26, 27 November, 1851.
58 *Ibid.*, 8 December, 1851.
59 *Ibid.*, 10 December, 1851.
60 *Ibid.*, 16, 18 December, 1851.
61 Macdonald Papers, vol. 538, Harcourt Vernon to Pope, 19 May, 1892.
62 Haight, *Country Life in Canada Fifty Years Ago*, pp. 297-298.

CHAPTER EIGHT: *The Liberal-Conservative Coalition*

(Pages 174 to 207)

1 *Leader* (Toronto), 25 August, 1852.
2 *Patriot* (Toronto), 25 August, 1852; *Montreal Gazette*, 29 October, 1852.
3 *Montreal Gazette*, 18 August, 1852.
4 *Patriot*, 15 September, 1852.
5 *Globe*, 12 October, 1852.
6 *Montreal Gazette*, 29 October, 1852.
7 *News*, 20 October, 1852.
8 Macdonald Papers, vol. 539, Macdonald to Louisa Macdonald, 13 October, 1852.
9 *Journals of the Legislative Assembly of the Province of Canada* (1852-1853), p. 313.
10 His name appears on the division lists for the first time on 8 March, and for the last time on 4 May, 1853. See *Journals of the Legislative Assembly of the Province of Canada* (1852-1853).
11 *Patriot*, 24 September, 1852.
12 *Globe*, 14 October, 1852.
13 *Ibid.*, 21 October, 1852.
14 *Ibid.*, 14 April, 1853.
15 *Ibid.*, 12 April, 1853.
16 *Journals of the Legislative Assembly of the Province of Canada* (1852-1853), p. 539.
17 *Globe*, 15 March, 1853; *Leader*, 23 March, 1853.
18 *Patriot*, 4 September, 1852.
19 *Journals of the Legislative Assembly of the Province of Canada* (1852-1853), p. 143.
20 *Patriot*, 24 September, 1852.
21 Clarke Papers, Thomson to Clarke, February, 1853.
22 *Patriot*, 25 August, 1852.
23 *Patriot*, 21 February, 1853.
24 *Ibid.*, 8 September, 1852.
25 *Montreal Gazette*, 13 September, 1852; *Patriot*, 23 February, 1853.
26 *Montreal Gazette*, 20 August, 1852.
27 *Patriot*, 17 March, 1853.
28 *Globe*, 22 March, 1853.

29 *Montreal Gazette*, 16 March, 1853.

30 *Patriot*, 18 March, 1853.

31 *Ibid.*

32 *Globe*, 24 March, 1853.

33 *Ibid.*

34 Clarke Papers, McDougall to Clarke, 2 February, 1853.

35 *Globe*, 2 April, 1853.

36 *Ibid.*, 14 May, 1853.

37 *Ibid.*

38 Macdonald Papers, vol. 194, Campbell to Macdonald, 8 March, 1855.

39 G. M. Trevelyan, *Garibaldi's Defence of the Roman Republic, 1848-9* (London, 1928), Chapter V.

40 Alessandro Gavazzi, *Six Lectures delivered in the Round Room of the Rotunda, Dublin, with a Biographical Sketch of the Author* (Toronto), 1853.

41 *Globe*, 2, 4 June, 1853.

42 *Ibid.*, 9 June, 1853.

43 *Ibid.*, 14 June, 1853.

44 *Ibid.*, 18 June, 1853.

45 *Montreal Gazette*, 15 July, 1853.

46 *Ibid.*, 18 August, 1853.

47 *Ibid.*, 19 August, 1853.

48 R. S. Longley, *Sir Francis Hincks, a Study of Canadian Politics, Railways, and Finance in the Nineteenth Century* (Toronto, 1943), pp. 238-239.

49 *Leader*, 28 February, 1854.

50 *Montreal Gazette*, 20 September, 1853.

51 Clarke Papers, McDougall to Clarke, 17 September, 1853.

52 *Globe*, 27 February, 1854.

53 Macdonald Papers, vol. 336, Macdonald to Strachan, 9 February, 1854.

54 *Ibid.*

55 *Globe*, 2 February, 1854.

56 *Leader*, 5 May, 1854.

57 *Globe*, 24 June, 1854; Public Records and Archives of Ontario, Buell Papers, Cameron to Buell, 21 June, 1854.

58 *Leader*, 27 June, 1854.

59 *Journals of the Legislative Assembly of the Province of Canada* (1854), pp. 29-30.

60 *Leader*, 30 June, 1854.

61 *Globe*, 24 June, 1854.

62 *Ibid.*, 14 July, 1854.

63 *Leader*, 8 August, 1854.

64 *Globe*, 7 August, 1854.

65 *Montreal Gazette*, 19 July, 1854.

66 *Ibid.*, 11 August, 1854.

67 *Leader*, 14 July, 1854.

68 *Globe*, 3 July, 1854.

69 *News*, 18 July, 1854.

70 *Ibid.*, 20 July, 1854.

71 *Ibid.*, 28 July, 1854.

72 *Leader*, 11 August, 1854.

73 Macdonald Papers, vol. 194, Campbell to Macdonald, 8 March, 1855.

[74] O. D. Skelton, *The Life and Times of Alexander Tilloch Galt* (Toronto, 1920), pp. 187-192.

[75] *Montreal Gazette*, 9 September, 1854.

[76] C. B. Sissons, *Egerton Ryerson, his Life and Letters* (Toronto, 1947), vol. 2, p. 281.

CHAPTER NINE: *The Victory of the Progressive-Conservatives*

(Pages 208 to 237)

[1] *Journals of the Legislative Assembly of the Province of Canada* (1856), Appendix 30.

[2] *Ibid.* (1854-1855), p. 144.

[3] *Globe*, 16 October, 1854.

[4] *Ibid.*, 13 September, 1854.

[5] *Leader*, 15 September, 1854.

[6] Macdonald Papers, vol. 336, Thompson to Macdonald, 22 September, 1854, Gowan to Macdonald, 25 September, 1854.

[7] *Globe*, 19 October, 1854.

[8] *Leader*, 19 October, 1854.

[9] *Globe*, 23 October, 1854.

[10] *Journals of the Legislative Assembly of the Province of Canada* (1854-1855), p. 194.

[11] *Leader*, 25 October, 1854.

[12] Macdonald Papers, vol. 336, Gowan to Macdonald, 13 December, 1854.

[13] Thompson, *Reminiscences of a Canadian Pioneer*, pp. 336-338.

[14] *Globe*, 2 October, 1847.

[15] Macdonald Papers, vol. 336, Macdonald to Strachan, 9 February, 1854.

[16] *Globe*, 9 November, 1854.

[17] *Ibid.*, 10 November, 1854.

[18] *Journals of the Legislative Assembly of the Province of Canada* (1854-1855), p. 385.

[19] *Quebec Gazette*, 21 December, 1854.

[20] Macdonald Papers, vol. 539, Macdonald to Louisa Macdonald, 21 February, 1855.

[21] Public Archives of Canada, Brown Chamberlin Papers, vol. 2, Macdonald to Chamberlin, 2 February, 1855.

[22] W. A. Langton (ed.), *Early Days in Upper Canada, Letters of John Langton* (Toronto, 1926), p. 216.

[23] Macdonald Papers, vol. 194, Campbell to Macdonald, 8 March, 1855.

[24] University of Toronto Library, John Langton Papers, Langton's Estimate of Macdonald, 1855.

[25] *Globe*, 12 March, 1855.

[26] Macdonald Papers, vol. 539, Macdonald to Louisa Macdonald, 21 February, 1855.

[27] *Globe*, 23 April, 1855.

[28] *Ibid.*, 12 March, 1855.

[29] *Ibid.*

[30] Sissons, *Egerton Ryerson*, vol. 2, pp. 328-331.

[81] J. G. Hodgins, *The Legislation and History of Separate Schools in Upper Canada: From 1841 until the Close of the Reverend Doctor Ryerson's Administration of the Education Department of Ontario in 1876* (Toronto, 1897), p. 93.

[82] *Globe*, 6 June, 1855.

[83] *Ibid.*, 11 June, 1855.

[84] *Leader*, 9, 13, 18 October, 1855.

[85] Macdonald Papers, vol. 539, Macdonald to Louisa Macdonald, 21 September, 1855.

[86] *Brown's Toronto General Directory, 1856* (Toronto, 1856), p. 323.

[87] Macdonald Papers, vol. 539, Williamson to Pope, 10 October, 1892.

[88] *Ibid.*, Macdonald to his Mother, 26 January, 1856.

[89] Brown Chamberlin Papers, vol. 2, Macdonald to Chamberlin, 7 August, 1855.

[40] *Ibid.*, Macdonald to Chamberlin, 21 January, 1856.

[41] Macdonald Papers, vol. 539, Macdonald to his Mother, 4 February, 1856.

[42] *Leader*, 28 February, 1856; *Globe*, 27 February, 1856.

[43] *Journals of the Legislative Assembly of the Province of Canada* (1856), p. 116.

[44] Macdonald Papers, vol. 336, John Ross to Macdonald, 23 August, 1855.

[45] Brown Chamberlin Papers, vol. 2, Macdonald to Chamberlin, 21 January, 1856.

[46] *Leader*, 20 February, 1856.

[47] *Ibid.*, 8 April, 1856.

[48] *Globe*, 11 March, 1856.

[49] *Journals of the Legislative Assembly of the Province of Canada* (1856), p. 144.

[50] *Leader*, 25 March, 1856.

[51] Thompson, *Reminiscences of a Canadian Pioneer*, p. 294.

[52] *Globe*, 27 March, 1856.

[53] *Leader*, 8 April, 1856.

[54] *Globe*, 30 May, 1856.

[55] Macdonald Papers, vol. 539, Macdonald to his Mother, 17 March, 1856.

[56] *Ibid.*, Macdonald to his Mother, 21 April, 1856.

[57] *Ibid.*, Macdonald to his Mother, 17 March, 1856.

[58] *Leader*, 17 April, 1856.

[59] Langton, *Early Days in Upper Canada*, p. 257.

[60] *Ibid.*

[61] Macdonald Papers, vol. 539, Macdonald to his Mother, 17 March, 1856.

[62] *Journals of the Legislative Assembly of the Province of Canada* (1856), pp. 322-330.

[63] *Ibid.*, p. 514.

[64] *Ibid.*, p. 522.

[65] *Ibid.*, pp. 538-539.

[66] *Globe*, 27 May, 1856.

[67] Public Archives of Canada, G10, vol. 2, Head to Labouchere, 23 May, 1856; G12, vol. 66, Head to Labouchere, 24 May, 1856.

[68] *Journals of the Legislative Assembly of the Province of Canada* (1856), pp. 554-555.

[69] *Globe*, 24 May, 1856.
[70] *Ibid.*, 30 May, 1856.

CHAPTER TEN: *Double Shuffle*
(Pages 238 to 272)

[1] J. B. Brebner, "Joseph Howe and the Crimean War Enlistment Controversy between Great Britain and the United States", *Canadian Historical Review*, vol. 11 (Dec. 1930), pp. 300-327.

[2] C. P. Stacey, *Canada and the British Army, 1846-1871, a Study in the Practice of Responsible Government* (London, 1936), pp. 98-99.

[3] D. G. G. Kerr, "Edmund Head, Robert Lowe, and Confederation", *Canadian Historical Review*, vol. 20 (Dec. 1939), pp. 409-420.

[4] *Ibid.*

[5] *Journals of the Legislative Assembly of the Province of Canada* (1857), Appendix 17, Labouchere to Head, 4 December, 1856.

[6] *Globe*, 9 January, 1851.

[7] Public Archives of Canada, G9, vol. 32, Head to Labouchere, 3 September, 1856.

[8] Sir Arthur Hardinge, *The Life of Henry Howard Molyneux Herbert, Fourth Earl of Carnarvon, 1831-1890* (Oxford, 1925), vol. 3, pp. 92-93.

[9] National Library of Scotland, Ellice Papers, first instalment, bundle 29a, Ellice to Rose, 6 October, 1856.

[10] *Ibid.*, Rose to Ellice, 15 December, 1856.

[11] *Journals of the Legislative Assembly of the Province of Canada* (1857), Appendix 17, Order-in-Council, 17 January, 1857.

[12] *Ibid.*, Order-in-Council, 16 February, 1857.

[13] Macdonald Papers, vol. 539, Macdonald to his Mother, 27 January, 1857.

[14] *Ibid.*, Macdonald to his Mother, 4 February, 1857.

[15] *Ibid.*, Macdonald to Louisa Macdonald, 17 March, 1857.

[16] *Globe*, 20 March, 1857.

[17] *Ibid.*, 26 March, 1857.

[18] Public Record Office, London, C.O.42, vol. 609, Head to Labouchere, 28 March, 1857, minute by Merivale, 13 April, 1857.

[19] G. P. de T. Glazebrook, *A History of Transportation in Canada* (Toronto and New Haven, 1938), pp. 179-180.

[20] *Globe*, 30 April, 1857.

[21] *Ibid.*, 13 May, 1857.

[22] Macdonald Papers, vol. 539, Macdonald to Louisa Macdonald, 27 April, 1857.

[23] C.O.42, vol. 609, Head to Labouchere, 23 March, 1857.

[24] Public Archives of Canada, Canada, Executive Council Minutes, State Book R, Order-in-Council, 18 July, 1857.

[25] C.O.42, vol. 610, Eyre to Labouchere, 12 July, 1857.

[26] Ellice Papers, first instalment, bundle 29a, Rose to Ellice, 3 July, 1857.

[27] Macdonald Papers, vol. 539, Macdonald to his Mother, 28 July, 1857.

[28] *Ibid.*, Macdonald to his Mother, 31 July, 1857.

[29] *Ibid.*, vol. 120, Memorandum on the Intercolonial Railway, August, 1857.

[30] *Ibid.*, Macdonald to Provincial Secretary, 1 February, 1858.

[31] Ellice Papers, first instalment, bundle 29a, Ellice to Rose, 9 August, 1857.

[32] *Ibid.*, Ellice to Rose, 1 August, 1857.

[33] Macdonald Papers, vol. 539, Macdonald to his Mother, 11 August, 1857.

[34] *Ibid.*, Macdonald to his Mother, 21 August, 1857.

[35] C.O.42, vol. 610, Head to Labouchere, 26 November, 1857.

[36] Macdonald Papers, vol. 336, Cayley to Macdonald, 11 November [1857].

[37] Skelton, *Galt*, p. 229.

[38] *Ibid.*, pp. 229-230.

[39] Macdonald Papers, vol. 293, Vankoughnet to Macdonald, n.d.

[40] *Ibid.*, vol. 539, Macdonald to his Mother, 30 November, 1857.

[41] *News*, 9 December, 1857.

[42] *News*, 11 December, 1857.

[43] *Ibid.*, 17 December, 1857.

[44] *Ibid.*, 18 December, 1857.

[45] Thompson, *Reminiscences of a Canadian Pioneer*, pp. 338-339.

[46] *News*, 29 December, 1857.

[47] Pope, *Memoirs*, vol. 1, p. 180.

[48] Macdonald Papers, vol. 539, Macdonald to Margaret Williamson, 20 March, 1858.

[49] Public Record Office, London, P.R.O. 30/6 (Carnarvon Papers), vol. 69, *Papers Relative to the Seat of Government of Canada*, October, 1857.

[50] Royal Archives, Windsor, P22, Draft Memorandum by General Grey, October, 1857.

[51] *Ibid.*, Labouchere to the Queen, 16 October, 1857.

[52] G1, vol. 143, Labouchere to Head, 31 December, 1857.

[53] *Leader*, 20 July, 1858.

[54] *Journals of the Legislative Assembly of the Province of Canada* (1858), p. 931.

[55] *Leader*, 29 July, 1858.

[56] *Assembly Journals* (1858), pp. 931-932.

[57] *Globe*, 30 July, 1858.

[58] *Atlas* (Toronto), 6 August, 1858.

[59] Pope, *Memoirs*, vol. 1, Appendix 3, pp. 339-341; E. A. Forsey, *The Royal Power of Dissolution of Parliament in the British Commonwealth* (Toronto, 1943), pp. 50-52.

[60] *Atlas*, 6 August, 1858.

[61] *Assembly Journals* (1858), pp. 935-936.

[62] C.O. 42, vol. 614, Head to Lytton, 9 August, 1858.

[63] Pope, *Memoirs*, vol. 1, p. 200.

[64] C.O. 42, vol. 614, Head to Lytton, 18 August, 1858.

[65] *Atlas*, 6 August, 1858.

[66] *Ibid.*

[67] C.O. 42, vol. 615, Head to Lytton, 22 October, 1858.

[68] *Assembly Journals* (1858), p. 1043.

[69] Canada, Executive Council Minutes, State Book T, Order-in-Council, 9 September, 1858.

CHAPTER ELEVEN: *The Humiliation of George Brown*

(Pages 273 to 314)

[1] Hughenden Manor, Beaconsfield Papers, bundle 13, Lytton to Disraeli, 14 December, 1858.

[2] Hardinge, *Carnarvon*, vol. 1, p. 119.

[3] C.O. 42, vol. 614, Head to Lytton, 16 August, 1858, minute by Lytton.

[4] *Ibid.*, Head to Lytton, 9 August, 1858, minute by Carnarvon.

[5] P.R.O. 30/6, vol. 69, Lytton to Head, 24 September, 1858, printed in *Question of the Federation of the British Provinces in America* (Colonial Office, Nov. 1858).

[6] C.O. 42, vol. 614, Head to Lytton, 16 August, 1858, minute by Carnarvon, 1 September, 1858.

[7] *Ibid.*, minute by Blackwood, 30 August, 1858.

[8] *Ibid.*, minute by Lytton.

[9] *Ibid.*, minute by Merivale, 31 August, 1858.

[10] *Ibid.*, vol. 615, Head to Lytton, 22 October, 1858, minute by Carnarvon, 8 November, 1858.

[11] *Ibid.*, vol. 614, Head to Lytton, 31 July, 1858, minute by Lytton.

[12] G1, vol. 146, Lytton to Head, 10 September, 1858.

[13] P.R.O. 30/6, vol. 69, Sutton to Lytton, 29 September, 1858, printed in *Question of Federation of the British Provinces in America.*

[14] *Ibid.*, Sutton to Lytton, 2 October, 1858.

[15] C.O. 42, vol. 614, Head to Lytton, 16 August, 1858, minute by Merivale, 31 August, 1858.

[16] P.R.O. 30/6, vol. 69, T. F. Elliot, *Memorandum on the Question of the Federation of the British Provinces in North America*; R. G. Trotter, "The British Government and the Proposal of Federation in 1858", *Canadian Historical Review*, vol. 14 (September, 1933), pp. 287-292.

[17] P.R.O. 30/6, vol. 69, *Memorandum for the Cabinet*, 10 November, 1858.

[18] G1, vol. 146, Lytton to Head, 26 November, 1858.

[19] Beaconsfield Papers, bundle 13, Lytton to Disraeli, n.d.

[20] *Globe*, 20 November, 1858.

[21] *Ibid.*, 23 November, 1858.

[22] *Ibid.*, 20 December, 1858.

[23] *Ibid.*

[24] *Ibid.*

[25] Ellice Papers, first instalment, bundle 29a, Rose to Ellice, 3 January, 1859.

[26] *Ibid.*

[27] C.O. 42, vol. 617, Head to Lytton, 8 January, 1859.

[28] *Ibid.*, Head to Merivale, 12 February, 1859.

[29] Beaconsfield Papers, Lytton to Disraeli, n.d.

[30] *Ibid.*, Lytton to Disraeli, 19 December, 1858.

[31] G1, vol. 146, Lytton to Head, 24 December, 1858.

[32] Canada, Executive Council Minutes, State Book T, Order-in-Council, 6 January, 1859.

[33] *Leader*, 2 February, 1859.

[34] C.O. 42, vol. 615, Head to Lytton, 9 September, 1858.

[35] G1, vol. 145, Lytton to Head, 20 August, 1858.

[36] C.O. 42, vol. 615, Head to Lytton, 9 September, 1858.

[37] C.O. 42, vol. 618, Head to Lytton, 7 May, 1859.

[38] *Leader*, 30 April, 1859.

[39] Macdonald Papers, vol. 539, Macdonald to his Mother, 2 October, 1858.

[40] Horsey, *Macdonald, His School Days and Law Offices*, p. 5.

[41] Pope, *Memoirs*, vol. 1, p. 206.

[42] *Leader*, 10 February, 1859.

[43] *Ibid.*, 16 April, 1859.

[44] *Ibid.*, 12 February, 1859.

[45] J. M. S. Careless, "Who was George Brown?", *Ontario History*, vol. 52 (April, 1950), pp. 57-66.

[46] G. W. Brown, "The Grit Party and the Great Reform Convention of 1859", *Canadian Historical Review*, vol. 16, (September, 1935), pp. 245-256.

[47] Macdonald Papers, vol. 336, Spence to Macdonald, 14 October, 1859.

[48] Pope, *Memoirs*, vol. 1, pp. 215-216.

[49] Macdonald Papers, vol. 539, Macdonald to Louisa Macdonald, 1 September, 1859.

[50] Brown, "The Grit Party and the Great Reform Convention".

[51] Macdonald Papers, vol. 336, Lindsey to Macdonald, 24 November, 1859.

[52] J. M. S. Careless, "The Toronto Globe and Agrarian Radicalism", *Canadian Historical Review*, vol. 29 (March, 1948), pp. 14-39.

[53] G10, vol. 2, Head to Newcastle, 1 December, 1859.

[54] Canada, Executive Council Minutes, State Book U, Order-in-Council on federation, 22 November, 1859.

[55] *Ibid.*, Galt to Colonial Secretary, 18 January, 1860.

[56] G1, vol. 150, Newcastle to Head, 27 January, 1860.

[57] Canada, Executive Council Minutes, State Book U, Order-in-Council on federation, 13 February, 1860.

[58] *Leader*, 30 April, 1860.

[59] *Thompson's Mirror of Parliament, being a Report of the Debates in both Houses of the Canadian Legislature* (Quebec, n.d.), no. 19, pp. 6-7.

[60] Macdonald Papers, vol. 260, Ross to Macdonald, 14 April, 1860.

[61] *Ibid.*, vol. 188, Macdonald to Lindsey, 19 April, 1860.

[62] *Thompson's Mirror of Parliament*, no. 31, pp. 6-8, no. 32, pp. 1-4.

[63] Ellice Papers, first instalment, bundle 29a, Rose to Ellice, 26 April, 1860.

[64] *Thompson's Mirror of Parliament*, no. 4, pp. 1-7.

[65] Sir Sidney Lee, *King Edward VII, a Biography* (London, 1925), vol. 1, p. 88.

[66] Ellice Papers, first instalment, bundle 29a, Rose to Ellice, 26 April, 1860.

[67] *Globe*, 18 August, 1860.

[68] *Ibid.*, 21 August, 1860.

[69] Robert Cellem, *Visit of His Royal Highness, the Prince of Wales, to the British North American Provinces and the United States in the Year 1860* (Toronto, 1861), p. 113.

[70] Royal Archives, Z466, Bruce to the Prince Consort, 14 August, 1860.

[71] *Globe*, 22 August, 1860.

[72] *Ibid.*, 3 September, 1860.

[73] Royal Archives, Z461, Prince of Wales to Prince Consort, 6 September, 1860.

[74] Macdonald Papers, vol. 297, Kirkpatrick's Memorandum on the Brockville Interview, September, 1860.

[75] *Ibid.*, Campbell's Memorandum on the Brockville Interview, September, 1860.

[76] Royal Archives, Z467, Newcastle to the Queen, 6 September, 1860.

[77] Macdonald Papers, vol. 260, Ross to Macdonald, 10 September, 1860.

[78] Pope, *Memoirs*, vol. 1, pp. 226-227.

[79] *Globe*, 20 September, 1860.

[80] Macdonald Papers, vol. 297, Campbell to Macdonald, 30 September, 1860.

[81] *Leader*, 12 November, 1860.

[82] *Ibid.*, 16, 17, 21, 22, 26, 30 November, and 1, 3, 8, 11, 12 December, 1860.

[83] *Journals of the Legislative Assembly of the Province of Canada* (1861), pp. 19-20.

[84] *Leader*, 21 March, 1861.

[85] *Census of the Canadas, 1860-61* (Quebec, 1863), vol. 1, pp. 42-43, 78-79.

[86] *Globe*, 11 April, 1861.

[87] *Montreal Gazette*, 24 April, 1861.

[88] *Leader*, 25 April, 1861.

[89] *News*, 24 April, 1861; *Globe*, 22 April, 1861.

[90] Macdonald Papers, additional, vol. 1, Macdonald to Amsden, 31 May, 1861.

[91] *News*, 8 June, 1861.

[92] *Ibid.*, 11 June, 1861.

[93] *Ibid.*, 12 June, 1861.

[94] *Ibid.*, 13 June, 1861.

[95] *Ibid.*, 11 June, 1861.

[96] *Address of the Hon. John A. Macdonald to the Electors of the City of Kingston with Extracts from Mr. Macdonald's Speeches delivered on various occasions in the Years 1860 and 1861*, p. viii.

[97] *News*, 12 June, 1861.

[98] *Ibid.*, 24 June, 1861.

[99] *Ibid.*, 3 July, 1861.

CHAPTER TWELVE: *Impasse*

(Pages 315 to 353)

[1] Macdonald Papers, vol. 337, Allen to Macdonald, 5 September, 1861.

[2] *Ibid.*, Feebar to Macdonald, 29 July, 1861.

[3] *Ibid.*

[4] *Ibid.*, vol. 253, Morrison to Macdonald, 1 December, 1861.

[5] L. B. Shippee, *Canadian-American Relations, 1849-1874* (New Haven and Toronto, 1939), pp. 114-116; Skelton, *Galt*, pp. 307-311.

[6] *Montreal Gazette*, 24 April, 1861.

[7] *News*, 14 May, 1861.

8 *Leader*, 18 April, 1861.

9 Sissons, *Egerton Ryerson*, vol. 2, p. 426.

10 *Leader*, 15 June, 1861.

11 Macdonald Papers, vol. 336, Spence to Macdonald, 14 October, 1859.

12 *Ibid.*, vol. 539, Macdonald to Louisa Macdonald, 18 October, 1860.

13 *Ibid.*, Macdonald to Louisa Macdonald, 11 April, 1861.

14 Skelton, *Galt*, pp. 314-316.

15 Lord Newton, *Lord Lyons, a Record of British Diplomacy* (London, n.d.), p. 48.

16 Stacey, *Canada and the British Army*, pp. 120-121.

17 C.O. 42, vol. 628, Monck to Newcastle, 19, 27 December, 1861.

18 Canada, Executive Council Minutes, State Book W, Order-in-Council, 28 December, 1861.

19 Macdonald Papers, vol. 99, Provincial Secretary to Macdonald, 28 January, 1862.

20 *Ibid.*, vol. 337, Gowan to Macdonald, 4 February, 1862.

21 *Ibid.*, vol. 194, Campbell to Macdonald, 13 December, 1861.

22 *Globe*, 19 March, 1862.

23 Macdonald Papers, vol. 337, Cameron to Macdonald [23 March, 1862].

24 *Globe*, 31 March, 1862.

25 *Ibid.*, 3 April, 1862.

26 *Ibid.*, 2 April, 1862.

27 *Journals of the Legislative Assembly of the Province of Canada* (1862), pp. 33-36.

28 Macdonald Papers, vol. 337, Campbell to Macdonald, 1 April, 1862.

29 Pope, *Memoirs*, vol. 1, pp. 234-235.

30 Macdonald Papers, vol. 99, *Report of the Commissioners Appointed to Prepare a Plan for the better Organization of the Department of Adjutant General of Militia, and the Best Means of Reorganizing the Militia of this Province and to Prepare a Bill Thereon* (Quebec, 15 March, 1862).

31 *Globe*, 9 May, 1862.

32 *Ibid.*, 7 May, 1862.

33 John Martineau, *The Life of Henry Pelham, Fifth Duke of Newcastle, 1811-1864* (London, 1908), p. 310.

34 Ellice Papers, first instalment, bundle 29a, Rose to Ellice, 23 May, 1862.

35 Martineau, *Newcastle*, p. 310.

36 *Globe*, 14 May, 1862.

37 *Ibid.*, 20 May, 1862.

38 *Ibid.*

39 *Ibid.*, 21 May, 1862.

40 Macdonald Papers, vol. 539, Macdonald to Margaret Williamson, 23 May, 1862.

41 John Sandfield Macdonald Papers, Watkin to Macdonald, 28 June, 1862.

42 Macdonald Papers, additional, vol. 1, Macdonald to Amsden, 30 July, 1862.

43 *Ibid.*, vol. 188, Shaw to Brown, 28 July, 1862.

44 *Ibid.*, Brown to Shaw, 3 September, 1862.

45 *Ibid.*, additional, vol. 1, Macdonald to Amsden, 30 July, 1862.

46 *Ibid.*, vol. 161, Adderley to Macdonald, 26 December, 1862.

47 *Ibid.*, additional, vol. 1, Macdonald to Amsden, 23 February, 1863.

48 *Globe,* 20 February, 1863.
49 Macdonald Papers, vol. 188, McWhinnie to Macdonald, 27 February, 1863.
50 *Ibid.,* vol. 188, Cameron to Macdonald [16 March, 1863].
51 Ellice Papers, first instalment, bundle 29a, Rose to Ellice, 3 March, 1863.
52 *Globe,* 20 March, 1863.
53 Macdonald Papers, vol. 338, Patton to Macdonald, 20 April, 1863.
54 *Globe,* 6 May, 1863.
55 *News,* 21 May, 1863.
56 Macdonald Papers, vol. 338, Duggan to Macdonald, 26 May, 1863.
57 *News,* 13 June, 1863.
58 Macdonald Papers, vol. 338, Patton to Macdonald, 10 June, 1863.
59 *Ibid.,* Cook to Macdonald, 14 June, 1863.
60 *Ibid.,* Daly to Macdonald, 1 July, 1863.
61 *Ibid.,* Cauchon to Macdonald, 27 June, 1863.
62 *Ibid.,* additional, vol. 1, Macdonald to Amsden, 5 August, 1863.
63 *Ibid.,* Macdonald to Amsden, 14 September, 1863.
64 *Ibid.,* vol. 215, Foley to Macdonald, 24 November, 1863.
65 Chamberlin Papers, vol. 2, Macdonald to Chamberlin, 20 November, 1863.
66 Macdonald Papers, vol. 338, Alleyn to Macdonald, 29 December, 1863.
67 *Ibid.,* Jones to Macdonald, 1 January, 1864.
68 *Ibid.,* vol. 191, Brydges to Macdonald, 16 January, 1864.
69 *Globe,* 30 January, 1864.
70 Macdonald Papers, vol. 247, Macpherson to Macdonald, 27 February, 1864.
71 *Ibid.,* vol. 338, Patton to Macdonald, 19 November, 1863.
72 *Ibid.,* vol. 191, Brydges to Macdonald, 24 February, 1864.
73 *Ibid.,* Brydges to Macdonald, 22 February, 1864.
74 *Ibid.,* vol. 539, Macdonald to Louisa Macdonald, 24 February, 1864.
75 *Globe,* 15 March, 1864.
76 Macdonald Papers, vol. 338, O'Reilly to Macdonald, 25 March, 1864.
77 *Globe,* 1 April, 1864.
78 *Journals of the Legislative Assembly of the Province of Canada* (1864), pp. 387-390.

CHAPTER THIRTEEN: *British North America in Conference*
(Pages 354 to 390)

1 *Globe,* 16 June, 1864.
2 Pope, *Memoirs,* vol. 1, appendix 5, pp. 344-350.
3 *Journals of the Legislative Assembly of the Province of Canada* (1864), pp. 383-384.
4 Pope, *Memoirs,* vol. 1, appendix 5.
5 *Globe,* 18 June, 1864.
6 Pope, *Memoirs,* vol. 1, appendix 5.

7 W. M. Whitelaw, *The Maritimes and Canada before Confederation* (Toronto, 1934), pp. 211-217.

8 Public Record Office, C.O. 217, vol. 234, MacDonnell to Cardwell, 18 July, 1864.

9 *Ibid.*, vol. 230, Mulgrave to Newcastle, 21 May, 1864, minute by Newcastle.

10 British Museum, Additional MSS. 44118 (Gladstone Papers), Gladstone to Cardwell, 25 July, 1864.

11 Public Record Office, P.R.O. 30/22 (Russell Papers), vol. 27, minute by Palmerston on Cardwell's draft dispatch to Monck, 29 July, 1864.

12 Stacey, *Canada and the British Army*, pp. 160-161.

13 Public Record Office, P.R.O. 30/48 (Cardwell Papers), vol. 39, Gordon to Cardwell, 10 April, 1865.

14 C.O. 217, vol. 234, MacDonnell to Cardwell, 18 July, 1864, minute by Fortescue, 4 August, 1864.

15 Public Archives of Canada, Nova Scotia Dispatches, vol. 108, pt. 2, Cardwell to MacDonnell, 9 August, 1864.

16 C.O. 42, vol, 642, Monck to Cardwell, 26 August, 1864, minute by Cardwell, 1 October, 1864.

17 *Montreal Gazette*, 1 September, 1864.

18 Canada, Executive Council Minutes, State Book AA, Order-in-Council, 29 August, 1864.

19 *Islander* (Charlottetown), 9 September, 1864.

20 *Morning Telegraph* (Saint John), 5 September, 1864, quoted in *Islander*, 9 September, 1864.

21 *Examiner* (Charlottetown), quoted in *Globe*, 20 September, 1864.

22 *Islander*, 9 September, 1864.

23 J. H. Gray, *Confederation; or the Political and Parliamentary History of Canada, from the Conference at Quebec in October, 1864, to the Admission of British Columbia, in July, 1871* (Toronto, 1872), vol. 1, p. 30.

24 *Globe*, 21 September, 1864.

25 *Ibid.*

26 *Morning Chronicle* (Halifax), 10 September, 1864.

27 *Islander*, 16 September, 1864.

28 *Ibid.*, 23 September, 1864.

29 *Morning Chronicle*, 12 September, 1864.

30 Macdonald Papers, vol. 51, Macdonald to Taché (draft), 12 September, 1864.

31 *Globe*, 21 September, 1864.

32 *Ibid.*

33 *Evening Express* (Halifax), 14 September, 1864.

34 *Montreal Gazette*, 19 September, 1864.

35 *Morning News* (Saint John), 19 September, 1864.

36 Macdonald Papers, vol. 51, Macdonald to Tupper (draft), 22 September, 1864.

37 Canada, Executive Council Minutes, State Book AA, Order-in-Council, 23 September, 1864.

38 Whitelaw, *The Maritimes and Canada*, p. 230.

39 P.R.O. 30/48, vol. 39, Cardwell to Gordon, 1 October, 1864.

[40] *Globe*, 10 October, 1864.

[41] *Ibid.*, 11 October, 1864.

[42] W. M. Whitelaw, "Reconstructing the Quebec Conference", *Canadian Historical Review*, vol. 19 (June, 1938), pp. 123-137.

[43] Macdonald Papers, vol. 46, p. 13.

[44] *Ibid.*, p. 14.

[45] *Ibid.*, p. 27.

[46] *Ibid.*, pp. 21, 24-25.

[47] *Ibid.*, pp. 29-38.

[48] *Globe*, 12 October, 1864.

[49] Macdonald Papers, vol. 46, pp. 51-57.

[50] A. G. Doughty (ed.), "Notes on the Quebec Conference, 1864", *Canadian Historical Review*, vol. 1 (March, 1920), pp. 26-47.

[51] *Globe*, 15 October, 1864.

[52] Macdonald Papers, vol. 46, pp. 64-70.

[53] *Ibid.*, pp. 65-72.

[54] Doughty, "Notes on the Quebec Conference", pp. 36-37.

[55] Macdonald Papers, vol. 46, pp. 142-149.

[56] *Ibid.*, p. 161.

[57] Joseph Pope, *Confederation, being a Series of hitherto unpublished Documents bearing on the British North America Act* (Toronto, 1895), pp. 84-85.

[58] Macdonald Papers, vol. 46, pp. 167-168.

[59] *Globe*, 28 October, 1864.

[60] *Ibid.*, 29, 31 October, 1864.

[61] *Ibid.*, 2 November, 1864.

[62] C.O. 42, vol. 643, Monck to Cardwell (confidential), 7 November, 1864.

[63] *Globe*, 9 November, 1864.

[64] Canada, Executive Council Minutes, State Book AA, Order-in-Council, 16 November, 1864.

[65] C.O. 42, vol. 643, Monck to Cardwell, 27 October, 1864.

[66] P.R.O. 30/22, vol. 38, Lyons to Russell, 24 October, 1864.

[67] *Ibid.*, Lyons to Russell, 28 October, 1864.

[68] Stacey, *Canada and the British Army*, pp. 165-166.

[69] Canada, Executive Council Minutes, State Book AA, Order-in-Council, 16 November, 1864.

[70] Macdonald Papers, additional, vol. 1, Macdonald to Amsden, 1 December, 1864.

[71] Sir Joseph Pope, *Correspondence of Sir John Macdonald* (Toronto n.d.), pp. 13-15, Macdonald to Tupper, 14 November, 1864.

[72] *Ibid.*, pp. 17-18, Tupper to Macdonald, 13 December, 1864.

[73] Macdonald Papers, vol. 51, Tilley to Macdonald, 23 November, 1864.

[74] British Museum, Additional MSS. 44118, Cardwell to Gladstone, 27 October, 1864.

[75] P.R.O. 30/48, vol. 39, Cardwell to Gordon, 26 November, 1864.

[76] P.R.O. 30/22, vol. 31, Russell to Newcastle, 12 June, 1862.

[77] P.R.O. 30/48, vol. 39, Cardwell to Gordon, 12 November, 1864.

[78] Royal Archives, P 22, Monck to Cardwell, 14 November, 1864.

[79] P.R.O. 30/48, vol. 39, Cardwell to Gordon, 14 October, 1864.

Chapter Fourteen: *Checkmate*

(Pages 391 to 430)

1 F.O. 5, vol. 963, Burnley to Russell, 21 November, 1864.

2 C.O. 42, vol. 643, Monck to Lyons, 12 November, 1864, enclosed in Monck to Cardwell, 12 November, 1864.

3 Shippee, *Canadian-American Relations*, p. 148.

4 Pope, *Correspondence*, p. 19, Macdonald to Swinyard, 19 December, 1864.

5 Shippee, *Canadian-American Relations*, pp. 177-179.

6 Pope, *Correspondence*, pp. 19-20, Macdonald to Swinyard, 19 December, 1864.

7 *Ibid.*, p. 18.

8 P.R.O. 30/22, vol. 38, Burnley to Russell, 27 December, 1864.

9 Macdonald Papers, vol. 510, Macdonald to Brydges, 1 January, 1865.

10 *Ibid.*, Macdonald to Swinyard, 1 January, 1865.

11 Pope, *Correspondence*, pp. 24-26, Tupper to Macdonald, 9 April, 1865.

12 Macdonald Papers, vol. 51, Tupper to Macdonald, 4 January, 1865.

13 J. A. Roy, *Joseph Howe, a Study in Achievement and Frustration* (Toronto, 1925), p. 259.

14 J. A. Chisholm, *The Speeches and Public Letters of Joseph Howe* (Halifax, 1909), vol. 2, pp. 268-295.

15 Macdonald Papers, vol. 51, Tupper to Macdonald, 4 January, 1865.

16 *Ibid.*, vol. 510, Macdonald to Fisher, 24 March, 1865.

17 P.R.O. 30/48, vol. 39, Gordon to Cardwell, 15 January, 1865.

18 *Ibid.*, Gordon to Cardwell, 10 April, 1865.

19 *Ibid.*, Gordon to Cardwell, 24 October, 1864.

20 Public Archives of Canada, New Brunswick, C.O. 189, vol. 2, Gordon to Cardwell, 2 January, 1865.

21 Public Record Office, C.O. 188, vol. 143, Gordon to Cardwell, 16 January, 1865.

22 *Ibid.*, Tilley to Gordon, 30 January, 1865, enclosed in Gordon to Cardwell, 30 January, 1865.

23 *Globe*, 21 January, 1865.

24 *Parliamentary Debates on the Subject of the Confederation of the British North American Provinces* (Quebec, 1865), p. 33.

25 *Ibid.*, p. 42.

26 *Ibid.*

27 *Ibid.*, p. 41.

28 Macdonald Papers, vol. 51, Tilley to Macdonald, 13 February, 1865.

29 *Ibid.*, Macdonald to Tilley, 20 February, 1865.

30 G. E. Buckle (ed.), *Letters of Queen Victoria* (London, 1926), Series 2, vol. 1, pp. 248-249, Palmerston to the Queen, 20 January, 1865.

31 G1, vol. 161, Cardwell to Monck, 21 January, 1865.

32 *Globe*, 6 March, 1865.

33 *Ibid.*, 7 March, 1865.

34 *Confederation Debates*, p. 648.

35 *Ibid.*, p. 669.

36 *Ibid.*, pp. 649-650.

37 *Globe*, 22 March, 1865.

[38] Macdonald Papers, vol. 339, Chamberlin to Macdonald, 22 March, 1865.

[39] Pope, *Correspondence*, p. 25, Tupper to Macdonald, 9 April, 1865.

[40] *Debates and Proceedings of the House of Assembly of Nova Scotia* (1865), p. 203.

[41] Pope, *Correspondence*, p. 24, Macdonald to Gray, 24 March, 1865.

[42] *Globe*, 10 March, 1865.

[43] Shippee, *Canadian-American Relations*, p. 134.

[44] Macdonald Papers, vol. 511, Macdonald to Gray, 27 March, 1865.

[45] *Ibid.*, Macdonald to Watkin, 27 March, 1865.

[46] A. Mackenzie, *The Life and Speeches of George Brown* (Toronto, 1882), p. 233.

[47] *Ibid.*, pp. 233-234.

[48] *The Times* (London), 28 April, 1865.

[49] Skelton, *Galt*, pp. 379-380; *Times*, 17 May, 1865.

[50] British Museum, Additional MSS. 44320 (Gladstone Papers), Gladstone to Gordon, 11 July, 1865.

[51] *Ibid.*

[52] Stacey, *Canada and the British Army*, pp. 185-186.

[53] Skelton, *Galt*, pp. 383-386.

[54] Pope, *Memoirs*, vol. 1, pp. 283-284.

[55] *Illustrated London News*, 3 June, 1865, pp. 526-527.

[56] British Museum, Additional MSS. 44118, Gladstone to Cardwell, 23 May, 1865.

[57] Macdonald Papers, vol. 161, Observations on the Answer to our Memo. of Yesterday, 2 June [1865].

[58] *Ibid.*, vol. 539, Macdonald to Louisa Macdonald, 17 June, 1865.

[59] *The Times*, 22 June, 1865.

[60] *Jackson's Oxford Journal*, 24 June, 1865.

[61] Macdonald Papers, vol. 74, Monck to Macdonald, 7 July, 1865.

[62] Pope, *Memoirs*, vol. 1, p. 285.

[63] Macdonald Papers, vol. 74, Monck to Macdonald, 3 August, 1865.

[64] Pope, *Memoirs*, vol. 1, Appendix 9, pp. 362-364.

[65] *Ibid.*, pp. 365-366, Macdonald to Brown, 5 August, 1865.

[66] *Globe*, 16 August, 1865.

[67] Macdonald Papers, vol. 539, Macdonald to Louisa Macdonald, 23 August, 1865.

[68] C. P. Stacey, "Fenianism and the Rise of National Feeling in Canada at the Time of Confederation", *Canadian Historical Review*, vol. 12 (September, 1931), pp. 238-261.

[69] Macdonald Papers, vol. 511, Macdonald to Monck, 18 September, 1865.

[70] P.R.O. 30/48, vol. 39, Cardwell to Gordon, 13 May, 1865.

[71] Public Archives of Canada, New Brunswick, Dispatches Received, vol. 45, Cardwell to Gordon, 24 June, 1865.

[72] P.R.O. 30/22, vol. 26, Cardwell to Russell, 22 July, 1865.

[73] *Ibid.*, vol. 31, Russell to Cardwell, 4 September, 1865.

[74] *Ibid.*, vol. 26, Cardwell to Russell, 15 August, 1865.

[75] Macdonald Papers, vol. 51, Fisher to Macdonald, 13 August, 1865.

[76] *Globe*, 4 September, 1865.

[77] Macdonald Papers, vol. 51, Tilley to Macdonald, 13 September, 1865.

[78] *Globe*, 27, 29 September, 1865.

[79] Pope, *Memoirs*, vol. 1, p. 291, Macdonald to Louisa Macdonald, 28 September [1865].

[80] Macdonald Papers, vol. 51, Fisher to Macdonald, 11 November, 1865.

[81] New Brunswick, C.O. 189, vol. 2, Gordon to Cardwell, 20 November, 1865.

[82] Macdonald Papers, vol. 51, Monck to Macdonald, 22 November, 1865.

[83] P.R.O. 30/48, vol. 39, Gordon to Cardwell, 20 November, 1865.

[84] Pope, *Memoirs*, vol. 1, appendix 11, pp. 370-371.

[85] Pope, *Correspondence*, p. 30, Monck to Macdonald, 20 December, 1865.

[86] *Reports of the Debates of the House of Assembly of the Province of New Brunswick During the Session of 1866, First Session*, p. 34.

[87] Macdonald Papers, vol. 51, Tilley to Macdonald, 13 February, 1866.

[88] New Brunswick C.O. 189, vol. 2, Gordon to Cardwell, 21 February, 1866.

[89] *Journal of the House of Assembly of the Province of New Brunswick* (1866—First Session), pp. 12-13; *New Brunswick Assembly Debates*, 1866, pp. 23, 34, 62-64.

[90] Macdonald Papers, vol. 51, Mitchell to Macdonald, 7 April, 1866.

[91] Public Archives of Canada, G13, vol. 2, Gordon to Monck, 10 April, 1866.

CHAPTER FIFTEEN: *Triumph*

(Pages 431 to 465)

[1] Pope, *Correspondence*, p. 32, Macdonald to Mitchell, 10 April, 1866.

[2] Public Archives of Canada, G13, vol. 12, Macdonald to Monck, 11 April, 1866.

[3] P.R.O. 30/48, vol. 39, Cardwell to Gordon, 1 July, 1866.

[4] Macdonald Papers, vol. 51, Tilley to Macdonald, 17 April, 1866.

[5] *Ibid.*, Monck to Macdonald, 23 April, 1866.

[6] *Ibid.*, Tilley to Macdonald, 21 April, 1866.

[7] *Ibid.*, Tilley to Macdonald, 20 April, 1866.

[8] *Ibid.*, vol. 191, Brydges to Macdonald, 17 January, 1866.

[9] *Ibid.*, vol. 51, Tilley to Macdonald, 17, 20 April, 1866.

[10] *Ibid.*, Monck to Macdonald, 23 April, 1866.

[11] P.R.O. 30/48, vol. 39, Gordon to Cardwell, 14 January, 1866.

[12] Macdonald Papers, vol. 51, Monck to Macdonald, 18 April, 1866.

[13] *Ibid.*, Monck to Macdonald, 17 April, 1866.

[14] *Ibid.*

[15] Pope, *Memoirs*, vol. 1, p. 306, Macdonald to Tilley, 8 October, 1866.

[16] Macdonald Papers, vol. 237, McMicken to Macdonald, 12 March, 1866.

[17] Stacey, "Fenianism and the Rise of National Feeling in Canada", p. 244.

[18] Pope, *Correspondence*, p. 33, Macdonald to Mitchell, 10 April, 1866.

[19] *Journal of the House of Assembly of the Province of New Brunswick* (1866—First Session), p. 217.

[20] Macdonald Papers, vol. 51, Tilley to Macdonald, 21 April, 1866.

[21] Stacey, "Fenianism and the Rise of National Feeling in Canada", p. 252.

[22] Macdonald Papers, vol. 51, Tupper to Macdonald, 17 June, 1866.

[23] *Ibid.*, Tupper to Macdonald, 19 June, 1866.

[24] *Ibid.*, Monck to Macdonald, 21 June, 1866.

[25] Pope, *Memoirs*, vol. 1, pp. 300-302, Macdonald to Monck, 22 June, 1866.
[26] P.R.O. 30/48, vol. 40, Cardwell to Monck, 7 July, 1866.
[27] Macdonald Papers, vol. 51, Tupper to Macdonald, 14 July, 1866.
[28] Pope, *Memoirs*, vol. 1, p. 304, Monck to Williams, 14 July, 1866.
[29] Macdonald Papers, vol. 51, Tilley and Tupper to Macdonald, 19 July, 1866.
[30] *Ibid.*, Macdonald to Tupper, 19 July, 1866.
[31] P.R.O. 30/48, vol. 40, Carnarvon to Cardwell, 14, 19, 20 July, 1866.
[32] *Ibid.*, Cardwell to Carnarvon, 19 July, 1866.
[33] *Ibid.*, Cardwell to Carnarvon, 27 July, 1866.
[34] *Ibid.*, Carnarvon to Cardwell, 28 July, 1866.
[35] Macdonald Papers, vol. 51, Tilley to Galt, 9 August, 1866.
[36] *Ibid.*, vol. 512, Macdonald to Mowat, 13 August, 1866.
[37] Pope, *Memoirs*, vol. 1, p. 307, Macdonald to Tilley, 8 October, 1866.
[38] Macdonald Papers, vol. 512, Macdonald to Mayor of Cornwall, 2 July, 1866.
[39] *Ibid.*, vol. 513, Macdonald to McMicken, 25 August, 1866.
[40] Beaconsfield Papers, bundle 12, Carnarvon to Disraeli, 27 August, 1866.
[41] *Ibid.*, Carnarvon to Disraeli, 30 August, 1 September, 1866.
[42] Pope, *Correspondence*, pp. 34-35, Macdonald to Michel, 28 August, 1866.
[43] Macdonald Papers, vol. 74, Monck to Macdonald, 29 August, 1866.
[44] *Globe*, 17, 22 August, 5 September, 1866.
[45] G10, vol. 1, Howe and Annand to Carnarvon, 3 October, 1866.
[46] Macdonald Papers, vol. 51, Brydges to Macdonald, 8 October, 1866.
[47] *Ibid.*, Monck to Macdonald, 11 October, 1866.
[48] *Ibid.*, vol. 513, Macdonald to White, 20 October, 1866.
[49] *Ibid.*, vol. 51, Monck to Macdonald, 12 October, 1866.
[50] *Ibid.*, vol. 47, pp. 3-4.
[51] Skelton, *Galt*, p. 408.
[52] Pope, *Confederation Documents*, p. 122.
[53] P.R.O. 30/48, vol. 40, Carnarvon to Cardwell, 19 July, 1866.
[54] Pope, *Memoirs*, vol. 1, pp. 316-317, Macdonald to Louisa Macdonald, 27 December, 1866.
[55] Macdonald Papers, vol. 47, pp. 46-52.
[56] *Ibid.*, vol. 51, Macdonald to Carnarvon, 24 December, 1866.
[57] *Ibid.*, Monck to Macdonald, 31 December, 1866.
[58] Pope, *Memoirs*, vol. 1, pp. 314-315.
[59] Macdonald Papers, vol. 51. Carnarvon to Macdonald, 23 January, 1867.
[60] Hardinge, *Carnarvon*, vol. 1, p. 303-304.
[61] Macdonald Papers, vol. 51, Macdonald to Carnarvon, 30 January, 1867.
[62] G. E. Marinden (ed.), *Letters of Frederic, Lord Blachford, Under-Secretary of State for the Colonies, 1860-1871* (London, 1896), pp. 301-302.
[63] Macdonald Papers, vol. 51, Macdonald to Carnarvon, 2 February, 1867.
[64] Pope, *Confederation Documents*, pp. 158-176.
[65] Pope, *Correspondence*, p. 451, Macdonald to Knutsford, 18 July, 1889.
[66] *The Congressional Globe: Containing the Debates and Proceedings of the Second Session of the Thirty-Ninth Congress* (Washington, 1867), p. 1617.
[67] Shippee, *Canadian-American Relations, 1849-1874*, p. 196.
[68] Royal Archives, B23, Carnarvon to the Queen, 4 February, 1867, Carnarvon to Grey, 6 February, 1867.

[69] *Ibid.*, Carnarvon to Grey, 7 February, 1867.

[70] *The Times*, 21 February, 1867.

[71] *Hansard's Parliamentary Debates* (London, 1867), third series, vol. 185, p. 576-b.

[72] Macdonald Papers, vol. 51, Carnarvon to Macdonald, 21 February, 1867.

[73] Hardinge, *Carnarvon*, vol. 1, pp. 346-347.

[74] G. E. Buckle, *The Life of Benjamin Disraeli, Earl of Beaconsfield* (London, 1916), vol. 4, p. 498.

[75] *Hansard*, third series, vol. 185, pp. 1016-1017.

[76] Pope, *Memoirs*, vol. 1, p. 338, Macdonald to Louisa Macdonald, 21 March, 1867.

[77] *Hansard*, third series, vol. 185, p. 1184.

[78] Macdonald Papers, vol. 75, Monck to Macdonald, 2 March, 1867.

[79] *Ibid.*, vol. 51, Macdonald to Carnarvon [5 March, 1867].

[80] *Ibid.*, Adderley to Macdonald, n.d.

EPILOGUE—*The First of July, 1867*

(Pages 466 to 484)

[1] Macdonald Papers, vol. 51, Macdonald to Fisher, 30 May, 1867.

[2] *Ibid.*, Macdonald to Tilley, 30 May, 1867.

[3] *Ibid.*, vol. 513, Macdonald to Shea, 3 June, 1867.

[4] *Ibid.*, Macdonald to Godley, 1 June, 1867.

[5] *Journal des Trois Rivières*, quoted in *La Minerve* (Montreal), 6 July, 1867.

[6] *Ottawa Times*, 3 July, 1867.

[7] *Morning News* (Saint John), 3 July, 1867.

[8] *British Colonist* (Halifax), 2 July, 1867.

[9] *La Minerve*, 8 July, 1867.

[10] *News* (Kingston), 2 July, 1867.

[11] *Observer* (Sarnia), 5 July, 1867.

[12] *Montreal Gazette*, 3 July, 1867.

[13] Pope, *Correspondence*, p. 46, Monck to Macdonald, 24 May, 1867.

[14] Macdonald Papers, vol. 513, Macdonald to Morris, 1 July, 1867.

[15] *Ibid.*, vol. 51, Macdonald to Archibald, 30 May, 1867.

[16] *Ibid.*, Tilley to Macdonald, 5 June, 1867.

[17] *Ibid.*, vol. 513, Macdonald to Mitchell, 1 June, 1867.

[18] *Ibid.*, vol. 230, McDougall to Macdonald, 5 June, 1867.

[19] Pope, *Correspondence*, p. 43, McGee to Macdonald, 9 April, 1867.

[20] Macdonald Papers, vol. 51, Monck to Macdonald, 26 June, 1867.

[21] *Ibid.*, vol. 188, Brown to Macdonald, 15 August, 1864.

[22] *Ibid.*, vol. 51, Macdonald to Monck, 5 April, 1867.

[23] *Ottawa Times*, 29 June, 1867.

[24] *Ibid.*, 3 July, 1867.

[25] Canada, Privy Council Minutes, 1 July, 1867.

[26] Royal Archives, B23, Buckingham and Chandos to Pakington, 22 June, 1867.

[27] *Leader* (Toronto), 2 July, 1867.

[28] *Grand River Sachem*, 10 July, 1867.

[29] *Northern Advance* (Barrie), 4 July, 1867

INDEX

Abbey, Dorethus, 65, 67-8

Aberdeen, George Hamilton Gordon, 4th Earl of, 186

Act to Protect the Inhabitants of this Province against Lawless Aggressions from the Subjects of Foreign Countries at Peace with Her Majesty, An, 62

Act of Union, 436

Adams, Charles Francis, 385, 388, 410

Adderley, Sir Charles Bowyer, 338, 456, 465

Adolphus Reach, 12

Adolphustown, 9, 12; John Hughes's school at, 13

Alabama, cruiser, 421

Albert, Prince, 299, 324

Allen, George, 317

Allen, John Campbell, 422

Alleyn, Charles, 249, 345

Alwington House, Kingston, 73, 78, 81

Ameliasburgh, 9

American Civil War, 318, 358

American "sympathizers", 49, 50

Anglin, Timothy W., 426, 440

Annand, William, 448, 460

Appomattox Court House, 410

Archibald, Adams George, 395, 472

Arthur, Sir George, Bart., 60; issued proclamation, 60

Ashburton Treaty, 392

Ashley, John, 56, 57, 58

Ashley vs. *Dundas*, 58

Aylwin, Thomas Cushing, 108

Badgeley, William, 103

Bagot, Sir Charles, Bart., 83, 86, 89

Baldwin, Robert, 81, 86, 106, 109, 123, 129, 130, 151, 166, 167: planned non-sectarian provincial university, 93

Bank acts, the, 28; Colonial Office threatens to disallow, 28

Bank of Montreal, 346

Bank of Upper Canada, 24, 28; capital stock increased, 24

Barclay, John, 17

Baring, Thomas, 163

Bath, 9

Battle of the Alma, 211

Battle of Gettysburg, 347

Baxter, George, 14, 16

Bay of Quinte, 9, 12, 25

Beaconsfield, Benjamin Disraeli, 1st Earl of, 274, 462, 464

Belleau, Sir Narcisse Fortunat, 300, 419

Belleville, 9, 305

Bellevue, 132

Benjamin, George, 195, 308, 328

Bernard, Hewitt, 372

Bernard, Susan Agnes, 455, 456

Birge, John W., 66

Blackwood, Arthur, 276

Blair, Fergusson, 351

Blake, William Hume, 136, 137, 151

Bonsecours Market, 140

Bothwell, George Brown's farm at, 289

Boulton, Henry John, 28, 71, 103, 123, 130, 138

Boulton, William Henry, 109, 116, 161, 162

Bowes, John G., 196, 212

Brantford, 305

Brass, William, 43

Bright, John, 463, 464

British American League, 141, 149; Kingston convention of, 142-146; Toronto convention of, 149-150

British Colonist, 209, 213, 259

British Columbia on union, 380

British Corn Laws, repeal of, 127, 134, 139

British North America federation, carried, 375; delegates, 445; Bill, 459, 460

British Whig, Kingston, 79, 89

Brockville, steamer, 61, 62

Brown, George, 158, 159, 167, 170, 181, 183, 187, 189, 190, 191, 195, 198, 203, 213, 221, 229, 259, 261, 263, 271, 280, 281, 289, 304, 307, 336, 339, 343, 349, 350, 354, 355-8, 366, 377, 381, 382, 384, 400, 404, 411, 415, 416, 419, 427: Free Kirkers led by, 98; and Grand Trunk Railway, 251-3; constitutional resolutions of, 297-8

Brown-Dorion government, 267, 289

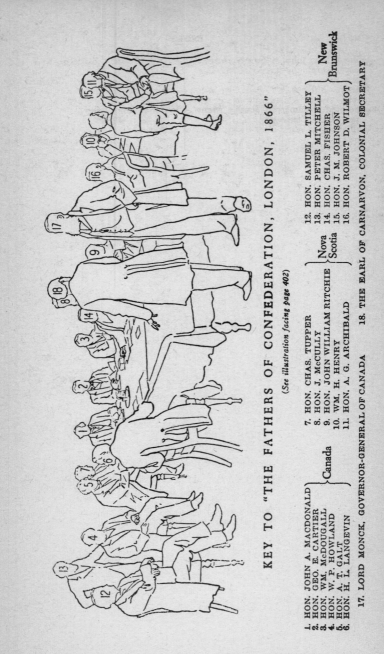

KEY TO "THE FATHERS OF CONFEDERATION, LONDON, 1866"

(See illustration facing page 402)

1. HON. JOHN A. MACDONALD
2. HON. GEO. E. CARTIER
3. HON. WM. McDOUGALL
4. HON. W. P. HOWLAND
5. HON. A. T. GALT
6. HON. H. L. LANGEVIN
} Canada

7. HON. CHAS. TUPPER
8. HON. J. McCULLY
9. HON. JOHN WILLIAM RITCHIE
10. WM. H. HENRY
11. HON. A. G. ARCHIBALD
} Nova Scotia

12. HON. SAMUEL L. TILLEY
13. HON. PETER MITCHELL
14. HON. CHAS. FISHER
15. HON. J. M. JOHNSON
16. HON. ROBERT D. WILMOT
} New Brunswick

17. LORD MONCK, GOVERNOR-GENERAL OF CANADA   18. THE EARL OF CARNARVON, COLONIAL SECRETARY

PROPOSED WINDOW FOR THE
PARLIAMENT BUILDING

*(From Bengough: "Caricature History of Canadian
Politics." Public Archives)*